D0143082

Essentials of Strategic Intelligence

Essentials of Strategic Intelligence

Loch K. Johnson, Editor

Praeger Security International Textbook

 PRAEGER

AN IMPRINT OF ABC-CLIO, LLC
Santa Barbara, California • Denver, Colorado • Oxford, England

Copyright 2015 by Loch K. Johnson

Library of Congress Cataloging-in-Publication Data

Essentials of strategic intelligence / Loch K. Johnson, editor.
  pages cm. — (Praeger security international)
ISBN 978-1-4408-3227-7 (hardback) — ISBN 978-1-4408-3228-4 (ebook) —
  ISBN 978-1-4408-3352-6 (paperback) 1. Intelligence service.   I. Johnson, Loch K.,
1942—.
UB250.E77 2015
327.12—dc23   2014028349

ISBN: 978-1-4408-3227-7
EISBN: 978-1-4408-3228-4
Paperback ISBN: 978-1-4408-3352-6

19 18 17 16 15   1 2 3 4 5

This book is also available on the World Wide Web as an eBook.
Visit www.abc-clio.com for details.

Praeger
An Imprint of ABC-CLIO, LLC

ABC-CLIO, LLC
130 Cremona Drive, P.O. Box 1911
Santa Barbara, California 93116-1911

This book is printed on acid-free paper ∞

Manufactured in the United States of America

Contents

Preface

Loch K. Johnson

IN 2007, PRAEGER SECURITY INTERNATIONAL PUBLISHED A LANDMARK in the study of intelligence: a five-volume work, entitled *Strategic Intelligence*, which presented a comprehensive array of articles on espionage activities written by top scholars from around the world. Thirty years before, one would have been hard-pressed to find enough good articles on the subject to fill two volumes, let alone five. In those three decades since 1975, however, the study of intelligence had grown considerably and allowed such an ambitious compilation of original essays. Today, several first-rate professional journals exist in the field, including the premier publications *Intelligence and National Security* (published in the United Kingdom), *International Journal of Intelligence and Counterintelligence* (the United States), and *Studies in Intelligence* (the Central Intelligence Agency, in both a classified and an unclassified form). In just the past ten years, bulging anthologies on the general topic of "strategic intelligence" have appeared, along with various "handbooks" on intelligence, a more specialized work on "intelligence and ethics," and, in 2014, a richly textured "companion to intelligence studies"—not to mention a tidal wave of books and articles on one aspect or another of this subject. (See Chapter One that follows this preface for specific citations.)

To bring greater focus to this wide literature, the volume offered here gathers together and updates several of the key articles published initially in the Praeger Security International five-volume series. For this new single volume, the chapters include revisions of the earlier work to take into account more recent intelligence issues. Here in one place, designed specifically for classroom use, are 21 core articles on strategic intelligence by some of the leading researchers in the field.

The Rise of Intelligence Studies as an Academic Discipline

The recent flowering of research on intelligence has been an academic phenomenon. Except in times of scandal (Watergate in 1973, CIA domestic spying in 1974, the Iran-*contra* affair in 1987), one could find in this earlier era relatively little media coverage of intelligence activities, so tightly held were these operations by the United States and other governments. Now, fueled by terrorist attacks of September 11, 2001, the erroneous prediction in 2002 that Iraq was developing and stockpiling weapons of mass destruction (WMD), and the latest controversy involving massive "metadata" collection on American citizens by the National Security Agency (NSA), hardly a week goes by without several reports on intelligence in the *New York Times* and other leading media outlets. These days, even America's top literary magazines, the *Atlantic Monthly* and the *New Yorker*, visit the subject with some regularity.

Moreover, an Intelligence Studies Group has been founded within the American Political Science Association as a forum for the presentation of papers and panel discussions on the subject of intelligence at the APSA's annual convention; and within the International Studies Association, an Intelligence Studies Section offers some 20 panels on intelligence topics each year at the ISA's annual meeting. Professional associations of intelligence scholars have formed in the United Kingdom, Canada, Germany, Australia, New Zealand, and elsewhere. Further, courses on intelligence have proliferated across the United States, the British Commonwealth, and in Europe, with evidence that this topic is catching on as an academic pursuit in other regions of the world as well. Clearly, intelligence studies has come of age.

A Roadmap to This Anthology

As with the earlier five-volume work, the chapters in this book display a breadth of inquiry. Presented here are empirical studies, historical treatments, theoretical frameworks, memoirs, case studies, legal analyses, comparative essays, and ethical assessments. The authors come from the ranks of academe, the intelligence agencies, think tanks, the world of diplomacy, and the legal world; and they represent a wide range of scholarly disciplines, including history, international affairs, law, political science, public policy studies, and strategic studies. The end result of this mix is a landscape illuminated by a variety of methods and appreciations—a research trove that examines the key aspects of modern-day intelligence, all condensed into one volume.

Understanding the Hidden Side of Government

The book is organized according to the major topics of study in the field. The first section, entitled "Understanding the Hidden Side of Government," introduces the reader to the "state of the discipline," beginning with a bibliographic essay by the editor and continuing with an examination of specific approaches scholars have adopted in their inquiries into this especially difficult discipline, where doors are often shut against outsiders.

In the bibliographic essay that opens the volume, I indicate how the literature on intelligence has mushroomed over the past 40 years. Some of this literature is unreliable, but much of it is of high quality. Amy B. Zegart follows my chapter with an important caveat: the literature may be more voluminous these days, but intelligence studies as an academic field has yet to be accepted as a central part of national security scholarship. The mainstream journals of history, international affairs, and political science still regard the study of intelligence as a marginal pursuit. As Zegart points out, there is a major disconnect between academic scholarship and those who make decisions and rely on intelligence in Washington, London, Berlin, and other capitals around the world. Rounding out this introduction, in Chapter Three, Michael Warner looks at methodologies scholars have used to study intelligence.

The Intelligence Cycle

In the second section, entitled "The Intelligence Cycle," the book shifts from a broad overview of intelligence to a more detailed examination of its core mission: the collection, analysis, and dissemination to policymakers of information gathered from around the world. The National Security Act of 1947, which created America's modern intelligence establishment, made it clear that this mission would be the primary duty of the intelligence agencies. As stated by Allen Dulles—the most famous director of Central Intelligence, or DCI (America's top intelligence official, until this title changed to director of National Intelligence or DNI in 2004)—the intelligence agencies were expected "to weigh facts, and to draw conclusions from those facts, without having either the facts or the conclusions warped by the inevitable and even proper prejudices of the men whose duty it is to determine policy."[1] The collection and interpretation of information, through espionage and from the public record (open-source intelligence), would be the main responsibility of America's secret agencies.

At the heart of this mission lies the so-called intelligence cycle. Professional intelligence officers define the cycle as "the process by which information is acquired, converted into intelligence, and made available to policymakers."[2] The cycle has five phases: planning and direction, collection, processing, production and analysis, and dissemination. Former CIA officer Arthur S. Hulnick notes in Chapter Four, however, that the idea of a "cycle" fails to capture the complexity of how intelligence is actually collected, assessed, and distributed by intelligence officers. Despite its abstract, theoretical nature, the concept of an intelligence cycle does nevertheless provide an overview of the key steps involved as information moves from the field where it is collected to the high councils of government where decisions are made.

Chapter Five in this section leads the reader into the world of the "ints," that is, the specialized "intelligences" (methods or tradecraft) used by intelligence officers to collect information. One important method is gathering information through the use of human agents ("assets") guided by case or "operational" officers working overseas for the CIA or the Defense Department—the topic of human intelligence, or HUMINT, presented by Frederick P. Hitz, a former CIA inspector general.

Other chapters in this volume discuss the method of signals intelligence, or SIGINT, a generic term used to describe the interception and analysis of telephone calls and other communications intelligence, as well as electronic emissions—everything from wiretapping telephones to studying the particles emitted by missiles in test flights. Sometimes these methods can be abused, as when they are used to spy on Americans without proper judicial warrants. SIGINT collection became a topic of national debate in 2013–2014, stirred by revelations by an inside government leaker (Edward J. Snowden, who fled to Russia) that the NSA had adopted "metadata" programs within the United States to collect information about the communications contacts of American citizens. Several authors examine this scandal later in the book.

A further "int" of significance is IMINT, or imagery intelligence, often known by the acronym GEOINT (geospatial-intelligence). In simple terms, IMINT or GEOINT refer chiefly to photographs taken by surveillance satellites and reconnaissance airplanes, either piloted or unpiloted. The interception of telephone conversations (SIGINT) can be revealing, but as the old saying goes, a picture can be worth a thousand words. Measurement and signature intelligence (MASINT) provides yet another method for learning about the activities of America's adversaries overseas. Here the focus is primarily on the weapons capabilities of a foreign nation or terrorist organization, which can be clandestinely examined through the use of technical procedures. One MASINT approach is to secretly place a form of litmus-paper near the target to determine, say, if a factory is producing aspirin or sarin nerve gas.

Not all the information needed by policymakers is acquired through HUMINT, SIGINT, GEOINT, or MASINT; indeed, the overwhelming majority—sometimes as much as 95 percent of the information that appears in classified government reports—is already in the public domain. This open-source intelligence (OSINT) must be sorted through, organized, and integrated with the secretly gained information. The ultimate objective of all the ints is to provide a nation's leaders with a "decision advantage" in world affairs—a motto inscribed on the walls of the DNI's headquarters in northern Virginia. One of the most difficult challenges in the complex process of collection, analysis, and dissemination of information comes in the final step: at the intersection between intelligence professionals and policymakers—two groups of individuals who often have sharply different training, aspirations, and cultures. Jack Davis, a seasoned CIA analyst, sheds light in Chapter Six on the heart and soul of the intelligence trade: the analysis or interpretation of information gathered through a synergistic combination of all of the ints. He also probes the sometimes turbulent relationship between intelligence officers and the policymakers they serve, the vital intelligence producer–consumer linkage that is further explored by James J. Wirtz in Chapter Seven. In hopes of extracting lessons on intelligence collection and analysis from recent intelligence disasters, British scholar Peter Gill dissects in Chapter Eight the failures associated with the 9/11 attacks and the poor judgments made by intelligence and policy officials about alleged Iraqi WMD.

Covert Action

The third section, entitled "Covert Action," enters an especially controversial compartment of intelligence: the means by which the United States attempts not just to gather and analyze information from around the world—hard enough—but to manipulate global events through secret activities in the advancement of America's best interests. An ambiguous passage of the National Security Act of 1947 charged the National Security Council (NSC), the group of bosses—the president, vice president, secretary of defense, and secretary of state—in charge of the sixteen U.S. secret agencies (see Appendix), to "perform such other functions and duties related to intelligence [over and beyond collection-and-analysis] affecting the national security as the National Security Council may from time to time direct."[3] The phrase "other functions and duties" left the door ajar for launching the CIA (and more recently the Pentagon) on a wide range of covert actions around the world.

Covert action (CA), sometimes referred to as the "quiet option," is based on the supposition that this secret approach to foreign affairs is likely to be less noisy and obtrusive than sending in the Marines. Sometimes professional practitioners also refer to covert action as the "third option," a foreign policy alternative situated somewhere between diplomacy, on the one hand, and open warfare, on the other hand. As former Secretary of State and National Security Adviser Henry Kissinger once put it, "We need an intelligence community that, in certain complicated situations, can defend the American national interest in the gray areas where military operations are not suitable and diplomacy cannot operate."[4] Still others prefer the euphemism "special activities" to describe covert action. Whatever the variation in terminology, the goal of covert action remains constant: to influence events overseas, secretly, in support of American foreign policy.

Covert action operations are often grouped according to four broad categories: propaganda, political, economic, and paramilitary (PM) activities. An example of a propaganda operation was the CIA's use of Radio Free Europe during the Cold War to transmit anti-communist themes into nations behind the Iron Curtain. An illustration of a political covert action during the Cold War was the CIA's clandestine funneling of funds to the anti-communist Christian Democratic Party in Italy. An economic example: the CIA attempted to destroy electric power stations in Nicaragua during the 1980s as a means of undermining the Marxist-oriented Sandinista regime in that Central American nation. PM operations can include everything from assassination plots against foreign heads of state or terrorist leaders to arming and guiding pro-American insurgent armies in one country or another. Little wonder this has been a controversial subject.

Gregory F. Treverton introduces the reader to the ins and outs of covert action in the first entry of this section (Chapter Nine). His essay is followed by William J. Daugherty's look at political and economic examples of covert action (Chapter Ten); Jennifer D. Kibbe's exploration of the Defense Department's entry into this domain (Chapter Eleven); Judge James E. Baker's legal analysis of covert action (Chapter Twelve); and, winding up this section, former diplomat John D. Stempel's contrast between America's use of covert action and diplomatic initiatives (Chapter Thirteen).

Counterintelligence

A third intelligence mission—after collection-and-analysis and covert action—is counterintelligence (CI) and its associated activity, counterterrorism (CT). They are the focus in Part IV of the book, entitled "Counterintelligence." Like covert action, CI went without specific mention in the National Security Act of 1947. By the early 1950s, however, it had similarly achieved a status of importance as an intelligence mission. Counterintelligence specialists soon waged nothing less than a secret war against antagonistic intelligence services (especially the Soviet foreign intelligence and military intelligence services, the KGB and the GRU, respectively); and after the end of the Cold War in 1991, CT specialists would focus on efforts to block terrorists who target the United States and its allies. Explaining why the missions of counterintelligence and counterterrorism evolved, a CI expert has pointed out that "in the absence of an effective U.S. counterintelligence program, [adversaries of democracy] function in what is largely a benign environment."[5]

The practice of counterintelligence consists of two matching halves: security and counterespionage. Security is the passive or defensive side of CI, involving such methods as background investigations, fences, sentries, alarms, badges, watchdogs, cybersecurity, and polygraphs (lie detection machines). Counterespionage (CE) is the offensive or aggressive side of CI. The most effective CE operation is the infiltration of an American agent or "mole" into the enemy camp, whether a hostile intelligence service or a terrorist cell—a ploy called a penetration. Thus, the practice of security is, according to one of America's top counterintelligence experts, "All that concerns perimeter defense, badges, knowing everything you have to know about your own people," whereas the CE side "involves knowing all about intelligence services—hostile intelligence services: their people, their installations, their methods, and their operations."[6]

Stan A. Taylor addresses these issues in the first essay in this part of the book (Chapter Fourteen). Then, in Chapter Fifteen, Athan Theoharis lays out the various challenges involved in keeping the United States free of foreign spies and terrorists. In the next two essays (Chapters Sixteen and Seventeen), Richard L. Russell and Jennifer Sims discuss the ups and downs of trying to establish an effective U.S. counterterrorism response, an objective complicated by the fragmentation of authority and widely differing cultures among America's intelligence agencies.

Intelligence and Accountability

The chapters in Part V, entitled "Intelligence and Accountability," stem from a concern that secret power might be misused by those in high office. This danger was underscored in 1975 when Congress discovered that U.S. secret agencies were guilty of spying against law-abiding American citizens; and again in 1987 during the Iran-*contra* affair, when some elements of the intelligence community violated the public trust by ignoring intelligence laws related to covert actions in Iran and Nicaragua.

The United States has been one of the few nations in the world to conduct an ongoing experiment in bringing democratic accountability to secret government activities. Democracy and spying don't mix together well. Secrecy runs counter to democratic openness, while at the same time openness possesses a threat to the success of espionage operations. Democracies need intelligence agencies to acquire information that may protect citizens, but these same citizens must be concerned about the possibility that secret agencies may be used against them for political objectives by unethical leaders. Until 1975, the nation's remedy for the tension between intelligence gathering and democracy was to place trust in the intelligence agencies and hope for the best. Elected officials treated the secret services as exceptional organizations, immune from the checks and balances envisioned by the framers of the Constitution. Lawmakers were content with this arrangement because if an intelligence operation went awry (like the CIA's paramilitary invasion of Cuba in 1961), they could duck responsibility. When James R. Schlesinger, DCI in 1973, attempted to inform John Stennis (D, Mississippi, a key member of the Senate Armed Services Committee) about an approaching CIA operation, the senator stopped him short: "No, no, my boy, don't tell me. Just go ahead and do it, but I don't want to know."[7]

This attitude on Capitol Hill—overlook rather than oversight—underwent a dramatic turnabout in December of 1974, however, when the *New York Times* reported on allegations of CIA spying at home and questionable covert actions in Chile. Congress might have waved aside the revelations about Chile as just another Cold War necessity in the struggle against regimes leaning toward Moscow, but spying on American citizens—voters—was another matter altogether. In January 1975, President Gerald R. Ford created a presidential Commission on CIA Activities within the United States (the Rockefeller Commission, led by his vice president, Nelson Rockefeller). Later that month, the Senate established a select committee to investigate intelligence activities. The committee was headed by Frank Church, a Democrat from Idaho, and became known as the Church Committee (I served as Church's assistant). A counterpart House committee, led by Representative Otis Pike, a Democrat from New York, began a separate investigation the following month.

These panels found many more improprieties than they had expected. Not only had the CIA engaged in domestic spying in violation of its charter (Operation CHAOS), so had the FBI and several military intelligence units. Furthermore, the FBI had carried out secret operations, known collectively as COINTELPRO, against thousands of civil rights activists, as well as members of the Ku Klux Klan and Vietnam War dissenters. The objective was to make the lives of these individuals miserable by disrupting their marriages and employment. The Bureau even attempted to blackmail Dr. Martin Luther King Jr., America's top civil rights leader, into committing suicide. Church Committee investigators also discovered CIA assassination plots against foreign leaders, along with efforts to topple President Salvador Allende of Chile—even though he had been democratically elected.

These revelations convinced lawmakers that the time had come to bring accountability into the dark recesses of America's government. Congress established intelligence oversight committees in both chambers—the Senate Select Committee on Intelligence (SSCI) in 1976 and the House Permanent Select Committee on Intelligence (HPSCI) in 1977. Further, with the Intelligence Oversight Act of 1980, lawmakers required advanced (*ante facto*, as opposed to *ex post facto*) reports on all secret intelligence operations so that Congress could evaluate the clandestine initiatives *before* they were implemented. The new committees pored over intelligence budgets, held regular hearings (mostly in closed session to protect spy sources and methods), and seriously examined the performance of America's intelligence agencies. The committees even enjoyed subpoena powers that allowed them to demand testimony from executive branch officials and other witnesses. No other nation has ever so thoroughly applied democratic principles to its secret services, although a number of foreign capitals are now beginning to follow the leadership of the United States in the direction of greater intelligence supervision.

Since 1975, this effort toward greater intelligence accountability in the United States has evolved in fits and starts. Sometimes lawmakers have insisted on close supervision of the secret agencies, as when they enacted the Oversight Act of 1980 with its stringent prior reporting requirements for covert operations, or when a series of laws in the 1980s (the Boland Amendments, named after their chief sponsor, Edward P. Boland, a Democrat from Massachusetts and the first HPSCI chair) sought to end covert actions in Nicaragua. At other times, members of Congress have loosened the reins of accountability—for example, repealing in 1985 a prohibition against covert action in Angola. On still other occasions, Congress has concentrated less on legislative restrictions than on helping the intelligence agencies improve their security and performance, as with the Intelligence Identities Act of 1982 that prohibited exposing the names of undercover intelligence officers.

The Iran-*contra* scandal of 1987 produced a major setback to this new oversight, as the Reagan administration bypassed most of the accountability rules and statutes in its conduct of a covert war in Nicaragua against the will of Congress as expressed in the Boland Amendments. The scandal was an alert to lawmakers. They responded by enacting the Intelligence Oversight Act of 1991, which further tightened intelligence supervision by clarifying reporting requirements and defining "covert action" in greater detail. Lawmakers also set up a more rigorous Office of Inspector General (IG) in the CIA, confirmed by and accountable to Congress.

This pulling and tugging has continued, most recently over whether President George W. Bush violated the Foreign Intelligence Surveillance Act (FISA) of 1978 by conducting warrantless wiretaps as part of the war against terrorism in the aftermath of the 9/11 attacks. The FIS legislation required warrants; but the White House claimed (when the secret operation leaked to the *New York Times* in 2005) that the law had become too cumbersome and, besides, the president had inherent authority—so claimed the second Bush administration—to conduct the war against terrorism as the White House saw fit. In 2006 and 2008, lawmakers approved a diluted set of restrictions related to the NSA's gathering of intelligence inside the United States. In 2013, however, the public began to react against the bulk collection of metadata on the communications practices of American citizens, and in 2014, a full-fledged national debate on the subject began to unfold. The NSA hoped through its metadata programs to ferret out terrorists by a collection dragnet thrown over the entire United States. Critics viewed this approach as anathema to democratic principles and ineffectual as well, while NSA officials maintained that massive surveillance of this kind (a form of "big data") was a useful tool for catching terrorists inside the United States.[8]

This debate aside for the moment (several authors address the issue in this volume), one thing is certain: the intelligence agencies in the United States are now very much a part of the nation's system of checks and balances. Americans want and deserve both civil liberties and a secure defense against threats; therefore, the search continues for an appropriate mix of liberty and security, democracy and intelligence effectiveness—precisely the topic of this section in the book.

The set of chapters on intelligence accountability are introduced with an essay (Chapter Eighteen) by David M. Barrett, the foremost authority on the history of accountability in the early years of modern U.S. intelligence (1947 to 1963). Next, Glenn Hastedt takes the reader into the counterterrorism thicket in Washington, DC, revealing how politics and America's avant-garde experiment in accountability influence both counterintelligence and counterterrorism (Chapter Nineteen). The premier scholarly expert on the National Security Agency, Matthew M. Aid, reviews the problems and the benefits associated with SIGINT and reveals the dilemmas of accountability posed by this super-secret agency (Chapter Twenty). Lastly, Mark Phythian brings the book to a close with a chapter on the British experience with intelligence accountability (Chapter Twenty-One).

Here, then, is what the reader will find in this comprehensive look at strategic intelligence. The contributors and the editor hope the book will help educate the public about the importance of intelligence activities, as well as stimulate scholars around the world to join this vital field of scholarship. I am pleased to acknowledge my gratitude to Steve Catalano, the editor at ABC-CLIO who helped nurture the project forward from conception to completion; to Leena S. Johnson for her indispensable encouragement and support; to the authors of these essays for their outstanding scholarship and their cooperation in keeping the publishing train running on time; and to the teams at BookComp, Inc. and ABC-CLIO for all their help.

This book is dedicated to the memory of Harry Howe Ransom (1922–2014), mentor, friend, and leader on the road toward advancing the scholarly study of strategic intelligence.

Notes

1. Quoted by Sen. Frank Church (D, Idaho), in *Congressional Record* (January 27, 1976), p. 1165.

2. *Fact Book on Intelligence* (Washington, DC: CIA Office of Public Affairs, April 1983), p. 17.

3. National Security Act of 1947, signed on July 26, 1947 (P.L. 97-222; 50 U.S.C. 403, Sec. 102).

4. Comment, *Evening News*, NBC (January 13, 1978).

5. My interview with an FBI counterintelligence specialist, Washington, DC (May 16, 1975).

6. My interview with Raymond Rocca, CIA/CI specialist, Washington, DC (November 23, 1975).

7. My interview with James R. Schlesinger, Washington, DC (June 16, 1994).

8. For a flavor of the debate, see Loch K. Johnson, "Restoring the Balance: Privacy, Security and the NSA," *World Politics Review* (November 2013), pp. 10–15; and General Michael V. Hayden (a former NSA and CIA director), "Beyond Snowden: An NSA Reality Check," *World Affairs Journal* (January–February 2014): http://www.worldaffairsjournal.org.

Part I: Understanding the Hidden Side of Government

CHAPTER ONE

An Introduction to the Intelligence Studies Literature

Loch K. Johnson

Before the "Year of Intelligence"

IN 1975, PROFESSOR HARRY HOWE RANSOM OF Vanderbilt University, a top intelligence researcher and a pioneer in the field noted, that he had been going after the subject with a pick and shovel for years, when—all of a sudden—various government investigative panels began to use bulldozers to unearth a mountain of new information.[1] He was referring to the inquiries conducted by the Church Committee in the U.S. Senate (led by Frank Church, D, Idaho), the Pike Committee in the U.S. House (led by Otis Pike, D, New York), and the Rockefeller Commission in the Ford White House (led by Vice President Nelson Rockefeller), all stimulated by *New York Times* revelations in 1974 that the Central Intelligence Agency (CIA) had spied on American citizens over the past decade.[2] These investigative panels had indeed added significantly to the extant literature on America's secret agencies, with the reports from the Church Committee alone rising in a stack some five feet high.[3]

This "Year of Intelligence" (1975, less affectionately known by some intelligence officers as the "Intelligence Wars") did represent a watershed in a number of ways. For example, before 1975 the Congress permitted the CIA and its sister agencies in the "intelligence community" to carry out operations at home and abroad without much legislative supervision. The allegations by the *New York Times* of domestic spying changed all that, as lawmakers scurried to prevent future intelligence abuses and allay the fears of folks back home (voters) that the CIA had become an American gestapo. The government of the United States began its ongoing experiment in intelligence accountability, now widely emulated in countries around the world.[4] The goal was to seek a better balance between security concerns, on the one hand, which require the existence of efficient intelligence agencies, and liberty, on the other hand, which rests upon safeguards against the abuse of secret power.

The year 1975 was a watershed in another sense, too, related to the extent of research documents and studies available on intelligence. As Professor Ransom's comment suggests, before this *annis mirabilis,* the intelligence studies cupboard was, if not bare, then scantily stocked.[5] The most noteworthy efforts since the creation of the modern American intelligence system after World War II came from Sherman Kent, a Yale University history professor known for his keen intellect and salty tongue, and who would later become an important organizing force inside the CIA for the development of its analytic capabilities; from Lyman B. Kirkpatrick Jr., another CIA official; from Professor Ransom, a professor at Harvard University when he first became interested in intelligence studies and who did much to inform the general public as well as scholars about intelligence in those early years; from Roger Hilsman, a government official and political scientist; and from journalists David Kahn and David Wise.[6]

Other significant works consisted chiefly of memoirs and biographies of various spies and spymasters,[7] along with examinations of intelligence successes and failures,[8] the difficulties of disseminating intelligence to busy and sometimes blinkered policy officials,[9] studies of Soviet intelligence operations against the United States,[10] exposés (of uneven reliability),[11] sporadic academic books or scholarly journal articles in the spirit of Kent and Ransom,[12] the rare textbook that devoted serious attention to the subject,[13] and the occasional newspaper article providing an in-depth look into one of the secret agencies.[14]

Both before and after 1975, much of the literature on intelligence has been speculative, unreliable, and sometimes wholly without merit; the reader and researcher have to be especially wary about books and articles claiming to understand the secret machinations of government agencies hidden behind guarded buildings and barbed-wire fences, not to mention multiple veils of classification. Since 1975, though, the availability of reliable documentation and research findings on intelligence has expanded dramatically—one could say exploded—and this chapter outlines some (but by no means all) of the notable features of this new research terrain.

After the "Year of Intelligence"

The literature on intelligence in 1975 is vast and difficult to capture in a chapter, even one that concentrates only on the literature in English. Indeed, this bibliography should be viewed more as a sampler than any effort to be comprehensive; many a good work will not be mentioned because of space limitations, and the reader is encouraged to consult literature reviews of greater length.[15] The objective here is simply to give the reader a sense of the chief topics and some of the major works that have addressed them.

On top of a stunning proliferation of books and articles on intelligence since the watershed year, the field has also witnessed the emergence of credible scholarly journals dedicated to intelligence studies.[16] To facilitate an examination of this literature, this chapter groups an array of studies into the following four broad categories: intelligence history, structure, and theory; intelligence missions (collection-and-analysis, counterintelligence, and covert action); intelligence accountability, ethics, and reform; and intelligence leadership and management.

Intelligence History, Structure, and Theory

British scholars have been particularly adept at offering insightful histories of intelligence within both the United Kingdom and the United States, as well as for other countries. The leaders have been the Cambridge University historian Christopher Andrew and King's College, London, professor Lawrence Freedman,[17] but they have enjoyed good company with Aldrich;[18] Cradock, who provides a practitioner's point of view;[19] Davies;[20] Foot;[21] Hennessy;[22] Jackson;[23] Jeffreys-Jones;[24] Ranelagh;[25] Shukman;[26] Stevenson;[27] and West.[28]

American, Canadian, and German scholars have provided useful intelligence histories, too. Samples include, on the U.S. side, works by Corson,[29] Gaddis,[30] Handel,[31] Leary,[32] May,[33] Naftali,[34] Richelson,[35] Rudgers,[36] Smith,[37] Troy,[38] Warner,[39] Winks,[40] and Zegart;[41] on the Canadian side, Charters and Ferris,[42] as well as Farson, Stafford, and Wark, plus Farson (joined by British scholars Gill and Phythian, as well as the Israeli scholar Shpiro);[43] and on the German side, Krieger.[44] Two government reports contain reliable histories of the CIA, prepared by Karalekas and by McNeil;[45] and, for histories of one of the most traumatic years in American intelligence, 1975, see Johnson, and Smist.[46]

Organizational blueprints ("wiring diagrams") usually fail to reveal much about how intelligence organizations actually function, but they are a starting point. With respect to the United States, Lowenthal and Richelson have laid out the linkages among America's sixteen intelligence agencies[47]—although new intelligence managers are inclined to change the names of various component parts, which makes the writing on this aspect of intelligence highly perishable. Cline outlined the evolution of the CIA as an organization from 1947 to 1981, and Absher, Desch, and Popadiuk trace the history of the President's Intelligence Advisory Board (PIAB).[48] Hastedt and Zegart examined organizational influences on intelligence failures, while Rob Johnston probed into the question of how institutional cultural norms affect America's intelligence agencies.[49] Andrew published studies on the organization of both British and Soviet intelligence, and Jeffrey also published on British intelligence.[50] A significant structural question is the relationship between the intelligence services of different nations. In one important example of research in this area, Richelson and Ball have explored ties between the United Kingdom and the United States.[51]

Theories have been difficult to construct in the intelligence field because the empirical data base for constructing and testing theories still remains relatively thin. Nonetheless, a number of scholars have made tentative forays into this uncertain terrain. Illustrations include the work of Betts,[52] Davies,[53] Handel,[54] Herman,[55] Hulnick,[56] Loch K. Johnson,[57] Rob Johnson,[58] Kahn,[59] Laqueur,[60] Robertson,[61] Shulsky,[62] and a special issue of *Intelligence and National Security* edited by Len Scott and Peter Jackson.[63] The question of transparency, the flipside of secrecy, is addressed by Lord and Finel.[64] Overall, the studies on intelligence theory find that the discipline remains in its infancy, holding great promise for scholars interested in blazing new trails.[65]

Intelligence Missions

Intelligence may be sorted into three primary missions: the collection and interpretation ("analysis") of information; the protection of government secrets against hostile intelligence services and other threats ("counterintelligence"); and the clandestine manipulation of events in foreign lands on behalf of a nation's interests, through the use of propaganda, political activities, economic disruption, and paramilitary operations (collectively known in the United States as "covert action" or "special activities"). Each of these missions has attracted the attention of intelligence scholars, especially collection, analysis, and dissemination—the heart and soul of intelligence.

Collection, Analysis, and Dissemination

The collection of intelligence relies on technical means (satellites and reconnaissance airplanes, for example—so-called technical intelligence or

TECHINT, in the professional acronym); on human means (classic espionage or human intelligence—HUMINT); and on the sifting of information available in the open literature (newspapers, public speeches, and the like—sometimes referred to as open-source intelligence or OSINT). In the U.S. experience, many of the best contributions from spy machines have come from relatively inexpensive unmanned aerial vehicles (UAVs), notably the Predator, which in 2003–2006 proved effective for scouring the Iraqi and Afghani countryside in search of insurgents. On occasion, far more costly surveillance satellites have demonstrated their value, too, by intercepting revealing telephone conversations among terrorists and other enemies (a method known as "signals intelligence" or SIGINT, a term for describing the capture of communications from one person or group to another, as well as other forms of electronic transmissions—such as emissions from rockets as they fly in the air).

Moreover, satellite photographic images or other photographs ("imagery intelligence" or IMINT, known also as "geospatial intelligence" or GEOINT) of, say, Russian and Chinese missile sites or North Korean troop movements, continue to be valuable for the security of the United States. Still, in the case of terrorism, it would be more advantageous to have a human agent well placed inside the upper reaches of the Al Qaeda organization; such a HUMINT agent ("asset") would be worth a dozen multibillion-dollar satellites.

Aim, Bamford, Kahn, and Keefe have examined the arcane technology of SIGINT in the United States;[66] Burrows writes on space surveillance;[67] and Richelson offers insights into a broad range of TECHINT developments in U.S. intelligence.[68] While chronicling its successes and failures since 1947, Hitz spells out many of the key dilemmas in America's practice of HUMINT,[69] and Gerecht provides a persuasive critique that the United States has ignored the use of nonofficial cover (NOC) for HUMINT operational officers overseas, thereby missing many opportunities to understand foreign societies by having personnel out in the field rather than inside U.S. embassies.[70] In the United States, leading experts on OSINT are Bean, Mercado, and Steele; and, in the United Kingdom, Gibson.[71]

At the core of intelligence is the challenge of analysis. Here the goal is to bring insight to the information that has been collected and processed. The method is straightforward: hire smart people to sift through all the information available in an attempt to predict what events may happen next in the world. Jervis has published influential research about the difficulties of carrying out analysis.[72] So has his colleague at Columbia University, Betts, who cautions—in one of the most widely read pieces on intelligence analysis—that when it comes to predicting events in the world, one must develop a "tolerance for disaster."[73] A CIA analyst, Jack Davis, has explored the perspective of policymakers on the analytic process in an in-depth interview of a key U.S. ambassador and recipient of many intelligence reports over the years;[74] Knorr has authored a case study of CIA analysis prior to the Cuban missile crisis in 1962;[75] Bar-Joseph and Kahana, additional case studies on the Yom Kippur War of 1973 (from the Israeli perspective);[76] Prados, a study on U.S. intelligence assessments of the Soviet Union;[77] and Russell, a report on the performance of intelligence analysts before and during the first Persian Gulf War.[78] For an exploration of unconventional analytic topics that have come before the U.S. intelligence agencies in the aftermath of the Cold War (for example, environmental and global health intelligence), see Johnson (2000).[79]

Once information is analyzed, it is ready to be passed along to policy officials. This task is known as "dissemination." Perhaps the greatest paradox of intelligence is that so much effort and funding go into the gathering of information for policymakers, only to have them ignore it. Some of the best assistant secretaries of defense and state have conceded that they spent, at best, five minutes a day scanning intelligence reports; they were simply too overwhelmed with other obligations. These pressures would be even more constraining for men and women higher up the policy hierarchy. The first challenge of dissemination, then, is to catch the attention of busy leaders, and this is why the marketing of intelligence is critical.

In marketing their products to consumers, the secret agencies confront several potential obstacles. Policymakers may choose to twist ("cook" or "spin") intelligence to fit their own political views or ideological predispositions, a distortion of information known as "politicization." Intelligence officers themselves may succumb to the temptation to slant information to suit the needs of policymakers as a way of advancing their careers by attracting favorable attention from powerful political figures—a phenomenon known as "intelligence to please." Fortunately, this temptation on the analyst's side of the equation occurs infrequently, because most analysts are imbued with a sense of professional ethics that shuns the practice of twisting information to please politicians.

More common is politicization on the consumer side: policymakers bending the facts to support policy objectives. Speaking truth to power is a notoriously difficult endeavor. Those in power often do not want to hear information that runs counter to their policy preferences; hence, they sometimes distort intelligence reports. An illustration is "cherry-picking," whereby decision makers select from intelligence reports only those snippets of information and analysis that uphold their stated policy positions, ignoring countervailing facts or conclusions.

Some government officials have been known to dismiss entire intelligence reports, as President Lyndon B. Johnson did with CIA analyses that came to a dismal prognosis about the likelihood of U.S. military victory in the Vietnam War, or as the second Bush administration did with CIA reports that found no connections between Al Qaeda and Saddam's regime in Iraq. In such instances, the unenviable but vital responsibility of intelligence managers is to call policy officials to account for their distortions, publicly if necessary.

Writings by Lowenthal,[80] Ransom,[81] and Wirtz[82] reveal the importance of understanding the issues of intelligence dissemination. They point to the need to maintain a high wall between policy officials and intelligence officers. Such a wall is necessary not in the sense of preventing communications between the two groups about intelligence collection and analysis priorities, which is important but, rather, to curb political ties between the two groups and the twisting of intelligence to meet policy objectives. The need for a wall notwithstanding, there is a sense among intelligence scholars that intelligence officers and law enforcement officials do need to reach out to each other and work together more closely in protecting the United States against security threats.[83]

Exploring still another angle of consumer–producer relations, Hastedt has written on the question of "public intelligence"—how intelligence goes beyond the narrow consumer–producer domain to enter the realm of public discussion.[84]

Counterintelligence

Protecting a nation's secrets—everything from the names of agents overseas to the methods used for spying on others—is the domain of counterintelligence. Some of the leading research here focuses on failures to stop the infiltration of "moles" into one's own intelligence services. For example, the journalist David Wise has devoted much of his professional career to the preparation of case studies on American moles, most recently the CIA traitor Aldrich H. Ames and the Federal Bureau of Investigation (FBI) traitor Robert Hanssen; and James J. Wirtz has explored the challenge of deception operations.[85]

A British writer, Tom Mangold, offers the most thorough study to date of America's premier spy catcher during the Cold War, James J. Angleton, chief of Counterintelligence at the CIA from 1954 to 1974.[86] Taylor and Snow examine more broadly the questions of why intelligence officers become traitors and how they are uncovered;[87] Peake looks at counterintelligence and the Office of Strategic Services (OSS), exploring the extent to which the United States was infiltrated by Soviet spies during World War II;[88]

Batvinis, Olmsted, and Sibley each explore the presence of communist spies inside the United States at the beginning of the Cold War.[89] West brings together a valuable overview on the subject of spy catching, and Glees looks at East German intelligence operations aimed at the United Kingdom.[90]

A subset of the counterintelligence literature is comprised of studies on counterterrorism. This field is vast and growing exponentially since the attacks of September 11, 2001. Another survey like the one in this chapter could be prepared for the counterterrorism literature alone, but for starters, see Gressang; Mahadevan; Mayer; Von Knop, Neisser, and Van Creveld; and Shultz and Dew.[91]

Covert Action

Covert action may be defined as those activities carried out by the CIA to secretly influence and manipulate events abroad. This approach is often referred to as the "third option"—in between sending in the Marines, on the one hand, and relying on the diplomatic corps to achieve one's goals on the other. The use of military force is "noisy" and likely to draw a quick reaction from adversaries, as well as stir widespread debate at home; and diplomacy can be notoriously slow and often ineffectual. Thus, covert action has had a special appeal to some presidents and their aides. With this tool, they can move rapidly and in relative quiet, avoiding lengthy public discussions over tactics and broader objectives (hence, the "quiet option" is another euphemism for covert action).

In the United States, covert action has often failed, as with the Bay of Pigs operation against Cuba in 1961 and the Iran-*contra* scandal in 1986. The latter especially discredited covert action because the Reagan administration carried out CIA paramilitary operations against Nicaragua despite strong congressional opposition and a law preventing such activities in that Central American nation. After the Iran-*contra* episode, the budget for covert action plummeted to its lowest levels: less than 1 percent of the CIA's annual budget. It would take the terrorist attacks against the United States on September 11, 2001, to stimulate a renewed interest in this approach to secret foreign policy. After 9/11, funding for covert action began a rapid rise in the name of combating world terrorism. In 2001–2002, the use of CIA paramilitary operations against the Taliban regime in Afghanistan, in tandem with overt military operations by the indigenous Northern Alliance and U.S. bombing missions, opened a new—and, in this case, quite successful—chapter in America's reliance on paramilitary covert actions.

Covert action is particularly hard to research because most of the archives on this subject remain locked up in the vaults of the CIA.

Nevertheless, in the United States, scholars have been able to ferret out enough information to provide a fairly good sense of this super-secret domain. Among the leading researchers are Coll,[92] Daugherty,[93] Godson,[94] Immerman,[95] Johnson,[96] Knott,[97] O'Brien,[98] Prados,[99] Reisman and Baker,[100] Treverton,[101] Weissman,[102] and Wyden (on the Bay of Pigs fiasco).[103] Valuable, too, are the hearings and reports of the Church Committee, published in 1975 and 1976,[104] as well as revealing case studies of covert action in Latin America, written by Grow, by Roosevelt, and by Wise and Ross.[105] Overviews by CIA insiders can be found in Baer, Crumpton, Scheuer, Rositzke, and Shackley;[106] and journalist Bob Woodward has given his impressions of the CIA and covert action during the Reagan years.[107] Two prominent members of Congress have recalled their experiences during the Iran-*contra* investigation into covert action in Nicaragua.[108] And on the relationship between CIA covert action and military special operations, see Kibbe.[109]

Accountability, Ethics, and Reform

In democracies, there is a belief that even secret agencies—perhaps most especially secret agencies—ought to be held responsible for their actions, as an important check on possible abuses of power. The means by which they are held responsible is known as accountability or "oversight"—the review of executive branch programs by lawmakers, judges, inspectors general, and special investigative panels. The literature in this subfield of intelligence studies is growing, just as in all the other subfields. In the United States, among the chief examples are Barrett (covering the early years of the Cold War),[110] Hitz,[111] Johnson,[112] Kaiser,[113] Koh,[114] Olmsted,[115] Oseth,[116] and Treverton;[117] and, with special attention to the question of civil liberties, Commager,[118] Donner,[119] Elliff,[120] Morgan,[121] Schwarz,[122] Theoharis,[123] and Wise.[124] Snider looks at relations between the CIA and Congress; Manget has explored the neglected topic of judicial oversight in the United States.[125] On intelligence oversight in the United Kingdom, Gill and Phythian have been leading researchers, along with Glees, Davies, and Morrison.[126] Whitaker examines the threat to individual liberty and privacy posed by growing government surveillance in modern societies.[127] Recently, scholars studying accountability have tried to incorporate a systematic comparative dimension into their work, contrasting the systems of oversight in different countries (see Born, Johnson, and Leigh[128]).

The overall conclusion reached by most studies on intelligence accountability is that oversight is often overlooked by lawmakers, who perceive few incentives for laboring behind closed doors to review intelligence programs when their re-election depends on a more public display of legislative activity.[129] The unfortunate end result of this inattention is an absence of checks on the secret agencies, which can result in intelligence failures like 9/11 and the Iraqi weapons of mass destruction (WMD), scandals like the CIA/FBI domestic spying finally revealed by the media and Congress in 1974–1975, and the Iran-*contra* affair disclosed in 1986.

Less researched is the ethical dimension of intelligence—an oxymoron for some who believe that no bright lines should exist between the safety of a nation and the gathering of intelligence or the use of covert action to advance national interests. Among the most thoughtful offerings in this area have been from Barry, Godfrey, and Herman, each of whom demonstrates that bright lines do, and should, exist for intelligence (just as with a nation's war-making powers).[130]

Intelligence reform has long been a topic of interest to scholars and citizens alike. Since the CIA was established in 1947, the reform literature in the United States has steadily commented on the need to improve various aspects of American intelligence. These commentaries have usually been in the form of reports from numerous congressional investigative panels and presidential commissions through the years that have dealt with intelligence issues.[131] Beyond these official government critiques are several analyses by U.S. scholars, many stimulated by the tragic 9/11 intelligence failure.[132]

The conclusion reached by most of these studies is that the United States needs a strong director of National Intelligence (DNI), not the weak one yielded by legislation in December 2004 (the Intelligence Reform and Terrorism Prevention Act); and that America's intelligence agencies must work together more closely to share information about threats facing the United States, eschewing their cultural proclivities toward parochialism. In a phrase, intelligence consolidation must replace the current dispersal of authority.

Intelligence Leadership and Management

As the consensus view on the need for stronger leadership for the U.S. intelligence "community" suggests, scholars and reformers alike see leadership and management as important dimensions of intelligence. A few scholarly studies exist on this topic.[133] By and large, though, the most insightful explorations of intelligence leadership and management have come from the experiences of the individuals who have led the intelligence agencies—memoirs by America's directors of Central Intelligence (DCIs, the title of the nation's intelligence chief from 1947 until the 2004 law that replaced this office with a DNI) or other key officials in the world of espionage.[134] One portrait that emerges from these insider accounts is of a secret world where intelligence bureaucrats enjoy considerable discretionary powers, with intelligence managers finding it difficult to rein in the offices and bureaus beneath them in the organizational hierarchy. The classic case is the Operations Directorate in the CIA—notoriously resistant to supervision by managers on the Agency's Seventh Floor.[135]

An important aspect of intelligence management is the question of government secrecy. Reformists have written extensively about the excessive use of secrecy in the United States, which they consider anathema to the fundamental principles of a democratic, open society.[136]

The Future Research Agenda for Intelligence Studies

As this bibliographic chapter indicates, the field of intelligence studies is broad and increasingly insightful; yet, from the point of view of trying to understand how to make intelligence less prone to failure, much research remains to be done. For scholars who may be interested in helping establish a new field of study, as well as aiding the democracies in protecting themselves more effectively against hostile forces, few fields of study can match this one in fascination and challenge.

Notes

1. Comment to me, Washington, DC (December 20, 1975).

2. See J. Leiper Freeman, "Investigating the Executive Intelligence: The Fate of the Pike Committee," *Capitol Studies* (Fall 1977), pp. 103–117; Loch K. Johnson, *Season of Inquiry* (Lexington: University Press of Kentucky, 1985) and "Congressional Supervision of America's Secret Agencies: The Experience and Legacy of the Church Committee," *Public Administration Review* 64 (January/February 2004), pp. 3–14; and Frank J. Smist Jr., *Congress Oversees the United States Intelligence Community* (Knoxville: University of Tennessee Press, 1976). On the leaks to the *New York Times* that led to the intelligence investigations of 1975, see John Prados, *The Family Jewels: The CIA, Secrecy, and Presidential Power* (Austin: University of Texas Press, 2013).

3. For the Church Committee reports, see especially Select Committee to Study Governmental Operations with Respect to Intelligence Activities, Final Report, 94th Cong., 2d Sess. Sen. Rept. No. 94-755, 6 vols. (Washington, DC: Government Printing Office, 1976), "Alleged Assassination Plots Involving Foreign Leaders," Interim Report, S. Rept. No. 94-465 (Washington, DC: Government Printing Office, November 20, 1975), and Anne Karalekas, "History

of the Central Intelligence Agency," Supplementary Detailed Staff Reports on Foreign and Military Intelligence, S. Rept. No. 94-755, vol. 4 (Washington, DC: Government Printing Office, April 23, 1976), pp. 1–107. The top-secret Pike Committee Report was leaked by a still unknown source and can be found in "The Report on the CIA That President Ford Doesn't Want You to Read," *Village Voice* 21 (1976). For the Rockefeller Commission Report, see Commission on CIA Activities within the United States, Report to the President (Washington, DC: Government Printing Office, June 1975).

4. Hans Born, Loch K. Johnson, and Ian Leigh, eds., *Who's Watching the Spies? Establishing Intelligence Service Accountability* (Washington, DC: Potomac Books, 2005).

5. This chapter does not address the writing on intelligence from the early master strategists, but their enduring observations on intelligence deserve to be read, e.g., Carl von Clausewitz, *On War*, edited by Anatol Rapoport (New York: Pelican, 1968).

6. Roger Hilsman, *Strategic Intelligence and National Decisions* (Glencoe: Free Press, 1956); David Kahn, *The Codebreakers: The Story of Secret Writing* (New York: Macmillan, 1967); Sherman Kent, *Strategic Intelligence for American World Policy* (Princeton: Princeton University Press, 1949, revised in 1965), and "Estimates & Influence," *Foreign Service Journal* (April 1969); Lyman B. Kirkpatrick Jr., *The Real CIA* (New York: MacMillian, 1968) and *The U.S. Intelligence Community* (New York: Hill and Wang, 1973); and Harry Howe Ransom, *Central Intelligence and National Security* (Cambridge: Harvard University Press, 1958), "How Intelligent Is Intelligence?" *New York Times Magazine* (May 22, 1960), pp. 20, 77–79, "Secret Mission in an Open Society," *New York Times Magazine* (May 21, 1961), pp. 20, 77–79, *The Intelligence Establishment* (Cambridge, MA: Harvard University Press, 1970), and "Strategic Intelligence and Foreign Policy," *World Politics* 27 (October 1974), pp. 131–146; David Wise and Thomas Ross, *The Invisible Government* (New York: Random House, 1964); David Wise, *The Espionage Establishment* (New York: Random House, 1967) and *The Politics of Lying* (New York: Random House, 1973). For one of the earliest scholarly studies on U.S. intelligence, see Henry M. Wriston, *Executive Agents in American Foreign Relations* (Baltimore: Johns Hopkins University Press, 1929).

7. For instance: Stewart Alsop and Thomas Braden, *Sub Rosa: The OSS and American Espionage* (New York: Reynal and Hitchcock, 1946); Allen Dulles, *The Craft of Intelligence* (Westport, CT: Greenwood, 1977); Arnold Kramish, *The Griffin: The Greatest Untold Espionage Story of World War II* (Boston: Houghton Mifflin, 1986); Jefferson Morley, *Our Man in Mexico: Winston Scott and the Hidden History of the CIA* (Lawrence: University Press of Kansas, 2007); Bayard Stockton, *Flawed Patriot: The Rise and Fall of CIA Legend Bill Harvey* (Washington, DC: Potomac Books, 2006); and Greville M. Wynne, *The Man from Moscow: The Story of Wynne and Penkovsky* (London: Hutchinson, 1967).

8. Anthony Cave Brown, *Bodyguard of Lies* (New York: Harper & Row, 1975), on World War II British intelligence operations; Sir John Masterman, *Double Cross*

System of the War of 1939–45 (New Haven: Yale University Press, 1972), another look at British intelligence; Seth W. Richardson, "Why Were We Caught Napping at Pearl Harbor?" *Saturday Evening Post* (May 24, 1947), pp. 79–80; and Roberta Wohlstetter, *Pearl Harbor: Warning and Decision* (Stanford: Stanford University Press, 1962), a study on intelligence with rare theoretical sensitivities.

9. Thomas L. Hughes, "The Power to Speak and the Power to Listen: Reflections in Bureaucratic Politics and a Recommendation on Information Flows," in *Secrecy and Foreign Policy*, edited by Thomas Franck and Edward Weisband (New York: Oxford University Press, 1974).

10. For example, John Barron, *KGB: The Secret Work of Soviet Agents* (Pleasantville, NY: Reader's Digest, 1974).

11. Samuel Adams, "Vietnam Cover-Up: Playing War with Numbers," *Harper's* 250 (May 1975), pp. 41–44, questioning the possible distortion of intelligence reporting from Vietnam; Philip Agee, *Inside the Company: CIA Diary* (Harmondsworth, Eng.: Penguin, 1975), a controversial "outing" of CIA officers and programs by a disgruntled former CIA officer; Richard Blum, ed., *Surveillance and Espionage in a Free Society* (New York: Praeger, 1972); Stuart H. Loory, "The CIA's Use of the Press: 'A Mighty Wurlitzer,'" *Columbia Journalism Review* (September/October 1974), pp. 8–18; Patrick J. McGarvey, *CIA: The Myth and the Madness* (New York: Saturday Review Press, 1972); Victor Marchetti and John D. Marks, *The CIA and the Cult of Intelligence* (New York: Knopf, 1974), a widely read, authoritative, and influential book at the time of its publication, written by two disgruntled former intelligence officers (with Marchetti highly perched in the CIA); Fletcher L. Prouty, *The Secret Team: The CIA and Its Allies in Control of the United States and the World* (Englewood Cliffs, NJ: Prentice Hall, 1973); and Sol Stern, "NSA and the CIA," *Ramparts* 5 (March 1967), pp. 29–38.

12. Gordon B. Baldwin, "Congressional Power to Demand Disclosure of Foreign Intelligence Agreements," *Brooklyn Journal of International Law* 3 (1976), pp. 1–30; Paul W. Blackstock, "The Intelligence Community Under the Nixon Administration," *Armed Forces and Society* 1 (February 1975), pp. 231–51; William J. Barnds, "Intelligence and Foreign Policy: Dilemmas of a Democracy," *Foreign Affairs* 47 (January 1969), pp. 281–95; Lawrence M. Baskir, "Reflections on the Senate Investigation of Army Surveillance," *Indiana Law Journal* 49 (Summer 1974), pp. 618–653; Ray Cline, "Policy Without Intelligence," *Foreign Policy* 17 (Winter 1974–1975), pp. 121–135; Chester Cooper, "The CIA and Decision-making," *Foreign Affairs* 50 (January 1972), pp. 223–236; Robert F. Ellsworth and Keith L. Adelman, "Foolish Intelligence," *Foreign Policy* 36 (Fall 1971), pp. 147–159; Stanley Levell, *Of Spies and Strategems* (New York: Prentice-Hall, 1963); Richard Harris Smith, *OSS: The Secret History of America's First Central Intelligence Agency* (Berkeley: University of California Press, 1972); Sanford Ungar, *FBI* (Boston: Atlantic Monthly, 1975); Jerrold L. Walden, "The C.I.A.: A Study in the Arrogation of Administrative Powers," *George Washington Law Review* 39 (October 1970), pp. 66–101; and F. W. Winterbotham, *The Ultra Secret* (New York: Dell, 1975).

13. The best example is Richard C. Snyder and Edgar S. Furniss Jr., *American Foreign Policy* (New York: Rhinehart, 1954).

14. For example, Tom Wicker, et al. "C.I.A. Operations: A Plot Scuttled," *New York Times* (April 25, 1966), p. A1.

15. See, for instance, Mark Lowenthal, *The U.S. Intelligence Community: An Annotated Bibliography* (New York: Garland, 1994), as well as his popular text *Intelligence: From Secrets to Policy*, 6th ed. (Washington, DC: CQ Press, 2014); the references in Loch K. Johnson and James J. Wirtz, ed., *Intelligence: The Secret World of Spies*, 3rd ed. (New York: Oxford University Press, 2014), as well as Loch K. Johnson, ed., *Handbook of Intelligence Studies* (New York: Routledge, 2007), *The Oxford Handbook of National Security Intelligence* (New York: Oxford University Press, 2010), and *Intelligence* (New York: Routledge, 2011), a four-volume compilation of classic essays on intelligence; Russell A. Miller, ed., *US National Security, Intelligence and Democracy: From the Church Committee to the War on Terror* (New York: Routledge, 2008); as well as Robert Dover, Michael S. Goodman, and Claudia Hillebrand, eds., *Routledge Companion to Intelligence Studies* (New York: Routledge Press, 2014); Loch K. Johnson and Allison M. Shelton, "Thoughts on the State of Intelligence Studies: A Survey Report," *Intelligence and National Security* 24 (February 2013), pp. 109–120; and Gregory Moore, ed., *The Encyclopedia of U.S. Intelligence* (New York: Routledge, 2015).

16. The key journals in the field are *Intelligence and National Security* and the *International Journal of Intelligence and Counterintelligence*, both established in the mid-1980s and both currently published by the Taylor & Francis Group in London. Important, too, is a journal published by the CIA's Center for the Study of Intelligence, entitled *Studies in Intelligence*. It is printed in both a classified version for cleared government officials and, with a different set of articles, an unclassified version for the outside reader. The National Military Intelligence Association also publishes, irregularly, a journal called the *American Journal of Intelligence*. The mainstream scholarly journals in history, political science, international affairs, strategy, and public administration will occasionally carry an article on intelligence, but they are rare. The *American Political Science Review*, for example, has only one article on this subject in its entire history dating back to the early 20th century. For the first college textbook on American foreign policy to place intelligence at the heart of this subject, see Loch K. Johnson, *American Foreign Policy and the Challenges of World Leadership: Power, Principle, and the Constitution* (New York: Oxford University Press, 2014). Also, Loch K. Johnson, *Seven Sins of American Foreign Policy* (New York: Longman, 2007).

17. Christopher Andrew and Vasili Mitrokhin, *The Mitrokhin Archive*, vol. 1: *The KGB in Europe and the West* (New York: Penguin/Basic Books, 1999); Christopher Andrew, *For the President's Eyes Only: Secret Intelligence and the American Presidency* (London: HarperCollins, 1995); Christopher Andrew and Oleg Gordievsky, *KGB: The Inside Story* (London: Hodder & Stoughton, 1990); Christopher Andrew and David Dilks, eds., *The Missing Dimension: Governments and Intelligence Communities in the Twentieth Century* (Urbana: University of Illinois

Press, 1984). Among Professor Freedman's many works on intelligence are *U.S. Intelligence and the Soviet Strategic Threat* (Princeton: Princeton University Press, 1986) and "The Politics of Warning: Terrorism and Risk Communications," *Intelligence and National Security* 20 (September 2005), pp. 379–438.

18. Richard Aldrich, *The Hidden Hand: Britain, America and Cold War Secret Intelligence* (London: John Murray, 2001).

19. Percy Cradock, *Know Your Enemy: How the Joint Intelligence Committee Saw the World* (London: John Murray, 2002).

20. See, for example, Philip H. J. Davies, "Ideas of Intelligence," *Harvard International Review* (Fall 2002), pp. 62–66.

21. M. R. D. Foot, *SOE in France* (London: Cass, 2004).

22. Peter Hennessy, *The Secret State: Whitehall and the Cold War* (London: Allen Lane Penguin Press, 2002).

23. See, for example, Peter Jackson, "The Politics of Secret Service in War, Cold War and Imperial Retreat," *Contemporary British History* 14 (2003), pp. 423–431.

24. Rhodri Jeffreys-Jones, *The CIA & American Democracy* (New Haven: Yale University Press, 1989), *Cloak and Dollar: A History of American Secret Intelligence* (New Haven: Yale University Press, 2002), and *In Spies We Trust: The Story of Western Intelligence* (London: Oxford University Press, 2013).

25. John Ranelagh, *The Agency: The Rise and Decline of the CIA* (New York: Simon & Schuster, 1986).

26. Harold Shukman, ed., *Agents for Change: Intelligence Services in the 21st Century* (London: St. Ermin's Press, 2000).

27. William Stevenson, *A Man Called Intrepid* (Basingstoke and London: Macmillan, 1976).

28. Nigel West, *MI6: British Secret Intelligence Operations, 1909–1945* (London: Weidenfeld & Nicholson, 1983). See also Robert Dover and Michael S. Goodman, eds., *Spinning Intelligence: Why Intelligence Needs the Media, Why the Media Needs Intelligence* (New York: Columbia University Press, 2009); and Robert Dover and Michael S. Goodman, eds., *Learning from the Secret Past: Cases in British Intelligence History* (Washington, DC: Georgetown University Press, 2011); Michael S. Goodman, *Spying on the Nuclear Bear: Anglo-American Intelligence and the Soviet Bomb* (Stanford, CA: Stanford University Press, 2007); and Sir David Omand, *Securing the State* (New York: Columbia University Press, 2010).

29. William R. Corson, *The Armies of Ignorance: The Rise of the American Intelligence Empire* (New York: Dial, 1977).

30. John Lewis Gaddis, "Intelligence, Espionage, and Cold War Origins," *Diplomatic History* 13 (Spring 1989), pp. 191–212. See also Christopher Andrew, "Intelligence and International Relations in the Early Cold War," *Review of International Studies* 24 (1998); and Douglas T. Stuart, *Creating the National Security State: A History of the Law That Transformed America* (Princeton, NJ: Princeton University Press, 2008).

31. Michael Handel, *War, Strategy and Intelligence* (London: Cass, 1987).

32. William M. Leary, *Perilous Mission: Civil Air Transport and CIA Covert Operations in Asia* (Tuscolusa: University of Alabama Press, 1984).

33. Ernest R. May, ed., *Knowing One's Enemies: Intelligence Assessment Before the Two World Wars* (Princeton: Princeton University Press, 1985).

34. Aleksandr Fursenko and Timothy Naftali, *"One Hell of a Gamble": Khrushchev, Castro, Kennedy and the Cuban Missile Crisis, 1958–1964* (London: John Murray, 1997). See also David E. Murphy, Sergei A. Kondrashev, and George Bailey, *Battleground Berlin* (New Haven: Yale University Press, 1999); and Richard Breitman, Norman J. W. Goda, Timothy Naftali, and Robert Wolfe, *U.S. Intelligence and the Nazis* (Cambridge: Cambridge University Press, 2005).

35. Jeffrey T. Richelson, *A Century of Spies* (New York: Oxford University Press, 1995).

36. David F. Rudgers, *Creating the Secret State: The Origins of the Central Intelligence Agency* (Lawrence: University Press of Kansas, 2000).

37. Bradley F. Smith, *The Shadow Warriors: OSS and the Origins of the CIA* (London: André Deutsch, 1981).

38. Thomas F. Troy, *Donovan and the CIA: A History of the Establishment of the Central Intelligence Agency* (Washington, DC: Center for the Study of Intelligence, Central Intelligence Agency, 1981), and *Wild Bill and Intrepid: Donovan, Stephenson, and the Origin of the CIA* (New Haven, CT: Yale University Press, 1996); also, Douglas Waller, *Wild Bill Donovan: The Spymaster Who Created the OSS and Modern American Espionage* (New York: Free Press, 2011).

39. Michael Warner, ed., *The CIA Under Harry Truman, CIA Cold War Records* (Washington, DC: History Staff, Center for the Study of Intelligence, Central Intelligence Agency, 1994). See also Michael Warner, *The Rise and Fall of Intelligence: An International Security History* (Washington, DC: Georgetown University Press, 2014); Arthur B. Darling, *The Central Intelligence Agency: An Instrument of Government, to 1950* (University Park, PA: Pennsylvania State University Press, 1990); and, for a history of CIA officers who have fallen in duty, Ted Gup, *The Book of Honor: Covert Lives and Classified Deaths at the CIA* (New York: Doubleday, 2000).

40. Robin Winks, *Cloak and Gown: Scholars in the Secret War* (New York: William Morrow, 1987).

41. Amy B. Zegart, *Flawed by Design: the Evolution of the CIA, JCS, and NSC* (Stanford: Stanford University Press, 1999). Also, for a detailed account of the state of U.S. intelligence on the eve of the 9/11 attacks, see Loch K. Johnson, *The Threat on the Horizon: An Insider's Account of America's Search for Security After the Cold War* (New York: Oxford University Press, 2010). For three insightful books by *New York Times* reporters with an intelligence beat, see Tim Weiner, *Legacy of Ashes: The History of the CIA* (New York: Doubleday, 2007), a beautifully written book but tilted with a strong bias against the CIA; Mark Mazzetti, *The Way of the Knife: The CIA, A Secret Army, and A War at the Ends of the Earth* (New York: Penguin, 2013), a close look at recent CIA and Pentagon paramilitary operations in Southwest Asia; and James Risen, *State of War: The Secret History of the CIA and the Bush Administration* (New York: Free Press, 2006).

42. David A. Charters, "British Intelligence in the Palestine Campaign," *Intelligence and National Security* 6 (January 1991), pp. 229–239; John Ferris, "Intelligence," in R. Boyce and J. Maiolo, eds., *The Origins of World War Two: The Debate Continues* (Basingstoke: Palgrave, 2003).

43. A. Stuart Farson, David Stafford, and Wesley K. Wark, eds., *Security and Intelligence in a Changing World: Perspectives for the 1990s* (London: Cass, 1991); Stuart Farson, Peter Gill, Mark Phythian, and Shlomo Shpiro, eds., *PSI Handbook of Global Security and Intelligence: National Approaches*, Vols. 1 and 2 (Westport, CT: Praeger Security International, 2008). See also Wesley K. Wark, ed., *Espionage: Past, Present, Future?* (London: Frank Cass, 1994).

44. Wolfgang Krieger, "German Intelligence History: A Field in Search of Scholars," *Intelligence and National Security* 19 (Summer 2004), pp. 185–198.

45. Karalekas, History of the Central Intelligence Agency, *op. cit.*; and Phyllis Provost McNeil, "The Evolution of the U.S. Intelligence Community—An Historical Perspective," in *Preparing for the 21st Century: An Appraisal of U.S. Intelligence*, Report of the Commission on the Roles and Capabilities of the United States Intelligence Community (the Aspin-Brown Commission, led by former Secretaries of Defense Les Aspin and, subsequently, Harold Brown), March 1, 1996, Appendix A.

46. Loch K. Johnson, *Season of Inquiry*, *op. cit.*; Smist, *op. cit.* For an examination of the top one hundred U.S. government inquiries since 1945 that rates the Church Committee in first place for its effectiveness, see Paul C. Light, *Government by Investigation: Congress, Presidents, and the Search for Answers 1945–2012* (Washington, DC: Brookings Institution, 2014).

47. Mark M. Lowenthal, *U.S. Intelligence: Evolution and Anatomy*, 2nd ed. (Westport, CT: Praeger, 1992); Jeffrey T. Richelson, *The U.S. Intelligence Community*, 6th ed. (Boulder: Westview Press, 2012). See also Loch K. Johnson, *Secret Agencies: U.S. Intelligence in a Hostile World* (New Haven: Yale University Press, 1996); and, on the connection between the intelligence agencies and outside contractors (outsourcing), see Tim Shorrock, *Spies for Hire: The Secret World of Intelligence Outsourcing* (New York: Simon & Schuster, 2008). Brad Westerfield gathered together and edited several outstanding articles written by CIA insiders that provide a wealth of information on organizational matters: *Inside the CIA's Private World: Declassified Articles form the Agency's Internal Journal, 1955–1992* (New Haven, CT: Yale University Press, 1995). For a somewhat overheated and hastily prepared examination of the U.S. intelligence agencies that nonetheless received considerable fanfare, given the *Washington Post* credentials of the two writers, see Diana Priest and William Arkin, *Top Secret America: The Rise of the New American Security State* (New York: Little, Brown and Co., 2012), which argues that the community is bloated in size and funding.

48. Ray S. Cline, *The CIA under Reagan, Bush, and Casey: The Evolution of the Agency from Roosevelt to Reagan* (Washington, DC: Acropolis, 1981); Kenneth Michael Absher, Michael C. Desch, and Roman Popadiuk, *Priviledged and Confidential: The Secret History of the President's Intelligence Advisory Board* (Lexington: University Press of Kentucky, 2012).

49. Glenn Hastedt, "Organizational Foundations of Intelligence Failure," in Alfred C. Maver, Marion D. Tunstall, and James M. Klagle, eds., *Intelligence Policy and Process* (Boulder: Westview Press, 1985), pp. 140–156; Amy B. Zegart, "September 11 and the Adaptation Failure of U.S. Intelligence Agencies," *International Security* 29 (Spring 2005), pp. 78–111; Rob Johnston, *Analytic Culture in the US Intelligence Community: An Ethnographic Study* (Langley, VA: CIA Center for the Study of Intelligence, 2005).

50. Christopher Andrew, *Secret Service: The Making of the British Intelligence Community* (London: Sceptre, 1991), and *The Defence of the Realm: The Authorized History of MI5* (London: Penguin, 2009); as well as Andrew and Gordievsky, *op. cit*; Keith Jeffrey, *The Secret History of MI6* (London: Penguin, 2010).

51. Jeffrey T. Richelson and Desmond Ball, *The Ties That Bind: Intelligence Cooperation Between the UK/USA Countries* (Boston: Allen and Unwin, 1985). See also David Staffaord and Rhodri Jeffreys-Jones, eds., "American–British–Canadian Intelligence Relations, 1939–2000," special issue of *Intelligence and National Security* 15 (2000); and Bradford Westerfield, "America and the World of Intelligence Liaison," *Intelligence and National Security* 11 (1996), pp. 523–560.

52. For example, Richard K. Betts, "Warning Dilemmas: Normal Theory vs. Exceptional Theory," *Orbis* 26 (Winter 1983), pp. 829–833.

53. Davies, *Harvard International Review, op. cit.*

54. Michael I. Handel, "The Study of Intelligence," *Orbis* 26 (Winter 1983), pp. 817–821.

55. Michael Herman, *Intelligence Power in Peace and War* (Cambridge: Cambridge University Press, 1996); this important book is an example of solid research that could fit into many categories in this chapter (history, for instance), but it is placed under theory because it provides a seminal blending of intelligence history and the author's understanding of public administration—all tempered by the hands-on experience of a former insider in British intelligence.

56. Arthur S. Hulnick, "The Intelligence Producer-Policy Consumer Linkage: A Theoretical Approach," *Intelligence and National Security* 1 (May 1986), pp. 212–233.

57. Loch K. Johnson, "Bricks and Mortar for a Theory of Intelligence," *Comparative Strategy* 22 (Spring 2003), pp. 1–28; *America's Secret Power: The CIA in a Democratic Society* (New York: Oxford University Press, 1989); and *National Security Intelligence: Secret Operations in Defense of the Democracies* (Cambridge, UK: Polity Press, 2012).

58. Rob Johnson, *Analytic Culture in the U.S. Intelligence Community: An Ethnographic Study* (Washington, DC: Center for the Study of Intelligence, CIA, 2005).

59. David Kahn, "An Historical Theory of Intelligence," *Intelligence and National Security* 16 (2001), pp. 79–92.

60. Walter Laqueur, *A World of Secrets: The Uses and Limits of Intelligence* (New York: Basic, 1985).

61. Kenneth G. Robertson, ed., *British and American Approaches to Intelligence* (Basingstoke: Macmillan, 1987).

62. Abram Shulsky, *Silent Warfare—Understanding the World of Intelligence* (London: Brassey's, 1993).

63. *Intelligence and National Security* 19 (Summer 2004); see especially in this volume: Len Scott and Peter Jackson, "The Study of Intelligence in Theory and Practice," pp. 39–169; and Christopher Andrew, "Intelligence, International Relations and 'Under-theorization,' " pp. 170–184.

64. Kristin M. Lord and Bernard I. Finel, "The Surprising Logic of Transparency," *International Studies Quarterly* 43 (1999), pp. 315–339.

65. See Peter Gill, Stephen Marrin, and Mark Phythian, eds., *Intelligence Theory: Key Questions and Debates* (New York: Routledge, 2009); and Stephen Marrin, "Intelligence Analysis Theory: Explaining and Predicting Analytic Responsibilities," *Intelligence and National Security* 22 (2007), pp. 821–846. For an example of an innovative studies linking intelligence to other aspects of international affairs, see John Stempel, "The Impact of Religion on Intelligence," *International Journal of Intelligence and Counterintelligence* 18 (2005), pp. 280–295; and Steve Tsang, ed., *Intelligence and Human Rights in the Era of Global Terrorism* (Westport, CT: Praeger Security International, 2007).

66. Matthew M. Aid, *The Secret Sentry: The Untold History of the National Security Agency* (New York: Bloomsbury Press, 2009); Matthew M. Aid and Cees Wiebes, eds., *Secrets of Signals Intelligence During the Cold War and Beyond*, Special Issue of *Intelligence and National Security* 16 (2001); James Bamford, *The Puzzle Palace* (Boston: Houghton Mifflin, 1984), and *The Shadow Factory: The Ultra-Secret NSA from 9/11 to the Eavesdropping on America* (New York: Doubleday, 2008); David Kahn, *The Codebreakers* (New York: Macmillan, 1967); Patrick R. Keefe, *Chatter* (New York: Random House, 2005). See also Mavis Batey, *Dilly: The Man Who Broke Enigmas* (London: Dialogue, 2009).

67. William E. Burrows, *Deep Black: Space Espionage and National Security* (New York: Random House, 1986).

68. Jeffrey T. Richelson, *The Wizards of Langley* (Boulder: Westview Press, 2002). See also David Robarge (the CIA Chief Historian), *Archangel: CIA's Supersonic A-12 Reconnaissance Aircraft*, Center for the Study of Intelligence (Washington, DC: Central Intelligence Agency, 2007); David H. Sharp, *The CIA's Greatest Covert Operation: Inside the Daring Mission to Recover a Nuclear-Armed Soviet Sub* (Lawrence: University Press of Kansas, 2012); and Michael Warner, "Reflections on Technology and Intelligence Systems," *Intelligence and National Security* 27 (February 2012), pp. 133–153.

69. Frederick P. Hitz, *The Great Game: The Myth and Reality of Espionage* (New York: Knopf, 2004).

70. Reuel Marc Gerecht, "A New Clandestine Service: The Case for Creative Destruction," in Peter Berkowitz, ed., *Future of American Intelligence* (Palo Alto, California: Hoover Institution Press, 2005), 103–138.

71. See, for example, Hamilton Bean, *No More Secrets: Open Source Information and the Reshaping of US Intelligence* (Westport, CT: Praeger Security International); Stephen C. Mercado, "Sailing the Sea of OSINT in the Information Age," *Studies in Intelligence* 48 (2004), pp. 45–55, reprinted in Loch K. Johnson and James J.

Wirtz, eds., *Intelligence: The Secret World of Spies*, 3rd ed. (New York: Oxford University Press, 2014); Robert David Steele, "Relevant Information and All-Source Analysis: The Emerging Revolution," *American Intelligence Journal* 19 (1999), pp. 23–30; and Stevyn D. Gibson, "Open Source Intelligence (OSINT): A Contemporary Intelligence Lifeline," PhD thesis, Cranfield University. For an overview of intelligence collection, see Robert M. Clark, *Intelligence Collection* (Washington, DC: CQ Press, 2013).

72. Robert Jervis, "Intelligence and Foreign Policy," *International Security* 2 (1986–1987), pp. 141–161, and *Why Intelligence Fails: Lessons from the Iranian Revolution and the Iraq War* (Ithaca, NY: Cornell University Press, 2010). See also Robert M. Clark, *Intelligence Analysis: A Target-Centric Approach* (Washington, DC: CQ Press, 2010); Roger Z. George and James B. Bruce, eds., *Analyzing Intelligence: Origins, Obstacles, and Innovations* (Washington, DC: Georgetown University Press, 2008); Loch K. Johnson, "A Framework for Strengthening U.S. Intelligence," *Yale Journal of International Affairs* 2 (February 2006), pp. 116–131; James P. Pfiffner and Mark Phythian, eds., *Intelligence and National Security Policymaking on Iraq: British and American Perspectives* (Manchester, UK: Manchester University Press, 2008); Paul R. Pillar, *Intelligence and U.S. Foreign Policy: Iraq, 9/11, and Misguided Reform* (New York: Columbia University Press, 2011); Jennifer E. Sims and Burton Gerber, eds., *Transforming U.S. Intelligence* (Washington, DC: Georgetown University Press, 2005); Michael A. Turner, *Why Secret Intelligence Fails* (Dulles, VA: Potomac Books, 2005); and Timothy Walton, *Challenges in Intelligence Analysis: Lessons from 1300 BCE to the Present* (New York: Cambridge University Press, 2010).

73. Richard K. Betts, "Analysis, War and Decision: Why Intelligence Failures Are Inevitable," *World Politics* 3 (1978), pp. 961–988, and *Enemies of Intelligence: Knowledge & Power in American National Security* (New York: Columbia University Press, 2007). Also: Richard L. Russell, *Sharpening Strategic Intelligence: Why the CIA Gets It Wrong and What Needs to Be Done to Get It Right* (New York: Cambridge University Press, 2007).

74. Jack Davis, "A Policymaker's Perspective on Intelligence Analysis," *Studies in Intelligence* 38 (1995), pp. 7–15.

75. Klaus Knorr, "Failures in National Intelligence Estimates: The Case of the Cuban Missiles," *World Politics* 16 (April 1984), pp. 456–475.

76. Uri Bar-Joseph, *The Angel: Ashraf Manwan, the Mossad and the Yom Kippur War* (Or Yehuda: Zmora-Bitan, 2011); Ehraim Kahana, "Early Warning Versus Concept: The Case of the Yom Kippur War, 1973," *Intelligence and National Security* 17 (Summer 2002), pp. 81–104.

77. John Prados, *The Soviet Estimate: U.S. Intelligence Analysis and Russian Military Strength* (New York: Dial, 1982); see also Donald P. Steury, ed., *Intentions and Capabilities: Estimates on Soviet Strategic Forces, 1950–1983* (Washington, DC: CIA, 1996).

78. Richard L. Russell, "CIA's Strategic Intelligence in Iraq," *Political Science Quarterly* 117 (Summer 2002), pp. 191–207.

79. Loch K. Johnson, *Bombs, Bugs, Drugs, and Thugs: Intelligence and America's Quest for Security* (New York: New York University Press, 2000).

80. Mark M. Lowenthal, "Tribal Tongues: Intelligence Consumers, Intelligence Producers," *Washington Quarterly* 15 (Winter 1992), pp. 157–168.

81. Harry Howe Ransom, "The Politicization of Intelligence," in a valuable anthology edited by Stephen J. Cimbala, *Intelligence and Intelligence Policy in a Democratic Society* (Dobbs Ferry, NY: Transnational, 1987), pp. 25–46.

82. James J. Wirtz, "Intelligence to Please? The Order of Battle Controversy during the Vietnam War," *Political Science Quarterly* 106 (Summer 1991), pp. 239–263.

83. See, for example, Stewart A. Baker, "Should Spies Be Cops?" *Foreign Policy* 97 (1994–1995), pp. 36–52.

84. Glenn Hastedt, "Public Intelligence: Leaks as Policy Instruments—The Case of the Iraq War," *Intelligence and National Security* 20 (September 2005), pp. 419–439.

85. David Wise, *Nightmover* (New York: Random House, 1992); James J. Wirtz, "Hiding in Plain Sight: Denial, Deception and the Non-State Actor," *SAIS Review of International Affairs* 28 (2008), pp. 55–63; see also David Wise, *Spy: The Inside Story of How the FBI's Robert Hanssen Betrayed America* (New York: Random House, 2002); John Barron, *Breaking the Ring* (Boston: Houghton Mifflin, 1987); and David C. Martin, *Wilderness of Mirrors* (New York: Harper and Row, 1980).

86. Tom Mangold, *Cold Warrior* (New York: Simon & Schuster, 1991).

87. Stan A. Taylor and Daniel Snow, "Cold War Spies: Why They Spied and How They Got Caught," *Intelligence and National Security* 12 (April 1997), pp. 101–125.

88. Hayden B. Peake, "OSS and the Venona Decrypts," *Intelligence and National Security* 12 (July 1997), pp. 14–34.

89. Raymond J. Batvinis, *The Origins of FBI Counterintelligence* (Lawrence: University Press of Kansas, 2007); Kathryn S. Olmsted, *Red Spy Queen: A Biography of Elizabeth Bentley* (Chapel Hill: University of North Carolina Press, 2002); Katherine A. S. Sibley, *Red Spies in America: Stolen Secrets and the Dawn of the Cold War* (Lawrence: University Press of Kansas, 2004).

90. Nigel West, ed., *The Faber Book of Espionage* (London: Faber & Faber, 1993); Anthony Glees, *The Stasi Files: The UK Operations of the East German Intelligence and Security Service* (New York: Simon & Schuster, 2003).

91. Daniel S. Gressang IV, "Audience and Message: Assessing Terrorist WMD Potential," *Terrorism and Political Violence* 13 (2001), pp. 83–106; Prem Mahadevan, *The Politics of Counterterrorism in India: Strategic Intelligence and National Security in South Asia* (London: I.B. Tauris, 2012); Jane Mayer, *The Dark Side: The Inside Story of How the War on Terror Turned into a War on American Ideals* (New York: Doubleday, 2008); Richard H. Shultz Jr. and Andrea J. Dew, *Insurgents, Terrorists, and Militias: The Warriors of Contemporary Combat* (New York: Columbia University Press, 2006); and Katherina von Knop, Heinrich Neisser, and Martin van Creveld (Hrsg.), *Countering Modern Terrorism: History, Current Issues and Future Threats* (Bielefeld, Germany: W. Bertelsmann Verlag, 2005).

92. Steve Coll, *Ghost Wars: The Secret History of the CIA, Afghanistan, and Bin Laden* (New York: Penguin, 2004).

93. William J. Daugherty, *Executive Secrets: Covert Action and the Presidency* (Lexington: University Press of Kentucky, 2004).

94. Roy Godson, ed., *Intelligence Requirements for the 1980s: Covert Action* (Washington, DC: Transaction Books, 1981).

95. Richard H. Immerman, *The CIA in Guatemala: The Foreign Policy of Intervention* (Austin: University of Texas Press, 1982).

96. Loch K. Johnson, "Covert Action and Accountability: Decision-Making for America's Secret Foreign Policy," *International Studies Quarterly* 33 (March 1989), pp. 81–109; *National Security Intelligence, op. cit.*; and "The Myths of America's Shadow Wars," *Atlantic Monthly Online* (January 31, 2013).

97. Stephen F. Knott, *Secret and Sanctioned: Covert Operations and the American Presidency* (New York: Oxford University Press, 1996).

98. Kevin A. O'Brien, "Interfering With Civil Society: CIA and KGB Covert Political Action During the Cold War," *International Journal of Intelligence and Counterintelligence* 8 (Winter 1995), pp. 431–456.

99. John Prados, *Presidents' Secret Wars: CIA and Pentagon Covert Operations From World War II Through Iranscam* (New York: Quill, 1985), *Lost Crusader: The Secret Wars of CIA Director William Colby* (New York: Oxford University Press, 2002), and *Safe for Democracy: The Secret Wars of the CIA* (Chicago: Ivan R. Dee, 2006).

100. W. Michael Reisman and James E. Baker, *Regulating Covert Action: Practices, Contexts, and Policies of Covert Coercion Abroad in International and American Law* (New Haven: Yale University Press, 1992).

101. Gregory F. Treverton, *Covert Action: The Limits of Intervention in the Postwar World* (New York: Basic Books, 1987); see also his *Intelligence for an Age of Terror* (New York: Cambridge University Press, 2009).

102. Stephen R. Weissman, "CIA Covert Action in Zaire and Angola: Patterns and Consequences," *Political Science Quarterly* 94 (Summer 1979), pp. 263–286 and his "An Extraordinary Rendition," *Intelligence and National Security* 25 (April 2010), pp. 198–222.

103. Peter Wyden, *Bay of Pigs: The Untold Story* (New York: Simon & Schuster, 1979).

104. See "Covert Action," Hearings, Select Committee to Study Governmental Operations with Respect to Intelligence Activities (the Church Committee), Washington, DC (October 23, 1975); Church Committee, "Alleged Assassination Plots," *op. cit.*; and Church Committee, Final Report, *op. cit.* On the question of assassination, see also Jeffrey Richelson, "When Kindness Fails: Assassination as a National Security Option," *International Journal of Intelligence and Counterintelligence* 15 (2002), pp. 243–274. For Senator Church's views on covert action, see his "Covert Action: Swampland of American Foreign Policy," *Bulletin of the Atomic Scientists* 32 (February 1976), pp. 7–11.

105. Michael Grow, *U.S. Presidents and Latin American Interventions: Pursuing Regime Change in the Cold War* (Lawrence: University Press of Kansas, 2008);

Kermit Roosevelt, *Countercoup: The Struggle for Control of Iran* (New York: McGraw-Hill, 1981); David Wise and Thomas B. Ross, *The Invisible Government* (New York: Random House, 1964).

106. Robert Baer, *See No Evil* (New York: Crown, 2003); Henry A. Crumpton, *The Art of Intelligence: Lessons from a Life in the CIA's Clandestine Service* (New York: Penguin, 2012); Harry Rositzke, *The CIA's Secret Operations: Espionage, Counterespionage, and Covert Action* (New York: Reader's Digest Press, 1977); Michael Scheuer, *Imperial Hubris* (Washington, DC: Brassey's, 2004); and Theodore G. Shackley, *The Third Option: An American View of Counter-insurgency Operations* (New York: Reader's Digest Press). See also Duane R. "Dewey" Clarridge, with Digby Diehl, *A Spy for All Seasons: My Life in the CIA* (New York: Scribner's, 1997); and Gary Berstsen, *Jawbreakers* (New York: Crown, 2006).

107. Bob Woodward, *VEIL: The Secret Wars of the CIA, 1981–1987* (New York: Simon & Schuster, 1987).

108. William S. Cohen and George J. Mitchell, *Men of Zeal: A Candid inside Story of the Iran-Contra Hearings* (New York: Viking, 1988). For the official government report on the Iran-*contra* affair, see Senate Select Committee on Secret Military Assistance to Iran and the Nicaraguan Opposition and House Select Committee to Investigate Covert Arms Transactions with Iran, *Hearings* and *Final Report* (Washington, DC: Government Printing Office, 1987).

109. Jennifer D. Kibbe, "The Rise of the Shadow Warriors," *Foreign Affairs* 83 (2004), pp. 102–115.

110. David M. Barrett, *The CIA and Congress: The Untold Story from Truman to Kennedy* (Lawrence: University Press of Kansas, 2005).

111. Frederick P. Hitz, "Unleashing the Rogue Elephant: September 11 and Letting the CIA Be the CIA," *Harvard Journal of Law & Public Policy* 25 (2002), pp. 756–781.

112. See, for example, Loch K. Johnson, "Congressional Supervision of America's Secret Agencies: The Experience and Legacy of the Church Committee," *Public Administration Review* 64 (January/February 2004), pp. 3–14.

113. Frederick M. Kaiser, "Congressional Rules and Conflict Resolution: Access to Information in the House Select Committee on Intelligence," *Congress and the Presidency* 15 (Spring 1988), pp. 49–73, and "Impact and Implications of the Iran-Contra Affair on Congressional Oversight of Covert Action," *International Journal of Intelligence and Counterintelligence* 7 (1994), pp. 205–234.

114. Harold Hongju Koh, "Why the President (Almost) Always Wins in Foreign Affairs: Lessons of the Iran-Contra Affair," *Yale Law Journal* 97 (June 1988), pp. 1255–1342.

115. Kathryn S. Olmsted, *Challenging the Secret Government: The Post-Watergate Investigations of the CIA and FBI* (Chapel Hill: University of North Carolina Press, 1996).

116. John M. Oseth, *Regulating United States Intelligence Operations: A Study in Definition of the National Interest* (Lexington: University Press of Kentucky, 1985).

117. Gregory F. Treverton, "Intelligence: Welcome to the American Government," in Thomas E. Mann, ed., *A Question of Balance: The President, the Congress, and Foreign Policy* (Washington, DC: The Brookings Institute, 1990), pp. 70–108.

118. Henry Steele Commager, "Intelligence: The Constitution Betrayed," *New York Review of Books* (September 30, 1976), pp. 32–37.

119. Frank J. Donner, *The Age of Surveillance: The Aims and Methods of America's Political Intelligence Surveillance* (New York: Vintage, 1981).

120. John T. Elliff, *The Reform of FBI Intelligence Operations* (Princeton: Princeton University Press, 1979).

121. Richard E. Morgan, *Domestic Intelligence: Monitoring Dissent in America* (Austin: University of Texas Press, 1980).

122. Frederick A. O. Schwarz Jr. [chief counsel for the Church Committee], "Intelligence Activities and the Rights of Americans," New York Bar Association meeting, New York City (November 16, 1976), reprinted in Congressional Record (January 28, 1977), pp. 51, 627–651.

123. Athan G. Theoharis, *Spying on Americans: Political Surveillance from Hoover to the Huston Plan* (Philadelphia: Temple University Press, 1978). See also Douglas M. Charles, *J. Edgar Hoover and the Anti-Interventionists: FBI Political Surveillance and the Rise of the Domestic Security State, 1939–1945* (Columbus: Ohio State University Press, 2007).

124. David Wise, *The American Police State: The Government Against the People* (New York: Random House, 1976). See also Michael Allen, *Blinking Red: Crisis and Compromise in American Intelligence After 9/11* (Dulles, VA: Potomac Books, 2013); Simon Chesterman, *One Nation Under Surveillance: A New Social Contract to Defend Freedom without Sacrificing Liberty* (New York: Oxford University Press, 2011); David Cole and James X. Dempsey, *Terrorism and the Constitution: Sacrificing Civil Liberties in the Name of National Security* (New York: The New Press, 2006); Louis Fisher, *9/11 and the Constitution* (Lawrence: University Press of Kansas, 2008); Jack Goldsmith, *The Terror Presidency: Law and Judgment Inside the Bush Administration* (New York: Norton, 2007); and Frederick A. O. Schwarz Jr. and Aziz Z. Huq, *Unchecked and Unbalanced: Presidential Power in a Time of Terror* (New York: The New Press, 2007).

125. Frederic F. Manget, "Another System of Oversight: Intelligence and the Rise of Judicial Intervention," *Studies in Intelligence* 39 (1966), pp. 43–50; L. Britt Snider, *The Agency and the Hill: CIA's Relationship with Congress, 1946–2004*, Center for the Study of Intelligence (Washington, DC: Central Intelligence Agency, 2008). See also Loch K. Johnson, "Ostriches, Cheerleaders, Skeptics, and Guardians: Role Selection by Congressional Intelligence Overseers," *The SAIS Review* 28 (Spring 2008), pp. 93–108.

126. For example: Peter Gill, "Reasserting Control: Recent Changes in the Oversight of the UK Intelligence Community," *Intelligence and National Security* 11 (April 1996), pp. 113–331; Mark Phythian, "Still a Matter of Trust: Post-9/11 British Intelligence and Political Culture," *International Journal of Intelligence and*

Counterintelligence 18 (2005–2006), pp. 653–681. See also the excellent overview of intelligence studies: Peter Gill and Mark Phythian, *Intelligence in an Insecure World*, 2nd ed. (Cambridge, UK: Polity Press, 2012); Glees, Anthony, "The Future of Intelligence Studies," *Journal of Strategic Security* 6 Suppl. (2013), pp. 124–127; Anthony Glees, Philip H. J. Davies, and John N. L. Morrison, *The Open Side of Secrecy: Britain's Intelligence and Security Committee* (London: Social Affairs Unit, 2006); and Philip H. J. Davies, *Intelligence and Government in Britain and the United States*, Vols. 1 and 2 (Santa Barbara, CA: Praeger, 2012).

127. Reginald Whitaker, *The End of Privacy: How Total Surveillance Is Becoming a Reality* (New York: New Press, 1999).

128. Born, Johnson, and Leigh, *op. cit.* See also Hans Born, Ian Leigh, and Aidan Wills, eds., *International Intelligence Cooperation and Accountability* (London: Routledge, 2011).

129. See, for example, Loch K. Johnson, "Accountability and America's Secret Foreign Policy," *Foreign Policy Analysis* 1 (Spring 2005), pp. 99–120, and "Supervising the Secret Foreign Policy: A Shock Theory of Congressional Oversight for Intelligence," in David P. Forsythe, Patrice C. McMahon, and Andrew Wedeman, eds., *American Foreign Policy in a Globalized World* (New York: Routledge, 2006), pp. 259–277. Also: Stuart Farson and Mark Phythian, eds., *Commissions of Inquiry and National Security: Comparative Approaches* (Santa Barbara, CA: Praeger Security International, 2011).

130. James A. Barry, "Covert Action Can Be Just," *Orbis* 37 (Summer 1993), pp. 375–390; E. Drexel Godfrey Jr., "Ethics and Intelligence," *Foreign Affairs* 56 (April 1978), pp. 624–642; Michael Herman, "Modern Intelligence Services: Have They a Place in Ethical Foreign Policies?" in Shukman, *op. cit.* On the ethical issue of protecting U.S. sources abroad, see Frank Snepp, *Decent Interval* (London: Allen Lane, 1980). See also Jan Goldman, ed., *Ethics of Spying: A Reader for the Intelligence Professional* (Lanham, MD: Scarecrow Press, 2006); and the *International Journal of Intelligence Ethics*, based in Washington, DC, which made its publication debut in 2010.

131. Among the most prominent of these commission and committee studies in the United States were the reports produced by the Aspin-Brown Commission, *op. cit.*; by the Kean Commission (led by former New Jersey governor Thomas Kean), *The 9/11 Commission Report*, the National Commission on Terrorist Attacks upon the United States (New York: Norton, 2004); and by the Silberman-Robb Commission (led by Judge Laurence H. Silberman and former Sen. Charles S. Robb), *Final Report*, Commission on the Intelligence Capabilities of the United States Regarding Weapons of Mass Destruction (Washington, DC, 2004). With respect to the controversy over faulty intelligence judgments about WMDs in Iraq, the British government produced two influential reports: Lord Butler's *Review of Intelligence on Weapons of Mass Destruction* (London, 2004) and Lord Hutton's *Report of the Inquiry into the Circumstances Surrounding the Death of Dr. David Kelly* (London, 2004). See also "Joint Inquiry Into Intelligence Community Activities Before and After the Terrorist Attacks of September 11, 2001," *Final Report*, U.S.

Senate Select Committtee on Intelligence and U.S. House Permanent Select Committee on Intelligence, the Graham-Goss Committees, led by Sen. Bob Graham, D, Florida, and Representative Porter J. Goss, R, Florida (Washington, DC: December 2002); and *Report on the U.S. Intelligence Community's Prewar Intelligence Assessments on Iraq*, Select Committee on Intelligence, U.S. Senate (Washington, DC: 2004).

132. John H. Hedley, "The Intelligence Community: Is It Broken? How to Fix It," *Studies in Intelligence* 39 (1996), pp. 11–19; Arthur S. Hulnick, *Fixing the Spy Machine* (Westport, CT: Praeger, 1999), and *Keeping Us Safe: Secret Intelligence and Homeland Security* (Westport, CT: Praeger, 2004); Allan E. Goodman, Gregory F. Treverton, and Philip Zelikow, *In From the Cold* (New York: Twentieth Century Fund, 1996); Loch K. Johnson, "The Failures of U.S. Intelligence and What Can Be Done about Them," *Yale Journal of International Affairs* 2 (February 2006); Lt. Gen. William E. Odum, *Fixing Intelligence* (New Haven: Yale University Press, 2002); Jennifer E. Sims and Burton Gerber, *Transforming U.S. Intelligence* (Washington, DC: Georgetown University Press, 2005); and Michael A. Turner, *Why Secret Intelligence Fails* (Washington, DC: Potomac, 2004).

133. See, for instance, Stafford T. Thomas, "The CIA's Bureaucratic Dimensions," *International Journal of Intelligence and Counterintelligence* 12 (Winter 1999), pp. 399–413.

134. See William E. Colby and Peter Forbath, *Honorable Men: My Life in the CIA* (New York: Simon & Schuster, 1978); Allen Dulles, *The Craft of Intelligence* (Westport, CT: Greenwood, 1977); Robert M. Gates, *From the Shadows* (New York: Simon & Schuster, 1996); Richard Helms, with William Hood, *A Look Over My Shoulder: My Life in the Central Intelligence Agency* (New York: Random House, 2003); Admiral Stansfield Turner, *Burn before Reading: Presidents, CIA Directors, and Secret Intelligence* (New York: Hyperion, 2005); and George Tenet with Bill Harlow, *At the Center of the Storm: My Years at the CIA* (New York: HarperCollins, 2007). See also John L. Helgerson, *Getting to Know the President: CIA Briefings of the Candidates, 1952–1992* (Washington, DC: CIA Center for the Study of Intelligence, 1996); and Douglas F. Garthoff, *Directors of Central Intelligence as Leaders of the U.S. Intelligence Community, 1946–2005* (Washington, DC: CIA Center for the Study of Intelligence, 2005). On British intelligence, see the elegantly written memoir of a former chair of the Joint Intelligence Committee, Cradock, *op. cit.*; and on Soviet intelligence, Oleg Kalugin with Fen Montaigne, *The First Directorate: My 32 Years in Intelligence and Espionage against the West* (London: Smith Gryphon, 1994). The best biographies of American intelligence chiefs are: Peter Grose, *Gentleman Spy: The Life of Allen Dulles* (Boston: Houghton Mifflin, 1994); and Thomas Powers, *The Man Who Kept the Secrets: Richard Helms and the CIA* (New York: Washington Square Press, 1981). For revealing interviews with intelligence managers and operatives, see Ralph Edward Weber, *Spymasters: Ten CIA Officers in Their Own Words* (Wilmington: SR Books, 1999); and for one legendary CIA operative's recollections, Ted Shackley with Richard A. Finney, *Spymaster: My Life in the CIA* (Dulles: Potomac Books, 2005). See also A. Denis Clift, *Clift Notes:*

Intelligence and the Nation's Security (Washington, DC: Joint Military Intelligence College, 2000); Loch K. Johnson, "James Angleton and the Church Committee," *Journal of Cold War Studies* 15 (Fall 2013), pp. 128–147; and Evan Thomas, *The Very Best Men: Four Who Dared: The Early Years of the CIA* (New York: Simon & Schuster, 1995).

135. See, for instance, Admiral Stansfield Turner, *Secrecy and Democracy: The CIA in Transition* (Boston: Houghton Mifflin, 1985).

136. One example: Daniel Patrick Moynihan, *Secrecy: The American Experience* (New Haven: Yale University Press, 1998).

CHAPTER TWO

Cloaks, Daggers, and Ivory Towers

Why Political Science Professors Don't Study U.S. Intelligence

Amy B. Zegart

U.S. INTELLIGENCE AGENCIES HAVE NEVER BEEN MORE important. Throughout the Cold War, the United States faced one principal adversary, and everyone knew it. The Soviet Union had territory on a map and troops wearing uniforms, paraded its nuclear missiles through Red Square, and operated on five-year plans. Today, critical threats to U.S. national security no longer come from a single great power with a return address and massive military might, but from more disparate and fast-changing adversaries that are harder to identify, quantify, and combat. Weak states now endanger strong ones. Small bands of transnational terrorists driven by fanaticism and hidden from view can strike far from home and continue to seek the world's deadliest weapons. And in our ever-increasing cyber-connected world, "attacks" no longer have to be kinetic to be debilitating. While information about enemy capabilities and intentions has always been essential, during the Cold War, the first and last line of defense was military firepower. Now it is intelligence.

Yet since September 11, 2001, questions about the competence, adaptability, and accountability of U.S. intelligence agencies have abounded. Why did the CIA and FBI fail to capitalize on numerous opportunities to disrupt the 9/11 plot?[1] Why did the intelligence community produce such flawed assessments about Iraq's weapons of mass destruction capabilities? The congressional intelligence committees,[2] the 9/11 Commission,[3] the Silberman-Robb Commission,[4] and a seemingly endless parade of press reports examined these questions and raised troubling doubts about the effectiveness of the Central Intelligence Agency (CIA), the Federal Bureau of Investigation (FBI), and the 14 other agencies of the U.S. intelligence community after the twin failures of 9/11 and the Iraq War. More recently, the creation of the Office of the director of National Intelligence, the CIA's expanded role in targeted killing, and the disclosure of highly classified information released by former National Security Agency (NSA) contractor Edward Snowden have raised a host of new questions. These include: What are the appropriate roles and missions of the CIA? How could individuals like Edward Snowden and Bradley Manning so systematically and easily undermine our intelligence apparatus? Are the NSA's massive data collection and data mining programs striking the right balance between security and privacy? How can intelligence oversight be improved to enhance the public trust in secret agencies that is essential in a democracy?

Political science professors have been strikingly absent from the debate. This chapter explores why. I begin by presenting the evidence of absence, showing how little attention political scientists at leading U.S. research universities pay to teaching and research about intelligence. Next, I examine the barriers in both academia and the political realm that prevent career political scientists from studying intelligence issues. Finally, I examine the consequences of neglect for the public's understanding of intelligence and for prospects of intelligence reform.

Missing Intelligence on Campus

Major research universities devote surprisingly little attention to the study of U.S. intelligence. In 2012, just seven of the top 25 U.S. universities ranked by *U.S. News & World Report* offered undergraduate courses on U.S. intelligence agencies or issues. In fact, undergraduates at America's elite universities had greater opportunities to learn about the rock band U2 than the spy plane by the same name; more than twice as many of the top 25 U.S. universities offered courses on the history of rock and roll than U.S. intelligence.[5]

Scholarly inattention is even more glaring in academic publishing. Between 2001 and 2012, the three most highly regarded academic journals in political science—the *American Political Science Review*, the *American Journal of Political Science*, and *Journal of Politics*[6]—published a total of 1,966 articles. Only three articles discussed topics even tangentially related to intelligence.[7]

International relations journals—which are considered less prestigious but are more targeted to an audience of international relations scholars and practitioners—are not much better. Since 2001, the top four international relations field journals—*International Organization*, *World Politics*, *International Studies Quarterly*, and *International Security*—have published more than 1,400 articles.[8] Only 14 articles, or 1 percent of the total, have covered intelligence topics. These figures suggest an astounding disconnect between policymakers and academics. At precisely the time that intelligence issues have dominated headlines and policymaker attention, 99 percent of the best articles produced by political scientists have been discussing research about other topics.

Finally, although the September 11 terrorist attacks have spawned a book-publishing frenzy about intelligence problems and the war on terrorism, nearly all of these post-9/11 books have been penned by policymakers and journalists, not by professors. Well-known public officials-*cum*-authors include former White House counterterrorism czar Richard Clarke,[9] former CIA Director George Tenet[10], former FBI Director Louis Freeh,[11] former CIA bin Laden Unit chief Michael Scheuer,[12] former Senate Intelligence Committee Chairman Bob Graham,[13] and Circuit Court Judge Richard A. Posner.[14] Journalists have been equally prolific. Among the legions of current and former reporters, producers, freelance writers, and editors who have published books about the U.S. intelligence community since 9/11 are James Risen, Thom Shanker, and Eric Schmitt from the *New York Times*;[15] Steve Coll, Bob Woodward, and Joby Warrick from the *Washington Post*;[16] Bill Gertz of the *Washington Times*;[17] Terry McDermott of the *Los Angeles Times*;[18] and *ABC News* reporter John Miller.[19] A more recent crop of policymakers, such as former CIA lawyer John Rizzo,[20] and journalists, such as Mark Mazzetti of the *New York Times*,[21] have documented how intelligence agencies evolved after 9/11. Only a handful of career academics have joined the fray.[22] Nearly everyone, it seems, has something to say about U.S. intelligence after 9/11 except professors.

Two Barriers to the Study of Intelligence

Why is this the case? Two types of barriers are to blame. The first lies inside the ivory tower and involves the professional norms and incentives that drive political science professors to research certain topics and not others. The second exists in the real world and involves the impediments to wresting facts from secret agencies.

The Perils of Academic Theory and Research Methods

At first glance, political science appears to be a natural home for conducting research about the U.S. intelligence community. But looks are deceiving. Political science is driven by abstract theoretical questions, not real-world policy questions, and by quantitative research methods that prize large datasets, formal models, and randomized experiments far more than qualitative approaches like historical case studies that are usually best suited to examining intelligence questions.

When it comes to theory, the study of U.S. intelligence has always existed in a no-man's-land, caught between the political science fields of international relations and American politics. For international relations scholars, the most interesting theoretical terrain covers relations between states, not what goes on inside them. Do states balance against great powers or bandwagon with them? Do they seek absolute increases in power, prosperity, and other benefits or care more about their relative position in the international pecking order? What makes threats between states credible? Under what conditions do nuclear weapons make interstate conflict more or less likely? Why is it that democracies do not fight each other? These are some of the enduring questions in international relations theory. Although some have studied inside-the-state variables and issues,[23] even the most popular arguments in international relations—such as Joseph Nye's work on "soft power" and Samuel Huntington's "Clash of Civilizations"—still gaze beyond national borders, at how American values or conflicts between civilizations shape international dynamics, rather than looking within them, at how a country's intelligence agencies operate.[24]

On the other hand, American politics scholars do look at the bureaucracy, but they focus almost exclusively on *domestic policy* agencies, and regulatory agencies in particular. Here too, theoretical agendas explain why. The central concern driving most research in American politics is the delegation of political power—understanding when and why elected officials voluntarily give some of their own authority to unelected government bureaucrats. The answers have varied, but all of them place great weight on the role of organized interests and the electoral incentives of legislators. This theoretical focus has naturally led scholars to examine domestic regulatory agencies like the Federal Trade Commission, Interstate Commerce Commission, and the Environmental Protection Agency, where interest groups are strong and where legislators have powerful reasons to care about what those groups want. In the 1970s and 1980s, the rage was capture theory, which argued that private industry designed and operated government agencies for its own benefit.[25] More recently, political scientists have used transaction cost economics to argue that Congress designs and oversees the bureaucracy in surprisingly efficient ways. This work, called the new institutionalism, has taken new ideas but continued applying them to the same old agencies.[26] In the quest to build theory, scholars have paid inordinate attention to domestic regulatory agencies and ignored the rest of the bureaucratic universe.

Political science is also driven, to a large extent, by research methods. In the quest to become more scientific over the past 20 years, the discipline has become much more quantitative. Large original datasets, formal mathematical models, and increasingly, randomized experiments involving hundreds of participants are considered the gold standard for what constitutes "good research." This quantitative bent, though promising for some topics, is deadly to others like intelligence—because it unavoidably skews research to questions where "evidence" consists of numbers that can be crunched, not history that can be traced, documents that can be unearthed, or people that can be interviewed. Case study research has fallen so far out of favor, Stanford's political science department, which is one of the best in the nation, no longer offers any doctoral courses on how to do it.

These abstract debates about theory and research methods have real consequences, creating powerful social norms about what constitutes "important work" and career incentives that direct scholarly attention in some directions and away from others. The process starts early, in graduate school. In top political science PhD programs, doctoral students are taught the canon of important theoretical work in class, are often expected to critique theoretical debates in comprehensive field exams before beginning their dissertations, and are ultimately judged by how much and how well their dissertation research contributes original insights to existing academic debates. The best doctoral programs also expect their graduates to have sophisticated quantitative skills and research agendas that make good use of them. Degrees are awarded, jobs are gotten, grants are won, tenure is secured, and reputations are made more often by producing the most theoretically interesting and methodologically sophisticated research, not by examining the most important government agencies or policy challenges.

The Perils of Secrecy

Features unique to academia make the benefits of studying U.S. intelligence low. At the same time, features unique to intelligence make the costs of studying intelligence exceptionally high.

No organization is easily studied from the outside. In private firms, nonprofit organizations, and government agencies, the formal mission and structure often reveal little about the "real" inner workings of the organization. Intelligence agencies, however, are particularly difficult for outsiders to study for two reasons.

The first and most obvious reason is classification—or, more precisely, the over-classification of information. The current classification system arose during the Cold War, when government officials kept paper records, managed information by hand instead of computers, and erred on the side of classifying more rather than less. By the 1990s, this system had become unmanageable. In 1997, the Commission on Protecting and Reducing Government Secrecy, chaired by the late Sen. Daniel Patrick Moynihan, found that roughly three million people in government and industry had the ability to classify information, and all of them were operating without consistent guidelines or statutory standards. "Apart from aspects of nuclear energy subject to the Atomic Energy Act," the commission concluded, "secrets in the Federal Government are whatever anyone with a stamp decides to stamp secret."[27]

The result has been an intelligence system where much remains inaccessible to the outside. Those interested in studying environmental policy, for example, can access more than 30 years of detailed budgetary data from the Environmental Protection Agency. By contrast, intelligence officials only began to release the grand total for the U.S. intelligence community budget beginning in 2007. Prior to that time, the budget had been publicly released only twice before, in fiscal years 1997 and 1998. Even now, these top-line budget figures still provide no insight into the budgets and priorities of the 17 individual agencies that comprise the U.S. intelligence community.

The Freedom of Information Act (FOIA), first passed in 1966, allows any person to request the release of classified documents, and by law, federal agencies must respond to all requests within 30 business days.[28] In reality, however, the FOIA process is time-consuming, cumbersome, and riddled with uncertainty. For starters, "response" means providing a status report of the request, not resolving it. More often, the actual processing period to determine whether a document will be released lasts months, even years. Since 1996, all federal agencies have been required to report statistics about their handling of FOIA requests. According to the CIA's records, the agency in 2012 handled 808 "complex" FOIA requests with a median processing time of 217 days.[29] The worst recorded year was 2001, when the median response time was 605 days, or nearly two and half years.[30] And of course, the median means that half of these requests took longer than 605 days to resolve—in some cases, much longer. According to a 2003 audit by the National Security Archive at George Washington University, the oldest pending FOIA requests were filed during the Cold War. In one, for example, a University of Southern California graduate student, William Aceves, requested Defense Department records on the

U.S. "Freedom of Navigation" program. He sent the request in 1989. When the National Security Archive conducted its audit 14 years later, Aceves had become a full professor, was still interested in the records for his research, and was still waiting to hear whether he would ever receive them.[31]

His is by no means an isolated case. Another National Security Archive audit found that in 2010, the CIA's oldest request had been pending for 12 years, since October 1998. The National Security Agency's oldest request was from May 1996. And the Defense Intelligence Agency's oldest request was from August 1993.[32] It may be that academic researchers can obtain classified information about a host of subjects more quickly and easily than these figures suggest. The problem, however, is that they can never be sure. There is no way to know ahead of time whether any particular FOIA request will take days, weeks, months, or years to process. The uncertainty inherent in the declassification system, in short, provides strong incentives for academics to steer clear of intelligence. Few career-minded professors are willing to risk their futures that newly declassified research materials are on the way.

The second reason that career academics have a hard time studying intelligence is closely related to the first: Classification has engendered a culture of secrecy inside the intelligence community that makes even unclassified information difficult for outsiders to obtain. Evidence is the lifeblood of research, and it comes in three forms: data sets, documents, and people. All are exceptionally difficult to find in the U.S. intelligence community.

Consider what at first glance would seem to be the easiest information to gather: the number of congressional hearings about different intelligence issues over time. It turns out that even this information is not so easily found. Intelligence is handled by at least eight major congressional committees, each of which provides whatever information it wants in whatever form it desires on its own website. No one, apparently, has thought to consider what minimum information should be provided consistently—say, an annual, updated list of committee hearing dates, topics, and a designation of whether hearings are open or closed to the public. Transcripts of open hearings are often not available to the public until months or years after the date of the hearing. The intelligence committees do release annual reports that list the number of closed and open hearings they held that year, but those lists provide little insight into the topic of the hearings and are sometimes inconsistent with hearing information provided on the committees' own websites. My point is not that committee hearing information is impossible to find but that it is far more difficult to find than it should be, particularly in a research area where everything else is even more inaccessible.

As one might expect, obtaining executive branch documents is more challenging. This is because intelligence agencies still retain a great deal of discretion over what information they release, to whom, and when. This gatekeeping role, combined with the intelligence community's natural penchant for holding information closely rather than sharing it broadly, has created a universe of information that is unclassified but effectively off limits to outsiders. In November 2004, for example, I called the FBI director's office and requested two sets of documents: an unclassified version of the Bureau's 1998 strategic plan and historical data about which FBI officials had won presidential rank awards—the government's highest civil service honor—between 1991 and 1998. I was quickly sent to the Bureau's office of public affairs, which advised that a Freedom of Information Act request would probably have to be filed. When I pointed out that the documents were not classified, that the Bureau had in fact referred to presidential rank awards in some of its own public documents,[33] and that the names of all winners from 1998 to 2004 were publicly listed on another federal government website,[34] I was told the information would be forthcoming. The FBI eventually sent me a large packet in the mail, but none of my requested documents were in it. Instead, the "data" inside consisted of photocopies of the Bureau's public web pages. I finally obtained the documents I needed months later by interviewing dozens of other officials and finding one who was willing to give me his own copy of the 1998 strategic plan and another who just happened to save paper copies of the programs from all the FBI's presidential rank award ceremonies during the 1990s.

People, finally, are crucially important for understanding the inner workings of U.S. intelligence agencies. But even locating the right people to interview is far more challenging in intelligence than in most other policy areas. Scholars interested in interviewing key EPA personnel for official business need only search the agency's online personnel directory. The State Department also puts its telephone directory online.[35] In comparison, at the CIA, the total number of employees is classified, and no online directory exists for officials without undercover responsibilities. Even the CIA's director of Public Affairs has no direct contact information posted online.

What's more, intelligence security procedures still strongly discourage contact with outsiders, even when it benefits the intelligence community. In 2004, for example, the CIA's Office of Security called a senior intelligence official and asked why he had been speaking with so many academics and other external contacts. The official explained that communicating with outside experts was part of his official job responsibilities set out by the director of Central Intelligence. He was brought in for questioning anyway and spent four hours the next day taking a polygraph test. "I didn't care," he later reflected. "But imagine if I were a GS-13. No way would I be talking to anybody again. We keep hiring people and giving them titles like director of Outreach. But nobody's told the security guys."[36]

In short, classified information is hard to get, and unclassified information is not much better: When it comes to the intelligence business, "public" does not mean "accessible." Over 50 years, the community's classification system, cultural affinity for secrecy, and reliance on bureaucratic procedures have produced a thicket through which information does not pass easily.

Enterprising academics certainly can overcome these barriers. But most never try, because doing so is costly and more attractive alternative research topics are plentiful. Indeed, gathering information about U.S. intelligence issues and agencies requires the one thing in shortest supply for most academics: time. The well-worn image of tweedy professors lounging in coffeehouses, pouring over old books, and pondering endlessly is nowhere close to the reality now confronting professors in major research universities. A more accurate view is captured by the phrase "publish or perish." Young professors are given between seven and ten years to make their scholarly mark in the world, or they are denied tenure and fired, often with little hope of landing another academic job any time soon. Most universities, in fact, operate with tight restrictions about the timing, expertise, and number of faculty appointments, creating a job market that is inefficient and incapable of hiring to meet surging educational needs or snatching good people when they are cast adrift in the tenure process elsewhere. The ticking tenure clock creates strong incentives for rising academics to research topics with data that is readily available so that publications can be produced quickly. Those topics are found more often and more reliably outside the U.S. intelligence community.

In sum, it should come as no surprise that intelligence has not been a hot topic in academia. U.S. intelligence agencies have been largely ignored because they are too domestic for international relations theorists and too foreign for scholars of American politics, because social norms and incentives discourage most political science scholars from venturing too far from the main intellectual currents or research methods of their fields, because it is exceptionally difficult for academics to get their hands on intelligence information for their work, and because plenty of other topics are easier to study.

Why Professors Matter

Some readers may be wondering, "So what if professors neglect the study of intelligence?" The short answer is that it matters a great deal. Academic teaching and research have the potential to shape public perceptions about how intelligence agencies actually work and influence policy choices about how to make intelligence agencies work better.

Public Perceptions: Fact versus Fiction

Most Americans' understanding of U.S. intelligence agencies is based more on fiction than fact. Tom Clancy spy novels, James Bond movies, and hit television shows like *Alias*, *24*, and *Homeland* are wildly popular but not wildly accurate. Even so-called realistic Hollywood portrayals veer far from reality. The 2013 blockbuster *Zero Dark Thirty*, for example, declared in its opening frame to be "based on first-hand accounts of actual events," and its director repeatedly called the movie a "reported film."[37] Yet *Zero Dark Thirty's* central claim—that torture was the key to getting the name of the courier that led to bin Laden—has been flatly contradicted by CIA Director Leon Panetta, Acting CIA Director Michael Morrell, and Senate Intelligence Committee Chairwoman Dianne Feinstein, among others. As Morrell noted in a statement to CIA colleagues, "the film takes significant artistic license, while portraying itself as being historically accurate." The film, he adds, "creates the strong impression that the enhanced interrogation techniques that were part of our former detention and interrogation program were the key to finding bin Laden. That impression is false."[38]

The CIA's own website acknowledges the misperception problem generated by spy-themed entertainment. Its homepage for high school students begins by noting, "A lot of people still think that our employees lurk around in trench coats, send coded messages, and use exotic equipment like hidden cameras and secret phones to do their job. (You know, all those things you see in the movies or read about in spy novels.) There is a little of that, but that's only part of the story."[39]

These examples may seem frivolous, but the danger is real. Polls show that American knowledge of intelligence is generally poor. In a 2012 national poll I commissioned with *YouGov*, 93 percent of Americans did not know how much of a typical intelligence report comes from secrets (the answer is less than 25 percent).[40] In my follow-up October 2013, national *YouGov* poll, I found that only 43 percent of Americans could correctly identify the director of National Intelligence from a list of names, while 74 percent could identify Miley Cyrus as the person who twerked at the MTV

Video Music awards that year. Nearly a third of Americans wrongly believed the National Security Agency conducts operations to capture or kill foreign terrorists, and another 39 percent of Americans simply didn't know if NSA activities included capturing or killing terrorists. Meanwhile, even in the midst of the Snowden revelations, half of Americans had no idea the NSA is responsible for breaking other countries' codes, and 39 percent wrongly believed that the NSA's phone "metadata" program—which was receiving widespread press coverage at the time—included the content of phone calls. As the Intelligence Science Board concluded, spy-themed entertainment is adult education.[41] Americans are steeped in misconceptions about what U.S. intelligence agencies actually do and misplaced expectations about how well they can do it. James Bond always gets his man, and Jack Bauer always saves the United States each television season, but real intelligence officers live in a different world. "On a weekly basis, we are always wrong about something," notes Mark M. Lowenthal, former Assistant Director of Central Intelligence for Analysis and Production. "That's why we have intelligence agencies, because we don't know."[42]

When public perceptions diverge so much from reality, two problems arise. The first is that the public may judge the intelligence community a failure—even when it may be working well—because perfection is an impossible goal to meet. The second problem is exactly the opposite: The public's confidence in the power and effectiveness of U.S. intelligence agencies may be so overblown that policymakers cannot garner support for intelligence reforms, even when they are desperately needed. Ultimately, the gap between public perceptions and policymaking imperatives may become impassable, with the public believing that intelligence agencies are overly powerful and should be restrained, and policymakers believing that they are too weak to protect U.S. citizens and interests and must be strengthened. Academic research and teaching are vital for bridging this gap—providing a realistic and dispassionate view of the capabilities that U.S. intelligence agencies have, the constraints and authorities under which they operate, and the challenges that they face.

Individuals versus Organizations: The Intelligence Reform Debate

Academics also have the potential to shape intelligence policy debates in Washington by analyzing problems in ways that others do not. Most often, intelligence policy discussions are dominated by policymakers and the journalists who cover them. For most officials and reporters, individuals are the heart of the matter: Intelligence successes and failures are all about who's on top, what skills different people bring to their jobs, who knows whom, and who fell down on the job. As Bob Woodward wrote in *The Commanders*, "Decision making at the highest levels . . . is a complex human interaction. . . . This human story is the core."[43]

Career academics, by contrast, find the human story is almost always less important than we think. Political scientists are taught to avoid "it depends on the person" arguments, for good reason. Explanations that chalk up outcomes to individual personalities, rivalries, and mistakes are easy to conjure and impossible to test or falsify in any scientific way. Perhaps more important, attributing outcomes to these kinds of idiosyncratic factors creates a narrative that every historical case is unique, blinding us to the possibility that there are other, important, underlying forces that make historical cases alike. Instead of searching for specificity, professors are trained to seek generality, to develop explanations that can account for outcomes across specific times, places, and individual leaders. Theirs is a quest for analytic power, not detailed description. Their goal is to identify root causes, not ephemeral ones. For academics, the most important determinants of intelligence success and failure are not individuals, but the forces that transcend them. This academic orientation to focus on general causes is far more likely to generate broader, and better, policy solutions. After all, if individuals are always to blame, then "throwing the bums out" is the best we can do.

The difference between these approaches is most usefully seen by examining accounts of 9/11. In the years since the World Trade Center and Pentagon attacks, the prevailing wisdom propagated by policymakers and journalists has attributed the tragedy to the failures of individuals. Former Clinton National Security Advisor Samuel Berger, former Secretary of State Madeline Albright, and former White House counterterrorism czar Richard Clarke, among others, have faulted President Bush and his administration for giving terrorism short shrift compared to missile defense and other foreign policy issues. Others, including Secretary of State Condoleezza Rice and Vice President Richard Cheney, have charged the Clinton administration with failing to develop an effective counterterrorism strategy and emboldening bin Laden by responding weakly to earlier terrorist attacks. Journalistic accounts, too, have focused on the role of individuals—on the personalities and personal battles behind the scenes that led to disaster.

These accounts are both understandable and misguided. We are left to think that if only a few important people had connected a few obvious dots, tragedy could have been averted. What is missing is a sense of context, of the underlying constraints and forces that made it likely that talented people would make poor decisions.

An organizational analysis, by contrast, finds three such constraints at work before 9/11: (1) cultural pathologies that led intelligence agencies to resist new technologies, ideas, and tasks after the Cold War ended; (2) perverse career incentives that rewarded intelligence officials for all of the wrong things; (3) and structural weaknesses dating back decades that prevented the U.S. intelligence community from working together as a coherent whole. With technology-phobic FBI agents keeping case files in shoeboxes rather than putting them into computers, with CIA operatives clinging to old systems designed for recruiting Soviet officials at cocktail parties rather than Jihadists in caves, with career incentives that rewarded intelligence officials for staying cloistered in their own agencies rather than sharing information across agency lines, and with a 40-year-old intelligence structure that gave no person the power to knock bureaucratic heads together, the U.S. intelligence community did not have a fighting chance against Al Qaeda.[44] According to this view, U.S. intelligence agencies failed to stop the terrorist attacks not because individuals made mistakes, but because individual mistakes were the inevitable result of the debilitating organizational deficiencies that had afflicted America's intelligence community for years. Fixing these organizational problems, not firing individuals, is the key to improving intelligence in the future.

I do not mean to suggest that university professors corner the market when it comes to offering penetrating analysis of the past and bright ideas for the future. What I am suggesting is that the day jobs of policymakers and journalists require different tools and time horizons than professors have, and these differences lead them to very different explanations and solutions. For policymakers and journalists, deadlines are tight, individuals matter, and success hinges on specifics—the details of the treaty, the intricacies of policy, the nuances of the story. As a result, policymakers and journalists tend to exaggerate the role of individual leaders in assessing past failures. They rely on anecdotal evidence that can be collected quickly instead of studying a single problem in systematic detail over a number of years. And they tend to favor reforms that address specific failings of the past. Professors, in contrast, are paid to search for general cause-and-effect relationships. They are trained to gather comprehensive evidence to support or refute hypotheses. And they naturally gravitate toward reforms that address the general problems they find. Thus, even when professors, journalists, and government officials examine the same problem, they are likely to focus on separate pieces of the puzzle, offer differing explanations, marshal distinct kinds of evidence, and suggest different implications.

Conclusion

The U.S. intelligence community needs help. With declining budgets and rising threat complexity, intelligence agencies in many respects face the worst of all worlds: They are still hobbled by the structures and ideas of the past and by new, still-weak institutions of the present, making it difficult to adapt to an uncertain future.

Sixty years ago, at the dawn of the Cold War, academics played a vital role in developing new organizations and new ideas for U.S. national security. Professors on leave from elite universities became some of the CIA's first analysts.[45] On campus, academic research on game theory provided key insights into the logic and workings of nuclear deterrence. Today, the demand for new thinking is just as great, but the obstacles to providing it are greater. More than a decade after September 11, at a time when intelligence is playing a more critical role in national security and foreign policy than it ever has before, professors are not flocking to learn about or work inside the U.S. intelligence community. The reasons have less to do with political views about the CIA or other intelligence agencies than with the professional incentives that career academics face. Restrained by theory and research methods on one side and secrecy on the other, political science professors are unlikely to be delving into the world of intelligence any time soon.

Notes

1. Together, the CIA and FBI missed 23 opportunities to potentially disrupt the September 11 attacks. See Amy B. Zegart, *Spying Blind: The CIA, the FBI, and the Origins of 9/11* (Princeton, NJ: Princeton University Press, 2007).

2. Report of the U.S. Senate Select Committee on Intelligence and U.S. House Permanent Select Committee on Intelligence, *Joint Inquiry Into Intelligence Community Activities Before and After the Terrorist Attacks of September 11, 2001*, 107th Cong., 2d sess., December 2002.

3. The National Commission on Terrorist Attacks upon the United States, *The 9/11 Commission Report* (New York: W. W. Norton, 2004).

4. The Commission on the Intelligence Capabilities of the United States Regarding Weapons of Mass Destruction, Report to the President of the United States (Washington, DC: Government Printing Office, March 31, 2005).

5. Based on analysis data from 2011–2012 *U.S. News & World Report* rankings and analysis of online university course catalogs conducted June–August, 2012.

6. Polling of political scientists reveals substantial consensus about the top three general disciplinary journals. For more, see James C. Garrand and Micheal W. Giles, "Journals in the Discipline: A Report on a New Survey of American

Political Scientists," *PS: Political Science and Politics*, April 2003, pp. 293–308. The seven universities offering undergraduate courses were Brown, Georgetown, Princeton, Rice, Stanford, the University of Southern California, and Yale. Data do not include summer or inter-term courses. "U.S. News Best Colleges 2012," *U.S. News & World Report*, 2012 Edition, September 20, 2011.

7. Based on analysis of abstracts from January 2001 through July 2012. The three intelligence-related articles were: Darren W. Davis and Brian D. Silver, "Civil Liberties vs. Security: Public Opinion in the Context of the Terrorist Attacks on America," *American Journal of Political Science* 48 (January 2004), pp. 28–46; Robert Powell, "Defending against Terrorist Attacks with Limited Resources," *American Political Science Review* 101 (2007): 527–541; Tiberiu Dragu, "Is there a Trade-off between Security and Liberty? Executive Bias, Privacy Protections, and Terrorism Prevention," *American Political Science Review* 105 (2011): 64–78.

8. The exact total is 1,453 articles, based on analysis of issues of *International Organization* from January 2001 through January 2014; *World Politics* from January 2001 through January 2014; *International Studies Quarterly* from January 2001 through December 2013; and *International Security* from January 2001 through fall 2013.

9. Richard A. Clarke, *Against All Enemies: Inside America's War on Terror* (New York: Free Press, 2004).

10. George Tenet, *At the Center of the Storm: My Years at the CIA* (New York: HarperCollins, 2007).

11. Louis J. Freeh, *My FBI: Bringing down the Mafia, Investigating Bill Clinton, and Fighting the War on Terror* (New York: St. Martin's, 2005).

12. Michael Scheuer, *Imperial Hubris: Why the West Is Losing the War on Terror* (Dulles, VA: Brassey's, 2004).

13. Bob Graham with Jeff Nussbaum, *Intelligence Matters: The CIA, the FBI, Saudi Arabia, and the Failure of America's War on Terror* (New York: Random House, 2004).

14. Richard A. Posner, *Preventing Surprise Attacks: Intelligence Reform in the Wake of 9/11* (Stanford, CA: Hoover Institution Press, 2005); Richard A. Posner, *Remaking Domestic Intelligence* (Stanford, CA: Hoover Institution Press, 2005). A number of other, less well-known, former officials have also produced major books. See, for example, Jennifer Sims and Burton Gerber, eds., *Transforming U.S. Intelligence* (Washington, DC: Georgetown University Press, 2005); Gregory F. Treverton, *Reshaping National Intelligence for an Age of Information* (New York: Cambridge University Press, 2003); Arthur S. Hulnick, *Keeping Us Safe: Secret Intelligence and Homeland Security* (Westport, CT: Praeger, 2004); Bruce Berkowitz, *The New Face of War: How War Will Be Fought in the 21st Century* (New York: Free Press, 2003).

15. James Risen, *State of War: The Secret History of the CIA and the Bush Administration* (New York: Free Press, 2006); Eric Schmitt and Thomas Shanker, *Counterstrike: The Untold Story of America's Secret Campaign Against Al Qaeda* (New York: Times Books, 2011).

16. Steve Coll, *Ghost Wars: The Secret History of the CIA, Afghanistan, and Bin Laden, from the Soviet Invasion to September 10, 2001* (New York: Penguin, 2004); Bob Woodward, *The War Within: A Secret White House History 2006–2008* (New York: Simon & Schuster, 2009); Bob Woodward, *Plan of Attack* (New York: Simon & Schuster, 2004); Bob Woodward, *Bush at War* (New York: Simon & Schuster, 2002); Joby Warrick, *The Triple Agent: The al-Qaeda Mole who Infiltrated the CIA* (New York: Vintage, 2012).

17. Bill Gertz, *Breakdown: How America's Intelligence Failures Led to September 11* (Washington, DC: Regnery, 2002).

18. Terry McDermott, *Perfect Soldiers: The 9/11 Hijackers: Who They Were, Why They Did It* (New York: HarperCollins, 2005).

19. John Miller and Michael Stone with Chris Mitchell, *The Cell: Inside the 9/11 Plot, and Why the FBI and CIA Failed to Stop It* (New York: Hyperion, 2002).

20. John Rizzo, *Company Man: Thirty Years of Controversy and Crisis in the CIA* (New York: Scribner, 2014).

21. Mark Mazzetti, *The Way of the Knife: The CIA, a Secret Army, and a War at the Ends of the Earth* (New York: Penguin Press, 2013).

22. See, in particular, Loch K. Johnson, *Bombs, Bugs, Drugs, and Thugs: Intelligence and America's Search for Security* (New York: New York University Press, 2002); Loch K. Johnson and James J. Wirtz, eds., *Strategic Intelligence: Windows into a Secret World* (Los Angeles: Roxbury Press, 2004); Richard K. Betts and Thomas G. Mahnken, eds., *Paradoxes of Strategic Intelligence: Essays in Honor of Michael I. Handel* (London: Frank Cass, 2003); Robert Jervis, *Why Intelligence Fails: Lessons from the Fall of the Shah and Iraqi WMD* (Ithaca: Cornell University Press, 2011).

23. See, for example, Graham Allison, *Essence of Decision: Explaining the Cuban Missile Crisis* (Boston: Little, Brown, 1971); Morton H. Halperin, *Bureaucratic Politics and Foreign Policy* (Washington, DC: Brookings, 1974); James Fearon, "Domestic Political Audiences and the Escalation of International Disputes," *American Political Science Review* 88 (September 1994), pp. 577–592; Kenneth Schultz, *Democracy and Coercive Diplomacy* (New York: Cambridge University Press, 2001).

24. Joseph S. Nye Jr., *Soft Power: The Means to Success in World Politics* (New York: Public Affairs, 2004); Samuel P. Huntington, *The Clash of Civilizations and the Remaking of the World Order* (New York: Simon & Schuster, 1996).

25. George J. Stigler, "The Theory of Economic Regulation," *Bell Journal of Economics and Management Science* 2 (1971), pp. 3–21; Sam Peltzman, "Toward a More General Theory of Regulation," *Journal of Law and Economics* 19 (1976), pp. 211–240; Gary Becker, "A Theory of Competition Among Pressure Groups for Influence," *Quarterly Journal of Economics* 98 (1983), pp. 371–400.

26. See, for example, Barry Weingast and Mark Moran, "Bureaucratic Discretion or Congressional Control? Regulatory Policymaking by the Federal Trade Commission," *Journal of Political Economy* 91 (October 1983), pp. 775–800; Mathew D. McCubbins, "The Legislative Design of Regulatory Structure," *American*

Journal of Political Science 29 (November 1985), pp. 721–748; Lawrence S. Rothenberg, *Regulation, Organizations, and Politics: Motor Freight Policy at the Interstate Commerce Commission* (Ann Arbor: University of Michigan Press, 1994).

27. *Report of the Commission on Protecting and Reducing Government Secrecy* (The Moynihan Commission), 103rd Cong., March 3, 1997 (Washington, DC: Government Printing Office, 1997), p. xxii.

28. Usually, agencies have only 20 working days in which to respond. An additional ten-day extension is available for "unusual circumstances." For a thorough discussion of FOIA, see United States Government Accountability Office, Information Management: Implementation of the Freedom of Information Act, Testimony before the Subcommittee on Government Management, Finance, and Accountability, U.S. House Committee on Governmental Reform, May 11, 2005, GAO 05-648T.

29. Central Intelligence Agency, Freedom of Information Act Annual Report, Fiscal Year 2012, p. 22, available at http://www.foia.cia.gov/sites/default/files/CIA .FY12.Final_.pdf (accessed February 5, 2014).

30. Central Intelligence Agency, Freedom of Information Act Annual Report, Fiscal Year 2001, p. 8.

31. The National Security Archive, George Washington University, "Justice Delayed Is Justice Denied: Freedom of Information Act Audit: The Ten Oldest Pending FOIA Requests," November 17, 2003, available at http://www.nsarchive .org (accessed February 4, 2014), pp.1–2.

32. The National Security Archive, George Washington University, "Eight Federal Agencies Have FOIA Requests a Decade Old, According to Knight Open Government Survey," July 4, 2011, available at http://www.nsarchive.org (accessed February 4, 2014).

33. See, for example, FBI press releases announcing the appointments of Sheri A. Farrar as assistant director of the FBI's Administration Services Division, October 30, 2001, available at http://www.fbi.gov/news/pressrel/press-releases/fbi-appoints-sheri-a.-farrar-as-assistant-director-of-the-fbis-administration-services-division-at-fbi-headquarters (accessed February 4, 2014) and the appointment of Gary M. Bald as head of the FBI's new National Security Branch, August 12, 2005, available at http://www.fbi.gov/news/pressrel/press-releases/fbi-announces-leadership-of-national-security-branch (accessed February 4, 2014).

34. A list of winners of presidential rank awards from 1998 to 2004 was published by the Office of Personnel Management (OPM) and was available on the OPM website as of March 2006.

35. See, for example, http://www.state.gov/documents/organization/112065 .pdf (accessed February 4, 2014).

36. Confidential interview by author, May 2004.

37. Amy Zegart, "Not Just another Movie: Zero Dark Thirty Lies. End of Story," *Foreign Policy*, January 1, 2013, available at http://www.foreignpolicy.com /articles/2013/01/30/not_just_another_movie_zero_dark_thirty (accessed March 4, 2014).

38. Message from the Acting Director: "Zero Dark Thirty," December 21, 2012, available at https://www.cia.gov/news-information/press-releases-statements/2012-press-releasese-statements/message-from-adcia-zero-dark-thirty.html (accessed March 4, 2014).

39. https://www.cia.gov/kids-page/6-12th-grade/who-we-are-what-we-do/our-mission.html (accessed February 4, 2014).

40. Amy B. Zegart, "Real Spies, Fake Spies, NSA, and More: What My 2012 and 2013 National Polls Reveal," *Lawfare,* November 7, 2013, available at http://www.lawfareblog.com/2013/11/real-spies-fake-spies-nsa-and-more-what-my-2012-and-2013-national-polls-reveal/#.UvQh5mSglUs (accessed February 4, 2014).

41. Intelligence Science Board, National Defense Intelligence College, "Educing Information: Interrogation: Science and Art," Phase I Report (December 2006), available at http://www.fas.org/irp/dni/educing.pdf (accessed March 5, 2014), p. ix.

42. Remarks, Regional Intelligence Conference, University of Southern California and the Center for the Study of Intelligence, Los Angeles, CA, February 2, 2006.

43. Bob Woodward, *The Commanders* (New York: Simon & Schuster, 2002), p. 34.

44. Amy B. Zegart, "September 11 and the Adaptation Failure of U.S. Intelligence Agencies," *International Security* Vol. 29 (Spring 2005), pp.78–111.

45. Loch Johnson, "The CIA's Weakest Link," *Washington Monthly* (July/August 2001), pp. 9–14.

CHAPTER THREE

Searching Where the Light Shines?

An American View of Methods for the Study of OSINT and the Other Intelligence"Ints"

Michael Warner

REFLECTIONS ON AN "AMERICAN VIEW" of studying intelligence should not be confused with any particularly "American method" for doing so. Indeed, there is no distinctly American form of intelligence. The craft of intelligence work has been performed according to its own seemingly immutable principles since ancient times, wherever sovereign powers have fought each other or remained ready to do so. The deadly realities of inter-dynastic (even if not quite inter-national) conflict have always made rulers and commanders desire to keep and steal secrets and to employ the clandestine arts to strengthen their friends and weaken their adversaries.

Nonetheless, there are American "idioms" for the practice of intelligence. It emerged as a professional discipline in the United States during and after World War I, developing from three prior disciplines: diplomacy, reconnaissance, and law enforcement. The dividing lines between it and these fields have remained ambiguous and porous. At least since World War II, intelligence in the United States has been conducted in ways that are comparatively large scale, expensive, technological, and ad hoc. Intelligence in America tends to be pragmatic, crafting solutions and then only later examining them for principles that made them work. American intelligence also tends to be comparatively visible, in that many of its secrets do not remain hidden for long, whether from institutional or political rivals, Congressional and media monitors, and ultimately the public. That openness—intended and unintended—has made the U.S. Intelligence Community the world's most studied.

Intelligence scholarship in America has proceeded on similar lines. The United States came late to the professional practice of intelligence, but researchers in America developed the study of intelligence at least as fast as scholars in other nations. The scholar of it must know something of both war and diplomacy—particularly how states defend themselves and employ their "levers of national power"—to understand intelligence. Historical scholarship on this topic in the United States has been based on two trends: on the episodic employment of official historians (and the later release of their studies), and on the investigative and sometimes unilateral declassification (often driven by political motivations) of reports, documents, and sometimes files relating to certain controversial episodes. If there is anything like an American method of studying intelligence, it would represent the collectivity of the particular methods employed in utilizing those resources. It would thus also be influenced, at least indirectly, by the source materials that have been made available.

What follows is not a bibliographical or archival guide to records holdings in the United States. It is not possible in one article to survey the collections of the National Archives and the holdings of the agencies of the U.S. Intelligence Community. Even for researchers, such a survey would have the ironic disadvantages of being both too detailed and too vague. It would also be quickly out of date as new files are released and disclosed. This essay is, rather, a reflection on the types of sources that are available and, more important, on the ways in which they influence the methods employed by scholars of American intelligence.

Intelligence and Scholarship

Intelligence can be thought of as that which states do in secret to support their efforts to mitigate, influence, or merely understand other nations (or at least their enemies). By its nature as an activity that risks the loss of fragile sources of information or other means of understanding and influence—and that can affect the lives of troops, subjects, and even leaders—intelligence is treated by its practitioners as sensitive and confidential. Even the accidental disclosure of some analytical, informational, or operational advantage over a rival is presumed to be tantamount to the loss of that advantage while it is still potentially useful. Thus the penalties for disclosure have always been severe (and those for espionage even harsher).

Wherever such life-and-death stakes obtain—and the United States is no exception—intelligence is done with some full or partial cloak of secrecy, and the documentary record of it is typically unavailable to onlookers.

Intelligence thus by definition resists scholarship, but in the United States there are countervailing forces in the nation's culture and polity that have mitigated the secrecy that customarily surrounds the discipline. First, Americans seem almost congenitally predisposed to distrust government in general and secret dealings in particular. Second, the nation's citizens and institutions practically relish holding officials accountable for their stewardship of the public's trust and resources; this phenomenon is magnified by large news and popular media industries competing for scoops and gripping tales for retail sale. The nation's two-party polity, furthermore, breeds mutual suspicion of anything resembling partisan or ideological interference with public institutions. Finally, the Constitution's implicit endorsement of strong executive branch departments (and its comparative silence on mechanisms to coordinate their efforts) fosters an institutional culture of independence and self-subsistence among the Cabinet-level departments, with each seeking to provide for its own needs in a variety of fields, including intelligence (not infrequently in duplicative ways).

These anti-secrecy trends and inclinations sometimes interact to convince administrations, Congresses, and intelligence agency heads that they must release various historical intelligence documents. Even when such decisions are taken, however, the compartmented organization of the executive branch usually ensures that declassification proceeds on a piecemeal, agency-by-agency basis—instead of being undertaken in a way that illuminates the workings of the entire intelligence system.

Scholarship has trended accordingly. Over the last 60 years, scholars in the employ of the U.S. Government have episodically sought to understand the experiences of the nation's intelligence services. Various Cabinet departments and intelligence agencies have hired professional historians or appointed chroniclers from their own ranks to write narratives of their recent activities. The Office of Strategic Services, for instance, gave this job to operative Kermit Roosevelt after World War II; the fledgling Central Intelligence Agency lured Arthur Darling from Yale; the Armed Forces Security Agency tapped the U.S. Navy's Cmdr. Laurance Safford.[1] In addition, the armed services' histories of their efforts in World War II—most notably the U.S. Army's "Green" series, but also the less-ambitious though still-substantial efforts by the other services—discussed intelligence matters as well at greater or lesser length. This tradition of ad hoc, in-house scholarship has endured to the present day, and over the last generation it has been supplemented by more strongly professional and institutionalized efforts in the Intelligence Community, the military, and the State Department (via the *Foreign Relations of the United States* series). The results of all these efforts have been uneven, but they have been real, and in places they have laid a solid foundation of fact that can support serious theoretical inquiry.

The federal government has not been content with allowing cleared, official historians to read its intelligence records. The United States, having performed little clandestine work overseas before 1941, has been comparatively liberal in opening up the files of actual intelligence offices up to the middle of the 20th Century. The best such pre-Cold War collection is that of the Office of Strategic Services (OSS), which Director of Central Intelligence William Casey had declassified in the 1980s. That process took several years longer than Casey might have anticipated, but now virtually all OSS files are available at the National Archives, and the rather haphazard collection (reflecting OSS' chaotic administrative practices) has been given an improved set of finding aids. The OSS files were and are important in themselves, being the first nearly complete records of the birth, maturity, and demise of a modern intelligence agency (from a nation that had not been conquered and occupied) to be made available to scholars. OSS was a sprawling agency, moreover, practicing several intelligence disciplines and engaging in hundreds of individual operations, and thus a researcher can read in its files documents on a wide variety of activities.

The release of OSS files has been accompanied by the broad declassification of diplomatic, military, and internal security files up to the mid-20th Century. Most records of the State, War, and Navy Departments up to that point (and sometimes beyond) are now available, including their intelligence files (except where those identify foreign sources or cryptologic methods). Many files of the Federal Bureau of Investigation from before the Cold War have been declassified as well, though case files on individuals are available (if at all) through Freedom of Information Act requests. The holdings of the Franklin D. Roosevelt presidential library are virtually all available, while the Harry S. Truman Library holds only a dwindling set of files in classified storage.

The net effect of these releases has been to make it possible for academic and private researchers to see all but a few of the extant documents on American intelligence up to 1946 and many of those documents for several years thereafter. In dealing with intact files, like those of OSS and other agencies, researchers use methodologies that are quite similar to those employed by official historians doing research in still-classified records. Both the "inside" and the "outside" historians work primarily from the office and operational files, from cable traffic and budget data, and from interviews (where living memory endures), artifacts, and other sources, to identify and assemble the clues to what happened and what it meant. The result can be a detailed and insightful appraisal of U.S. intelligence capabilities and performance, such as Katherine Sibley's *Red Spies in America* (on Soviet industrial espionage in the 1940s).[2]

The first place for the researcher to look is always "the file." Like virtually all governmental organizations from the late-19th Century onward, intelligence agencies are hierarchies, and their officers at multiple levels have created and preserved files on their activities. Just as the sources for intelligence history are often the same as those used by military and diplomatic historians, the methods for using them are similar as well. The sort of files that get saved at the State Department or one of its military counterparts—and eventually made available to historians—tend to be archived by office first, by subject next, and then sometimes by operation or activity, according to the records protocols governing the larger department or organization in which they are embedded. The independent intelligence agencies of the United States adapted their filing schemes from the State and War Departments (with minor adjustments to fit their specific needs). The FBI adopted its filing system from the Department of Justice.

The more expensive the activity or topic, the more places one finds files on it. Costly activities and projects ordinarily require more personnel and logistical expenses, hence more accounting and security controls—and more legal counsel—and thus more files. An agency's legal, financial, logistical, and security offices can be expected to keep their own files on larger activities. The director of the agency may have a file on it if it demands his attention or a briefing for higher authorities. Something really important will merit files in other agencies and in the Presidential libraries as well. These can be quite valuable for the researcher because they provide a different (if not always more objective) perspective on the activity.

Not all important incidents, projects, issues, or events are well documented. Here is a quandary in intelligence research: what to infer from a situation in which there are few or no files? That can happen in two circumstances. The first is when events are happening too quickly for everything to be documented by the people on the spot. In such cases the documentation will typically come in the form of summary cables and after-action reports, which are not always as accurate and complete as a researcher might wish. The second case is when the head of the agency or one of its units was specifically ordered to keep the "paper trail" as short as possible. Such instances are rare, but the exceptions that prove the rule (like the CIA's "Track II" in Chile in 1970) are notorious.[3] One reason there were not more such exceptions, even at the height of the Cold War, is the difficulty of doing anything of consequence in a bureaucracy without written authorizations and regular funding streams. When an exception is made, typically some extraordinary aspect will be added to an operation already under way, as with the abortive assassination plotting in the CIA's Guatemala coup operation in 1954.[4] Such operational annexes would usually have been authorized orally.

The next place to look for records, especially if the activity took place overseas, is in the cable traffic. Intelligence agencies live by their official communications channels, and the messages routed along them are meticulously preserved and organized. Cables are supposed to be terse and clear, for the safety and success of the operation and the people involved, not to mention the expense of sending them. Indeed, when compared with staff memoranda produced at a comparatively leisurely pace in the home offices, cables generally seem both laconic and articulate. Cables could take many hours to reach their recipients, however, and not a few cabled instructions had been overtaken by events by the time their addressee finally read them.

Files and cables, where available, allow the researcher to establish accurate chronologies. Where chronology is not, or cannot be, established, the conclusions drawn from the evidence must be regarded as tentative or even as suspect. Chronology is a vital clue in sorting causes and effects, and more than one "urban legend" circulated among intelligence officials (and even among scholars) has been debunked by the simple method of carefully charting events along a reliable time sequence.

A third key source for researchers is budget data. Budgets are sure indicators of the priorities of an organization and of that organization's priority in the larger scheme of policy implementation. They are also an index for comparison in looking at operations themselves, indicating as they do the relative size of the operation in relation to other activities. Agency-wide budgets serve another purpose—that of giving the researcher a benchmark for the quality and challenges of leadership. Declining budgets are a severe test of a leader's ability. Tough decisions are forced on a leader in such times; he or she has to trim somewhere to preserve other priorities, and such choices generally result in disagreements and even bitterness among the managers whose projects and offices lose out. On the other hand, growing budgets allow him to throw money at problems, and many directors are tempted to do just that, often with meager and short-lived results.

Another help, sometimes, is the personnel file of someone involved in an activity. If it contains performance evaluations for the time in question or names of other people involved, such a file gives a researcher important reference points. It also provides clues to the orientation of the officer in question—his professional training and background—that may have had a bearing on the decisions or operation in question. Knowledge of the personnel involved also helps in surmounting the difficulties posed for intelligence scholarship that are caused by secrecy and compartmentation. One cannot assume that an event that was prior in time helped to cause a later one, or that a prior report caused a subsequent decision, since the personnel involved may have had no access to such information. Sometimes it is possible to show that someone involved in an earlier operation was in a position to have had a role in a later one. The converse is true as well—sometimes two things that looked similar were really independent, with no common personnel.

This discussion of sources for official research in intelligence must seem quite elementary to any historian working in the documentary record of 20th century military or diplomatic history. That is no coincidence, for military and diplomatic history is precisely what historical research in intelligence is. Intelligence is not some privileged realm where the usual rules of organizational dynamics and group behavior do not apply; thus it is no exception to the rules of historical scholarship. One gathers the records and facts and arranges them according to the time-honored ways of archival practice and scholarship. An intelligence service will possess more secrets, and sometimes more colorful characters, but its job is to assist the making and the implementing of a nation's strategic decisions. Its records therefore exist in the same milieu and the same patterns as the diplomatic and military ministries that intelligence serves.

Independent Scholarship

Works on American intelligence by independent researchers are in some ways more interesting than the official histories because their authors faced a more difficult task. Where few records have been released, the researcher has to appraise his or her sources in the knowledge that they are surely fragmentary. He has to word his judgments accordingly, erring always on the side of caution, and building to generalizations only on stable bases of fact. Intelligence studies in academia have nevertheless quickened over the last three decades in the fields of history and political science, as more scholars of the diplomatic and military arts grasp the importance of intelligence for their own disciplines and gain familiarity with the relevant documentation. The methods of these "outside" scholars can, in skilled hands, bring their practitioners to genuine historical understanding.

Writing about intelligence in the absence of hard archival sources is a labor that strongly resembles the writing of ancient history. Much of the best writing in this genre is heavily literary in character, rather than historical in the Rankean sense of depicting events *wie es eigentlich gewesen war* ("as they actually happened"). This is not meant as a criticism. Livy, Tacitus, and Thucydides, to name three classical scribes, sought, by the portrayal of fascinating but flawed characters against the backdrop of grand narratives, to illustrate the larger themes of nature, society, and Man himself.[5] The intelligence histories that have been written along different but not dissimilar lines tend to be entertaining and insightful about the characters that populate their narratives.

Where histories of American intelligence aspire to be more Rankean than literary, they tend to resemble in some ways the works of modern historians writing about ancient times. They have to rely on fragments, not files. Their chronologies are sometimes hazy. Rumor and myth are everywhere, often so intertwined with fact that, in some cases, just beyond the reach of living memory, truth and fiction can no longer be separated. The one obvious advantage that intelligence historians have over ancient historians is in the opportunity to interview their subjects—when they will talk (which is sometimes at considerable length). Acquiring the real documents, when one does not have the files they came from, is only the beginning of the task for academic and private researchers. It can be tricky to match them up with the accreted legends that both informed and were themselves formed by an earlier body of literature written without any access to the sources (historians of ancient Greece have a similar chore in squaring the tangible discoveries of modern archeology with the narration of Herodotus, for instance).

A careful non-official researcher tracks down any official documents, studies, reports, and histories that might be available on his or her topic. Congressional testimony and floor debates and (in recent years) the committee reports accompanying the annual Intelligence Authorization Acts, are particularly good sources. The Central Intelligence Agency (where this author once worked) has released several dozen monographs and compilations on its history, and the National Security Agency's release efforts are equally extensive. The armed service intelligence offices have done their share of publishing as well. Such official releases have their distinct limitations. Especially when written by long-serving agency officers (as opposed to professional historians), they typically display a lack of methodological ambition, being straightforward, chronological organizational or operational narratives. They are straitened by the scope of their charters, by the rigors of the declassification process, and by the aptitudes and curiosity of their authors. Nonetheless, they provide an important touchstone of accepted fact that the researcher can use as a platform for further inquiry, or at least a landmark along the way.

The reports of blue-ribbon study commissions and investigative panels can also be illuminating and even crucial to the researcher's work. A watershed for scholars of the U.S. Intelligence Community came with Congress's publication of the *Final Report* of the Senate's special committee that met under the leadership of Sen. Frank Church in 1975–1976. It is no exaggeration to say the "Church Committee's" seven volumes laid the foundation for public knowledge of American intelligence. The Committee's survey of the history of the Central Intelligence Agency from its founding to the mid-1970s is particularly valuable in being comprehensive, insightful, and reliable (in large part because it was based on several dozen still-classified histories produced or held by the CIA's History Staff).[6] There are also examples of official inquiries that made it to the public via extra-legal routes, like the Department of Defense's historical compilation relating to the Vietnam War (the "Pentagon Papers," 1971) and the report of the House of Representative's select committee on intelligence that was rejected by the full House in 1976 (the "Pike Report").[7]

The researcher next looks for the declassified documents themselves. Independent researchers have typically found the sources available to them were typically piecemeal and incomplete. Many of the records sent to the National Archives after 1950 represent "finished" intelligence products—that is, disseminated intelligence analysis. Few policy or administrative documents, and even fewer operational records, have been released. Complete files are rarer still. The spotty official documentation available to academic and private researchers makes their task difficult, though not impossible. The Central Intelligence Agency and the National Security Agency have linked quantities of records to the historical and Freedom of Information Act sections of their public websites. In some cases, the government has released extensive records on particular controversial incidents or topics. Although several of these large-scale declassifications were undertaken for the purpose of clearing the air on certain events, others were related to Congressional investigations or even criminal prosecutions; in both of these latter cases there were political or legal motivations (and sometimes both) for releasing the material. The releases themselves range from the work done by U.S. authorities to track (and occasionally exploit) Nazis and the assets they looted in World War II to the flap over the intelligence on Saddam Hussein's weapons of mass destruction. Other examples include the early-Cold War effort to read Soviet intelligence communications and capture Russian agents ("Venona"); efforts to destabilize the governments of Guatemala (1954), Cuba (1959–1964), Chile (1970–1973), and Nicaragua (1983–1986); intelligence on the assassination of President Kennedy; and analysis and operations related to al Qaeda before the attacks of September 11, 2001. It should be noted that these releases also have the larger, penumbral effect of setting precedents that encourage the subsequent release of other and related materials as well.

The timing of these releases is a critical factor in judging the reliability of scholarly work on U.S. intelligence. Knowing not only the sequence of intelligence activities and events but also the timing of the production and subsequent release of (both internal and public) information about them helps one judge the value of secondary reference materials (and even of some primary sources). It is crucial to understand how much material was and was not available to the author of a history or the drafter of a memo. Anything written about intelligence against Germany in World War II, for instance, must be read with particular care if it was published before the revelation of the ULTRA secret in 1974. Similarly with works on certain Cold War espionage cases in the United States, if published before the public release in 1995 of the "Venona" cables (the decryptions of Soviet intelligence telegrams sent to and from foreign posts, mostly during World War II). It is even a factor to consider when reading histories written by government historians. Several early official histories of U.S. intelligence, for example, were written without access to the mysteries of signals intelligence or the outlines of important human intelligence operations. This reality does not falsify the arguments or discredit the facts cited in works published before these key releases, but it does make them incomplete in important ways.

Much documentation continues to come out through official responses to private requests for documents. The main avenue for such releases has been the Freedom of Information Act (often referred to by its acronym, FOIA). Although not unreasonably scorned by some researchers and declassification advocates as hopelessly slow and haphazard, FOIA requests have nonetheless cumulatively resulted in the release of millions of pages. A requester needs to describe what he or she wants with a fair degree of precision and then to be very patient, but such virtues are sometimes rewarded. Peter Grose's *Operation Rollback* on early covert action programs and Kathryn S. Olmsted's *Red Spy Queen* on Soviet spy-turned-informant Elizabeth Bentley are two recent examples of important works based largely on documentation obtained through FOIA requests.[8]

A handful of researchers have availed themselves of Section 4.4 of Executive Order 13526 (and its predecessors), which allows agency heads to grant scholars engaged in meritorious "historical research projects" limited access to still-classified files. Evan Thomas's *The Very Best Men* is an example of what can be accomplished via this route; Benjamin Weiser's *A Secret Life* on the CIA's Polish asset Col. Ryszard Kuklinski is another.[9]

Some researchers have taken unconventional but still productive paths to a deeper insight on the evolution of the American intelligence system. David M. Barrett, for instance, mined Congressional records, many of them in the papers of former members tucked away in local college libraries or historical societies (and holding a surprising amount of records that would be classified if residing in agency or departmental files).[10] American intelligence can also be studied through its relations with foreign intelligence services, as Jim Beach, Jay Jakub, and Richard J. Aldrich have demonstrated.[11]

News reports that are contemporaneous with the activity under scrutiny can be useful, when read with care. They are fragmentary and often wrong, but they have a certain vitality and immediacy, and they not infrequently touch on ground truth (sometimes better than reporters know). Hints of many intelligence operations show up in the newspapers during or shortly after they take place. A famous example is the Chicago *Daily Tribune's* story on June 7, 1942, that suggested that the Americans had excellent intelligence (and perhaps even broken Japanese naval codes) in time to assist the U.S. Navy's defense of Midway Island three days earlier.[12] Parts of the *Tribune* article were shockingly accurate, but happily Tokyo either missed or ignored it. Indeed, the trouble for any outside observer is that of determining which of the myriad press reports accurately reflect real activities. This can be all but impossible to do, even for friendly intelligence officers reading in the papers about contemporary operations to which security compartmentation gave them no formal access.

Journalists who cover intelligence matters sometimes write histories of recent events—with mixed results. These tend to rely on anonymous sources whose motivations are left unexamined, to lack fastidious chronologies, and to seek to influence live policy debates. Not infrequently, moreover, they touch briefly on important issues or events but have little inkling of their true significance. Thus, these "instant histories" usually do not hold up well over the decades, and after a time they come to be viewed by scholars as being worth little more than extended newspaper articles. They may provide a flavor of their times and some authentic detail, but they are not scholarship.

Memoirs of intelligence professionals, and of decision makers who relied on them, are often useful, especially if the researcher reminds herself that no memoirist loses an argument in his own memorandum-for-the-record.

There are very few "inside" memoirs produced by a serving officer and written as part of his official duties. Occasionally, a senior official will be given limited access to the files some years after her retirement, and her manuscript will be sanitized to remove any classified information before it is published. Two such memoirs by former directors of Central Intelligence (Robert Gates and George Tenet) are noteworthy for their candor and the light they shed on contemporary events as well as on the workings of the CIA.[13] More typical is the memoir produced with no access at all. A handful of memoirs are themselves small-scale intelligence operations—witness Kim Philby's *My Silent War*, published in 1968 while Philby was a pet of the KGB in Moscow.[14] His subtle mockery of CIA counterintelligence chief James Angleton—to name but one example—must be viewed according to how it may have served the KGB's interests to embarrass a pillar of its Main Enemy's defenses.

Oral histories should be heard in a similar light. There are a surprising number of former intelligence officers at large who can be (but usually have not been) interviewed. Indeed, at the time of this writing, there are some intelligence veterans of World War II still alive. This continuity (sometimes) allows researchers to have their drafts commented on by participants in the historical events, or at least by people who knew "how it felt" to do intelligence work in 1954, or 1964, or 1984. Oral history, however, falls in the same historiographical genre as the memoir literature and has to be judged by basically the same rules (indeed, when the subject of an oral history can no longer be asked what he or she really meant to say, the transcript of his or her interview is for all intents and purposes an informal memoir). The advantages and pitfalls of oral history are well known, however, and need not be reviewed here at greater length.

Methods for the Digital Age

The problem of writing history from the daily news resembles another development that is gradually transforming the scholarship on U.S. intelligence. While our knowledge of the Intelligence Community and its forebears before the 1970s is fairly good, many researchers in American intelligence history are interested in the latter periods of the Cold War and, increasingly, the War on Terror. Not entirely by coincidence, the last decade of the Cold War saw a key technological change in the accelerating digitization of communications, and hence of official records. This development has had two effects on intelligence scholarship. First, it has dramatically increased the volume of records available to official historians, while making their searches of those records both more and less difficult. Second, the comparative ease of purloining large quantities of such electronic records has resulted in several well-publicized dumps of files onto the public Internet, resulting in a different but ironically analogous dilemma for independent researchers.

Official historians now have hitherto undreamt-of riches, if they can gain the access to them. Modern government offices keep fewer paper files, storing their documents in electronic files and their communications in e-mails. The serving historian who knows which folders to query—and has the necessary permissions to do so—will find more records than he can ever read. Indeed, it is possible to narrow an entire office's output to a just a few days and even view multiple drafts of a memo or briefing as it evolves through coordination and editing. The problem is more the surfeit than the lack of documentation. Few records are destroyed, as few offices have the surplus talent to dedicate to the task of patiently saving the wheat and deleting the chaff. Instead, old office folders live on and on, in increasingly obscure places. Search engines for efficiently mining office-level shared folders either do not exist or are not available. When the stars align, however, an official historian can enjoy marvelous documentation.

Independent scholars face an analogous feast-or-famine situation. Recent headlines have shown that a single trusted individual can abscond with thousands of documents and make them available to the press or the public. This has compounded every disadvantage faced by independent scholars mentioned above—especially the burdens of partisanship and unrepresentative sampling. What has become available through these unilateral, unauthorized disclosures has been a contextless grab bag of odds and ends on operations and programs. Those that have been publicized have mostly been the spectacular ones (which sell newspapers and generate advertising revenue). The revelations also mean that independent scholars have a great deal more information than ever before, and despite the problems with this bonanza, it seems unlikely that any of the scholars mining it would prefer it were somehow taken back and re-classified by the relevant authorities. For those patient enough to connect it to the past of intelligence in America and the world, the long-term result will be a comparatively reliable historical picture of the recent past of the U.S. Intelligence Community.

Conclusion

Recent decades have seen rapid progress in the methods of historical inquiry in intelligence in the United States. During this time, the U.S. government has declassified millions of pages related to intelligence, a collectivity that is surely greater, both relatively and absolutely, than that which any other nation has released on this subject. The two trends are related. Declassification has allowed historical scholarship of intelligence to make real strides, and scholarship has assisted declassification. The net result is that a large portion of the available "case studies" examined by scholars searching for the basic patterns of intelligence work tend to be American ones.

This is mostly a good thing, but it has its risks. Any researcher works with what he or she has; thus, the available sources will largely determine the research methods that can be employed. A great deal of reliable knowledge is being produced on U.S. intelligence for all phases of its existence—but the picture that has emerged is by no means a complete or balanced one. The material that has been declassified shows the controversies, not the daily grind and thus is a little skewed toward the extraordinary, just as reading only the morning newspaper could convince one that human life is an unending round of political controversies, violent crimes, movie openings, stock trades, and sporting events. Thus also with intelligence studies in the United States.

The results produced by the scholars working with these sources might well be expected to be quite insightful and detailed about particular incidents but not necessarily as learned about the whole sweep of American intelligence. It should not surprise anyone that documentation that emphasizes "human intelligence" activities (as opposed to, say, imagery intelligence), controversial collection methods, analytical (vice operational) matters, and happenings in Washington (as opposed to events in the field) gives rise to research that also concentrates on such matters. Academic and private scholars tend to focus on scandals, human intelligence (both espionage and covert action), and analytical debates. Their colleagues in the employ of the intelligence agencies not infrequently follow the example of their academic mentors and friends. The fact that the official researchers are employed by single agencies further weakens the incentive to do multi-agency research or to attempt to judge how well their agency and others worked together in advancing the national interest. There are fewer scholarly writings, with a less finely developed methodology, on the functioning of U.S. intelligence as a whole.

Such a judgment is not meant as a criticism of anyone engaged in the hard work of understanding U.S. intelligence history. What has happened is not the fault of outside scholars—it is the predictable corollary of official secrecy. Saying that, moreover, is not a condemnation of official secrecy, which is and must remain a reality. It is more an appeal to think beyond the sources and the secrecy and learn how to hunt for the proverbial car keys even in places where the streetlight does not shine. What these methods amount to is a constant need to search for the impact that intelligence made on events. The researcher, both inside and outside the organization, must constantly ask what it was that an intelligence agency actually accomplished with the mission, resources, and authorities allotted to it. How well did it serve decision makers in their deliberations and the conduct of their offices? These are tricky questions to answer even with full access. Determining how well an agency worked with what was given to it is the intelligence scholars' contribution to achieving the ultimate goal of all intelligence scholarship: learning how intelligence made a difference.

Notes

The opinions voiced in this article are the author's own and do not represent those of the Department or any other U.S. Government entity.

1. Kermit Roosevelt, ed., *War Report of the OSS*, two volumes (New York: Walker, 1976). Arthur B. Darling, *The Central Intelligence Agency: An Instrument of Government, to 1950* (University Park, PA: Pennsylvania State University Press, 1990). Laurance F. Safford, "A Brief History of Communications Intelligence in the United States," National Security Agency, 1952. This can be read at http://www.fas.org/irp/nsa/safford.pdf.

2. Katherine A.S. Sibley, *Red Spies in America: Stolen Secrets and the Dawn of the Cold War* (Lawrence, KS: University Press of Kansas, 2004).

3. See Kristian C. Gustafson, "CIA Machinations in Chile in 1970," *Studies in Intelligence* 47 (2003).

4. See Gerald Haines's addendum on this plot in Nicholas Cullather, *Secret History: The CIA's Classified Account of its Operations in Guatemala, 1952–1954* (Stanford, 1999).

5. "My purpose is not to relate at length every motion, but only such as were conspicuous for excellence or notorious for infamy. This I regard as history's highest function, to let no worthy action be uncommemorated, and to hold out the reprobation of posterity as a terror to evil words and deeds." Tacitus, *Annals*, III:65.

6. This Church Committee volume was drafted by Anne Karalekas and later republished in a volume edited by William M. Leary, *The Central Intelligence Agency: History and Documents* (University, AL: University of Alabama Press, 1984).

7. *New York Times*, eds., *The Pentagon Papers as Published by the New York Times* (New York: Quadrangle, 1971). "The CIA Report the President Doesn't Want You to Read," *Village Voice*, supplements (February 11 & 23, 1976).

8. Peter Grose, *Operation Rollback: America's Secret War behind the Iron Curtain* (New York: Houghton Mifflin, 2000). Kathryn S. Olmsted, *Red Spy Queen: A*

Biography of Elizabeth Bentley (Chapel Hill, NC: University of North Carolina Press, 2002).

9. Evan Thomas, *The Very Best Men: Four Who Dared—The Early Years of the CIA* (New York: Simon & Schuster, 1995). Benjamin Weiser, *A Secret Life: The Polish Officer, His Covert Mission, and the Price He Paid to Save His Country* (New York: Public Affairs, 2004).

10. David M. Barrett, *The CIA and Congress: The Untold Story from Truman to Kennedy* (Lawrence, KS: University Press of Kansas, 2005).

11. Jim Beach, "'Intelligent Civilians in Uniform': The British Expeditionary Force's Intelligence Corps Officers, 1914–1918," *War and Society* 27:1 (May 2008). Jay Jakub, *Spies and Sabotuers: Anglo–American Collaboration and Rivalry in Human Intelligence Collection and Special Operations* (New York: St. Martin's, 1999). Richard J. Aldrich, *The Hidden Hand: Britain, America and Cold War Secret Intelligence* (London: John Murray, 2001).

12. Subsequent legal and Congressional attention to the matter that summer exposed the fact of the codebreaking coup. See Gordon W. Prange (with Donald M. Goldstein and Katherine V. Dillon), *Miracle at Midway* (New York: McGraw-Hill, 1982), p. 367.

13. Robert M. Gates, *From the Shadows: The Ultimate Insider's Story of Five Presidents and How They Won the Cold War* (New York: Simon & Schuster, 2006 [1996]). George Tenet with Bill Harlow, *At the Center of the Storm: The CIA during America's Time of Crisis* (New York: Harper, 2008 [2007]).

14. Kim Philby, *My Silent War* (New York: Grove, 1968).

Part II: The Intelligence Cycle

CHAPTER FOUR

What's Wrong with the Intelligence Cycle?

Arthur S. Hulnick

NO CONCEPT IS MORE DEEPLY ENSHRINED IN the literature than that of the "intelligence cycle." I studied the intelligence cycle as an undergraduate in Sherman Kent's book on strategic intelligence and then later when I attended the U.S. Air Force Intelligence School in 1957.[1] In 1965, in the training courses required by the Central Intelligence Agency (CIA), I studied it yet again. When it came time to start writing about intelligence, a practice I began in my later years in the CIA, I realized that there were serious problems with the intelligence cycle.[2] It is really not a very good description of the ways in which the intelligence process works. Additionally, it ignores two main parts of intelligence work, counterintelligence and covert action. There is an alternative view.

The First Step

The intelligence cycle is so nicely described elsewhere that there seems no need to go over it here. So, let us start at the beginning and look at what is wrong. The notion that policymakers, or intelligence consumers, as they are sometimes called, provide guidance to intelligence managers to begin the intelligence process is not correct. Policy consumers do sometimes indicate their main concerns to intelligence managers, but often they assume that the intelligence system will alert them to problems or provide judgments about the future. Consumers will sometimes tell intelligence managers what they are worried about or the direction in which they intend to take policy—but not always.

Still, it is usually not too difficult for intelligence managers to learn what policymakers are up to, but the managers often have to take the initiative to obtain the information. If intelligence managers at various levels are in touch with their policy counterparts, this sharing of information may work quite well. Over the years, intelligence managers have tried to systematize this process by asking policy officials to provide specifics on their concerns. In the Carter administration, for example, a system of National Intelligence Topics (NITs) was created as a way of soliciting guidance for intelligence. Later, they were called Key Intelligence Questions (KIQs). In some cases, when policy consumers failed to submit NITs or KIQs, managers had to resort to sending policy officials a list of topics, asking them to cross out the ones they thought were not necessary or adding those they wanted to add to the list. Even then, the lists were sometimes ignored.

In the end, intelligence managers have to make decisions about the subjects that ought to be covered. Often, this is driven by world events. But none of this provides guidance for intelligence collection. The guidance comes from within the system. Secretary of Defense Donald Rumsfeld, in the George W. Bush administration, is reported to have once said that "we don't know what we don't know," but that is usually not the case. Intelligence managers often know what gaps exist in the intelligence data base derived from intelligence collectors and analysts. Filling the gaps is what drives the intelligence collection process, not guidance from policymakers. Thus, the first step in the intelligence cycle is incorrect in reality.

The Second Step

The second step is equally incorrect. Collection managers cannot wait for guidance in regard to gaps in the intelligence data base to begin the collection process. The gaps will be filled once the collection process is under way. For example, in running espionage operations, commonly called HUMINT (for human intelligence), it may take months or years to find a person who has access to the information needed and is willing to be recruited as a spy. The same may be true for technical collection sensors. Satellites in space, which make up many of the sensor platforms, are not nearly as flexible as managers would wish. Thus, anticipating the intended targets cannot be overlooked. For example, during the British confrontation with Argentina over the Falkland Islands, the United States could not help the British with space imagery because the satellite, programmed to observe the Soviet Union at that time, only passed over the Falklands at night.

Of course, with the use of unmanned aerial vehicles, imagery collection has become more easily refocused on targets of opportunity, but the unmanned aircraft may still not be in the right place when they are needed. Even open source intelligence (OSINT), which has been given new life in recent years because of the proliferation of information on the Internet and the establishment of the Open Source Center, requires planning to ensure access to needed material. Intelligence managers need sophisticated software to mine the data because there is so much of it.

The Real Drivers

— Intelligence managers collect, not policy officials

For all these reasons, intelligence managers, and not policy officials, are the real drivers of the intelligence collection process. Clearly, intelligence moves from collection to analysis, as the intelligence cycle holds, but analysts do not always need new intelligence material to understand world events. The data base is already so large that a competent analyst could write about most events without any more than open sources to spur the process. The incremental addition of new intelligence from human sources or technical sensors may modify the analytic process but rarely drives it. *[analysis driven w/out info]*

The job of the analyst is, in part, to evaluate raw material and put it in perspective. The analyst receives intelligence material from a variety of sources, including media reports, official reports from other government agencies, as well as reports from the intelligence collection process. In my experience as a practicing analyst in the military and in the CIA, raw reports from human sources or technical sensors are sometimes fragmentary, biased, contradictory, or just plain wrong. In order to analyze the data, the analyst compares the new material with the existing data base and previous analysis. Hanging a finished product—whether it is current reporting or a longer-range estimate—on one source usually does not work well. This is apparently what happened in the case of the estimate on weapons of mass destruction (WMD) in Iraq that helped trigger the invasion of that country. The estimate was based, in part, on the reporting of one rather poor and unreliable source. The estimate turned out to be quite wrong, as we now know.[3]

Operating in Parallel

Collect & analysis together

A better way of looking at the relationship of intelligence collection and intelligence analysis is to think of the two processes as operating in parallel rather than sequentially. The two processes are co-equal in terms of utility. It is important to note as well that raw reporting from the collection process, set up into standardized formats, usually goes to policy officials as well as to analysts at about the same time. Though this may not always be true in other intelligence systems, it is certainly true in the United States. Whereas senior policy officials may not see a great deal of the raw reporting, there are usually watch centers at the various policy agencies that screen the raw reporting and send forward the most interesting ones.

Unfortunately, as I have already noted, some of this raw intelligence may be incomplete, contradictory, or just wrong. Policy officials sometimes take the reporting as having been judged and evaluated. Thus, I have heard officials say that the CIA has reported an event, when in fact what the officials have seen is an unevaluated agent report passed along to them by their watch centers. It is not possible to stop this flow of raw reporting. As Bob Gates, the former director of the CIA once noted to me, once the spigot is opened, it is not possible to close it, even though allowing consumers to have raw reporting at about the same time as the analysts receive them creates some serious problems for the analysts. Collection managers often take a different view. They believe they are doing a great service to the policy community by providing this raw reporting. If the intelligence cycle really worked, the circulation of raw reports to policy officials would not happen.

A Major Problem

Since intelligence collection and intelligence analysis operate in parallel and should be co-equal, one would expect that there would be a great deal of information sharing between the two. Regrettably, this is not always the case. Because of restrictions of information sharing, psychological barriers, fears of compromising sources, and security concerns, the intelligence collection process and the intelligence analytic process not only operate in parallel, they are sometimes quite independent of each other. This is a major problem.

When I first joined the CIA, I was assigned on a temporary basis to an office in the Directorate of Plans (DDP), later renamed the Directorate of Operations (DO), and in 2005, renamed yet again as the National Clandestine Service (NCS). My job was to deal with incoming reports from the field. When an interesting report came in one day, I asked my boss if we should alert the relevant analyst about it. He rejected the idea, saying that our job was to send reports like it to the White House, not to the Directorate of Intelligence, since analysts were not worth the attention. I was shocked. Later, when I became an analyst, I did my best to establish good relations with my operational colleagues, but there were issues.

Barriers to Communication

In those days there were physical barriers, manned by armed guards, to prevent analysts and operations officers from visiting each other's offices. Later, the physical barriers were removed, but the psychological ones remained. Operations people feared that somehow analysts would mishandle reports from the field and reveal the identity of clandestine sources. Analysts mistrusted operations officers because they were thought to be devious and untrustworthy. This mistrust was kindled in part because analysts in those days tended to be introverts who found the extroverted personality of the typical operations officers to be abrasive. Operations people tended to think that the introverted analysts were "wimps."

Over the years, these stereotypes have largely been overcome, but efforts to increase communication between analysts and operators by colocating them have not always been successful. Agency managers have pushed analysts to take tours overseas with field stations, but it is more difficult for an operations officer to serve a tour as an analyst. Similar issues may not arise in other intelligence agencies unless they have co-equal collection and analysis components.

The Defense Intelligence Agency (DIA), for example, was immune to this sort of "stovepipe" problem because it was mostly an analytic rather than collection agency. As Defense HUMINT grows, perhaps the same problem will arise. The National Security Agency (NSA) and the National Geo-Spatial Intelligence Agencies (NGIA) are devoted mostly to collection, but they tend to be tightly compartmentalized, creating a different kind of "stovepipe" problem. In theory, all the intelligence agencies should share raw data and coordinate analysis, but for a variety of reasons, they do not always do so. This was one of the main critiques of both the 9/11 Commission and the commission investigating the intelligence failure surrounding the estimate on WMD.

A Mixed Bag

There is a tendency among intelligence agencies to hold back the most sensitive and exciting reports until the agency's leaders have been able to deliver the reports to senior policy officials, thus highlighting the skill and cleverness of their people and "scoring points" with the officials. One effort to spur interagency communications has been the establishment of centers, where all the agencies have representation and where their representatives can easily talk with their counterparts, even informally, to discuss events and incoming intelligence. The establishment of these centers has been something of a mixed bag. We know from the 9/11 investigations that the then-existing counterterrorism center (CTC) was not a place where all information was shared.[4]

Now, efforts at intelligence reform have "morphed" the CTC into a National Counterterrorism Center (NCTC), controlled by the director of National Intelligence (DNI). Will that spur the agencies into more easily sharing their best and most sensitive data? It would be nice to think so, but experience shows that this does not always happen, even at the highest level.

–dont want to share data

The Final Stages

In the final stages of the intelligence cycle, finished intelligence, broken down into a variety of products, emerges from the analytic process. It is supposed to be delivered to policy officials—the literature refers to this delivery as dissemination—and then policy officials either make decisions or create further requirements and the cycle starts over again. This, too, is a distortion of what really happens. Much of this depends on the kind of intelligence product that is being delivered. These products include warning intelligence, in which consumers are alerted to "breaking news," current intelligence to update consumers on world events on which they already have some knowledge, in-depth studies on particular situations or issues, and forecasts of the future, the estimate. All products are received and used in a different way, but none of them really drive the policy process.

Warning intelligence is supposed to alert policy officials to breaking world situations, especially those for which they may have to take action. Both intelligence managers and policy consumers hate surprise. It is embarrassing for intelligence when the system misses an event about which it should have had information. For example, the CIA failed to detect the fact that the Indian government planned to conduct a nuclear test in 1998. Later investigations revealed that this was both a collection and an analysis failure. The CIA had no assets it could tap in India at that time, and the Indian analyst at the CIA had somehow missed the fact that the Indian prime minister had declared his intention to hold the tests. Despite the fact that there was little the U.S. government could do to stop the tests, policy officials were nonetheless outraged at this failure.[5]

Even greater outrage was directed at the entire intelligence community for its failure to detect the 9/11 terrorist attack on the United States. This has been exhaustively examined and has led to the restructuring of the intelligence system. Yet, there is considerable evidence that there was little that might have been done to avert the disaster. But it illustrates the point that policy officials expect the intelligence system to be all-knowing, all-seeing, and always correct. As Richard Betts pointed out many years ago, intelligence failure is probably inevitable.[6] Warning of crisis should come early enough so that policy officials can have time to develop some kind of considered response. Unfortunately, the warning may come so late that it is really an alert that the crisis has already begun. Using a system that is composed of warning centers at major military commands, tied in to warning centers at all the intelligence agencies and in policy departments in Washington, and taking advantage of the proliferation of 24-hour TV and Internet outlets, the warning network rarely misses the start of a crisis, and it is then able to reach out to decision makers quite rapidly. When the decision makers ask intelligence officers how they should respond to the crisis, typically intelligence officers decline to provide advice, thus staying clear of the policy process.

The Most Useful Product

Current or daily intelligence is the most ubiquitous of all types of intelligence products, delivered at all levels and usually first thing in the morning. It is designed to supplement the media, based on the assumption that policy officials have already gotten their media inputs from newspapers or television news. It is the most popular of all intelligence products because current intelligence is an "easy read," short, and to the point. For those policy officials who only have ten or fifteen minutes a day to absorb intelligence products—and consumer surveys consistently show that this is about all the time policy officials have for such things—current intelligence is rated as the most useful product from the intelligence community. The idea of this product is to summarize events, explain how they fit into some context, and suggest what might happen next. It is a very journalistic methodology.

Unlike warning intelligence that may lead to policy action, as the intelligence cycle suggests, current intelligence hardly ever leads to policy decisions—and it is not meant to do so. Instead, it gives generalists at senior levels a chance to find out about events outside their main areas of responsibility. Specialists often complain that the daily intelligence flow does not provide the level of detail they would need to make policy, but the current intelligence products are not designed for specialists. In fact, it would be quite likely that specialists would have seen a great deal of the raw intelligence data that lay behind the current intelligence product anyway.

During the 9/11 investigation, much was made of the fact that one daily publication, the *President's Daily Brief* (PDB), had on August 6, 2001, reported the possibility that terrorists might use commercial aircraft as cruise missiles to attack commercial or government buildings within the United States.[7] Critics of the president took this to have been a warning the president and his senior staff had missed, but normally the PDB would not have been the kind of intelligence product used for warning. The warning would have been delivered in a much more specific document devoted entirely to the subject. Intelligence managers have never expected the PDB or similar publications to be more than educational in nature. Certainly, these publications do not drive the intelligence process.

In-Depth Studies

The same might be said for the myriad in-depth intelligence studies churned out by the analytic components. These studies have proliferated in recent years, although they were rarely attempted at the beginning of the Cold War. These studies are designed to provide in-depth analysis on specific subjects and are meant more for policy officials at working levels rather than senior decision makers, who rarely have the time to read them. These studies help in forcing analysts to come to grips with a specific subject, provide useful information to consumers within the intelligence system, and support policymakers as they design policy initiatives.

The production of these studies grew over the years as a way of giving analysts a vehicle for attacking a problem in more depth than was possible in a daily or weekly publication and without the fuss and bureaucracy involved in producing the more formal national estimate. Policy officials sometimes request these in-depth studies, along the lines suggested by some versions of the intelligence cycle, but in many cases, the studies are produced because analysts are directed by intelligence managers to write them, or analysts themselves believe they should be written. When Robert M. Gates took over the Directorate of Intelligence (DI) at the CIA during the early days of the Reagan administration, he decreed that analysts should produce at least two of these in-depth studies every year. Gates was fond of pointing out that the DI produced about 5,000 of these studies one year. It was not clear, however, how many of them were actually read.

In recent years, these studies have been more carefully tailored to the needs of policy officials. The same might be said for the Defense Intelligence

Agency products, which are geared to military needs, or those coming from the State Department's intelligence and research unit, which has always focused its analysis on foreign policy issues. The fourth category of product, the estimate, is the one most likely to drive the policy process, at least in theory. But the reality is often different.

The Reality of Estimates

The estimate is a creature of the Cold War, but it has its roots in World War II. It is supposed to be a forecast of the future that decision makers can use to build policy, just as the intelligence cycle proposes. The estimate is supposed to be drawn by analysts from all the producing agencies, coordinated by the analysts among themselves to reach an agreed forecast, with dissenting views included. Then it is blessed by the agency leaders; is signed off at the top; is sent to the president, the National Security Council, and staffs; and serves as the basis for policy discussions. There are actually cases where this has happened, where decision makers have waited for the intelligence community's views as embodied in the estimate, but these cases are rare.

The reality is that policy officials often know what they want to do even before they receive the estimate and hope that this product will confirm in some way the wisdom of the path they have already chosen. When the estimate conflicts with their views, policy consumers may dismiss it as uninformed, useless, or even obstructionist. When it agrees with what they think they already know, then they may see it as confirming, irrelevant, or again useless. Although one would think that policymakers would want to know when they were heading in the wrong direction, this is not usually the case. Policy consumers do not welcome intelligence that is non-confirming, perhaps because the large egos that brought them into positions of power do not permit admissions of ignorance.

The WMD Case

There is no better example of what can go wrong in the estimates process than the experience with the problems related to Iraq and Saddam Hussein's alleged possession of weapons of mass destruction in 2003. We now know how the intelligence system politicized the estimate to meet the needs of the George W. Bush administration. The estimate on WMD was flawed from the beginning. It was based on the reporting of only a few unreliable sources. Then analysts made several faulty assumptions about the weapons Saddam Hussein had or used before the first Gulf War. Finally, policy officials used the estimate to convince both Americans and other nations that Saddam was about to develop nuclear weapons. All of this was wrong.[8]

According to James Risen, intelligence officials in both the collection and analysis arms of the CIA, as well as those in other agencies, knew the sources were poor and the conclusions wrong, but they could not fight senior managers who wanted to satisfy the political needs of the White House. Even more corrupting, it appears that Secretary of Defense Rumsfeld, fearing that the estimate would not support the already planned invasion of Iraq, sent his own officials, neither of them intelligence officers, to find the "correct" information.[9] All these steps were perversions of the estimates process. One can only hope that such antics will not take place in the future.

For all the reasons cited, it seems clear to me that trying to learn how intelligence works by using the intelligence cycle model will lead to misunderstandings about what really happens in the intelligence world. Collection and analysis are really parallel processes. The key to their effective functioning lies in the extent to which there is good communication between the two processes. There needs to be, as well, good communication between intelligence managers and policy consumers throughout the intelligence process. At the same time, however, intelligence managers must stand up to policy officials when they seek to make the intelligence judgments conform to political needs.

Intelligence and Policy

In the early days of the Cold War, the founders of the CIA debated the extent to which intelligence should be close to policy. Sherman Kent, a Yale professor who went on to establish the national estimates system in the CIA, and one of the early thinkers about the intelligence process, believed, as did "Wild Bill" Donovan and others, that if intelligence became enmeshed in the policy process, it would lose its value. Kent argued that the best way to avoid politicization of intelligence was to remain distant and aloof. Later, Roger Hilsman, one of the intelligence chiefs at the State Department, took a different view. Hilsman thought that intelligence had to be close to policy to remain relevant.[10] The experiences of the Bush era suggest that Kent may have been right all along.

Nonetheless, other studies have shown that there must be good communication between policy consumers and intelligence managers if intelligence is to be on target and meet the needs of decision makers. At the same time, intelligence managers have to stand up to efforts by policy officials to skew intelligence judgments when the conclusions are at variance with the political proclivities of partisan officials. No one said this would be easy. It is a constant challenge to provide "truth to power." Intelligence must deliver the unvarnished bottom line. Policy officials can go elsewhere for politicized information if they wish, but at their own peril.

Looking at Counterintelligence *[handwritten: not part of intelligence cycle]*

Leaving aside the collection and analysis processes in intelligence, one cannot understand the entire intelligence system without looking at counterintelligence. Counterintelligence is largely defensive in nature, and it is not part of the traditional intelligence cycle—although some writers have tried to adapt the cycle into a counterintelligence model.[11] In my view, counterintelligence follows an entirely different and unique path, with a model of its own. It is certainly worth studying, because counterintelligence is a major function of intelligence, consists of both active and passive components, and has become as controversial as any aspect of the intelligence function in government.

In its earliest forms, counterintelligence usually meant counterespionage—stopping enemy, adversary, or even friendly spies from stealing a country's own secrets. Of course, the target country might very well be carrying out espionage against the enemies, adversaries, or friends at the same time as it tries to defend against similar sorts of spying. Thus, stealing secrets for one's country is good and necessary; having one's secrets stolen is dangerous and despicable. U.S. intelligence officers, for example, are rewarded for their successes in gathering information from their targets, even though some of what they do may be illegal in the countries they target. At the same time, other U.S. intelligence officers are heralded for their ability to root out foreign spies and are castigated when they fail to do so. After all, espionage is illegal in the United States and must be stopped.

More Diverse

Today, counterintelligence has become much more diverse than just stopping spies. It now means countering terrorism, narcotics flows, global organized crime, and subversion. Whatever the threat, however, the patterns of intelligence activity in fighting all of them are similar. It has nothing to do with the intelligence cycle. Instead, there is a counterintelligence methodology that is unique. *[handwritten: nothing to do with the intelligence cycle]*

First, in countering national security threats, counterintelligence units must identify and locate the evil-doers. This might be foreign intelligence operatives working for a hostile intelligence service, a terrorist cell, a unit of a crime "army," or a group of narcotics pushers. There are several proven intelligence methods for identifying the "bad guys," including the use of: penetrations, or "moles," to get on the inside of the groups or services; surveillance, either physical or technical; informants; and intelligence derived from captured or detained individuals. All have both positive and negative aspects.

Based on the Cold War experience, we know that it is possible to recruit officials of a foreign intelligence service to turn coat and betray some of the activities of their operatives. There are several known cases where the United States was able to place a mole inside a foreign service, and there were a number of U.S. intelligence officers—such as Aldrich Ames, John Walker, and Robert Hanssen—who gave away U.S. secrets to the Soviets. The FBI seemed quite capable of recruiting penetrations of crime groups such as the Sicilian Mafia. Penetrating a terrorist cell is far more difficult and dangerous. Terrorist cells are usually made up of a handful of people, all of whom may be bonded by family or religious ties. Even if a terrorist cell member wanted to become a "double agent," the first hint of disloyalty to the cell could result in death. *incorp into cycle?*

Physical or electronic surveillance is another proven method of identifying counterintelligence targets. Overseas, this kind of surveillance can be mounted against potential targets as a result of decisions by intelligence managers. In the United States, however, the rules are more strict. Counterintelligence officials would, in most circumstances, be required to go through a legal process and obtain a warrant before employing surveillance against a U.S. citizen, a resident alien, or a U.S. person. This issue became front-page news early in 2006 when the *New York Times* revealed that President George W. Bush had authorized surveillance of communications without warrant, arguing that Congress had given the president the authority to do so.[12] The scandal involving former NSA contractor Edward Snowden's release of volumes of classified information about electronic surveillance focused even more attention on the issue. This may not be resolved until a court case is brought or new legislation is passed defining the parameters of surveillance use domestically.

Using Informants

Informants can be very useful in identifying counterintelligence targets. Informants are not recruited agents but, rather, people who see something amiss and report their suspicions to authorities. In hostage situations, informants may be able to point out where unusual activity is taking place. For example, prior to 9/11, flight school managers reported to the Federal Bureau of Investigation (FBI) their concerns about Middle Eastern men seeking flight training only to steer aircraft, rather than learn to take off and land. Unfortunately, FBI senior officials refused to grant field agents permission to interview the informants, claiming that there was no probable cause to do so.[13]

Informants can also cause a lot of wasted effort. During the sniper crisis in Washington, DC, in 2002, in which two men were able to terrorize the area by random attacks on innocent targets, requests for information resulted in more than 100,000 inputs, of which 40,000 were worth investigating.[14] People who have experience in fielding informant reports note that, often, the reports are used to denounce spouses, parents, or unpleasant neighbors and provide no useful intelligence. Nonetheless, informants can prove to be helpful in identifying bad guys.

Intelligence from Interrogation

After 9/11 a good deal of controversy arose over the use of intelligence gained from the interrogation of detainees, either overseas or here at home. In the wake of 9/11, some men of Middle Eastern Muslim extraction, who were not U.S. citizens, were required to register with the federal government. Some of these people had irregularities in their visas, had overstayed their stay in the United States, or were in the United States illegally. They were detained in somewhat harsh conditions and, in some cases, badly mistreated. It did not appear, however, that much effort was made to find out if any of them had ties to terrorism.

At the same time, as the United States geared up to take down the Taliban government in Afghanistan, some Taliban fighters or people associated with Al Qaeda were captured, turned in by informants, or sold to the United States by Afghan warlords. These people, dubbed "enemy combatants" by the Bush administration, were shipped to the Guantanamo Naval Base in Cuba, where U.S. authorities said U.S. legal rules did not apply to them. These people were interrogated using what some described as harsh methods, or even torture, according to press reports.

After the United States invaded Iraq in 2003, more detainees were captured on the battlefield. These fighters were imprisoned in Iraq at some of Saddam Hussein's former prisons, including the infamous one at Abu Ghraib. It was at this location that the worst abuses took place. Apparently, unschooled, unscreened, untrained guards were turned loose to abuse the prisoners in the mistaken belief that this would "soften them up" for interrogation. All of these situations involving detainees were handled badly.

Long experience has taught that there are effective ways to interrogate prisoners, using methods that do no harm to the subjects while producing useful intelligence. Unfortunately, those lessons were not applied effectively in the post-9/11 situations. The literature on interrogation methods, on training interrogators, and on handling subjects should have been readily available to anyone involved in trying to extract intelligence from detainees. Anyone who has been involved in intelligence-style interrogations knows that torture is ineffective and counterproductive, as well as ·abhorrent and illegal. Since those experiences, the rules have been changed to exclude such behavior by U.S. officials.

A good interrogation may yield only bits and pieces of information, but if intelligence collectors are careful, they may be able to piece together a broader picture from a series of subjects. The main aim, of course, is to try to learn something about the cells, or units, that the subjects have come from, especially about their plans for future operations.

Stopping the Bad Guys

After the "bad guys" have been identified, then a decision has to be made about the kinds of operations that will be mounted to stop whatever kind of plan or activity might be under way against U.S. interests. This creates a dilemma. Usually, intelligence officers will press to extend or broaden the collection effort to make sure that all the bad guys have been identified and located. At the same time, law enforcement officials are eager to bring the bad guys to justice. This creates a serious problem, often described as the "cops and spies" dilemma.[15]

The divisions between law enforcement and intelligence in the United States have deep roots. Unlike many other industrialized countries, the United States does not have a domestic intelligence service, such as the MI-5 in Great Britain or the DST in France. Instead, the United States has relied for many years on the FBI—which is really a law enforcement organization—to gather counterintelligence and then act to bring lawbreakers to justice. In other countries, the domestic intelligence services collect and analyze counterintelligence in parallel with counterpart foreign intelligence organizations that work beyond the country's borders. When suspected criminal behavior is uncovered, the domestic intelligence services may turn to national police organizations to carry out law enforcement operations against the suspects.

Intelligence versus Law Enforcement

In the United States, however, where no domestic intelligence service has existed, there have been both legal and procedural barriers between the national intelligence services, whose focus has been almost exclusively abroad, and the FBI, which has always had a role in domestic counterintelligence. Traditionally, counterintelligence collected abroad was passed to the FBI, which then determined, usually in consultation with the Justice Department, whether there was probable cause to open a criminal investigation. This would be used to gather evidence that could be brought if a court case arose. This was different from the gathering and analysis of intelligence data, which traditionally was not treated or handled as evidence.

Because of cover considerations and the need to protect the identity of intelligence officers, intelligence managers did not want their people to have to appear in court and wanted as well to protect the sources and methods used to collect intelligence. The FBI was under no such strictures, but the evidence they gathered had to be backed by appropriate warrants and protected according to legal standards. The Aldrich Ames case is a perfect example of how this system used to work.

A joint CIA and FBI team was able to track down Ames and identify him as a Soviet mole in the CIA. Then the FBI obtained a warrant under the Foreign Intelligence Surveillance Act (FISA) to be certain that they had the right target. Once that was done, a second FBI team, with a criminal warrant, took over the investigation and gathered evidence that might be used to prosecute Ames. In the end, Ames agreed to a plea bargain and the case never came to court, but it illustrates how a firewall was in place to separate the counterintelligence investigation from the criminal one.[16]

Taking down Barriers   *COPS & Spies dilemma*

Since 9/11 some of the barriers between intelligence and law enforcement have been weakened, but the cops and spies dilemma still exists. Under the new rules, the FBI may levy requirements on the U.S. intelligence services to collect information specific to their domestic needs. It is not yet clear if such intelligence would be used as evidence in court cases. More likely, the FBI would ask that intelligence be gathered to support its newly created National Security Branch, which combines the FBI's older counterterrorism and counterintelligence units with its newer intelligence bureau, created after 9/11.

At the same time, the CIA and the FBI have drawn more closely together with a strong push from Congress. FBI agents have been assigned to the CIA for counterintelligence purposes for many years, and more recently, to fight terrorism. CIA officers are reportedly working closely with FBI field offices where antiterrorism task forces have been created. While this may break down traditional barriers between the two agencies, there is still some resentment among CIA officers about the growing role of FBI attachés serving abroad and FBI concerns about the reluctance of CIA officers to share information.

The Counterintelligence Model

So, when one looks at the pattern of counterintelligence functions, it does not look at all like the intelligence cycle. Instead, it may be seen as follows:

Identification; Penetration; Exploitation; Interdiction; Claim Success. In this pattern, exploitation is the process of learning as much as possible about the bad guys before moving against them. Interdiction means either arresting the lawbreakers or pre-empting their operations. Though political leaders often talk about bringing the enemy to justice, suggesting that they would be arrested and taken to trial, convicted, and punished in the fight against terrorism, pre-emption may be the preferred course of action, especially overseas. In one case, for example, a U.S. *Predator* with a missile on board was reportedly used to strike a terrorist leader in Yemen, killing him and his associates while they were driving in the desert.[17] One might argue that this was punishment before trial, or alternatively, that this was necessary to prevent the terrorist from leading a strike against the United States.

The downside of pre-emption is that sometimes innocent victims are slain along with the intended targets. That was apparently what happened when the Bush administration launched a missile from a drone aircraft against Ayman al-Zawahiri, Osama bin Laden's deputy, early in 2006. The missile killed 17 people, according to press reports, but not the intended target, who later broadcast an attack on Mr. Bush, equating him with Adolf Hitler. Despite the failure to kill Zawahiri, the Bush administration later said that the attack had indeed killed an important terrorist leader and was worth the cost.[18]

Exploitation before Interdiction

In the counterintelligence model, exploitation comes before interdiction, meaning that as much intelligence as possible should be gathered before the case or operation is turned over to law enforcement. Of course, in cases in which there is pressure to stop the enemy or adversary, exploitation may come before the intelligence is fully gathered. For example, in the case of the "Lackawanna Six," exploitation was cut short because of the need for political leaders to show that they were cracking down on terrorism. The Six were Yemeni immigrants living outside Buffalo, New York, who went to Afghanistan before 9/11 in the misguided belief that training with the Talilban fighters was going to be something of a lark.[19]

When they discovered that the Taliban were really training terrorists, the Yemeni immigrants returned to the United States. After 9/11, they turned themselves in to authorities to explain what they had done. They were quickly arrested and eventually jailed. No one at the time seemed to realize that at least one or two of them might have been sent back to Afghanistan as double agents to penetrate Al Qaeda. Even an effort to learn more about their experiences was cut short by the pressure to achieve quick convictions to show that the government was moving swiftly against terrorism.

Claiming Success

Finally, in the last step of the counterintelligence process, authorities often make public claims of success, a rare step in intelligence work. Normally, intelligence managers try very hard to keep successes secret so that they might be repeated. An oft-quoted CIA saying is, "The secret of our success is the secret of our success."[20] In cases in which intelligence has been gathered successfully, it is critical to protect sources and methods. In counterintelligence, however, the claim of success, made when the case has ended, could be used to convince the public that the government is ever watchful and actually doing something with the billions of dollars spent on intelligence. During his tenure as FBI director, J. Edgar Hoover made a fine art out of going public with counterintelligence success. His senior agents all received training in public relations, and the FBI was made to look good, even when serious mistakes had been made.[21]

Whereas intelligence is usually carefully hidden (except for the counterintelligence cases), intelligence failure quickly becomes public. This is a serious problem for intelligence managers. In the early days of the CIA, there was no public affairs function even to deal with the public or the media. When Admiral Turner became director in 1977, however, he instituted a Public Affairs Office, much to the chagrin of many old-timers. Since then, the CIA has had to wrestle with the appropriate response when media queries arise. This is especially true when a spy case, such as the capture of Aldrich Ames, becomes public knowledge or when a covert action surfaces.

information becoming public

More forthcoming CIA directors, such as George Tenet, have had the Public Affairs Office respond generously to media questions. Under the successor regime of Porter Goss as CIA director, however, the CIA seemed to return to a more conservative approach. In such cases, it would not be uncommon for the media to receive the standard answer to questions about intelligence. This says that the CIA "can neither confirm nor deny allegations of intelligence activity," which is little more forthcoming than "no comment." Nonetheless, enterprising reporters, such as Bill Gertz of the *Washington Times* and James Risen of the *New York Times*, seem to be quite successful in learning about inside stories at the CIA and other intelligence agencies.

Defensive Counter Intelligence

There are defensive measures in counterintelligence that do not fit into either the traditional intelligence cycle or the model just described. These measures are often lumped together as various aspects of security. They include careful background checks on prospective employees, including the use of polygraph interviews to verify the information candidates submit on their applications and continuing monitoring of employees throughout their careers. Facilities used for intelligence and other governmental functions are extensively guarded and patrolled, monitored with alarm and surveillance devices, and protected by barrier entry devices to keep out unwanted visitors.

Some facilities have protective systems in roadways and parking areas that can be activated to stop suicidal vehicle bombers. Buildings may be shielded electronically to prevent an adversary's use of listening devices or electronic surveillance to intercept and steal secrets. Most important, employees are trained in security awareness, so that they can report anything that seems to be a threat. They are taught to protect the secrets with which they have been entrusted, and this responsibility lasts even after they leave their employment.

For example, those of us who were once inside the system and signed secrecy agreements are obligated to submit their published materials, including this chapter, to their agencies for review before they are given to their editors and publishers. This is not censorship but, rather, a system to ensure that no secret information is inadvertently released. Some CIA authors have taken advantage of this system to include blacked-out passages in their books, demonstrating that they really were prepared to release sensitive information but were stopped by the review process. This tends to sell more books and can be a clever marketing ploy.

The Covert Action Function — not in Intelligence cycle

The last function of intelligence—and again one not included in the intelligence cycle—is that of covert action, or special operations. This activity is not really intelligence in its traditional role of gathering and analyzing information but, rather, the use of intelligence resources to carry out the national security policy of the state using surreptitious methods. Intelligence agencies around the globe carry out such operations because they have the necessary secret facilities and personnel. All through the Cold War, it was covert action that drew most of the attention and most of the criticism of American intelligence.

General Jimmy Doolittle, one of the notable heroes of World War II, after taking a hard look at intelligence in the immediate postwar period, concluded that the United States would have to be more clever, more tricky, and more devious than our Communist adversaries if we were to overcome their bid for world domination. He stated that Americans would just have to accept this "repugnant" policy.[22] When the CIA became involved in trying to overthrow governments in Guatemala, Iran, Indonesia, and Cuba and was severely criticized in some quarters for having done so, it became clear that there were limits to what the American people were prepared to accept.

Much has been written about the nature and limits of covert action, and there seems no need to repeat that here.[23] Although covert action does not fit into the intelligence cycle, there is a pattern to this function worth outlining. This pattern is similar to other aspects of policy development and implementation, except that covert action is supposed to be secret and to disguise the role of the United States.

Policy Formulation

The pattern of policy formulation looks a bit like the intelligence cycle, but in reality it is quite different. In the first step of the policy process, policy officials within the national security bureaucracy recognize and identify a problem they must address. Theoretically, the identification of the problem comes from intelligence, but in reality, policy officials often see this at about the same time as intelligence officials because both receive the incoming data at about the same time, as explained earlier.

In the next step, policy officials begin to seek options for dealing with the problem, assuming some role for the United States is necessary. At this point, one of the options might well be a covert action. We know from long experience with covert action that it only makes sense as an adjunct to policy and should not be the policy itself.[24] Thus, the choice of using covert action remains with decision makers and is not chosen by intelligence. The conventional wisdom in some circles during the Cold War was that intelligence managers decided to mount covert actions independent of policy officials. (This notion that the CIA was a "rogue elephant" running amok was debunked during the famous investigations of intelligence held by Sen. Frank Church in the 1970s. Church learned that all CIA covert actions had been directed in some way by the White House and funded in secret by members of Congress.)[25]

Finally, decision makers at the top choose the option they desire and direct its implementation. In the case of covert action, this requires that the president issue a written finding that the covert action is needed. Then the appropriate intelligence official must brief the Intelligence Oversight Committees of Congress, in secret, about the policy "on a timely basis." Congress has often pressed presidents to issue the findings before the option is implemented, but presidents have usually chosen to ignore this, claiming that it infringes on their freedom of action.[26]

The pattern looks like this:

Problem Recognition
Option Creation
Option Selection
Implementation

Intelligence analysis should feed into the process at all stages, but we know that the options that policy officials choose are driven by many things. Intelligence is not always at the top of the list.

Consequences of Covert Action

Covert action has both short- and long-term consequences. This is true of all kinds of policy choices, but because covert action is kept secret, the normal debate about policy choices takes place among a relatively small group of people. The result is that short-term solutions, which may seem attractive at the time they are chosen, may prove to have unintended consequences in the long run. There are too many examples to cover here, and the literature on covert action is voluminous. It is sufficient to say that U.S. governments rarely think about the long-term consequences of policy choices, and, in that regard, covert action is no different from more open kinds of policies.

There is a long tradition in intelligence that intelligence officers do not offer policy recommendations to decision makers. Though this may be true for the delivery of finished intelligence products, it is not so in regard to covert action. As Dr. James Steiner, a former CIA officer, has pointed out, in covert action, especially in the war on terrorism, the attempt to be policy-neutral does not apply.[27] For many years, a senior CIA officer has been assigned to the White House staff to help work out the details of covert action when policymakers decide to have such operations.

This officer's role is to make sure that requested covert actions are feasible and supportable. Thus, the officer is as much a policymaker as an intelligence official.[28]

It is argued elsewhere in this chapter that one way to address the short-term versus the long-term consequences of covert action is to set up a center, much like the other interagency centers in U.S. intelligence. This center, however, should include both intelligence and policy officials. Its goal would be to analyze how a covert action might work and what its impact would be. The intelligence officers assigned to such a center should come from both the analytic and the operational units of the CIA. Traditionally, covert action has been kept compartmentalized within operations units, without the benefit of analytic inputs.

It seems pretty clear that presidents will always want to have the option of using some form of covert action against enemies and adversaries. No presidents in living memory, even those who were suspicious of covert action, have ever said that they would not use it. Therefore, the intelligence agencies that might be involved in such operations—primarily the CIA in the present U.S. intelligence community—must be prepared to be tasked to carry out covert action and must maintain the capability to do so.

A Flawed Vision

I suspect that, despite my preaching about alternatives to the traditional intelligence cycle, it will continue to be taught both inside government and elsewhere. Nonetheless, it would be encouraging to think that those so deeply wedded to the flawed concept of the intelligence cycle would, in the course of studying this volume, realize that there is an alternative to the traditional view of how intelligence works. Perhaps they might even consider it for discussion. Yet we know that people tend to look for confirming rather than disconfirming data. They will seek to defend the intelligence cycle rather than consider the alternatives. Nonetheless, the intelligence cycle is a flawed vision and, thus, poor theory. One need only ask those who have toiled in the fields of intelligence.

Notes

1. Sherman Kent, *Strategic Intelligence for American World Policy* (Princeton: Princeton University Press, 1966). I studied an earlier version published in 1948.

2. See, for example, Arthur S. Hulnick, "The Intelligence Producer-Policy Consumer Linkage: A Theoretical Approach," *Intelligence and National Security* 1 (May 1986).

3. James Risen, *State of War: The Secret History of the CIA and the Bush Administration* (New York: Free Press, 2006).

4. *The 9/11 Commission Report* (New York: W.W. Norton, 2003), pp. 339–360.

5. Arthur S. Hulnick, *Fixing the Spy Machine: Preparing American Intelligence for the 21st Century* (Westport, CT: Praeger, 1999), p. 59.

6. Richard K. Betts, "Analysis, War, and Decision: Why Intelligence Failures Are Inevitable," *World Politics* 31 (1978).

7. Arthur S. Hulnick, *Keeping Us Safe: Secret Intelligence and Homeland Security* (Westport, CT: Praeger, 2004), p. 16.

8. Risen, *State of War*.

9. Hulnick, *Keeping Us Safe*, pp. 85–86.

10. Roger Hilsman, *Strategic Intelligence and National Decision* (Glencoe, IL: Free Press, 1956).

11. "CSIS and the Security Intelligence Cycle," available at http://www .csis-scrs.gc.ca (accessed 1 April 2004).

12. Risen, *State of War*, pp. 39–60.

13. *9/11 Report*.

14. Arthur S. Hulnick, "Indications and Warnings for Homeland Security: Seeking a New Paradigm," *International Journal of Intelligence and Counterintelligence* 18 (Winter 2005–2006).

15. Hulnick, *Keeping Us Safe*, pp. 103–118.

16. See, for example, Pete Earley, *Confessions of a Spy: The Real Story of Aldrich Ames* (New York: G.P. Putnam's Sons, 1997).

17. Hulnick, *Keeping Us Safe*, p. 72.

18. Craig Whitlock and Walter Pincus, "Qaeda Deputy Mocks Bush," *Washington Post*, 31 January 2006.

19. Hulnick, *Keeping Us Safe*, pp. 126–127.

20. Hulnick, *Fixing the Spy Machine*, p. 81.

21. Ronald Kessler, *The Bureau: The Secret History of the FBI* (New York: St. Martin's Press, 2002).

22. Harold M. Greenberg, "The Doolittle Commission of 1954," *Intelligence and National Security* 20 (December 2005), pp. 687–694.

23. See, for example, Abram Shulsky and Gary Schmitt, *Silent Warfare* (Washington, DC: Brassey's, 2002).

24. James E. Steiner, "Restoring the Red Line between Intelligence and Policy on Covert Action," *International Journal of Intelligence and Counterintelligence* 19 (Spring, 2006), pp. 156–165.

25. See, for example, Rhodri Jeffreys-Jones, *The CIA and American Democracy*, 3rd ed. (New Haven, CT: Yale University Press, 2003).

26. Christopher Andrew, *For the President's Eyes Only* (New York: Harper Collins, 1995).

27. Steiner, *op. cit.*

28. Hulnick, *Fixing the Spy Machine*, pp. 82–83.

CHAPTER FIVE

The Importance and Future of Espionage and Intelligence Liaison

Frederick P. Hitz

WHEN PRESIDENT TRUMAN SIGNED THE NATIONAL SECURITY ACT of 1947 into law, creating the Central Intelligence Agency (CIA), he believed not that he was creating a new espionage organization for the United States but, rather, that he was greatly improving the manner in which important national intelligence would find its way to his desk. Earlier he had disestablished the Office of Strategic Services (OSS), the wartime foreign intelligence collection and analytical entity, declaring that he did not want an American Gestapo in peacetime. By 1947, he had changed his mind on the need for a civilian intelligence organization for three principal reasons. First and most important, the lessons of the 1941 Pearl Harbor attack strongly suggested the need for greater early warning of a future surprise attack on the United States. Second, he needed a centralizing intelligence organization that would gather and analyze all the intelligence reports headed for the Oval Office and attempt to make something coherent out of them so he would not have to do it himself. It is not clear that he wanted the new organization to go out and collect intelligence information on its own, as this had been tasked primarily to the Armed Services and to the Federal Bureau of Investigation (FBI). Third, he was convinced by Secretary of the Navy James Forrestal and others in his Cabinet that the U.S.S.R. would become a problem now that the Nazis were defeated, and that he needed a window into Stalin's thinking and imperial ambitions, especially in Western Europe. The Cold War was beginning.

The CIA got off to a slow start. Its early directors were military men who had a limited idea of the coordinating role the CIA was intended to play and were aware of the bureaucratic sharks circling them, representing the parochial interests of the military departments, the FBI, and the State Department, all of which wanted to maintain their direct access to the president on intelligence matters. Two events conspired to change this modest approach. George F. Kennan penned his famous "Long Telegram" from Moscow, alerting Washington in 1946 to Stalin's imperialist designs on that part of Europe not already under Soviet control, and recommending a policy of "containment" by the United States. At the very least, this would require affirmative action by the United States in funding democratic political parties, labor unions, student groups, and cultural organizations in Italy, France, and Western Germany to oppose the communist elements seeking to dominate these entities. In addition, to be most effective, the hand of the United States should remain hidden. The military were not the appropriate weapon to oppose clandestine Soviet infiltration, and the State Department rejected the assignment, so the fledgling CIA got the job. Luckily, there was language in the 1947 Act creating the CIA that directed it to perform, with the authorization of the president, vice-president, and secretaries of defense and state acting as the National Security Council, "such other functions and duties related to intelligence affecting the national security as the National Security Council may from time to time direct." Thus was created the covert action responsibility of the CIA that grew enormously from 1948 to 1952 under the leadership of Frank Wisner. Wisner's so-called Office of Policy Coordination (OPC) was lodged ostensibly in the Department of State, but in reality it was an operational element of the CIA.

The second major development was the arrival on the scene of two savvy directors of Central Intelligence (DCI). Air Force Lieutenant General Hoyt S. Vandenberg and retired Army General Walter Bedell Smith (who had been Eisenhower's wartime chief of staff) knew what the organization required to move up to the big leagues and were prepared to fight for it. Vandenberg was responsible for securing for future DCIs the requisites to do their job. The National Security Acts of 1947 and 1949 that he had lobbied for (and that had also shown the handiwork of an outside commission appointed by President Truman in 1949 that included Allen Dulles) gave the DCI unparalleled authority in Washington. They gave Vandenberg and his successors as DCI the power to hire and fire his subordinates; spend money on their own say-so without further justification; short-circuit the federal government's cumbersome procurement authorities in order to perform the intelligence mission; and act across the range of intelligence collection, analysis, and dissemination responsibilities. The scope of authority was to include activities from classic espionage to special operations (covert action) to all-source analysis to briefing the president's National Security Council. In short, Vandenberg got the CIA, and the DCI especially, off to a running start before he returned to the Air Force. Bedell Smith took the new organization the rest of the way.

Bedell resuscitated the CIA's estimative intelligence, a function that had earned its stripes during the wartime OSS period but had lain dormant upon the OSS's demise. Estimative intelligence looks out to the future, attempting to foresee problems of concern to the president that may be coming down the line. With Truman's go-ahead, Bedell created a Board of National Estimate reporting to the DCI, led by the same Harvard history professor, William Langer, who had put it together for General Donovan during World War II. Professor Langer managed to convince a number of wise men from the nation's best universities to work for him and Bedell, tasking them with tracking the future course of the Cold War rivalry with the U.S.S.R.

DCI Smith also made it clear that covert action and special operations existed in a chain of command extending from the DCI and in coordination with the other espionage capability that the DCI oversaw for the president, the Office of Special Operations (OSO). He thus contrived to bring Wisner's OPC into the CIA in fact.

The OSO's responsibility was to gather foreign intelligence information by secret means (that is, classic espionage). It was often stumbling over or wandering into operations conducted by the OPC, because the foreign actors who stole the secrets were often the same ones who could manage the propaganda or organize the political meetings for the OPC. This is an important historical point. If the CIA did not take the field to secretly oppose Soviet propaganda, backdoor electioneering, and subversion in Western Europe, several of the United States' most important allies might have been in jeopardy. Furthermore, intelligence activity that connoted "action" was very much in the American character. It drew many adherents in the early CIA both because there was a perceived need (as the constant stream of national security directives from the president and National Security Council attested) and because, if successful, you could see the results. At the same time, the slow, painstaking process of recruiting spies to report on happenings behind the Iron Curtain and in the Soviet Union itself had to be undertaken. In the late 1940s and 1950s, this was difficult and dangerous work, new to Americans, of whom very few spoke the relevant languages: Russian, Polish, Czech, and Hungarian. It required a patience and professionalism in terms of tradecraft that the OPCers sometimes overlooked or made fun of. The spy recruiters and handlers (of whom DCI-to-be Richard Helms was a prominent representative) were dubbed "the prudent professionals" and were not as esteemed or promoted as quickly as the OPC "action" types. Bedell tried to end all that by making of the OSO and OPC one clandestine service, directed by one chief, Allen Dulles, who reported to him. Over time, it worked. The two skill sets became a little more interchangeable, although DCI Smith noted in his farewell remarks to President Truman that he thought the CIA was expending far too little effort with too meager results in acquiring intelligence penetrations of the Soviet Union.

Bedell was, of course, succeeded by DCI Allen Dulles, who jumped on the Eisenhower administration's desire to contain the Soviet Union by mounting covert action programs rather than confronting it with U.S. military force. As Supreme Commander, Allied Forces, Europe, in World War II, General Eisenhower had been a consumer of Britain's ENIGMA German code-breaking successes and knew both the role and the limitations of intelligence. As president, he believed strongly that the Soviet worldwide advance had to be stopped, if not rolled back, and covert action operations seemed a cheap and relatively low-risk way to do it. Enamored of early successes in overthrowing regimes in Iran (1953) and Guatemala (1954), the president and his advisors at the CIA grew accustomed to pushing the envelope in operations, overlooking close shaves and longer-term backlash.

However, this extraordinary progress in spying on the U.S.S.R. and containing its influence during the Eisenhower years encountered several highly public setbacks as well. The revelation in May 1960, initially denied by President Eisenhower, that the Soviets had shot down a U-2 surveillance aircraft flying over Soviet territory, disrupted the Paris summit. The plan to secretly train Cuban exiles to land on Cuban soil to overthrow the Castro regime—later adopted by President Kennedy and put into practice half-heartedly in an indefensible location at the Bay of Pigs—abruptly ended a run of successes by the CIA. Kennan's X article had alerted Washington to the bitter adversities ahead in confronting as politically hardened a foe as the Soviets, so it was naturally only a matter of time before a handful of poorly conceived or blighted operations gave the CIA an enduring notoriety and taint abroad and dispelled the aura of the Agency's infallibility around Washington. The Bay of Pigs disaster triggered the replacement of Allen Dulles by John McCone, whose signal innovation as DCI was to put the analytical consensus within his own Agency under intense personal scrutiny.

The tattered doctrine of plausible deniability, however, still held an occasionally disproportionate allure for Kennedy and later presidents. After a national wake-up on the shores of Cuba's Bay of Pigs, JFK raised the CIA's operational arm from the ashes, only to shoot for the moon all over again in *Operation Mongoose*, which saw the Agency embark on a rash of sometimes frantic missions to overthrow a now-entrenched Fidel Castro.

Despite the evident hazards of the profession, presidents relied substantially on CIA spies in Berlin to counter Soviet pressure there. The Eisenhower-Kennedy years were the beginning of the era of America's greatest technical intelligence successes as well, with spies and electronics working hand-in-glove in Berlin and elsewhere; with the construction of the U-2 high-altitude photo-reconnaissance aircraft; and with the refinement, beginning in the 1960s, of overhead satellite surveillance, eventually able to communicate images and intercepted electronic signals to Washington in real time. Nonetheless, it was on Cuba, in the October missile crisis in 1962, that U.S. intelligence showed that it had arrived at a position of sufficient maturity in its collection systems to be able to support President Kennedy with intelligence from all three principal collection branches: SIGINT, IMINT, and HUMINT. The U-2 flyovers were the first to supply photographs of Soviet medium-and intermediate-range ballistic missiles being transported to, unloaded, and installed in Cuba. Signal intercepts pointed to a heavy buzz of communications around the part of the island where the missiles were being installed, and human sources witnessed the transfer of mysterious long tubes on highways too small to accommodate them. Although there were many details that human sources were unable to provide, our principal spy, Oleg Penkovsky, from his vantage point at the pinnacle of Soviet military intelligence, reported on the ranges and characteristics of the IRBMs and MRBMs that were being installed. He also revealed that General Secretary Khrushchev was way out in front of his Politburo in thus challenging the United States so close to its home territory.

The fact that President Kennedy had Penkovsky's insights into Khrushchev's overexposure, confirming the observations of his own former ambassador to the U.S.S.R. Llewelyn Thompson, meant that JFK was prepared to give up the strategic advantage of a surprise attack on the installation and, in a masterstroke of statecraft, give General Secretary Khrushchev an opportunity to escape from the corner into which he had painted himself. In my view, this was the apex of U.S. intelligence support to the president during the Cold War. After October 1962, prosecution of the Vietnam War became the overriding national security concern of Presidents Kennedy, Johnson, and Nixon. The CIA built up its presence in South Vietnam and collected useful human intelligence, from captured Vietcong and North Vietnamese prisoners especially, that permitted it to report consistently that the Government of South Vietnam (GOSVN) was unlikely to prevail in the war unless it took a more active role in the fighting and was able to win over greater support in the Vietnamese countryside. The CIA's rejection of the validity of high body counts that were held by American military intelligence to signal attrition in the North Vietnamese capacity to wage the war is reminiscent of today's intelligence controversy about the import of the nonexistence of weapons of mass destruction (WMD) in Iraq.

In the case of Vietnam, the CIA more or less stuck to its guns that North Vietnam was not being defeated in 1968 despite its loss of manpower, whereas it was "dead wrong" in its assessment of the existence of chemical and biological weapons stores in Iraq in 2003, according to the Silberman-Robb Presidential Commission Report. In both cases, the requirement of good, on-the-ground, contemporaneous human source reporting was critical to CIA intelligence judgments. In Vietnam we had it, whereas in Iraq we did not. Silberman-Robb found that the critical National Intelligence Estimate of October 2002 on Iraqi WMD was based on unilateral spy reporting that dated from 1991 and UN weapons inspection reporting that dated to 1998. There was no direct, on-the-ground HUMINT after that before the outbreak of the war. Over the decades, the NIE process had taken on its share of taxing intelligence puzzles, but it was clearly compromised and out of date in this one.

It is ironic that, as today, the great blows to the quality and competence of CIA human source reporting in the 1970s were delivered during a Republican presidency, on the watch of a national security establishment that valued and to some extent depended on good intelligence for its activist foreign and defense policy. Although Richard Nixon privately disparaged the Ivy Leaguers at Langley whom he believed had favored his opponent in the 1960 presidential race against JFK, he needed good intelligence on Vietnam to support the Paris peace talks Secretary of State Henry Kissinger was conducting with the North Vietnamese and also his overtures to China. Indeed, when it looked as if an unabashed Marxist, Salvador Allende, was poised to win the Chilean presidential election of 1970, it was to the CIA that President Nixon turned, improperly bypassing the rest of his foreign policy establishment and the U.S. Congress to mount a coup against a democratically elected Latin American leader.

Watergate and the Nixon resignation turned the tide against this manifestation of executive imperialism, while the CIA caught a fair measure of popular and congressional backlash. Investigative reporter Seymour Hersh wrote a series of articles in the *New York Times* in December 1974 setting forth the ways in which the CIA (and the FBI) had illegally spied on

American anti-Vietnam War protesters, opened people's mail, tested hallucinogenic substances on unwitting subjects, and otherwise acted outside the bounds of an already broadly demarcated charter without the knowledge of Congress or the American people.[1]

Congressional reaction was swift and severe. The U.S. Senate and House of Representatives each convened investigating committees to hold extensive public hearings on CIA abuses. Sen. Frank Church, a Democrat from Idaho who was running for president, tried to lock then-DCI William Colby into admissions that the Agency had attempted to assassinate several world leaders such as Fidel Castro, Patrice Lumumba of the Congo, Rafael Trujillo of the Dominican Republic, and Salvador Allende without a president's authorization, claiming that the CIA was a "Rogue Elephant." In the end, the Church Committee was unable to substantiate these allegations. There was some assassination plotting at the CIA, directed by presidents, but none was shown to have been carried out successfully.

However, the Senate's inquiry caused President Ford to create a blue ribbon panel headed by Vice-President Rockefeller to look into the matter and to preempt Congress's certain desire to legislate restrictions on U.S. intelligence activity. Thus was born the effort to establish greater executive and legislative branch oversight of the intelligence community. President Ford promulgated Executive Order 11905 in February 1976, which banned assassination of foreign political leaders by U.S. intelligence operatives or their surrogates, among other restrictions. The order contained a number of additional dos and don'ts that were binding on the intelligence community, and it was reissued by Ford's successors, Carter and Reagan, in substantially the same form. After several years of trying to pass legislation establishing more comprehensive and binding charters for intelligence community agencies such as the FBI, CIA, NSA, and NRO, real-world dangers posed to the United States by the Soviet Union caused the public and Congress to regain some equilibrium on the subject of further restraining U.S. intelligence gathering capabilities, and the effort was dropped. Congress settled for one paragraph in the Intelligence Authorization Act of 1980. It required the DCI and the president to keep Congress "fully and currently informed" of all intelligence activities, including covert action, consistent with the president's constitutional authorities and the DCI's duty to protect "sources and methods from unauthorized disclosure."

Congress believed it could settle for this paragraph instead of the several-hundred-page charter bill, because it had established in 1975 and 1976 permanent oversight committees of the House and Senate to review intelligence community programs and operations, just as every other department and agency in the executive branch is reviewed.

Some argue that since the creation of the House Permanent Select Committee on Intelligence (HPSCI) and the Senate Select Committee on Intelligence (SSCI), with rotating memberships after seven years' service, the CIA has never been the same aggressive collector of human intelligence that it was during the height of the Cold War. I disagree. The world had changed by 1975. Although the Soviets still maintained a nuclear arsenal pointed at America's heartland, it was on the downhill side of the slope economically and politically. It had an aging leadership and an increasing inability to provide for the needs and wants of its people. The United States was receiving more volunteers as spies from the Soviet Union as its high-ranking cadres became increasingly gloomy about the country's future prospects. In the United States, Vietnam had exploded the postwar consensus surrounding U.S. foreign policy, and a stronger demand for oversight and accountability for all of America's overseas activities had emerged.

When this era of intelligence reform ended, the full-time housecleaners who worked at Langley and the FBI had managed to stay out of the headlines for the most part. Spying against private citizens clearly violated the 1947 Act but made for no more than a sideshow when compared to spy-hunting inside the U.S. government. Light almost never shines on this most sensitive area of surveillance, counterespionage, but in this domain of intelligence work especially, tumult has been virtually inseparable from tradecraft. Penetrations and double-crosses can be expected in the competition among major intelligence services, but the integrity of intelligence operations rests on how well very fragmentary and circumstantial clues about possible security breaches can be read. Moles were often uncovered only years after their work got started. Indeed, when the Cold War did end abruptly, counterespionage work was not ready to wind down but was putting itself in high gear, as Americans were making inroads into the former Warsaw Pact services, shedding light on turncoats here at home.

American intelligence contended with a number of notorious penetrations in the Cold War, and most spectacular of these was the early discovery that the Soviets had recruited the top British liaison official in America, Kim Philby. Philby had until then been regarded as one of MI6's best men—a man in line to be its next director, a brilliant and affable character, and a mentor to many of Langley's rising stars. The United States had depended heavily on him personally for many of our early postwar efforts in Europe. Philby had been in a position to alert Moscow to many of the biggest and most sensitive intelligence exploits under way: the development of the atomic bomb and the VENONA project, through which the NSA was attempting to break encrypted communications from the Soviet embassy and the New York consulate during World War II. But he could not prevent the NSA from discovering an old code-name, Homer, referring to a British mole in the UK embassy in Washington. Homer was one member of the entire Cambridge Five spy ring, another of whom was quickly tied to Philby, as a friend boarding at Philby's home. In 1951, Philby's official career effectively ended. But it took another decade's worth of revelations for his career as a double-agent to be sufficiently understood to put him in criminal jeopardy, whereupon he defected.

James Jesus Angleton, the CIA's master spy hunter, was one among many of Philby's former friends on whom his treachery left a lasting impression. Angleton's occupation at the CIA was actually not widely known. He was simply "the Ghost of Langley," the man who showed up unannounced at the DCI's office for an immediate, private audience with the boss. A classics major and poet at Yale who moved in the same circles as T.S. Eliot and Ezra Pound, Angleton was picked toward the beginning of his career to run the counterintelligence operation in Rome, during the crucial 1947 elections that kept the Italian Communist Party out of power. Angleton's early career also solidified CIA liaison operations with other services, including those of Britain and Israel. And he worked alongside the Mafia during his Rome posting. The Mafia had operated on behalf of the OSS in wartime Italy and had helped to perfect some of the more lethal aspects of the CIA's tradecraft.

Angleton's cunning instincts came to the attention of Allen Dulles, who asked him in 1954 to head the CIA's counterspy operations. By 1959, Angleton had unearthed Jack Dunlap as a mole in the NSA who had reached high-level "no inspection" clearances. But in retrospect, though the Philby affair had ignited Angleton's imagination, it had not furnished the CIA with the kind of tradecraft lessons that would shed a much clearer light on future penetration controversies. In 1961 Angleton seemed to be nearing more breakthroughs, having been given personal charge of debriefing a defecting KGB major, Yuri Golitsyn, but Golitsyn became increasingly problematic for the CIA over time. In addition to the key information he did betray, he was willing to speculate endlessly about other penetrations of U.S. intelligence and spun out theories that Angleton showed himself ready to embrace. Among the most troubling questions he raised was the identity of the mole Sasha, a code-name that sparked the most tortuous inquisition that the Agency would ever launch: These investigations had such disproportionate impact on work at the Agency that their records remain completely restricted to this day. And Golitsyn insisted with some vehemence to CIA officers, after each subsequent defector surfaced, that anyone to follow him would almost certainly be a plant, blunting the CIA counterintelligence staff's instincts. The name of one of those subsequent defectors, Yuri Nosenko, was much later cleared of being a Soviet double agent, but Nosenko fell afoul of his own glaring penchant for fabrication and at first cast the most severe suspicions upon himself. Working on Angleton's behalf, J. Edgar Hoover's FBI went to extremes to try to extract a confession from Nosenko but was ultimately unsuccessful. Meanwhile, Nosenko had languished in solitary confinement for three years. In the aftermath, Hoover judged Angleton poisonously misguided, and the debacle helped to drive a permanent wedge between the FBI and CIA, from which neither agency extricated itself until after September 11.

Angleton put at least 50 intelligence officers under surveillance during his career and removed at least 16 from the service. Problems at the CIA became more severe as his views darkened into clinical paranoia over the course of the 1960s. The only personal trust Angleton was ultimately able to sustain was in his closest circle. Meanwhile he elaborated plots with Golitsyn's help. As facts became hunches, and his hunches increasingly bordered on the absurd, he came into permanent conflict with the Agency's leadership. Finally, he could not find a distinction between political loyalty and personal allegiance to his theories. He was barred from direct contact with Golitsyn in 1968 by DCI Dick Helms and ushered into retirement in 1974 by DCI Bill Colby, while the Hersh revelations of domestic spying were in the headlines. His counterintelligence staff was diminished from 300 to 80.

The counterespionage underworld that defends against other powerful foreign intelligence agencies is a reality in which things remain extraordinarily indeterminate. A myriad of conceivable avenues might lead to operational betrayal. Angleton's version of reality was to adopt the premise that the most successful Soviet campaigns were those of knowingly false information—disinformation—that could operate at a great remove from the Agency's headquarters. Penetrations were less important than the false tracks onto which the CIA could be lured. But in truth, the kinds of judgment calls are so immensely difficult that spy hunters must make sure to arrive at breakthroughs in cases of penetration. Major revelations might never come down the road. And surveillance might fail to turn up any mole at all. Moreover, in the life-or-death stakes of the Cold War, there was always the potential that too broad or intrusive a mole hunt would leave more self-inflicted damage to CIA operations than unearthing a mole would stanch. Nevertheless, crucial countermeasures still had to be taken, and in counterespionage it was often the effort to run down trails of minor lifestyle and procedural misconduct that kept operations secure.

Philby was the result of a relatively spectacular breakthrough, but the Aldrich Ames and Robert Hanssen penetrations during the 1980s and 1990s remained almost entirely invisible for years after the investigations got rolling. Ames and Hanssen did their damage over a period of time when CIA attitudes about lifestyle and procedural misconduct had remained too lax for too long. The Agency lost the distinction between operations in the outside world and the life of discipline required inside. Most espionage operations are carried out in the gray areas of administrative procedure, but over the years, these moles built microcosms of that mission right in the offices that they ran at the CIA and FBI. Like all other skilled professions, intelligence officers have to accept a high level of personal autonomy in those they rely upon, but the basics of tradecraft, on-time reporting, and drug and alcohol-free behavior are important too. Over the long haul, the maintenance of strict operational routine and personal integrity goes a fair way toward assuring the success of the intelligence community in its operational mission.

Within the CIA, the chaos that followed Operation CHAOS (the controversial CIA domestic mail-opening program revealed in 1974) lasted well into the Carter presidency and the tenure of DCI Stansfield Turner. President Carter put the CIA back on the offensive in his changing attitude to the Sandinistas in Nicaragua and the covert action he instigated to oppose the Soviet takeover of Afghanistan in 1979. Still, it remained for Ronald Reagan to initiate an across-the-board revitalization of both U.S. defense and intelligence resources that would reverse the post-Vietnam War drawdown and counter ongoing outbreaks of Soviet aggression. President Reagan authorized a covert action to train and reinforce the *contra* resistance to the Marxist Sandinista revolution of 1979 in Nicaragua and a second covert program to build up the *mujahedeen* factions opposing the Soviet-controlled government in Afghanistan. At the same time, he initiated a research program to intercept incoming missiles in space. The Kremlin began to believe the United States was trying for a first-strike capability against the U.S.S.R. and initiated a worldwide intelligence alert called Project Ryan to report on indicators confirming such an effort. At the same time, old age and sickness were removing Soviet premiers at a record rate. In March 1985, a completely new figure ascended to power in the Kremlin, Mikhail Gorbachev, who was focused on curtailing Soviet commitments to defend communism everywhere (the Brezhnev Doctrine) and reforming the economy to provide a better response to the needs of the Soviet people. Meanwhile the Reagan administration was having a difficult time keeping the U.S. Congress on board for the operation to support the *contras*. After the second amendment curtailing CIA support for the *contras* passed Congress—and was signed into law by the president because it was attached to an omnibus year-end appropriations bill—some members of the administration on the National Security staff and in the CIA concocted a scheme to sell embargoed weaponry to Iran in exchange for information about terrorists who had abducted Americans in the Middle East, using the proceeds from the sales to supply weapons illegally to the *contras*. The Iran-*contra* scheme finally blew up in the press in fall 1986, sending the Reagan White House and William Casey's CIA into a tailspin.

It took the appointment in 1987 of Judge William Webster as DCI, a former director of the FBI and U.S. Court of Appeals judge, to restore legitimacy and integrity to CIA operations after the Iran-*contra* fiasco. Meanwhile, CIA covert operators got congressional approval to supply Stinger missiles to the Afghan *mujahedeen*, a policy that proved pivotal to driving the Soviets out of Afghanistan. As unintentionally transparent as the Nicaraguan covert action was to the world, so the cooperation by the CIA with the Pakistani intelligence service to supply armaments to Afghani and Arab guerillas in Afghanistan was painted as a state secret within the boundaries of "plausible deniability." The Soviets knew where the weaponry, especially the Stingers, was coming from, but they were in no position to do much about it, despite the concerns of Pakistan's nervous chief of state, Mohammed Zia-ul-Haq.

To date, the Afghan covert action has been the last big successful clandestine political operation mounted by the CIA in which the U.S. hand did not show to an impermissible degree. By and large, the CIA officers involved kept their promise to Pakistan's rulers that they would physically stay out of Afghanistan and work through the Pakistani intelligence service, the ISI. The advent of both round-the-clock cable news programming and instant worldwide communications via the Internet have successfully impinged upon the United States' ability to maintain the necessary secrecy of a major covert political operation. This was made manifest in the administration of President George H. W. Bush, when the president, despite his tour of duty as DCI and his appreciation for the role of intelligence, turned instead to the American military to deal with both Manuel Noriega in Panama in 1989 and Saddam Hussein in the first Gulf War in 1991. When President Clinton sought to make use of covert action in overthrowing Saddam in the mid-1990s, he found it was impossible. Congress had gained an appetite for micromanaging an operation that could have high domestic stakes, and the CIA had too few covert assets to bring it off.

By the same token, viewed in retrospect, in the mid-1980s it would turn out that the United States had suffered unprecedented high-level penetrations of its intelligence services, through the handiwork of Aldrich Ames in the CIA and Robert Hanssen in the FBI. Ames began his espionage for Soviet handlers in March 1985 in order to get $50,000 to buy himself out of debt. He was a 30-year spy in the CIA's operations directorate who had specialized in Soviet matters, arriving at a senior level even though he had a mediocre record—which included numerous episodes of alcohol abuse, security violations, and a chronic inability to get his financial accountings and contact reports about meetings with Soviet officials in on time. In short, Ames probably should never have been permitted to be on the front line, meeting and assessing Soviet officials one-on-one. But he was. And he used his position and his knowledge of how both the Soviet and U.S. intelligence systems operated to betray, over a period of nine years, every agent working for the United States against the U.S.S.R., details of numerous U.S. operations against the Soviets, and the names of his colleagues who were engaged in the effort. Ames's betrayal led to the certain execution of ten U.S. spies and probably more, along with the compromise of hundreds of U.S. intelligence operations. The arrest of Aldrich Ames in 1994 provoked a wave of disillusionment and dismay in the American public and among the congressional oversight committees that such a sloppy and seemingly inept spy could betray so much over such a long period, not only without being caught, but without the CIA having mounted a serious effort to track him. The damage to the Agency's reputation was nothing short of devastating.

For the FBI, no less damaging was the tale of Robert Hanssen, a dour misfit who had used his superior information technology skills to eventually burrow into the deepest corners of the Bureau's counterintelligence operations against the U.S.S.R. Hanssen managed to turn over vast amounts of operational detail and names of U.S. agents to the Soviets in an on-again off-again career of espionage that began in the late 1970s and continued until his arrest in February 2001. Hanssen's case was a tougher one to crack than Ames's because Hanssen had been careful never to meet with his Soviet handler, conducting all his business with the Soviets through dead drops in a park near his home in Northern Virginia. Furthermore, Hanssen had compromised many of the same spies named by Ames or by Edward Lee Howard, another CIA turncoat of the period, so it took an analysis of operations that had gone sour that could not have been compromised by Ames or Howard, and also the help of a Soviet source, before Hanssen's own activities could be distinguished and an arrest finally made.

At the same time that these spy wars were taking place between the Soviet and U.S. intelligence services, the CIA was beginning to enjoy real success in running Soviet and Bloc volunteer spies who were supplying vast amounts of useful intelligence information about Soviet and Warsaw Pact war-fighting plans in Europe and Soviet military research and development (R&D). In the former case, Ryszard Kuklinski, a high-ranking member of the Polish General Staff, passed the CIA all of the Warsaw Pact plans that crossed his desk from 1972 until his defection in 1981; in the second case, Adolph Tolkachev provided his U.S. case officer with the latest Soviet military R&D on stealth technology and air defense missilery from the late 1970s until 1985, saving the U.S. taxpayer millions of dollars in unnecessary defense expenditure. These successful Soviet spy volunteer recruitments at the end of the Cold War, and others like them, proved the value of a vigorous human source collection program at the time that the Soviet regime was under severe internal stress.

The need for espionage did not disappear with the dismantling of the Berlin Wall in 1989 and the dismemberment of the U.S.S.R. in 1991. The successor Russian government kept its intelligence officers in the field and the West at bay on a number of important issues. Yet, over time, the threats targeted by American intelligence agencies began to shift. As authoritarian regimes calcified or collapsed over the decade of the 1990s—frequently ex-Cold War client governments—the new threats would become proliferating weapons of mass destruction and emerging nonstate terrorist factions, exemplified by Osama bin Laden and Al Qaeda.

In a series of bold and ever-more sophisticated attacks, beginning with that on the Khobar Towers, a U.S. Air Force billet in Saudi Arabia in 1997, followed by the bombings of U.S. embassies in Dar es Salaam and Nairobi in 1998, and the attack on the USS *Cole* in 2000, this affluent Saudi veteran of the *mujahedeen* effort against the Soviets in Afghanistan, Osama bin Laden, showed he was capable and desirous of inflicting unacceptable damage on the United States in order to drive it out of the Muslim holy places of the Middle East. His organization, known as Al Qaeda, or the Franchise, had in 1991 volunteered to lead the Islamic effort to force Saddam Hussein to leave Kuwait, but his offer was overlooked by the Saudi royals. Subsequently in exile in the Sudan, and after 1995 in Afghanistan as a guest of the Taliban regime, Osama preached Islamic unity and defiance in opposing the West's continued military basing in the region and the support it was giving to autocratic and selfish rulers in Saudi Arabia, Egypt, and the Gulf who were doing nothing to provide for their populations. The CIA, in particular in the U.S. intelligence community, became alarmed at the growing strength, sophistication, and appeal of Osama's rhetoric against the United States' role in the Middle East, which targeted it as the "far enemy." After President Clinton's weak and ineffective response to the African embassy bombings, the CIA established a task force to track Osama and Al Qaeda, but it was never able to deliver the knockout punch on his compound in Afghanistan or stop his continuing deadly momentum during the Clinton years, even though then-DCI George Tenet "declared war" on Al Qaeda in an attempt to bring focus to American intelligence's counterterrorist strategy.

In 2001 the CIA began receiving heightened liaison reporting from U.S. allies in Europe and the Middle East that Al Qaeda was planning something big. But where—in the region or against a U.S. installation overseas—was unknown. This was becoming Osama's trademark: long months of preparation and then a sudden strike. But just like the U.S. government's previous experience with a massive surprise attack on U.S. territory at Pearl Harbor, we were not prepared nor really expecting an attack in the continental United States. September 11, 2001, was an unforeseen and life-shattering wake-up call on the capacity of nonstate, religious-inspired terrorism to threaten stable societies like the United States and our European allies. It took President George W. Bush minutes to declare that the United States was involved in a war against terror and that all the military and intelligence resources of the United States would be deployed to win it.

What were those intelligence resources? In late 2001, in what condition did the intelligence community find itself to take on Osama bin Laden, Al Qaeda, and the challenge of religious-based international terror? With the passing of the Cold War, the CIA had been downsized and had in addition witnessed the dramatic departure of large numbers of expert spy handlers and analysts whose skills had been shaped by the challenge of the Soviet Union and who did not have much interest in or familiarity with the milieu of terrorism, drugs, crime, and weapons proliferation, issues which would be the meat and potatoes of Presidential Decision Directive 35 that set the blueprint for intelligence community targeting after the Cold War ended. So they retired and took with them their knowledge of spy tradecraft and of foreign languages. On top of that, as the 9/11 post-mortems would show, the intelligence agencies had grown into mature bureaucracies without much initiative, imagination, or creativity. They faced a target that operated in the shadows of nation-states but wasn't one; that had low overhead and a tight network of collaborators that it deployed with iron-handed discipline; and that possessed one unassailable attribute: Many of its adherents were willing to commit suicide for the cause and would strap on a bomb just to take civilian bystanders with them.

Other problems beset the intelligence agencies in 2001 as well. A division between domestic and international spheres of terrorism no longer existed. A plot that could begin in a Hamburg mosque or a Madrid suburb could be planned for immediate execution in New York or Washington. The divided responsibilities between the FBI and CIA that historical accident and concern about domestic civil liberties had spawned in the aftermath of World War II were hindrances in the 21st century to the kind of instant information sharing and teamwork that cell phones and Internet access in the hands of our terrorist attackers demanded. Compartmentalization and "need to know" take on sinister meanings when the effect is to deny intelligence to a sister agency equally charged with the responsibility to pre-empt a terrorist act.

Some of the more egregious barriers to intelligence sharing and teamwork between the intelligence agencies were struck down in the USA-PATRIOT Act passed in October 2002 and in the Intelligence Reform Bill, passed in December 2004. Now, wiretap permissions, when granted, run to the individual who is the target of the surveillance, not the instrument by which he intends to communicate. Grand jury testimony in terrorist cases can be shared among the law enforcement and intelligence entities having an interest in the matter. The Foreign Intelligence Surveillance Act (FISA) has been amended to include among the parties against whom the U.S. government may seek authorization for electronic surveillance from the special Foreign Intelligence Surveillance Court not just spies but terrorists as well, and the standard for authorizing surveillance has been broadened to encompass those as to whom terrorism is "a principal purpose" of their activity and not "the" purpose. There are additional sections in the 2001 Act that beef up the anti-money laundering provisions of federal statute and enhance the "sneak and peek" possibilities open to law enforcement, as well as enable more Internet intrusion of suspected terrorists. It is possible that some of the more aggressive portions of the USA-PATRIOT Act may be modified somewhat to include a greater measure of accountability.

The intended changes included in the Intelligence Reform Act of 2004 date back to the Church Committee era but trespassed on more turf and would only see the light of day three years after September 11, with some of the most intense bureaucratic lobbying of any intelligence bill. In the Act, there has been a concerted effort to remedy one of the principal perceived deficiencies in the performance of the intelligence agencies prior to 9/11, namely the absence of "an attending physician" who could treat the patient as a whole and be responsible for the work of all the specialists racing around performing tests on the patient on their own. That metaphor, used by the 9/11 Commission to sway Congress and the president, was the premise behind creating the new position of director of National Intelligence (DNI). The DNI was intended to be the intelligence czar, a Cabinet officer holding both managerial and budgetary authority over the entire intelligence community. He would also be the president's principal intelligence adviser.

When the dust settled after passage of the Act, the DNI's lines of command were not as clear as the Commission hoped for. The Defense Secretary and the Department of Defense (DOD) continue to share many of the DNI's management and budgetary authorities relating to the intelligence agencies under the command of the DOD. The DOD intelligence agencies—NRO, NSA, DIA, and NGA—account for 80 percent of the intelligence budget. There is also the matter of information sharing, which the Act seeks to encourage by requiring the DNI to have a subordinate responsible for creating an information sharing environment in the intelligence community.

The 2004 Act also treats the intelligence community's self-inflicted wounds, represented by the failures to warn of the 9/11 attacks and to accurately account for the weapons of mass destruction stockpiled by Saddam Hussein since 1991—believed ready for dispersal to terrorists by Saddam at some point if the UN embargo of Iraq was not lifted. The existence of Iraqi WMD was one of the principal reasons cited by the Bush administration for preparing to go to war against Iraq. A seemingly authoritative National Intelligence Estimate (NIE) circulated by the CIA in October 2002 detailed the supposed holdings of chemical and biological weapons by the Iraqi Ba'athist regime and the efforts of the regime to make nuclear weaponry advances. Furthermore, United Nations testimony drawn from the NIE by Secretary of State Colin Powell in February 2003, on the eve of the Iraq War, was used to sweep aside Allied opposition to the invasion. It has become painfully clear since then that Saddam suspended his WMD programs after 1991 to get out from under the UN-sponsored embargo. There were no WMD stockpiled in Iraq prior to the war, as Saddam had destroyed them.

What made the U.S. intelligence community's views on Iraqi WMD so objectionable was not that they held such preconceptions (most other knowledgeable intelligence services held identical views—the UK, Russia, Germany, France, and Israel), but that the NIE sought to justify the weapons' existence on outdated and unconfirmed reporting. The proprietary data dated from 1991, reports from UN inspectors stopped in 1998, and assessments rested heavily on unilateral sources like "Curveball," whose credibility was in question. The analytical tradecraft employed by the CIA on the critical NIE was fatally deficient.

At the same time, the president's decision to spread the war from Afghanistan to Iraq sounded alarm bells for quite a few veteran intelligence officers within the ranks. A number of these in-house critics believed the move into Iraq would instantly squander goodwill that the American government had gained in the Islamic world as a result of the September 11 attacks. Some intelligence officers subscribed to the view, later corroborated in the post-invasion Iraq Survey Group's two reports, that the inspections broken off in 1998 and the sanctions in place after had already boxed in Saddam.

Moreover, although DCI George Tenet had gained the confidence of the hawks on the president's war cabinet, both Vice President Cheney and Defense Secretary Donald Rumsfeld made it known in the press that they harbored deep distrust of the CIA's analysis of Iraq. The Defense Secretary had steered the 1998 Rumsfeld Commission that took the CIA to task to sharpen its poor nonproliferation reporting against a backdrop of two missed calls at the agency in five years—Saddam Hussein's startling WMD advances up to the 1990 Gulf War and India's clandestine nuclear tests in 1996. The vice-president possessed quite the opposite disposition, misappropriating even dubious raw intelligence leads to hype the imminent threat from the Ba'athist regime. Analysts at Langley found themselves frozen out of most White House planning. The war cabinet opened a small ad hoc shop within the Defense Department to cherry-pick intelligence reporting from across the community to be seeded in the media to reinforce two bogus claims: (1) that Iraq's Ba'athists had entered into an active pact with bin Laden's network, and that (2) the Ba'athists were on the verge of going nuclear. The Secretary was known to scorn the DIA's Iraq analysis as well, and he overruled pointed warnings issued by the Army Chief of Staff that the U.S. military could not occupy the country without a contingent of 300,000 soldiers. Amidst rising tensions and mounting controversy over Saddam's alleged possession of nuclear weaponry, Tenet balked too, sending a formal request to the Department of Justice to begin a criminal investigation to identify the source of a leak of a CIA operative's identity (a career officer who was unwittingly dragged into the dispute over the war's strained *casus belli*), even though it was sufficiently clear that the leaker would have to have been a senior White House official.

As the war wore the military down until it was an occupation in disarray, disgruntlement surfaced publicly. First, Richard Clarke, the former counterterrorism czar at the National Security Council, made searing statements against the administration at the 9/11 Commission hearings, and then the departing National Intelligence Officer for the Middle East, Paul Pillar, spoke out:

If the entire body of official intelligence analysis on Iraq had a policy implication, it was to avoid war—or, if war was going to be launched, to prepare for a messy aftermath. What is most remarkable about prewar U.S. intelligence on Iraq is not that it got things wrong and thereby misled policymakers; it is that it played so small a role in one of the most important U.S. policy decisions in recent decades.[2]

The overlord at the DIA for Iraq planning, Spider Marks, told a reporter at the *Times* that prewar misjudgments had been made in many quarters, not just in the Cabinet leadership. "We lost our finger on the pulse of the Iraqi people and built intelligence assessments from a distance."[3] Out in Langley, the CIA has been under a pall.

The blunt consensus in the 9/11 Commission report and on Capitol Hill in the Intelligence Reform Act of 2004 to downgrade the CIA was probably not ill-advised. The Agency now has the leeway to be loyal at arm's length during domestic imbroglios, and in principle it has a new referee in the DNI. This has hardly been an auspicious time, however, to watch the demoralization at the CIA, with constant leaking of sensitive intelligence information and the hemorrhaging of experienced intelligence officers into lucrative private-sector security jobs or retirement. Where does that now leave the CIA and the intelligence community, who bear the preponderant responsibility to inform the president about terrorists and their targets *before* these attacks occur? Future performance alone will provide the answer. The intelligence community has weathered its share of crises in the past. Yet there are some systemic reasons to be concerned.

To start with, the intelligence agencies allowed their capabilities to attenuate markedly during that ten-year period between the disintegration of the Soviet Union and September 11, 2001. There are still too few intelligence officers who have studied and understand Arabic civilizations or who have lived in the Middle East at some point in their careers. Moreover, many of the collection techniques of the Cold War have been rendered obsolete by cell phones, the Internet, and other aspects of changing technology. The CIA cannot continue to operate as it did in the pre-Iraq period, largely excluded from the hard targets that the United States is up against. Where it has no physical presence, the Agency has historically relied for HUMINT primarily on defectors, detainees, legal travelers, opposition groups, and foreign government liaison services, but these sources divulge their secrets at some distance in time and space from the ongoing developments inside the target they are reporting on. Getting inside the adversary's organization is thus a higher priority than it was even in the Cold War. Yet even though the Directorate of Operations budget is now more than double its pre–September 11 levels, an estimated 80–90 percent of intelligence information about Al Qaeda still comes in as SIGINT.[4] The whereabouts, goals, and tactics of terrorists are thus available only imprecisely and intermittently.

In the HUMINT area, American intelligence is still behind other services in having linguists who speak the hard languages of the Middle East, Central Asia, or Southeast Asia. In addition, this assignment is becoming less appealing to spy runners from the standpoint of safety and quality of life. Increasingly, CIA operatives will bring back key intelligence only by acting with the flexibility, the skills, and the cover it takes to run operations unlinked with an official installation—under nonofficial cover. Consequently, the problems spies face conducting espionage will be more dangerous. Families, too, will be divided, as many overseas tours in areas of prime concern to the intelligence agencies are not safe for young children.

Furthermore, there has been an especially rocky post-Tenet transition for the current director of the Central Intelligence Agency (DCIA), former Congressman Porter Goss. Mr. Goss has been criticized for bringing a number of hostile and inexperienced congressional staffers with him to Langley, making for even more precipitous erosion from the ranks among senior officers with substantial field experience. This will hinder the CIA's ability to take full advantage of the uptick in personnel recruitment, because so many experienced officers appear to be leaving. Goss announced that rebuilding the operations directorate would be the overriding priority of his tenure, but an irony thus far has been the number of critics comparing the present impasse to DCI Stansfield Turner's first year, marked by some of the most severe confrontations and mishandled purges the Directorate had ever experienced. By the end of 2005, Goss had lost one Directorate of Operations head, two deputy directors, and more than a dozen department, division, and station heads.[5]

An equally fundamental point is that Americans are not the "good guys" anymore in many areas of the Middle East. This sounds simplistic, yet much of U.S. intelligence success during the mature stages of the Cold War occurred because Soviet and Soviet Bloc officials volunteered to work for the American or British intelligence services as a way to oppose the corruption and misery of their own lives behind the Iron Curtain. That motivation appears less prevalent in the Middle East today. The United States is perceived as a threatening, non-Islamic outside force, only interested in the region's petroleum resources. Perhaps the hard push by the United States for democratic governments in the region will alter this attitude. It will be a hard sell.

The upshot of pervasive suspicions in the region about American aims is that, to be successful, the CIA and the other intelligence community HUMINT collectors will have to work indirectly, and multilaterally, through the good offices of friendly intelligence services, the operational channels called intelligence liaison. Since September 11, the CIA has been doing that in a major way, trading superior resources and technology for on-the-ground intelligence information about terrorist threats. The CIA has built a formalized network of over two dozen liaison offices, and DOD has gotten into the game as well, with less formal and even lower-profile liaison and reconnaissance missions for the special forces. These DOD operations do not fill the need for nonofficial cover and penetrations, but they do have a tactical yield.

The difficulty liaison relationships present, however, is that we are no longer in complete control of the spy operation. Our liaison intermediaries will influence both whom we target and how we manage the take. The result is bound in many cases to be a dilution of the product and a diminished timeliness. But the most worrisome deficiency will be a lack of confidence that one is getting the full picture, with the ongoing potential to leave the United States vulnerable and the region unstable. It is worth remembering the lessons of the Pakistani ISI's control over our access to the *mujahedeen* during the 1980s and 1990s in Afghanistan or the heavily slanted read of the opposition that the Shah's SAVAK presented the CIA in Iran's prerevolutionary decades. Nevertheless, liaison operations account so far for nearly all of the 3,000 suspected terrorists who have been captured or killed outside the Iraq theater.[6]

Disruptions in these liaison relationships come with the territory, but the CIA's experiences in Latin American counternarcotics operations have provided a number of relatively useful lessons for working with less-corruptible, more-trustworthy elite units in the more-questionable partnerships with foreign services. Porter Goss has rightly pronounced himself wary of leaning too far toward liaison operations. There are, however, elements of liaison operations that cannot be replaced by CIA HUMINT work. The first of these is legal access: To carry out targeted killings in a foreign country, it becomes prudent to give and receive assurances from other sovereign governments. Kidnapping also is best avoided wherever the local service is willing to kick down the door for us. And shutting down nearly endlessly re-routable financing pipelines to terrorists requires a willingness to do so on the part of many sovereign partners simultaneously.

The intelligence community's technical collection programs may not be in much better shape than its HUMINT. Signals intelligence gathering is hindered by inadequate translation capabilities, while a wary target will be more willing to communicate by word of mouth, cleft stick, and carrier pigeon than by telephone or more modern means. From an operational standpoint, the fallout from the brouhaha over warrantless surveillance by the NSA of communications from potential terrorists abroad with individuals in the United States that arose in early 2006 may further limit the gathering of useful intelligence. Actually, it appears that most Al Qaeda instructions are moving through Arabic websites on the Internet, which intelligence services worldwide are not yet recovering or translating in a comprehensive or timely fashion.

When all is said and done, counterterrorism and counterproliferation intelligence gathering follows a new paradigm. It is less about classic espionage than persistent tracking of terrorists and their potential weapons by good detective work and perceptive mining of reams of open sources. This is no longer back-alley skulking in a trench coat. It is down-and-dirty police investigative work, tracing radicals and their bomb-making materials, and recruiting informants to watch mosques and radical meeting sites. That is why in the United States it is so important for the CIA to work well with the FBI, with Customs, with Immigration and Naturalization, and with local police first responders. Intelligence gathering in the 21st century is now less about James Bond or George Smiley than it is a Frankenstein composite of law enforcement, spies, and forensics.

At the same time, nearly ten years after publication of the 9/11 Commission Report and passage of the Intelligence Reform and Terrorism Prevention Act of 2004 (IRTPA) that created the National Counterterrorism Center and the Director of National Intelligence (DNI), it is possible to make some relevant observations about their effect on the Intelligence Community (IC).

Ret. General James Clapper is the fourth DNI to serve during this period. His office continues to expand, along with its staff, in an effort to monitor and direct the intelligence gathering and analytical efforts of 16 separate intelligence departments, most of them located in the Department of Defense. The goal of the legislation was to give the DNI real budgetary authority over the 16, and that has never been realized, but Clapper still plays the role of principal spokesperson for the IC. The director of the Central Intelligence Agency (DCIA) reports to him after a fashion, as does the director of the National Security Agency (DIRNSA), but as a practical matter, these two principals run their own shows.

As near as one can discover, the CIA has had little success recruiting human sources among the terrorist groups active in the Middle East, but it has pursued a more active role in the Predator drone program, seeking out and assassinating terrorist principals in Afghanistan, Pakistan, Yemen, and

Somalia. This and signals intelligence are largely what account for the approximately $16–17 billion spent on counter-terrorism annually by the USG.

This rate of expenditure is unlikely to continue. The US is not the vulnerable country it was on 9/11. It has locked the doors literally and figuratively to cockpits in the nation's airlines. It has invested enormous resources across the country to help local police and federal officials to pursue reports on terrorist activity in cooperation with local authorities. Although there has not yet been another attack in the U.S. on the scale of 9/11, the public remains wary and worried. The departing inaugural director of the NCTC, Michael Leiter, observed in 2012 that the US needed to develop a resiliency to the possibility of future terrorist attacks because it is probably not possible to plug every hole 100 percent of the time. Nonetheless, the notion of "if you see something, say something" has taken hold in the US, and the homeland has been surprisingly without major incident for over ten years.

As to the need to effectively collect foreign intelligence beyond the parameters of counter-terrorism, while the Administration pivots toward Asia, the performance and prospects are unclear. The United States remains challenged linguistically as it seeks to gather human intelligence abroad, but it remains formidable in its electronic, visual, and signals interception capabilities, as the recent furor over the U.S. coverage of the NSA demonstrates. Whether the NSA's wings are to be clipped because of the Edward Snowden revelations of 2013 remains to be seen, but it is safe to assume that, barring another massive 9/11-style attack, espionage and the role of intelligence will revert to a quieter, less expensive norm.

Notes

The author wishes to express his gratitude to Princeton Woodrow Wilson School PhD candidate Martin Stein, who assisted significantly in the preparation of this chapter.

1. Seymour Hersh, "Huge CIA Operation Reported in U.S. Against Antiwar Forces, Other Dissidents During Nixon Years," *New York Times* (December 22, 1974); Hersh, "President Tells Colby to Speed Report on CIA," *New York Times* (December 24, 1974); Hersh, "3 More Aides Quit in CIA Shake-Up," *New York Times* (December 30, 1974).

2. Paul R. Pillar, "Intelligence, Policy, and the War in Iraq," *Foreign Affairs* 85 (March/April 2006), pp. 15–27, at 16.

3. Michael R. Gordon, "Catastrophic Success: Poor Intelligence Misled Troops about Risk of Drawn-Out War," *New York Times* (October 20, 2004).

4. Dana Priest, "Foreign Network at Front of CIA's Terror Fight," *Washington Post* (November 18, 2005).

5. Dafna Linzer, "A Year Later, Goss's CIA Is Still in Turmoil," *Washington Post* (October 19, 2005).

6. Ibid.

CHAPTER SIX

Intelligence Analysts and Policymakers

Benefits and Dangers of Tensions in the Relationship

Jack Davis

THIS CHAPTER WAS ORIGINALLY OCCASIONED by public interest in reported tensions between Central Intelligence Agency (CIA) analysts and policymaking officials of the administration of President George W. Bush regarding the significance of ties between the Saddam Hussein regime and Al Qaeda terrorists, an important factor in the U.S. decision to invade Iraq in 2003. No evaluation of the latter case is provided. The chapter addresses, instead, general patterns of tensions between intelligence analysts and policy officials in order to provide a context for public assessment of the Iraq-Al Qaeda incident when the public record is more complete as well as provide enhanced understanding of similar future instances of tension.

Over the years, most of the tens of thousands of written and oral assessments produced by CIA analysts in an effort to support the policymaking process have been received by policy officials with either appreciation or silence. Many of the assessments are in response to policymaker tasking, usually a sign of expectation of useful insights. Many consist of briefings and exchanges via telephone or teleconferencing, where the fact that policy officials invest the time to elicit and discuss analysts' assessment of an important national security issue is testimony to the value the officials expect to receive. Many assessments, as to be expected considering the volume of production, miss the mark for the targeted officials in terms of relevancy, timing, or fresh insights, and thus evoke no reaction.

That said, tensions in the relationship between CIA intelligence analysts and administration policymakers are a common occurrence—an essentially normal by-product of the two camps' distinctive professional missions. The analyst's *main* professional commitment is to assess national security issues without bias for or against the outcomes sought by the incumbent presidential administration; the policymaker's professional commitment is to articulate, advocate, and advance the administration's national security agenda.

Often, the resultant tension in the relationship helps both camps to deal more effectively with the challenges of analytic and policymaking uncertainty that usually attend complex national security issues. Under policymaker criticism or questioning of judgments, analysts tend to revisit their initial views of the soundness of assumptions about what drives the issue and the implications of incomplete, ambiguous, and contradictory evidence. In response, policy officials often are moved to recalculate the elements of their own assessments of threats to and opportunities for advancing U.S. interests.

At times, though, tensions take a turn that does not serve well sound analysis, effective policymaking, or the national interest; charges of politicization or analytic distortion to support or undermine a policy initiative issue forth from one or both camps. These cases usually arise when policy officials repeatedly reject the analysts' studied interpretative judgments on the status of or outlook for a complex national security issue, especially when such judgments are seen to complicate policy initiatives that are politically important to an administration.

If tensions are a normal occurrence, and their elimination both impractical and unwise, recommendations of ground rules to enhance benefits and curb dangers would seem called for. But first one should make a closer assessment of the roots and branches of the tensions.

Tensions in analyst–policymaker relations in the United States can be traced back at least to the establishment in 1941, under the auspices of the Office of Strategic Services (OSS), of the first bureaucratically independent cadre of intelligence analysts. Sherman Kent, who later played a major role in setting professional standards for CIA analysis, came away from his World War II experience in the OSS with the conviction that relations between producers and consumers of intelligence assessments are not naturally harmonious, despite the common goal of advancing U.S. national security interests. Kent did not much change his views about inherent strains in the relationship during his years of analytic service with the CIA (1951–1967).

Why not harmonious? The character of the policy issue at stake, personalities in both camps, the degree of contention about policy direction among administration leaders, and the role of Congress as a third party to the policymaking process from time to time have contributed to the onset and intensity of analyst–policymaker tensions. The underlying constant, though, is the aforementioned difference in perspective on professional mission between the producers of intelligence analysis and their policymaking clients.

The Analyst's Perspective

CIA analysts are concentrated in the Directorate of Intelligence (DI), which takes pride in its organizational independence from the president, the secretaries of State and Defense, and the other policymakers its intelligence assessments are intended to serve. The conceit that DI assessments are free of policy and political influence or bias comes across in the slogans by which the analysts and their leaders usually define their professional mission: objective analysis, carrying truth to power, telling it like it is.

Over the decades, on many critical and controversial national security issues—for example, Soviet strategic arms, the Vietnam War, Central American insurgencies—considerable substantive expertise, much sweat equity, and tough-minded assessment of assumptions and evidence have gone into the analysts' interpretation of past and ongoing events. The usual bureaucratic result was and is a readiness among analysts to defend key judgments against criticism, even though they are aware of gaps and other flaws in their information.

Regarding prediction of future developments, where unexpected intermediate events can throw seemingly sound forecasts off course, analysts also have confidence in their expertise and work ethic, and they take pride in their belief in the independence of their judgments from policy and political influences.

Concerted public criticism of flawed analytic performance on major national security issues spawns intervals of analytic humility for the DI as an organization, its leaders, and usually the analysts directly involved. But for the most part, confidence, even overconfidence, in substantive judgments is a staple of the analyst's environment. Especially the more experienced DI analysts tend to see themselves as the best informed on the issues they follow as well as the most objective national security professionals in the U.S. government. Over the decades, on many issues, they probably have been.

Analysts vary in their experiences with and attitudes toward policy officials. That said, a common first reaction to criticism of their assessments by policy officials is to suspect that either politics or the critics' lack of requisite substantive expertise is at work. Digging in at the heels in defense of the original assessment at times follows. Probably more often, the analysts undertake a reappraisal of their assumptions, evidence, and argumentation, though a substantial change in judgments does not necessarily result.

The Policymaker's Perspective

Policy officials, for their part, also vary in their experiences with and attitudes toward CIA analysts. A good number of career policy officials over the decades have considered the DI analysts on their accounts not only the best informed among the governmental community of intelligence analysts but also the quickest to respond to requests for analytic assistance. This subset of policy officials also appreciates that CIA assessments, unlike those issued by analysts in policymaking departments, are rarely skewed to support a party to the bureaucratic politics that usually colors the policy-analysis process on national security issues.

The tendency among officials closest to the president runs differently. These essentially political appointees, because of their own partisan cast, can be quick to attribute partisan motivation to CIA analysts. Especially when a political party has been out of power for some years, newly appointed Republican officials tend to see the Agency as dominated by holdover liberal Democrats, whereas new Democratic officials tend to see the strong influence of Republican conservatives. Many top-level appointees have served in previous presidential administrations and have requisite confidence in their own analytic skills and substantive knowledge of the issues. Some carry over from previous service critical views of the competence of Agency analysts as well as of their perceived propensity to an anti-administration bias.

Regarding professional mission, both career officials and political appointees see themselves as action officers as well as policy analysts. Their job is to get accomplished their vision of the president's national security agenda—the goals, strategies, and tactics that emerge from policy analysis.

Unlike intelligence professionals, policy officials are little pained by a merger of an administration's interests in domestic U.S. politics and foreign policy goals. As a rule, to policy officials, especially presidential appointees, government is politics as well as policy. The merger of policy and political advocacy at times requires building a "yes case" or a "no case" amidst inconclusive evidence of the soundness of a policy initiative and the uncertain implications for policy success of daily developments involving, for example, U.S. diplomatic or military campaigns.

This does not mean administration officials are ready to ignore CIA assessments that, say, would give political opponents in Congress ammunition to criticize policy. Often policy officials will ask analysts to "unpack" their assessment, revealing what is fact and what is opinion, or they will call for a briefing and an exchange of views either to enlighten or to leverage analysts.

In sum, at root, tensions, when they occur, represent a collision between the analyst's mission-driven belief that policymaker criticism of carefully crafted assessments reflects politics or limited substantive command of issues and the policy official's mission-driven belief that CIA assessments that complicate a well-deliberated initiative reflect anti-administration bias or poor analysis.

The Analytic Branches of Tension: Opinions, Facts, Evidence

Though difficult to untangle in actual cases of analyst–policymaker tensions, separating the varieties of analytic production into three branches—opinions, facts, and evidence—serves to clarify both the character of strains in the relationship and potential ground rules for managing tensions.

Regarding estimative judgments or opinions on issues of high uncertainty (for example, multiyear projections of political developments in unstable foreign countries, or prediction of the outcome of protracted U.S. military and diplomatic engagements in violence-prone regions), even well-informed policymakers at times gain insights from intelligence analysts' well-argued estimative judgments.

But when analysts' bottom-line judgments are seen as implicit criticism of and potentially harmful to policy agendas, administration officials are prone to dismiss them as "opinions."

Then-Secretary of Defense Donald Rumsfeld, in an October 24, 2002, press briefing, went to great lengths to define the limits of the analysts' opinions in such circumstances: "If you think about it, what comes out of intelligence is not fixed, firm conclusions. What comes out are a speculation, an analysis, probabilities, possibilities, estimates. Best guesses."[1] Further, policy officials claim, often with justification, that the opinions regarding future developments spawned by policy analysis are sounder than analysts' opinions, if only because they are able to take fuller account of the weight of carrots and sticks the United States may be ready to deploy.

More than once, policy officials have let it be known, in particular, that they are little interested in whether analysts think U.S. initiatives will succeed. The analyst's main job, according to critics, is to provide assessments that enable policy analysts to reach sound judgments about what actions to take to implement policy, despite the uncertainty that fogs complex world events. The analyst's focus should be on strengths and weaknesses of foreign players, their tendencies, motivations, and risk calculations that would help policy officials identify potential dangers and U.S. leverage points.

Regarding facts, tensions are infrequent and usually involve competing methods of determining facts. Here a fact is defined as something concrete and reliably detected and measured: what a foreign adversary said in a recorded speech or intercepted conversation, as opposed to what he or she meant or actually intends to do.

A prominent official once observed, regarding facts, that policymakers are like surgeons. "They don't last long if they ignore what they see once they cut the patient open."[2]

When policy officials are hesitant to accept as fact a condition or development reported by analysts that could complicate political goals or policy implementation, they tend to challenge the sources and methods the analysts relied on in their determination of facts. During military engagements, for example, military officials have preferred to determine battlefield damage to the enemy as recorded in post-flight reports by U.S. pilots and to dismiss the analyst's usually more modest calculations of damage that were based on, say, overhead imagery.

The most noteworthy tensions between CIA analysts and policy officials usually are over differences about the meaning of available evidence—that is, differences over what to conclude about something knowable but not conclusively known to either intelligence or policy professionals.

On the issues that give rise to major tensions, first, there are gaps in information because of secrecy and collection limitations. Second, the available evidence reflects a body of reporting parts of which are of questionable reliability and are contradictory and ambiguous. Concerning, for example, the dispute between CIA analysts and prominent administration officials over the Saddam Hussein regime's connection to the U.S. war on terror: What will history show the burden of the evidence to have been regarding the nature of Iraq's prewar ties to Al Qaeda terrorists—a minor or major threat to U.S. interests?

Regarding the meaning of inconclusive evidence, former CIA Director and Cabinet member William Casey (1981–1987), in a dispute with analysts over the Soviet role in International terrorism, set forth his standard for keeping a policy-sensitive issue on the table: "Absence of evidence is not evidence of absence."[3] In effect, if a development or relationship is plausible, analysts cannot prove a negative to the satisfaction of officials with minds and agendas of their own.

In disputes with analysts about the meaning of inconclusive evidence, policymakers can insist on raising as well as lowering the bar of proof regarding judgments that could have a negative impact on their agendas. Once, when an analyst averred that reliable evidence had become available that indicated a suspected development that undermined an administration policy initiative was "almost certainly taking place," a policy critic retorted that the analyst "couldn't get a murder-one conviction in an American court with [his] evidence."[4]

The Critic's Challenges to DI Tradecraft

Policy officials have been generous in spelling out the elements of their criticism of Agency analysis. In doing so, the officials at times were motivated principally to improve the quality of support they receive for the demanding task of policy analysis and implementation. At times, the motivation also included an effort to defang or discredit politically unhelpful assessments. And at times the objective was to shape an intelligence deliverable into a tool that would lend political support to administration policy.

It is worth noting that policy officials who have been generally complimentary of the analyst's performance as well as those long dissatisfied with performance table similar criticisms.

Part of the analyst–policymaker tension in evaluating evidence reflects a difference in professional attitude toward odds. To an analyst, the judgment that the evidence indicates that a development favorable to U.S. interests is unlikely usually means the odds against the existence or emergence of the development at issue are roughly 4 to 1. Given such odds, the busy analyst as a rule is ready to go forward with his or her assessment and move on to the next assignment.

In contrast to a policymaker with an agenda to advance, the same starting odds of roughly 1 in 5 can make it promising as well as politically necessary to stay on the case. Moreover, on politically important issues, the official will not overlook the prospect that the analyst's pessimistic judgment could be off base because, first, they are insufficiently informed about the current state and potential fluidity of foreign forces at play and, second, because they do not appreciate the impact on developments of U.S. carrots and sticks, if a policy initiative gathers backing.

The reluctance of critical policy officials to rely on what they see as unhelpful assessments on issues important to an administration goes beyond professionally necessary "positive thinking" on their part. Critics also point out what they see as systemic weaknesses in the analyst's tradecraft (that is, analytic methodologies).

First, since cognitive bias is pervasive, analysts, like all observers, tend to see more quickly and vividly what they expect to see and, conversely, tend not to see and properly credit information that would undermine their prior judgments. Critics contend that analysts delude themselves if they think they are exempt from this so-called confirmation bias because of their claims to "objectivity."

Critics have made this point over the decades in defending requests that analysts take another look at their interpretation of the evidence regarding the rate of success of the strategic hamlet program in Vietnam (1960s), the seriousness of Soviet plans for winning a nuclear war (1970s), the battlefield successes of U.S.-backed insurgents in Nicaragua (1980s), and after September 11, 2001, the significance of Iraqi-Al Qaeda connections to the war on terror.

The analyst's phrase "we have no evidence that X exists" is judged particularly unhelpful by those officials dedicated to either blunting the threat or seizing the policy opportunity in question. The critics note that analysts rarely admit they have no evidence that X does not exist. Besides, one critic averred, "policymaking is not [done] in a court of law."[5] A similar criticism is that analysts are too tied to the specific reports that reach their "inbox" and do not take sufficient account of the inherent aggressiveness, ruthlessness, and duplicity of U.S. adversaries.

Policymaking critics also complain that analyst training and incentives place too much emphasis on "straight line, single outcome" analysis on complex and uncertain issues. Critics say this "make the call" approach is both unhelpful to sound decision making and prone to error.

Former Deputy Secretary of Defense Paul Wolfowitz, long a critic of Agency analysts, observed in an interview conducted in 1994 that analysts' assertiveness in the face of uncertainty can turn an Agency assessment on complex issues into a weapon for one policymaking camp to use against another. In contrast, by tabling alternative interpretations, analysts would provide a tool useful to all participants in policy debates and decision making.

Further, the critics aver that, especially when policy stakes are high, analysts should expend much more effort evaluating what they don't know and why they don't know it before issuing estimative judgments downplaying dangers on which policy officials are focused. For example, could gaps in information that lead analysts to discount the likelihood of potentially harmful developments of concern to U.S. officials be caused by denial and deception (D&D) operations, or inadequate U.S. collection, or flawed assumptions about which pathways and relationships an adversary is pursuing to effect the feared development?

The 1999 report of a commission chaired by the future Secretary of Defense Donald Rumsfeld, after noting past intelligence failures on timely detection of foreign ballistic missile developments, cautioned analysts not to be quick to conclude that absence of evidence indicated absence of vigorous weapons programs by potentially hostile countries. The report, instead, charged analysts with pursuing alternative plausible explanations for "particular gaps in a list of [program] indicators."[6]

In truth, policy officials may prize the analyst who can come quickly to a crisp conclusion on issues surrounded by uncertainty that supports their agenda. But policy officials who see CIA judgments as obstacles to their agenda are themselves quick to connect the make-the-call culture to the analyst's record of analytic failures from the Cuban missile crisis to the Iraqi invasion of Kuwait.

Perhaps most important, according to the critics, it is the duty of responsible policy officials to ask probing questions; to insist on critical review of the evidence; to send analysts back to the drawing board for another look; in effect, to pull any loose thread in an unhelpful intelligence assessment.

Then-Secretary of Defense Rumsfeld, in his October 24, 2002, press briefing, referred to the importance of engagement and criticism: "to the extent there's no feedback coming from . . . a user of intelligence, then one ought not expect that the level of competence . . . on the part of people supplying the intelligence will be as good . . . as if there's an effective interaction."[7] Granted, political overtones often color these criticisms. But in tradecraft terms, they represent reasonable standards for policy officials to levy on analysts charged with providing distinctive value added to U.S. policymaking efforts.

Defining Professional and Unprofessional Analysis

The doctrinal basis for a response to criticism by administration officials should reflect definitions of professional and unprofessional standards for intelligence analysts as agents both of the national interest and of the policymaking process. Thus, a definition of analytic professionalism should posit as equally important standards both of objectivity (defined as tough-minded evaluation of evidence and other sound analytic practices) and utility (defined as distinctive data and insights policy officials find useful for managing threats to and opportunities for advancing U.S. interests).

Neither objectivity without utility nor utility without objectivity would meet the test of the author's following definition: The mission of intelligence analysts is to apply in-depth substantive expertise, all-source information, and tough-minded tradecraft to produce assessments that provide distinctive value-added to policy clients' efforts to protect and advance U.S. security interests. The analyst's long-held standard of analytic objectivity has helped to promote an institutional ethic of pursing independence from all biases, including policy and political influences, in making judgments in the face of substantive uncertainty. But studies, including those commissioned by the Agency, indicate that substantive biases (experience-based mindsets) are all but essential for effectiveness in an environment of high-volume production and tight deadlines. In such circumstances, the effect on production of an "open mind" is akin to the burden of an "empty mind." In addition, cognitive biases (especially seeking confirmation for experience-based assumptions amidst inconclusive evidence), in effect, are hardwired mental traits.

Pursuit of the defined mission regarding objectivity, then, comes down to an effort to minimize bias by critical review of the assumptions driving the analyst's mindset and of the adequacy of the available evidence to draw any meaningful judgment and, if so, the content of the judgment.

Also to fulfill the defined professional mission, analytic deliverables must be seen by policy officials to have utility as they define their professional agenda, which, as previously indicated, is to posit and enact an administration's politically colored policy agenda. The analysts who would produce an assessment with high potential for utility to the policy-making process can no more ignore the political context in which their clients operate than they can ignore where the latter are on their learning curves (for example, how much background information is needed) and decision-making cycles (for example, planning stage or implementation stage).

To take account of the politics of policymaking is not a license for intelligence professionals, as analysts, to become policymakers, or their speechwriters or spear carriers. But if an analyst is not close enough to the process to feel the political pressures affecting policymaking, he or she probably is not close enough to produce professionally crafted deliverables that provide distinctive value added.

Thus, there will always be a danger that analysts, in constructing their written assessments and oral commentary, will introduce a policy or political slant—either deliberately or through disregard of analytic standards.

Analysts have done so in the past and likely will do so from time to time in the future.

A politicized and therefore unprofessional assessment can be defined as an analytic deliverable that reflects either (1) the analyst's motivated effort to skew building-block assumptions, evaluation of the evidence, and bottom-line judgments to support—or oppose—a specific policy, political entity, or general ideology, or (2) a conspicuous disregard for analytic standards that produces unmotivated but similarly distorted outputs that could affect the policymaking process.

From the policymakers' agenda-oriented perspective, it makes little difference whether what they see as analytic bias is motivated or unmotivated. One senior official, for example, complained that every assessment that indicated or implied that an administration initiative was flawed constituted analytic policymaking because it provided ammunition for Congress to oppose funding the initiative.

As long as policymakers' criticism of the objectivity, soundness, or utility of analysis reflects a legitimate tradecraft concern, they are not necessarily putting pressure on analysts to engage in unprofessional behavior. Policy officials have the license to change the intelligence question in search of insights in addition to those embedded in the analyst's initial assessment, to ask that assumptions and evidence be examined more thoroughly, and to request customized follow-on assessments. That is part of their job description, whether they are seeking fresh insights or analytic support for their established views.

Thus, it is not unprofessional behavior for analysts, on their own or when requested, to provide assessments that set out to make the case for an alternative view to their unit's agreed interpretations of ambiguous evidence of ongoing developments and estimative projections of complex trends. The only professional requirements are that such efforts at, say, devil's advocacy, be clearly labeled and vested with appropriate analytic standards for crafting a challenge to the mainline views on an issue embedded with substantive uncertainty.

Additionally, it is not unprofessional behavior for an analyst, when requested, to address matters clarifying tactical policy options for dealing with specific threats to and opportunities for an established general policy. The key to sound "action" or "implementation" analysis is for the analyst to identify plausible initiatives and evaluate them in cost-benefit terms, and for the policymakers to choose what course to pursue and bear responsibility for their decisions.

Finally, for a manager to tighten tradecraft standards on a politically sensitive policy issue before an analyst's assessment goes forward under a corporate DI seal is not necessarily a signal of unprofessional behavior. Painful to the analyst, yes. Politicization of his assessment, no.

Analysts and their managers and leaders must be vigilant in identifying, deterring, and decrying unprofessional assessments as herein defined; when engaged in analysis, they are and must remain intelligence professionals, not policy or political aides—or critics. If an analytic cadre is to deserve its vaunted organizational independence, it must be ready to hold its ground, in the name of the national interest, against pressures for politicization, no matter the source, the intensity, or the circumstances.

But analysts must also take seriously the "cry wolf" danger of levying charges of politicization whenever their authority to control the key judgments of an assessment is abridged.

More to the point, if ever teamwork must prevail over turf warfare and over the individual analyst's sense of entitlement to determine what "call" to make on a matter of substantive uncertainty, it is when the analytic corps is constructing assessments on politically contentious policy issues. Over the decades, many analysts who have made adjustments to initial assessments that maintained objectivity while enhancing utility have felt the sting of colleagues' unreasonable charges of politicization.

The Analyst's Response to Policymaker Criticism: Best Practices

The challenge for analysts, then, is to turn tensions to professional advantage by maintaining rigorous analytic tradecraft standards while enhancing the utility of their assessments to policymakers. Despite a popular reputation for flawed performance, CIA analysts regularly meet this demanding standard. To turn on its head an observation on policy success and failure attributed to President Kennedy after the 1961 Bay of Pigs debacle: Analytic failures draw a thousand critics; analytic successes are orphans.[8]

Call them "ground rules," call them "best practices"; lessons can be learned from both failures and successes, and recommendations made for how analysts should respond to policymaker criticism. The underlying concept behind the recommendations that follow is that analysts carry the heavier burden of managing tensions in policymaker relations in a manner that advances the national interest.

The main reason is that the policymaking camp is the more powerful of the two. Policy officials have many alternative sources to Agency analysts for information and insight, including their own staffs and departmental analytic organizations; the academic, research, and business communities; the media and the Internet. In contrast, Agency analysts have no comparable alternative market that would justify the large size of their cadre and high volume of production of assessments. Congress demands and receives a steady stream of oral briefings from Agency analysts but is rarely seen as an equal to administration officials as a client for written assessments.

The central theme of the recommendations is that analysts are professionally required to take the tradecraft elements of policymaker criticism seriously, no matter how much they may perceive that the politics of policy advocacy also are at play. Analysts, thus, should respond to criticism with a reassessment not only of the argumentation and judgments of the original assessment but also of whether it provided utility or distinctive value for the policymaking community. The goal is to take tradecraft issues off the table, so to speak, in an effort to isolate and then defuse any politically motivated elements of policymaker criticism.

First, become expert on the policymaker's world. Analysts should commit to learning as much about the U.S. policymaking process and their key policymaking clients as, say, a national security correspondent for a major newspaper or other media outlet is expected to command. Analysts, starting from year one, have to spend quality time analyzing how Washington works, warts and all, even if this slows down the pace of grasping how Baghdad, Beijing, or Buenos Aires work. In particular, analysts should understand their client's role as action officer as well as policy analyst. This investment will enable analysts to role-play the policy clients who have criticized an assessment, not to mortgage analytic integrity but to evaluate tradecraft performance through a different set of eyes.

Second, become accomplished at understanding and managing substantive uncertainty. Analysts are taught and are generally aware that their judgments on complex issues are based on thoughtful but fallible assumptions that in turn color their evaluation of fragmentary, contradictory, ambiguous, and otherwise inconclusive evidence. They have been cautioned about mindset and confirmation bias. Yet the norm is to rely on these powerful but vulnerable mental processes to get their assessments out under tight deadlines, and with a confident judgment.

Usually the resultant assessment holds up well against both the expectations of policymaking clients and the subsequent course of events. Usually. But what to do when a policy official conveys doubts or outright criticism?

Here, without being too quick to jettison original argumentation and judgment, the analysts should move from passive to active awareness of the limitations of their analytic craft. More active attention to the perils of analysis amidst substantive uncertainty entails taking a more thorough accounting of plausible alternative explanations and outcomes that were discarded or downplayed during the crafting of the assessment that drew criticism.

Casual re-examination of an assessment by its author and production unit to take the measure of alternatives at times is helpful, but the process of "talking about alternatives" is prone toward defense rather than critical evaluation of the original argumentation. More structured and external-ized challenges to the assessment hold greater promise of fresh insights that either strengthen confidence in, or point to useful modifications of, the assessment that drew criticism.

Tested approaches to alternative or challenge analysis include devil's advocacy, key assumptions check, quality of information review, and argu-ment mapping. Still another technique, known as analysis of competing hypotheses, tests which of several plausible explanations for a complex event or trend stands up best against a battery of relevant information.

Third, become adept at role-playing. At times, as indicated, analysts will be well positioned to prepare a professional response to criticism by un-dertaking an open-minded assessment of the policy critic's paradigm (that is, mental model) on a contentious issue. However colored by political considerations it may at first seem to the analysts, deconstruction will help identify the critic's assumptions, evaluation of evidence, and calculations of likelihood. Once this information is at hand, the analysts may see a path toward revision of their own assessment that both protects objectivity and enhances utility.

Fourth, lean forward professionally with action analysis. Analysts should not hesitate to respond to criticism about unhelpful analysis by changing the question from the one they initially believed should be ad-dressed to one policy critics call for—again a possible path to both objec-tivity and utility. Often the shift, as previously indicated, is from what is the most likely interpretation of an event or relationship or the most likely future path of development to depiction of the direct and indirect leverage the United States has to reduce dangers and seize opportunities.

In most cases, analysts can be professionally comforted by assuming savvy administration officials, despite a politically required public opti-mism, know their policy initiative is facing heavy obstacles, even before the CIA assessment elaborated the point. What is now in demand are intel-ligence insights for doing something about the obstacles.

An analyst once tabled an assessment that placed emphasis on the gen-eral political dynamics in country Z, including both domestic reform ten-dencies promoted by the United States and a deliberate show of independence from Washington on certain international issues. The word came back that the high-level U.S. official who had asked for the assessment "wanted to leverage the president of country Z, not love him."[9]

Fifth, master techniques for evaluating inconclusive evidence. More deliberate analyst attention to evaluating evidence on contentious policy issues is another promising avenue for stripping tradecraft complaints from policymaker criticism of analytic performance. Careful consideration of alternative meanings of gaps in information, especially regarding suspected programs to develop weapons of mass destruction (WMD), can help build credibility with critics.

Analysts can organize and assess what is known and unknown to determine, for instance, whether the gaps in expected indicators more likely represent limited U.S. collection and substantial D&D, an innovative approach to WMD development, or nonexistence of a concerted development effort. The aforementioned analysis of competing hypotheses is well suited to provide an externally structured (that is, minimally subjective) competition to see which explanation is the most and least compatible with available related information.

Sixth, use estimative terminology carefully. Analysts have a professional obligation in maintaining integrity while supporting the policymaking process to avoid compounding substantive uncertainty with linguistic confusion. This is essential to managing tensions on sensitive issues. To deter both misunderstanding and manipulation of judgments, analysts should avoid vague estimative phrases such as "real possibility" and "good chance." Though not without risk of an exaggerated precision, analysts should aim to set boundaries to key judgments (for example, "we judge the likelihood of development Z to be low—on the order of 10 to 20 percent"). On controversial issues, analysts should also avoid nonfalsifiable judgments such as "it is possible," "suggests that," and "according to reports." They should provide instead an evaluation of the authenticity, adequacy in terms of completeness and consistency, and significance of the evidence. And when no confident judgment can be made, analysts should say so directly.

As previously indicated, policy officials tend to stick to initiatives even against long odds. An assessment that calculates an estimated probability of a development at, say, roughly 80 percent, is making transparent a roughly 1-in-5 prospect of being wrong. An assessment that develops the longshot case using plausible alternative assumptions and evaluations of the evidence, as well as the analyst's preferred 4-in-5 prospect, can serve professionally to provide distinctive value added to policymakers without sacrifice of analytic integrity.

Seventh, be responsive to criticism but not at the cost of objectivity. As long as an analytic unit believes it has done its homework in evaluating evidence and in considering alternative explanations and projections, it should stand by its estimative judgments, even if policymaker criticism persists or intensifies. But the unit should also work to ensure continued access to and credibility with critical clients by varying the focus and perceived utility of its deliverables. Analysts should consider the following "1-3-1" approach to an issue of critical policy import on which they are engaged in producing nearly daily assessments.

Once a week, issue an assessment that features a net judgment, whether or not the one favored by policy officials. Include a credible accounting of the impact of recent developments and reports.

Several times a week, put the net judgment approach aside and employ action analysis to address tactical dangers and policy opportunities on which direct and indirect U.S. leverage could be applied.

Once a week, change the question via the tradecraft of alternative analysis, in order for both analysts and policymakers to examine the issue from another angle—for example: what-if analysis (what policymakers would see, if the likelihood of development X increased), risk–benefit analysis (the adversary's estimated calculations affecting its motivation for and ability to engage in development X), and if–then analysis (implications of the advent of a high-impact, low-probability development regarding X).

Finally, what of the danger that analysts' efforts to curb their own substantive and cognitive biases will generate deliverables that provide unwarranted support to the clients' biases and political agenda while weakening respect for the production unit's professional judgment?

There may be no win-win answer to the vulnerability of unintended consequences of attempts at professional accommodation of the tensions attending policymaker criticism of analysis. Policymakers, for example, have been known to tear off the cover page (literally and figuratively) explaining the main view of the analysts and the context for presenting an alternative view—and then citing the latter as the Agency's judgment.

But avoidance of the initiatives recommended above for professional accommodation of criticism and instead countering policymaker exaggeration of certitude with analyst exaggeration will help neither camp. As a rule, a blending of deliverables that indicates an openness toward alternative interpretations with regular affirmation of what analysts believe to be sound, if vulnerable, judgments will protect analytic professionalism, maintain credibility with and access to the policy clients, and best serve the national interest.

Analysts and production units unsure of how to proceed when confronted with policymaker criticism with political overtones should engage the Agency's Ombudsman for Politicization and other detached veteran practitioners for help in identifying the best professional response. Agency training courses that include case studies on managing tensions would also help prepare analysts and managers for their initial exposure to friction with their policymaker clients.

Largely as a result of internal as well as external reviews of flawed analytic performance regarding judgments about Iraqi WMD arsenals and programs under the Saddam Hussein regime, many recommendations for dealing with criticism of analysis by policy officials similar to those outlined above have been adopted or reinforced as tradecraft doctrine by CIA's senior leadership. The difficult transformation from doctrine to practice is now well under way.

Policymaker Prerogatives—and Their Limits

The preceding two sections of the chapter addressed: (1) analysts' professional prerogative to stick to their best judgment after testing it for soundness, no matter the intensity of policymaker criticism; (2) their obligation to mitigate tensions via alternative means of support to policy clients, such as action analysis; and (3) the breach of professionalism entailed in both deliberate and unintentional politicization of analysis.

What about the rights and wrongs of the admittedly more powerful policymaking camp? The national interest is best served when the two camps work together to combine sound intelligence analysis with sound policy analysis. That said, when the two camps clash, what are the prerogatives of policy officials, and what actions should be considered a breach of their professional obligations?

The questions and answers that follow are an attempt by the author, long an observer of the relationship but a member of the analytic camp, to set ground rules for policy officials that would enhance the benefits and temper the dangers of tensions in analyst–policymaker relations.

1. Are policymakers entitled professionally to reach, publicize, and act upon estimative judgments that diverge from intelligence assessments on a national security issue?

Yes. As indicated throughout this chapter, intelligence analysis, especially inherently fallible interpretative and predictive analysis, is an input to and not a substitute for policy analysis. Policymakers as analysts take account of other providers of information and judgment, and also bring their own, often considerable, experience, insights, and biases to the difficult tasks of policy formulation and implementation, for which they must take ultimate responsibility.

2. Are policy officials professionally entitled to ask intelligence analysts to take another look at their estimative judgments (for example, to review assumptions, evidence, and argumentation)?

Yes. Policymakers are commissioned to devise, promote, and enact the president's national security agenda. They know when a policy consensus is taking shape and the time for action is approaching on issues, despite intelligence assessments that sound a caution. Yet officials, especially those with an appreciation for the distinctive role of intelligence analysis, hesitate to ignore intelligence findings and estimative judgments that call into question the underpinnings for U.S. initiatives. One response in these circumstances is to ask analysts to go back to the drawing board. Furthermore, from the point of view of the national interest, well-articulated criticism of analysis is much preferable to inadequate guidance for the execution of intelligence deliverables and scant attention to the assessments once delivered.

3. Are policymakers professionally entitled to urge analysts to review and revise their confidence levels in analytic judgments?

Yes. For the same, usually healthy, reasons one analyst or intelligence agency challenges another's conclusions on whether a shrouded current relationship or indeterminate future development is nearly certain, probable, or unlikely, policymakers may ask analysts to rethink their degree of confidence in a judgment. Once again, the answer assumes estimative judgments are inherently subject to error and that policymakers' criticism of analysis is more useful to sound performance than their ignoring of analysis. Needless to say, intelligence analysts are professionally bound to stick to judgments on probability that survive their critical review, and intelligence professionals must take care not to allow the pressure of a process of repeated requests for revision to move the bottom line further toward one supportive of policy than the analysts' tradecraft would justify.

4. Are policymakers professionally entitled to ask analysts to provide well-argued alternatives to their studied bottom-line judgments (for example, devil's advocacy)?

Yes. Policy officials are at least as wary of the consequences of policy failure as analysts are of intelligence failure. They are professionally entitled to task analysts to use their skills and resources to present for consideration alternative or multiple views of a complex and uncertain issue. At times a call for, say, devil's advocacy may be a caution against the perils of groupthink, especially in cases in which policymakers agree with the analysts' judgments. At times the policymaker's motive will be to move Agency analysis to closer alignment with his or her own thinking. As long as rigorous analytic tradecraft norms are adhered to for whatever form of alternative analysis is solicited, and the analyst's preferred bottom-line judgment is firmly attached to the deliverable, intelligence professionals should welcome the opportunity for customized service to their policymaking counterparts.

5. Are policymakers professionally entitled to ask analysts to change the question they address (say, from whether a development is likely to how it might occur)?

Yes. Once an administration adopts an initiative, policymakers tend to move forcefully into their action-officer mode and have limited interest in analysts' views, based on the latter's reading of the evidence, on whether the policy is likely to succeed, much less whether the policy was wise to undertake. Policy officials have a job to do—to make the policy work. They are professionally entitled to ask intelligence analysts to provide action or implementation analysis—that is, expert assessment of opportunities for moving the policy forward and of specific dangers to be avoided, taking account of insights into the adversary's strengths, weaknesses, and "game plan."

6. Are policymakers professionally entitled to seek analytic judgments from sources other than the CIA and other U.S. professional intelligence organizations?

Yes. No matter how strongly intelligence professionals would prefer otherwise, policy officials, in pursuit of their policymaking and political goals, have a right to rely on whatever sources of information and insight they choose, either to supplement or to substitute for the support they get from intelligence professionals. This includes use of business, academic, and other nongovernmental sources; their own staffs, whether configured as a policymaking or intelligence unit; and also, as has happened, foreign intelligence services. Policymakers, in short, are entitled to reap the benefits of as complete and varied a set of substantive inputs as they can command as they undertake the arduous task of managing an uncertain and often perilous national security issue. If policymakers use different sources of analytic support simply because they want more cordial answers than those provided by intelligence professionals, then the policy officials must bear the burdens of self-deception, policy failure, and political censure when such outcomes prove to be the case.

7. Are policymakers professionally entitled to attribute to intelligence analysts judgments that overstate or understate analysts' confidence levels?

No. Once a studied, clear, and (if challenged) revisited statement of likelihood regarding a development, relationship, threat, or opportunity is established by Agency analysts, policy officials can attribute it to intelligence in order to buttress their own views or reject it in favor of their own alternative statement of likelihood. But they do not have the authority to attribute to intelligence professionals an estimative judgment the latter do not hold.

8. Are policymakers professionally entitled to force analysts to alter their best estimative judgments?

No. As already acknowledged, policy officials are entitled professionally to reject intelligence assessments and reach and promote their own estimative judgments (Question 1, above) and are also entitled to urge analysts to rethink and recast Agency intelligence judgments (Question 3, above). That clarified, under no circumstances are policy officials professionally entitled to force intelligence analysts to change estimative judgments. Obviously, there are risks to treating as inviolate intelligence judgments that are contrary to policy preferences. Events may prove the analysts to be wrong. Congressmen may complicate the funding and execution of an administration's strategy and tactics by using intelligence findings and estimative judgments to block or modify policy initiatives. Unauthorized leaks to the media of intelligence positions may create an untimely public debate over policy. These circumstances can cause a run-up in immediate costs, ranging from embarrassment of the administration to the thwarting of what history may judge to have been a sound policy initiative. But the long-term costs to the integrity and morale of intelligence professionals of forcing them to change their judgments will likely cause much greater harm to the national interest by weakening a vital arm of the national security establishment.

9. Are policy officials professionally entitled to use the media to criticize intelligence analysts' competence in an effort to protect an administration from congressional and public criticism of a policy initiative?

No. As argued in this chapter, policy officials are entitled, indeed encouraged, to criticize through government channels either a specific body of analysis or intelligence tradecraft generally. Furthermore, as policy professionals, they are entitled to raise publicly their criticism of analysis as long as it is couched in analytic terms and is not, in effect, a politically motivated ad hominem attack. That is, as policy professionals, they are not entitled to criticize publicly a careful body of intelligence work and the credentials of the analysts who produced it merely to relieve themselves of the burden of credible defense of their own contrary judgments. In principle, nearly all parties to the uniquely American system for making national security policy proclaim the value of maintaining the integrity of intelligence analysis. A practice of trying to leverage a congressional vote or public debate on a policy initiative by criticizing the credentials of analysts who produce uncongenial analysis undermines the principle.

10. Are policy officials professionally entitled to apply pressure on Agency leaders to remove from a production unit a manager or analyst responsible for assessments with judgments policymakers see as biased, wrong, or otherwise unhelpful?

No. Analysts and their managers should be judged by Agency leaders solely in terms of professional credentials and adherence to analytic tradecraft norms, including good-faith efforts to respond to tradecraft criticisms by policy officials through the various means outlined earlier in this chapter (for example, key assumptions check, devil's advocacy). The challenge of reaching sound analytic judgments amidst the perils generated by substantive complexity and uncertainty should not be compounded by a requirement for "political correctness" or fears about job security.

11. Are policy officials professionally entitled to request Agency analysts to engage in policy advocacy, for example, to produce a "white paper" that is released as an intelligence product?

No. Agency analysts may assist by providing information for the production of a white paper, but this and other formats of policy advocacy must be issued under the seal of a policymaking department or staff. The role of Agency analysts is to provide analytic support to policy planning and implementation by administration officials—and not to make, advocate, or criticize policy. Again, the long-term importance to the national interest for Agency analysis to be and be seen as a source of substantive objectivity as well as policy utility far outweighs any short-term political advantage gained from using an adulterated form of intelligence analysis to gain public or congressional support for a policy initiative.

Concluding Thoughts

What about enforcement of these or any other set of ground rules aimed at moderating tensions in analyst–policymaker relations? U.S. experience has shown that presidents and their inner circles from time to time will play by their own rules. Agreed prerogatives and constraints and authoritative calls of "foul" might nonetheless serve well over the long haul, if only to evoke second thoughts about ignoring a transparent set of rules for improving both intelligence analysis and national security policymaking.

Presidential administrations already have an instrument in place for monitoring the adequacy and quality of intelligence analysis, along with all other intelligence functions. The President's Intelligence Advisory Board (PIAB) is well situated, both to help shape the ground rules and to monitor for analyst compliance. Over the decades, PFIAB members—former administration officials, members of Congress, and military and business leaders—collectively have commanded formidable knowledge about analysts and policymakers. And as a rule, PFIAB staff reports on analytic performance have been noted for both independence and insight.

For the Agency, the Ombudsman for Politicization has served since the early 1990s to educate new analysts about professional standards, to monitor for politicization, and to counsel analysts about the concerns they raise on the issue. Over the years, the Ombudsman, selected by and serving at the pleasure of the director for Intelligence, has been a highly qualified former intelligence manager serving part-time as an independent contractor.

The following recommended changes relating to the Ombudsman are intended to strengthen both the educational and protection functions, including participation in shaping ground rules and more active monitoring for compliance on the part of policy officials as well as intelligence professionals.

- Change the position name to Ombudsman for Analytic Professionalism (OAP). The professional obligations for analysts in the management of tensions involve more than the avoidance of policy or political bias.
- Provide the OAP with a small staff. The rise in importance to U.S. national security of countering weapons proliferation and terrorism—issues on which conclusive evidence will be a rarity—is likely to increase tensions over the meaning of available information and thus the demands on the OAP.
- To ensure the independence of and enhance analyst confidence in the OAP, have the newly instituted director of National Intelligence nominate and Congress confirm the title holder to serve a fixed term of five years.
- To help hold policymakers as well as analysts accountable in their management of tensions, require the OAP to provide the intelligence oversight committees of Congress with periodic reports on the compliance of both camps with agreed ground rules.

This chapter, by design, has mentioned Congress only briefly, although it is the third side of the triangle that constitutes the U.S. system for making and implementing national security policy. Yet for any set of ground rules for governing analyst–policymaker relations to have a lasting impact, Congress, on its own or in response to public demand, must take action to promote and monitor such an initiative. The goal, one last time, would be to ensure that the inevitable tensions between Agency analysts and administration officials are managed to the benefit of the national interest.

Notes

All statements of fact, opinion, or analysis expressed are those of the author and do not reflect the official positions or views of the CIA or any other U.S. government agency. Nothing in the contents should be construed as asserting or implying U.S. government authentication of information or Agency endorsement of the author's views. The material has been reviewed by the CIA to prevent the disclosure of classified information.

1. Quoted in "Rumsfeld on New DoD Intelligence Team," *Early Bird* (newsletter), Department of Defense (October 25, 2002), available at http://www.defenselink.mil/news/Oct2002/t10242002_t1024sd.htm

2. Author's interview with Paul Wolfowitz, "Paul Wolfowitz on Intelligence-Policy Relations," *Studies in Intelligence* 39 (Langley, VA: Central Intelligence Agency, 1996).

3. Author's interview with CIA analysts present when the remark was made at CIA Headquarters, Langley, VA, in 1982, cited in Jack Davis, "Tensions in Analyst-Policymaker Relations: Opinions, Facts, and Evidence," *Occasional Papers*, CIA, Kent Center 2 (2003), p. 3.

4. Comment made to the author in April 1980, CIA Headquarters, Langley, VA, cited in Davis, "Tensions," p. 3.

5. Author's interview with Paul Wolfowitz, "Paul Wolfowitz."

6. Intelligence Side Letter [to Congress and the director of Central Intelligence], Report of the Commission to Assess the Ballistic Missile Threat to the United States (March 18, 1999).

7. Quoted in "Rumsfeld on New DoD Intelligence Team," *Early Bird*.

8. Editor's note: After the Bay of Pigs failure in 1961, President Kennedy observed, "There is an old saying that victory has a hundred fathers and defeat is an orphan," cited in Arthur M. Schlesinger Jr., *A Thousand Days: John F. Kennedy in the White House* (Boston: Houghton Mifflin, 1965), p. 289.

9. Author's recollection of a 1973 incident, cited in Davis, "Tensions," p. 6.

CHAPTER SEVEN

The Intelligence-Policy Nexus

James J. Wirtz

Introduction

THE INTELLIGENCE–POLICY NEXUS IS A CRITICAL PART of modern government. Policymakers rely on intelligence professionals for data about broad international trends and their potential consequences, information about the intentions and capabilities of friends and foes alike, and specific warnings needed to avert disaster. Intelligence managers and analysts look to the policy establishment for their raison d'être. The intelligence community exists solely to provide policymakers with the information and analysis needed to formulate effective public policies. Few relationships in government are as symbiotic as the intelligence–policy nexus. One might thus expect that it would be relatively easy for intelligence professionals and policymakers to maintain smooth and productive working relations. Yet, few relationships are as challenging or produce as much controversy as the interaction between policymakers and intelligence professionals. The modus vivendi that governs their work is fragile, and disagreements that originate deep within the bureaucracy can easily find their way into tomorrow's headlines. The accusation that the Bush administration manipulated finished intelligence to support the decision to launch a preventive war against Iraq in 2003, for example, is the latest contentious issue in the history of the intelligence–policy nexus in the United States.

A variety of problems can emerge to bedevil relations between the intelligence and policymaking communities. The best-known pathology, politicization, occurs when policymakers place overt or subtle pressure on intelligence analysts and managers to produce intelligence estimates that support current political preferences or policies. Other issues, however, have received far less attention in the literature on intelligence. For example, there is no consensus about what constitutes best practices when it comes to intelligence–policy interaction, which can lead to acrimony as intelligence managers attempt to institute reforms. The information revolution also is creating new points of friction as intelligence analysts and policymakers interact using informal channels of communication, creating new challenges for those charged with monitoring the contents of finished intelligence—formal written reports that reflect a deliberate judgment made by analysts.

This chapter explores the tensions and pressures that shape interaction between intelligence professionals and policymakers as they go about the business of informing, making, and executing foreign and defense policy. The first section describes the two normative theories that offer competing explanations of how relations between intelligence professionals and policymakers should be organized. It also explores the intelligence pathologies that can emerge if either of these theories is applied with too much stringency. The second section explores the origins and consequences of politicization. The third section examines how the information revolution is transforming the relationship between analysts and officials, producing benefits as well as unintended consequences. Although technology has always shaped the intelligence cycle—setting intelligence requirements, collecting data, analyzing information and producing finished intelligence, and communicating information to people who can put it to good use— the information revolution might actually be altering the intelligence– policy nexus, creating an entirely new dynamic in relations between the intelligence and policymaking communities.

A Theory of the Intelligence–Policy Nexus?

Two normative theories animate the debate about best practices in the intelligence–policy nexus. One, most closely associated with the work of Sherman Kent, focuses on ensuring the independence of intelligence analysts when it comes to providing information to policymakers.[1] Kent's thinking, which shaped the formation and early evolution of the U.S. intelligence community, identifies the importance of political and policy detachment when it comes to producing relevant and effective finished intelligence. The other operational framework, most closely associated with the reforms instituted in the mid-1980s by then director of Central Intelligence Robert M. Gates, focuses on providing "actionable" intelligence, information of immediate and direct use to policymakers.[2]

To produce actionable intelligence, analysts have to maintain close working relationships with policymakers, literally looking into officials' inboxes to make sure finished intelligence addresses important policy issues of the day. These frameworks appeal to different groups within the government, produce specific benefits, and exhibit unique intelligence pathologies.

The Kent Approach

Sherman Kent's approach to the intelligence–policy nexus is based on the premise that effective intelligence is independent intelligence. Analysts must maintain their distance from current policy and policymakers to prevent their reports from being shaped by their customers' preferences. In Kent's view, intelligence managers and analysts should be free to set intelligence requirements and production plans for finished intelligence products, deciding which projects best support policymakers. This approach guards against politicization because it creates real procedural and even physical barriers that prevent policymakers from influencing the questions addressed and answers presented in finished intelligence. Analysts often champion this model of the intelligence–policy nexus because it provides them with the intellectual freedom to pursue their interests within the relatively broad guidelines created by intelligence managers.

At the core of the Kent approach is a grand bargain between policymakers and intelligence professionals. The intelligence community is master of its own house, but analysts and intelligence managers must avoid becoming embroiled in political decisions or commenting publicly or even privately on current policy or political issues. This division of responsibility is especially important because it gives intelligence analysts a special cachet in the U.S. political system, where the intelligence community is often seen as an objective source of information that is beyond the reach of partisan influence. Intelligence professionals take this bargain seriously. The organizational culture of the Central Intelligence Agency (CIA), for instance, reinforces this bargain through formal and informal norms and rules against political or policy commentary in the products produced by the Agency. Finished intelligence analysis also is scrubbed clean of policy content or obvious political bias that might have inadvertently crept into the work of analysts.

The strength of Kent's approach is that it preserves the independence of analysts by separating the intelligence community from the overt pressure or organizational and interpersonal incentives that can shape intelligence to conform to current policy or the personal and political biases of policymakers. Yet, by creating a strong barrier against politicization, Kent's prescriptions can separate intelligence too completely from policymakers, leading to other problems. For instance, policymakers are "inbox driven": They only have the time and energy to deal with their areas of responsibility or issues of immediate importance. Thus, weighty research papers offering reviews of broad issue areas or regions are likely to be ignored by policymakers. Those who are not responsible for the issues or regions covered will not read the paper, while those with a professional interest in the topic will seek more detailed analyses. Similarly, in-depth reports are likely to be ignored by most policymakers who have no responsibility for the issue surveyed. Without a good understanding of the issues that preoccupy specific policymakers, high-quality finished intelligence might be viewed as useless by intelligence consumers because it covers the wrong topics, arrives too late to be of use, lacks the proper level of detail, or addresses the wrong facet of the problem at hand. In fact, without some sort of collaboration between analysts and policymakers, the arrival of timely, relevant, and useful finished intelligence would depend on luck.

Organizational pathologies also can emerge if intelligence managers and analysts become too detached from the needs of policymakers. Analysis can take on a life of its own as the personal or bureaucratic agendas of intelligence professionals begin to take precedence over the needs of their consumers. For instance, critics charged that the CIA's Office of Soviet Analysis (SOVA), especially its division specializing in the study of the Soviet economy, became increasingly scholastic as the Cold War progressed. Because the command economies of the Communist bloc had little in common with those of the capitalist West, the CIA was forced to create an entirely new academic discipline to understand Soviet economic performance and capability.[3] Promising academics were recruited from the best graduate schools and given specialized training, journals were founded to cultivate new methodologies and to provide a forum for theoretical debate, and analysts worked hard to gain insights into Soviet economic performance, a state secret of the Communist regime in Moscow. As analysts sought to sharpen their methodological skills and improve the sophistication of their theories, however, they began to lose sight of the big picture, especially the fundamental question that suggested itself to policymakers in the early 1980s. Could the Soviet command economy compete over the short term with the capitalist economies of the West, or was the regime in Moscow built upon an economic house of cards?

Actionable Intelligence

When Robert Gates, then deputy director for analysis at the CIA, became frustrated with the unwillingness of CIA analysts to provide intelligence to meet the specific requirements of administration officials, actionable intelligence was born. Under Gates's system, analysts might have been asked, for example, when—not if—the Soviet economy would collapse. Intelligence professionals cried foul, noting that by posing specific and pointed questions, Gates was attempting to shape the analysis to suit the expectations of policymakers. In response, Gates suggested that he was trying to make analysts less academic so that they would produce relevant and timely finished intelligence that responded to the needs of administration officials.

The core assumption behind actionable intelligence is that analysts must be aware of the needs of policymakers and that intelligence managers have an obligation to task analysts so that they produce useful intelligence for their clientele. According to Gates:

> My view has been all along from the very beginning of my career—and perhaps due to the fact that I have served on the National Security Council—that the Intelligence community has to be right next to the policymaker, that [the analyst] has to be at his elbow—that he has to understand what is on his mind. He has to understand what his future concerns are. He has to understand what his agenda is. He has to understand some of the initiatives that he is thinking about taking. He has to be willing to ask the policymaker what he's working on, or what came of his last conversation with a world leader so that the intelligence can be made relevant; so that the Director, or the office director, or what can go back and give guidance to the analysts.[4]

From this perspective, policymakers already have a reasonable idea of what they need—information to help them implement their policies. Most of the support they require from the intelligence community is largely technical in nature: demographic, geographic, political, economic, and military data about the issue at hand and how allies and adversaries are responding to U.S. policies. Some observers have even noted that as crises emerge, policymakers should communicate with analysts directly to increase the flow of information and the timeliness of analysis. Under these circumstances, analytic debates within the intelligence community are counterproductive and actually reduce the confidence policymakers have in finished intelligence. When the chips are down, officials want information they can use to solve problems, not competitive analysis designed to highlight various theoretical or methodological approaches to the issues of the day.[5] In fact, some policymakers have discovered that the intelligence community can actually serve as an extension of their office staff, providing a ready source of analysis and information tailored to meet their personal interests and agendas.[6]

In reality, much of the finished intelligence produced by analysts takes the form of actionable intelligence: The information supplied to policymakers often is matter-of-fact data about what is occurring in a specific part of the world, the state of a foreign economy or industry, or the capability of a weapons system. Moreover, elected officials usually enter office with a pre-existing worldview and policy agenda; they look to the intelligence community to help them implement their policies. If intelligence professionals fail to recognize this political and policy reality, they risk becoming irrelevant.

Nevertheless, following the Gates model too closely can create its own set of problems. There is a possibility that policymakers will pose biased questions to the intelligence community to guarantee that analysis favorable to their positions will emerge, or that they will fail to pose the correct questions, leading to an incomplete understanding of the challenges they face. If analysts also concentrated only on actionable intelligence, they might lack the time to conduct the independent, in-depth research needed to uncover threats and trends not on current policy agendas. When they initially took office, for instance, members of the Bush administration had not placed Al Qaeda on the top of their foreign and defense policy agendas. Instead, they were more concerned with improving Russian–American relations, deploying a U.S. missile defense system, and reducing U.S. military commitments overseas. It was up to the intelligence community to increase the salience of the terrorist threat to the United States among senior officials.

Normative theory and practice thus highlight the competing priorities that animate the intelligence–policy nexus. Analysts need some leeway, unconstrained by the preference of policymakers or even intelligence managers, to pursue their hunches and interests, regardless of current political or policy preferences. Without this freedom, policymakers would lack independent information and insight into current and emerging international issues. For their analysis to be relevant and timely, however, intelligence professionals must possess a keen awareness of policymakers' current interests and responsibilities. What policymakers require is information and finished intelligence reports that address the issues found in their inboxes. They also would benefit from long-term research that highlights emerging problems before they become crises or sources of embarrassment.

Politicization

Politicization, the effort of policymakers to shape intelligence to conform to their policy or political preferences, can emerge in both overt and subtle ways. Although the term suggests that intelligence analysts are victims when policymakers manipulate intelligence to suit their needs, intelligence professionals can themselves politicize intelligence when they allow bureaucratic or personal incentives to influence their estimates and reports. Intelligence managers and analysts can "pander" to policymakers by presenting them with information and analysis that meets their expectations and confirms their chosen policies. Intelligence estimates also can appear to be politicized when they are effective—that is, when they actually have a policy or political impact.

Overt politicization occurs when policymakers deliberately pressure analysts to produce estimates that support their policies or to shape the intelligence cycle to confirm current policy or political preferences. The act of deliberately shaping intelligence estimates would have to be driven by expediency or desperation because policymakers run a grave risk by preventing accurate, if unpleasant, information and finished intelligence from informing national policy. In extreme cases of politicization, senior officers or policymakers can even retaliate against analysts for providing them with information that contradicts their existing beliefs or plans. In the days leading up to Operation Market Garden, the Allied airborne-armor operation to seize the Rhine River crossings in September 1944, Major Brian Urquhart, chief of Intelligence for the British I Airborne Corps, detected signs that Nazi armored divisions were actually bivouacked in Arnhem, that last objective of the Allied advance. When Urquhart relayed to his superiors this information, which called into question the feasibility of the entire operation, he was visited by a senior medical officer who placed him on sick leave.[7]

Overt politicization, however, is difficult to keep concealed, because analysts and intelligence managers will go to great lengths to resist what they believe are illegitimate efforts to influence their finished intelligence reports. In the aftermath of the Vietnam War, for instance, Samuel Adams, a former CIA analyst who helped develop estimates of enemy troop strength during the war, charged that senior intelligence officials and military officers deliberately suppressed his findings because they gave the Viet Cong greater strength than had been reported in previous intelligence estimates. The controversy over the incident only increased in the aftermath of the conflict and became the subject of a CBS news documentary and libel litigation between General William C. Westmoreland (retired), who was the former head of the Military Assistance Command in Vietnam, and CBS.[8] Some controversies boil over even more quickly. Following the second Gulf War, accusations emerged that the members of the George W. Bush administration had tried to undermine the credibility of Ambassador Joseph Wilson, who investigated reports that Iraqi agents had attempted to purchase yellowcake, a nuclear material, from Niger. Wilson had turned in a memo to intelligence officials in February 2002, explaining why the alleged Iraqi activity was probably a hoax. When the president claimed in his 2003 State of the Union Address that Iraq had sought uranium in Africa, Wilson went public in a July 6, 2003, editorial in the *New York Times*, stating that the Bush administration knowingly lied about the status of Iraq's nuclear program. In retaliation, Bush administration officials allegedly "outed" Valerie Plame, Wilson's wife, effectively ending her career as a clandestine CIA officer.[9]

Although they make headlines, charges that policymakers deliberately engage in politicization are relatively rare. Instead, policymakers and intelligence managers can shape analysis in more subtle, and sometimes even inadvertent, ways. Those who bring positive news can be rewarded with praise in front of colleagues, whereas those who bring unwelcome information can be chastised or criticized in front of their coworkers. "Positive" estimates are more likely to be rewarded with promotions, increases in pay, or sublime inducements important to bureaucrats—a larger office, new furniture, travel. "Negative" estimates are unlikely to be rewarded; in fact those with an eye for finding potential trouble in a generally positive situation are often avoided by policymakers whose workday is often spent responding to a never-ending series of crises, problems, or complaints. Loss of access to policymakers can take the form of *bureaucratic death*, a situation in which intelligence officials are no longer invited to important meetings because of their history of providing contradictory or discouraging reports.[10] Only the smartest and toughest policymakers encourage their staffs to take steps to avoid sending inadvertent signals to subordinates and intelligence managers to prevent analysis from being shaped to meet their expectations or to emphasize the positive aspects of every situation. Indeed, some observers have noted that the ability to literally pressure subordinates to provide honest assessments is a key to success in politics and war.[11]

Without knowing it, however, efforts to encourage analysts to provide their honest opinions can have unintended consequences. During the Vietnam War, for example, General Westmoreland was provided with a negative assessment of his command's ability to hold the marine position at Khe Sanh, the findings of an estimate that he had personally requested.

After hearing the report, which was delivered to his entire staff, he thanked the analysts for their best estimate and then stated that he would no longer tolerate gloomy evaluation of the marine's prospects at Khe Sanh. Years later, Westmoreland's chief of intelligence, Major General Philip Davidson (retired) remarked that he had never heard a negative prediction for the outcome at Khe Sanh. In what was an apparent effort to bolster morale, Westmoreland had told his command that he no longer wanted negative reports about the situation at Khe Sanh. It is not surprising that his staff complied.[12]

When intelligence has an effect on important foreign and defense policy debates, charges of politicization often emerge. Ironically, when intelligence analysts offer timely and relevant estimates to policymakers, they are sometimes accused of meddling in political affairs because their reports have an impact, favoring one side in a political dispute over another. As issues become increasingly a matter of heated partisan politics or less focused on technical issues, the role played by intelligence analysts as neutral purveyors of information and analysis increases. Moreover, if the finished intelligence in question was not backed by a clear analytical consensus, there always will be intelligence "dissenters" ready to take their case to elected officials or the media. As Richard Betts has noted, this is exactly the situation that emerged in the controversy over enemy strength during the Vietnam War: The effort to shape an analytical consensus spilled over into acrimony that lasted for years and became a matter of public and political debate.[13]

The Information Revolution and the Intelligence–Policy Nexus

The information revolution has broken down barriers of space and time by virtually eliminating the costs of communication, even at intercontinental distances. The computer and the Internet have provided individuals with an ability to organize and analyze information that was unheard of only a few decades ago. The Internet itself is a positive-sum institution: The more people who have access to the Internet and this virtually free means of communication, the more powerful the tool becomes for all concerned.[14] The real power of new computing and communication architectures is that they can potentially allow people everywhere and anywhere to find and interact with each other in real time.

As with any technology, the information revolution contains its own embedded ideology, so to speak: People will find that it should be employed in a particular way, regardless of the intentions of its designers. In fact, the inventor of a machine is often unaware of the logic inherent in the technology he or she is creating. Gutenberg was a Catholic, but his printing press made the Protestant reformation possible because printing facilitated the dissemination of competing ideas (that is, heresy).[15] The automobile transformed America—dispersing extended families and building suburbs and new American cultures.[16] The automobile's effects, however, were perceived only when the transformation of society was well under way.

The information revolution also is transforming society. It is an egalitarian technology that breaks down social, economic, political, and bureaucratic barriers and allows people direct access to each other's very personal "inboxes," for the most part facilitating frank communication even across hierarchical organizations. At the same time, the information revolution also documents human interaction as it channels not just formal, but informal, communication into what amounts to official or corporate records. In a sense, people have to convert private interactions into a public record to participate in the information revolution, but they seem to accept this as the price of entry for using the new technology.

The information revolution is having both a profound and a subtle impact on the intelligence–policy nexus. The "digitization" of everyday life has burst upon the public's consciousness in a profound way with Edward Snowden's revelations about the U.S. intelligence community's use of social media to apparently gather domestic and foreign intelligence. The information revolution has empowered the intelligence community, allowing it to monitor virtually everything moving across the World Wide Web. At the same time, however, the information revolution has enabled individuals within the intelligence community, in this case Snowden, to make their objections known to current government policy by providing the details of highly classified programs to the media or by placing that material directly on the Internet. The ubiquity of modern data storage and transmission also enables politically or policy motivated leakers to move data on a *massive* scale.[17] Put somewhat differently, the information revolution threatens the grand bargain at the core of the intelligence–policy nexus because it beckons to disgruntled analysts to directly shape policy by bringing their concerns to the public.

Because we use information revolution technologies on a daily basis, we also overlook the more subtle changes it is bringing to well-understood bureaucratic practices. In terms of the intelligence–policy nexus, for example, the information revolution has reframed the opportunities for interaction between intelligence analysts and policymakers in ways that are not well captured by either the Gates or Kent frameworks. The barriers to interaction assumed by the Kent model, which are supplied by intelligence managers or by the process of crafting formal intelligence estimates, are completely broken down by the information revolution. Policymakers and their staffs can now easily communicate on a daily basis directly with analysts. It is increasingly difficult for analysts to stand above the fray of politics or policy if they are bombarded with a barrage of questions about current policy, calls for data, or requests for commentary or supplemental information about media coverage of some international event. Moreover, as the volume of this informal interaction between policymakers and analysts increases, it can begin to drown out the message carried by the formal estimates offered by intelligence organizations. Because of the sheer volume of interaction between analysts and policymakers, it also might be nearly impossible for intelligence managers to monitor this informal communication, and any effort to restrict analysts' access to this communication technology would be resisted on both personal and professional grounds. The information revolution has created a new medium for interaction between analysts and policymakers that, by its very nature, flies in the face of the norms suggested by Kent's framework.

Policymakers' access to analysts is so great that it can overwhelm them, degrading their ability to provide significant actionable intelligence called for by the Gates model. It might be difficult for individuals outside of government or the military to understand, but as members of a "service industry," intelligence analysts must place the immediate needs of administration officials ahead of other important professional or organizational objectives. Questions or requests for information, no matter how trivial, must receive a prompt and complete response. Additionally, because service is part of the ethos of the intelligence community, performance metrics are focused on measuring responsiveness to policymakers' demands, not the quality or thoroughness of the response given or the opportunity costs created by setting aside long-term research projects. Because everyone within the policymaking and intelligence communities is virtually free to task analysts, intelligence managers are no longer able to set production priorities or timelines. In fact, because managers are judged by the same production metric as analysts, they have little incentive to intervene in informal communications to protect analysts from being endlessly besieged with questions by policymakers.

The information revolution offers more opportunities for intelligence analysts to interact with officials while making it increasingly difficult for analysts to hold their attention. Because policymakers have ready access to nongovernmental sources of information provided by 24-hour cable television and Internet news services, intelligence analysts have to hold the attention of policymakers by providing catchy titles to reports that exaggerate the importance or the certainty underlying estimates. The Silberman-Robb

Commission, which investigated the intelligence community's account of Iraq's weapons of mass destruction program prior to the second Gulf War, found that the *President's Daily Brief* (PDB)—a tightly held piece of finished intelligence that is read by a few select senior officials on a daily basis—suffered from various flaws and created several problems.[18] PDBs tended to contain bold statements and judgments that were probably intended to engage the reader but failed to convey a sense of the qualifications, judgments, or assumptions that were embedded in the analysis. Commissioners were concerned that a daily exposure to PDB briefings might "create, over time, a greater perception of certainty about their judgments than is warranted." Questions posed to PDB briefers are answered in future PDBs or in a Senior Executive Memorandum, which are distributed to all those who receive the PDB. Commissioners believed that the volume of reporting that could be produced by a question of clarification, for example, could create a false impression among PDB recipients that the president was intensely interested in a subject, thereby shaping priorities and policy.[19]

The commissioners also searched in vain for evidence of politicization in the intelligence community's reporting on Iraqi weapons of mass destruction programs. What they uncovered, however, was evidence of the impact of the information revolution—especially the breakdown of hierarchy. The CIA Ombudsman for Politicization told the commissioners, for example, that analysts on Iraqi issues worked under more "pressure" than any other analysts in the history of the CIA. For months they were required to provide enormous amounts of both formal and informal reporting directly to the highest officials in the U.S. government. These officials also questioned analysts directly about their work to explore the assumptions and data that were used. Policymakers are justified in asking these types of questions, regardless of their motivations, but the fact that senior officials apparently scrutinized analysts directly probably affected subsequent analysis. Analysts also were under pressure "to answer the mail quickly," which in itself can be detrimental to calm contemplation of complicated issues.[20] Cutting and pasting is not a measured reassessment of first principles or even secondary assumptions, and it unfortunately occurs when timeliness takes precedence over depth in the information age.

Conclusion

Intelligence reform is cyclical. Sometimes scholars and other observers warn that analysts are too detached from policymakers' concerns and are producing finished intelligence that is dated or irrelevant. At other times, concerns about politicization emerge; observers worry that intelligence analysts and managers are no longer serving as an independent source of information for policymakers and that the intelligence cycle has been corrupted by all sorts of political or bureaucratic considerations. Since the early 1980s, the pendulum has been swinging in favor of producing "actionable" intelligence, but in the aftermath of a series of intelligence setbacks leading up to and following the September 11, 2001, terror attacks, observers have had second thoughts about the status of the U.S. intelligence community. Intelligence reform, based on organizational change, is the order of the day.

It is extraordinarily difficult to strike a balance between detachment and responsiveness in the intelligence–policy nexus. As Betts noted, fixing one type of intelligence problem only exacerbates other types of problems.[21] For instance, providing all available information to analysts would overwhelm them; by contrast, restricting the flow of information creates the risk that they will not receive critical bits of information needed to make sense of emerging threats. Because the correct balance of detachment and responsiveness depends upon the specific issue or problem confronting intelligence analysts and policymakers, it is virtually impossible ex ante to fine-tune the intelligence–policy nexus.

In a sense, those interested in intelligence reform are addressing a moving target. The proper balance in the relationship between intelligence professionals and policymakers is shaped by external and internal factors. Externally, the changing threat environment and issue agenda create different types of challenges for the intelligence community. Reporting on developments within nation states requires different collection and analytical capabilities than does reporting on terrorist networks or super-empowered individuals. Internally, new communication and information processing capabilities—combined with the way analysts and policymakers actually use these novel capabilities—are creating new modes of interaction within the intelligence–policy nexus. Recent massive leaks of classified information also demonstrate that the grand bargain at the heart of the intelligence–policy nexus is becoming increasingly fragile; the information revolution has given analysts an easily accessible tool to shape policy to their liking. It might be too early to sound the death knell for the Kent and Gates models, but in the future it will probably become increasingly difficult to capture the reality of the intelligence–policy nexus within these competing theoretical frameworks.

Notes

1. Sherman Kent, *Strategic Intelligence for American World Policy* (Princeton: Princeton University Press, 1946).

2. H. Bradford Westerfield, "Inside Ivory Bunkers: CIA Analysts Resist Managers' 'Pandering'—Part II," *International Journal of Intelligence and Counterintelligence* 10 (Spring 1997), pp. 19–54; Richard K. Betts, "Politicization of Intelligence: Costs and Benefits," in Richard K. Betts and Thomas Mahnken, eds., *Paradoxes of Strategic Intelligence* (London: Frank Cass, 2003), pp. 59–79.

3. David M. Kennedy, *Sunshine and Shadow: The CIA and the Soviet Economy* (Cambridge: Harvard University, JFK Case Program, 1991).

4. Gates quoted in Westerfield, "Inside Ivory Bunkers."

5. William Odom, *Fixing Intelligence: For a More Secure America* (New Haven, CT: Yale University Press, 2003).

6. Jack Davis, "A Policymaker's Perspective on Intelligence Analysis," *Studies in Intelligence* 39 (1995), pp. 7–15.

7. Sir Brian Urquhart, who was under-secretary-general of the United Nations (UN) from 1974 to 1986, played a leading part in the development of UN peace-keeping operations throughout the Cold War. Urquhart was eventually knighted for his service to the United Nations.

8. James J. Wirtz, "Intelligence to Please? The Order of Battle Controversy during the Vietnam War," *Political Science Quarterly* 106 (Summer 1991), pp. 239–63.

9. "Then & Now: Joseph Wilson," CNN, 19 June 2005, available at http://www.cnn.com/2005/US/03/07/CNN25.tan.wilson/index.html.

10. Mark Lowenthal, *Intelligence: From Secrets to Policy* (Washington, DC: CQ Press, 2003), p. 148.

11. Eliot Cohen, *Supreme Command* (New York: Free Press, 2002).

12. Phillip Davidson, Interview II by Ted Gittinger, June 30, 1982, Oral History Collection, LBJ Library, Austin, Texas, pp. 23–24; and William C. Westmoreland, *A Soldier Reports* (Garden City, NY: Doubleday, 1976), p. 338.

13. Betts, pp. 73–74.

14. Bill Gates, *The Road Ahead* (New York: Penguin, 1996).

15. Printing increased literacy because it provided common people with something to read. Without printing, Martin Luther could not have encouraged people to read the Bible themselves.

16. George F. Kennan, *Around the Cragged Hill* (New York: W.W. Norton, 1994).

17. Daniel Ellsberg's leak of a 7,000-page secret history of the Vietnam War, known as the Pentagon Papers, pushed the limits of 1970s technology. A hard copy of the materials had to be physically removed from a classified storage facility and then photocopied for dissemination. By contrast, Private Bradley Manning, a low-level analyst serving in Iraq, was able to transfer about a half million classified documents and a quarter million diplomatic cables to the WikiLeaks website, a feat that was beyond imagination in the 1970s. See James C. Goodale, *Fighting for the Press: The Inside Story of the Pentagon Papers and Other Battles* (New York: CUNY Journalism Press, 2013), p. 211.

18. Commission on the Intelligence Capabilities of the United States Regarding Weapons of Mass Destruction, "Report to the President of the United States," 31 March 2005.

19. Ibid., pp. 160–81.

20. Ibid., pp. 187–89.

21. Richard Betts, "Analysis, War, and Decision: Why Intelligence Failures Are Inevitable," *World Politics*, 21 (October 1968), pp. 61–89.

CHAPTER EIGHT

9/11 and Iraqi WMD

Intelligence Failures?

Peter Gill

THE SEPTEMBER 11, 2001, ATTACKS ON New York and Washington (9/11) and the lack of the predicted weapons of mass destruction (WMD) in Iraq apparently represent two highly significant intelligence "failures," especially in the United States, with the best-endowed intelligence community in the world, but also, in the case of Iraq, for the United Kingdom.

If journalists provide the first draft of history, and, sometimes, official inquiries provide the second, then it falls to academics to provide a third. This is distinguished from the first two, in part, by facing fewer deadlines, but also, it is to be hoped, by providing an analysis rooted in the previous literature of the subject. Journalists will probably not have the time and may not have the expertise to do this, and the objective of governmental inquiries is determined largely by their timescale and terms of reference. Congress has investigated both 9/11 and Iraq, as have special commissions,[1] and the Iraq WMD issue has been investigated by various UK parliamentary, judicial, and special inquiries.[2]

This chapter places 9/11 and Iraq in a broader context of the literature on previous intelligence failures in order to answer some key questions:

- What do we mean when we talk of intelligence failure?
- To the extent that these were failures, what caused them?
- Were they, in fact, political as well as intelligence failures?

What Is Intelligence Failure?

The clear limits to intelligence are easily demonstrated by reference to a few of the defining events of the last century that U.S. and other intelligence services failed to anticipate. Any such list would include failures to predict the Soviet testing of its first atomic bomb, the North Korean invasion of South Korea, the construction of the Berlin Wall, an apparent string of failures over Vietnam, the Soviet invasion of Czechoslovakia in 1968 and of Afghanistan in 1979, the Iranian revolution of the same year, the Polish crisis of 1980–1981 and, more centrally, given that its primary focus for over 40 years was the USSR, the end of the Cold War.

Formally, intelligence exists to inform policy. States gather information at home and abroad regarding national security threats, establish structures for its analysis, and then disseminate the resulting intelligence to those in executive or policymaking positions for them to act on. The "idealist" view is that intelligence should, where possible, speak truth unto power so that politicians do not act based on misunderstandings of their position. Intelligence "tells it like it is," and if the politicians do not like it, then that is their problem (and maybe ours). The "realist" approach is that intelligence serves power; it must retain a close relationship with policymakers and meet their requirements for intelligence so as not to lapse into irrelevance.[3]

Either way, "failure" occurs when intelligence gets it wrong so that misleading information is presented to executives resulting, possibly but not inevitably, in unsuccessful policy. (Intelligence may be wrong, but superior power may nevertheless enable an adversary to be overcome.) Although failures may occur on different timescales, there are essentially two forms: false negatives (type 1) and false positives (type 2). In the first, there is a failure to apprehend something that is a threat, with the result that a surprise attack is suffered; in the second, a threat is perceived but turns out to be baseless. Clearly, 9/11 in the United States (and July 7, 2005, in the United Kingdom) represent the first, and the misapprehension of Iraqi WMD represents the second. Although there may be common factors in the explanation of these different types of failure, it is important to bear in mind that there are also key differences.

We need to be careful as to how we delineate failure. It is the thankless task of intelligence to seek to prevent nasty surprises, but we must be realistic. It is simply not feasible to construct a security intelligence process that can guarantee freedom from all surprise attacks. George Orwell imagined how such a society would look in his novel *1984*. Despite some exaggerated post-Snowden accounts,[4] neither the U.S. nor UK have become

Orwellian states despite their futile attempt at "total surveillance." Driven by technological possibility and organizational desire, this is doomed to failure, based as it is on a naïve belief that "collecting everything" will reveal threats. It only makes sense to judge failure in the context of what we might reasonably expect security agencies to know, given their size, resources, etc. But though the sheer diversity and complexity of the world means that surprises will always be a possibility, surely we should be able to organize better to ensure that "type 2" failures do not occur. For example, these are less urgent: if there is no actual attack (because there is, in reality, no threat), then there will be more time for analysis (though anxious politicians may not perceive things that way).

There is another complication, however, as evidenced in the Iraqi failure. We may hope that intelligence exists to inform policy, but this textbook relationship may not pertain in the messy world of government. Governing politicians and other executives do not sit patiently by while intelligence officials contemplate the nuances of their analyses—they want to act and, given their survival skills, often believe that their own information, contacts, senses, and judgments are at least as good as those of officials. Consequently, their policies are as likely to be informed by their own beliefs, ideologies, and perceptions as they are by official intelligence reports.[5]

To put this more conceptually, the relationship between intelligence and policy is a subset of the more general relationship between information and power: any individual, organization, or government seeks information in order to inform better its actions, including attempts to exert influence or power. However, this "rational actor" ideal type may not describe what actually happens in the world. The relationship between information and power may be reversed, so that what our actor actually determines to be relevant information depends on what she wants to do or how she wants to do it. In life and government, not only does what you see depend on where you sit (a matter of perception) but also on what you want to do (a matter of power). Thus, at whatever level of power and decision making we are interested— individual, group, corporate, governmental—people will not only pay more attention to information that supports their preferred position but also will discredit anything that contradicts it as mischievous or deception.

So, in the cases of 9/11 and Iraq, we can identify three main possibilities: they were examples of intelligence failure, in which the professionals in the relevant agencies failed to collect sufficient information and/or analyze it correctly so that their governments were misinformed; they were examples of political failure, in which governments' actions or inactions were based on pre-existing beliefs, judgments, or ideologies and the role for intelligence was to provide *post hoc* rationalization for those decisions in order to sell them to skeptical publics; or, these cases represent a messy mixture of both professional and political failures.

What Causes Intelligence Failure?

Michael Herman identifies two general conclusions from a survey of the literature: first, the weak link is not so much a failure to collect information as to analyze it, and, second, the weakness is intellectual rather than administrative:

> People interpret data through images, historical analogies, personal experiences and other hypotheses. There is a cognitive rigidity about the way they fit information into these patterns. They see what they expect to see; they come to conclusions too early and stick to them for too long.[6]

There was a direct echo to this in the conclusion of the 9/11 Commission that one of the main contributory factors was a failure of imagination.[7]

Fundamental are the problems of overload and complexity. The very sophistication of modern information-gathering systems produces the problem of overload. Intelligence systems may demand ever more data in the empirical illusion that it will solve the mysteries and secrets when, in fact, they are likely to suffer the fate of the thirsty individual who tries to drink from a fire hose. As the 9/11 Report noted:

> One can see how hard it is for the intelligence community to assemble enough of the puzzle pieces gathered by different agencies to make some sense of them. . . . Accomplishing all this is especially difficult in a transnational case. We sympathize with the working-level officers, drowning in information and trying to decide what is important.[8]

Yet we now learn that the drive to "collect everything" increased after 9/11. NSA has been constructing a new facility in Utah for the storage and analysis of everything collected.[9] In a public statement challenging a Snowden-related press story as to the extent of NSA surveillance, the NSA and ODNI said that, using all its authorities, the agency "touches" 1.6 percent of Internet traffic and that analysts "look at" 0.00004 percent.[10] Although the agencies have not earned a reputation for complete openness in recent months, these figures look plausible: if up to 2 billion records a day are "collected,"[11] the 1.6 percent that are "selected" amount to 32 million, which far exceeds anything that could realistically be "analyzed." So, about 80,000 will be "looked at," which sounds barely plausible if one accepts that "analysis," however clever the software in use, ultimately requires a human being to decide what the communication means. For certain, this facility has not solved the problem of "overload."

Analysis itself is prone to intellectual shortcomings such as "mirror-imaging,"[12] "groupthink," and the "paradox of expertise"[13] and may be compounded by internal administrative obstacles, which have been variously characterized in the literature as "distortions"[14] or "pathologies."[15] Specialization is a key feature of the Weberian bureaucracy and serves many useful purposes, but maximizing the efficiency of information flows and encouraging imagination are not prominent among them. In intelligence bureaucracies there are additional hurdles that, again, may be soundly based, but further hinder the flow—notably secrecy and compartmentalization of information.[16] This may occur both within and between organizations: for example, analysts may be in complete ignorance of information that would be important for their work because they are perceived not to "need to know" aspects of specific operations. This may be compounded by the existence of different databases; if they cannot be linked, the information is effectively hidden from analysts.[17] The 9/11 Commission showed how, given the poor state of the Federal Bureau of Investigation's (FBI) information systems, analysts' ability to access information depended largely on whether they had a personal relationship with anyone in the squad where the information resided.

Finally, in addition to cognitive and bureaucratic obstacles to analysis, we must remember that those states, organizations, groups, or people who are the targets of intelligence operations are unlikely to remain passive. They have their own objectives and deploy their own techniques to counter attempts to discover their secrets. These may be just defensive but may also attempt to deliberately mislead and thus disrupt an opponent's operations. Therefore, as analysts seek to manage overload and complexity, they must not forget that some of the information they obtain may be intended to mislead them.

Collection and Analytical Failures on Iraq

The absence of expected WMD in Iraq has become the most investigated failure of all time. In the United States, both the Senate Select Committee on Intelligence (SSCI) and the Silberman-Robb Commission reported; in the United Kingdom, no fewer than five inquiries have taken place, and Australia had two. Surely, therefore, we have the definitive picture of what went wrong. Well, arguably, no. Certainly, the combined output of these inquiries has provided enough raw materials for a future avalanche of scholarly discussions of *intelligence* failure, because they picked over in minute detail the performance of the professionals, but by comparison, the issue of policy or political failure has been rather neglected.

The SSCI inquiry into the U.S. intelligence community's prewar intelligence assessments on Iraq, beginning in June 2003, set out to consider the quantity and quality of intelligence on Iraqi weapons of mass destruction programs and ties to terrorist groups; "the objectivity, reasonableness, independence, and accuracy of the judgments reached"; whether these were properly disseminated to the executive and legislative branches; and whether any political pressure affected these assessments.[18] In February 2004, the committee announced that the second phase of its report, including the more politically contentious issues of the extent to which, if at all, government statements had exaggerated the intelligence, would appear only after the 2004 presidential election. In the event, it did not appear until 2008, after the Democrats took over the chairmanship of SSCI in the wake of their mid-term election victory.

The overall SSCI conclusion on the national intelligence estimate (NIE) on Iraqi WMD, produced quickly in October 2002, is damning. "Most of the major key judgments," it concluded, were "either overstated, or were not supported by, the underlying intelligence reporting. A series of failures, particularly in analytic trade craft, led to the mischaracterization of the intelligence."[19] The failure is firmly located as being overwhelmingly one of analysis, with some failures in collection, all compounded by poor management and an environment that seemed to militate against information sharing.[20] In short, the report assigns responsibility for the failure first to analysts, second, to managers and bureaucratic structures and, third, to failures in collection.[21]

On collection, the SSCI criticized the heavy reliance during the 1991–1998 period on United Nations weapons inspectors (UNSCOM) and the fact that the intelligence community did not use the period of the inspections to establish human intelligence (HUMINT) sources that could replace the inspectors in the event of their departure. Incredibly, in light of the certainty of the conclusions contained in the October 2002 NIE, after 1998 the intelligence community did not have any HUMINT source of its own reporting on Iraqi WMD.[22] Similarly, none of the United Kingdom's human sources were able to report directly on WMD.[23] Interestingly, given the amount of money expended on it, there is very little comment in the SSCI Report and none at all in Butler on the absence of any signals intelligence (SIGINT) regarding WMD.

The SSCI found that the assessment that Iraq "is reconstituting its nuclear program" was not supported by information that dual-use equipment

was being purchased because it failed to show that it was c
Iraqi nuclear program. As with the British government's Se̟
dossier, judgments that Iraq "has chemical and biological w
stated conclusions that could be safely reached on the basis o
intelligence.[24] On chemical and biological weapons (CBW), suspicions
based on Iraq's past technological capabilities in this area, deception prac-
ticed against UNSCOM, and past failure to satisfactorily account for all
CBW holdings and precursors could have supported a conclusion that Iraq
may have had such weapons, but the leap to asserting that it actually had
them was not justified by the raw information.

The claim that Iraq was "vigorously trying to procure uranium ore and
yellowcake" via Niger exaggerated the existing state of knowledge.[25]
Moreover, even after it emerged that claims as to Iraqi attempts to procure
material via Niger were based on forged documents, both the CIA and the
Defense Intelligence Agency (DIA), "continued to publish assessments that
Iraq may have been seeking uranium from Africa," and the CIA "continued
to approve the use of similar language in Administration publications and
speeches, including the State of the Union."[26] In the United Kingdom,
Butler concluded that there was evidence that Iraq had sought uranium
from Africa although there was no evidence that it had obtained any.[27]

Excessive compartmentalization of HUMINT inhibited the production
of effective analysis. The committee concluded that the process by which
the intelligence community "calculates the benefits and risks of sharing
sensitive human intelligence is skewed too heavily toward withholding
information."[28] However, the committee found that the problem of information sharing went further and that there was a tendency for the CIA to
deny information to more specialist agencies that could have allowed for
input that challenged existing presumptions.[29] Known dissenting views
from other parts of the intelligence community were not always included
in assessments where they would have challenged the dominant assumption—as, for example, over the debate concerning the purpose of aluminum tubes. In some cases assessments that conformed to the dominant
assumption bypassed specialist agencies that were in a position to challenge them.[30] The UK Butler report made precisely the same criticism.[31]

An important contextual factor was the failure a decade earlier to identify the active nuclear weapons program that did then exist in Iraq and
which was destroyed after 1991. Similarly, the UK Butler inquiry concluded that there was a "tendency for assessments to be coloured by overreaction to previous errors."[32] The then-recent avalanche of criticism at the
agencies' failures to prevent 9/11 was another. So strong was this dynamic,
according to the SSCI, that managers shared the same groupthink

presumptions and so did not utilize established mechanisms to challenge them. "Red teams" or "devil's advocate" approaches were simply not used. The report concluded that managers "did not encourage analysts to challenge their assumptions, fully consider alternative arguments, accurately characterize the intelligence reporting, or counsel analysts who lost their objectivity."[33]

This dominant assumption that Iraq possessed and was concealing WMD led directly to serial errors: it meant that information collection was driven not only by the desire to "fill in the gaps" about WMD programs but also to find the "evidence" of the links between Saddam Hussein and al Qaeda that formed the other leg of the neocon case for war.[34] This "led Intelligence Community analysts, collectors and managers to both interpret ambiguous evidence as conclusively indicative of a WMD program as well as ignore or minimize evidence that Iraq did not have active and expanding weapons of mass destruction programs."[35] "Absence of evidence may not be evidence of absence," but in the case of Iraq, it was mistakenly taken as "evidence of presence."

The Silberman-Robb Commission reached the same conclusion:

> Collectors and analysts too readily accepted any evidence that supported their theory that Iraq had stockpiles and was developing weapons programs, and they explained away or simply disregarded evidence that pointed in the other direction.[36]

As Michael Herman noted, no one was asking the question: "Could it be because there are no WMD at all?"[37] But if anyone thought so, "no one wanted to say that because so much intelligence would have to be discounted."[38]

Failure to Disseminate Intelligence

If the resources devoted to analysis pales in comparison with those given to collection, the same may be said of dissemination. Again, this can contribute to failure because, at the risk of stating the blindingly obvious, if intelligence is not communicated to someone who can do something with it, the so-called intelligence process may be reduced to a self-serving cycle of collecting and storing information. For Christopher Andrew, "The historical record suggests . . . that the points at which the intelligence cycle most frequently breaks down are in the assessment process and the policy interface rather than in collection."[39] Obstacles to sharing information with other agencies are extensive; they may reflect the choice of the agency not to share the information or simply a lack of awareness that anyone outside would be interested. There can be problems even within agencies; for example, handlers may be reluctant to admit their own doubts about their sources' veracity, whereas analysts need to know the credibility of the sources of the information with which they are dealing.

Much criticism after 9/11 concentrated on this failure to share information. In some cases this rightly criticized failure to share is based on nothing more than ignorance or poor understandings, but there are legitimate reasons. For example, all agencies jealously guard their sources and methods, not because they are short-sighted, but because they fear their compromise if information they provide is used unwisely. Recipients outside the community may not appreciate that the publication of an item of intelligence can enable a target to identify and eliminate its source—in some cases a person. Nevertheless, the 9/11 Commission described clearly the failures of sharing information between U.S. agencies prior to the attacks[40] and recommended that the Cold War assumption that intelligence can only be shared with those who need to know must be replaced by a need-to-share culture of integration.[41] Only time will tell, however, if the post-9/11 attempts to implement this survives the fallout from Bradley (now Chelsea) Manning's plundering of the DoD's top secret intranet and Edward Snowden's ability, as a computer system administrator with Booz Allen, to appropriate thousands of NSA and GCHQ files of the highest classification.

Dissemination within the community is an important factor in the quality of final products, but it is dissemination outside of the community that establishes the credibility and utility of intelligence. The primary consumers of intelligence are the "doers"—political or corporate. How intelligence conclusions are presented is important: specifically, how does it present degrees of uncertainty? The use of language is crucial; indeed it determines what, in the end, is considered to be the knowledge upon which policy may be based or by which it is rationalized. Intelligence seeks to improve knowledge by reducing uncertainty but is only ever partially successful. The way in which different national systems seek to convey this uncertainty varies. For example, U.S. NIE incorporated footnotes recording the dissents of particular agencies from the main conclusions, and the CIA provides percentage probabilities of success in possible future operations.[42] The SSCI found that the language used throughout the NIE "did not accurately portray the uncertainty of the information," and instead "portrayed what intelligence analysts thought and assessed as what they knew and failed to explain the large gaps in the information on which the assessments were based."[43] Policymakers were denied the context that open acknowledgment of the gaps in the intelligence picture would have provided. The unusually short time in which the NIE was prepared—three weeks—meant that it contained little by way of new analysis or expertise and, being the product of three separate drafters, lacked overall coherence.[44]

Moreover, where uncertainty was expressed (as was also the case in the United Kingdom and Australia), it was used to suggest that Iraq's WMD were even more extensive than indicated but that clever Iraqi denial and deception techniques, refined since 1991, had effectively concealed the scale. In the United Kingdom the Joint Intelligence Committee (JIC) eschewed dissenting footnotes, and the Butler Review described how the JIC accommodated uncertainty. When the intelligence was unclear or inadequate, the JIC reported alternative interpretations as long as the membership agreed they were viable,[45] but minority hypotheses were not produced. So it normally attempted to reach a consensus in the assessment, and the section of Key Judgements would often include warnings as to the thinness of the evidence. Inevitably this search for consensus "may result in nuanced language." Subtleties such as "the intelligence indicates" rather than "the intelligence shows" may escape the untutored or busy reader. We also came across instances where Key Judgements unhelpfully omitted qualifications about the limitations of the intelligence that were elsewhere in the text."[46] But if language is nuanced in order to satisfy those who are producing it, the subtleties of what they mean may well escape those who receive it. If, as Butler noted, not even the producers are themselves clear as to the significance of the language, what hope is there for the reader?

> We have been told that some readers believe that important distinctions are intended between such phrases as "intelligence indicates . . .", "intelligence demonstrates . . .", and "intelligence shows . . .", or between "we assess that . . .", "we judge that . . .", and "we believe that . . .". We have also been told that there is in reality no established glossary, and that drafters and JIC members actually employ their natural language.[47]

Butler did not suggest any particular way of trying to deal better with this problem—it is indeed inherent in any process involving language—but recommended that the intelligence community review their conventions.[48] The government's response was that the guidance to staff on use of language had been reviewed and reissued (we might also hope that politicians are inducted into them) and that JIC minutes are now to include "alternative and minority hypotheses or uncertainties."[49]

In the broadest sense, all intelligence provides warnings, but states and corporations alike view warnings of nasty surprises as the central intelligence function. During the Cold War, sophisticated systems were developed for the surveillance of indicators that an attack might be pending. For example, during 1950–1975, the United States had a watch committee and National Indications Center and Soviet military intelligence (GRU), and the KGB maintained similar systems for indications of Western attacks.[50] Now that the fear of attacks from non-state actors has replaced these, the process of providing appropriate indicators is much more difficult, and the judgments to be made in issuing warnings are acute. The 9/11 Commission noted that, with the exception of the analysis of Al Qaeda attempts to obtain WMD, the U.S. intelligence community failed to apply warning methodologies to the potential threat of a terrorist attack on the United States.[51]

At the same time, analysts' fears about the possibility of an attack on the United States were not reaching the right people, or, perhaps, they were not listening. The commission reported: "Most of the intelligence community recognized in the summer of 2001 that the number and severity of threat reports were unprecedented." However, despite the number of fragments, there were too few specifics to point to a named target. Moreover, the 9/11 planning fell into "the void between foreign and domestic threats," which made it harder to make sense of the fragments:

> The foreign intelligence agencies were watching overseas, alert to foreign threats to US interests there. The domestic agencies were waiting for evidence of a domestic threat from sleeper cells within the United States. No one was looking for a foreign threat to domestic targets. The threat that was coming was not from sleeper cells. It was foreign—but from foreigners who had infiltrated into the United States.[52]

Chapter 8 of the 9/11 Commission report effectively conveys the same story that former Clinton and Bush administration terrorism coordinator Richard Clarke had already told of serial warnings to which there was no policy response.[53] In part this reflected the still-dominant Cold War assumptions of the foreign policy experts, upon whom the new president relied, that threats came essentially from states. The key document in alerting the administration should have been a *President's Daily Brief* (PDB) from August 6, 2001, containing an item headed "Bin Laden Determined to Strike in U.S." It was the thirty-sixth PDB item relating to Bin Laden or Al Qaeda in 2001.[54] The analysts who produced the item were responding to an inquiry by the president about whether any threats to the United States existed, and to them "represented an opportunity to communicate their view that the threat of a Bin Laden attack in the United States remained both current and serious." The president told the inquiry that the report "was historical in nature" and that "if his advisers had told him there was a cell in the United States, they would have moved to take care of it." However, the PDB contained a number of potential warnings, including the fact that FBI information "indicates patterns of suspicious activity in this country consistent with preparations for hijackings or other types of attacks, including recent surveillance of federal buildings in New York."[55]

The "Political" Failure

Intelligence is inevitably about conveying uncertainties and probabilities. But even if collection is as effective as possible and analysis gets it right, the professionals may fail if their product does not convince policymakers of the need to act accordingly. Just as there are various causes of intelligence failure, so there are varieties of political failure: executives may fail to maintain an environment within which critical analysis can be conducted, they may manipulate the production of particular kinds of intelligence, or they may just select that which supports their predispositions while ignoring or rejecting anything that does not.[56]

Richard Betts has argued:

> In the best-known cases of intelligence failure, the most crucial mistakes have seldom been made by collectors of raw information, occasionally by professionals who produce finished analyses, but most often by the decision makers who consume the products of intelligence services. Policy premises constrict perception, and administrative workloads constrain reflection. Intelligence failure is political and psychological more often than organizational.[57]

There is an inevitable tension here: in democratic societies it is elected politicians, not salaried officials, who make policy decisions. Inevitably, policymakers have their own preferences based on their own backgrounds, experiences, interests, and worldviews, and they (like the rest of us) have a tendency to resist information that conflicts with those. Therefore, analysts face an uphill task:

> Intelligence is part of the government system, and has to have empathy and credibility with the policy-makers it serves. It cannot adopt an Olympian objectivity, or detach itself completely from government's policies and preconceptions. It has to sell its product, and has to be sensitive to its audience to do so.[58]

But, in selling their product, the very problem for analysts is that it rarely meets the level of certainty that politicians, as men and women of action, demand. But if analysts struggle to sell their work to the policymakers, the latter may also struggle to sell their policies to the public.

Compared to Iraq, there has been little discussion of whether 9/11 was a political rather than intelligence failure. As indicated at the start of this chapter, 9/11 seems to have been a false negative—there was a real threat that was missed. But, as Steve Marrin has argued, the growing reality of al Qaeda's *strategic* threat was well understood by the agencies and communicated to the relevant decision makers so that it was well understood, except by the early Bush administration. But by the late 1990s, there was a general recognition that existing counter terrorist policies in response to earlier attacks were not working and few domestic defensive measures had been taken. Marrin reminds us that policymakers may not act for a variety of reasons: they may think it is impractical, undesirable, and unnecessary or just cannot think what to do and so, in order to understand the influence of intelligence on policy, or lack thereof, we must study policy, not intelligence.[59]

The president's style of governance and level of engagement with the material was a contributory factor to the 9/11 failure. No NSC meetings were called to discuss the threat outlined in the August 6th PDB, and the Commission could find "no indication of any further discussion before September 11 among the President and his top advisers of the possibility of a threat of an al Qaeda attack in the United States." One reason for this is that the president retired to his Texas ranch for the summer. Director of Central Intelligence (DCI) Tenet visited him there on August 17th but "did not recall any discussions with the President of the domestic threat during this period."[60] The report saw "little evidence that the progress of the plot was disturbed by government action. The US government was unable to capitalize on mistakes made by Al Qaeda. Time ran out."[61]

On Iraq, the initial SSCI Report absolved policymakers of responsibility for the intelligence failure, concluding that it found "no evidence that the IC's mischaracterization or exaggeration" on Iraqi WMD was "the result of political pressure."[62] Further still, it blames the intelligence community for not "accurately or adequately" explaining to policymakers the uncertainties that lay behind the catalogue of erroneous judgments contained in the NIE.[63] The section of the second report published in June 2008 produced some examples of key prewar public statements that were unsubstantiated by intelligence at the time, but it was far from unanimous.[64]

However, the groupthink identified by the SSCI—"examining few alternatives, selective gathering of information, pressure to conform within the group or withhold criticism, and collective rationalization"[65]—may itself have been the consequence of individual perceptions of political pressure. Yet the regular visits to CIA headquarters by Vice President Dick Cheney, a key advocate of the case for war between September 2001 and February 2003, were not held to have influenced the thrust of analysis on Iraq.[66] Nor is it clear that the managerial failure to utilize mechanisms designed to test analyses was attributable solely to a shared set of presumptions rather than, at least in part, to their close proximity to policymakers who had been making the case for a developing and threatening Iraqi WMD program for months prior to the drafting of the October 2002 NIE. In this respect, "managerial failure" could be interpreted as a euphemism for "politicization." Moreover, the SSCI had to reconcile the fact that, anonymously, a number of officials had been prepared to voice concerns but were unwilling to be publicly identified.[67] Ironically, it is not at all clear that, in this area of inquiry, the SSCI itself adopted the best analytical practices it identified as being absent from the intelligence effort on Iraq.

Silberman-Robb was not authorized to investigate how policymakers used the intelligence they received, but it still dismissed charges of politicization and, like the SSCI, criticized the intelligence community for failing to communicate effectively with policymakers.[68] Nevertheless, in dismissing charges of politicization, it did come far closer than the SSCI to recognizing the pressures emanating from the White House, to the extent that its conclusion on politicization can be regarded as somewhat contradictory:

> We closely examined the possibility that intelligence analysts were pressured by policymakers to change their judgments about Iraq's nuclear, biological, and chemical weapons programs. The analysts who worked Iraqi weapons issues universally agreed that in no instance did political pressure cause them to skew or alter any of their analytical judgments. That said, it is hard to deny the conclusion that intelligence analysts worked in an environment that did not encourage scepticism about the conventional wisdom.[69]

The detailed investigations into Iraq have shown clearly that there were failures within intelligence processes—in terms of collection, analysis, and dissemination. However, the official diagnosis of the problem, as represented in the official inquiries referred to here, is incomplete. This conclusion results from a combination of the following factors: the obvious desire of UK/ U.S. governments to present the case for war as though the intelligence left them no option but to disarm Iraq forcibly and the failure of official oversight bodies to identify clearly the extent to which intelligence (processes and products) were misused in order to mislead the public. All governments are prone to present their chosen course of action in definite terms; having made decisions, they are reluctant to invite further public debate and criticism. But, in this case, the stakes were much higher, involving military invasion, and there is a growing body of evidence that this gulf reflected not just politicians' customary "oversimplification and exaggeration"[70] and shows that the intelligence could never sustain the policy upon which the governments had determined at least a year before the invasion.

Space does not allow a detailed dissection of this, but the job has already been done by John Prados with respect to the United States.[71] He took a series of key documents (several of which were also the basis for the SSCI's 2008 Report referred to above), for example, the CIA White Paper on Iraq's WMD of October 2002, President Bush's Cincinnati speech of October 2002, his State of the Union address of January 28, 2003, and Secretary of State Powell's remarks to the UN Security Council of February 5, 2003, subjected them to detailed scrutiny in terms of the then available intelligence, and demonstrated the growing gulf between them.

Thanks to the Butler Review in the United Kingdom, we can make a similar comparison.[72] In March 2002—one year before the invasion—the Joint Intelligence Committee (JIC) provided an assessment that "intelligence on Iraq's WMD and ballistic missile programmes is sporadic and patchy." On nuclear weapons, "there is very little intelligence." Similarly, "there is very little intelligence relating to [Iraq's chemical warfare programme]."[73] Six months later the JIC said: "Intelligence remains limited and Saddam's own unpredictability complicates judgments about Iraqi use of these weapons. Much of this paper is necessarily based on judgment and assessment."[74]

But, in Blair's foreword to the September 2002 dossier, we read: "What I believe the assessed intelligence has established *beyond doubt* is that Saddam has continued to produce chemical and biological weapons. . . . I am in no doubt that the threat is serious and current."[75] And, in the Commons on September 24, 2002, Blair said: "The intelligence picture . . . is *extensive, detailed and authoritative.*"[76] This was clearly highly misleading.

Thus the far greater failure was political. As we know now, Blair's foreign policy adviser, David Manning, met with Condoleezza Rice in March 2002 and assured her that Blair would not budge in his support for regime change.[77] Blair told Bush the following month that the United Kingdom would support military action to achieve regime change in Iraq, and from summer onward, bombing of Iraq was increased steadily in order to try to provoke Saddam Hussein into some response that would provide a pretext for war.[78] In July, C (head of SIS) reported back to Downing Street on his recent Washington talks:[79]

There was a perceptible shift in attitude. Military action was now seen as inevitable. Bush wanted to remove Saddam, through military action, justified by the conjunction of terrorism and WMD. But the intelligence and the facts were being fixed around the policy.[80]

But the only possible legal justification for invasion was Iraq's failure to disarm in line with UN resolutions passed after the first Gulf War. Since Blair knew that he could not carry his party with him without such legal justification, the crucial role for intelligence was to support or rationalize the case regarding WMD.

So, power (the policy decision to invade Iraq) clearly led to external and internal pressures on the U.S. agencies during 2002 that resulted in judgments "firmed up" beyond what the evidence would bear, or it was simply ignored. As Scott Lucas has argued, the key point is not to seek for specific points at which politicization occurred but, rather, to see prewar intelligence "as part of a bureaucratic battle for influence and control."[81] But what was selected for public presentation and its delivery by political leaders amounted to a clear deception. James Pfiffner concluded that:

Insofar as President Bush misled the Congress and the citizenry, either from deliberate misstatements or through creating an atmosphere in which he was not well informed by his advisers, he undermined the crucial trust upon which the nation depends.[82]

We await the outcome of a fifth UK inquiry into Iraq established by then Prime Minister Gordon Brown under John Chilcot in 2009. It finished taking evidence in 2011 and has examined all aspects of UK policy until the withdrawal of UK troops in July 2009; most of the evidence received has been published.[83] But publication of the report, expected to be one million words, is still delayed as of February 2014 by the reluctance of the Cabinet Office to allow the publication of certain documents that the Inquiry has seen and wants to publish. These relate to cabinet-level discussions and notes of conversations between Blair and Bush, and some between Brown and Bush.[84] If and when published, these should enlighten us further on the extent of the political failure that was Iraq.

Conclusion

The case of 9/11 illustrates elements of both intelligence and political failure, though it is difficult with this kind of surprise attack to imagine how intelligence might have been structured to prevent it. As an analytical device, we can ask the "what if" question. For example, even if President Bush had reacted to the August PDB and all the disparate pieces of information that we now know about had been connected, the intelligence would still have amounted only to a general warning of possible hijacks within the United States at some unspecified future time. Assuming that the airline security and law enforcement communities then responded to this warning, their procedures would not have been sufficiently robust to prevent the seizure of all four planes on September 11. In the case of Iraq, what if the actual uncertainties regarding the presence of WMD had been accurately and regularly communicated to the decision makers— would they have not invaded Iraq? Here, the evidence suggests strongly that it would have made no difference because the U.S. and UK governments were determined on regime change by spring 2002 despite the weak intelligence then existent. Thereafter, the contribution of intelligence was as a tool to be utilized in selling that policy to skeptical publics, other countries, and ultimately the UN, and this was the context within which it was steadily "firmed up." Therefore, although Iraq may also represent a messy mixture of intelligence and political failure, the latter was more serious and primarily responsible for the subsequent costly debacle in Iraq.

As a result of these commissions and inquiries, there has been a great debate, primarily in the United States, as to how intelligence might be reformed in order to prevent a recurrence of failures. Even if one acknowledges that changes must include policy and practices, not just structures,[85] we must note that the potential for reform is seriously limited. The combination of cognitive and organizational pitfalls endemic within information and intelligence processes should alert us to the probability that reforms will have no effect.[86] Betts argues:

> Observers who see notorious intelligence failures as egregious often infer that disasters can be avoided by perfecting norms and procedures for analysis and argumentation. This belief is illusory. Intelligence can be improved marginally, but not radically, by altering the analytic system. The illusion is also dangerous if it abets overconfidence that systemic reforms will increase the predictability of threats.[87]

Of course, no extent of organizational reforms within intelligence can have the slightest impact on the possibility of political failures.

Finally, these events and subsequent inquiries indicate an enormous need for public education and vigorous oversight. Given the long history of secrecy within which security intelligence has operated, it is not surprising that the public misunderstands its role. Now that intelligence is (partly) out of the box, it will not be possible to get it back in. Therefore, the task of explaining the potential and limits of intelligence is an urgent one for governments, practitioners, oversight committees, and scholars. It is a fundamental expectation of governments that they will provide public security, and, in their urge to reassure the public, even well-intentioned politicians may be tempted to exaggerate the possibility that they can do so. If, as in the case of Iraq, governments exaggerate threats and misuse intelligence in order to bolster their claims, they are culpable of serious dereliction of duty. Since 9/11 there has been some soft-pedalling on oversight because of the false perception that this will somehow hinder greater intelligence efficiency; the Iraq debacle has reinforced the need for energetic oversight to reduce, though it cannot eliminate, the likelihood of future intelligence and political failures.[88]

Notes

1. Respectively, T. H. Kean and L. H. Hamilton, *The 9/11 Report: The National Commission on Terrorist Attacks Upon the United States* (2004), available at http://www.9-11commission.gov/report/index.htm; L. H. Silberman and C. S. Robb, *Report* (Washington, DC: Government Printing Office for the Commission on the Intelligence Capabilities of the United States Regarding Weapons of Mass Destruction, 2005), available at http://www.wmd.gov/report/report.html.

2. The most significant one that is discussed here is Butler, *Review of Intelligence on Weapons of Mass Destruction*, HC898 (2004), available at http://www.butlerreview.org.uk/report/.

3. Cf. D. Omand, *Securing the State* (London: C. Hurst & Co., 2010), pp. 178–182.

4. A. Rusbridger, "These technologies are formidable. They are beyond what Orwell could have imagined." In N. Watt *et. al.*, "Debate Grows over "Orwellian" NSA Technology," *The Guardian* (October 10, 2013), p.4.

5. For example, S. Marrin, "Intelligence Analysis and Decision-Making: Methodological Challenges," in P. Gill, S. Marrin, and M. Phythian (eds.), *Intelligence Theory: Key Questions and Debates* (London: Routledge, 2009), pp.131–150.

6. M. Herman, *Intelligence Power in Peace and War* (Cambridge: Cambridge University Press, 1996), p. 228.

7. Kean and Hamilton, *op. cit.*, pp. 339–348.

8. Ibid., p. 355.

9. James Bamford, "The NSA is Building the Country's Biggest Spy Center (Watch What You Say)," *WIRED*, http://www.wired.com/threatlevel/ (March 15, 2012). Accessed July 7, 2013.

10. Joint Statement: NSA and Office of the Director of National Intelligence, August 21, 2013, www.nsa.gov.

11. As they are by the GCHQ Tempora programme, according to G. Greenwald, "How NSA Can See 'Nearly Everything You Do Online,'" *The Guardian* (August 1, 2013), pp.1–2.

12. M. M. Lowenthal, *Intelligence: From Secrets to Policy*, 2d ed. (Washington, DC: CQ Press, 2003), pp. 92–93.

13. Kent Center for Analytic Tradecraft, *Making Sense of Transnational Threats*, Sherman Kent School, Occasional Papers (3:1, October, 2004), p. 4.

14. R. Mandel, "Distortions in the Intelligence Decision-Making Process," in S. J. Cimbala, *Intelligence and Intelligence Policy in a Democratic Society* (Ardsley-on-Hudson, NY: Transnational Publishers, 1987), pp. 69–83.

15. L. K. Johnson, *America's Secret Power: The CIA in a Democratic Society* (New York: Oxford University Press, 1989), pp. 76–99.

16. Mandel, *op. cit.*, p. 73.

17. For a discussion of current efforts to increase information sharing by means of web-based technologies see P. Gill and M. Phythian, *Intelligence in an Insecure World*, 2nd edition (Cambridge: Polity, 2012), pp.108–111.

18. SSCI, *Report on the U.S. Intelligence Community's Prewar Intelligence Assessments on Iraq* (Washington, DC: Government Printing Office, 2004), available at http://intelligence.senate.gov/iraqreport2.pdf 1.

19. Ibid., p. 14.

20. Ibid., p. 15.

21. For the view of some former insiders see R. Kerr, T. Wolfe, R. Donegan and A.Pappas, "Intelligence Collection and Analysis on Iraq: Issues for the Intelligence Community," in J.P. Pfiffner and M. Phythian (eds.), *Intelligence and National Security Policymaking on Iraq* (Manchester: Manchester University Press, 2008), pp.153–161.

22. SSCI, 2004, *op. cit.*, p. 25.

23. Butler, *op. cit.*, paras 402–405.

24. SSCI, 2004, *op. cit.*, p. 14.

25. Ibid., p. 75.

26. Ibid., pp. 77, 80–81.

27. Butler, *op. cit.*, paras 490–503.

28. SSCI, 2004, *op. cit.*, p. 26.

29. Ibid., pp. 27–28.

30. Ibid., pp. 128–129.

31. Butler, *op. cit.*, paras 566–578. See also B. Jones, *Failing Intelligence: The True Story of How We Were Fooled into Going to War in Iraq* (London: Biteback Publishing, 2010), esp. pp 90–94.

32. Butler, ibid., para 458.

33. SSCI, 2004, *op. cit.*, pp. 23–24.

34. Kerr, Wolfe et. al., *op. cit.*, p.155; P. R. Pillar, "Intelligence, Policy, and The War in Iraq," in Pfiffner and Phythian (eds.), pp. 233–243 at 236–240; S. Lucas, "Recognising Politicization: The CIA and the Path to the 2003 War in Iraq," in Pfiffner and Phythian (eds.), *Intelligence and National Security* (26:2–3, 2011) pp. 203–227 at 211–213.

35. SSCI, 2004, *op. cit.*, p. 18.

36. Silberman and Robb, *op. cit.*, p. 10.

37. BBC, "A Failure of Intelligence," *Panorama*, BBC1, broadcast 11 July, 2004.

38. B. Woodward, *Plan of Attack* (New York: Simon & Schuster, 2004), p. 197.

39. C. Andrew, "Intelligence, International Relations and 'Under-theorisation,'" *Intelligence and National Security* 19 (2004), p. 172.

40. Kean and Hamilton, *op. cit.*, pp. 353–360.

41. Ibid., p. 417.

42. For example, see ibid., p. 143; also Lowenthal, *op. cit.*, pp. 100–101.

43. SSCI, 2004, *op. cit.*, p. 17.

44. Kerr, Wolfe et. al., *op. cit.*, 159.

45. Butler, *op. cit.*, para. 45.

46. Ibid., para. 603.

47. Ibid., para. 45, fn. 13.

48. Ibid, para 604. D. Omand, *op. cit.*, pp. 200–204 describes post-2004 changes.

49. Foreign and Commonwealth Secretary, *Review of Intelligence on Weapons of Mass Destruction: Implementation of Its Conclusions*, Cm6492 (London: Her Majesty's Stationary Office, 2005), paras. 29–30.

50. Herman, 1996, *op. cit.*, p. 235; A. N. Shulsky and G. J. Schmitt, *Silent Warfare*, 3d ed. (Washington, DC: Brassey's, 2004), p. 59.

51. Kean and Hamilton, *op. cit.*, pp. 344–348.

52. Ibid., p. 263.

53. R. A. Clarke, *Against All Enemies: Inside America's War on Terror* (London: Simon & Schuster, 2004).

54. Kean and Hamilton, *op. cit.*, p. 366.

55. Ibid., pp. 261–262.

56. G.Treverton, 2008, discusses politicisation forms from "hard" to "soft." "Intelligence Analysis: Between "Politicization" and Irrelevance," in R. G. George and J. B. Bruce (eds.), *Analyzing Intelligence: Origins, Obstacles and Innovations* (Washington, DC: Georgetown University Press, 2008), pp. 91–104 at 93–96.

57. R. K. Betts, "Analysis, War, and Decision: Why Intelligence Failures Are Inevitable," *World Politics* 31 (1978), p. 61.

58. M. Herman, "Threat Assessments and the Legitimation of Policy?" *Intelligence and National Security* 18 (2003), p. 177.

59. S. Marrin, "The 9/11 Terrorist Attacks: A Failure of Policy Not Strategic Intelligence Analysis," *Intelligence and National Security* (26:2–3, 2011), pp.182–202.

60. Kean and Hamilton, *op. cit.*, p. 262.

61. Ibid., p. 277.

62. SSCI, 2004, *op. cit.*, p. 16.

63. Ibid.

64. SSCI, Report on whether public statements regarding Iraq by U.S. Government Officials were substantiated by Intelligence Information, June 5, 2008. http://www.fas.org/irp/congress/2008_rpt/statements.pdf Accessed February 1, 2014.

65. SSCI, 2004, *op. cit.*, p. 18.

66. Ibid., pp. 275–276, 285.

67. Ibid, p. 272.

68. Silberman and Robb, *op. cit.*, p. 5.

69. Ibid., p. 11.

70. R. Aldrich, "Whitehall and the Iraq War: The U.K.'s Four Intelligence Enquiries," *Irish Studies in International Affairs* 16 (2005), p. 74.

71. J. Prados, *Hoodwinked: The Documents That Reveal How Bush Sold Us a War* (New York: New Press, 2004).

72. A fuller analysis is provided in P. Gill, "Keeping in Touch With 'Earthly Awkwardness': Failures of Intelligence Analysis and Policy in the U.K.," in T. C. Bruneau and S. C. Boraz (eds.), *Reforming Intelligence: Obstacles to Democratic Control and Effectiveness* (Austin: University of Texas Press, 2007), pp.96–120.

73. Butler, *op. cit.*, paras. 270–275.

74. Ibid., para. 295.

75. Her Majesty's Government, *Iraq's Weapons of Mass Destruction: The Assessment of the British Government* (September 24, 2002), available at http://www.the-huttoninquiry.org.uk/ (emphasis added).

76. Butler, *op. cit.*, para. 464. Emphasis added by Butler.

77. D. Manning, "Your Trip to the U.S.," Memo to the Prime Minister (March 14, 2002), available at http://slate.msn.com/id/2120886/ June 20 2005.

78. M. Danner, "The Secret Way to War," *New York Review of Books* (June 9, 2005), pp. 70–74; M. Smith, "Blair Hit by New Leak of Secret War Plan," *Sunday Times* (May 1, 2005).

79. This is described in J. Risen, *State of War: The Secret History of the CIA and the Bush Administration* (London: Free Press, 2006), pp. 113–115.

80. M. Rycroft, "Iraq: Prime Minister's Meeting, 23 July 2002," available at http://slate.msn.com/id/2120886/ June 20 2005.

81. Lucas, *op. cit.*, 207.

82. J. P. Pfiffner, "Did President Bush mislead the country in his arguments for war with Iraq?" in Pfiffner and Phythian, *op. cit.*, pp. 59–84 at p.79.

83. http://www.iraqinquiry.org.uk/transcripts.aspx.

84. Letter from John Chilcot to David Cameron (November 4, 2014). http://www.iraqinquiry.org.uk/media/54976/2013-11-04_Chilcot_Cameron.pdf.

85. J. E. Sims and B. Gerber, "Introduction," in J. E. Sims and B. Gerber (eds.), *Transforming U.S. Intelligence* (Washington DC: Georgetown University Press, 2006), pp. ix–xvi.

86. For example, Herman, 1996, *op. cit.*, p. 230.

87. Betts, *op. cit.*, p. 61. See also Robert Jervis, "The Politics and Psychology of Intelligence and Intelligence Reform," in Pfiffner and Phythian (eds.), *op. cit.*, pp.162–171.

88. These arguments are developed in more detail in Gill and Phythian (2012), *op. cit.* pp. 200–208.

Part III: Covert Action

CHAPTER NINE

Covert Action

Forward to the Past?

Gregory F. Treverton

MY INTRODUCTION TO COVERT ACTION WAS A fascinating one, moving as a graduate student and then freshly minted PhD to Washington to work for the original Senate Select Committee on Intelligence—often called the Church Committee after its chair, Sen. Frank Church (D-ID).[1] The investigations, hard on the heels of Watergate and allegations of covert U.S. intervention in Chile, were the nation's first ever look behind the green wall of intelligence. I had written about presidential decision making and expected to work on the role of intelligence analysis in those decisions.

In fact, I spent virtually all my time on covert action, and much of that on Chile.[2] That stint in Washington was exhilarating and frustrating, and it produced one of very few "aha!" moments I've had researching in deeply classified documents. Press accounts had attributed to Henry Kissinger, then the National Security Advisor, the line: "I don't see why the United States should stand by and watch Chile go communist merely due to the stupidity of the Chilean people." The quote rang true enough, but I hadn't seen a source and didn't expect to. Then, we received a spate of highly classified documents, including minutes from the 40 Committee, the administration's interagency committee for reviewing covert actions.[3]

Kissinger, previously a scholar, had changed the committee's record keeping from the terse notations of previous administrations—"CIA project 123 is approved," with no mention of operation or country—to those of a recording secretary. So there it was at the end of the notes on one meeting: "The chairman [Kissinger] closed the meeting by observing that he didn't see why. . ."

When I reflected some years later on covert action, what struck me was how much the targets of U.S. covert action had changed from the 1940s to the 1990s.[4] Many of the CIA's early postwar targets, like Iran's Mossadeq or Guatemala's Arbenz, wanted, almost pleadingly, not to be enemies of the United States. However, for later targets, like Nicaragua's Sandinistas or Iran's Khomeini, the United States was more useful as an enemy than a friend. Cuba's Castro bridged the two periods, with America-as-foe becoming the best thing he had going for him.

By the end of the 1990s, a second theme was also apparent: major American "secret" operations, from Nicaragua and Angola to Cambodia and Afghanistan, were not very secret. They had become "overt" covert action, in that actions became public not just when their results were known but while they were in progress. Support for the Nicaraguan rebels, or contras, the most controversial example, was openly debated and openly funded. Neither opponents nor supporters had reason to keep it secret; for its part, the Reagan administration regarded covert action as good policy and good domestic politics, a key element of the Reagan Doctrine, which was intended to challenge Marxist-Leninist states around the world. Indeed, when the Reagan administration decided to sell arms to Iran and keep the operation secret, it turned inward, to the White House staff.[5] In embroidering that operation to divert money for the contras, White House aides apparently kept the president ignorant to protect him—providing him with plausible denial of the sort the CIA had long since abandoned.

Now, the United States has come full circle. After 9/11, not only have most covert actions not been very secret, they have been mostly paramilitary actions in support of broader, mostly military counterterrorism operations. The campaign against terror has thrown CIA covert operators and Pentagon special forces together in new ways. The successes of that cooperation, in Afghanistan and Iraq, was impressive. Because the operations are not very secret and because they are part of the broader campaign against a fearsome foe—transnational terrorism—the questions of how to square them with America's values are less evident. Yet the process is making for less clarity about who does what and why. More important, it is complicating who *authorizes* lethal force and on what basis.

This chapter first reviews the early history that set the pattern for U.S. covert action in the half a century after World War II and enquires into how the success or failure of covert actions should be judged. It then looks at the circumstances, both at home and abroad, that changed covert action to "overt covert," and it argues for a bias toward acting openly, not covertly. If covert action is to be employed, what lessons emerge from the history? It then asks how those lessons apply in current circumstances, and it concludes with a coda on how the oversight of intelligence, especially covert action, by Congress has functioned.

Early Successes Set the Pattern

Spying may be the world's second oldest profession, but for the United States, it was only the Cold War, coming on the heels of America's wartime experience with secret operations conducted by the Office of Strategic Services, that led to the creation of an intelligence service in peacetime and to covert operations. Notice that spying—human intelligence or HUMINT, in the jargon of the trade—and covert action are superficially similar but in fact quite different. Both involve secret relationships between U.S. intelligence officers and foreigners. But the point of spying is information; the U.S. officer is relatively passive, and the process is designed to protect the foreign spy's link to the United States. For covert action, by contrast, the purpose is doing something; the U.S. officer is active, and the process carries inherent risks of being blown—the riskier it is, the more ambitious the action.

Wartime success and postwar threat: these were the backdrop for the creation of the Central Intelligence Agency (CIA). In a few years America plunged from the euphoria of victory in World War II to the confrontation with a looming Soviet threat, when Western Europe seemed to teeter in the balance. The first line of American response to the onset of the Cold War was overt: the surge of assistance to Europe through the Truman Doctrine and the Marshall Plan. But the second line was renewed interest in what was then called covert psychological warfare—what we could now call propaganda—as a way to respond to the Soviet Union by means that were less than war but more than nothing.

In this atmosphere, the National Security Council approved NSC 1012, a plan that had originated with George Kennan, then director of the State Department's Policy Planning Staff and the author of the famous X article outlining the policy of containment of the Soviet Union. NSC 1012 was the turning point for covert action, expanding it from propaganda to direct intervention. In the words of the document, covert action comprised:

> propaganda, economic warfare; preventive direct action, including sabotage, anti-sabotage, demolition and evacuation measures; subversion against

hostile states, including assistance to underground resistance movements, guerrillas and refugee liberation groups, and support of indigenous anti-communist elements.[6]

NSC 1012 also codified the notion of plausible denial: operations were to be "so planned and executed that any U.S. Government responsibility for them is not evident to unauthorized persons and that if uncovered the U.S. Government can plausibly disclaim any responsibility for them."

The fledgling CIA's first success came that same year, in 1948, when its covert support to the Italian Christian Democrats helped them beat back an electoral challenge from the Italian Communist Party. By 1950 the United States had succeeded in the covert struggle in Western Europe; in Eastern Europe its covert operations wound down to propaganda and intelligence gathering. The center of the battle against communism moved, as Washington saw the world, away from Europe to small, weak countries. Europe had put the CIA into the business of covert political action, but Asia got the agency into secret paramilitary operations in the Korean War, a pattern repeated a decade later in another Asian war, Vietnam.

The incoming Eisenhower administration called for a more active response to the Soviet threat than the passive containment of the Truman administration. CIA operators soon registered two successes that set the pattern for the next two decades. On August 21, 1953, after a week of turmoil in the streets of Tehran, the Iranian prime minister, Mohammed Mossadeq, who had nationalized that country's oil industry, surrendered. Three days later the shah, who had fled Iran the previous week with his queen, returned to the capital. At his palace a few days later, he offered a toast to Kermit "Kim" Roosevelt, the chief of the CIA's Near East and Africa Division and the man who had improvised Mossadeq's downfall: "I owe my throne to God, my people, my army—and you!"[7]

The next year, on June 16, 1954, Guatemalan Colonel Carlos Castillo Armas crossed the border into his country from Honduras with a few hundred men trained and armed by the CIA. Pilots under CIA contract flew air cover. The president of Guatemala, Jacobo Arbenz Guzmán, was deserted by his air force and his army, which refused his order to arm workers and peasants. The American ambassador hastily arranged a transfer of power to the chief of the armed forces. (In a moment of tragicomedy, that man immediately pledged that he would continue the struggle against Castillo Armas, America's designated successor to Arbenz. Only after complicated negotiations led by the ambassador did Castillo Armas emerge as president.)[8]

The Iran and Guatemala operations—code-named TPAJAX and PBSUCCESS, respectively—coming within a few years of the CIA's success in Western Europe, made the agency's reputation and set the pattern for covert action in the years ahead. Small, cheap, fast, and tolerably secret, they encouraged Washington to think other covert actions could be likewise. When the next administration decided to confront revolution in Cuba, its covert response was the same as in Guatemala. So were the CIA officers who carried it out.

The blush of short-run success amidst the Cold War obscured several warnings. In the early 1950s, both Iran and Guatemala were eminently vulnerable to manipulation by an outside power, particularly the United States. In both, contending political forces were in close balance. Those balances might have tipped against Mossadeq and Arbenz even if the CIA had not intervened. So it appeared that relatively small operations were enough to tip the balance. Yet in both cases, limited interventions might have failed. In fact, Kermit Roosevelt's first plot did fail; CIA Director Allen Dulles was ready to roll up the operation and bring the troops home. And the CIA officers who ran PBSUCCESS were under no illusions: if their deceptions failed and Arbenz were able to get his military into combat, the invaders would be overwhelmed.

Thus, success was purchased at the price of enlarging the intervention. American purposes did not change, but the operational requirements of achieving them did. Once the United States was committed, in secret and in a small way, the stakes increased, and the CIA took the next step. The effort to intimidate Arbenz became a paramilitary campaign, if a small one. In the process, plausible deniability became more tenuous.

Six years later at the Bay of Pigs, deniability evaporated entirely. "How could I have been so stupid, to let them go ahead?"[9] The words were from John Kennedy. When the CIA-trained invasion force of Cuban exiles hit the beach in the early dawn hours of April 17, 1961, everything went wrong: the lives of brave Cubans were spent; the United States was seen to be intervening; and the intervention failed. Once the plan had changed (without anyone outside the CIA quite noticing it) from a guerrilla operation into a full-fledged amphibious invasion, the chance of keeping it tolerably secret diminished to the vanishing point.

Judging Success

Evaluating covert action in retrospect is speculative, for it is bedeviled by the imponderable of what might have been; history permits no reruns. Failures, such as the Bay of Pigs invasion, are apparent, but successes are harder to judge. Consider the CIA intervention in the Angolan civil war of 1975. On the surface it was a failure: the Cuban- and Soviet-supported faction, the MPLA (Popular Movement for the Liberation of Angola), was installed while the U.S. role in trying to prevent that outcome was being exposed. If, however, the initial purpose was more limited—for instance, to raise the price of victory for the MPLA and its Soviet and Cuban backers—then Angola might be counted a short-run success. Yet American officials did not convey the impression that their aims actually were so limited, either at the time or later.

When, on the one hand, covert actions have succeeded in their short-run purposes, it may be that the action, though marginal, was just the bit of "support for our friends" that tipped the balance in the internal politics of a foreign country. On the other hand, it may be that the American support was entirely superfluous, and the same successful outcome would have ensued without the U.S. involvement. If this is so, all the covert action accomplished was to implicate the United States and tarnish the success by labeling it "made in America" when the existence of the covert action became known.

A case in point was covert American support to opposition political parties and media in Chile during the presidential tenure of Salvador Allende (1970–1973), a self-proclaimed Marxist. There is no question that those parties and media were under pressure from the Allende government.[10] The opposition forces survived to fight another day, but there is no telling whether CIA support for them was decisive or irrelevant.

What is clear is the signal conveyed to history by the revelations of American covert action. In retrospect, most reasonably objective observers conclude that Allende's experiment in Chile would have failed on its own terms.[11] Yet history's lesson is not that Allende fell of his own accord but that the United States overthrew him in 1973. That is the public perception, even though this lesson is untrue in the narrow sense: Washington did not engineer his coup, nor did the CIA or the American military participate in it. The very fact of American covert action meant that at a minimum, "it is fair to say that the United States cannot escape some responsibility for [Allende's] downfall."[12]

In a longer perspective, neither the Iran nor the Guatemala operations can fairly be given too much credit—or too much blame—for what happened afterward in Iran and Guatemala. On one hand, TPAJAX restored the shah of Iran to his throne, where he remained for nearly a quarter century, a pro-Western bastion in a turbulent region. Twenty-five years of stability is no mean feat in international affairs. On the other hand, American covert action identified the shah's Iran more closely with the United States than was good for either of them.

In any case, however, the aspects of U.S. policy that loomed so large in the shah's downfall in 1979 were overt, not covert. They were his image as an American client, the waste and corruption associated with his massive U.S. arms purchases, and his own dependence on the United States. These factors owed much more to American policy during the 1970s than to the event of 1953.

A similar conclusion also applies to Guatemala in 1953. If, in retrospect, the "success" of PBSUCCESS also looks more ambiguous than it seemed at the time, most of the blame or credit lies with American foreign policy, not with covert action. PBSUCCESS did not make it inevitable that Washington would then forget about Guatemala; it only made it possible. David Phillips, a CIA officer who worked on PBSUCCESS, the Bay of Pigs, and Chile, laments that "Castillo Armas was a bad president, tolerating corruption throughout his government and kowtowing to the United Fruit Company more than his own people." But he argues that the United States "could have prevented this with the vigorous exercise of diplomatic pressure . . . to assure that he pursued social reform for the many rather than venal satisfaction for a few. Instead, Washington breathed a collective sigh of relief and turned to other international problems."[13]

Several covert operations of the 1950s remained secret for a long time. For example, the CIA's assistance to Tibetans resisting the domination of their land by the People's Republic of China, regarded in intelligence lore as a successful holding action, is still a little-discussed operation, especially because it is an embarrassment now that Sino-American relations have thawed. In another example, the effort to unseat President Sukarno of Indonesia, who had earned Washington's opposition for his espousal of nonalignment, ranged from covert political action to a paramilitary operation; it is not much better known than the Tibetan operation.[14]

Even in the 1960s, several brief and limited interventions—small in terms of numbers of people involved, though not in terms of purpose—remained secret for some time. So-called Track II—a secret effort to touch off a military coup in 1970 to prevent Allende from being seated as Chile's president, an operation run without the knowledge of the State or Defense Departments—was not revealed for five years after it happened. And the sad plots in the 1960s to assassinate Fidel Castro stayed buried for over ten years.[15]

Changing Targets, Changing Times

Yet times changed. Major covert actions became likely to become public knowledge—sooner rather than later, perhaps even before the operation was over. In 1986, the arms sales to Iran became public even though the leak did not initially come from Washington but from an article published in Beirut in Arabic. Americans became more skeptical of their government, of its information, and its capacity, a skepticism that is a legacy of the long history beginning with the label "Watergate." By 1986, when Ronald Reagan, the most popular president in generations, first denied that his administration had traded arms sales to Iran for the release of American hostages in Lebanon, most Americans did not believe him.

This skepticism has been reinforced by the prominence of investigative journalism; every cub reporter aspires to be Woodward or Bernstein of Watergate fame. The media now contain more people asking hard questions, even of secret operations, and probing for leaks; and there are fewer who are prepared to take the government at its word. New media have multiplied the numbers of people probing and dramatically accelerated the process of moving secret information—real or fanciful—to a huge audience. Moreover, new technology has empowered leakers in a way hard to imagine 20 years ago: a Bradley Manning or an Edward Snowden could get out information it would have taken a Cold War spy a lifetime to photocopy. We used to say that the ship of state is like no other, for it leaks from the top. That is still true, but now it also can break apart at the bottom.

Not every exposé, however, has created a controversy. Even now, not every covert action is controversial. Of the 40 or so covert actions under way in the mid-1980s, at least half had been the subject of some press account.[16] Yet only several were controversial enough that the original leaks developed into continuing stories. Most of the rest were open secrets, more unacknowledged than unknown; most members of Congress thought they made sense, as did most Americans who knew or thought about them—and, no doubt, most of the journalists who reported them. Save for the controversy over drone strikes, the same was true of most of the covert war against terror after 2001.

Before September 11, 2001, the biggest open secret, or overt covert operation, was U.S. aid to those in Afghanistan resisting Soviet occupation of their country. Former CIA Director William Colby characterized the reaction to revelations of American assistance to the resistance in Afghanistan: "Afghanistan was a two-column headline in *The Washington Post* for one day, then almost nothing."[17] Americans in and out of Congress broadly supported the cause of the rebels, or *mujahedeen* (often called freedom fighters at the time, which became a cruel irony on 9/11), and the aid was a way to increase the cost of the Soviet occupation. American assistance reportedly begun in a small way in the last year of the Carter administration escalated sharply to reach as much as a half billion dollars a year by the late 1980s.[18]

Like the covert war against terror in the 2000s, the secret was an open one; the American role was not so much covert as unacknowledged, by tacit agreement. Then, the reason for circumspection was the delicate position of the Pakistan government, the conduit for the American supplies to the rebels. Pakistan was prepared to support the rebels but was unwilling to be too visible in doing so lest it antagonize its powerful neighbor, the Soviet Union. In those circumstances, resorting to the CIA, rather than the American military, was more a matter of being discreet than of keeping the whole affair secret.

Certainly there will be cycles in American attitudes toward international threats, as there have been before. In the early 1980s, most Americans evidently shared their president's concern with the Soviet threat, and their congressional representatives went along with huge increases in defense spending—and in covert action. Ronald Reagan was able to rebuild considerable authority and discretion in the American presidency, the Iran-*contra* debacle notwithstanding. After September 11, 2001, George W. Bush had at least as much of both support and authority. Most Americans enthusiastically supported the war in Afghanistan, and they were prepared, initially at least, to support the war in Iraq as a front in a longer fight against terrorism.

Still, if the changes in American domestic politics since the mid-1970s have made it more difficult for the United States to achieve its purposes secretly, other changes make it harder now than in the 1950s for the United States to intervene successfully at all, covertly or openly. Despite the controversy and mystique that surrounded covert action (and to some extent still do), history suggests that there is no magic to it. It means providing foreigners secretly with money, weapons, or training as tokens of American support.

With the passage of time, however, a little money here, a few weapons there became less likely to achieve grand foreign policy purposes. Castro was a target of a different order than Arbenz. To think in 1975 that a few million dollars might alter the fate of Angola was a faint hope at best and an illusion at worst, especially given that the CIA recognized that the Soviet Union and other external actors might counter American support with more assistance of their own. Even the CIA officials who planned the Bay of Pigs covert action knew that to delay the invasion until Cuba had received deliveries of advanced Soviet fighter planes would be to condemn the plan to certain failure.

Also, notice the contrast between two Central American cases three decades apart—Guatemala and Nicaragua. Castillo Armas's liberators numbered no more than several hundred. Their "invasion" was more conjured than real. Yet they had control of the air, in large part because Arbenz, unsure of the loyalty of his air force, was unwilling to risk putting his own pilots in the air. *Sulphates*—Spanish for "laxatives," the name Guatemalans gave to the invaders' bombs—plus rumors exaggerating the size of the invasion were enough to induce Arbenz to capitulate. In the case of Nicaragua, the contras numbered about 10,000 by the mid-1980s, yet not even the most ardent advocates of U.S. assistance to them argued that they were about to induce the Sandinistas to say uncle, much less that they posed a threat sufficient to overthrow the regime by sheer force of arms.

The makers of revolutions learned their own lessons from history, including the history of American covert action. They were determined not to repeat the mistakes of Arbenz and Mossadeq. They sought to assure themselves the loyalty of the army or to build revolutionary cadres of their own. Before the fall of communism, they also learned that if the United States threatened them, there were other sources of support to which they could turn. And, unlike Arbenz or Mossadeq, they turned to those sources sooner rather than later. Moreover, they learned that the United States could be very useful as an enemy. Arbenz, Mossadeq, and even Allende sought Washington's approval, or at least its acquiescence. By contrast, if the United States was of use to Castro, the Sandinistas, and the Ayatollah Ruhollah Khomeini, it was primarily as a foreign demon against which their revolutions could rally—even though the Sandinistas were prepared to accept American aid as long as it was forthcoming, and the revolutionary Iranians were not above seeking American spare parts for their military. In 1979 Iranians took Americans hostage and released them only when they ceased to be useful counters in the bargaining within the revolution. Suffice it to say that no one learned the value of America-as-enemy better than Osama bin Laden.

Values and Instruments

In all likelihood, the record shows, covert operations will become known, and America will be judged for having undertaken them. Thus, the practical lessons lead into moral issues. These issues are muted now by the fearsomeness of the terrorist threat. They are hardly unique to covert intervention, though they are powerfully present there, and they risked—and may still risk—being obscured in policymaking by the presumption that covert actions will remain secret. Overt interventions, such as the American invasions of Grenada in 1983 or Panama in 1989, or the bombings of Sudan and Afghanistan in 1998, not to mention the war against Iraq in 2003, raise similar moral and instrumental concerns. These concerns are not absolute; they must be considered against the gravity of the threat and the adequacy of other available responses.

In December 1976, when I was in Washington working with several old friends who were making arrangements for the transition between the Ford National Security Council (NSC) and the Carter NSC, we had decided to retain the basic structure of the Ford operation, with its network of sub-Cabinet committees for particular purposes. Yet of course, as a new administration, it was necessary to change the names of those committees, and so we joked about naming options. The 40 Committee, the Ford administration's group for discussing covert action, would become the "If They Can Do It, So Can We" Committee.

Yet, "if they can do it, so can we" did not seem, even then, to be an unacceptable rationale on either moral or instrumental grounds. What the Soviet Union or other nations did could not settle the issue, nor can how terrorists act. We consider ourselves different from them and imagine that the difference is not only basic to what we are as a people but also a source of American influence in the world, part of this country's moral armor.

We also believe that the example of democracy is powerful, one toward which peoples all over the world will gravitate if given the chance. Believing that, we must also believe that the example is a powerful part of our external behavior, not just of our internal arrangements. If people will choose democracy when given the chance, then democracy is demeaned, perhaps doomed to fail, if it is imposed from the outside. There is something incongruous about helping overthrow governments—especially ones that come to power through elections that we would define as tolerably fair (as in Chile in 1970)—in the name of democracy.

In this view, some of the successes of covert action seem, on the one hand, ambiguous or transient in retrospect, accomplished at significant cost to what we hold dear as a people and to America's image in the world. On the other hand, the world is a nasty, complicated place. The fight against terror has driven home that lesson. In that regard, Americans' historical ambivalence between the high moral view and the feeling that international politics is a dirty business is understandable.

Terrorism aside, nations affect each others' politics in so many ways that any too-tidy definition of "intervention" is suspect. In all the examples cited, covert action formed only part of American policy. The United States decided whether to grant economic aid to Cuba, Chile, or Angola, and whether to release Iranian assets held in the United States. Most of these decisions were based on explicitly political criteria. Even if similar decisions toward other countries are not so clearly political, the decisions in any case have political effects on the country in question; foreign political leaders have no doubt of that fact.

The same is true of actions by private American actors. U.S.-based businesses either invest or do not invest in a country, and that decision too has not just an economic but also a political effect. That is the case even if the decision is not "political" in any narrow sense of the term. Most of the businesses or banks that chose not to invest in Chile under Allende probably did not make that choice for any specific political reason, despite Washington's pressure. Rather, their decision was a business one, based on the climate in Chile. They saw that judgment as an economic one, though political instability surely was a factor in it.

In this context, if a unilateral self-denying ordinance against all intervention—open or covert—seemed too restrictive when the Soviet threat existed, it surely does now in an era of terrorism. Some threats to American national security require responses. Some American friends deserve support. What is imperative to keep in mind is the long-term costs of intervention for a government that is not notable for attending to long-term considerations.

Given that "covert" action is not likely to remain secret, why not act openly? In the case of aid to the FNLA and UNITA in Angola, covert rather than overt aid spared the first identification with the United States for only a few months; as for aid to the contras in Nicaragua, the "covert" form made not one whit of difference. The operation quickly became known, and the same was true of aid to the *mujahedeen* in Afghanistan. Nor is it obvious in most of these cases that the recipients of American largesse minded the source of the money being known. There is also the risk that covertness creates a self-fulfilling prophecy: If the United States only aids its friends secretly, then any link to the United States may seem sinister, portending much more than is actually the case.

The scope for doing openly what might earlier have been done covertly has increased dramatically since the 1970s. Sovereignty has become less absolute, and international law has come to recognize people, not just nation-states. In that sense, international law has moved in a very "American" direction, even if Americans do not always like the results, as with the creation of the International Criminal Court. But international practice (if not law) has come to recognize that some behavior by national leaders justifies external intervention, even with force of arms.

American radio stations broadcasting into Eastern Europe and the Soviet Union from Munich, *Radio Free Europe* and *Radio Liberty*, were private organizations in form; advertisements exhorted Americans to contribute to them. In fact, they were created and financed covertly by the CIA as propaganda vehicles. When that support was disclosed in 1967, the radio stations nevertheless continued to operate; they became supervised by a board and supported openly by appropriations from Congress.

In the 1980s, the Reagan administration was moved to create the National Endowment for Democracy (NED) on the model of the (then West) German party foundations, like the Konrad Adenauer Stiftung. They are instruments of the major parties but are supported openly by government money. They have openly assisted kindred parties and labor movements around the world. The NED, whose core budget reached $40 million in 2003, channels money to institutes of the two American political parties plus an AFL-CIO group and a business group, which then make grants in support of democratic institutions in a number of countries around the world.[19]

So far, the record of the endowment is mixed but hopeful. Its grants, and those of its four constituent institutes, began by being cautious and close to government policy. It remains an open question whether, given American politics, public funding is compatible with creative (and thus controversial) acts by private groups. The original NED budget was only an eighth of that of the German party foundations. Over the years, Congress has put a variety of restrictions on the endowment. For instance, in 1985 Congress halved the endowment budget and denied any funding to the Republican and Democratic institutes, although that prohibition was relaxed the next year. It may still be easier for the CIA to get money from Congress secretly than for another institution to get it openly—even if the purposes of the two are broadly similar. Funding for the CIA remains wrapped in the cloak of national security, so members of Congress may be prepared to fund particular activities but prefer not to be seen to vote for them openly.

Still, the endowment organizations have become more venturesome as the international and domestic climate has changed. More important, the endowment now works with scores of kindred organizations, both from other governments and from the private sector. For instance, before Slobodan Milosevic fell from power in 2000, the endowment and other U.S. government sources openly funded opposition parties and groups to the tune of some $25 million.[20] Indeed, the whole operation was almost a carbon copy, done overtly, of what the United States had done earlier covertly in Chile, for instance. In the instance of Serbia, the main difference other than overtness was that U.S. government agencies had lots of company from other countries and private nongovernmental organizations (NGOs). In other respects, the post mortem could have been written by a

CIA operative about Chile. For instance: "Foreign assistance should focus not only on political parties but should continue to support a broad range of nongovernmental organizations, labor unions, think tanks, and media."

Acting openly, however, is not always easy or a complete substitute for covert action. It requires an explicitness about influencing the politics of a foreign country that is uncomfortable for Americans and hence likely to be controversial. Moreover, governments that feel threatened by that open assistance can act to prevent it more easily than if it were covert. Yet even that ability is diminishing; national borders are more porous. Milosevic's Serbia did try to limit the assistance to opposition organizations. It had some success keeping foreign advisors out but much less success stopping money flows, and thus ended, somewhat paradoxically, with the worst of outcomes from its perspective: the antigovernment effort was well funded but harder to tar with the epithet "foreign influence" than it would have been had scores of foreign advisors been present. To quote the post mortem again: "While foreign assistance helped to build and sustain the broad anti-Milosevic coalition, indigenous organizations and action were mainly responsible for driving events."

A bias toward openness has its limitations, but surely it is the right long-term direction for American policy. Openness would reflect the reality that, as the century ends, national boundaries are more and more permeable. Given this reality, moreover, those groups the United States would like to support may not be so chary of accepting help, even—perhaps especially—if it is open. The United States would say to them: "We are prepared to support you but only openly. We think that is better for you. In any case, we know it is better for us."

Choosing the Covert Option: Lessons from History

The history of covert action before September 11, 2001, suggests that in deciding whether to choose the covert option, prudent policymakers should ask themselves a careful series of "what if" questions. That injunction applies to all policies, foreign and domestic. But it applies with special force to covert action because of the presumption of secrecy.

The most obvious "what if" is "what happens if—or more likely, *when*—it becomes public? What if it becomes public in midstream?" This is the *New York Times* test. Large covert actions will not remain secret, a reminder that is easy to state but hard to embody in the making of policy when the pressures go in the direction of wishful thinking. Witness the reflections on the Bay of Pigs invasion by Richard Bissell, then head of the CIA's clandestine service:

> The argument was [not] made that this is now a very public business, and we'd better treat it as such, and either cancel it if we can't stand the publicity, or else do some of the things that will increase the chances of success if we are going to go forward with it.[21]

If the Iran operation of 1985–1986 had remained secret for several years after all the U.S. hostages in Lebanon had been released, that success might have outweighed the costs of being seen to have traded arms for hostages when the operations became public. Perhaps. We cannot know for certain. It did not, however, take a sophisticated analysis to show that a covert policy targeted on some Iranians was vulnerable to being publicized by opposing Iranian factions if and when it suited their political purposes. And it was equally likely that when the cover was blown, trading arms for hostages with a nation the United States had denounced as terrorist would be deemed unacceptable—by America's allies, much of the rest of the world, and most important, the American people.

Of course, whether a particular covert operation can bear the test of disclosure is apparent in retrospect but often far from obvious before the fact. Prudence suggests that presidents pay careful attention to such warning signals as the review process throws up—the views of Cabinet officers, people in the White House who attend to the president's interests, and congressional overseers who are surrogates for public reaction.

One warning signal, however, is evident in advance: Does the intervention contradict overt American policy? If it does, as with arms sales to Iran, it is especially improbable that the operation will withstand the test of disclosure. The arms sales were exactly the opposite of the administration's public policies, which had twisted the arms of America's allies not to sell arms to Iran, had sought an end to the Iran–Iraq war with neither a victor nor a vanquished, and had pledged not to bargain with terrorists over hostages, much less to sell arms to them.

A second "what if" is "what if the first intervention does not succeed? What then?" If covert action is to remain secret, most of the time it will have to be small. Small operations have often begun with grand purposes, objectives incommensurate with the instrument. When the goals could not be achieved, leaders were tempted to take the next step and the next. This happened in the Bay of Pigs invasion, Angola, and Iran in the mid-1980s. Sometimes a limited objective can be achieved, but its achievement makes it appealing to hope for more—witness Angola and perhaps Nicaragua, where the United States did seem to achieve its initial aim of cutting weapons supplies from Nicaragua to the antigovernment rebels in El Salvador. Answering this "what if" suggests, at a minimum, careful attention to the CIA's covert operators themselves, for signs of skepticism about whether operations as initially conceived can achieve their purposes. Such signs were present between the lines of Track II in Chile, Angola, and Nicaragua. Some risks are worth running, but few are worth running in ignorance.

A third set of "what if" questions is "what signal will be received, by whom and with what result?" These judgments are also easier with the benefit of hindsight, for they involve calculations of threat and of American interests. Intelligence assessments by the CIA or the State Department provide one set of indicators. In 1985–1986, for example, American intelligence on Iran was weak, but what there was offered precious little ground for believing there were moderates who might be detached from their revolutionary colleagues. Later U.S. intelligence cast doubt on the imminence of a Soviet threat to Iran, one of the original premises of the operation. These were cautions that the intended signals might go awry.

The nature of those who are to receive secret American assistance can provide another warning signal. Because their relationship to the United States is meant to be clandestine, the CIA is often in a weak position to compel them to act to suit American purposes, yet the United States inevitably will become associated with their actions, like it or not, if and when the fact of support becomes known. Aid to the contras was dogged by their origins in Somoza's hated National Guard and by charges of human rights violations. Similarly, support for resistance forces in Afghanistan could have been justified as a way to put strategic pressure on Soviet occupation of that country; but given the character of the resistance forces, it was hardly a way to bring democracy to Afghanistan—far from it.

The regional context, in particular the attitude of American friends in the region, is another source of guidance. In the instance of Afghanistan, American assistance to the resistance was supported, though with varying degrees of publicity, by nations ranging from Pakistan and Egypt to Saudi Arabia and China. In Central America this indicator was more ambiguous, for most of the nations of the region publicly expressed qualms about the aid to the contras while privately hoping the Sandinistas could be made to go away.

These rules of thumb amount to establishing a presumption against covert action. The guidance is mostly negative, a series of cautions. It is unwelcome to officials who are looking for something to do rather than something to avoid—a trait that runs deep in the American character and is reinforced by the circumstances in which covert action becomes an option. Yet given how both America and the world have changed over the postwar period, the circumstances in which major covert action makes sense as policy are sharply limited.

Guidelines akin to these were articulated in the 1970s by Cyrus Vance, later Secretary of State. For Vance, the criterion for covert action in the National Security Act of 1974—"affecting the national security"—was too loose. Instead, he recommended covert intervention only as an exceptional measure, when it was "absolutely essential to the national security" and when no other means would do.[22] Decisions would still be matters of judgment under this more restrictive guide, but no one has improved on the Vance standard.

Covert Action since September 11, 2001

How has covert action changed since 9/11? And how do those changes relate to the lessons from earlier operations? Most strikingly, 9/11 underscored all too dramatically another theme from the review of earlier covert actions—the problem of control. The very fact that the interventions are meant to be covert gives rise to special problems of control. The link between U.S. intentions and the actions of those foreigners is tenuous at best. They are acting; the United States is only helping. Their purposes may not be ours. They have every incentive to hear from their CIA liaisons what they want to hear or construe it to their own purposes. In the details of earlier operations, that meant that covertly supported groups sometimes engaged in a little unsanctioned drug dealing or killing along the way or tried to overturn regimes when the United States only thought it was keeping opposition forces alive.

In supporting the anti-Soviet *mujahedeen* in Afghanistan, however, the problem of control was strategic. To minimize the American role, the CIA provided mostly money. Most of the contact in Afghanistan with the *mujahedeen* was done by Pakistan's Inter-Services Intelligence (ISI). For its own and Pakistani reasons, ISI gave preference to the radical Islamists among the *mujahedeen*, and in doing so, sowed the seeds for the takeover of Afghanistan by the Taliban and the formation of Al Qaeda as a unified fighting force. "Their" purposes were manifestly not "ours." The two sets of purposes converged only so long as both wanted to expel the Soviet Union from Afghanistan.

In that sense, the problem of control merges with the more general problem of longer-term, unintended side effects, one that afflicts not only foreign policy but all of human action. In this case, however, as in most others, it seems unlikely that any amount of asking "what if" could have changed the decisions in the 1970s and 1980s. The "what if" was simply too iffy. The Soviet Union was there in Afghanistan. Getting it out, somehow, was more than U.S. policymakers at the time could hope for. No story about the trail from ISI support to the Taliban to Al Qaeda to collapsing towers could have been made vivid enough to change the decision. The most that might have been accomplished would have echoed David Phillips's comment about Guatemala a half century earlier: support for the *mujahedeen* didn't have to entail that the United States would forget about Afghanistan after the Soviet Union departed.

One big part of the change in covert action happened before 9/11, as Serbia illustrated. Given the end of the Cold War and the changing currents in international law and attitudes, the CIA seemed all but out of the business of Chile-style political actions to sustain opposition forces or overturn regimes. In 2006, the Bush administration proposed major funding in support of Iranian opposition groups, but it did so openly, through the State Department. There may arise cases in which covert funding seems imperative—it is hard to imagine supporting North Korean opposition elements at all, and surely impossible openly—but they should be rare. In promoting democracy, or even regime change, the world has transformed enough to allow the bias toward openness to prevail, along with the bias toward company.

To that extent, covert action became, post-9/11, primarily paramilitary, with the CIA operating either independently or, more often, with military special operators. Surely, the CIA's performance as the first Americans in Afghanistan was impressive.[23] Its operations were secret only in their tactical details and thus met the *New York Times* test. The national investigation of 9/11 lauded that CIA role and the Afghanistan precedent of joint CIA-military teams. It recommended, though, that the CIA cede responsibility for directing and executing operations to the military, with agency officers and capabilities integrated into military-directed teams, giving both the CIA and the Special Forces the opportunity to do what each does best.[24] The December 2004 intelligence reform bill was silent on this issue, and the CIA and the military decided that both would remain in the paramilitary operations business.

Which agency is responsible for conducting paramilitary operations has been at issue well before 9/11, driven by Vietnam and other episodes. The arguments for giving the military control have been, historically, the ones the 9/11 Commission cited: the requisite capabilities are military, the task has not been a continuous priority for the CIA, and it makes no sense for the nation to build two parallel capacities. Operations by the military would give those carrying them out the status of combatants under international law, at least if they were visibly soldiers. On the other side is the concern that the military was never very agile or discreet, let alone covert. That concern may have diminished, but not disappeared, as the Special Forces have developed a wide variety of units and types of operations.

Whatever else is occurring, the Special Forces and the CIA were thrust together, and the CIA was pushed into counterterrorism operations, both with the military and independently. Both kinds of operations raise thorny questions of authorization and accountability. The drone, or UAV (unmanned aerial vehicle), strikes began soon after 9/11. In 2002, CIA operatives killed five suspected Al Qaeda operatives, including one American citizen, in Yemen with a Predator missile fired from a drone. [25] After that, the drone strikes waxed and waned in numbers but accounted for over 95 percent of non-battlefield targeted U.S. killings by 2013.[26] They were a continual bone of contention with host countries, especially Pakistan, and opponents of the strikes, especially in the region, had reason to exaggerate the incidental deaths of innocents. There was also concern about whether their value in taking out terrorist leaders was outweighed by their "blowback" effect in validating the terrorists' narrative. By that narrative, the attacks were both cowardly and indiscriminate, killing innocent civilians with technology from the safety of an unmanned plane.

CIA covert operations require a presidential finding, one transferred in secret to the relevant committees of Congress.[27] Very broad existing counterterrorism findings apparently provided authorization for the CIA to conduct all the UAV attacks. By contrast, a similar operation conducted by military Special Forces could be set in motion simply by the chain of command from the president as commander-in-chief.

The 2011 raid on Osama bin Laden's compound was a CIA operation but one conducted mostly by military special operators. It was hardly covert. The reason for authorizing it through the CIA was, again, the delicate position of Pakistan, whose sovereign territory was breached. The raid, though, demonstrated the need to tidy up authorizations across Title 10 (military) and Title 50 (CIA). Deciding on operations with a handshake tends to suit, especially, the covert operators. It may not suit the nation, as it leads to unwise operations or, as likely, the foregoing of valuable opportunities.

Covert Action and Open Democracy

The United States will remain in the business of covert action. It will continue to confront the paradox of secret operations in a democracy, even if those operations are mostly paramilitary and counterterrorist in character. Unfortunately, the process of congressional oversight of intelligence, including covert action, so carefully crafted in the 1970s, is now regarded as something of a joke in Washington. Terrorism is frightening enough to the body politic to justify almost any action in response—though the controversy in 2006 over eavesdropping on Americans by the National Security Agency in the wake of the terrorist attacks of 9/11 emphasizes the "almost." The House and Senate oversight committees have not escaped the bitter partisanship that has come to afflict Congress as a whole, and for a variety of reasons, the stature of the committee members has declined, though with several sparkling exceptions.

The 9/11 Commission suggested that if a single national intelligence director is to oversee the entire intelligence community—and preside over funding for all of it—Congress also should concentrate its oversight. Accordingly, the commission called on Congress to renew its commitments from the 1970s, having either a single joint committee to oversee intelligence (on the model of the old Atomic Energy Committee) or single committees in each house. Like the House Homeland Security Committee after them, the intelligence committees were never given the monopoly that was intended at their creation, and through the years, even more committees have become involved.

The commission also sought to revamp ideas from the 1970s agreements in several other ways. To represent other committees with interests in the field, the new oversight committee or committees would revert to the practice of having a member who also serves on each of the following committees or subcommittees: Armed Services, Judiciary, Foreign Affairs, and Defense Appropriations. To promote continuity and expertise, oversight committee members should serve indefinitely on the new intelligence committees. The new committees should be smaller—perhaps seven or nine members in each chamber of Congress—so that each member feels a greater sense of responsibility and accountability for the quality of the committee's work.

Here, too, the arguments are of long standing, running back to the congressional investigations of the 1970s. However, changing times reshuffle the arguments. Surely the idea of having real focal points is the right one. The objective was identical in the 1970s, but it was never fully achieved and has eroded since then as more committees have gotten into the act. In those days, the model favored by the 9/11 Commission, a single committee for both houses on the Atomic Energy Committee model, was not in favor, for it was regarded as having become the captive of the agency it oversaw. That fear that permanent committee members might become too cozy with the agencies they oversaw also led Congress in the 1970s to give the intelligence committees rotating memberships.

Now, however, those memories are distant and the need for focal points more intense. To try to achieve those points, the commission also favored the 1970s practice of appointing members from other committees with stakes in intelligence to the oversight committees. So, too, by the lights of 2004, when the commission reported, the need for experience on the oversight committees outweighed concerns over cooption, and so the commission favored open-ended assignments to the committee or committees, not rotating ones. But these are details. The real challenge for Congress is not to lag too far behind the executive branch in its own reshaping for the intelligence challenges of the 21st century.

The Iran-*contra* affair two decades earlier showed how difficult it can be to manage the paradox of secret operations in an open society. When the president finally signed the finding in January 1986 for the Iran arms sales operation, that finding was explicit: do not tell Congress. The congressional overseers did not find out about the Iran operation until autumn— hardly the law's requirement of "fully and currently informed" by anyone's definition. Later on, the president himself apparently was not told when the Iran and *contra* operations crossed with proceeds from the arms sales to Iran used to fund the contras without congressional appropriation.

In another sense, however, the system worked. In deciding to sell arms to Iran, the president pursued a line of policy opposed by both his Secretaries of State and Defense, about which he was afraid to inform the congressional intelligence committees and which was liable to be revealed by Iranian factions when it suited them. It is hard to imagine any system providing more warning signals. When most of the government's senior foreign policy officials are opposed, it is likely that the policy is wrong. The president thus proceeded at his own peril.

With regard to the diversion of money for the contras, the lesson is a caution for presidents and those who advise them: do not run covert operations from the White House. Before the 1970s it would have been unthinkable for an administration to do so; then the reason was that presidents wanted to stay at arm's length from such things, even if they could not plausibly deny them in a pinch. Now, though, if covert actions are to be undertaken, they should be done by the agency of government constructed to do them—the CIA. It has both the expertise and the accountability.

Moreover, the history of covert action suggests that if the president's closest advisors become the operators, the president loses them as sources of detached judgment on the operations. The president's own circle become advocates, as Allen Dulles did in the Bay of Pigs invasion, not protectors of the president's stakes (even if he does not quite realize his need for protection). So it was with Reagan's National Security Advisors, Robert McFarlane and John Poindexter; once committed, they had reason to overlook the warning signals thrown up by the process. Excluding the designated congressional overseers also excluded one more "political scrub," one more source of advice about what the American people would find acceptable. And the chances increased that someone like Lt. Col. Oliver North would misguidedly interpret the president's interest after his own fashion.

William G. Miller, the staff director of the first Senate Intelligence Committee, reflected on the Iran-*contra* affair: "If clear lines hadn't been drawn a decade ago, there would have been no hue and cry now."[28] Now is the time to remember again those lines and draw them again, all the more so as the boundary between covert action and military special operations blurs.

Notes

1. For an assessment by a fellow staffer, see Loch K. Johnson, "Congressional Supervision of America's Secret Agencies: The Experience and Legacy of the Church Committee," *Public Administration Review* 64 (January 2004), pp. 3–14.

2. See *Final Report of the Select Committee to Study Governmental Operations with Respect to Intelligence Activities of the United States Senate*, 94th Congress, 2nd sess. (1976). For links to these reports, as well as to a rich range of other documents, both historical and contemporary, see www.icdc.com/~paulwolf/cointelpro/cointel .htm.

3. The "40" merely referred to the directive that had created the committee. At other times, in modest attempts at discretion, the committees had been named for the room in which they met.

4. Gregory F. Treverton, *Covert Action: The Limits of Intervention in the Postwar World* (New York: Basic Books, 1987). This chapter draws on an article produced from the book, Gregory F. Treverton, "Covert Action and Open Society," *Foreign Affairs* 65, no. 5 (Summer 1987).

5. For an authoritative account of the affair, see *Report of the President's Special Review Board* (the Tower Commission) (Washington, DC: Government Printing Office, 1987). The *Final Report of the Independent Counsel for Iran/Contra Matters* (1993) is available at http://www.fas.org/irp/offdocs/walsh.

6. Reprinted in William M. Leary (ed.), *The Central Intelligence Agency: History and Documents* (Tuscaloosa: University of Alabama Press, 1984), pp. 131–33.

7. Cited in Kermit Roosevelt, *Countercoup: The Struggle for the Control of Iran* (New York: McGraw-Hill, 1979), p. 199. Because Roosevelt's account is not independently documented, his recollections should be taken as evocative, not gospel truth.

8. The most authoritative account of the Guatemala intervention is Richard H. Immerman, *The CIA in Guatemala: The Foreign Policy of Intervention* (Austin: University of Texas Press, 1982), though additional details have been declassified more recently.

9. Quoted in Theodore C. Sorensen, *Kennedy* (New York: Harper & Row, 1965), p. 309.

10. The best account of covert action during this period is *Covert Action in Chile*, staff report to the Senate Select Committee . . . on Intelligence Activities, 94th Congress, 1st sess. (December 1975).

11. See, for example, Conor Cruise O'Brien, "How Hot Was Chile?" *The New Republic* (August 26, 1985) p. 37.

12. Author's press briefing on behalf of the Church Committee, Washington, DC, December 4, 1975.

13. David Atlee Phillips, *The Night Watch* (New York: Atheneum, 1977) p. 53.

14. For accounts of both, see chapters 8 and 9 of John Prados, *Presidents' Secret Wars: CIA and Pentagon Covert Operations Since World War II* (New York: Morrow, 1986).

15. Both Track II and the anti-Castro plots are detailed in *Alleged Assassination Plots Involving Foreign Leaders*, an interim report of the Senate Select Committee . . . on Intelligence Activities, 94th Congress, 1st see. (November 20, 1975).

16. This number is rough, based on my interviews at the time and on press accounts. In any case, the precise number does not mean very much because operations vary widely in cost, not to mention risk and degree of controversy.

17. Interview with author, Washington, DC (January 9, 1986).

18. See Steve Coll, *Ghost Wars: The Secret History of the CIA, Afghanistan, and Bin Laden, from the Soviet Invasion to September 10, 2001* (New York: Penguin Press, 2004).

19. The NED's website contains a careful history of the idea and organization, one that is self-aware of the constraints on NED's operations. See http://www.ned .org/about/nedhistory.html.

20. For this figure, the following quotes, and a nice summary of the Serbian case, see United States Institute of Peace, *Whither the Bulldozer: Nonviolent Revolution and the Transition to Democracy in Serbia*, Special Report 72 (August 6, 2001), available at http://www.usip.org/pubs/specialreports/sr72.html.

21. Interview, Columbia University Oral History Research Office (1967), p. 25.

22. Testimony before the Senate Select Committee . . . on Intelligence Activities (Dec. 5, 1975).

23. As usual in Washington, if success didn't have a thousand fathers, it surely did have a thousand chroniclers. Among many accounts of the CIA's role, see Gary C. Schroen, *First In: How the CIA Spearheaded the War on Terror in Afghanistan* (New York: Random House, 2005).

24. Formally, the National Commission on Terrorist Attacks upon the United States, *The 9/11 Commission Report* (Washington, DC, 2004), available at http:// www.9-11commission.gov (accessed August 2, 2004). The specific recommendations are summarized in the Executive Summary and spelled out in more detail in chapter 13, "How to Do It? A Different Way of Organizing the Government."

25. See Dana Priest, "U.S. Citizen among Those Killed in Yemen Predator Missile Strike," *Washington Post* (November 8, 2002), available at http://www-tech.mit.edu /V122/N54/long4-54.54w.html; Walter Pincus, "U.S. Strike Kills Six in Al Qaeda: Missile Fired by Predator Drone; Key Figure in Yemen Among Dead," *Washington Post* (November 5, 2002), p. A01, available at http://www.washingtonpost.com/ac2/wpd yn?pagename=article&node=&contented=A5126-2002Nov4&notFound=true (accessed April 25, 2005).

26. Micah Zenko, *Reforming U.S. Drone Strike Policies* (New York: Council on Foreign Relations, 2013).

27. The term "finding" comes from the Hughes-Ryan Act of 1974, which required the president to "find" a particular operation necessary to U.S. national security. Turned into a noun, that became a finding delivered in secret to relevant committees of Congress.

28. Interview with author, Washington, DC (January 16, 1987).

CHAPTER TEN

Political Action as a Tool of Presidential Statecraft

William J. Daugherty

THE INTELLIGENCE DISCIPLINE OF COVERT ACTION HAS been a policy staple of every post–World War II American president, Democrat or Republican, and most often employed against countries and organizations that were or are hostile toward the United States or U.S. interests. But covert action didn't start with the Cold War; indeed, a number of earlier presidents, going back to George Washington, also relied on what we would call covert action to achieve foreign policy objectives. Thus, covert action is traditionally a tool of presidential statecraft, the purpose of which is, simply stated, to influence a foreign audience either to do something, or to refrain from doing something, in a direction that coincides with American foreign policy objectives. Put differently, covert action is applied, by specific presidential direction, to compel the target audience to change its policies or its behavior. The target audience might be a foreign government, a foreign nation's general population or distinct part of a population, or members of a hostile nongovernmental organization, such as a narcotics cartel or terrorist group.

Individual covert action operations are managed very much like intelligence collection or counterintelligence operations in that foreign nationals are recruited and directed clandestinely to perform a specific mission, usually the provision of confidential information. The difference is that, whereas all aspects of a collection or counterintelligence operation are to remain secret, a covert action operation must ultimately produce some result that is clearly apparent, or overt, at least to the target audience (if not the wider public) if it is to have any influence or effect. Although the result must be visible, the sponsorship—for example, the government or intelligence service—of the persons or group that generated the apparent result must remain hidden so as not to undermine the result's credibility with the target audience. In sum, the identity of the sponsor is actually the secret, not the operation itself. For example, if a respected labor leader in a country whose population was generally unsympathetic to the United States were to organize a general strike to emphasize the incompetence of his government, neither he nor the strike would be credible if it were known that the U.S. government was secretly paying him to perform this act.

Purely clandestine operations that are run either to collect sensitive information or to serve a counterintelligence objective are legally considered as routine missions of the U.S. intelligence community. As such, the individual intelligence agencies within the community possess continuing legal authorities to conduct these operations, a great deal of institutional latitude in how they do it, and a fairly low level of congressional oversight. Conversely, covert action programs are not routine intelligence activities: they must have special authorizations to meet federal law requirements, they are denied a good deal of the policy and operational flexibility that other intelligence operations enjoy, and they receive intense oversight from not only Congress but also the National Security Council. Arguably, because they are implemented explicitly to support a president's foreign policy initiative, covert action programs are not even "intelligence" in nature, even though they are executed by the Central Intelligence Agency (CIA) and rely on clandestine methodologies. These differences ultimately remove covert action programs from the realm of general intelligence activities and transform them into highly sensitive instruments of presidential policy.

In essence, covert action programs are secret adjuncts to a particular foreign policy established by the president and employed to support overt policy implementation measures (for example, diplomacy, trade favoritism or sanctions, foreign aid, military force, training initiatives, and loan guarantees or grants). It is the president, advised by the National Security Council, who decides whether a policy will have a covert component and, if so, how that component will be used. For each covert action program, under which dozens or even hundreds of individual operations may be run, federal law dictates that the president sign a document declaring that he "finds" that the covert action program is necessary for national security purposes. This finding (as it is known in the parlance) spells out the objectives and implementation limits of each program, sets a program budget, defines the role of the CIA and any supporting agencies in executing the program, and includes a risk versus gain assessment. Furthermore, all findings must be sent to the intelligence oversight committees in Congress within 48 hours of the president signing the document. Once begun, covert action programs receive nearly continuous scrutiny from CIA senior management, Congress, and the president and his national security team. This oversight is conducted until the program is abolished, a move that again requires a presidential signature. These extra measures necessary to initiate, execute, and terminate covert action programs truly make them "presidential" in all respects.

Covert action programs fall under one of four general operational categories: propaganda, political action, information warfare, and paramilitary operations. Political action programs, the focus of this chapter, generally seek to achieve influence through covert activities that involve the manipulation, legitimate or otherwise, of a foreign nation's political and/or economic system, with the instigating hand of the U.S. government remaining hidden from view. Political action operations are always provocative to some degree, ranging from operations that slightly irritate (for example, paying a few individuals to carry protest signs in front of a government office or bribing public officials) to the highly antagonistic and hostile (for example, flooding a country with counterfeit currency or creating a major strike to cripple the economy and undermine the ruling regime). Regardless, political action operations, whether directed at a nation's political institutions or its economy (and often both), seek to change the behavior or policies of a government. Such meddling is contrary to international law and the United Nations Charter and may, if compromised with the sponsorship of the American government exposed, generate many problems, both political and practical, for the president at home and abroad.

But offsetting this risk—and hence its attractiveness to presidents—is the fact that operations that covertly manipulate a country's political processes or economic system are usually much less costly than other forms of pressure, especially military force. For example, if a covert political action program to oust Panamanian dictator Manuel Noriega in 1989 had been attempted and succeeded, the financial and political costs of such would have been far less than the costs (including humanitarian) of using the U.S. military to invade and occupy the country until Noriega was captured.

American history is replete with examples of presidents authorizing secret activities intended to foster and further American interests at the expense of foreign governments. In point of fact, George Washington used covert action programs in addition to intelligence collection operations during the American Revolution and continued doing so after his election to the presidency in 1791 to secure the fledgling democracy. Arguably, the first use of covert action in the new administration was not against an overseas government but against the sovereign governments of Native American tribes.

Once in office, Washington was abetted by his secretary of state, Thomas Jefferson, in implementing a covert action program—a classic example of a political action operation—intended to create confidence and goodwill with various tribes whose lands lay between the settled East Coast and the interior of the continent, awaiting further exploration. Jefferson's objective was to lay the foundation for the U.S. government eventually to acquire their lands for the development or construction of inland transportation systems, such as roads, bridges, and canals, an infrastructure vital to the movement of commercial goods and people within the country. The need to grow the economy was critical to sustaining the faith of the Americans in the newly created democracy, the permanence of which was by no means assured just because the U.S. Constitution was ratified. Quite simply, if Americans were not better off economically under the new Constitution, there would be little reason for them to continue to support it. Gaining access to tribal lands for the movement of goods, as well as to encourage the migration to and settlement of the West was, hence, an important part of Washington's economic policy.

The methods Washington and Jefferson employed are easily recognized as basic political action tactics. First, the secretary of War was given visible responsibility for this program, putatively acting autonomously to insulate the president and secretary of State from any negative consequences that might occur. The War secretary then proceeded, through the help of clandestine agents, to bribe tribal chiefs, selectively dole out financing for trading posts and other businesses, extend (or threaten to foreclose) loans granted to tribal leaders, and manipulate the chiefs' human foibles (here, greed) to run them into heavy debt. Owing monies that they had no way of repaying left the tribal leaders vulnerable to exploitation by government agents, who agreed secretly to swap tribal debts for treaties transferring Indian land titles to the United States.

When Jefferson acceded to the White House, he was bedeviled by the predatory actions of the Barbary pirates, seagoing thugs who plundered American commerce in the western Mediterranean and captured American sailors for ransom. Jefferson's solution was the same that later presidents, including Dwight D. Eisenhower, John F. Kennedy, and Richard M. Nixon, found so attractive—implementing a political action program to undermine covertly the offending government (the Tripolitan Pasha) and affect a change of regime by placing a rival on the throne. Jefferson's scheme also involved bribery, secret funding of opposition groups, and a small paramilitary operation conducted by U.S. Marines. The Pasha, seeing the writing on the wall, decided to deal with Jefferson, resulting in an accord that halted acts of piracy against the U.S. merchant fleet and released the American hostages, while allowing the Pasha to retain his throne.

Covert actions, particularly political/economic action programs, were employed through the mid-1800s as America expanded westward to gain land for the United States from European colonial powers and neighboring Mexico. Under James Madison's direction, two territorial administrators infiltrated secret agents into the Florida panhandle, at the time under Spanish control, to foment a rebellion that would appear to be the actions of local, pro-U.S. residents. The anticipated Spanish reaction would then provide the pretext for the president to order the occupation of the land by U.S. troops to protect lives and property, followed by a proclamation granting the locals their proclaimed wish for independence from Spain. The operation relied on individuals who, in today's intelligence lexicon, would be labeled "agents provocateur" and who were well supplied with secret funds and used a clandestine communications system to coordinate their schemes. A supposedly spontaneous insurgency against the Spanish did break out, with the rebels declaring independence and asking for assistance from the American government. Madison responded by proclaiming that west Florida was actually already a U.S. possession by dint of its (rather suspect) inclusion with the Louisiana Purchase, and soon the Stars and Stripes flew over Pensacola and Mobile.

Madison followed this land expansion with similar covert tactics (that is, a spontaneous uprising and call for independence) from pro-U.S. inhabitants in eastern Florida to acquire that territory before the British could seize it from the steadily weakening Spanish empire. His successors—James Monroe, John Quincy Adams, and Andrew Jackson—all employed elements of covert political action operations in their policies toward Mexico. Monroe maneuvered to reduce British influence with the Mexican regime, and Jackson attempted to induce the Mexicans to sell or cede land north of the Rio Grande to the United States. Bribery, support for underground opposition groups, inflammatory propaganda, the public dissemination of erroneous information (disinformation, in espionage parlance), and secret slush funds were all covert methods set in motion by these presidents. That Jackson was ultimately unsuccessful in gaining any Mexican land does not obviate the fact that he carefully and skillfully employed political action operations to further his overt foreign policy.

In an interesting parallel to a large covert political action program initiated in the 1980s under President Ronald Reagan that used a variety of means to deny sensitive emerging technologies to the Soviet Union, Abraham Lincoln established a clandestine network in Europe to prevent those nations from providing much-needed military supplies to the Confederate States during the Civil War. The complex program began with the collection of raw intelligence, the analysis of which identified individuals and companies secretly trading with the South. Political action operations were then run against the traders to disrupt the production of the war materiel, sabotage the factories, and intercept the materiel en route to the Confederate States. Knowing that the Union navy could not always snare the South's blockade runners, waging a covert interdiction campaign in Europe to prevent war materiel from being loaded on a Confederacy-bound ship in the first place proved an effective and economical way to deny the South vital war-making capabilities.

Prior to the Civil War, American presidents essentially used covert action in general and political action operations in particular to expand the land territory of the nation and protect American lives and commerce from foreign interference. But within two decades of the ending of the American insurrection, and well before the United States became a world military force, presidents began using these covert methodologies to strengthen foreign commercial ties, protect American economic interests, and expand international trade. In the 1880s, the American government became cognizant of the tremendous economic potential of Asia as a source of raw materials and a destination for the export of finished goods. It became the goal of presidents to open these markets to trade and to protect the markets once established. A concomitant objective was to reach agreements with Asian regimes for coaling stations for the U.S. Navy's growing Asiatic fleet. Korea drew the interest of the navy and, hence, of President Chester A. Arthur (not a president one usually associates with an aggressive foreign policy), early in that decade for both a trading partner and a refueling post. But Japan and China had squared off over which was to exercise the dominant political and economic influence over the Korean Peninsula, leaving Korea much like a fish caught between two cats. Arthur relied on covert political activities, particularly the supply of arms and funds to a Korean group interested in upsetting the pro-Chinese regime that held power (with the U.S. involvement remaining under the table), to drive a wedge between Tokyo and Beijing in hopes of creating and then filling a power void. A quick-rising squabble between France and China distracted the latter and provided a fortuitous opening for the American-supported clique, which then moved into power.

Under President Benjamin Harrison, America's annexation of Hawaii, whose natural port at Pearl Harbor was a matter of strategic import for the Asiatic fleet, was the consequence of a political action operation bearing similarities to Madison's grab of west Florida. It likewise involved, in 1893, the clandestine fomenting of a "popular" insurrection that portended bloodshed and justified intervention to protect American diplomatic facilities and citizens. Navy sailors and marines occupied Hawaiian government buildings, and the American ambassador soon thereafter declared the establishment of a provisional—and pro-American—government.

But it was, of course, the Cold War and the creation of the CIA that truly made covert political action a critical component of presidential statecraft. Throughout the Cold War, it was the fundamental objective of the United States to (1) counter Soviet expansionary policies; (2) support pro-West governments that were targets of Soviet subversion; and (3) weaken or undermine foreign governments that had fallen into the Soviet orbit. (Policies of transforming oppressive regimes into democracies had to wait until the presidencies of George H. W. Bush and his son, George W. Bush.) The attraction for American presidents in employing political and economic covert actions against the Russian bear was that it permitted the U.S. government to apply a varying degree of pressure against the Moscow regime but to do so without generating a clear and direct threat to core Soviet interests that might eventually invite a military response. Because covert action programs used a broad spectrum of capabilities that allowed presidents to calibrate the intensity of the pressure felt or perceived by the Soviet leadership, the interests of the United States were protected and advanced but without backing the Soviets into a corner that might have left them no recourse but war. (Of course, the Soviets were concurrently doing the same things against the United States, using the term "active measures" in place of covert action.)

Although at first rather reluctant to open an intelligence war against the Soviet Union, which had been, after all, America's ally in the recent world war, by 1947 President Harry S. Truman had become convinced that Soviet hostility toward the United States, the Western democracies, and capitalist systems would only increase, ultimately threatening democracies and nations seeking to become democratic. To counter Soviet subversive operations in regions considered vital to U.S. national security, Truman implemented overt policies such as the Truman Doctrine (for Greece and Turkey) in March 1947 and the Marshall Plan (for the reconstruction of Western Europe) just three months later. But overt programs intended to strengthen democratic political systems and rebuild devastated economies in Europe and the Near East were also judged to be insufficient when considering the scope and depth of Soviet covert machinations to undermine those same countries. Under Truman's personal initiative, his newly established National Security Council (NSC) drew up its first national security directive—an order for the CIA (created concurrently with the NSC by federal statute) to counter Soviet political and economic subversive programs in Italy and France, operations by which the Stalinist regime in Moscow sought to acquire control of those governments through manipulation of legitimate electoral processes.

To be sure, there were precedents from which one could learn. Elections in Eastern European countries following the war found the local Communist Parties legitimately winning seats in those parliaments, from which party members were then chosen to fill key Cabinet positions in the government. With covert assistance from Moscow, the democratic processes were subverted from within (Czechoslovakia was particularly instructive), resulting in the establishment of oppressive pro-Soviet communist regimes. In France and Italy, Soviet agents were likewise seeking to gain control of those elements of society that are fundamental to democracy—political parties, newspapers, labor unions, publishing houses, student groups, and more—through the provision of nearly unlimited funds and then employ these societal influences as front organizations for Soviet intelligence to use to corrupt the democratic processes.

NSC documents from 1947 and 1948 show that the Truman administration viewed a victory for the French and Italian Communist Parties as an unacceptable outcome and, should that happen, reached the conclusion that all governments in Western Europe would be menaced. The CIA was given the responsibility of countering the Soviet operations, in part by political action—the provision of secret funding to individual candidates for political office as well as to the multiple political parties. In this, neither the U.S. government nor the CIA had a preferred candidate or party. The funds, millions of dollars, were given liberally to groups, organizations, unions, and politicians across the political spectrum, from the far right to the left of center. It mattered, not so much who won, but who had to be defeated. Ultimately, between overt U.S. policies and the covert program, the Communists lost at the polls. Still, it terms of the role that political action operations played in the greater scheme of things, it is important to understand that the millions of dollars in covert funding constituted only a small percentage of the monies expended in the overt diplomatic programs meant to strengthen governmental institutions and to rebuild the economies devastated from war. Covert action programs, certainly including political and economic operations, are most effective when supporting well-established overt policies, and the operations in Italy and France are proof of this. The perceived need to secretly fund Italian politicians and parties continued through the administration of Lyndon B. Johnson, ending only in 1967.

Perhaps the most familiar—or notorious—political action operations are those in which the president directs the CIA to oust a foreign government or regime. Again, the idea is to make it appear as though local opposition groups act on their own initiative and through their own resources. Presidents Eisenhower, Kennedy, and Nixon each issued orders to the CIA to overthrow regimes deemed to be politically too close to the Soviet Union, but with varying degrees of success. Operations to reverse regimes in Iran and Guatemala managed to achieve their objective, but similar efforts in Indonesia, Cuba (after paramilitary operations failed in each), and Chile did not. Kennedy further toyed with the idea of ordering political action programs to unseat regimes in Santo Domingo and British Guyana, as did Reagan early in his administration with Surinam.

The covert overthrow of a foreign regime by the United States is never as easy as its proponents seem to believe, nor are successes truly positive or unalloyed in the long term. For many intelligence professionals, the overthrow of the Iranian regime of Mohammed Mossadeq in 1953 was a double-edged sword, for the ease with which it seemingly occurred served to mislead future presidents and CIA directors into attempting similar operations with less fortunate results. In the case of Iran, the fact is that the CIA itself did not cause the overthrow of Mossadeq. What the CIA did was to provide, in essence, a push at the margins of an already developed and much larger indigenous political movement unhappy with Mossadeq and his policies. It is unknown whether the anti-Mossadeq forces would have prevailed had the CIA not stepped in at a key moment, but it is beyond doubt that the CIA as an institution did not itself effect the change. Indeed, the operation at first appeared to be an abject failure, and it was only the fortuitous appearance of a popular Iranian general to rally the mobs at a critical moment that brought about the ouster of Mossadeq. It is not an oversimplification to say that the Americans contributed just the right amount of pressure, at just the right moment, with just the right people. Said differently, the operation succeeded mostly (or even only) because of luck.

Yet the lesson the CIA and the Eisenhower (and later Kennedy) administration took away from the Iranian program was that the reversal of hostile regimes was nothing particularly difficult; that American ingenuity and righteousness of purpose were enough to prevail. Interestingly, the one person who realized differently was the man who orchestrated the Iranian program, Kermit Roosevelt. Asked to lead the next such operation, the removal of Guatemalan leader Jacobo Arbenz, barely a year later, Roosevelt declined and left the agency. That the Guatemalan operation, a blend of paramilitary, political action, and propaganda operations, went well further solidified the belief in the Washington circle that the United States could replace governments at will and without fear of failure.

After the Guatemalan program, the Eisenhower administration took aim at the Indonesian government of Sukarno, who announced his intentions of allowing Communist Party members to hold positions in his Cabinet. Eisenhower, duly alarmed at the prospect of a pro-Soviet regime in that country, authorized a robust covert action program, including operations aimed at manipulating the political and economic processes, to remove Sukarno from power. This effort failed miserably, with the consequence that Sukarno's hold on power was stronger. An astute, objective student analyzing this program might have reached the conclusion that maybe, just maybe, political action operations to change an entrenched regime might not be as easy or as useful as thought. But with the apparent successes of Iran and Guatemala in the background, the lessons of Indonesia were lost.

It is instructive to note that the definition of "success" as applied to a political action program, especially one in which the change of a regime through subversive measures is the objective, can be elusive. Eisenhower, Kennedy, and Nixon each believed that success constituted the replacement of a pro-Soviet or potentially pro-Soviet government with a right-wing, pro-American regime. And in the short term, that was perhaps so. But over the longer run, arguably more harm was done. The hapless Mossadeq was replaced by a monarchy that grew more oppressive and dictatorial over the years, itself eventually overthrown by indigenous elements, transforming America's most important ally in the Middle East into a radical Islamic fundamentalist state that has now waged a war of terrorism against America for a quarter century. Although communist forces were thwarted in Guatemala in 1954, the resulting oppressive, right-wing military dictatorship murdered hundreds of thousands of its own citizens over the next 40 years, leaving an impoverished nation in its stead.

Chile was the target of covert electoral manipulations beginning with Kennedy, who sought to forestall socialist or communist regimes by directing the provision of secret funds to several Chilean political parties and, especially to one presidential candidate, Eduardo Frei. The program continued through President Nixon, who at one time toyed with instigating a military coup to prevent the election of socialist Salvador Allende. When this proved unfeasible and Allende was elected, Nixon turned his efforts toward destabilizing the new regime. Included in his bag of tricks were monies given to political parties and candidates, payments to various mass media outlets to produce political advertisements or messages, and funds to social and professional organizations—labor unions, student groups, women's clubs, and business and civic associations. In the end, the military acted unilaterally, instigating a coup that left Allende dead and the government in the hands of an oppressive, right-wing military cabal that endured for two decades.

But not all political action programs are failures. The CIA managed a number of covert political action operations against the Soviet Union, some for nearly the length of the Cold War. These programs picked up strength and importance during the administration of Jimmy Carter, including operations that fostered the printing and underground distribution within the Soviet Union of prohibited political tracts, the writings of banned Russian authors like Aleksandr Solzhenitsyn and Boris Pasternak, and religious works (Bibles and Korans). Along with the infiltration of printed materials, these political action operations provided, through secret channels, desktop publishing equipment to Soviet dissidents to print and disseminate their writings, known as "samizdat," within the Soviet Union. Additionally, operations funded Soviet exiles in Western Europe, enabling them to write and publish books, journals, and monographs that, though intended primarily for distribution within émigré circles, likewise found their way clandestinely to readers inside the Soviet Union. An adjunct initiative known as the Nationalities Program funded the printing and distribution of journals and pamphlets directed toward the non-Russian ethnic minorities in the Soviet Union, keeping alive their history, culture, and language at a time when the Soviet government was attempting to suppress them. Other CIA political action programs in Europe funded human rights and prodemocracy organizations as part of a larger effort to counter anti-Western Soviet propaganda. These programs and more were continued and expanded during the administration of Ronald Reagan, effectively and inexpensively applying pressures on the Soviet government that contributed to the ultimate demise of the Soviet Union.

But perhaps the most successful political action program ever was a broad-based effort to undermine the legitimacy of the Polish military government that came to power in 1980 while concurrently supporting the independence movement headed by Polish labor union Solidarity. If a critical attribute of any covert action program is that it would, if exposed, meet with the approval of the American public, this was one such program. Although much of the program remains classified, despite its overwhelming success, elements of it have come into the public eye.[1]

As the end of the Carter administration drew near, it was faced with the Soviet Union pressuring the Polish government to outlaw Solidarity and its supporters, as well as threatening to move its military across the border if the Polish power structure failed to contain the growing influence of the union. In response, Carter directed his National Security Advisor, Zbigniew Brzezinski, to advise the Vatican that the United States had clandestine intelligence resources available to aid Solidarity. Moreover, with European governments reluctant to openly confront the Soviet Union over its aggression, Brzezinski bluntly asked Pope John Paul II if he would consent to joining with the United States to isolate economically, culturally, and politically the Soviets if they openly intervened in Poland. The Pope would and did.

The Reagan administration thus inherited an expanding covert political action program that first deterred a Soviet military intervention in Poland (similar to the Soviet invasions of Hungary in 1956 and Czechoslovakia in 1968) and then enabled Solidarity and other underground organizations to survive and resist the martial law government of Gen. Wojciech Jaruzelski. But the CIA's covert operations did not end with just Poland: Reagan believed that if Poland was able to throw off the communist system and emerge as a free and democratic nation, the other five Eastern European countries would follow. The Polish program thus expanded into a worldwide confrontation of the legitimacy of the communist governments of Eastern Europe and the Soviet Union itself. Poland held its first free elections in 1989, and within two years, not only were Eastern European countries free of Soviet domination, but the Soviet Union as a political system disappeared into the dustbin of history. Of course, Eastern Europe did not gain its independence, nor did the Soviet Union collapse solely because of the covert action operations initiated by the Reagan administration, but these missions did fulfill their intended goal and then some, supporting a vast array of overt United States political, economic, and military policies that collectively made it impossible for Moscow to continue the Cold War.

This abbreviated introduction to covert political action programs operations is meant neither to convince the skeptical of their efficacy nor to provide support to those who see them as a solution to difficult or seemingly insoluble foreign policy issues.[2] Truman and Eisenhower employed political action operations against the Soviet threat with mixed results. Truman's use of covert action in Italy and France must be judged as highly successful, whereas the long-term consequences of the Iran and Guatemalan operations, as well as the clear failure of the Indonesian venture, place into question the wisdom of Eisenhower's decisions to use covert methods against those regimes. Kennedy's efforts in influencing the Chilean elections was successful only in the short term, with a socialist government eventually coming to power despite his efforts, as well as Johnson's, and Nixon's use of multiple political action operations to forestall it. Similarly,

Kennedy's intense efforts to overthrow the Cuban regime of Fidel Castro were not only unmitigated failures but might well have placed his administration in serious jeopardy, had the operations become public knowledge during his tenure in office. Unrecognized by many historians, Carter's reliance on covert programs, political action especially, was more successful than not, especially in that he laid the foundation for many of Reagan's programs against the Soviet Union directly and in countering Soviet interventions in places like Afghanistan and Central America.

Whether or not political action programs are an appropriate tool for the president in implementing foreign policies depends on a number of factors, not the least of which is the ability of the president and the national security team to recognize and accept the limits of any covert action program. Certainly it should be clear that these political action operations are not suitable for crisis resolution; rather, they are most wisely employed in consonance with a thoughtfully developed, comprehensive foreign policy with well-defined objectives implemented in a methodical manner. Successful foreign policies are never the responsibility of just one agency of government, and certainly not intelligence agencies. But covert actions that influence the political or economic systems of target audiences may, when wisely employed, serve a president and the country well.

Notes

The author thanks Matthew Easterwood, BA, JD, for his research assistance with this chapter.

1. Robert M. Gates, a former director of the CIA, has provided some detail in his memoir, *From the Shadows: The Ultimate Insider's Story of Five Presidents and How They Won the Cold War* (New York: Simon & Schuster, 1996), which was cleared for publication by the CIA. Other partial accounts have appeared in Zbigniew Brzezinski, *Power and Principle: Memoirs of a National Security Advisor 1977–1981* (New York: Farrar, Straus & Giroux, 1985); and Carl Bernstein and Marco Politi, *His Holiness, John Paul II and the Hidden History of Our Time* (New York: Doubleday, 1996), on which the CIA will not comment. This is unfortunate in that the story is generally now in the public domain, but also at a time when the CIA and the intelligence community are under serious attack, a story that is clearly a great success would only redound to the benefit of the CIA.

2. Mention of more recent covert programs, including political and economic action operations, which might provide more enlightenment for this chapter, is precluded by continuing classification of programs after the Reagan era and the CIA's requirement that this author clear his writings with them prior to publication.

CHAPTER ELEVEN

Covert Action and the Pentagon

Jennifer D. Kibbe

THE DECADE-PLUS SINCE THE TERRORIST attacks on September 11, 2001, saw a number of changes in the U.S. national security outlook, not the least of which was a renewed willingness to consider covert action as a policy option. During this same period, the single most significant change in the military services has been the dramatic expansion (in both size and responsibility) of its special operations forces (SOF). The concurrence of these two trends has led to a blurring of the distinction of whether or not military units are conducting covert operations and has raised questions about whether such covert operations are subject to adequate congressional oversight. These two trends have also led to a third phenomenon, known as "convergence": an increase in hybrid SOF/CIA operations which have the potential to increase the level of oversight but which could also serve to further blur some very indistinct lines.

"Covert action" is defined in U.S. law as activity that is meant "to influence political, economic, or military conditions abroad, where it is intended that the role of the United States Government will not be apparent or acknowledged publicly."[1] Covert actions are, thus, legally distinct from clandestine missions: "clandestine" refers to the tactical secrecy of the operation itself; "covert" refers to the secrecy of its sponsor. Although most often associated with the assassination of leaders or the overthrow of a government, the category of covert action can include a wide range of activity from propaganda and disinformation to political influence operations to training and support for foreign military forces to paramilitary operations. Historically, the Central Intelligence Agency (CIA) has been the main agent of U.S. covert action, but the significant growth of SOF, in terms of numbers, resources, and influence, and the increased use of them to conduct unacknowledged operations which would be called covert action if conducted by the CIA, have raised crucial questions not only about oversight and accountability, but also about congressional versus executive control of unacknowledged operations far from recognized battlefields.

Special Operations Forces

Special Operations Command (SOCOM) is comprised of both units that conduct overt or "white" operations and those that conduct "black" operations, including both covert and clandestine missions. Those involved in white special operations include Army Special Forces (Green Berets); most Ranger units; most of the Navy SEALs (Sea, Air, Land); and numerous aviation, civil affairs, and psychological operations units. These white special operators are largely involved in training selected foreign forces in counterterror, counterinsurgency, and counternarcotics tactics; helping with various civil government projects; and disseminating information to foreign audiences through the mass media. The black operators fall under JSOC, which commands the elite units of each service's SOF, including Special Forces Operational Detachment-Delta (Delta Force), Naval Special Warfare Development Group (DEVGRU, or SEAL Team 6), the Air Force's 24th Special Tactics Squadron, and the Army's 160th Special Operations Aviation Regiment and 75th Ranger Regiment. These units (also known as special mission units) specialize in direct action operations such as hunting terrorists and rescuing hostages. In addition, since 2003, JSOC has also formally included the highly classified Mission Support Activity (MSA), which was imported from the Army for the express purpose of gathering intelligence streamlined for the needs of JSOC's special mission units. Previously known as the Intelligence Support Activity (ISA), or more recently as Gray Fox and Intrepid Spear (its name changes regularly for security reasons), MSA has also reportedly conducted direct action missions in Somalia, Pakistan, and several other countries.[2]

From the beginning of his term in 2001, one of Secretary of Defense Donald Rumsfeld's chief priorities was to transform the military from a large conventional force built to face another superpower into a leaner and more flexible and agile force capable of fighting the less conventional conflicts that were dominating the post-Cold War period. Though his desire to expand special operations was part of that original overall goal, it received a huge boost when, at the beginning of the war in Afghanistan, the military's special operations units had to rely on CIA operatives to establish links to the Northern Alliance fighters. By all accounts, Rumsfeld was incensed at this lack of DOD control and was determined to build up his special operations capabilities to eliminate any future dependence on the CIA.

Over the next decade, that determination gradually led to significant increases in funding, personnel, and authority for SOF. At SOCOM's financial height, before budgetary pressures and the sequester kicked in, the Obama administration's FY2012 SOF budget request was $10.48 billion, roughly three times SOCOM's 2001 budget. Although it has decreased somewhat since then (the FY2012 budget request was $9.9 billion), most analysts, military and civilian alike, expect SOCOM to weather the belt-tightening period better than its conventional warfare colleagues. In terms of personnel, SOCOM has grown from 38,000 in 2001 to approximately 66,000 in early 2014, a 73 percent increase.[3]

In March 2004, after an intensive bureaucratic struggle, Rumsfeld was successful in his campaign to install SOCOM as the leader of the war on terror, ahead of the conventional forces whose leaders he perceived as too tentative. President Bush signed the new Unified Command Plan 2004, which designated SOCOM as the "lead combatant commander for planning, synchronizing, and as directed, executing global operations" in the war on terror (although it did leave the geographic commanders in charge of counterterrorism operations in their own theaters). SOCOM "receives reviews, coordinates and prioritizes all DOD plans that support the global campaign against terror, and then makes recommendations to the Joint Staff regarding force and resource allocations to meet global requirements."[4] This increase in SOCOM's institutional authority coincided with Rumsfeld's signing a secret order, the Al Qaeda Network Execute Order (AQN ExOrd), which gave JSOC broad new operational authority to conduct offensive strikes against al Qaeda in 15 to 20 countries, including Syria, Pakistan, Iran, the Philippines, and Somalia.[5]

An amendment to the FY2005 National Defense Authorization Act represented a further step along SOCOM's road to independence as Congress granted its forces the authority, for the first time, to spend money for counter terrorism missions for such activities as paying informants, recruiting foreign paramilitary fighters, and purchasing equipment or other items from foreigners (so-called Section 1208 funds). Previously, only the CIA had been authorized to disburse such funds, meaning that SOF had had to rely on the CIA to provide the funds for various operations. Congress originally granted SOF spending authority of $25 million, and that amount has since increased to $50 million, currently authorized through FY2015.

For his part, President Obama was initially reluctant to rely on SOF operations in countries outside the war zones until SEAL Team 6 rescued the captain of the *Maersk Alabama* from pirates in the Indian Ocean in April 2009, just three months into his first term.[6] The rescue mission demonstrated just how effective JSOC units could be, but it also highlighted some of the bureaucratic impediments in utilizing them when the plan encountered a delay in deploying the SEAL team. That experience, combined with the ongoing terrorist threat, led the Obama administration to enact several significant changes in terms of how JSOC was tasked for missions. Most importantly, JSOC was given standing authority to use whatever military resources it needed anywhere in the world in pursuit of its counterterrorist mission, thereby avoiding sometimes costly delays while the military bureaucracy processed its requests for use of a submarine, for instance, for a particular mission. The leaders of JSOC, Lt. Gen. Stanley McChrystal from 2003–2008 and Vice Adm. William McRaven from 2008–2011, had been slowly developing this authority for several years; Obama extended it and formalized it into policy during the summer of 2009.[7]

The Obama administration also granted the geographic combatant commanders, as well as the theater commanders in Iraq and Afghanistan, the authority to use SOF personnel, including JSOC, in forming task forces in their regions (rather than only SOCOM having that authority). One former top JSOC commander reportedly described the changes implemented during 2009 in stark terms: "Obama gave JSOC unprecedented authority to track and kill terrorists, to 'mow the lawn.'"[8] Personnel and authority since 9/11, JSOC has also acquired an impressive operational infrastructure, including an equipment and technology acquisition branch, a research arm, and "its own drones, its own reconnaissance planes, even its own dedicated satellites in its own space unit."[9] SOCOM's, and specifically JSOC's, growth in size, scope and influence, together with McRaven's envisioned Global SOF Network, raise the critical questions of whether JSOC is conducting any covert operations and of the degree and adequacy of congressional oversight of its activities.

Covert Action v. "Traditional Military Activities"

The Congressional oversight requirements for covert action are set forth in the 1991 Intelligence Authorization Act, which codified two requirements for any covert action. First, there must be a written presidential finding stating that the action is important to U.S. national security, which cannot be issued retroactively. Second, the administration must notify the intelligence committees of the action as soon as possible after the finding has been issued and before the initiation of the operation, unless "extraordinary circumstances" exist, in which case the president must fully inform the committees "in a timely fashion."[10]

The other significant feature of the 1991 Intelligence Authorization Act is that, in response to the Reagan administration's use of the National Security Council staff to conduct covert action in connection with Iran-contra, it expressly applied the requirements to "any department, agency, or entity of the United States Government." In other words, Congress no longer assumed that only the CIA could or would conduct covert operations. This would seem to indicate that where SOF are conducting unacknowledged operations in countries with which the U.S. is not at war, they are, in fact, acting covertly and should follow the same regulations for presidential findings and congressional notification that the CIA does.

The law also included, however, a few designated exceptions to the definition of covert action. Most relevant here, "activities the primary purpose of which is to acquire intelligence" and "traditional . . . military activities or routine support to such activities" are deemed not to be covert action and thus do not require a presidential finding or congressional notification. While the act itself does not define "traditional military activities" (TMA), the conference committee report presenting the legislative history states that the phrase is meant to include actions preceding and related to hostilities which are either anticipated to involve (conventional) U.S. military forces or where such hostilities are ongoing, whether U.S. involvement in the action is made public or not, as well as any military action where the U.S. role is apparent or to be acknowledged publicly.[11]

According to the conferees, the determination of whether or not unacknowledged activities are TMA depends "in most cases" upon whether they constitute "routine support" to such an operation. The conferees (referencing the Senate Intelligence Committee's report) considered "routine support" to be unilateral U.S. activities to provide or arrange for logistical or other support for U.S. military forces in the event of a military operation that is intended to be publicly acknowledged (even if that operation ends up not taking place). Examples cited by the Senate committee included caching communications equipment or weapons in an area where such a future military operation is to take place, acquiring property to support an aspect of such an operation, and obtaining currency or documentation for use in such an operation. "Other-than-routine" activities that would constitute covert action if conducted on an unacknowledged basis include: recruiting or training foreign nationals to support a future U.S. military operation, organizing foreign nationals to take certain actions during a future U.S. military operation, and targeting public opinion in the country concerned.[12]

The interpretation of the TMA exception has caused considerable controversy as first Bush and then Obama have relied increasingly on SOF, particularly JSOC, in the war on terror. Unacknowledged operations conducted by SOF during wartime clearly do not require a presidential finding and congressional notification. Despite the conference committee's efforts at clarification, however, the definition still leaves a gray area around the interpretation of the word "anticipated." It is most commonly thought of in the literal sense of "preparing the battlefield," a phrase the Pentagon has since expanded to "operational preparation of the environment." The conference committee report of the 1991 law defines "anticipated" as meaning that the president and the secretary of defense have approved both the activities and operational planning for hostilities.[13] However, as Robert Chesney has pointed out, it is important to understand what "operational planning" means in the context of the military: "The military has developed a rather elaborate process for the production of operational plans, embodied in a decision-making system called the Joint Operation Planning Execution System (JOPES). . . . The nature of the process is to anticipate circumstances that, though potentially quite unlikely, might foreseeably result in an order from the President to use armed force."[14] In other words, the "operational planning" standard is not restrictive at all. Indeed, during the Bush administration, the Pentagon interpreted that language as including events taking place "years in advance" of any involvement of U.S. military forces.[15] But the Pentagon's broad interpretation of "anticipated" raises an obvious and important question: in conducting counterterrorism operations, when SOF execute an unacknowledged operation in a country where U.S. troops are not already present, how can they "foresee" that it is in anticipation of involvement of the regular armed forces later on, and thus not a covert action that requires a presidential finding and congressional notification (particularly if it is "years in advance")?

Critics contend that the Bush and Obama administrations have been eager to shift more covert activity from the CIA to the military precisely because they see the TMA loophole as giving them more of a free rein. As one military intelligence official characterized the Pentagon's view:

> Everything can be justified as a military operation versus a [covert] intelligence performed by the CIA, which has to be informed to Congress. . . . [Pentagon officials] were aware of that and they knew that, and they would exploit it at every turn. . . . They were preparing the battlefield, which was on all the PowerPoints: "Preparing the Battlefield."[16]

Even some U.S. government officials have conceded having difficulty in distinguishing between covert action and some military operations. In his January 2009 nomination hearings to become the director of National Intelligence (DNI), Dennis Blair responded to a written question from the Senate Select Committee on Intelligence (SSCI) asking how he differentiated between "covert action, military support operations, and operational preparation of the environment," by acknowledging that "[t]here is often not a bright line between these operations. . . ."[17] Similarly, in answer to the same question as part of his nomination to be CIA director, Panetta admitted that "the line between covert actions under Title 50 and clandestine military operations under Title 10 has blurred" and expressed his concern that although Title 10 operations were "practically identical" to Title 50 ones, the former "may not be subjected to the same oversight."[18]

Expanding Legal Interpretations

Beyond using the TMA exception to limit congressional reporting requirements on their ever-increasing use of SOF outside of war zones, both the Bush and Obama administrations have relied on two other strands of domestic legal authority for those actions as well, interpreting both in a broad vein reminiscent of their TMA interpretations: the 2001 Congressional Authorization to Use Military Force (AUMF) and the president's Article II power as commander-in-chief.

Both administrations have most frequently pointed to the 2001 congressional Authorization to Use Military Force (AUMF) as supporting their actions. That resolution authorizes the use of "all necessary and appropriate force" against those parties the president "determines planned, authorized, committed, or aided" the 9/11 attacks.[19] Both administrations have interpreted the AUMF as granting them virtually unlimited authority as long as they "determined" that a particular target has some connection to al Qaeda. As more time has passed since 9/11, however, and as the U.S. military has been used against terrorist groups ever more tangentially connected to al Qaeda, first Bush's and now Obama's interpretations have met with increasing skepticism. Critics have asked how some of those targeted, such as al Qaeda in the Arabian Peninsula (AQAP) or al Shabaab, neither of which existed in 2001, could credibly be said to have been connected to 9/11 (as stipulated by the AUMF).

In response to the growing criticism, the Obama administration soon expanded its interpretation of the AUMF as allowing the targeting of al Qaeda, Taliban, and "associated forces." According to then-Department of Defense General Counsel Jeh Johnson, associated forces include those organized armed groups that have entered the fight alongside al Qaeda and are a co-belligerent with al Qaeda in the hostilities against the United States and its coalition partners.[20] Despite continuing controversy about the breadth of the AUMF, Congress expressly affirmed the administration's interpretation (with respect to detention authority) in Section 1021 of the National Defense Authorization Act for FY2012.[21]

Critics both inside and outside of government continued to express concern and lobbied for various remedies, including repealing or reforming the AUMF. The administration's assertion that knowledge of what groups were included under the rubric "associated forces" was classified only further intensified the criticism. These concerns led to an extraordinary hearing in May 2013 as the Senate Armed Services Committee (SASC) took up the question of what to do about the AUMF. It became apparent not only that the SASC members had little idea of just how broadly the Obama administration was interpreting the AUMF, but also that they had never seen a list of associated forces (it was unclear even whether such a list actually existed). In answer to questions from several senators, the Pentagon representatives agreed that the AUMF authorized lethal force against al Qaeda's associated forces in countries as disparate as Mali, Syria, Libya, Yemen, and the Congo. Sen. John McCain (R, Arizona), generally a supporter of a muscular approach to foreign policy, voiced the discomfort felt by many of the senators present: "But the fact is that this authority . . . has grown way out of proportion and is no longer applicable to the conditions that prevailed" when Congress originally passed it in September 2001. McCain added, ". . . I must say I do not blame you because basically you have got carte blanche as to what you are doing throughout the world. . . ."[22]

Just one week later, in a speech at the National Defense University, Obama proclaimed his intent to get America off a "perpetual war footing" and continued: "We must define the nature and scope of this struggle, or else it will define us. . . . Unless we discipline our thinking, our definitions, our actions, we may be drawn into more wars we don't need to fight, or continue to grant presidents unbound powers." In that vein, Obama pledged to "refine, and ultimately repeal" the AUMF.[23]

And yet, Obama's pledge and legislators' concerns notwithstanding, serious negotiations between Congress and the White House to effect some improvement in the AUMF had not begun by early March 2014.[24] Differing opinions in Congress about what needs to be done, if anything, and the executive branch's historic tendency to not voluntarily give up power to the Congress will continue to render any change extremely difficult.

Even if it were possible to repeal the AUMF, however, doing so would be no guarantee against the expansive use of SOF outside of war zones for missions that would be called covert action if conducted by the CIA. Whenever there has been any question about the executive's authority to act in counterterrorism situations, both the Bush and Obama administrations have ultimately relied on the president's Article II power as commander-in-chief to act in the nation's self-defense in the face of an "imminent" threat. Obama's lawyers, however, secretly expanded the definition of "imminence" to the point of rendering it virtually meaningless. According to a leaked Department of Justice memo, their concept of "elongated imminence" "does not require the United States to have clear evidence that a specific attack on U.S. persons and interests will take place in the immediate future." Indeed, where a terrorist in question "has recently been involved in activities posing an imminent threat of violent attack" against the U.S., "and there is no evidence suggesting that he has renounced or abandoned such activities," his previous actions "would support the conclusion that the member is an imminent threat."[25] The administration's expanded conception of imminence did not go unnoticed. As Georgetown University Law Professor Rosa Brooks explained, "[a]ccording to the Obama administration, 'imminent' no longer means 'immediate,' and in fact the very *absence* of clear evidence indicating specific present or future attack plans becomes, paradoxically, the basis for assuming that attack may *perpetually* be 'imminent.'" (emphasis in original) [26] Micah Zenko of the Council on Foreign Relations made the same point in fewer words, calling the administration's new definition "completely nonsensical."[27]

Congressional Oversight

Another facet of the question of whether there is adequate oversight of unacknowledged military actions far from a recognized battlefield concerns the situation on Capitol Hill. Legally, the ultimate arbiters of what does and does not constitute covert action are the House and Senate intelligence committees, which exert a type of veto through their control of the intelligence authorization process. However, that authority is circumscribed in several ways. First, if it is a SOF mission (as opposed to a CIA one), funding authorization in the Senate shifts from the intelligence committee to the Armed Services Committee, creating a crucial split on the Senate side between the authority to determine whether it is a covert action and budgetary control. In the House, funding authorization remains with the House Permanent Select Committee on Intelligence (HPSCI) assuming, of course, that the operation has been disclosed to the committee. Since the Pentagon usually defines SOF missions as traditional military activities, it tends to send its funding requests directly to the armed services committees.

Second, the armed services committees have ultimate control over the intelligence authorization process in any case, since they must sign off on intelligence authorization bills before they go to the full House and Senate for a vote. Third, appropriations for a SOF mission would fall to the defense subcommittees of the House and Senate Appropriations Committees. Finally, appropriations for nearly all intelligence activities are included as a classified section of the defense appropriations bill anyway, meaning that the real control over the entire intelligence purse also lies with the appropriations defense subcommittees.

All of this divided jurisdiction inevitably leads to bureaucratic turf wars, which are only exacerbated by the intelligence and defense committees' respective senses of ownership of their particular issues. As the lead intelligence authorizers, the intelligence committees want to be able to consider programs in the context of the entire intelligence budget and believe they should be privy to information about SOF programs that look, see, and feel like covert action. The defense committees, on the other hand, view SOF actions as part and parcel of the military and thus under their exclusive jurisdiction.

In its report on the Intelligence Authorization Act for FY2010, the House intelligence committee noted "with concern" that

> . . . [i]n categorizing its clandestine activities, DOD frequently labels them as 'Operational Preparation of the Environment' (OPE) to distinguish particular operations as traditional military activities and not as intelligence functions. The Committee observes, though, that overuse of this term has made the distinction all but meaningless."[28]

The committee further complained that

> . . . DOD has shown a propensity to apply the OPE label where the slightest nexus of a theoretical, distant military operation might one day exist. Consequently, these activities often escape the scrutiny of the intelligence committees, and the congressional defense committees cannot be expected to exercise oversight outside of their jurisdiction.[29]

At some point (it is unclear exactly when) the Obama administration did begin briefing the "appropriate" committees on "all lethal action" taken outside of Iraq and Afghanistan (it is also unclear just how extensive that briefing is).[30] Those briefings notwithstanding, in March 2012 Congress began to require that the Pentagon provide the armed services committees with quarterly briefings on its counterterrorism operations.[31] While this step (and, indeed, the Obama administration's briefings) are an improvement, it fails to sufficiently close the existing oversight gaps. First, while it does give the armed services committees a more thorough view of military operations, the measure does nothing to fix the fact that the key overseers of covert action, the intelligence committees, do not have a full view of what the U.S. is doing covertly around the world. Second, in a major difference from CIA covert actions, the measure does not by law require presidential approval of the military operations. Third, it is doubtful that this reporting requirement includes the military's SAPs, particularly the waived SAPs.[32] Even Sen. Dianne Feinstein (D-Calif.), chair of the Senate intelligence committee, who has referred approvingly to members of her committee being briefed monthly by the CIA on its drone strikes, has considered creating a FISA-like court to oversee the use of armed drone strikes. In February 2013, Feinstein noted that it was "very hard" to oversee the CIA's drone program "because it is regarded as a covert activity, so when you see something that is wrong and you ask to be able to address it, you are told no."[33]

There have been small moves made toward more coordination between the intelligence and defense committees (a few members serving on both, for example), but the crux of the problem remains: as long as the Pentagon is conducting unacknowledged operations far from any recognized war zone but creatively defining them as traditional military activities, and as long as the defense committees accept that definition, the U.S. could well be engaged in covert actions that are not subject to adequate scrutiny and risk assessment outside the executive branch.[34]

The Obama administration reportedly also increased the requirements for White House, NSC, and Pentagon review of JSOC operations outside of war zones,[35] efforts that led to the signing of a classified presidential policy guidance (PPG) in May 2013.[36] Over a year in the drafting, the PPG ostensibly laid out the guidelines for lethal action outside of war zones, by both the CIA and JSOC, including both drone strikes and other covert actions. Unfortunately, the president's speech about the guidelines was less than clear on several issues, and leaks to reporters yielded different assessments of whether the PPG actually tightened or loosened drone targeting, for example.[37]

The lack of clarity issue aside, a pledge to increase scrutiny within the executive branch does not obviate the need for legislative oversight. For one thing, even if there is stricter internal review now, that would not necessarily carry over to a different administration. More importantly, however, the real question is whether there is sufficient review of the procedures and operations by people outside the circle of officials who have a vested interest in the program and/or the administration. That is the central importance of requiring congressional oversight of covert operations. That is not to say that congressional oversight is always done well or is without its own problems and constraints, but requiring administration officials to explain and justify their covert action decisions to the legislative branch does increase the chances that potential problems will be identified before it is too late.[38]

When counterterrorism operations are emphasized to the degree that they have been, it is all the more important to have people outside the inner circle asking tough questions. As we have already seen in Pakistan and Yemen, lethal operations that go wrong can dramatically erode support for the U.S. among the local population—that is, after all, where the battle against terrorism is really being fought.[39]

Convergence

A new characteristic of the U.S.'s unacknowledged operations abroad that has evolved since 9/11 renders the whole picture, and congressional attempts to oversee that picture, even more complex. In the immediate aftermath of 9/11, the CIA was asked to smooth the way into Afghanistan and to pursue al Qaeda and its affiliates around the world with a paramilitary division that, having been decimated by post-Cold War budget cuts, was a shadow of its former self. As a result, the Agency borrowed or "opconned" (assumed operational control over) members of SOF to help with the workload. Even while Rumsfeld was fighting fierce bureaucratic battles against the CIA to ensure JSOC took the lead in counterterrorism, there were reports of how well CIA and JSOC operators on the ground were working together (Kibbe 2012).

As the so-called war on terror expanded, despite some lingering turf battles, their operators and missions became increasingly integrated. In discussing some of the operations that have taken place under the 2004 ExOrd, for instance, senior U.S. officials have described some of the military missions as having "been conducted in close coordination with the CIA" and explained how military commandos have "acted in support of CIA-directed operations."[40] Similarly, the Obama administration's campaign in Yemen was described in June 2011 as being "led by" JSOC and "closely coordinated" with the CIA.[41]

In 2009, the close relationship that existed between CIA Director Leon Panetta and McChrystal's successor as JSOC commander, Vice Adm. William McRaven, yielded an unprecedented agreement setting out rules for joint missions.[42] By mid-2011, this convergence of CIA and JSOC operators was "so complete that U.S. officials ranging from congressional staffers to high-ranking CIA officers said they often [found] it difficult to distinguish agency [CIA] from military personnel."[43]

Meanwhile, by 2006 there were indications that policymakers were thinking about how to combine what they saw as the political advantages of the two organizations. Michael Vickers, then with the Center for Strategic and Budgetary Assessments but soon to become the assistant secretary of Defense for Special Operations and Low Intensity Conflict, emphasized in a congressional hearing the "critical" nature of "making full use of authorities in the Global War on Terror," "particularly the flexible detailing and exploitation of the CIA's Title 50 authority."[44] Vickers' statement implied that in deciding which forces to use in an unacknowledged operation, the weighing process involves more than just the domestic legal differences between CIA and JSOC covert action; that is, the more stringent and clear oversight requirements for the former as opposed to the latter. The policy decision also involves consideration of the potential international implications and the reality that in a situation where a covert operation goes wrong, the diplomatic fallout is likely to be worse if the military is involved than if it is a CIA action. Even though both constitute a violation of sovereignty (assuming neither has the prior approval of the foreign power), most countries have intelligence agencies that conduct espionage and covert action (albeit not at the same rate as the U.S.), so while there might well be some form of protest about a CIA covert action, most governments accept it as a reality and want to preserve their own room for similar action.[45] But if U.S. military personnel are caught conducting covert operations in countries where the U.S. is not at war, such activities could be interpreted as acts of war under international law but, at a minimum, could attract far more negative attention.[46] It is for precisely this reason that Pakistan's government essentially looks the other way at CIA drone strikes on its territory while refusing to allow JSOC strikes or personnel on the ground.

Thus, by detailing JSOC personnel to the CIA, policymakers could leverage the CIA's wider international room to maneuver to conduct JSOC operations on a more wide-ranging basis, albeit at the apparent cost of having to inform Congress. This "flexible detailing" means that in each situation, the administration can weigh the trade-off between the domestic and international ramifications. Notably, according to all accounts, this was the way the bin Laden raid was conducted on May 2, 2011. It was, in all respects, a JSOC operation, but was nominally run under the CIA's imprimatur because Pakistan was kept in the dark. One administration official described the bin Laden strike as the "proof of concept" for the administration's new strategy in the fight against terrorism, implying that more such operations will be in the offing.[47] Sure enough, just five months later, the drone attack that felled the charismatic imam (and American citizen), Anwar al-Awlaqi, in Yemen was conducted by a combination of JSOC and CIA drones operating under CIA authority. There has even been discussion of exploiting the "flexible detailing" of the CIA's authority as one of the options being considered for post-pullout Afghanistan: putting JSOC troops in the country under CIA control after 2014 so that Washington could claim that U.S. troops were no longer present.[48]

The problem, however, is that if an operation is really just a JSOC raid being run under the CIA's Title 50 covert action authority, as opposed to a CIA raid run with some help from JSOC personnel, then the distinction between the two blurs even further than it already has. And, in fact, the CIA's authority over the bin Laden raid seems to have been a bit contrived. Even CIA Director Panetta said that although he was formally in charge because the president had chosen to conduct it as a covert operation, ". . . I have to tell you that the real commander was Admiral McRaven because he was on site, and he was actually in charge of the military operation that went in and got bin Laden."[49] The problem with blurring or ignoring the differences between the CIA and JSOC is that the ostensible plausible deniability that is seen as the virtue of CIA operations becomes precariously thin. Moreover, while such detailing could improve oversight (assuming the CIA notifies Congress appropriately), it is unclear whether in such a situation the CIA would have sufficient insight into the operation's planning to be able to brief Congress adequately.[50]

Drone Policy Developments

The Obama administration's evolving drone policies provide an interesting case study of many of the issues laid out above. In early 2013, administration officials began to discuss phasing the CIA out of the drone war and shifting operations to the Pentagon. The reasons given included Obama's belief in the principle that the military should be responsible for taking direct lethal action even outside traditional war zones and the desire to re-focus the CIA on intelligence collection and analysis, which many felt had received short shrift as the agency devoted more and more resources to counterterrorism operations. Many observers applauded the goal on the basis of the assumption that military operations would provide more public transparency. Others, however, noted that since the military's drone attacks are conducted by JSOC (not the regular Air Force), and given the existence of waived SAPs, it was entirely unclear, and possibly quite unlikely, that such a move would lead to increased transparency.

Obama's intention also raised the thorny problem of conducting drone strikes in Pakistan. The latter had long been in the CIA's purview as a result of the Pakistani government's insistence that the U.S. military have no presence on its soil (or in its airspace). So, turning potential future Pakistan strikes over to JSOC does not appear to be an option. But neither does the administration seem ready to give up on being able to conduct future strikes in Pakistan, even if it has cut back on them. During negotiations in early 2014, when Afghan President Hamid Karzai remained unwilling to allow any U.S. troops to stay in Afghanistan beyond 2014, there were reports of U.S. officials making contingency plans to use air bases in Central Asia from which the CIA could conduct future Pakistani strikes (even if the drones are CIA, they still need military protection).[51] In recognition of the Pakistan problem, the classified policy guidance on drone rules issued in May 2013 reportedly established a "preference" for military-run drone strikes, but did allow for a continuing CIA role.[52]

Beyond Pakistan, though, the administration's intention to shift drones from the CIA to JSOC faced other obstacles as well. One was the question of which drone program was the most effective. When the Obama administration first decided in 2009 to use airstrikes in Yemen against the rising al Qaeda in the Arabian Peninsula (AQAP), the White House put JSOC firmly in charge. Two years later, however, JSOC's record included several instances of killing the wrong people, incurring civilian casualties, leaving behind shrapnel with U.S. military markings, and lots of scathing news reports. Eventually, the CIA began flying missions in Yemen as well from a secret new base in Saudi Arabia.[53] When Obama's intention to move all drones over to JSOC became clear in early 2013, many counterterrorism officials were still unsure the capability gap between the two agencies had been closed. Sen. Feinstein voiced similar concerns, saying she had seen the CIA "exercise patience and discretion specifically to prevent collateral damage" and that she "would really have to be convinced that the military would carry it out that well."[54] Those concerns still seemed pertinent after a JSOC strike in Yemen in December 2013 hit a wedding convoy. Although the U.S. claimed that all 12 people killed were militants, a Human Rights Watch investigation said the evidence indicated "some, if not all those killed and wounded were civilians."[55]

The administration's plan to shift drone strikes from the CIA to JSOC received another blow when several members of the House and Senate appropriations committees (it is unclear exactly which members) inserted wording into a classified annex to the federal budget approved in January

2014 that restricted the use of any funding to transfer drones or the authority to carry out drone strikes from the CIA to the Pentagon. The unusually direct move to exert control over such a sensitive national security program appeared to signal an intensification of the intra-congressional turf battle described above. The intelligence and armed services committees seem to be facing off with an eye toward controlling jurisdiction over armed drone operations in the future. It has been largely the Senate intelligence committee, and Feinstein in particular, that has focused on the reports of the CIA having better targeting success and incurring lower collateral damage. The armed services committees have largely backed the administration's plan and were furious at the appropriators' move.[56]

A few weeks later, the chairman of the Senate Armed Services Committee, Sen. Carl Levin (D, Michigan), attempted to hold a joint classified hearing with the Senate intelligence committee, intending to bring in both CIA and Pentagon officials to discuss the drone issue with both committees at the same time. The White House balked, however, at allowing CIA officials to testify about classified CIA programs in front of the 26 senators and 62 House members who sit on the armed services committees. The White House refused to issue the necessary security clearances for the members and instructed the CIA not to appear at the hearing. Moreover, few of the members of the intelligence committee attended the hearing either.[57]

Yet another complicating factor is the CIA's own bureaucratic imperative to hold on to an operational responsibility for which it has spent more than a decade developing expertise. Although there are many within the Agency (in addition to outside analysts) who are uncomfortable with the evolution of the Agency's role as an operator of large-scale lethal operations, the chief of the CIA's Counterterrorism Center, who has led its drone operations for the past seven years, is reportedly "fiercely opposed to giving up the agency's role."[58]

By late 2013, Obama's plan to shift drone strikes to the military had made little headway. As Rep. Adam Schiff (D, California) noted, the administration's goal of getting the CIA out of drone strike operations was "proving difficult to accomplish," and even if it happened, it would not entail a clean break. Indeed, Pentagon and CIA officials were engaged in talks aimed at "finding a way to merge key aspects of the CIA's drone operations with those of JSOC, so that both sides are deeply and simultaneously involved in nearly every strike," using a "find, fix and finish" process that features seamless cooperation and robust integration between CIA and DOD.[59]

Conclusion

It is clear that the current law governing congressional notification and oversight of covert action needs to be updated. It was written in 1991, so its authors could not have foreseen how the issue would change in the ensuing 20 years, in terms of actors (with the growth of SOF),[60] issues (with the rise of terrorism), and technology (with the advent of drones and advances in intelligence collection). Whether by updating the guidelines for the TMA exception to close what has become an obviously large loophole or by defining new categories of unacknowledged operations with similar reporting requirements, no matter the agency involved, Congress needs to be more involved in overseeing these operations and making sure the risks involved have been duly considered. The real problem is that doing so will involve negotiating several cross-cutting political battles: Congress against the White House, the intelligence agencies and the Pentagon; the intelligence and armed services committees against each other; and, to some lingering degree, the CIA against JSOC. It is hard to be optimistic.

Notes

1. 50 U.S.C. § 3093.

2. Marc Ambinder and D. B. Grady, *The Command: Deep Inside the President's Secret Army* (New Jersey: John Wiley & Sons, Inc., 2012): 883–907.

3. U.S. Special Operations Command, *Fact Book 2014* (Tampa, FL: USSOCOM, 2014), p. 12, available at: http://www.socom.mil/news/documents/ussocom_fact _book_2014.pdf (February 25, 2014).

4. U.S. Special Operations Command, About USSOCOM, available at: http:// www.socom.mil/Pages/AboutUSSOCOM.aspx (February 25, 2014).

5. Marc Ambinder, "Then Came 'Geronimo,'" *National Journal* (May 7, 2011); Jeremy Scahill, *Dirty Wars: The World is a Battlefield* (New York: Nation, 2013).

6. Ambinder, "Then Came 'Geronimo.'"

7. Marc Ambinder, "Obama Gives Commanders Wide Berth for Secret Warfare," *The Atlantic* (May 25, 2010), available at: http://www.theatlantic.com /politics/archive/2010/05/obama-gives-commanders-wide-berth-for-secret-warf are/57202/ (February 25, 2014); Jennifer D. Kibbe, "Conducting Shadow Wars" *Journal of National Security Law & Policy* 5(2012): 373–292.

8. Quoted in Ambinder, "Then Came 'Geronimo.'"

9. Priest and Arkin, *Top Secret America*, p. 225.

10. 50 U.S.C. § 3093.

11. H.R. Conf. Rep. No. 166, 102d Cong., 1st Sess., reprinted in 137 *Congressional Record*, No. 115, H5904-06 (daily ed. July 25, 1991), p. 5905–5906.

12. U.S. Senate, Senate Select Committee on Intelligence, *Authorizing Appropriations for Fiscal Year 1991 for the Intelligence Activities of the U.S. Government (accompanying S. 1325)* (S. Rept. 102-85). June 19, 1991; Jennifer D. Kibbe, "Covert Action, Pentagon-style," in Loch Johson (ed.), *The Oxford Handbook on National Security Intelligence* (New York: Oxford University Press, 2010), pp. 569–586.

13. H.R. Conf. Rep. No. 166, 102d Cong., 1st Sess.

14. Robert Chesney, "Military-Intelligence Convergence and the Law of the Title10/Title 50 Debate," *Journal of National Security Law and Policy* 5 (2012): 599–600.

15. Jennifer D. Kibbe, "The Rise of the Shadow Warriors." *Foreign Affairs* 83 (March/April 2004): 102–115; Kibbe, "The Military, the CIA and America's Shadow Wars."

16. Quoted in Jeremy Scahill, "The Secret US War in Pakistan," *The Nation* (December 7, 2009); Kibbe, "Conducting Shadow Wars."

17. U.S. Senate Select Committee on Intelligence, *Questions for the Record for Admiral Dennis Blair upon Nomination to be Director of National Intelligence, Select Committee on Intelligence* (January 22, 2009), p. 15.

18. U.S. Senate Select Committee on Intelligence. *Questions for the Record, Nomination of the Honorable Leon E. Panetta to be Director, Central Intelligence Agency*, available at: http://intelligence.senate.gov/090205/panetta_post.pdf (accessed February 18, 2014); Kibbe, "Conducting Shadow Wars."

19. Authorization to Use Military Force, P.L. 107-40, 115 Stat. 224 (2001) [S.J. Res. 23].

20. Hon. Jeh Charles Johnson, General Counsel, U.S. Department of Defense, "The Conflict Against Al Qaeda and its Affiliates: How Will It End?," Speech Before the Oxford Union, November 30, 2012, available at http://www.lawfareblog.com/2012/11/jeh-johnson-speech-at-the-oxford-union/ (February 15, 2014).

21. "National Defense Authorization Act for Fiscal Year 2012," Public Law 112-81, Sec. 1021, December 31, 2011.

22. U.S. Senate, Committee on Armed Services, *Hearing to Receive Testimony on the Law of Armed Conflict, the Use of Military Force, and the 2001 Authorization for Use of Military Force*, May 16, 2013, p. 16.

23. President Barack Obama, Remarks by the President at the National Defense University (May 23, 2013).

24. Michael Hirsh and James Oliphant, "Obama Will Never End the War on Terror," *National Journal* (February 27, 2014).

25. U.S. Department of Justice White Paper, *Lawfulness of a Lethal Operation Directed against a U.S. Citizen Who is a Senior Operational Leader of Al-Qai'da or an Associated Force*

26. Rosa Brooks, *The Constitutional and Counterterrorism Implications of Targeted Killing*, Testimony Before the Senate Judiciary Subcommittee on the Constitution, Civil Rights, and Human Rights (April 23, 2013), p. 13.

27. Jonathan S. Landay, "Leaked U.S. Justification for Drone Killings Assailed as Rewriting Definition of 'Imminent Threat,'" *McClatchy Newspapers* (February 5, 2013).

28. U.S. House of Representatives, *Intelligence Authorization Act for Fiscal Year 2010 (accompanying H.R. 2701)* (H. Rept. 111–186), June 26, 2009, p. 48.

29. Ibid., p. 49; Kibbe, "Conducting Shadow Wars."

30. Barack Obama, "Remarks by the President at the National Defense University," National Defense University, Washington D.C. (May 23, 2013), available at: http://www.whitehouse.gov/the-press-office/2013/05/23/remarks-president-national-defense-university (accessed February 15, 2014).

31. Craig Whitlock, "Lawmaker Wants Military to Promptly Alert Congress about Drone Strikes," *Washington Post* (May 8, 2013).

32. Kibbe, "The Military, the CIA and America's Shadow Wars."

33. "Sens. Feinstein, Leahy Push for Court Oversight of Armed Drone Strikes," *The Hill* (February 10, 2013).

34. Kibbe, "The Military, the CIA and America's Shadow Wars."

35. Ambinder, "Obama Gives Commanders Wide Berth for Secret Warfare"; Karen DeYoung and Greg Jaffe, "U.S. 'Secret War' Expands Globally as Special Operations Forces Take Larger Role," *Washington Post* (June 4, 2010); Mazzetti, "US Is Said to Expand Secret Actions in Mideast."

36. Peter Baker, "In Terror Shift, Obama Took Long Path," *New York Times* (May 27, 2013).

37. Micah Zenko, "Confront and Confuse," *Foreign Policy National Security* (May 28, 2013), available at: http://www.foreignpolicy.com/articles/2013/05/28/confront_and_confuse_obama_drone_speech (January 18, 2014); Kibbe, "The Military, the CIA and America's Shadow Wars."

38. Jennifer D. Kibbe, "Congressional Oversight of Intelligence: Is the Solution Part of the Problem?" *Intelligence and National Security* 25 (2010): 30; Amy Zegart, "The Domestic Politics of Irrational Intelligence Oversight," *Political Science Quarterly* 126 (2011): 1–25.

39. Kibbe, "Conducting Shadow Wars."

40. Eric Schmitt and Mark Mazzetti, "Secret Order Lets US Raid Al Qaeda," *New York Times* (November 9, 2008).

41. Mark Mazzetti, "U.S. Is Intensifying a Secret Campaign of Yemen Airstrikes," *New York Times* (June 8, 2011); Kibbe, "Conducting Shadow Wars."

42. Kibbe, "Conducting Shadow Wars."

43. Greg Miller and Julie Tate, "CIA Shifts Focus to Killing Targets," *Washington Post* (September 1, 2011).

44. U.S. House, *Assessing U.S. Special Operations Command's Missions and Roles: Hearing before the Subcommittee on Terrorism, Unconventional Threats and Capabilities Subcommittee of the House Committee on Armed Services, US House of Representatives.* 109th Cong., 2d Sess. (June 29, 2006).

45. Col. Kathryn Stone, *"All Necessary Means" —Employing CIA Operatives in a Warfighting Role alongside Special Operations Forces*, U.S. Army War College Strategy Research Project (July 4, 2003).

46. Kibbe, "The Rise of the Shadow Warriors"; Kibbe, "Conducting Shadow Wars."

47. Siobhan Gorman and Julian E. Barnes, "Spy, Military Ties Aided bin Laden Raid," *Wall Street Journal* (May 23, 2011).

48. Kimberly Dozier, "Building a Network to Hit Militants," *Associated Press* (January 5, 2011).

49. Leon Panetta, "Interview with Leon Panetta," *PBS Newshour* (26, May 3, 2011).

50. Kibbe, "The Military, the CIA and America's Shadow Wars."

51. Ken Dilanian and David S. Cloud, "U.S. Seeks New Bases for Drones," *Los Angeles Times* (February 16, 2014).

52. Peter Baker, "Pivoting from a War Footing, Obama Acts to Curtail Drones," *Washington Post* (May 23, 2013).

53. Greg Miller, "Obama's New Drone Policy Leaves Room for CIA Role," *Washington Post* (May 25, 2013).

54. Miller, "Obama's New Drone Policy Leaves Room for CIA Role."

55. Greg Miller, Report: Deadly Drone Strike in Yemen Failed to Comply with Obama's Rules to Protect Civilians," *Washington Post* (February 20, 2014).

56. Eric Schmitt, "Congress Restricts Drones Program Shift," *New York Times* (January 16, 2014).

57. Ken Dilanian, "Sen. Levin's Bid to Boost Drone Oversight Falters in Congress," *Los Angeles Times* (February 12, 2014).

58. Greg Miller, "CIA Remains behind Most Drone Strikes, Despite Effort to Shift Campaign to Defense," *Washington Post* (November 25, 2013).

59. Miller, "CIA Remains behind Most Drone Strikes."

60. A further complicating factor that needs to be accounted for in any updating of the covert action legislation is the increasing role being played by private contractors. See Laura A. Dickinson, "Outsourcing Covert Activities," *Journal of National Security Law & Policy* 5 (2012): 521–537.

CHAPTER TWELVE

From Cold War to Long War to Gray War

Covert Action in U.S. Legal Context

James E. Baker

Introduction

COVERT ACTION HAS HISTORICALLY INCLUDED activities on a continuum from diplomacy to acts of war undertaken to conceal the national footprint or plausibly permit deniability.[1] As a result, these activities are undertaken without the ordinary mechanisms of internal policy preview and external validation. Thus, while the law pertaining to covert action permits and prohibits, most of all it regulates its use by creating substantive thresholds triggering statutory and executive processes for authorizing and then appraising covert activities. These processes are intended to ensure that the means to effect covert actions are lawful, but also to ensure that the policy choices are sound and that the gain from action exceeds the pain, both in the short and long run.

Although covert action has historically played a small part in the intelligence budget and as an intelligence function, it has played a disproportionate role in defining public perceptions of the intelligence instrument, in shaping congressional oversight, and in policy impact.[2] The same is true with the development of U.S. intelligence law. This was true during the

Cold War, and it has proven true during the "Long War" to counterterrorism in the wake of the September 11th attacks. And it will remain true going forward in what one might describe as the "Gray War," the effort to counter terrorism and the proliferation of weapons of mass destruction (WMD) capabilities to state and non-state actors. These threats command response from all the instruments of national security power, including covert action. Knowledge of law and legal policy regarding covert action is therefore imperative to those who wield national security power as well as those who would appraise their efforts.

This chapter is divided into two sections. The first section analyzes five core aspects of covert action in the U.S. legal context. Part A examines the relevant constitutional authorities of the president and Congress. Part B addresses the statutory context for covert action, taking into account the most recent changes in the United States Code. Part C explores the intricacies of executive process and review. Part D then looks at the sources of legal permits and constraints on covert action. Finally, Part E illuminates the practical application of national security law.

The second section raises three legal policy questions: (1) Is the statutory definition of "covert action" effective as a legal threshold to identify those activities whose risks, consequences, and benefits warrant covert review, approval, and appraisal? (Part A); (2) Is the measure of executive preview and review adequate to address the policy and legal risks inherent in covert action, as well as those activities that bear comparable risks? (Part B); and (3), Are the existing mechanisms for external appraisal of covert action effective? (Part C).

I. Legal Framework—A Thumbnail Sketch

Analysis of U.S. covert action law, like national security law generally, starts with the Constitution. This reflects the fact that the president's authority in this area derives directly from the Constitution. It also reflects the fact that many legal issues that arise in this area involve the separation of powers between the political branches, including matters of notification and reporting as well as the extent to which Congress can otherwise delimit presidential assertions of constitutional authority.

Beyond the Constitution, the most important law in this area is found in the National Security Act of 1947, as amended, and in Executive Directives, including Executive Orders 12333 and 13470. However, as discussed below, the fact that an action is taken under covert action authority does not exempt that action from U.S. law. Therefore, Title 18, Title 50, and Title 10, among other United States Code provisions, are also relevant to the legal regulation of covert action in context. So too, because covert action necessarily engages all the intelligence functions—collection, analysis and dissemination, counterintelligence, and potentially liaison. One cannot execute an effective action without first collecting and analyzing the intelligence upon which it is based. Neither can one hope to preserve deniability without the prudent exercise of counterintelligence capacity. Thus, a practitioner in this field requires a broad-based understanding of the intelligence mechanism.

A. Constitutional Context

The president's intelligence powers are found in the president's enumerated constitutional authority as commander-in-chief and chief executive and in the area of foreign affairs. Constitutional authority is also derived or implied from these enumerated authorities. For example, the word "intelligence" is not referenced in the text of the Constitution. However, because the president could not effectively exercise his enumerated authorities without intelligence capacity, presidential lawyers and most scholars imply or derive an intelligence authority from Article II's enumerated powers as well as the executive authority generally found in Article II.

Authority is also implied from long-standing executive practice as well as in those few Supreme Court decisions that address intelligence.[3] At least in times of war, the Supreme Court has recognized this inherent authority, including the actual conduct of intelligence operations. In the case of *Totten*, for example, the Court held that as commander-in-chief, President Lincoln had authority to "employ secret agents to enter the rebel lines and obtain information respecting the strength, resources, and movements of the enemy."[4] The fact that an 1876 case is still good law demonstrates that Courts are hesitant if not loath to resolve differences of constitutional view where the intelligence function is concerned.

A recurring question is just how far the president's intelligence authority extends in authorizing covert action and keeping it secret. The extent to which the president's inherent authority is magnified as commander-in-chief in times of conflict is a matter of debate. However, there is surely a wartime "gloss" that attaches to the exercise of executive authority during conflict overseas. There is a wider debate on whether, or how, such a gloss applies at home. This was the focus of the *Youngstown* decision as well as the more recent cases regarding detainees.[5] Whether such a gloss might also apply in contexts like the external gray of counterterrorism and nonproliferation operations will be a recurring question in the years ahead.

Congress's authority over the intelligence function is found in its funding power, its general legislative power, as well as the broad range of enumerated authorities it possesses over national defense. In parallel fashion to the president, Congress also derives or implies additional authority that is "necessary and proper" to exercise its legislative functions. Nonetheless, Congress has recognized the president's special role and authority with respect to covert action. The National Security Act of 1947, as amended, for example, requires the president to approve covert action in writing and authorizes the CIA to "perform such other functions and duties related to intelligence affecting the national security" a phrase understood since 1947 to include covert action.[6] Moreover, the Act provides for congressional notification of covert action as opposed to consultation or approval. However, in constitutional practice, strong legislative resistance can shape or even lead to the termination of a covert action or program. Congress's leverage increases where a program requires the authorization and appropriation of new money as opposed to presidential authorization to spend existing funds.

B. Statutory Context

Definition

The National Security Act of 1947, as amended, remains the bedrock of United States intelligence laws, including in the area of covert action. This Act, in some manner or another, has served as statutory authorization for covert activity since 1947.[7] However, it was not until 1991, in the wake of the Iran-Contra affair, that Congress defined covert action in the Intelligence Authorization Act of 1991.[8] "Covert action" is defined as:

> an activity or activities of the United States Government to influence political, economic, or military conditions abroad, where it is intended that the role of the United States Government will not be apparent or acknowledged publicly. . . .[9]

It is also defined by what it is not. Through negative definition, covert action does not include:

(1) activities the primary purpose of which is to acquire intelligence, traditional counterintelligence activities, traditional activities to improve or maintain the operational security of United States Government programs, or administrative activities;

(2) traditional diplomatic or military activities or routine support to such activities;

(3) traditional law enforcement activities conducted by United States Government law enforcement agencies or routine support to such activities; or,

(4) activities to provide routine support to the overt activities (other than activities described in paragraph (1), (2), or (3)) of other United States Government agencies abroad.[10]

This definition was intended to capture activities that Congress determined should be channeled through a particularized process of executive authorization and congressional notification because of the nature of and risk inherent to the activities involved. The definition was also intended to capture existing practice. The legislative history states: "It is not intended that the new definition exclude activities which were heretofore understood to be covert actions, nor to include activities not heretofore understood to be covert actions."[11] As a result, historical practice is particularly relevant to legal interpretation. The legislative history and practice are also particularly important in determining what, if any, activities are "traditional" and thus exempt from the definition's reach.[12]

Notably, the definition is act-based, not actor-based. This means that the law does not just apply to the Central Intelligence Agency, but also to the Department of Defense, the Federal Bureau of Investigation, and so on, provided the contemplated activity fits the positive definition of covert action and is not otherwise "traditional." However, identity of the agency involved is surely relevant in determining whether an activity is "traditional." For example, certain activities like raids might be "traditional" if undertaken by military actors in uniform during armed conflict but not if undertaken by non-attributable U.S. surrogates in peacetime.

Findings

Under the National Security Act, covert action must be authorized in the form of a finding signed by the president. This reflects the president's direct responsibility for covert action. It also reflects the law's requirement that the president find that, "an action is necessary to support identifiable foreign policy objectives of the United States and is important to the national security of the United States. . . ."[13] This is a low substantive threshold. It does not take much imagination to see how a counterterrorism, nonproliferation, or other national security endeavor might be "important to national security." That makes the procedural requirements of the law that much more important, as it is through a rigorous process that important substantive issues and differences may be identified, addressed, and mitigated.

Findings must be in writing "unless immediate action by the United States is required," in which case a contemporaneous notation of the president's decision shall be made and a written finding produced within 48 hours.[14] As a policy matter, this language addresses concerns about exigent circumstances. As a legal matter, it obviates the constitutional argument that Congress cannot impede the president's authority to respond to immediate security threats through imposition of a written process. Findings must also specify the Department or agencies authorized to fund or participate "in any significant way" in an action as well as specify whether the participation of third parties (for example, third countries or persons) is contemplated.[15] This language responds to the use of surrogates, like Brunei and the NSC staff, to circumvent CIA funding and reporting requirements during the Iran-Contra affair.

Reporting

The Act also requires the president to ensure that findings are reported to the intelligence committees "as soon as possible after such approval and before the initiation of the covert action. . . ."[16] The ordinary process of notification is in writing to the full committees. In practice, this means not only to the members but also designated staff with an oral briefing accompanying the underlying document. However, "to meet extraordinary circumstances affecting vital interests of the United States," the president may limit notification to the so-called Gang of Eight (the chairmen and vice chairmen of the congressional intelligence committees and the majority and minority leaders of each house of Congress) "and such other member or members of the congressional leadership as may be included by the President."[17] Exercise of this option requires a statement from the president indicating why the action in question warrants limited notification. The president may, of course, authorize notification to additional members of Congress, or staff, something between the full committee and Gang of Eight.

Finally, the Act implicitly authorizes the President to withhold notification altogether by stating that: "Whenever a finding is not reported pursuant to paragraph (1) or (2) of this section, the President shall fully inform the congressional intelligence committees in a timely fashion and shall provide a statement of the reasons for not giving prior notice."[18]

Memoranda of Notification. In addition to reporting findings, "significant change[s] in" or "significant undertaking[s] pursuant to a previously approved action," must be reported "in the same manner as findings are reported."[19] This language is implemented through presidential Memoranda of Notification (MONs), which supplement, amend, or clarify previously approved findings. Thus, it is in the form of a MON that the president authorizes significant undertakings and changes to existing findings. It follows that MONs are reported to Congress using one of the three mechanisms specified for reporting findings. The triggering threshold for significant undertakings or changes has been the subject of internal executive debate as well as debate with Congress and within Congress. The 1990–1991 legislative history gave two examples.

> This would occur when the President authorizes a change in the scope of a previously approved finding to authorize additional activities to occur. The second type of change specified in this subsection pertains to significant undertakings pursuant to a previously approved finding. This would occur when the President authorizes a significant activity under a previously approved finding without changing the scope of the finding concerned.[20]

However, in 2010, Congress amended the law to make the criteria for subsequent reporting explicit.[21] This suggests a difference of view in law exposed through practice between Congress and the Executive on when an MON, and thus additional congressional notification, was required. The legislative history is more direct. "There have nonetheless been serious disputes over the implementation of these practices—and over the meaning of the provisions on which they are based—with respect to notification regarding certain intelligence activities."[22] The law now states:

> In determining whether an activity constitutes a significant undertaking . . . the president shall consider whether the activity—
>
> (A) involves significant risk of loss of life;
> (B) requires an expansion of existing authorities, including authorities relating to research, development, or operations;
> (C) results in the expenditure of significant funds or other resources;
> (D) requires notification under section 3094 [funding of intelligence activities] of this title;
> (E) gives rise to a significant risk of disclosing intelligence sources and methods; or
> (F) presents a reasonably foreseeable risk of serious damage to the diplomatic relations of the United States if such activity were disclosed without authorization.[23]

Of course, these are some of the very issues a rigorous internal process of review should identify in any case.

Ongoing Activities. In addition to reporting findings and MONs authorizing significant undertakings or changes to existing findings, the Act includes a third reporting requirement. The president "shall ensure that the congressional intelligence committees are kept fully and currently informed of the intelligence activities of the United States, including any significant anticipated intelligence activity as required by this subchapter[,]" a term understood to include covert activities.[24] Likewise, the director of National Intelligence and the heads of all other government entities involved in covert action:

> To the extent consistent with due regard for the protection from unauthorized disclosure of classified information relating to sensitive intelligence sources and methods or other exceptionally sensitive matters . . . shall keep the congressional intelligence committees fully and currently informed of all covert actions which are the responsibility of, are engaged in by, or are carried out for or on behalf of, any department, agency, or entity of the United States Government, including significant failures. . . .[25]

These are important provisions. At the higher levels of the political branches, program initiation receives more attention and consideration than program administration. Policy level oversight also tends to focus on moments of crisis or failure and less on ensuring that programs are on track and in fact accomplishing what they were intended to achieve and in the manner contemplated and represented to the president. Moreover, if an activity is effective, or even if it is not, it is intended to influence events. As a result, when events are influenced, the Executive should assess those changes and consider whether policies and programs should change as well. This makes the process of internal Executive review all the more important, including the requirement contained in Executive Order 13470 that "the NSC shall. . . conduct a periodic review of ongoing covert action activities, including an evaluation of the effectiveness and consistency with current national policy of such activities and consistency with applicable legal requirements."[26]

Assessment. For a number of years, the National Security Act successfully served as an agreed-upon mechanism between branches for addressing covert action. The Act incorporated the ultimate constitutional positions of both branches (prior reporting and no reporting) without either side conceding ultimate authority. The Act left the political branches to work through the constitutional principles and tensions in an informal and contextual manner. In this way, the statute played an overlooked but important constitutional role by defining expectations and suggesting limits; that is, it set constitutional "rules of the road" between the president and Congress on the meaning and reporting requirements for covert action. Thus, while the president and Congress disagreed on an important point of law at the time of passage, they also agreed to disagree and work out accommodations. For example, when President Bush signed the 1991 Intelligence Authorization Act into law, he stated his constitutional view that he was not required to report findings in advance or at all, but in a side letter to the chairmen of the congressional intelligence committees undertook as a matter of practice not to withhold notification to Congress beyond a few days after signing a finding, understood on the Hill as within 48 hours.[27]

However, the public record reflects discord between the branches in the decade following the 9/11 attacks regarding the thresholds for authorizing and reporting covert action. This discord was manifest in the debate following the disclosure of the president's Terrorism Surveillance Program, which was not covert action, but was reported using Gang of Eight methodology.[28] As noted above, Congress in 2010 added detail to the law on the reporting threshold for MONs. It required notification to the full Committee when the president makes a limited notification. It also required the president to validate periodically the continuation of a limited notification. Each of these amendments was cast as a compromise in the legislative history, again signaling a need to resolve differences of view through practice.

Those who find national security advantage, or necessity, in preserving a limited notification mechanism or who favor the flexibility of a process where the president need not authorize every modification of a program should note that often, the enduring consequence of failing to keep the intelligence committees meaningfully informed is even more detailed reporting requirements.

C. Executive Process and Review

Public consideration of the Executive Branch intelligence process should start with Executive Order 13470, which amended Executive Order 12333. Executive Order 13470 designates the National Security Council as the highest Executive Branch entity for the review and direction of intelligence policies and activities.[29] With respect to "Covert Action and Other Sensitive Intelligence Operations," it further directs:

> The NSC shall consider and submit to the President a policy recommendation, including all dissents, on each proposed covert action. . . .[30]

The definition of "covert action" found in section 4(g)(b) of Executive Order 13470 is the same as that found in the National Security Act. Thus, the statutory definition is used as the Executive predicate to trigger specific processes of executive review.

Although these internal processes are generally classified, a number of prior disclosures indicate what a process of review might look like. In the wake of the Iran-Contra scandal, President Reagan issued and released NSDD-286, "Approval and Review of Special Activities," describing at a point in time a process of review beginning at the working group level and moving to the Deputies Committee and to the Principals Committee before concluding with the president.[31] The public record also reflects that President Clinton in establishing his National Security Council system directed that "the Attorney General shall be invited to attend meetings pertaining to his jurisdiction, including covert actions."[32]

Where the president has directed that a particular process of review occur, he must authorize any deviation from that process or otherwise delegate his authority to do so. Directed or not, the president should be informed when important or relevant views and perspectives are omitted from NSC consideration of covert action. Finally, the special relationship between the president and covert action is as evident in directive as it is in statute. While the U.S. role in a covert action may not be apparent or acknowledged publicly, lawful covert action may only be conducted with the written approval of the president. This observation should not be lost on intelligence officials who disagree with policy or commentators who disagree with the acts of commission or omission placed at the CIA's door rather than in the Situation Room or the Oval Office.

D. Legal Permits and Constraints

In addition to authorizing covert activities, the law—by which I mean the Constitution, statutes, and directives—imposes certain constraints on their conduct. Of course, much of the relevant law is found in classified presidential and executive directives (for example, Attorney General Guidelines and Intelligence Directives, which are referenced in Executive Order 13470).

Duty to Follow the Law

Under 50 U.S.C. § 3093 "[a] finding may not authorize any action that would violate the Constitution or any statute of the United States."[33] Therefore, contrary to popular perception, covert action does not allow the American government to violate domestic law or act extralegally. All covert activity must comply with U.S. law, including criminal law, unless the law is not applicable, perhaps because it exempts the government or an intelligence entity of the government. This constraint includes international law to the extent it is incorporated into U.S. law. For example, the law of armed conflict is found in, among other places, Section 2441 of Title 18 of the United States Code. Similarly, implementation into U.S. law of the United Nations Convention against Torture and Other Cruel, Inhuman, or Degrading Treatment or Punishment is through Section 2340A of Title 18 of the Code.[34]

The Law of Armed Conflict

The law of armed conflict (LOAC) with respect to both the resort to force as well as the means and methods of using force has become integral to the overt and covert use of lethal force against terrorists.[35] This was first evident when the United States placed the threat posed by Al-Qaeda into a LOAC paradigm in the late 1990s. It was at this point the United States government first publicly stated that its actions against Al-Qaeda were conducted in self-defense and anticipatory self-defense and that figures like Osama bin Laden were lawful military targets of attack. This LOAC paradigm is also evident in the president's instructions conveyed by CIA officers to certain Afghan "tribals" as paraphrased by the 9/11 Commission. The instructions reference some of the staples of the law of armed conflict that one might find on a military rules of engagement card, involving distinction, necessity, proportionality, and the humane treatment of prisoners. Specifically, the report noted:

> The United States preferred that Bin Laden and his lieutenants be captured, but if a successful capture operation was not feasible, the tribals were permitted to kill them. The instructions added that the tribals must avoid killing others unnecessarily and must not kill or abuse Bin Ladin or his lieutenant if they surrendered.[36]

Subsequent administrations embraced this LOAC analysis and built upon the 1990s framework, making the law of armed conflict even more apparent as both a permit and a constraint on the conduct of covert action in the years after September 11th.

The application of the LOAC might now be intuitive in the context of the armed conflicts in Iraq and Afghanistan. However, at least two factors have magnified the impact and role of this law on the conduct of covert action generally. The first has been the advent of the UAV, or drone, as a weapons platform that can be remotely piloted and covertly reach almost any target location in the world. The second is the determination that the United States is engaged in ongoing hostilities with armed groups of

Al-Qaeda and its allied or associated forces; that is, the United States is engaged in an armed conflict outside the operational theaters of Afghanistan. This means that the president, and others, could authorize the resort to overt, secret, and covert force not just on an episodic basis in anticipation of and against imminent threats (anticipatory self-defense), but in the course of ongoing hostilities. As such, force could be used on a continuing basis, without an independent decision to resort to force, against those having the status of lawful or unlawful combatants or persons engaged in direct participation in hostilities (DPH). Of course, one challenge in the counterterrorism context is to determine who in fact has the status of a lawful or unlawful combatant or as a direct participant in hostilities. The United States government has not publicly defined the meaning of "DPH" in the counterterrorism context or, for that matter, any other context. This leaves it to others to assert and define its meaning in customary international law.

This posture was, of course, reinforced by the Joint Resolution Authorization for Use of Military Force (AUMF) in the wake of the September 11th attacks. The AUMF, as a matter of U.S. domestic law, authorizes the president

> to use all necessary and appropriate force against those nations, organizations, or persons he determines planned, authorized, committed, or aided the terrorist attacks that occurred on September 11, 2001, or harbored such organizations or persons, in order to prevent any future acts of international terrorism against the United States by such persons or organizations.[37]

The authorization came without geographic limitation. The resolution has also been interpreted to apply to elements and groups associated with Al-Qaeda not just at the time of the September 11th attacks, but anyone subsequently aligned with the Al-Qaeda objectives. Nor is there an apparent or declared distinction between overt and covert force. Thus, in covert context, the president's inherent authority to employ the law of armed conflict in the defense of the United States is reinforced by Congress's express authorization to use "all necessary and appropriate force."

Due Process

The targeting of U.S. persons in the context of counter-terrorism operations has also raised the potential applicability of the due process clause to actions that might entail the targeting of U.S. persons. A Department of Justice (DOJ) draft White Paper, "Lawfulness of a Lethal Operation Directed against a U.S. Citizen Who is a Senior Operational Leader of

Al-Qa'ida or an Associated Force," dated November 8, 2011, and made public in February 2013, states: "The Department assumes that the rights afforded by Fifth Amendment's Due Process Clause as well as the Fourth Amendment attach to a U.S. citizen even while he is abroad."[38] The application of the Bill of Rights to certain covert actions is not altogether a novel one. In the context of rendition, for example, the United States has long considered the limitations, if any, imposed by the Fifth Amendment on U.S. conduct. In some contexts, the Courts have done so as well (United States v. Yunis) or chosen not to do so on the basis that the operation was secret (El-Masri v. United States).[39]

What is novel is the DOJ's qualified application of the due process clause to targeted killing.[40] However, it is not clear whether the U.S. government has definitively applied this clause as opposed to applying it on a qualified or cautionary basis. Nor is it evident that the government has applied the clause in a manner that meaningfully moves beyond the ordinary process of military targeting decision. In the same White Paper, for example, the DOJ stated:

> [T]he "realities" of the conflict and the weight of the government's interest in protecting its citizens from an imminent attack are such that the Constitution would not require the government to provide further process to such a U.S. citizen before using lethal force.[41] Nonetheless, consideration of the due process clause, and related law, is now integrated in U.S. legal process as a potential contextual constraint.

Assassination Prohibition

Additional constraints are found in executive orders, most notably the prohibition on assassination originally promulgated by President Ford in 1976, and currently in force pursuant to Executive Order 12333, as amended by Executive Order 13470.[42] This order continues in force, subject like other executive orders to classified presidential interpretation, amendment, or suspension. However, what is acknowledged publicly is that the targeting of legitimate military targets consistent with the law of armed conflict is not considered "assassination" under the Executive Order. As former National Security Advisor Samuel Berger testified before the 9/11 Commission with respect to the (overt) August 1998 missile strikes in Afghanistan:

> [W]e received rulings in the Department of Justice—[that the] executive order [did] not prohibit our ability—prohibit our efforts to try to kill Bin Laden because it did not apply to situations in which you are acting in

self-defense or you're acting against command and control targets against an enemy, which he certainly was.[43]

As evidenced by parallel executive statements, similar conclusions were reached at the time of the 1986 U.S. air strikes on Tripoli, which included a compound and perhaps a tent used by Colonel Qaddafi, and in April 2003 when the United States targeted buildings where Saddam Hussein was thought to be located.

Domestic Impact/Blow-Back

In addition, "[n]o covert action may be conducted which is intended to influence United States political processes, public opinion, policies, or media."[44] In the vernacular of intelligence law, the prospect of U.S. covert propaganda influencing the U.S. media and public is known as "blow-back," an enhanced risk in a global world with 24/7 Internet news cycles. As criminal lawyers will recognize, the critical term in the prohibition is "intended," defining the restriction as one of specific intent. Of course, lawyers might find that the United States should be deemed to have intended something that is a predictable and logical consequence of its actions.

Regardless of legal argument, as a matter of legal policy, decision makers must evaluate the consequences of U.S. covert activities "blowing-back" even where such a result is not intended. United States policy and public understanding of U.S. policy is not well served if it is based on false or false-flagged information. To pick a safe Cold War example, the covert recruitment and insertion of a "rebel force" may lead unwitting policy observers to make unfounded conclusions about the strength of the opposition to a regime if they are unaware of the force's pedigree. Likewise, were the United States to covertly place favorable news articles in the foreign press, a historical mechanism for disseminating propaganda during the Cold War, the potential for blow-back might hinge on whether the material was disseminated in English and/or in a forum likely to be covered by the U.S. media. One can imagine the permutations that might arise in the context of the Internet, social media, and a 24-hour news cycle expectant of immediate response.

II. Legal Policy, Context, and Issues

During the Cold War, the United States (and the Soviet Union) engaged in multiple covert actions, a number of which were "overt-covert actions," such as landing at the Bay of Pigs, supplying the Contras, and providing support to the Afghan Mujahedeen.[45] Such "covert" mechanisms allowed proxies to engage in hot war, while the great power conflict remained "cold." Resort to covert action also reflected the strategic view that the threat posed by communism warranted resort to all the instruments of national policy. Consider the words of the 1954 Doolittle Committee report to President Eisenhower on CIA covert activities:

> It is now clear that we are facing an implacable enemy whose avowed objective is world domination by whatever means at whatever cost. . . . There are no rules in such a game. Hitherto acceptable norms of human conduct do not apply.[46]

This past may be prologue in the 21st century. Covert action is well suited to address the threats of terrorism, proliferation, and cyber-attack.

In a conflict with terrorists intent on conducting acts of terrorism with high intensity consequences, the United States should be expected to utilize all available national security instruments. Covert action is well suited to address a non-state opponent acting outside the laws of armed conflict without a particular territory, base, or chain of command, including in territories whose governments are unable or unwilling to effectively intervene. This is evident whether U.S. counterterrorism activities are viewed within the prism of armed conflict and a Long War or as something more akin to a Gray War between war and peace. Consider the 2008 warning of then CIA Director Michael Hayden, which echoed that of the Doolittle Committee:

> Never before have we faced an enemy so completely committed to our destruction and so completely irresponsible with human life. Al-Qa'ida is willing to sacrifice both its own operatives and the Muslims for whom it professes to fight. This enemy, unprecedented in our history, requires a response that also has no model in our past.[47]

However, because counterterrorism is also a contest between values—including legal values—and because this contest requires intelligence alliance, the when, why, where, and how of covert action takes on added importance.

Covert action also offers a range of tools to disrupt proliferation supply chains. Indeed, where non-state and state access to and control of weapons of mass destruction is the present threat, intelligence in all its dimensions is the essential tool. In the words of Director Hayden, "We identify the illegal sellers and buyers of technology and expertise. And we use covert action to disrupt illicit transfers."[48] There are distinctions between

Cold War covert action and today's covert action. First, the signature covert action of the 21st century to date is the offensive counterterrorism operation—a missile strike or a rendition—rather than the foreign policy coup. Second, today's covert operations are conducted with more regulated procedural oversight within the executive branch than those authorized decades ago. What hasn't changed is that covert action, in theory, in law, and sometimes in practice, is fast, flexible, and secret. That makes it a preferred tool where the intended policy effect will be lost if the U.S. hand is apparent, the cost will outweigh the gain if the United States is held to account, or the opportunity is lost if the target is alerted. In addition, covert action allows "assisting states" to otherwise deny complicity in necessary but locally unpopular actions.

However, covert action magnifies some of the negative pathologies of national security decision making. A terrorist target of opportunity may come and go in the wink of a Predator's electronic eye. Therefore, speed and secrecy are necessarily emphasized both in the field and as part of the Washington process of approval and validation. Speed and secrecy can increase the risk of mistake. The imperative to act is also intense. This imperative comes in two forms. First, there is the innate tendency within the government to focus on the immediate threat or necessity in contrast to the enduring consequences, as Justice Jackson observed in *Youngstown*.[49] Second, where the national security threat is greatest, the pressure to push to the limit of the law is also greatest, as it should be. Such pressures can exacerbate those already derived from the rapid, secret, and truncated process of authorization triggered by the definition of covert action.

A. Is the Definition of Covert Action Functional and Effective?

As discussed in section one, the definition of covert action was intended to address a threshold question: What is covert action? A number of legal and process results flow from that answer. The critical legal policy question, however, is whether the definition covers what it should without reaching what it should not. More specifically:

> Does the law guide inherently risky operations or those that bear special foreign policy consequence to an appropriate level of review and accountable decision?

Alternatively, does the law encourage the use of analytic rubrics designed to avoid internal and external process, or that nonetheless have that result?

Four areas warrant ongoing and conscious evaluation to ensure the lines are drawn in a lawful and prudent manner. These are described as areas because they address the nexus between covert action and, in turn, liaison, cyber space, military operations, and overt activities. In each area, the distinguishing lines may be uncertain. Thus, lawyers and policymakers have opportunity to interpret and apply the law so as to select preferred options and outcomes. It is essential that the choices made are conscious, wise, and part of a legal policy framework rather than a series of ad hoc efforts to get to yes.

Covert Action and Liaison

Liaison involves the formal and informal ties between allied, or merely like-minded, intelligence services. Thus, liaison can occur on an ongoing basis with a close ally or on an episodic or even a singular basis where the national security interests of two countries, or perhaps only two services, momentarily align.

As an intelligence function, liaison lies somewhere between collection and covert action. Whereas most liaison entails the routine passage of information that one might expect between allies, closer to the edge there can be a thin line between liaison and an effort to influence events overseas that is more comparable to covert action. This line is in sight where, for example, U.S. information may not just inform a liaison partner but predictably result in the partner taking action on the basis of the intelligence provided. In other circumstances, where the United States is engaging in coordinated action—for example, a rendition with the participation of the host nation—the activity may fall outside the construct of covert action because the U.S. role is acknowledged, at least to the assisting government.

The legal question, in context, is: How much is too much U.S. involvement such that liaison activities should be considered covert action? The legal policy question is: Are such activities subject to a measure of preview and review commensurate with their influence overseas and their policy benefits and risks regardless of whether they are covert action or something else?

Covert Action in Cyberspace

A second area that warrants ongoing and conscious definitional review involves the application of covert action law to cyberspace, a forum that would seem to especially lend itself to the non-attribution aspects of covert action. At least three questions warrant consideration. First, are the definitional thresholds for covert action adequate to identify that subset of putative cyber activity that should be treated as covert action because of the intended result? In short, does the definition make sense and work when applied to cyberspace? Second, do the law and internal executive processes serve to guide operators and decision makers to preferred and lawful options? Third, whether internally or externally (which means in Congress), are the expectations between critical actors shared? And if not shared, are they articulated so as to avoid surprises and later disputes as to whether and how the law applies?

With respect to each of these questions, one might consider if the law is nimble or subtle enough to address the distinctions in cyber operations between offense, offensive-defense, and defense. The same question arises with respect to cyber strategies that could be used to accomplish multiple missions using the same technical capacity—collection, defense, or proactive influence on events overseas.

Overt-Covert Operations

History is full of covert actions that were secret at the time of their undertaking but later revealed. There are also examples of covert activities in U.S. practice that were generally known at the time of their undertaking, at least on a strategic level if not on a tactical level, by which I mean the fact of a program if not its details. These might be called "overt-covert actions." They tend to be strategic in nature because strategic covert action is more prone to disclosure. It generally takes place over time and is larger in scale. Overt-covert actions are nonetheless covert actions because, while the role of the United States may be apparent, the program is not publicly acknowledged—plausible deniability is maintained for both the United States and any government that may be witting, complicit, or perhaps targeted. During the Cold War, this was (at times) an important distinction. Preserving the veil of deniability through the use of proxies helped to alleviate the pressure one side or the other might have otherwise felt to respond overtly, or be seen responding overtly, to an action. Likewise, in a counterterrorism context today, a targeted-killing program for example, it might be important to the host state (within whose territory the action is taking place) to maintain a veneer of plausible deniability for reasons of national sovereignty and pride and to avoid public outcry.

What becomes of a covert action when it becomes known or de facto overt? Does it matter? Are over-covert actions lawful? On the one hand, if it is the genuine intent of the U.S. government that the action not be apparent or acknowledged publicly, the legal answer appears a clear "yes." The government can decide whether to authoritatively acknowledge an action at the time. Moreover, the plain language of the National Security Act on its face would appear to permit at least the CIA to continue such activities, whether covert or not, if directed by the president pursuant to 50 U.S.C. §3036(d)(4) and buttressed by any independent constitutional authority a president might also bring to bear.

On the other hand, it is possible that the law, or perceptions of the law, may encourage dysfunctional results. This might occur where policymakers feel constrained from responding to what is on a strategic level obvious in order to preserve what is on a tactical level covert. Likewise, in order to preserve the capacity to fund and conduct activities pursuant to covert action mechanisms, government actors may deny the obvious and thus diminish U.S. credibility in contexts where the values of transparency and law matter as much as tactical results. In the case of targeted killing, for example, there would seem to be a meaningful distinction between the general knowledge and acknowledgment of a program, which is overt; and tactical knowledge of where, when, and with what support, which is covert and would cause national security harm if acknowledged. Foreign support or acquiescence might be lost and potential targets alerted were tactical knowledge revealed.

What is less clear is whether it is the law, perceptions of the law, or bureaucratic culture that discourages the government from transparently discussing the policy and legal basis behind targeted killing, or whether the law is being used as a shield by those who want to limit discussion lest their statements limit future options or necessitate response from those governments that may then feel compelled to respond. If it is the law that forbids discussion of targeted killing at a policy level, then the law should be changed to distinguish more subtly between that which is necessarily secret and covert and the policy and legal underpinnings of policies implemented through covert means.

Military Activities and Covert Action

As noted in Part B, the definition of "covert action" is "act" rather than "actor" based. Whereas the 1974 Hughes-Ryan amendment to the Foreign Assistance Act of 1961 required the president to sign a finding to authorize covert action by the CIA and to notify the intelligence committees of that finding, the 1991 amendments to the National Security Act contemplate covert activities conducted by other executive agencies.[50]

The most visible manifestation of this language in practice is, of course, the 2010 bin Laden raid undertaken by Navy SEALS under CIA authority.[51] Two legal questions arise:

Has the law's exception for traditional military activities distorted its intended purpose by guiding inherently risky operations with foreign policy impact to a particularized process of review, approval, and notification?

Further, in the case of blended operations like the bin Laden raid, which incorporate covert and non-covert options and elements, does the law push decision-makers to particular outcomes so as to avoid covert processes or notification procedures as opposed to the selection of the most appropriate and effective tool for foreign policy and implementation purposes?

Uniformed military operations have historically not been considered or treated as covert activities. Thus, even if the definition is action based, the exception for "traditional military activities" may effectively remove some, many, or all clandestine military operations from its reach.

Whether an activity is conducted as a military or intelligence operation has both legal and policy consequences. It will determine the process of authorization and approval, which is to say whether the operation is considered using the operational military chain of command or the executive process for covert action. As noted above, in the case of covert action, the president *must* approve an action in the form of a finding or MON unless it can be said that an activity falls under an existing authority. In the case of a military operation, it *may* involve the president as commander-in-chief giving a verbal order or signing off on a memo. The process used will also determine the normative participants to include operators, policy-makers, and lawyers. As illustrated by the bin Laden raid, a choice between military and covert action will influence how command and control for an action is exercised, although the assignment of command is ultimately a matter of presidential discretion. The decision will also determine whether, how much, and from where funding is available. Finally, the decision may determine whether the Congress is notified, which committee(s), in what form, and whether such notification takes place in advance, if at all.

Those who wield the power of the law should constantly consider whether they are invoking a particular law or process because it is the most efficacious way to accomplish the mission or whether they are doing so for bureaucratic reasons, perhaps to avoid a level of review, a reporting requirement, or "the lawyers." If the latter, why? If the process is deemed too slow, then change it. To turn Whit Griswold's phrase about the answer to a bad idea being a good idea, the answer to bad process is good process (not no process), which is the subject of the next section.[52]

B. The Nature and Scope of Review

With respect to activities that are encompassed within the definition of covert action, two legal policy questions linger: How much executive process is appropriate before a finding or MON is signed or authorization for a specific operation given? How much detail should be specified in these documents beyond that necessary to satisfy the statutory requirements?

Process and Appraisal

In the view of some, "process" itself is a euphemism for "bureaucracy," pejorative meaning intended.[53] Bureaucracy can delay, if not lose, operational opportunity. Bureaucracy increases the prospect of security breach. Sometimes it brings layers of lawyers with it. At the same time, national security is not subject to the same processes of internal, external, or public evaluation that occurs in other policy areas. National security programs, and certainly compartmented intelligence programs, are secret. Limits on external appraisal also derive from certain functional and structural aspects of national security decision making and the presidency, especially during war. Where national security is concerned, the policy pressure to succeed is at its greatest. As Madison observed, "safety from external danger is [indeed] the most powerful director of national conduct."[54] For presidents this responsibility is real, immediate, and sincere. As a result, as Justice Jackson observed of executive deliberation, "[t]he tendency is strong to emphasize transient results upon policies . . . and lose sight of enduring consequences upon the balanced power structure of our Republic."[55] Further, for a presidency conditioned to crisis and command, which is to say the modern presidency, appraisal is difficult to implement. There is also less opportunity for appraisal because where national security activities are subject to external review, they are subject to doctrines of judicial and political deference.

Process can be good or bad. Good process should be viewed as a source of policy strength in an area historically prone to foreign policy risk. Good process alerts decision makers to the pros and cons of contemplated action, including the benefits and risks of accomplishing the task covertly. Process also helps to ensure that secret policies are consistent with overt policies, and where they are not, there is good reason for any divergence. In addition, in an area where U.S. actions are intended to be kept secret, policymakers and those who may become aware of the underlying acts, if not their impetus, must be made aware of their existence to avoid blowback or inadvertent disclosure.

For sure, streamlined executive decision has advantages in speed and secrecy. Speed comes in part from the absence of objection or dissent. But there can be advantages to considering objections and dissent. Because the conflict with Islamic terrorists is a conflict fought over values with words and not just territory with weapons, careful review also allows policymakers to balance the benefits and costs represented by both the means and ends of action.

In the context of intelligence operations using military means, such as the use of the Predator to attack the enemy, whether covert or not, the value of rigorous process is obvious. The military, for example, uses multiple-tiered computer modeling to assess the potential for collateral damage. Targets are validated through a tested and recognized staff process. In short, rigorous but timely process can demonstrate confidence in policy choice, legal arguments, and a willingness to account for effect.

Specificity

Policymakers and lawyers must also consider the measure of detail to include in a finding or MON. There exists a tension between the generic authorizing instrument that provides flexibility but uncertain direction and the too-specific instrument, which may need amendment with change in the field. From the standpoint of legal policy, such documents should be crafted with sufficient specificity so that it is clear to the president what he is approving and the policy implications and risks of doing so. Specificity results in accountability. Where flexibility may be required—for example, where the geographic foci of activity may shift—there should also be sufficient authority to adjust in the field or a viable process to garner prompt policy consideration. This might come in the form of approval by the Principals or Deputies Committees or an appropriate subset of the Committees.

Field operatives can also benefit from sufficient detail so that the policy intent is clear and operatives are protected from the second guessing that comes with failure. Where authority is clear and clearly invoked, operators will take greater risks in the field. Where the risks of action are known to decision makers and acknowledged, operators will take greater risks as well because they operate with the confidence of authority and diminished risk of second guessing after the fact.

C. Are the Processes of External Appraisal Effective and Trusted?

The 9/11 Commission and the WMD Commission recommended that Congress reform intelligence oversight.[56] In particular, the Commissions were critical of the episodic and reactive nature of oversight as well as the disparate sources of congressional input into the design and funding of intelligence.

Congressional oversight is selective. Few members of Congress outside the intelligence committees possess the background to address intelligence issues. Moreover, even the intelligence committees operate with the inherently inductive knowledge that comes from periodic briefings rather than daily contact with operators and policymakers. Members see only part of the picture, and then only that part contained in executive talking points that have survived layers of editing and are designed to fend off partisan attack. Where members do follow intelligence closely, their interest tends to flow toward high profile areas and not to areas like computer interoperability and funding audits, where appraisal may be needed most. Recall that approximately 85 percent of intelligence funding is directed to the Department of Defense.[57]

Public discourse following the Snowden disclosures suggests there is another problem with the oversight of intelligence—a lack of public trust. In the case of the NSA, an important segment of the public appears not to trust or is unwilling to defer to the oversight mechanisms established in law. To many, it seems not to have mattered that the institutions the law intended review these programs in fact did so, including relevant committees of Congress and the Foreign Intelligence Surveillance Court.

Yet congressional appraisal of covert action remains an important source of democratic legitimacy as well as perspective, in part because it may be the only source of external perspective available. This is not a matter of constitutional idealism but a matter of national security efficacy. In a system of shared powers and separate branches, Congress can provide a source of legitimacy and sometimes check on intelligence activities that are conducted outside the reach of public knowledge. At times, committee members may be the only persons outside the NSC process and relevant intelligence agencies aware of an activity and, certainly, the only persons without a direct policy stake in the success or funding of the activity. While the president alone has the authority to wield the covert action tool and the bureaucratic wherewithal to do so effectively, he acts at the zenith of his authority when acting pursuant to congressional authorization as well as his own authority, or, in the case of covert action, where he acts with the meaningful involvement and validation of the Congress.[58] Those who believe in the necessity of executive action to preempt and respond to security threats should favor a legal policy of meaningful oversight that maximizes presidential authority.

The inclusion of an independent check on executive action also reduces the potential for mistake. That is because the executive takes particular care in what it tells Congress. War Powers Reports may be bland, but they do necessitate an internal process before they are submitted that causes senior officials to check their assumptions and arguments one more time before they send the report to the president and Congress. In similar fashion, in notifying Congress of covert action, executive branch actors are even more likely to consider whether they have, in fact, covered all the angles and addressed or mitigated divergent views. It is worth noting that, at least according to the legislative history, "the primary purpose of prior notice is to permit the intelligence committees, on behalf of Congress, to offer advice to the President."[59]

Finally, risk-taking in the field increases where the government exercises shared authority. Though this statement is hard to demonstrate empirically, the concept is nonetheless real. As reflected in statements made to the 9/11 Commission, there is a cultural perception in the intelligence community that there is danger in acting too aggressively when the authority to do so is unclear or subject to political change. Where authority is embedded in a written finding provided to Congress, there can be no legitimate debate as to what was or was not authorized (unless the finding is itself ambiguous). Therefore, there can be no legal excuse for not leaning forward in execution. Nor does the inclusion of the legislative branch necessarily undermine the requirements for speed and secrecy. One of the most significant intelligence secrets briefed to the Gang of Eight in the terrorism context—the U.S. effort to capture or kill Osama bin Laden in the late 1990s and beyond—did not leak.

The question then becomes whether there are ways to improve the process of external appraisal and validation, which will also enhance public confidence. Security specialists and not merely lawyers committed to the constitutional framework should care that the process works for three reasons. First, the effort to counter terrorism and control the proliferation of weapons will not be won with a singular event or victory. At best, it will be contained through one tactical success after another over time. An effective process of external validation can contribute to sustained public support and congressional funding. Second, an effective mechanism of external appraisal can help to ensure that finite national security tools are used wisely and thus essential resources, including public confidence, are not squandered on ill-advised programs or controversial programs. Third, the counterterrorism and counter-proliferation activities implicated by each of the questions posed above involving liaison, cyberspace, military operations, and overt-covert operations raise issues at the factual and constitutional nexus between security and liberty. New issues of due process, for example, have arisen in the context of rendition and targeted killing. Moreover, many activities that might occur in cyber space will present novel and complex questions of law, policy, and impact.

"Trust us" will not work. Courts want to see the argument behind the assertion of a secrecy privilege. Many in the public want to see the reasoning and not just the result. And where internal actors lack confidence in the process of appraisal, we may find that unauthorized disclosure increases as a de facto method of taking external appraisal directly to the public.

Conclusion

Why should we care about covert action? Because it is an essential tactical tool to address the 21st-century challenges of terrorism, weapons proliferation, and rogue states and failed states, as well as the advent of cyberspace as a critical national security arena. Why should we care about covert action law? Because national security law plays three critical purposes, each of which will advance national security if the law is wielded effectively. Law provides substantive authority to act. It facilitates process, both between branches of government and within each branch. And it conveys fundamental legal as well as policy values, as reflected in the Constitution's commitment to the principles of liberty and to providing for the common defense.

This is true in the area of covert action. First, the law provides substantive authority to act. This comes in the form of the president's inherent constitutional powers as well as the implicit and subsequently express grant of authority in the National Security Act of 1947, as amended, for the president to authorize covert action.

The second purpose of law is to provide a framework for essential process and decision making. Because the substantive threshold for acting is low, rigorous internal and external process is necessary to validate the resort to covert action. Covert action as an instrument of national security is neither inherently good nor inherently bad. Whether its invocation is wise will depend in large measure on the ability of decision makers to effectively and faithfully follow a process that is at once timely, contextual, and meaningful. Moreover, because covert action is an instrument invoked to address extraordinary national security challenges, there are extraordinary pressures on decision makers and operators that can distort process. These pressures include the necessity of speed, the allure of secrecy, and the imperative to confront immediate security challenges. An effective process addresses these national security pathologies.

Third, and finally, the law embodies U.S. legal and policy values at home and abroad. These values are reflected in the authorities and constraints the law places on the exercise of covert action. Foremost is the general principle, found in the National Security Act, that covert action is subject to the law: "A finding may not authorize any action that would violate the Constitution or any statute of the United States."[60] However, the law sometimes serves as both a value permit and a constraint, as in the case of the law of armed conflict. The modern covert action regime is also founded on the principle of accountability. This is an essential democratic legal value, but it is also a policy value, embedding as it does the judgment that with accountability come both more informed decision making and judicious risk taking.

Understanding these purposes, lawyers will be better prepared to withstand the pressures of practice and articulate to decision makers why law can serve to advance actual national security concerns as opposed to only being followed as a matter of principle. In turn, policymakers will better understand that the law is not just a series of random obstacles. Rather, the meaningful and timely application of law leads to wiser and more enduring security results.

Notes

The views expressed herein are those of the author and do not necessarily represent the views of the United States government or any organization within the United States government. The author acknowledges and thanks Mattie Godzala, Nan Mooney, and Lala Qadir for their thoughtful comments and helpful suggestions regarding this chapter.

1. For a historical overview, see Gregory F. Treverton, *Covert Action: The Limits of Intervention in the Postwar World* (1987) and Reisman & Baker, *supra* note 4.

2. Robert M. Gates, "The CIA and American Foreign Policy," *Foreign Affairs* (Winter 1987–1988). Covert action is one of the five intelligence functions along with collection, analysis and dissemination, liaison, and counterintelligence. See James E. Baker, *In the Common Defense: National Security Law for Perilous Times* 137 (2007).

3. See, e.g., Totten Administrator v. United States, 92 U.S. 105, 106 (1875); Curtiss-Wright Export Corp. v. United States, 299 U.S. 304, 320 (1936); United States v. Nixon, 418 U.S. 683, 685 (1974); Tenet et al. v. Doe et ux, 544 U.S. 1, 1–2 (2005); see also W. Michael Reisman & James E. Baker, *Regulating Covert Action* 117–118 (1992).

4. *Totten*, 92 U.S. at 106.

5. Youngstown Sheet & Tube Co. v. Sawyer, 343 U.S. 579 (1952).

6. 50 U.S.C. § 3036 (Supp. I 2013) (authorizing the director of the Central Intelligence Agency to "perform such other functions and duties related to intelligence affecting the national security as the president or Director of National Intelligence may direct"), available at http://uscode.house.gov/view.xhtml?req =granuleid:USC-prelim-title50-section3036&num=0&edition=prelim.

This provision was previously codified as amended at 50 U.S.C. § 403-4a(d) (4) (2006), but was editorially reclassified to 50 U.S.C. § 3036, effective May 20, 2013. For the purposes of this chapter, subsequent citations to relevant provisions of the National Security Act, as amended, and associated statutes will reference the editorially reclassified code. These will eventually be published in Supplement I (2013) to the 2012 United States Code.

7. *Id.*; *see also* Reisman & Baker, *supra* note 4, at 118.

8. Intelligence Authorization Act, Pub. L. 102-88, 105 Stat. 429, 443 (1991) (codified as amended at 50 U.S.C. § 413b(e) (2006)) (editorially reclassified at 50 U.S.C. § 3093(e) (Supp. I 2013)), available at http://uscode.house.gov/view .xhtml?req=granuleid:USC-prelim-title50-section3093&num=0&edition=pre lim; *see also* Baker, *supra* note 3, at 148–154.

9. 50 U.S.C. § 3093(e).

10. *Id.*

11. S. Rep. No. 102–185, at 235 (1991).

12. For a discussion of the etymology of "national security," see Mark Shulman, *The Progressive Era Origins of the National Security Act*, 104 Dick. L. Rev. 289, 290–293 (Winter 2000).

13. 50 U.S.C. § 3093(a) (Supp. I 2013), available at http://uscode.house.gov/view .xhtml?req=granuleid:USC-prelim-title50-section3093&num=0&edition=prelim.

This provision was previously codified as amended at 50 U.S.C. § 413b (a) (2006) but was editorially reclassified to 50 U.S.C. § 3093(a), effective May 20, 2013.

14. 50 U.S.C. § 3093(a)(1) (Supp. I 2013), available at http://uscode.house .gov/view.xhtml?req=granuleid:USC-prelim-title50-section3093&num=0 &edition=prelim.

This provision was previously codified as amended at 50 U.S.C. § 413b(a)(1) (2006), but was editorially reclassified to 50 U.S.C. § 3093(a)(1), effective May 20, 2013.

15. 50 U.S.C. § 3093(a)(3)-(4) (Supp. I 2013), available at http://uscode .house.gov/view.xhtml?req=granuleid:USC-prelim-title50-section3093&num =0&edition=prelim.

This provision was previously codified as amended at 50 U.S.C. § 413b(a)(3)- (4) (2006), but was editorially reclassified to 50 U.S.C. § 3093(a)(3)-(4), effective May 20, 2013.

16. 50 U.S.C. § 3093(c)(1) (Supp. I 2013), available at http://uscode.house .gov/view.xhtml?req=granuleid:USC-prelim-title50-section3093&num=0 & edition=prelim).

This provision was previously codified as amended at 50 U.S.C. § 413b(c)(1) (2006 & Supp. V 2011), but was editorially reclassified to 50 U.S.C. § 3093(c)(1), effective May 20, 2013.

17. 50 U.S.C. § 3093(c)(2) (Supp. I 2013), available at http://uscode.house .gov/view.xhtml?req=granuleid:USC-prelim-title50-section3093&num=0& edition=prelim.

This provision was previously codified as amended at 50 U.S.C. § 413b(c)(2) (2006), but was editorially reclassified to 50 U.S.C. § 3093(c)(2), effective May 20, 2013.

The "Gang of Eight" limited notification has migrated to other areas of intelligence practice as reflected by disclosure of the president's so-called Terrorist Surveillance Program. However, as a matter of law, the "Gang of Eight" notification mechanism is a covert action procedure heretofore not adopted by Congress as a general or routine mechanism for reporting intelligence matters. Alfred Cumming, Cong. Research. Serv., R40691, Sensitive Covert Action Notifications: Oversight Options for Congress 7 (2009).

18. 50 U.S.C. § 3093(c)(3) (Supp. I 2013), available at http://uscode.house.gov /view.xhtml?req=granuleid:USC-prelim-title50-section3093&num=0&edition =prelim).

This provision was previously codified as amended at 50 U.S.C. § 413b(c)(3) (2006), but was editorially reclassified to 50 U.S.C. § 3093(c)(3), effective May 20, 2013.

19. 50 U.S.C. § 3093(d)(1) (Supp. I 2013), available at http://uscode.house .gov/view.xhtml?req=granuleid:USC-prelim-title50-section3093&num=0 &edition=prelim.

This provision was previously codified as amended at 50 U.S.C. § 413b(d)(1) (2006 & Supp. V 2011), but was editorially reclassified to 50 U.S.C. § 3093(d) (1), effective May 20, 2013.

20. S. Rep. No. 102-85, at 235 (1991); see also Approval and Review of Special Activities, National Security Decision Directive 286 (Oct. 15, 1987), available at http://www.fas.org/irp/offdocs/nsdd/ [hereinafter NSDD-286].

21. 50 U.S.C. § 413b(d)(2) (2010) (editorially reclassified at 50 U.S.C. § 3093(d) (2) (Supp. I 2013)), available at http://uscode.house.gov/view.xhtml?req =granuleid:USC-prelim-title50-section3093&num=0&edition=prelim.

22. S. Rep.111–223, at 19 (2010).

23. 50 U.S.C. § 3093(d)(2) (Supp. I 2013), available at http://uscode.house. gov/view.xhtml?req=granuleid:USC-prelim-title50-section3093&num=0&edition =prelim.

This provision was previously codified as amended at 50 U.S.C. § 413b(d)(2) (2006 & Supp. V 2011), but was editorially reclassified to 50 U.S.C. § 3093(d) (2), effective May 20, 2013.

24. 50 U.S.C. § 3091(a)(1)(Supp. I 2013), available at http://uscode.house .gov/view.xhtml?req=granuleid:USC-prelim-title50-section3091&num=0 &edition=prelim.

This provision was previously codified as amended at 50 U.S.C. § 413(a)(1) (2006), but was editorially reclassified to 50 U.S.C. § 3091(a)(1), effective May 20, 2013.

25. 50 U.S.C. § 3093(b) (Supp. I 2013), available at http://uscode.house.gov /view.xhtml?req=granuleid:USC-prelim-title50-section3093&num=0&edition =prelim.

This provision was previously codified as amended at 50 U.S.C. § 413b(b) (2006 & Supp. V 2011), but was editorially reclassified to 50 U.S.C. § 3093(b), effective May 20, 2013.

26. Exec. Order No. 13,470, 73 Fed. Reg. 45,325 (July 30, 2008) [hereinafter E.O. 13,470].

27. S. Rep. No. 102-85, at 233 (1991).

Dear Mr. Chairman: I am aware of your concerns regarding the provision of notice to Congress of covert action. . . . I anticipate that in almost all instances, prior notice will be possible. In those rare instances where prior notice is not provided, I anticipate that notice will be provided within a few days. Any withholding beyond this period will be based upon my assertion of authorities granted this office by the Constitution.

For an example of a president withholding notification before these provisions were enacted, see Turner, *supra* note 20.

28. Letter from Senator Jay Rockefeller to Vice-President Richard Cheney (July 17, 2003).

29. E.O. No. 13,470, *supra* note 29. Special activities are "activities conducted in support of national foreign policy objectives abroad which are planned and executed so that the role of the United States Government is not apparent or acknowledged publicly . . ."; in other words, covert action. Exec. Order No. 12,333, 46 Fed. Reg. 59,941 (Dec. 4, 1981), *amended by* Exec. Order No. 13,470, 73 Fed. Reg. 45,325 (July 30, 2008) [hereinafter E.O. 12,333].

30. E.O. No. 13,470, *supra* note 29.

31. NSDD-286, *supra* note 23.

32. Organization of the National Security Council, Presidential Decision Directive No. NSC-2 (Jan. 20,1993), available at http://www.clintonlibrary.gov /pdd.html.

33. 50 U.S.C. § 3093(a)(5) (Supp. I 2013), available at http://uscode.house .gov/view.xhtml?req=granuleid:USC-prelim-title50-section3093&num=0 &edition=prelim.

This provision was previously codified as amended at 50 U.S.C. § 413b(a)(5) (2006), but was editorially reclassified to 50 U.S.C. § 3093(a)(5), effective May 20, 2013.

34. 18 U.S.C. § 2340A (2001).

35. U.S. Dep't of Justice, Lawfulness of a Lethal Operation Directed against a U.S. Citizen Who is a Senior Operational Leader of Al-Qa'ida or an Associated

Force (draft Nov. 8, 2011) [hereinafter DOJ White Paper], available at www .justice.gov/oip/docs/dept-white-paper.pdf.

36. The 9/11 Commission Report, Final Report of the National Commission on Terrorist Attacks upon the United States 123 (2004); see also Richard Posner, "The 9/11 Report: A Dissent," *N.Y. Times* (Aug. 29, 2004), available at http://www .nytimes.com/2004/08/29/books/the-9-11-report-a-dissent.html.

37. Authorization for Use of Military Force § 2, Pub. L. 107-40, 115 Stat 224 (2001).

38. DOJ White Paper, *supra* note 38.

39. United States v. Yunis, 859 F.2d 953 (D.C. Cir. 1988); El-Masri v. United States, 479 F.3d 296 (4th Cir. 2007).

40. DOJ White Paper, *supra* note 38.

41. *Id.*

42. E.O. No. 12,333, *supra* note 32.

43. *Joint Inquiry into Intelligence Community Activities before and after the Terrorist Attacks of September 11, 2001*, 107th Cong. 248 (2002) (testimony of Hon. Samuel R. Berger, former Assistant and Deputy Assistant to the President for Nat'l Sec. Affairs).

44. 50 U.S.C. § 3093(f) (Supp. I 2013), available at http://uscode.house.gov /view.xhtml?req=granuleid:USC-prelim-title50-section3093&num=0&edition =prelim.

This provision was previously codified as amended at 50 U.S.C. § 413b(f) (2006), but was editorially reclassified to 50 U.S.C. § 3093(f), effective May 20, 2013.

45. *Id.*

46. James H. Doolittle, William B. Franke, Morris Hadley, & William D. Crawley, Report on the Covert Activities of the Central Intelligence Agency 2 (1954), available at http://www.foia.cia.gov/sites/default/files/document_convers ions/5829/CIA-RDP86B00269R000100040001-5.pdf.

47. Michael Hayden, Dir., Cent. Intelligence Agency, Remarks at the Atlantic Council (Nov. 13, 2008).

48. Michael Hayden, Dir., Cent. Intelligence Agency, Remarks at the Los Angeles World Affairs Council (Sept. 16, 2008).

49. Youngstown Sheet & Tube Co. v. Sawyer, 343 U.S. 579, 635–36 (1952) (Jackson, J., concurring).

50. Exec. Order 13,470, *supra* note 29.

51. Siobhan Gorman & Julian Barnes, "Spy, Military Ties Aided bin Laden Raid," *Wall St. J.* (May 23, 2011), available at http://online.wsj.com/news/articles /SB10001424052748704083904576334160172068344.

52. Alfred Whitney Griswold, Essays on Education 96 (1954).

53. John Lehman, "Getting Spy Reform Wrong," *Wash. Post* (Nov. 16, 2005), available at http://www.washingtonpost.com/wp-dyn/content/article/2005/11/15 /AR2005111501316.html.

54. The Federalist No. 8 (Alexander Hamilton).

55. Youngstown Sheet & Tube Co. v. Sawyer, 343 U.S. 579, 634 (1952) (Jackson, J., concurring).

56. The 9/11 Commission Report, Final Report of the National Commission on Terrorist Attacks upon the United States 419–423 (2004); The Commission on the Intelligence Capabilities of the United States Regarding Weapons of Mass Destruction, Report to the President of the United States 337–341 (2005).

57. Richard A. Best Jr., Alfred Cumming, & Todd Masse, Cong. Research Serv., RS22112, Director of National Intelligence: Statutory Authorities 2 (2005); Commission on the Roles and Capabilities of the Intelligence Community, Preparing for the 21st Century: An Appraisal of U.S. Intelligence 49 (1996), available at http://www.gpo.gov/fdsys/pkg/GPO-INTELLIGENCE/content-detail.html.

58. *Youngstown*, 343 U.S. at 635–636.

59. S. Rep. No. 102-85, *supra* note 30, at 232.

60. 50 U.S.C. § 3093(a)(5) (Supp. I 2013), available at http://uscode.house .gov/view.xhtml?req=granuleid:USC-prelim-title50-section3093&num=0 &edition=prelim.

This provision was previously codified as amended at 50 U.S.C. § 413b(a)(5) (2006), but was editorially reclassified to 50 U.S.C. § 3093(a)(5), effective May 20, 2013.

CHAPTER THIRTEEN

Covert Action and Diplomacy

John D. Stempel

COVERT ACTION AND DIPLOMACY HAVE HAD a long and checkered career to-gether for over two millennia. From the earliest organized governments, when functions were not sufficiently differentiated, clandestine operations were standard practice in international relations. Beginning with the Achaemenid Persians between the sixth and fourth centuries BCE, the organization of intelligence as part of government was developed to a very high degree and copied by Arabs, Turks, Afghans, Mongols, and Hindus over the following centuries. Activities that we now consider covert action—assassination, co-opting the king's counselor (or mistress), para-military support for insurgencies, and propaganda—were common. There was little or no distinction between "intelligence" and "covert action" until the 19th and 20th centuries. That developed in the West as a result of the evolution of Westphalian diplomacy in the 15th and 16th centuries.[1]

The emergence of Western diplomacy was driven by the disastrous desolation caused by the Thirty Years' War. Crude but temporary diplomatic missions began in the 15th century in Venice and the Italian states and spread to Europe. Intelligence and eventually secret operations were an integral part of these activities, though they were fairly simple by modern standards. In the Elizabethan period, British covert action multiplied the effective power of England, especially when the use of gold and Protestant mercenaries as diplomatic weapons saved the Protestant cause in France and the Low Countries.

By the end of the Napoleonic Wars in 1815, the Treaty of Vienna included the regulation of diplomatic ranks and began the formal organization of diplomacy under international laws regulating diplomatic rights and duties. It included the principles that diplomats are not to interfere in the internal affairs of states and an outright condemnation of espionage.[2] Of course, this did not stop spying, but it forced intelligence services to become more professional and began the differentiation between intelligence and diplomacy in terms of norms, objectives, and means and methods.

As other European societies followed Britain through the Industrial Revolution, and as continental European politics became more complex through the 18th and 19th centuries, intelligence services and capabilities grew. The United States entered the diplomatic arena in the late 18th century after winning its independence from Britain, but distance, communications, and time kept it from playing a serious role in European and world politics until nearly a century later. The 1898 Spanish–American War, coupled with World War I, brought the United States into the world arena.

Because of this history, America lagged behind the rest of the world in developing an organized intelligence capability. Throughout most of the 19th and early 20th centuries, both U.S. intelligence and diplomacy were ad hoc affairs, which included secret operations on occasion, where needed and possible. Roosevelt's maneuvers involving the acquisition of the Panama Canal are a good example. In fact, the United States had no professional diplomatic community until the Rogers Act of 1924, and until 1940, no formal intelligence organizations existed except the military service intelligence departments.

George Washington created his own informal intelligence network during the American Revolution, but it dissolved after the American victory at Yorktown. The U.S. Army began to develop intelligence units during and after the Civil War experiment with outsourcing intelligence to Allan Pinkerton's organization. Formal organizations were not created until the 1880s in the Army and Navy Departments.[3]

In World War I, the military services ran their own shows, and a civilian Committee on Public Information under George Creel focused largely on propaganda and internal security. During the interwar years (1919–1939), American intelligence lapsed back into previous peacetime routines, with the military service units dominating the field. American code-breaking efforts were terminated in 1929.

As the war clouds grew over Europe again in the late 1930s, President Franklin Roosevelt selected William O. Donovan to create the Office of the Coordinator of Information in June 1941, which became the Office of Strategic Services (OSS) the next year. This was the first organized American effort to conduct what became known within the next decade as covert activities—propaganda, political operations, economic operations, and paramilitary activities, as well as sabotage, espionage, and counterespionage during World War II.

When the OSS was disbanded in September 1945, President Truman transferred its intelligence functions to the State Department, where they became the Bureau of Intelligence and Research. He also created the Central Intelligence Group (CIG) a year later to keep the rest of the trained professionals, including covert action operators, together until the United States could sort out its postwar needs.[4]

Most of today's scholarly work cites the creation of the Central Intelligence Agency (CIA) in 1947 as part of the National Security Act as the real beginning of professionalized intelligence in American government.[5] The vast increase in technological capabilities—such as better communications and space photography—required a much greater concentration of resources and manpower to succeed. Cooperation with Allied intelligence services in World War II socialized Americans to international intelligence work. The imperatives of postwar politics and the rise of the Cold War made such an effort necessary on a continuing basis.[6]

The CIA has maintained its links with the State Department and the military in Washington. Abroad, U.S. and other countries' embassies often host resident personnel under "official" cover. However, the overall tension between the utility of covert action and the requirements of diplomacy and foreign policy continue to this day, breaking out in open hostility on occasion.

Covert Action: Methods and Operations

Covert action is formally referred to in presidential executive orders as "special activities." Perhaps the most inclusive general description is Jeff Richelson's:

> Covert action, also known as "special activities," includes any operation designed to influence foreign governments, persons, or events in support of the sponsoring government's foreign policy objectives while keeping the sponsoring government's support of the operation secret. Whereas in clandestine collection, the emphasis is on keeping the activity secret, in covert action the emphasis is on keeping the sponsorship secret.[7]

Such activities are aimed at keeping the sponsoring government's role secret, but they also do violate the diplomatic Vienna Convention injunctions against interference in the domestic affairs of the host country.

When a covert action is uncovered, the sponsoring country's relations with the target country are adversely affected. This generally brings diplomats back into the problem, because they are the ones who take the brunt of criticism and later raise the general foreign policy question of whether such actions were or are worth the cost. Before pursuing this discussion, the following section examines the types of actions and individual issues/problems. Although much is known about historical operations, details on present-day activities are scarce. This circumstance hampers a complete and fully informed discussion.

Propaganda, sometimes called "psychological warfare," or "psyops," has both overt and covert aspects. The press and cultural sections of embassies pass out overt, or "white," information that is attributed to official sources and represents the government's official view. "Gray," or partially concealed propaganda, and "black" propaganda that are attributed to someone else, such as falsified statements from a foreign government, are concealed variants. All these types of propaganda were used to influence the 1948 elections in Greece and Italy against the communists. The Soviets made heavy use of all three types from 1945 to the demise of the Soviet Union.[8] Other countries consistently use white propaganda (for example, the British Broadcasting Company and the French Press Agency).

Examples of black operations include the American establishment of a clandestine radio station in Guatemala that broadcasted news of a revolutionary army so convincingly that the procommunist president resigned. Soviet efforts to convince Africans that the United States was responsible for creating AIDS are similar black efforts. A similar clandestine operation publicized in late 2005 told of U.S. military officials paying to have stories placed in the Iraqi press lauding the role of American soldiers in trying to enhance security in Iraq.

For many years, *Radio Free Europe* and *Radio Free Liberty* dispensed gray information while covertly supported by the CIA as privately supported organizations. In 1973, Congress gave them independent status under the Board for International Broadcasting to "whiten" their offerings. Such activities are estimated to constitute about 40 percent of the CIA's covert activities.

Economic operations have been the least used covert activities by the CIA, accounting for only 10 percent of U.S. covert activities. Economic support in terms of goods shipments to support friendly governments or withholding trade with unfriendly countries occurs on both the overt and covert levels. Sanctions are overt; manipulating a national currency clandestinely is covert. Much of the action against the Allende government in Chile in the early 1970s involved economic issues, including inciting labor strikes and depressing the world copper price. Positive efforts include measures to restore Iraq's economy after the American defeat of Saddam Hussein in 2003 and shipments of food to friendly countries under the Public Law (PL) 480 program. Economic measures are often overt as well as covert, and these include foreign aid as well as favorable trade pacts. Efforts to beef up the cattle and food industries in Africa are normally overt, but given sensitivities in some areas to the HIV/AIDS problem, covert measures to give additional vaccines and medicines to people in certain places may be necessary.

Political action is a more diffuse and complex category, involving everything from financial support for key leaders to creating insurgencies. Such action accounts for about 30 percent of U.S. covert activities. Some known examples include payments to Jordan's King Hussein, giving money and campaign advice to the Solidarity movement in Poland in the 1980s, and supplying political organizational personnel and money to Afghan politicians since 2002.

In addition to major U.S. efforts in Western Europe in the 1940s, there were two campaigns in Chile in 1964 and 1970. The first was a solid success; the second failed to prevent Salvadore Allende from becoming president and led to a campaign to overthrow him that was a major trigger for the Church Commission's 1974–1975 investigation of the CIA.

Moving toward activities that present an even greater challenge to international norms, there are instances where both the United States and the Soviet Union supported coupes d'etat against foreign leaders. Soviet support for coups in Czechoslovakia in 1948 and in Afghanistan in 1978 are clear-cut cases of the exercise of Soviet political and eventually military power. The Soviets supplied political support to a number of other regimes including Cuba, Angola, Iraq, and Mozambique up to and including use of force over the past 60 years.

The U.S. has been identified with four other coups in addition to the Guatemalan and Chilean examples given. In 1953, some money and organizational skills were supplied to forces loyal to the shah, which brought down Prime Minister Mossadeq's government and restored the monarchy. The overthrow of the shah 25 years later drew substantially on Iranian anger at the earlier effort and raised the question of whether the 1953 coup was effective in protecting long-term U.S. interests. Successful U.S. efforts in 1961 to oust Trujillo from the Dominican Republic and acquiescence in an army coup that killed South Vietnamese President Ngo Dinh Diem in 1963 are other cases the Church Commission discussed. The United States also gave political support to those seeking to oust Philippines President Ferdinand Marcos in 1986 and political and active military support to oust the regime in Grenada in 1983, Panamanian President Manuel Noriega in 1989, and the Haitian military dictatorship in 1993–1994.

Paramilitary activities, including assassinations, often overlap with or are carried out in conjunction with political action operations. They generally involve more risk and controversy than any other type of covert action. The CIA's Special Operations Unit ran a "secret" war against the North Vietnamese puppet regime in Laos from 1963 until the United States withdrew from Vietnam in 1973. CIA support for other wars/guerilla operations has included action in 26 publicly identified countries, including the Ukraine, Poland, Albania, Hungary, Indonesia, China, Oman, Malaysia, North Korea, Venezuela, the Dominican Republic, Bolivia, Guatemala, Cuba, Nicaragua, El Salvador, Angola, Greece, Afghanistan, and Iraq. Soviet operations include at least that many countries over the 72 years of the regime's existence.

Some clandestine American activities involved support for or protection of other elements of the clandestine intelligence collection process, including the maintenance in Iran of monitoring stations to track Soviet missile launches and monitoring sites in Laos and Cambodia for following North Vietnamese troop movements. In the 1980s, American covert operations involving Pakistani aid to the Afghan rebels against the Soviet puppet regime there were major factors in the eventual Soviet withdrawal in 1989. As in most other large-scale operations, part of the activity was covert, the rest merely secret, much of which eventually became public.

The New Terrorism

One of the spillovers from American–Afghan operations in the 1980s and the Gulf War of 1990–1991 was the rise of Islamic terrorism, which eventually led to the destruction of the World Trade Center towers and damage to the Pentagon on September 11, 2001, when Al Qaeda–trained terrorists flew aircraft into these buildings. Subsequent military action in Afghanistan that destroyed Taliban rule there and chased Al Qaeda into Pakistan was greatly facilitated by both overt and covert operations that relied heavily on CIA cooperation with U.S. military forces, and paramilitary efforts were key to early success. Coordination between the CIA and Defense Department forces, however, did not remain uniformly good throughout and remains a subject of concern to intelligence reformers.[9] Failure to destroy or capture a significant number of Al Qaeda forces and leaders was one of the issues that led to the 9/11 hearings and intelligence reform in 2004–2005. A related issue was the use of intelligence in the decision to attack Iraq in March 2003. The misreading of Iraqi nuclear and chemical/biological capabilities and the limited American understanding of Iraq and its politics brought forth criticism on both counts.

The concentration on intelligence reform led to a reassessment of American intelligence capabilities and a reorganization of the intelligence community under a new director of National Intelligence (DNI).[10] Although the most intense focus centered on the more strenuous overt and secret activities, covert action has been affected as well. Information now available suggests there is more increased covert activity in support of penetrating terrorist cells and infrastructures. Support activities related to U.S. invasion and occupation of Iraq, and U.S. support of Afghanistan's democratic experiment post-2001, have grown dramatically. In these areas, paramilitary operations and support are crucial, overt or covert. This concentration suggests there are fewer resources for and less reliance on covert activities elsewhere, but this is speculative at this time (2014).[11]

Covert Action: Assessment

As covert action became a bureaucratized activity in U.S. foreign policy after World War II, rather than an ad hoc political or military event, it became controversial. For over 25 years after 1945, during the Cold war, Americans treated covert activities with a "don't ask, don't tell" mentality. This followed a familiar pattern: most nations do not now and never have openly discussed their covert activities. There have been some academic discussions of past efforts when material became available or when enterprising journalists uncovered unsuspected connections. However, these tended to be one-shot stories with little follow-up. This began to change in the United States in the early 1970s when U.S. involvement in Chile drew the attention of Senator Frank Church and others. In 1975–1976, a congressional commission investigated alleged intelligence abuses.[12] The Church Commission and subsequent government and scholarly efforts have focused on three issues: Is covert action effective? Is covert action under control? Is covert action moral?

Literature on effectiveness from both academic and professional sources stresses several negative points:

1. The "blowback" from failed operations—or even successful ones—damages U.S. foreign policy.
2. Americans are deficient in the cultural understanding necessary to successfully manipulate other cultures; hence covert action often ends badly.
3. Covert action is not an effective mechanism for resolving crises and has to be integrated as part of an effective policy to succeed.
4. Often, the objectives of the covert activity are not compatible with American values.

5. Often, unclear boundaries between covert action and military operations result in failures.
6. Short-term successes often lead to long-term disasters.[13]

Others, including some critics, concede that despite difficulties, covert action is something that can be useful if it is used properly: (1) if covert activities are integrated into coherent overall foreign policy; (2) if active coordination is maintained between all government agencies; and (3) if no overt options will accomplish the mission. Most agree that other options should be exhausted—much of the political and propaganda work should be done openly, and it must be done competently with a good chance of success. Like other choices for effective action, there are pitfalls as well as possibilities.[14]

The dispute over effectiveness spills over to the second issue: Is covert action under proper control? For Americans, this means conforming to relevant legislation and final presidential approval of such action. President Reagan's definition of "covert action," published in Executive Order 12333 in 1981 and still in effect today, covers

> . . . special activities conducted in support of national foreign policy objects abroad which are planned and executed so that the role of the United States Government is not apparent or acknowledged publicly . . . but which are not intended to influence United States political processes, public opinion, policies, or media and *do not include diplomatic activities or the collection or production of intelligence and related support functions* (emphasis added).[15]

The U.S. Congress found this definition acceptable and incorporated similar language in its 1991 Intelligence Authorization Act. The common theme was that covert action is not an intelligence activity, and the requirements for a presidential finding did not apply to diplomatic activities. Also, such special activities were not to be targeted at or designed to influence the American public or American politics.

The development of a working definition of "covert action" stemmed from the work of the Church Commission, which at first called the CIA a "rogue elephant" but then backed away from that view in its final report. No other country deals with covert action this way. In 1994, the Hughes-Ryan legislation, which required the presidential finding for covert action, also ended the doctrine of plausible deniability for the president.

The presidential finding combines a determination that the activity is important enough to U.S. national security that it should be undertaken despite the risks and possible exposure and that the purpose for which it is undertaken and the methods used would be approved should it become public—the risk should be worth it. In 1986, the Iran-*contra* scandal underscored the reason for such legislation when it broke. National Security Council officials John Poindexter and Oliver North concocted a scheme to sell weapons to Iran in return for the release of American captives in Beirut and then (illegally) use the proceeds to fund U.S. operations against the Nicaraguan Sandinista government by supporting the contras.

This operation was never a true covert action, because approval was never sought. Some CIA, diplomatic, and military officials were involved in these basically criminal activities that were kept from Congress's attention until the story was revealed abroad. A few were tried in court, others were fired, and some left government voluntarily. There was considerable anger among the professionals in the various agencies. President Reagan escaped serious censure when he apologized to the country in a televised speech following the scandal.[16]

Journalists and students of intelligence had a field day with the Church Commission's initial allegations about rogue elephants and with the Iran-*contra* scandal, as they often do when intelligence operations go awry.[17] Ever since the 1960s, periodic book and magazine exposés have vied with serious analysis for public attention when covert action is the subject. This highlights the continuing tension between the secrecy needed for covert action and intelligence activities and the requirements for democratic transparency in government. A few other democracies have begun to gently question intelligence activities, but in most nations this is a non-problem—these matters are simply not discussed.

The final question is whether covert action is moral. It is always justified as important or even vital for national security. It has been separated from diplomacy and discouraged in international law because it is not considered an acceptable part of international relations. Nevertheless, it persists—as do efforts to codify and extend international law.

Throughout the Cold War, America operated on the basis of the view developed by a panel appointed by President Eisenhower. Headed by retired Gen. Jimmy Doolittle, its report said that in view of Communism's win-at-all-costs approach to foreign affairs, the United States would have to reconsider its concepts of fair play and undertake to subvert, sabotage, and destroy our enemies.[18] America did not fully trade morals for Realpolitik, but it certainly erred on the side of a more vigorous covert action policy.

Beginning with the Carter administration and reemerging with the Clinton administration, the question of how moral our foreign policy was continued to bubble. The Reagan administration returned to the more forceful arguments for fewer limits on covert action, and so did the first President Bush; after 9/11, so did President George W. Bush. Key players in his administration consistently made the argument that the brutality and viciousness of the terrorists required the utmost response. However, the president's policy of bringing democracy to the Middle East, which justified the 2003 invasion of Iraq, also raised the question of whether covert actions by their very nature undercut strategies to promote democracy in Iraq and elsewhere.[19]

Several writers have made the argument that covert action must be considered in terms of just war theory and that covert action can be justified in some circumstances but should not be used as a "lazy country's way of avoiding hard diplomatic work."[20] Some former agents argue that collecting intelligence and covert action often involve working with amoral characters, especially when terrorists such as Al Qaeda are the targets.[21]

They have a point, and no one has said the choices are easy. Most thoughtful writers suggest that some form of the following guidelines would give a government a solid base for defending covert actions if they went bad and that most people would support covert action taken for the following reasons:

1. The president approves the covert action after organized deliberation within the executive branch and the legally required consultation with Congress.
2. The action's intentions and objectives are clear, reasonable, and just and are also part of a coherent foreign policy.
3. Overt means of advancing the policy will not work.
4. There is significant probability of success, with minimal damage to innocent people.
5. Damage inflicted should be proportional to the threat reduced or averted.

Of course, such assessments have and could turn out to be wrong, or actions could be botched or turn out badly. There is really no way of averting criticism or political damage, but a defense of just covert action will limit damage to the diplomacy of the country that can so defend itself politically if matters go badly.

Using such guidelines may also assist in minimizing organizational struggles and clashes within the intelligence, defense, and diplomatic communities. If all work from the same page, intra-governmental spats will be minimized because positions will have to be harmonized or adjusted before action can get under way. Legal issues would be minimized, and there will also be more markers for judging the effectiveness of covert action. Those who have put themselves above the requirements for control are those who caused real damage to the system. They have also raised the bar of distrust across both international as well as domestic dimensions.

Conclusion: The Future

Combining considerations of effectiveness, control, and morality has and will help governments assess and carry out special activities in a future that is coming at us with dizzying speed.

When the United States began its romance with covert action in the late 1940s and 1950s, leaders of developing new nations had not yet mobilized masses of people in the developing world for political action. Politics was still very much an elite game when Kermit Roosevelt helped restore the shah to power in 1953. The mobilization of Iran's Islamic population by Khomeini and others made covert action almost impossible. The OSS successes in France and Burma during World War II were difficult to repeat in the Eastern Europe of the 1940s and 1950s. Similarly, the triumph of mass movements in other African and Middle Eastern states in the 1960s increased the need for effective diplomacy while simultaneously reducing the productive scope of covert activities. Covert action in Afghanistan and Iran from 2001–2014 in this discussion so quickly became overt action that the term should probably not be used to describe most of the activities of the Iraq–Afghan wars.[22]

Similarly today, the explosion of cell phones, computers, and the Internet has complicated covert operations. The geometric increase in surveillance capacities and means for harming others has both helped and hindered covert actions, and foreign policy and intelligence become more complex and interlinked than they have ever been.

The result, certainly for the United States, has been a reassessment of intelligence and the creation of a new Office of the director of National Intelligence (ODNI). Covert action has come under renewed scrutiny. Paramilitary efforts were stepped up in the wake of 9/11. Efforts have been made to increase public diplomacy and bring politics activities into more transparent light.

All postwar presidents have used covert action with congressional approval since 1974 (the exceptions have resulted in disgrace and/or punishment for the culprits). It is not unreasonable to suggest that they will continue to do so in a dangerous world. To achieve success, however, they will have to keep in mind the pitfalls and problems connected with such activities, as well as the guidelines for success listed above.

Ultimately, all connected with such activities need to bear in mind the words of former National Security Agency Director William E. Odom: "Intelligence performance simply cannot be separated from foreign policy-making and military operations."[23]

Notes

Robert W. Pringle Jr. and Jennifer Griffin aided the author in identifying several sources.

1. For history on these points, see Keith Hamilton and Richard Langhorn, *The Practice of Diplomacy* (New York: Routledge, 1995); G. R. Berridge, *Diplomacy: Theory and Practice*, 3rd ed. (New York: Palgrave, 2002); and Adda Bozeman, *Strategic Intelligence and Statecraft* (Washington: Brassey's, 1992).

2. Berridge, *Diplomacy*, pp. 618ff.; for more detail see Garrett Mattingly, *Renaissance Diplomacy* (New York: Houghton Mifflin, 1995).

3. See Scott Breckinridge, *The CIA and the U.S. Intelligence System* (Boulder, CO: Westview Press, 1986), chap. 1; Jeff Richelson, *The U.S. Intelligence Community* (Boulder, CO: Westview Press, 1995), chap. 1.

4. Charles D. Ameringer, *U.S. Foreign Intelligence: The Secret Side of American History* (Lexington: Lexington Books, 1990). This is an excellent and readable, swift review of U.S. intelligence from the country's inception through the Reagan administration, including covert action.

5. Richelson, *Intelligence Community*; Rhodri Jeffreys-Jones, *The CIA and American Democracy* (New Haven, CT: Yale University Press, 1989), intro and chaps. 1, 2; Abram N. Shulsky, *Silent Warfare: Understanding the World of Intelligence* (Washington: Brassey's, 1991), chaps. 2 and 14.

6. Breckinridge, *CIA and U.S. Intelligence*, part 1.

7. Richelson, *Intelligence Community*, p. 3.

8. Christopher Andrews and Vasili Mitrokhin, *The World Was Going Our Way: The KGB and the Battle for the Third World* (New York: Basic Books, 2005), is an excellent review of Soviet activities.

9. Sean Naylor, *Not a Good Day to Die* (New York: Berkley Books, 2005); William E. Odom, *Fixing Intelligence* (New Haven, CT: Yale University Press, 2003), chap. 4 and conclusion.

10. Steve Strasser (ed.), *The 9/11 Investigations: Staff Reports of the 9/11 Commission* (New York: Public Affairs, 2004).

11. Paul Pillar, *Terrorism and Foreign Policy* (Washington: Brookings Institution, 2001); Strasser, *9/11 Investigations*; Odom, *Fixing Intelligence*, pp. 150–192.

12. Breckinridge, *CIA and U.S. Intelligence*, parts 2 and 3; Loch K. Johnson, *America's Secret Power: The CIA in a Democratic Society* (New York: Oxford University Press, 1989); Loch K. Johnson and James J. Wirtz (eds.), *Strategic Intelligence: Windows into a Secret World* (Los Angeles: Roxbury, 2004), part 8.

13. Excellent examples and discussions of these points may be found in William J. Daugherty, *Executive Secrets: Covert Action and the Presidency* (Lexington: University Press of Kentucky, 2004), chaps. 1–3; Chalmers Johnson, *The Sorrows of Empire* (New York: Metropolitan Books, 2004); Anonymous [Michael Sheuer], *Imperial Hubris: Why the West Is Losing the War on Terror* (Washington: Brassey's, 2004); Michael Sheuer, *Through Our Enemies' Eyes* (Washington: Brassey's, 2002);

Odom, *Fixing Intelligence*, chaps. 7 and 9; Johnson, *America's Secret Power*, chaps. 6–9; Kim Roosevelt, *Countercoup: The Struggle for Control of Iran* (New York: McGraw-Hill, 1979); Stephen Kinser, *All the Shah's Men* (Hoboken, NJ: Wiley, 2003); Naylor, *Not a Good Day to Die*. Of these authors, four are former intelligence professionals, two are academics, and two are journalists.

14. Daugherty, *Executive Secrets*, conclusion; Odom, *Fixing Intelligence*, chaps. 7–9; Johnson and Wirtz, *Strategic Intelligence*, chaps 17, 19, 21, 28.

15. Executive Order 12333, U.S. Intelligence Activities, December 4, 1981, 3 CFR 200 (1981, 46 FR 59955, as amended by Executive Order 12701, 14 February, 1990, 55 FR 59333).

16. Daugherty, *Executive Secrets*, pp. 34–37; Bob Woodward, *Veil: The Secret Wars of the CIA, 1981–1987* (Buccaneer Press, 1994).

17. David Atlee Phillips, *The Night Watch* (New York: Ballantine Books, 1982); Victor Marchetti and John Marks, *The CIA and the Cult of Intelligence* (New York: Knopf, 1974).

18. Johnson and Wirtz, *Strategic Intelligence*, chap. 22.

19. David Rieff, *At the Point of a Gun: Democratic Dreams and Armed Intervention* (New York: Simon and Schuster, 2005), pp. 173–176; Stephen M. Walt, *Taming American Power: The Global Response to U.S. Primacy* (New York: Norton, 2005), pp. 243–247.

20. The source of the quote is a former intelligence officer who also served with the Foreign Service. The same themes can be found in Johnson, *America's Secret Power*, pp. 261–262; Daugherty, *Executive Secrets*, pp. 67–70 and conclusion; Johnson and Wirtz, *Strategic Intelligence*, pp. 278–279.

21. Henry Crumpton *The Art of Intelligence: Lessons from a Life in the Clandestine Service* (New York: Penguin Group 2012).

22. Robert Baer, *See No Evil* (New York: Crown, 2002); James Risen, *State of War* (New York: Free Press, 2006).

23. Odom, *Fixing Intelligence*, p. 186.

Part IV: Counterintelligence

CHAPTER FOURTEEN

Definitions and Theories of Counterintelligence

Stan A. Taylor

Counterintelligence is to intelligence as epistemology is to philosophy. Both go back to the fundamental question of how we know things, both challenge what we are inclined to take most for granted and both offer heavy advantage in debate to those who are skeptical of appearances.

Thomas Powers[1]

THEORIES ARE DEVELOPED AND USED in science to present conceptual frameworks that allow one to understand and explain phenomena. Theories also generate questions that are useful in research. These frameworks normally consist of assumptions (often called hypotheses) and statements, usually described as necessary and sufficient, for both explanation and prediction. However, in social sciences, the explanatory function is somewhat more important than the predictive function of theory since all of the controls necessary for a predictive theory are not available. Theories in Social Sciences can be very useful in *explaining* phenomena but only moderately useful as *predictive* tools in what are called "post hoc" predictions that are much the same as explanations of historical events. This chapter presents a counterintelligence theory that explains to some extent the existence of counterintelligence practices in any state. The theory is drawn from broader intelligence theories of which counterintelligence is a part. This attempt to theorize about counterintelligence begins with a brief discussion of intelligence theories and then derives counterintelligence theories from them.[2]

Definitions and Theories of Intelligence

Intelligence scholars argue about definitions of intelligence, but the primary difference between these efforts is merely the expansiveness of the definitions. In its most expansive application, intelligence refers to:

- The process that begins when national decision makers identify what information is needed to help them make better informed decisions regarding any entity with which they must deal.
- The prioritization, collection, analysis, production, and use of that information.
- The organizations and groups that actually collect, analyze, and produce the information.
- The other activities of various groups who participate in the intelligence cycle.
- The information and insights that flow from this process.

As defined, "intelligence" differs from the general use of information by human beings in everyday social intercourse in, at a minimum, six ways.

1. The fate of ideologies, nations, economies, and people may depend on how effectively the information or intelligence is utilized.
2. The information desired is usually, although not always, information that other individuals, groups, and nations do not want revealed.
3. The information desired is about individuals, groups, or nations who often, although not always, are hostile or potentially hostile toward the collecting nation.
4. The collection of this information is usually, although not always, done clandestinely.
5. Individual, group, or national rights may be violated in the collection of this information.
6. The broader intelligence process may generate secret special activities meant to influence the foreign or domestic policies of other states without revealing the source of the influence.

The Latin origins of the word "intelligence" are revealing. The prefix "*inter*" means between or among. Thus, the term "international relations" refers to the relations between or among nations. The remainder of the word "intelligence" comes, in its earliest usage, from the Latin word "*leger*"—the gathering of fruit or vegetables. Over time, these two terms were combined into one word referring to the knowledge and skills necessary to distinguish between good and bad fruit and vegetables. Gradually, the meaning of the term "intelligence" came to connote the skills and aptitudes needed to make wise and productive choices about any aspect of one's life. It is used in this chapter to refer to the knowledge and information necessary to make informed decisions about statecraft.

While some scholars stress the difference between intelligence as used by psychologists and intelligence as used by national strategists, in reality they come from the same origins.[3] The word *intelligence* in "intelligence quotient" or IQ really refers to the human ability to process environmental information into usable and productive knowledge. That is not substantially different from the ability to collect and process information about the interstate environment as a necessary prelude to informed statecraft.

National Security and Intelligence

At the outset, it is useful to understand the relationship between security and intelligence. Two early pioneers in the analysis of state power, Harold and Margaret Sprout of Princeton University, argued that there were five functions or variables by which the power of any state could be analyzed or measured[4].

1. The information-providing function. How well do states define a need for information and then collect, analyze, and utilize that information?
2. The decision-making function. Can a nation coordinate all of its resources into an effective strategy?
3. The means-providing function. How well can states provide the elements of power needed to achieve strategic goals?
4. The mean-utilizing functions. How well can a government utilize or effectively organize all of the means it may possess?
5. The resistance-to-demands function. How resilient is a state to the demands and challenges of other states?

Intelligence operations, particularly counterintelligence (CI) are critical in the first function but also play a significant role in the fifth function. Demands are more easily resisted when the intentions and capabilities of a threatening state or other entity are known and when the threatening entity does not have access to U.S. intelligence. In sum, intelligence is a significant part of state power, and power—the ability to influence other states in a predictable way—is a crucial and critical key to national security.

Theories of Intelligence

Humans use theories to explain observed reality. They are necessary for the development of any discipline. However, only a few scholars have attempted to develop theories of intelligence; among them are David Kahn and Loch K. Johnson.[5] Kahn believes his theory meets the requirements of all theories—it is both explanatory and predictive. He begins with the assumption that all biological organisms, from amoeba to nation states, need to sense their environment sufficiently to protect their existence. This leads him to his notion that intelligence, by its very nature, is for protection or for defense. That is, it is "essential to survival, but not to dominance."[6] He discusses both the antiquity and ubiquity of intelligence but notes the changing relative importance between physical intelligence (for example, information about physical objects—tanks, troops, etc.), whose importance is in relative decline, and verbal intelligence (for example, captured communications that may reveal enemy plans), which is increasing in importance. Kahn believes intelligence is increasing in importance but acknowledges that it will never be perfect. He also believes that the greatest contemporary and future problem intelligence faces is to be accepted by generals and heads of state whose minds are often set before they view intelligence information.

Johnson's approach is less of a general theory and more specific to strategic intelligence—that is, intelligence needed to support foreign policy and national strategy. He modestly calls his effort a "preface" to a theory and addresses the question of how much of a nation's scarce resources should be devoted to intelligence. He argues that such variables as a nation's global involvement, foreign policy goals, perceived threats, number of intelligence targets, and its ability to "consume" intelligence information will need to be studied more closely in order to construct an explanatory and predictive theory of intelligence. Johnson's greatest contribution is his insistence that intelligence must be viewed in the overall context of a nation's global strategy and threats.

A third and more general theory of intelligence, one into which both Kahn's and Johnson's theories would fit quite comfortably, can be drawn from cybernetics, a discipline developed in 1947 by mathematician Norbert Weiner and others.[7] The word "cybernetics" comes from a Greek word meaning "helmsman" or "governor"—one who steers a ship. A helmsman must use skill, intuition, and constant feedback from the environment to permit accurate steerage of the vessel.

Cybernetics is a complex science drawn from biology, neural modeling, psychology, mathematics, and electrical engineering, as well as other disciplines. It is the science of feedback—the study of how information can maintain or alter any biological, social, mechanical, or artificial system. Cybernetics has contributed to the development of General Systems Theory, Artificial Intelligence, and Robotics, as well as to significant developments in psychology and learning theories.

It is a perfect paradigm or theory for the role of intelligence applied to statecraft. Decision makers are the helmsmen, the governors, who must use skill, intuition, and a constant flow of information or intelligence to optimize efficiency (defined as the most security at the least cost) for the state. Cybernetics is the iterative flow of information that allows thermostats to maintain temperature in a building, computers to manufacture goods, guided missiles to reach their targets, and human beings to function in an often hostile world. It is about goal-oriented behavior at all levels of living systems. It allows these systems to reach defined goals based on accurate information flows. It is a unifying theory that runs through all levels of human interaction. Though not frequently acknowledged, it played a role in the development of constructivism, particularly social constructivism—the notion that social institutions adapt through the constant processing of stimuli (information) from the environment.

"Intelligence," defined as process, product, or people, collects and analyzes stimuli from the international environment. This information is used by decision makers as they act as helmsmen in steering the ship of state through the hazardous waters of international politics.

It should be obvious that all theories of intelligence or counterintelligence are overlaid on the traditional Realist approach to international affairs. That is, it is the anarchic nature of global affairs that forces states to look out for their own interests, knowing that no others will look out for those interests for them. As long as states are sovereign, and as long as there is no ultimate authority among states, intelligence will be collected by all states and counterintelligence efforts will be taken to protect state secrets, prevent hostile penetrations, and to turn "the opponent's agents into double agents or by feeding them false information that they report home."[8]

Counterintelligence

Counterintelligence "refers to the efforts taken to protect one's own intelligence operations from penetration and disruption by hostile nations" or groups and to protect state secrets.[9] Its primary functions are to:

- Protect classified information from unauthorized disclosure.
- Collect information about foreign intelligence services in order to prevent them from obtaining classified information from your nation.
- Collect information about hostile or potentially hostile group or state sponsored intelligence services in order to prevent them from disrupting or

compromising your own operations through penetration, disinformation, or other means.

- Identify and recruit foreign intelligence agents in order to feed false and misleading information through them—that is, to "double" them and use them for your own purposes.

Counterintelligence Techniques

Several techniques, practices, and procedures are necessary in order to perform the above functions.[10]

1. Pre-employment Personnel Security

All intelligence community (IC) employees, as well as all people who handle classified information, are subject to background checks. These background checks begin with biographical information then go on to include interviews with people who have known the applicant. For many IC agencies, this background check may also involve a polygraph or lie detector test. Although some scholars doubt the validity of information obtained by polygraph, few doubt that the fear of "being put on the box" has a deterring effect. While the Central Intelligence Agency (CIA), the National Reconnaissance Office (NRO), the Defense Intelligence Agency (DIA), and the National Security Agency (NSA) have used the polygraph for many years, the Federal Bureau of Investigation (FBI) only began to polygraph employees after the disastrous Robert Hanssen case. Hanssen had spied for both the Soviet Union and Russia for about 22 years and would most likely have continued had his treason not been revealed by another spy who knew of his activities.

2. In-service Personnel Security

Each agency also monitors its own employees during their period of employment. Many require periodic polygraph tests, during which the employees are asked questions about their lifestyles as well as questions about foreign contacts and about classified material they have handled. Other aspects of employee lifestyles—dramatic changes in financial worth, changes in spending habits, aberrant sexual practices, etc.—are also observed independently and may provide questions for future polygraph sessions as well as act as warning signs to counterintelligence officers.

Counterintelligence officers who administer polygraph tests and who check the financial situations of employees need also to pay attention to job satisfaction. Of all the scholarly literature on betrayal, the role of dissatisfaction and disgruntlement needs to be mined for insight. The only government agency that does this well is the Defense Personnel and Security Research Center (PERSEREC). This Center has begun to include disgruntlement in its frequent aggregate study of U.S. traitors. Perhaps as this phenomenon is studied more, Human Resource personnel in the IC will become more involved in counterintelligence so that the earliest indications of disgruntlement and dissatisfaction can be addressed before they turn into acts of betrayal.

3. Facility Security

Successful counterintelligence is impossible if facilities where secrets are produced and stored are not secure. Every agency in the IC, as well as government offices, institutes, businesses, and contractors that handle classified information are responsible for facility security. Often this will also include computer security. Facility security varies widely from location to location, and some of America's worst security breaches have occurred at defense contractor facilities. It is the responsibility of IC counterintelligence officers to monitor security at all of these sites and to take actions when that security is lax.

There are two challenges to traditional facility security. The first is the dramatic rise in the number of outside contractors who do work for the intelligence community. Shockingly, 36 percent of all employees who have access to top secret information are private contractors, and 70 percent of the intelligence community's secret budget goes to private firms.[11] The second is the dramatic increase in the volume, velocity, vulnerability, and variety of the communications that travel in and out of these facilities and the ease by which these communications can be downloaded onto miniscule flash drives.

4. Communications Security

Overall communications security in the U.S. is the responsibility of the NSA, who provide, maintain, and verify secure communications equipment at most IC agencies and other offices that handle classified information. However, each agency also carries out some communications security functions within its own facilities. As noted above, the volume, velocity, vulnerability, and variety of these communications present a serious counterintelligence problem.

5. Classification and Compartmentation

Information that might reveal sensitive national security secrets is classified by the government. Information may be classified both vertically and horizontally. There are three horizontal levels of classified information—confidential (used with decreasing frequency), secret, and top secret. Top secret information may be divided into vertical divisions called codeword compartments. The information in each compartment usually comes from a unique and specific intelligence collection source. That is, top secret/codeword material derived from a particular human source will be classified top secret and given a unique codeword. Information derived from intelligence intercepts of encrypted Soviet government communications throughout the 1950s, for example, was classified as top secret/VENONA. A person's access to compartmented information is given on a need-to-know basis—that is, whether knowledge of the particular information is necessary for the performance of the person's official duties.

Issues of classification and compartmentation are continual thorns in the side of democratic governments. Virtually no one believes they protect classified information as they should, but virtually everyone agrees that governments have a legitimate right to keep sensitive national security information secret. A perfect line between these two poles, in all likelihood, will never be drawn.

Revealing properly classified information to unauthorized persons (called "leaking"), especially when a nation is a war, traditionally would be considered treason. It has historically been dealt with and seen as a serious problem. It is a problem that has become more complicated in recent years by the celebration of leakers and their leaked information than it was in a pre-technological age. In today's world, either patriots wanting to reveal government wrongdoing or charlatans merely wanting fame and glory may be the source of leaked information. The more it becomes seen as a source of fame or notoriety, the greater the problem becomes. The English essayist Joseph Addison once asked, ". . . is there not some chosen curse, some hidden thunder in the stores of heav'n, red with uncommon wrath to blast the man who owes his greatness [meaning notoriety] to his country's ruin?"[12]

6. Signals Intelligence

All available, primarily international, intercepted communications are searched for clues that might reveal foreign agents operating in the U.S. or that might reveal U.S. persons working under foreign control. For example, the VENONA project, mentioned above, was begun in 1941 by Army security and taken over by the NSA when it was created in 1952. The names of many well-known American and British traitors—Klaus Fuchs, Kim Philby, Alger Hiss, the Rosenbergs, just to name a few—were revealed through VENONA decrypted information. This practice is also complicated by the requirements of privacy.

The traditional tasks of signals intelligence have become dramatically more complicated with the opening of cyberspace as an interstate battle ground. This development will add as yet unforeseen and significant CI opportunities and vulnerabilities. And the digitization of virtually all electronic communications has already created both an additional complication and, as well, a rich source of CI information.

7. Prosecuting Traitors

Anti-espionage laws are not effective unless penalties exist for revealing or stealing secret information. Foreign agents in the U.S. who are caught stealing secrets or receiving classified information will be jailed, if they do not have official cover, or they will be declared *persona non grata* and deported if they are in the country as a representative of their governments under official cover. U.S. citizens or U.S. persons who are caught revealing classified information are subject to federal prosecution.

Catching foreign agents or their American assets is a complicated task primarily under the direction of the FBI. The FBI has a long history of detecting law breakers, gathering solid evidence against them, and then relying on the Department of Justice for prosecution. The CIA, on the other hand, prefers to detect traitors, monitor their activities, and use them as a lead to other traitors and spies of whom they might not be aware. Rather than prosecuting them, they might wish to "double" them or supply them with misleading information. The clash between these two cultures has created a strained relationship between these two intelligence agencies marked by an absence of collaboration and cooperation of legendary proportions. And as has often been said, the success of counterintelligence in America rises or falls with the level of cooperation between the FBI and the CIA.

Assumptions of Counterintelligence Theory

Counterintelligence arises from the existence of four conditions or assumptions. First, it assumes that a nation has a decision-making system that deals with information that, in the hands of hostile groups or nations, could jeopardize national security. Second, it assumes that a nation has one or more intelligence services that collect that information and then try to prevent it from falling into enemy hands. Third, it assumes that foreign intelligence services will attempt to obtain other nations' classified information through normal intelligence procedures (human intelligence and signals intelligence) as well as through attempting to identify some who possess classified information and enticing them to reveal it to them. And fourth, a theory of counterintelligence assumes a very low level of trustworthiness in virtually all people. This last assumption will be discussed at greater length below.

These four assumptions add up to a theory of counterintelligence that explains the existence of counterintelligence activities in the intelligence services in all internationally active nations or non-state groups. The first three of the above assumptions fit nicely into each of the theories of intelligence discussed earlier. Counterintelligence is primarily defensive—it attempts to protect national secrets from other groups or nations in whose hands that information might be harmful. Kahn's theory of intelligence stresses the defensive value of intelligence, a subsidiary function of which is counterintelligence. Johnson's theory of intelligence is also useful in understanding counterintelligence. Johnson's theory, among other things, suggests that the extensiveness of a nation's global involvements explains the extensiveness and the costs of intelligence services. And the scope and extensiveness of a nation's intelligence services also explains both the efforts and the funds necessary to protect the security of the information collected.

The Cybernetic Theory of Intelligence is what is called a "grand theory"—it explains a large variety of human behavior from which more narrow and specific activities can also be explained. As applied to the field of intelligence and counterintelligence, this theory also works very well. Nations require information so that decision makers can steer the ship of state safely through the hazardous waters of international politics. That information or intelligence diminishes in value if it is known to other nations or groups, particularly hostile ones. In fact, counterintelligence is essential in order for intelligence to be useful. Revealed classified information is more dangerous than the absence of information because it means that the steering of the ship of state may be based on false information, on information describing conditions that no longer exist, or on information deliberately revealed to deceive. Thinking of the helmsman metaphor again, uncertainty about a state's environment may be better than unwarranted certainty, and the illusion of security may be worse than the absence of any intelligence services at all. As Thomas Powers has written,

An insecure [intelligence] service is not merely useless; it is positively dangerous, because it allows a hostile agency to manipulate the penetrated organization, as the British, for example, manipulated German intelligence during World War II. MI 5 turned German agents in Britain, used them to feed false information to Germany, and thereby thoroughly confused the

Germans as to the probable site and nature of the invasion of Europe. The Germans would have done better with no agents in Britain at all. . . . It is better to have no intelligence service at all than to have one which is insecure.[13]

Trust

More must be said about the fourth assumption of counterintelligence—the absence of trust—since it is particularly critical to an understanding of counterintelligence. Were all people fully trustworthy, many counterintelligence functions would be unnecessary. Most elements of personnel security and certain aspects of facility security (checking briefcases and packages that leave secure facilities, for example) would be unnecessary and there would be few or no traitors to prosecute. Communication lines would still need to be made secure, and captured communications of other states would still have to be mined to see if foreign agents had penetrated any agencies or facilities. But it is the absence of trust that makes much of counterintelligence necessary.

This assumption is a human level application of Realism. It is based on that notion that, for whatever reasons, humans possess an inherent dark side that causes them to doubt the goodness of others. Human nature is flawed, as Niebuhr and other realists have argued. Thus, they must always take steps to see that they are not hurt by their trust of others. When 16-year veteran CIA officer Harold Nicholson attempted to justify his selling classified information to the Soviet Union, he explained that since his work had kept him away from his family and prevented him from being a good father, he thought he needed to look out for his own interests for once and earn some extra money for his family.

Not only is distrust the basis of much counterintelligence, but its very practice magnifies the presence of distrust. It is a curious conundrum—an automatic and self-feeding cycle that ultimately degenerates in paranoia and worse. The act of counterintelligence quite literally feeds feelings of suspicion which, in turn, create greater distrust. And a culture of distrust spawns disgruntled employees who are ripe for recruitment by foreign intelligence services. In his 1953 play, *Camino Real*, Tennessee Williams has the following dialogue.

John: "Why does disappointment make people unkind to each other?"
Marguerite: "Each of us is very much alone."
John: "Only if we distrust each other."
Marguerite: "We have to distrust each other. It is our only defense against betrayal."

As two former CIA employees have written, "The function of the counterespionage officers is to question and verify every aspect of CIA operations; taking nothing at face value, they tend to see deceit everywhere. In an agency full of extremely mistrustful people, they are the professional paranoids."[14] Counterintelligence officers must distrust their fellow employees, look suspiciously on (and even challenge) the good faith of defectors, and study foreign intelligence entities so thoroughly so they begin to "think" like foreign intelligence agencies and officers.

James Jesus Angleton, the legendary and controversial director of CIA counterintelligence for over 20 years, described the landscape of counterintelligence as "a wilderness of mirrors," an "ever-fluid landscape where fact and illusion merge. . . ."[15] It is not an easy environment in which to work. Rebecca West has noted that "people who work in a self-contained [counterintelligence] unit are apt to develop theories which develop none the better for never being subject to open discussion."[16]

It is widely believed that Angleton's culture of distrust pervaded the CIA for so long that counterintelligence gained a very bad reputation within the agency—a reputation that lingered long after Angleton's forced 1974 resignation. In reaction to this culture of distrust, employees tended to question the need for both counterintelligence functions and officers. They tended to believe that their fellow officers who had been vetted and cleared and were in the service of their country could be trusted. It was a notion somewhat like joining a community service or business club; once a Rotarian, for example, one could be trusted forever, at least by fellow Rotarians.

This anti-counterintelligence culture may have contributed to the failure to detect subsequent traitors throughout the entire IC. For example, the treason of Aldrich Ames, a CIA officer who spied for the Soviet Union and then for Russia for nine years, was nurtured partially by this culture. Information he sold to the Soviets resulted in the betrayal and death of nearly all of the CIA's most productive Soviet assets at the height of the Cold War. Time and time again, over nine years, a failure to take counterintelligence seriously, in part a reaction against the Angleton years, resulted in ignoring clear signals of Ames's treason.

On his just under $70,000 a year salary, Ames paid cash for a $540,000 home, purchased a $40,000 red Jaguar automobile (which he drove to work), and had money left over to purchase cosmetic dental surgery on his teeth. Ames once even cited Angleton's legacy as a reason for his decision to spy.[17] Whether Ames's statement is true or merely his attempt to blame someone else for his treason, it is undoubtedly true that counterintelligence was not taken as seriously as it should have been at that time.

Sources of Treason

This trust-distrust paradox was first stated by the 1st-century Roman philosopher and statesman Seneca in his *Letters to Lucilius*: "It is a vice to trust all, and equally a vice to trust none." But who can you trust? This dilemma has provoked many to study the causes of betrayal and treason. It turns out that while many traitors on both sides of the Iron Curtain, particularly during the early years of the Cold War, were motivated by ideology, money has been the primary motivation of treason since the mid-1970s.[18] But if one examines secondary motives, that is, motives that led to ideological betrayal or selling out for monetary gain, the role of disgruntlement is growing. If one "considers those who, though not completely disgruntled, were not entirely 'gruntled' (to borrow from Oscar Wilde), then disgruntlement becomes a more prevalent motive" for treason.[19]

If the "trust assumption" aspect of counterintelligence theory is correct, then it may well be that a substantial part of the defense against treason in the future may be played by the human resource personnel in each intelligence agency. The ability to keep personnel satisfied with their employment may be one of the better defenses against treason, particularly against treason for financial gain. How to accomplish that is not the purpose of this chapter; however, enlightened and responsive leadership and management; collegial work conditions; the absence of "cronyism" in salary and advancement decisions; and fair rewards for quality service, work equality, and employees who have "bought" into the mission of the agency for whom they work are certainly beginning points. Perhaps Andrew Roberts captured a glimpse of what was coming when he wrote in 1997, "Tomorrow's traitors are more likely to be driven to betray not from ideological convictions but from whining complaints about poor pension provisions or underfunded performance-related pay."[20]

The Edward Snowden Case

In late June of 2013, the most massive unauthorized release of government classified information in U.S. history became the intelligence failure *de jour* (*de annee?*) and had faded very little at the time of this writing. Edward Snowden, nominated for various public honors by some, yet vilified by others, was a different kind of traitor. As Mark Bowden points out, the classical leakers in contemporary American history (Mark Felt and Daniel Ellsberg, for example) released classified information to protest a specific act of wrongdoing—Watergate and deception in the Defense Department and the White House, respectively. But, argues Bowden, Snowden appears to be objecting to the very concept of government secrecy itself.[21] Felt and Ellsberg wanted to expose what they thought to be illegal and improper government behavior. The same cannot be said about Snowden and Manning. Both the statements accompanying their leaks, and the information leaked, seek solely to discredit all government secrets, even those that may enhance U.S. security. Their leaks want to shame intelligence agencies for doing what the White House, Congress, the Department of Justice, and even the American public had asked them to do. In response to widespread accusations that the IC had failed to "connect the dots" before 9/11, the NSA, finally and with wide support, was beginning to connect the dots yet found itself vilified at home and abroad for doing so.

The issue of Edward Snowden presents a case study for CI officials that can only be made when more information is available. Why did he pass the pre-employment interviews? Why could a young man who dropped out of high school, enrolled but did not attend a British university, and left the CIA with a negative job evaluation be hired and allowed to access highly classified information, first by the NSA and then by Booz Allen Hamilton, a global consulting company doing lucrative business with the NSA as well as other government and private organizations? The short answer is that he seemed to be very good at what he did.

This answer raises a classic CI question—does job performance trump loyalty? At this early stage of the Snowden affair, it appears that every CI technique listed above may have failed. Certainly pre-employment checks failed, in-service monitoring was flawed, and security at the CIA/Dell facility was lax, while at the same time, Snowden's own personal communication security was strong. One wonders why his voluminous downloading of data was not noticed, and, apparently, classification and compartmentalization failed to prevent access into areas where he had little justification to be. Interviews with four officials at Booz Allen Hamilton should have sent HR people running to Snowden's office, and it remains to be seen whether or not some CI office did not learn about his communications with journalists.

The final CI technique discussed above, punishment of traitors, remains to be tested. Justice Department officials would like to prosecute Snowden, if for no other reason than to deter future leakers. But, as of this writing, he remains secure (although probably not comfortable) in Russia. Were he to be returned to the U.S., Justice Department officials would have a difficult decision to make. Successfully prosecuting a person who has won or is being considered for a variety of prestigious awards from nations around the world, as well as adulation from several American newspapers, would be difficult. The government has the law on its side, but public opinion would create massive opposition to justice being served. One wonders if the old adage, "crime unpunished is crime encouraged" is still valid in the age of instant fame (or notoriety).[22] Applied to this case, one might say, "treason unpunished is treason encouraged." When the Duke of York, in Shakespeare's *Richard the Second*, discovers disloyalty in something hanging around his son's neck, his response is immediate and vociferous: "Treason!" he shouts, "foul treason!"[23]

A government case against Snowden might be helped if the government could demonstrate that the very practices Snowden revealed in his leaked documents were the same practices that have been used by NSA to identify people associated with terrorist attacks in the U.S., the U.K., Spain, and Germany.

Summary and Conclusion

This chapter began by defining intelligence and discussing how intelligence related to national security and then offered a brief review of three compatible and interrelated theories of intelligence. This was followed by a definition of counterintelligence, a summary of the primary functions of counterintelligence, and a review of counterintelligence techniques. Following that, four assumptions about counterintelligence were presented. These four assumptions provided a basis for a counterintelligence theory. At a general level of activity, this theory explains the existence of the practice of counterintelligence in virtually all states. The level of both intelligence and counterintelligence activities, as Johnson argues, depends on the extensiveness of a state's global activities and obligations.[24]

The necessary absence of trust within the Intelligence Community creates a conundrum in which CI is justified, but at the same time, treason becomes more likely. Yet it is that condition that provides the foundational assumption in the theory of counterintelligence. Were all people trustworthy, much counterintelligence work would be unnecessary. That being the case, those who guard government secrets need to devote more time and energy into developing and nurturing trustworthiness within their employees. And at the same time, a related effort needs to be made to reduce the rather high levels of disgruntlement among the custodians of national secrets.

This is a difficult task when, of necessity, the functions of counterintelligence are dispersed and decentralized throughout the IC and when the very practice of counterintelligence tends to alienate some employees. Clearly, the counterintelligence staff in every agency needs to take their work more seriously. Both routine as well as random security investigations need to be standard procedure rather than something done only when a traitor has been revealed. Perhaps the advice of the Countess to Bertram in Act I, Scene I, of Shakespeare's *All's Well That Ends Well* ought to be followed—"Love all, trust a few, do harm to none."

Counterintelligence personnel need to be well-trained. There is a tendency to assume that any intelligence professional can be moved in and out of counterintelligence without additional training. And counterintelligence needs to be done in the field as well as at the home office. CI officers need to be rewarded within their field of specialization. Many feel that they need to get out of CI and into better career tracks or even to leave their agency and work in the more profitable private security industry. Counterintelligence is taken seriously in America only after a traitor has been revealed. After FBI agent Robert Hanssen was caught, the FBI acknowledged that it did not take security seriously. After CIA officer Aldrich Ames was caught, CIA officials acknowledged the same.

Finally, counterintelligence is the most difficult of all intelligence work. It is a thankless task where practitioners are in a "lose-lose" situation. If spies are found within U.S. agencies, it is called a counterintelligence failure. If they are not found, it may also be called a counterintelligence failure. What is often called the Law of Invisible Phenomena must be kept in mind: The absence of evidence is not evidence of absence.

Notes

I wish to thank the following for their help at various stages of the writing of this chapter: Kara Norman, Eric Lindsay, and Victoria Taylor.

1. *The Man Who Kept the Secrets: Richard Helms & the CIA* (New York: Knopf, 1979), cited in Charles E. Lathrop, *The Literary Spy* (New Haven: Yale University Press, 2004), 54.

2. Any social science researcher must always keep in mind Roger Scruton's warning: "In general, scientific thinking involves theories that are borrowed from the context that gave rise to them and applied out of context, on the basis of slim analogies." "Scientism and the Humanities," Wheatley Forum Lecture, Brigham Young University, Provo, Utah (May 7, 2012).

3. See, for example, Douglas Wheeler, "A Note about Intelligence Historiography," *The Intelligencer: [A] Journal of U.S. Intelligence Studies* (Summer/Fall, 2011), 48.

4. Harold and Margaret Sprout, *Foundations of National Power: Readings on World Politics and American Security*, 2d ed. (New York: Van Nostrand, 1962), 167–175.

5. David Kahn's theory is found in his "An Historical Theory of Intelligence," *Intelligence and National Security* 16 (2001): 79–92; Loch K. Johnson's theory is

found in his "Preface to a Theory of Strategic Intelligence," *International Journal of Intelligence and Counterintelligence* 16 (2003–2004): 638–663.

6. Kahn, "An Historical Theory of Intelligence," 80.

7. This section is drawn from my "Security and Intelligence," Chapter 14 in Alan Collins (ed.), *Contemporary Security Studies* (Oxford: Oxford University Press, 2006).

8. Mark M. Lowenthal, *Intelligence: From Secrets to Policy*, 3d ed., (Washington, D.C.: CQ Press), 151.

9. Mark M. Lowenthal, *Intelligence: From Secrets to Policy*, 2d. ed., (Washington, D.C.: CQ Press), 113.

10. The best available list of all counterintelligence techniques is found in Frederick L. Wettering, "Counterintelligence: The Broken Triad," *Intelligence and National Security* 13 (2000): 265–300.

11. As reported by Robert O'Harrow Jr., Dana Priest, and Marjorie Censer, *The Washington Post* (June 13, 2013), p. 1.

12. Joseph Addison, *Cato* (Act 1, Scene 1), written 1712 and first performed in 1713.

13. Powers, *The Man Who Kept the Secrets*, as cited in Lathrop, *The Literary Spy*, 49.

14. Victor Marchetti and John Marks, *CIA and the Cult of Intelligence* (New York: Knopf, 1974), cited in Lathrop, *The Literary Spy*, 52.

15. The phrase actually comes from T. S. Eliot's 1920 poem, "Gerontion." It has also been used as the title of several books, including one by former CIA officer David Martin in 1980 about Angleton. The subsequent quotation comes from Norman Polmar and Thomas B. Allen, *Spy Book: The Encyclopedia of Espionage*, 2d ed. (New York: Random House Reference, 2004), 685.

16. *The New Meaning of Treason* (New York: Time, 1960) cited in Lathrop, *The Literary Spy*, 51.

17. Pete Early, *Confessions of a Spy* (New York: Putman's Sons, 1997), 146.

18. See Stan A. Taylor and Daniel Snow, "America's Cold War Spies: Why They Spied and How They Got Caught," *Intelligence and National Security* 12 (1997): 101–125. The best work on treason is done by the Defense Personnel Security Research Center (PERSEREC) in Monterey, California. See, for example, Susan Wood and Martin F. Wiskoff, *Americans Who Spied against the Country Since World War II* (Monterey: CA, 1994) and Lynn F. Fischer, "Espionage: Why Does It Happen," at http:/www.hanford.gov/oci/maindocs/ci_r_docs/whyhappens.pdf (accessed December 20, 2005), as well as Theodore R. Sabin and others, *Citizen Espionage: Studies in Trust and Betrayal* (Westport, CT: Praeger, 1994).

19. Taylor and Snow, "America's Cold War Spies," 110.

20. The *Sunday Times* (London, May 25, 1997), as cited in Lathrop, *The Literary Spy*, 398.

21. Mark Bowden, "What Snowden and Manning Don't Understand about Secrecy," at http://www.theatlantic.com/politics/archive/2013/08/bowden-manning -snowden/278973/, appearing on-line August 23, 2013. Accessed 24 August 2013.

See also Sean Wilentz, "Would You Feel Differently about Snowden, Greenwald, and Assange If You Knew What They Really Thought?" *The New Republic* (January 14, 2014), http://www.newrepublic.com/article/116253/ edward-snowden-glenn -greenwald-julian-assange-what-they-believe. Accessed February 19, 2014.

22. I have not been able to locate the origins of this saying, but it has been kept very much alive in Armenia since 1915.

23. Act 5, Scene 11, in *The Tragedy of King Richard the Second*.

24. Johnson, "Preface to a Theory of Strategic Intelligence," 638–663.

CHAPTER FIFTEEN

The Successes and Failures of FBI Counterintelligence

Athan Theoharis

RELYING ON DEPARTMENTAL CONTINGENCY FUNDS, ON June 29, 1908, Attorney General Charles Bonaparte established by executive order a special investigative force within the Department of Justice, the Bureau of Investigation (formally renamed the Federal Bureau of Investigation, FBI, in 1935). Bonaparte's decision in effect contravened recent congressional actions of 1907–1908 that first rejected the attorney general's request to fund a special agent task force and then barred the Justice Department from contracting for the services of Secret Service agents. Because his decision violated the intent of these actions (although the 1870 statute creating the Department of Justice authorized it to prosecute "and detect" federal crimes), Bonaparte was forced to assuage congressional concerns. During January 1909 testimony before a House Appropriations Subcommittee, the attorney general emphasized the need for such a force, stressed that it would only investigate violations of federal statutes, and pledged to monitor its operations closely to ensure that agents would not violate privacy rights or monitor political beliefs. The size of this agent force (34 in 1909) and Bonaparte's assurances deterred congressional opposition. Congress nonetheless approved appropriations in 1909 confining the Bureau of Investigation to "detection and prosecution of crimes against the United States."

Congress revisited this restriction in 1910, empowering the newly created Bureau to conduct "such other investigations regarding official matters under the control of the Department of Justice as may be directed by the Attorney General." This more permissive standard was triggered by the enactment that year of the Mann (or White Slave Traffic) Act criminalizing the transportation of women across state lines "for the purpose of prostitution, or for any other immoral purpose." Not only had Congress thereby expanded the definition of interstate commerce crimes, but a numerically larger force would be required with agents stationed outside Washington, D.C., subject to the supervision not of the attorney general but the bureau director.[1]

The belated (April 1917) U.S. military involvement in World War I did not fundamentally change the Bureau's role as a law enforcement agency. Its wartime investigations focused on alien residents, prominent antiwar critics, and radical activists. Those targeted included Socialist Party officials Charles Schenck and Eugene Debs, leaders of the radical Industrial Workers of the World Union, Senator Robert LaFollette, social reformer and pacifist Jane Addams, black nationalist leader Marcus Garvey, prominent Irish nationalist Eamon de Valera, and the anti-British and pro-Irish Hearst press and *Chicago Tribune*. The Bureau's most controversial actions, however, involved the arrests of hundreds of suspected "slackers" in New York City in 1918 and the arrests of 6,000–10,000 citizens and alien residents during dragnet raids of January 1920, the so-called Palmer raids. All were law enforcement operations, initiated on the suspicion that the targeted subject had violated either the Espionage Act of 1917, the Conscription Act of 1917, or the alien radical deportation provisions of the 1917 and 1918 immigration acts.[2]

Subsequent revelations that, in the postwar years, Bureau agents intensively monitored political and labor union activities and even investigated members of Congress instrumental in triggering a congressional investigation of the involvement of senior Harding administration officials in the Teapot Dome scandal led President Calvin Coolidge to dismiss Attorney General Harry Daugherty in 1924. Harlan Fiske Stone, Daugherty's successor, in turn fired Bureau Director William Burns and issued a series of orders to preclude future FBI abuses. These included banning wiretapping and restricting investigations to violations of federal statutes. Investigations of political activities, though scaled back, were not wholly abandoned. Bureau Director J. Edgar Hoover (Burns's successor) encouraged concerned citizens to continue reporting on such activities while the FBI's agents were to report such information as coming not from their investigations but "sources." Bureau files on organizations such as the American Civil Liberties Union and the Communist Party (for a time during the 1920s renamed the Workers Party) continued to be developed.[3]

The real shift in the FBI's role occurred in the mid-1930s when it began to conduct intelligence investigations having no direct law enforcement purpose. The catalyst to this new role stemmed from twin domestic and international crises: the Great Depression at home and the international policies of Nazi Germany and the Soviet Union. The devastating economic crisis of the Great Depression caused many Americans to question the nation's economic and political institutions, with some joining fascist and communist movements. Concurrently, as "subversive" powers committed to furthering their own international goals, German and Soviet officials sought to recruit American fascists and communists to conduct espionage.

President Franklin Roosevelt accordingly turned to the FBI to neutralize this perceived foreign-directed security threat. In May 1934, in a one-time response, the president directed the FBI to conduct "an intensive and confidential investigation of the [American] Nazi movement with emphasis on anti-American activities having any connection with German government officials." Then, in August 1936, he met with Hoover to discuss "the question of subversive activities in the United States, particularly Fascism and Communism." Roosevelt was particularly concerned that "some [domestic] organizations would probably attempt to cripple our war effort through sabotage." No U.S. agency was acquiring "general intelligence information" about such "subversive activities," Hoover responded, but then claimed that a 1916 appropriation statute would provide the authority allowing the FBI to conduct such investigations at the request of the State Department. Roosevelt orally concurred while emphasizing the need for secrecy (for domestic political as much as for security reasons).[4]

The sensitivity of intelligence investigations (which lacked any law enforcement purpose) ultimately posed a bureaucratic problem for FBI officials, because the 1916 statute required a State Department request to trigger them. In response to FBI pressure, on June 26, 1939, Roosevelt assigned to the FBI and military and naval intelligence sole responsibility for all such investigations. Then, in a series of delimitation agreements concluded with military and naval intelligence in 1940–1942, the FBI acquired a monopoly over all domestic intelligence investigations—with military and naval intelligence investigations confined to military personnel and base security (which would include weapons programs such as the Manhattan Project).[5] FBI officials also expanded authorized investigative techniques. To anticipate espionage and sabotage, Roosevelt secretly authorized FBI wiretapping in May 1940 during "national defense" investigations—even though the 1934 Communications Act banned wiretapping and the Supreme Court ruled in 1937 that this ban applied to federal agencies and in 1939 required the dismissal of any indictment based on evidence obtained through wiretaps. On his own, Hoover authorized FBI break-ins of targeted individuals and organizations to install microphones or photocopy records, a series of mail-opening programs (to intercept and open mail transiting through the United States from identified foreign countries), and the cooperation of telegraph and cable companies' access to cable traffic involving 13 identified foreign countries transiting to and from the United States.[6]

Roosevelt's concerns that German agents might seek to exploit anti-Yankee sentiments in Latin and South America also led him to expand the FBI's counterintelligence role. Dating from 1940, FBI officials worked out with William Stephenson, the head of the British Security Coordination (BSC) stationed in New York City, a liaison relationship to ensure that German agents active in Latin and South America would be closely monitored. Then, on June 24, 1940, Roosevelt authorized the FBI to conduct "foreign intelligence work in the Western Hemisphere on the request of the State Department." In response, Hoover created a Special Intelligence Service (SIS) with FBI agents assigned as "legal attachés" to U.S. diplomatic missions in the capitals of 18 nations in the region. The combination of the FBI–BSC liaison program and the FBI's SIS led to the detection during World War II of 832 German espionage agents, the apprehension of 336, and the shutting down of 24 clandestine radio stations used by German agents to communicate with Berlin and with other agents in Latin America.[7]

In contrast to its successful counterintelligence role in Latin and South America, FBI counterintelligence operations within the United States had mixed results—striking successes and major failures.

In 1938 FBI agents arrested Guenther Rumrich and three other members of a German-directed espionage ring operating out of New York City (although another 14 co-conspirators escaped arrest by fleeing to Germany). Dating from 1927, German intelligence operatives had recruited German American citizens and German alien residents to infiltrate defense plants (particularly those engaged in airplane and ship construction) and the U.S. military to obtain information about U.S. military technology and tactics, defense planning, and shipping operations in the port of New York. The acquired information was then relayed to Germany through couriers who were either passengers or employed in the shipping industry. In June 1941, moreover, FBI agents successfully shut down another German espionage operation, headed by Frederick Duquesne and involving 33 citizens and resident agents, that sought to relay sensitive defense information to Germany through a shortwave radio station in Centerport, Long Island. And in an even more dramatic success, FBI agents in 1942 arrested two four-man teams of German saboteurs, one that had landed in Amagansett, Long Island, and the second in Jacksonville, Florida. These teams' purposes were to sabotage American transportation and industrial facilities along the East Coast, an aluminum plant in Tennessee, and locks on the Ohio River.

The FBI's successes in the Rumrich, Duquesne, and German saboteur cases resulted more from good luck than FBI investigative prowess. In the Rumrich case, the original lead came in September 1935 when a customs officer apprehended William Lonkowski (a German agent sent to the United States in 1927) when boarding the liner *Europa* with film strips and letters concealed in a violin case. Alerted to German espionage plans, FBI officials received a further break when Rumrich blatantly attempted to obtain blank American passport forms in February 1938. Interviewed by military intelligence agents, Rumrich admitted his role. Military intelligence thereupon referred the matter to the FBI, and, in return for leniency, Rumrich identified the other participants in this operation. In the Duquesne case, German intelligence operatives had pressured William Se-bold (an American citizen of German descent), during a family visit to Germany, to serve as a spy. When returning to the United States, however, Sebold contacted the FBI and agreed to participate in an elaborate sting operation. FBI agents assisted him in setting up a shortwave radio station to relay to Germany information obtained by their recruited spies. The apprehension of the German saboteurs was equally fortuitous, the byproduct of the inadvertent discovery of the landing of one of the four-man saboteur teams by Coast Guardsman John Cullen when patrolling the beach near Amagansett. The saboteurs claimed to be fishermen and paid Cullen a bribe. Having overheard them speaking German, a suspicious Cullen returned the next morning to discover the equipment and uniforms that the four men had buried in the sand. He immediately brought this discovery to the attention of the FBI. In the interim, one of the four saboteurs, George Dasch, fearing discovery, approached the FBI and told agents the cover names and possible contacts of the other members of his team and the second team that had landed in Florida.[8]

Ironically, the most serious security threat was posed not by a wartime adversary, Nazi Germany, but a wartime ally, the Soviet Union. The FBI, however, failed to discover the scope of Soviet espionage activities during the prewar and wartime years. Dating from the late 1930s and continuing after the United States and the Soviet Union became military allies in 1941, FBI agents closely monitored Soviet embassy and consular officials stationed in the United States (as well as Soviets assigned to the wartime Soviet Government Purchasing Commission) and high-level American

Communist Party officials. The scope and intensity of this counterintelligence effort cannot be fully documented either because relevant FBI documents remain classified or, when released, are heavily redacted. At a minimum, the FBI wiretapped the Soviet embassy, the headquarters of the American Communist Party, and a host of radical labor union and political organizations; bugged meetings that Soviet officials or American communists attended; intercepted the mail of communist officials and activists; and broke into the offices and residences of prominent American communists and other radical activists. In these efforts, FBI agents sought to uncover activities "detrimental to the national defense of the United States with respect to espionage, propaganda activities and otherwise."[9]

Nonetheless, despite the intensity of FBI counterintelligence operations, the Bureau's agents failed to uncover the involvement of American communists and Soviet officials in espionage during the World War II era. These included the pilfering of FBI files by Judith Coplon, a communist employed in the Department of Justice; the atomic espionage activities of David Greenglass and Theodore Hall; and the pilfering of classified information for delivery to the Soviets by two rings of communists employed in various wartime agencies, one headed by Victor Perlo and the second by Nathan Silvermaster.[10]

The FBI, it must be emphasized, had not been deterred from seeking to learn about Soviet and American communist espionage activities by a Roosevelt administration indifferent to the employment of communists and motivated to sustain U.S.–Soviet cooperation, or because of the priority of German counterintelligence operations. In fact, Attorneys General Robert Jackson and Francis Biddle approved all FBI requests to wiretap the Soviet embassy and Communist Party headquarters and identified communist and radical activists. Furthermore, dating from 1940, FBI officials assured the White House that they had the situation in hand. In a 1941 report, for example, FBI Director Hoover claimed that the FBI's

> active and intensive [counterintelligence] operations are carried on in keeping under observation and constant study the operations of the German, Italian, Soviet and Japanese Agents. . . . The identification of all major representatives of the Governments specified are known and their activities are under constant scrutiny.

Earlier in 1940, Hoover reported that FBI agents were able to "maintain a careful check against the channels of communication, the sources of information, the methods of finance, and other data relative to" Soviet, German, French, and Italian agents.[11]

Hoover's 1940 and 1941 reports had been prepared at a time when the United States was neutral and when the Soviet Union and Germany still adhered to a 1939 nonaggression pact. FBI surveillance of Soviet officials and American communists, however, did not abate and instead intensified after the United States and the Soviet Union became allies following the Pearl Harbor attack. Indeed, in post-1941 reports to the White House, the FBI director emphasized the possibility of Soviet (and communist) subversion. Yet the only information that he reported about Soviet officials and American communists involved their efforts to influence either U.S. policy toward the Soviet Union, individuals of Baltic or Eastern European descent, or congressional legislation. Alternatively, Hoover cited communist efforts to influence labor union, youth, and civil rights movements.[12] This total failure to uncover the reality of Soviet espionage is documented by a December 1944 report on FBI "espionage and counter-intelligence operations" having "ramifications within the United States" that only cited the actions of German agents or double agents.[13]

Two cases in particular highlight this counterintelligence failure. The first is a massive FBI investigation of planned Soviet espionage activities, and the second is the response of senior FBI officials to the defection of Victor Kravchenko, a Soviet official employed in the Soviet Government Purchasing Commission.

Through a wiretap of Communist Party headquarters, FBI officials learned that Communist Party leader Earl Browder had alerted a West Coast Communist Party activist, Steve Nelson, about a forthcoming sensitive initiative. Bugging Nelson's residence in Oakland, California, FBI agents intercepted Nelson's meeting with Soviet embassy official Vassili Zubilin in April 1943, at which time Zubilin gave Nelson a large "sum of money" for the express "purpose of placing Communist Party members and agents in industries engaged in secret war production in the United States so that information could be obtained for transmittal to the Soviet Union." Thus alerted to a planned Soviet espionage operation involving the recruitment of American communists, FBI officials benefited further with the receipt in August 1943 of an anonymous letter to Hoover that identified by name a number of Soviet officials who were purportedly involved in espionage (some employed in the Soviet embassy and others in Soviet consulates, the Soviet trading company Amtorg, or the Government Purchasing Commission).

In response, Hoover ordered a massive FBI counterintelligence operation, code named COMRAP (Comintern Apparatus), one that had the advantage of focusing on identified Soviet and Communist Party officials. FBI agents followed these individuals and from them followed those with whom they were in contact, eventually totaling forty-six. Lasting two years, the FBI's COMRAP investigation (which extended beyond physical surveillance to include the extensive use of wiretaps, bugs, break-ins, and mail opening) failed to uncover a single instance of Soviet or American communist espionage. Indeed, a December 1944 report summarizing the results of this investigation claimed only that the suspects had distributed "pro-Russian propaganda" through the media and communist front groups to "influence the people and Government of the United States toward acceptance of Soviet foreign policy," to recruit new Communist Party members, to "collect political information of value to the USSR," to "secure information of value to the [Communist] Party," and to promote "the employment of Communists in Government work."[14]

This failure raises questions about FBI counterintelligence capabilities. In part, FBI efforts were neutralized by the safeguards adopted by Soviet officials, as trained professionals, to avert discovery. Equally important, FBI agents had focused on prominent communist leaders and not low-level functionaries (some of whom had severed contact with the Communist Party). FBI agents even failed to follow up on what could have been a promising lead—their discovery, through monitoring one of the COMRAP suspects, Louise Bransten, of her December 1944 meeting in Washington, D.C., with Nathan Silvermaster and Charles Flato. Silvermaster at the time was the subject of a Hatch Act investigation (authorizing the dismissal of any federal employee who was a Communist Party member). FBI officials first learned of Silvermaster's role as head of one of two Soviet espionage rings (and Flato's role as a contributing member) in November 1945 with the defection of the courier for these two rings, Elizabeth Bentley.[15]

A second FBI counterintelligence failure involved defector Victor Kravchenko. Alerted in February 1944 to Kravchenko's pending defection (formally announced in April 1944), FBI officials obtained Roosevelt's and Attorney General Francis Biddle's unqualified authorization to pursue this matter. (Hoover had sought such assurances in light of the potential impact on U.S.–Soviet relations.) Meeting with Kravchenko in March 1944, FBI agents learned that he was willing to brief them about the "espionage activity of Soviet representatives in the United States," about other "illegal conspiracies" between Soviet representatives and U.S. defense firms, about the "activities" of Soviet intelligence agents in the United States, and about the organization and plans of the Soviet Communist Party and the NKVD (the predecessor to the KGB). In return for this information, Kravchenko demanded personal protection (including transportation to a safe hiding place and a permit to carry a gun) and limited financial support (namely, "no monetary worries for about a year and a half"). Hoover immediately briefed Biddle about Kravchenko's demands. The attorney general again authorized the FBI director to proceed as he saw fit. Biddle had concurrently secured Secretary of State Cordell Hull's approval, because this defection could adversely affect already delicate U.S.–Soviet relations. At first hesitant Hull concurred, convinced that this was a "matter of internal security and might involve sabotage," could provide insights into "what the Russians were doing here," and could serve as a "convenient card" that he could use "when he next conferred" with Soviet officials.[16]

FBI officials, however, failed to exploit this opportunity to learn about ongoing and planned Soviet espionage activities. Instead, they launched an intensive investigation of Kravchenko and those Americans whom he contacted (all prominent anticommunists), suspecting that he "may be an agent" of the NKVD and thus "part of a NKVD scheme to check on the Bureau's activities and attempt to lay some predication for possible embarrassment of the Bureau." In this investigation that lasted until 1945, FBI agents used wiretaps extensively, conducted break-ins, and opened the mail of Kravchenko and his American contacts, in addition to monitoring their activities closely.[17]

The FBI's counterintelligence failures in part resulted from the difficulty of anticipating espionage, but just as important was the essentially political criteria employed to target suspected subversives. In guidelines issued in September 1936, Hoover ordered FBI agents to target "Maritime Industry, Government affairs, steel industry, oil industry, newspaper field, clothing, garment and fur industry, general strike activities, Armed Forces, educational institutions, general activities—Communist and Affiliated Organizations, Fascists, Anti-Fascist movements, and activities in Organized Labor organizations." This focus on radical labor union and political activists was not revised after U.S. military involvement in World War II. Among those targeted were the radical American Youth Congress (during a 1942 break-in of the organization's New York headquarters, FBI agents photocopied Eleanor Roosevelt's correspondence with its leaders); Mrs. Roosevelt's contacts with the International Student Association (another radical youth group); anti-Nazi refugees from Germany (Thomas Mann, Bertolt Brecht, Hanns Eisler, Ruth Berlau, Leonhard Frank, Berthold Viertel), suspect because of their Marxist political views; and communists employed in the Hollywood film industry (targeted in 1942 under a code-named COMPIC program). Ironically, the catalyst to the COMPIC investigation was Hollywood's production of antifascist and pro-Soviet films (such as *For Whom the Bell Tolls* and *Mission to Moscow*), confirming that FBI officials' underlying concern was that communists could influence the popular culture.[18]

The reality of Soviet espionage became publicly known with Elizabeth Bentley's congressional testimony in August 1948, with the congressional and grand jury testimony of another communist defector, Whittaker Chambers, in August/December 1948, with the arrest in March 1949 and subsequent trial of Judith Coplon, and with the arrest in 1950 and subsequent trial of the Rosenbergs.

These publicized Soviet espionage activities had occurred three to six years earlier in 1944–1945 (with the exception of Coplon, who remained a government employee at the time of her arrest). During the resultant investigations and media exposés, however, no question was raised about a seeming FBI counterintelligence failure. The FBI instead was credited with having ensured the convictions of Coplon, Alger Hiss, and the Rosenbergs. And although Coplon's conviction was reversed on appeal, owing to the failure of FBI agents to have obtained a warrant and to having wiretapped her, even this reversal did not raise questions about methods or capabilities. The debate over Soviet espionage operations instead centered on the actions of the Roosevelt and Truman administrations, with the main accusation leveled by McCarthyites that these administrations' "softness toward Communism" had enabled disloyal communists to obtain federal employment and had also hamstrung the FBI from uncovering Soviet espionage.

This public debate was misplaced. In reality, the Roosevelt and Truman administrations had given FBI officials wide latitude to conduct counterintelligence operations (with Roosevelt authorizing FBI intelligence investigations as early as 1936, in 1940 secretly authorizing "national defense" wiretapping, and in 1942, reaffirmed by Truman in 1947, authorizing FBI investigations to effect the dismissal of disloyal federal employees). Ironically, the very cases that raised public doubts about these Democratic administrations and that had fostered a positive assessment of the FBI's investigative prowess underscore the Bureau's counterintelligence deficiencies.

The Bentley case indirectly documents this. Her November 1945 detailed account of her role as a courier for two wartime Soviet espionage rings, whose members she identified, first alerted FBI officials to this wartime Soviet espionage operation. The participants in this conspiracy had been able to retain their governmental positions despite a government screening program instituted in 1942 to preclude the employment of disloyal employees. (Under this program, an individual could be denied employment or dismissed should the FBI have uncovered evidence of "a reasonable doubt as to his loyalty to the Government of the United States.") The head of one of these two rings, Nathan Silvermaster, had escaped a

Hatch Act firing and, in addition, Bureau agents did not launch an investigation to ascertain his involvement in espionage when learning of his (and Flato's) meeting with Bransten in December 1944.

Based on Bentley's disclosures in November 1945, FBI officials launched a massive investigation of those she identified as Soviet agents. A special squad of 200 agents intensively investigated her claims (concurrently urging her to renew her contact with her Soviet handler, Anatoly Gorsky). And because their main objective was to identify those involved in a suspected, ongoing espionage operation, FBI agents were authorized to employ a series of illegal investigative techniques: wiretaps, break-ins, and mail opening. Nonetheless, as recorded in a March 1970 FBI memorandum, despite having investigated Bentley's charges "over and over again," agents were unable to "substantiate and corroborate" them. An October 1946 report to the Truman White House, following up on the flurry of reports based on Bentley's November 1945 allegations that Hoover had sent to Truman administration officials between November 1945 and March 1946, offers further documentation of this failure. FBI officials then lamely justified their inability to corroborate Bentley's charges as due to the "time element," the alleged conspiracy having dated "back several years." This report continued, "The facts are strong in many instances and circumstantial in others principally because of the disparity in time between the date of these activities and the actual report of these activities to the authorities."[19] The FBI's "facts," however, only involved the confirmation that the accused individuals knew and met with each other, whether socially, at public meetings, or through correspondence—but not that they engaged in espionage.

In the final analysis, the FBI's failure was the product of bad luck. Soviet officials had been alerted to Bentley's defection by Kim Philby, a secret Soviet agent employed in British intelligence. Apprised by Philby of Bentley's defection, Soviet officials first ordered their operatives in New York and Washington to "cease immediately their connection with all persons known to Bentley in our work," "to warn the agents about Bentley's betrayal," and to return to Russia before they could be interviewed by the Bureau. The recruited American spies were also instructed to deny any involvement in espionage but to admit to having known Bentley because the FBI might already have observed such contact. Although the FBI had failed to confirm the involvement of those named by Bentley in espionage, Justice Department officials convened a grand jury in 1948 hoping to break one of the participants into admitting his involvement and implicating the others. This strategy failed; none of those identified by Bentley was indicted.[20]

FBI officials' immunity from critical scrutiny recurred in what was contemporaneously seen to be its most brilliant counterintelligence success—the uncovering of a Soviet conspiracy to steal atomic bomb secrets. At various times during 1950, FBI agents arrested the participants in this operation—Julius and Ethel Rosenberg, David Greenglass, Harry Gold, and Morton Sobell. Yet despite the fact that this espionage operation had occurred in 1944–1945, no question was then raised about this after-the-fact apprehension or about how this conspiracy was belatedly uncovered.

The identification of the participants in this Soviet espionage operation was the consequence not of FBI investigative efforts but a wartime military intelligence program, subsequently code-named VENONA. Military intelligence first intercepted Soviet consular messages sent from New York and Washington to Moscow during the years 1940–1948 and successfully deciphered them (with the important breakthrough occurring in 1949–1950). Because Soviet operatives had assumed that their communications to Moscow could not be deciphered, their reports at times included background information about their sources, which enabled military and FBI officials to identify the recruits (Greenglass, Rosenberg, Gold) even though these consular messages concealed their identities through code names. The FBI's principal contribution to the resultant prosecution of the Rosenbergs involved pressuring Greenglass, Gold, and Max Elitcher to admit their own involvement and implicating the Rosenbergs and then developing circumstantial information that corroborated their testimony in specific instances.

Military intelligence was responsible for vetting the individuals employed in the Manhattan Project. Nonetheless, under the wartime delimitation agreements, the FBI should have alerted military intelligence officials about all information that FBI agents had developed about the potential disloyalty of any of the Manhattan Project's employees. In this case, the FBI's failure was secondary. The intercepted VENONA messages, however, pinpoint a more serious FBI counterintelligence failure. In contrast to the Los Alamos project, where Julius Rosenberg's role was indirect (recruiting his brother-in-law David Greenglass, a military recruit assigned to Los Alamos), the VENONA messages confirm that Julius Rosenberg had personally stolen—and in addition had recruited two others, Joel Barr and Alfred Sarant, employed in defense-related industries, to steal—information about sensitive military technology for transmission to the Soviets. The classified information pilfered by these three included information about radar systems, jet engine designs, analog fire-control computers, and the proximity fuse. Barr and Sarant copied and transmitted 9,000 pages of secret documents relating to over 100 weapons programs and the entire

12,000-page design for a U.S. jet fighter while Rosenberg provided the design for the proximity fuse. Military intelligence was again responsible for vetting individuals employed in defense industries, but in this case the FBI failed to follow up when Barr and Sarant switched jobs when denied an earlier clearance. At no time, moreover, did FBI officials authorize investigations to ascertain whether either Rosenberg or Barr had engaged in espionage, even when discovering their employment in defense-related work.[21]

Portrayed as the crime of the century at the time, the Rosenberg case was not the sole known instance of Soviet atomic espionage. The deciphered VENONA messages also documented that Theodore Hall (and his friend Saville Sax, who served as his courier to the Soviets) had similarly provided the Soviets with atomic bomb secrets. FBI officials learned of Hall's and Sax's roles at the same time as the Rosenberg-Greenglass-Gold operation. Without assessing the significance of the information that Greenglass had provided the Soviets (he was only a high school graduate), Hall was a particularly valued recruit, having graduated from Harvard College with a degree in physics at the age of eighteen. On receipt of his submissions, Soviet officials in Moscow characterized them as of "great interest" and encouraged further submissions.

Alerted by military intelligence in 1950 to Hall's and Sax's espionage activities, FBI officials launched a massive investigation that included checking files on communist activities compiled during the 1930s and 1940s, breaking into their residences and opening their mail, and monitoring their contacts and activities in 1950–1951. Then, in 1951 FBI agents conducted aggressive separate interviews of Hall and Sax, hoping to break one or both of them to admit to their past conduct and implicate the other. In these interviews, FBI agents asked questions based on the documentation of their activities in the deciphered Soviet consular messages. Unlike Greenglass, Gold, and Elitcher, however, both Sax and Hall denied any involvement in espionage. Sax, moreover, brazenly explained why he had traveled to Albuquerque in 1945 (planning to apply for admission to New Mexico University) or why he had visited the Soviet consular office in New York in 1944 (to assist relatives in the Soviet Union through Russian War Relief). Because FBI agents could not break Sax or Hall, this investigation was closed in 1952. "All outside leads have been exhausted," an FBI official reported, and the "only indication we have" of Hall's and Sax's "espionage activity" came from VENONA and such information "cannot be disseminated outside the Bureau."[22]

The Bentley, Rosenberg, and Hall cases were not the FBI's sole counterintelligence failures. Another case, highly publicized during the Cold War era, involved former State Department employee Alger Hiss, indicted in

December 1948 on two counts of perjury (for denying to a federal grand jury having given classified State Department documents to a known communist, Whittaker Chambers, in 1938). FBI officials first learned of this espionage operation not when it occurred in 1936–1938 but when Chambers in November–December 1948 produced State Department documents that he claimed Hiss had given him.

Prior to this dramatic development, FBI officials had failed, first in 1941 and then in 1946, to pursue potential leads that could have uncovered the Hiss–Chambers relationship. In May–August 1941, an FBI informer, Ludwig Lore, told FBI agents of Chambers's "OGPU [Soviet intelligence] Activities in the United States" and his supervision of approximately 70 Soviet agents, and specifically of Chambers's contacts with two "private secretaries to Assistant Secretaries of State" and with another secretary employed by "one of the high officials of the Department of Commerce." Lore claimed that Chambers had obtained from the Commerce Department secretary "all necessary statistical data" and from the State Department secretaries "two extra copies" of the Roosevelt administration's diplomatic correspondence, which they had typed. FBI agents subsequently interviewed Chambers, who admitted only to having been in contact with an "underground group" of federal employees (identifying 20, including Hiss but no secretaries) whose purpose was to influence government policy. FBI agents did not press him on the differences between his account and that of Lore–Chambers having endorsed their conception of the threat: communist influence on New Deal policy.

Then, in 1946, pressured by an FBI agent about his knowledge of Hiss's activities (the FBI had launched an investigation of Hiss in 1945 based on the suspicion that he might have engaged in espionage, during the course of which Hiss's phone was tapped and his mail opened), Chambers only claimed that Hiss was "favorably impressed with the Communist movement." When the interviewing agent asked Chambers if he possessed any documentary evidence that Hiss had been a Communist Party member, Chambers responded that he did not and then emphasized that he had "never purposefully held out any information and had always been forthright in relaying any information that he had in which the Bureau had shown an interest."[23] Ironically, much like Hiss himself, FBI officials were blindsided when Chambers produced in November–December 1948 documentary evidence (typed and handwritten documents and microfilm copies of State Department documents), which he only then admitted to having acquired from Hiss in 1938.

The FBI's principal contribution to Hiss's indictment, moreover, stemmed from the grand jury testimony of an FBI expert that the typed documents produced by Chambers had been typed on the same typewriter owned by the Hisses. A further FBI effort to enhance Chambers's credibility to the grand jury (essential because he had abruptly changed his grand jury testimony between October and December 1948, in October denying any knowledge of espionage activity and then in December claiming that Hiss had regularly given him State Department documents since 1936) involved an attempt to identify the individual (known to Chambers only as Felix) who in 1936–1938 had photographed the classified documents that Chambers claimed to have received from his government sources. The result was a fiasco—an alleged Felix, Samuel Pelovitz, was produced in December 1948 as a grand jury witness. During his testimony, Pelovitz denied knowing Chambers or to having any photographic skills. Prosecutors then called Chambers, who at first identified Pelovitz as Felix but recanted this identification when called back before the grand jury, lamely explaining that Felix was not Jewish, but Pelovitz was. The FBI had produced the wrong man; Pelovitz coincidentally was a former communist and had resided (but not in 1936–1937) on the same street (Callow) and city (Baltimore) as Chambers's Felix.[24]

The Hiss case highlights the centrality of luck for FBI counterintelligence successes—in this instance the fact that a communist defector had since 1938 maintained what he described as a "life jacket." The limits of FBI capabilities are further highlighted by another seemingly successful FBI counterintelligence operation—the apprehension of Justice Department employee Judith Coplon as a Soviet spy.

As in the Rosenberg and Hall cases, Coplon's recruitment as a Soviet spy was discovered through the VENONA project. The deciphered messages confirmed that she had been recruited in 1944–1945 at the time of her employment in the Department of Justice. Coplon, however, had escaped discovery of her disloyalty whether in 1944–1945 or with the inception of the Federal Employee Loyalty Program in 1947. Having first learned of her disloyalty in 1949, FBI and senior Justice Department officials sought to ascertain whether she continued her espionage activities and to identify her Soviet contacts. In the course of this intelligence investigation, Bureau agents wiretapped both her office and home phones (and those of her parents in New York, with whom she frequently visited). Bureau and Justice Department officials eventually decided to launch a sting operation to ensure her conviction for espionage by making available to her carefully selected FBI records that would command her attention but would not compromise the nation's security. Coplon bit, and she was arrested in March 1949 when attempting to deliver 28 FBI records to Valentin Gubitchev, a Soviet intelligence operative assigned to the United Nations staff in New York.

Coplon's attorney petitioned the court during her first trial, demanding the submission of the 28 FBI reports as evidence. When the judge so ordered, FBI officials recommended dropping the case rather than honoring this order—claiming that their public release would harm the nation's security. Justice Department officials rebuffed this proposal. The released records, though not harming the nation's security, proved deeply embarrassing to FBI officials—confirming that agents monitored political activities and wiretapped extensively (15 of the reports were based on wiretaps). Coplon's attorney immediately demanded a hearing to ascertain whether his client had been tapped, a motion that the U.S. attorney prosecuting the case successfully rebuffed as a "fishing expedition." In Coplon's second trial, however, the presiding judge honored the defense's motion for a pretrial hearing resulting in the disclosure that Coplon's office and home phones had been tapped, that the FBI agent who denied any knowledge as to whether Coplon's phone had been tapped had in fact routinely received the results of these wiretaps, and that FBI officials had ordered the destruction of the Coplon wiretap logs "in view of the imminence of her trial." The combination of the revelations about FBI wiretapping activities and the failure of arresting agents to have obtained a warrant ultimately led to her conviction being overturned on appeal.[25]

The Coplon case underscores the problem of attempting to convict individuals when evidence had been illegally obtained through a counterintelligence operation. FBI and Justice Department officials were unwilling to disclose (in this case as in the cases of Hall and Sax) how they had learned of Coplon's espionage activities (and thus the reasonableness of the wiretaps and the failure to obtain an advance warrant). To do so would have publicly compromised the VENONA program.

These Cold War internal security cases had far-reaching political ramifications, lending support to a McCarthyite politics that blamed the Roosevelt and Truman administrations for Soviet espionage successes. Significantly, the McCarthyites never attempted to ascertain the reality of the FBI's responsibility and that FBI officials had been accorded broad latitude by both presidents. Just as important, Soviet recruitment of ideologically motivated federal employees had been foreclosed by the late 1940s, owing to the stricter standards governing federal employment instituted by Truman in March 1947 under the Federal Employee Loyalty Program. Henceforth, Soviet officials were compelled to rely on their own agents or to recruit sources based on greed, not ideology.

Soviet officials also employed "illegals," that is, individuals not assigned officially to Soviet consular or embassy offices. One such was Rudolf Abel, a colonel in the Soviet Union's intelligence service, the KGB, who entered the United States from Canada in November 1948 on a false passport. The KGB's resident agent in New York, Abel was uncovered in 1957 due to the defection of another Soviet illegal, Reino Hayhanen. Recalled to the Soviet Union, Hayhanen interrupted his return upon arriving in Paris in May 1957, approaching the U.S. consulate and then advising a CIA officer of his role as a Soviet agent and how he had entered the United States in 1952 under a false passport. In return for a promise of resettlement, Hayhanen described Soviet intelligence activities, identified one of his recruits (Roy Rhodes), and provided background information that eventually led to Abel's apprehension. Hayhanen did not know Abel's cover name or residence but remembered meeting him in a photo studio in Brooklyn. Based on this lead, FBI officials launched an intensive investigation that eventually led to Abel's arrest on June 21, 1957. Tried and convicted, Abel was released in 1962 in return for the Soviets' release of captured U-2 pilot Francis Gary Powers.[26]

Luck and solid investigation had led to Abel's apprehension. The same combination led to the FBI uncovering another Soviet espionage ring headed by retired naval communications officer John Walker Jr., who dating from 1968 had provided the Soviets with sensitive information relating to naval communications. Walker's motives for spying were strictly mercenary; he was quite conservative politically—indeed his political beliefs and background as a private investigator and businessman enabled him to receive security clearances. Walker, moreover, recruited his brother (Arthur), son (Richard), and a friend (Jerry Whitworth) to pilfer classified information. FBI agents uncovered Walker's espionage activities and those of his ring fortuitously in 1984—their first awareness of possible espionage derived from an anonymous letter (written by Whitworth) to the FBI's San Francisco office and then from reports to the FBI's Boston field office from Walker's former wife, Barbara, and daughter, Laura. FBI agents were at first unable to identify the writer of the San Francisco letter and did not immediately follow up on Barbara's and Laura's reports on Walker's espionage activities. An intrepid FBI supervisor finally acted on these reports, triggering an intensive investigation that culminated in the arrests in May 1985 and resulting conviction of John, Arthur, and Richard Walker and Jerry Whitworth.[27]

If the Abel and Walker cases highlight the importance of luck to FBI counterintelligence successes, the FBI's delayed apprehension of Aldrich Ames was primarily the responsibility of officials in the Central Intelligence Agency (CIA). A career CIA officer, Ames was appointed in 1983 the head of the Agency's counterintelligence branch on the Soviet Union and then in 1990 was assigned briefly to the Agency's Counterintelligence Center.

Disillusioned with the Agency and motivated by greed, in 1985 Ames approached the Soviets to sell secret information, particularly identifying Soviet officials whom the CIA had recruited as double agents. He continued thereafter, in return for large sums of money, to identify other double agents as well as providing sensitive CIA records. Troubled by the deaths (or disappearances) of these sources, CIA officials suspected a mole, although they did not focus on Ames until 1992 and only sought FBI assistance in 1991 to uncover the suspected spy—having ignored Ames's extravagant life style, sloppy work habits, and excessive drinking. When finally given free rein, the FBI's intensive investigation (including wiretapping and bugging Ames's residence, monitoring his credit card bills and trash, and following him) resulted in his arrest, on February 21, 1994, and conviction.[28]

FBI officials experienced similar embarrassment owing to their failure over a 21-year period to uncover another U.S. intelligence official who had also identified to the Soviets the Russians whom the FBI and CIA had recruited as double agents. This spy, Robert Hanssen, was employed in the FBI's counterintelligence division. After joining the FBI in 1976, Hanssen was assigned to the Bureau's counterintelligence division in 1979 and then in 1983 to that division's Soviet analytical unit, where he had access to sensitive information about FBI counterintelligence programs, the identities of 50 recruited Soviet double agents, and thousands of pages of classified FBI, CIA, and NSA documents. Dating from 1979 he provided much of this information to the Soviets in return for large sums of cash and diamonds. As the result of the death of one of the FBI's recruited double agents in 1986, Bureau officials launched an investigation to identify the mole. Nonetheless, Hanssen escaped detection until late 2000, in part because of the precautions he had taken as a skilled counterintelligence officer (including not disclosing his identity to his Soviet contacts and successfully diverting attention from himself). His arrest on February 18, 2001, was the byproduct of the November 2000 defection of a Russian intelligence officer who, in return for a $7 million payment, delivered to U.S. intelligence the Russian file on Hanssen. This file contained a tape of Hanssen's conversation with a Soviet official (enabling FBI agents to identify his voice) and a bag that he had used to provide documents to the Soviets that contained his fingerprints. Until acquiring this file, FBI investigators had focused on CIA officer Brian Kelley as the suspected mole.[29]

This narrative does not recount the totality of FBI counterintelligence operations. Because of continued classification restrictions, it is impossible to ascertain whether these and other known counterintelligence operations are representative.[30] Nonetheless, the known history of FBI counterintelligence successes and failures permits some qualified observations.

First, FBI failures were not due to incompetence but to the difficulty of identifying carefully trained spies (or, for that matter, terrorists) who had an obvious interest in precluding discovery of their plans. The cases cited herein highlight the importance of luck (most notably the defection of Soviet intelligence operatives). These cases further confirm the impossibility of achieving absolute security. This is highlighted by the recent FBI investigation of the sender(s) of anthrax letters in October–November 2001. Despite the intensity of an FBI investigation that lasted seven years, the sender of the anthrax letters, Bruce Ivins, remained unidentified until 2008. This delayed discovery occurred even though FBI investigators had three advantages: first, they knew that such letters had been sent (and did not need to anticipate this possibility); second, the sender had to have access to a lab and the expertise to weaponize anthrax; and third, FBI agents had the vastly expanded surveillance authority provided by the 2001 USA PATRIOT Act.[31]

The Ames and Hanssen cases further confirm the unreasonableness of an expectation of absolute security. Despite the repressive character of Soviet society, and although Soviet intelligence officials closely vetted potential recruits to ensure their ideological loyalty and were not constrained by a need to respect due process or privacy rights, FBI and CIA officials were nonetheless able to recruit Soviet intelligence officers to betray their nation's secrets.

The FBI's failure to anticipate planned threats to the nation's security was repeated in the aftermath of the 9/11 terrorist attacks, despite the radical expansion of the Bureau's surveillance powers authorized under the USA PATRIOT Act. At a minimum, FBI agents failed to anticipate and prevent three planned terrorists operations: a December 2009 plot to bomb a Detroit-bound airliner; a botched car-bombing attack of May 2010 targeting New York City's Times Square; and a successful April 2013 bombing attack targeting the Boston Marathon.[32]

Second, this history highlights that FBI agents either focused on the wrong suspects, ignored tantalizing leads, or (in the Kravchenko case) made unwarranted assumptions. The objective of anticipating espionage inevitably led to a form of profiling where suspects were targeted based on their politics and associations. This suspicion drove the COMRAP investigation and, more recently, underpinned a recommendation of FBI agent Kenneth Williams.

In a report of July 10, 2001, recommending that FBI headquarters launch a nationwide investigation focusing on Middle Eastern alien residents attending flight schools, Williams cited in particular an Al Qaeda sympathizer, Zakaria Soubra. Soubra had come to Williams's attention because of his public role in organizing demonstrations and meetings against U.S. and Israeli policy in the Middle East, his militant beliefs that the resort to violence in defense of Islam was justified, and his advocacy of a unitary Islamist state. When interviewing Soubra, Williams discerned in his apartment photographs of Osama bin Laden and Chechnyan *muhahedeen*. The FBI's subsequent (post-9/11) investigation of Soubra (and others whom Williams had identified in his July communication) uncovered no evidence that they either had advance knowledge of the September attacks or were co-conspirators. That radical political activism does not predict violence and that anticipating terrorism based on public political activities is nonpredictive is confirmed by Williams's failure to have identified Hani Hanjour as a prospective terrorist. Hanjour had, off and on over the previous five years, attended flight schools in the Phoenix area; but he was not a known public exponent of Islamist views. Yet on September 11, 2001, Hanjour (not Soubra) piloted one of the four commandeered jets, American Airline Flight 77, into the Pentagon.

The *President's Daily Brief* of August 6, 2001, captioned, "Bin Ladin Determined to Strike in the US," provides further evidence of the limitations of basing counterintelligence investigations on political criteria. The final paragraph of this document reported that the FBI was "conducting approximately 70 full field investigations throughout the US that it considers Bin Ladin related." None of these investigations, however, involved any of the 19 terrorists who engineered the 9/11 attack. A July 2, 2001, communication from the FBI's Counterintelligence Division to federal, state, and local law enforcement agencies warning of possible terrorist attacks by groups "aligned with or sympathetic to Usama Bin Ladin [an alternative spelling of the Al Qaeda leader's name, often used by the U.S. government]," moreover, starkly admitted that "the FBI has no information indicating a credible threat of terrorist attack in the United States."[33]

Political (and as well ethno-religious) profiling has serious limitations—and carries the additional risk that such investigations could lead to violations of civil liberties and privacy rights. Indeed, one byproduct of the FBI's counterintelligence investigations of the World War II and Cold War years was the acquisition of information about the political and personal conduct of suspected subversives. Although this information could not be used for legitimate prosecution or national security purposes, FBI officials in time (on the strict condition that recipients not disclose their actions) purposefully disseminated this information to "reliable" reporters, members of Congress, and congressional committees for the purpose of "influencing public opinion." These covert and extensive dissemination practices proved crucial to the promotion of a McCarthyite politics.[34]

Notes

1. Willard B. Gatewood, *Theodore Roosevelt and the Art of Controversy: Episodes of the White House Years* (Baton Rouge: Louisiana State University Press, 1970), pp. 236–247, 249–254, 257–287; Vern Countryman, "The History of the FBI: Democracy's Development of a Secret Police," in Pat Watters and Stephen Gillers (eds.), *Investigating the FBI* (Garden City, NY: Doubleday, 1973), pp. 33–38; Max Lowenthal, *The Federal Bureau of Investigation* (New York: William Sloane, 1950), pp. 3–17; Sanford Ungar, *FBI* (Boston: Atlantic Monthly/Little Brown, 1975), 38–41.

2. William Preston, *Aliens and Dissenters: Federal Suppression of Radicals, 1903–1933* (New York: Harper Torchbooks, 1966), pp. 6–7, 118–151, 208–238; Robert Murray, *Red Scare: A Study of National Hysteria, 1919–1920* (New York: McGraw-Hill, 1964), pp. 14, 18–32, 210–222; Charles McCormick, *Hopeless Cases: The Hunt for the Red Scare Terrorist Bombers* (Lanham, MD: University Press of America, 2005), pp. 14–141; Lowenthal, *Federal Bureau of Investigation*, pp. 24–35, 83–129, 147–198; Ungar, *FBI*, pp. 41–45; Curt Gentry, *J. Edgar Hoover: The Man and the Secrets* (New York: Norton, 1991), pp. 71–72, 79–105.

3. Athan Theoharis and John Stuart Cox, *The Boss: J. Edgar Hoover and the Great American Inquisition* (Philadelphia: Temple University Press, 1988), pp. 76–80, 82–86, 92–94; Gentry, *J. Edgar Hoover*, pp. 117–142; Ungar, *FBI*, pp. 45–49.

4. Ibid., Theoharis and Cox.

5. Ungar, *FBI*, p. 101; Theoharis and Cox, *The Boss*, pp. 148–154, 179–185.

6. Athan Theoharis, *Spying on Americans: Political Surveillance from Hoover to the Huston Plan* (Philadelphia: Temple University Press, 1978), pp. 97–99, 106, 125–126, 130; Gentry, *J. Edgar Hoover*, pp. 281–282.

7. Douglas Charles, "'Before the Colonel Arrived': Hoover, Donovan, and the Origins of American Central Intelligence, 1940–41," *Intelligence and National Security* 20, no. 2 (June 2005), pp. 225–237; Leslie Rout and John Bratzel, *The Shadow War: German Espionage and United States Counterespionage in Latin America during World War II* (Frederick, MD: University Publications of America, 1986), pp. 29–40, 454–456; Thomas Troy, *Wild Bill and Intrepid: Donovan, Stephenson, and the Origins of the CIA* (New Haven, CT: Yale University Press, 1996), pp. 33–40, 63–76; G. Greg Webb, "Intelligence Liaison Between the FBI and State, 1940–44," *Studies in Intelligence* 49, no. 3 (2005), pp. 25, 29–38.

8. Athan Theoharis, *The FBI and American Democracy: A Brief, Critical History* (Lawrence: University Press of Kansas, 2004), pp. 50–52; Francis MacDonnell, *Insidious Foes: The Axis Fifth Column and the American Home Front* (New York: Oxford University Press, 1995), pp. 49–61, 127–128, 131–133.

9. Athan Theoharis, *Chasing Spies: How the FBI Failed in Counterintelligence But Promoted the Politics of McCarthyism in the Cold War Years* (Chicago: Ivan Dee,

2002), pp. 49–50, 56–94; Theoharis and Cox, *The Boss*, pp. 9–11, 13–15; Athan Theoharis, "A Creative and Aggressive FBI: The Victor Kravchenko Case," *Intelligence and National Security* 20, no. 2 (2005), pp. 324–328.

10. Not all Soviet espionage successes were the consequence of FBI counterintelligence failures. Under a 1943 delimitation agreement, military intelligence had exclusive responsibility for all personnel employed in the Manhattan Project. This agreement prohibited the FBI from initiating any investigation of "persons connected with the Atomic Bomb Project," although the FBI did have the responsibility of forwarding to military intelligence any information its agents had obtained in the course of other investigations. Katherine Sibley, *Red Spies in America: Stolen Secrets and the Dawn of the Cold War* (Lawrence: University Press of Kansas, 2004), p. 145.

11. Theoharis, *Chasing Spies*, pp. 60–61.

12. A representative sample of such FBI reports to the White House includes: Letters, Hoover to Watson, October 24, 1942, August 3, 1943, September 30, 1943, October 27, 1943, August 7, 1944, and December 28, 1944, OF 10-B; all in Franklin Roosevelt Presidential Library, Hyde Park, NY.

13. Letter, Hoover to Hopkins, December 22, 1944, and accompanying Quarterly Report on Espionage and Counterintelligence Activities Having United States Connections, November 1, 1944, OF 10 B, Roosevelt Library.

14. Theoharis, *Chasing Spies*, pp. 62–78.

15. Ibid., pp. 47–49, 77.

16. Theoharis, *Chasing Spies*, pp. 50–53.

17. Theoharis, "A Creative and Aggressive FBI," pp. 321–331.

18. Theoharis, *Chasing Spies*, pp. 57–60, 151–155; Theoharis and Cox, *The Boss*, pp. 13, 191–193; Alexander Stephen, *"Communazis": FBI Surveillance of German Emigre Writers* (New Haven, CT: Yale University Press, 2000), pp. 2, 20, 35–36, 43–45, 50, 67, 76–77, 85, 89, 117–129, 138, 190–199, 253–269, 271, 275–276.

19. Theoharis, *Chasing Spies*, pp. 42–43.

20. Theoharis, *Spying on Americans*, pp. 197–198; Theoharis, *Chasing Spies*, pp. 41– 43, 54–55, 239–241; Allen Weinstein and Alexander Vassiliev, *The Haunted Wood: Soviet Espionage in America—The Stalin Era* (New York: Random House, 1999), pp. 103–107.

21. Theoharis, *Chasing Spies*, pp. 17–18, 31–32, 45–47, 81–83; Steven Usdin, "Tracking Julius Rosenberg's Lesser Known Associates," *Studies in Intelligence* 49, no. 3 (2005), pp. 13–19.

22. Theoharis, *Chasing Spies*, pp. 31–32, 81–84; Theoharis, *The FBI and American Democracy*, pp. 84–85. The FBI's voluminous file on this investigation, FBI 65-59122, documents the intensity of the investigation of Hall and Sax; the 1952 decision to close this investigation is Memo, name deleted to Branigan, May 8, 1953, FBI 65-59122-403.

23. Theoharis, *Chasing Spies*, pp. 114–141.

24. Ibid., pp. 36–41, 114–131.

25. Ibid., pp. 48–49, 84–93; Theoharis, *Spying on Americans*, pp. 100–105.

26. Nigel West, *The Illegals: The Double Lives of the Cold War's Most Secret Agents* (London: Hodder and Stoughton, 1999), pp. 116–126; Robert Lamphere and Tom Shachtman, *The FBI-KGB War: A Special Agent's Story* (New York: Random House, 1986), pp. 273–277.

27. John Barron, *Breaking the Ring* (Boston: Houghton Mifflin, 1987), pp. 3–22, 40–137.

28. Tim Weiner, David Johnston, and Neil Lewis, *Betrayal: The Story of Aldrich Ames, an American Spy* (New York: Random House, 1995), pp. 3–9, 13–17, 32–43, 81–99, 110–120, 128–166, 190–195, 200–252, 276–291; Mark Riebling, *Wedge: The Secret War between the FBI and CIA* (New York: Knopf, 1994), pp. 413–415, 430–433, 441–447.

29. David Wise, *Spy: The Inside Story of How the FBI's Robert Hanssen Betrayed America* (New York: Random House, 2002), pp. 3–4, 7–8, 18–22, 24–27, 37–42, 50–68, 74–84, 94–99, 107–108, 117–119, 122–142, 159–160, 162–247.

30. Other known cases include Erich Gimpel, William Colepaugh, Gaik Ovakimian, Andre Shevchenko, William Remington, Kaarlo Tuomi, Ann and Robert Baltch, Ivan and Alexandra Egorov, Morris and Lona Cohen, James Harper, Daniel Richardson, Allen Davies, Jonathan Pollard, Edward Howard, Ronald Pelton, Wen Ho Lee, Richard Miller, Thomas Kavanaugh, Larry Wu-Tai Chin, David Barnett, Karl Koecher, Sharon Screnage, Nelson Drummond, Joseph Garfield Brown, Valery Markelov, William Whalen, Herbert Boekinhaupt, Felix Bloch, Earl Pitts, Harold Nicholson, Stanislau Gusev, Katrina Leung, Brian Regan, Ana Montes, Gennadi Zakharov, Christopher Boyce, Marian Zacharski, and Stephan Lipka.

31. *New York Times* (September 17, 2005), p. A1; (April 23, 2010), p. A13; (February 16, 2011), p. A14.

32. *New York Times* (January 18, 2010), p. A1; (May 5, 2010), p. A1; (May 16, 2010), p. A1; (May 10, 2013), p. A1; (August 2, 2013), p. A13.

33. *The 9/11 Commission Report: Final Report of the National Commission on Terrorist Attacks upon the United States* (New York: Norton, 2004), pp. 225–227, 239, 258, 261–262, 272; U.S. Senate Select Committee on Intelligence and U.S. House Permanent Select Committee on Intelligence, *Report on Joint Inquiry into the Intelligence Community Activities Before and After the Terrorist Attacks of September 11, 2001*, 107th Cong., 2d sess. (2003), pp. 20–22, 325–335, Appendix: The Phoenix Electronic Communication (redacted text of Williams's July 10, 2001, report to FBI headquarters); *New York Times* (May 4, 2002), p. A10; (May 9, 2002), p. A22; (June 19, 2002), p. A18; (September 25, 2002), p. A12.

34. For examples of such uses, see Theoharis, *Chasing Spies*, pp. 139–234 and Theoharis, *Spying on Americans*, pp. 133–195.

CHAPTER SIXTEEN

The Intelligence War against Global Terrorism

Richard L. Russell

AMERICANS WERE HORRIFIED THAT THEIR INTELLIGENCE COMMUNITY (IC) failed to detect and disrupt the Al Qaeda surprise attacks of September 11, 2001. They rightly ask, "How is it possible that the intelligence community, which costs American taxpayers tens of billions of dollars per year, so miserably failed in protecting citizens and the homeland?"

The IC should have been better prepared to warn of Al Qaeda operations because the terrorist organization had been waging a war against the United States for some time. Al Qaeda bombed the American embassies in Kenya and Tanzania in 1998 as well as attacked the U.S.S. *Cole* in Yemen in 2000. These attacks should have signaled loud and clear that Al Qaeda had declared war on the United States, but American naiveté fueled the view that terrorist attacks were more a problem for law enforcement than for the military. Both civilian policymakers and the military hierarchy resisted moving the United States to a war footing to take head on the threat posed by Al Qaeda.[1] In response to the African embassy bombings, the United States could only muster half-hearted retaliatory cruise missile strikes against Al Qaeda–affiliated positions in Afghanistan and Sudan, which did little to blunt the network's capabilities to strike again against the United States.

The CIA, too, had not moved to a wartime footing to tackle Al Qaeda. Director of Central Intelligence George Tenet had warned in a December 1998 memorandum to his key lieutenants in the IC that the United States was at war with Al Qaeda and that he wanted no resources spared for the fight.[2] But Tenet's bravado was not matched by resources. The team inside the CIA's Counterterrorism Center (CTC) in the run-up to 9/11 only had five analysts assigned to track global Al Qaeda operations.[3] A handful of analysts is hardly commensurate with Tenet's call to "spare no resource." Within the CIA's Directorate of Operations (DO), responsible for collecting human intelligence, senior management believed that the Al Qaeda threat before 9/11 was being exaggerated and resisted assigning CIA resources to the problem, according to former White House official Richard Clarke.[4] The former head of the bin Laden unit in the CTC, Michael Scheuer, even believes that senior CIA officials "have made careers by keeping silent in the face of unfairness, avoiding risk, and refusing to make decisions." [5] The CIA's own inspector general has found senior CIA officials negligent for failing to competently orchestrate the Agency's resources against Al Qaeda prior to 9/11.[6]

But that, as they say, is all history. The challenge today for scholars, intelligence officers, policymakers, and the American public is to move beyond the blame game and take a hard, clear-eyed look at what went wrong. We need to find ways to sharpen the nation's intelligence capabilities for countering Al Qaeda—as well as loosely aligned affiliates and successor organizations that share a militant Islamic ideology and hatred of the United States, which they blame for most (if not all) of the failings of the Islamic world—in what regrettably promises to be a long-term struggle.

The term "terrorism" generates considerable debate and controversy, which sometimes boils down to the view that "one man's terrorist is another man's freedom fighter." Many observers in the United States tend to view operations conducted by terrorist groups against American military and diplomatic facilities and personnel as terrorist attacks, but they probably should be more accurately seen as insurgents using terrorist tactics to wage war. When American military forces were deployed to Iraq from 2003 to 2011, news headlines were dominated by Iraqi insurgent use of terrorist tactics, especially roadside bombings. But in the past, other insurgent groups have used terrorist tactics against the United States, sometimes with nation-state sponsorship. Hezbollah, for example, benefited from Syrian and Iranian support in the 1980s in its bombings in Lebanon, which killed 241 Marines and destroyed the American embassy in Beirut. The Saudi Hezbollah benefited from substantial assistance from Iran when it bombed the Khobar Towers in Saudi Arabia in 1996 and killed 19 American servicemen.[7] In short, Al Qaeda is not the first militant Islamic movement to use terrorism against the United States, and they are not likely to be the last. To steer clear of that thicket of debate on the differences between terrorism and insurgency, this chapter views terrorism as the use of violence by transnational groups or organizations that is directed principally against civilians for political purpose.

The CIA has traditionally played the leading role in the IC along three major lines to support the president in the war on terrorism. First, the CIA runs human intelligence operations needed to penetrate the walls of secrecy behind which terrorists plot and plan against the United States. Second, the CIA performs analysis of terrorist groups to inform presidential decision making. And third, the CIA is also tasked to mount covert actions against terrorist groups to disrupt, prevent, and preempt their operations. This chapter critically examines the CIA's past performance in each of these areas against the terrorist adversaries, draws some lessons learned, and makes recommendations for strengthening future performance. This chapter acknowledges that the CIA's traditional position as the premier intelligence service in the community has been eclipsed by the creation of the Office of the director of National Intelligence (ODNI) and will conclude with some thoughts on how the DNI should best orchestrate the reorganized IC.

Stealing the Terrorists' Secrets

The IC taps a wide and deep array of sources of information to understand international terrorism. The United States uses diplomats and defense attachés posted abroad to collect information. It relies on publicly available information, such as newspapers, periodicals, and websites, to analyze terrorist group memberships, propaganda, recruitment, and ideology. The IC also is able to use satellite imagery to identify terrorist training camps and state support for terrorist groups. The United States, for example, in 1998 used many of these sources of intelligence to identify Al Qaeda training camps in Afghanistan for retaliatory cruise missile strikes for the bombing of the two embassies in Africa.[8] The IC also clandestinely acquires information on terrorist groups and their plans from human sources (human intelligence, or HUMINT) and from intercepting communications such as radio, telephone, and email (signals intelligence, or SIGINT). The primary responsibilities for these HUMINT and SIGINT operations fall, respectively, to the CIA and the National Security Agency (NSA) in the IC.

The CIA's National Clandestine Service (NCS) is charged with running human intelligence operations intended to collect strategic intelligence on American adversaries.[9] The CIA's core human intelligence collection mission is to steal secrets that adversaries want to hide from the United States, secrets that could adversely affect American national interests.

The CIA's operational tradecraft for running human operations was honed during the Cold War. The Agency's operational officers working abroad under cover had used a method of spotting, accessing, developing, and recruiting Soviet diplomats and military officers primarily by trolling the diplomatic cocktail circuit. Though this is a proven method of human collection, the CIA's human operations against the Soviet Union were, on balance, less than impressive. Before the entire stable of CIA spies in the Soviet Union were exposed to the Soviet KGB by traitor Aldrich Ames, the Agency only had about a dozen spies inside the Soviet Union.[10]

The method is now deeply ingrained into the institutional culture at the CIA, and it has been difficult for the Agency to move toward contemporary international terrorists targets. A former CIA case officer who was in the Agency's training class as late as 1999, nearly a decade after the Cold War, recalls that it was still focused on trolling the diplomatic cocktail party circuit.[11] Unfortunately, and quite obviously, members of Al Qaeda, Hezbollah, Hamas, Islamic Jihad, and their state sponsors in Syria and Iran do not regularly participate in diplomatic cocktail parties. Nor, for that matter, do the scientists and technicians with experience in weapons of mass destruction (WMDs) programs, who might offer their talents to terrorist groups with or without the knowledge of their countries. Rogue Russian scientists trying to make a lucrative living are a particular problem on this score.

The CIA has done precious little to exploit alternative means of getting human intelligence information. Most notably, the Agency has a strong bureaucratic culture to run "agents in place," even though it has failed to do this with any consistency or reliability over a period of decades. The CIA and American security would be much better off if the Agency were sparing no expense or effort to encourage defections from countries with pervasive and oppressive internal security apparatus, called "hard target" countries. The United States, for example, should be offering money and perhaps resettlement in the United States or the West for disaffected Al Qaeda and Hezbollah members and scientists and technicians laboring in North Korea's and Iran's suspected nuclear weapons programs, all of whom could offer significant intelligence to the United States. Dozens of defections would give CIA analysts snapshots of terrorist groups and plans, intentions, and capabilities, as well as disrupt WMD-related activities.

The CIA also significantly suffers in human operations against Middle East terrorist groups such as Al Qaeda and Hezbollah because it suffers from shortages of Arabic and Farsi speakers. Former CIA case officer

Robert Baer lamented that he was one of only two Arabic speakers in the CTC when it was set up in the 1980s to track Hezbollah and Palestinian terrorist groups.[12] And judging from news reports today, the CIA is not gaining ground fast enough to address this gap. The chancellor of the University of California at Berkeley, for example, met with CIA officials to discuss language capabilities and came away from the meeting with the understanding that "their needs are desperate."[13]

The CIA is also overly dependent on foreign intelligence liaison service information. Because the Agency lacks foreign language capabilities, it relies on foreign intelligence services, which do have hard languages such as Arabic and ethnic backgrounds needed to penetrate terrorists cells. The Senate-House investigation into 9/11 determined that the CIA is overly dependent on liaison reports and fails to deliver its own or "unilaterally" acquired human intelligence. It found that

> the Intelligence Community depended heavily on foreign intelligence and law enforcement services for the collection of counterterrorism intelligence and the conduct of other counterterrorism activities. The results were mixed in terms of productive intelligence, reflecting vast differences in the ability and willingness of the various foreign services to target the Bin Ladin and al-Qa'ida network.[14]

Unilaterally acquired intelligence is essential to compare and check against the information provided by foreign liaison services as well as other American sources of information.

There can be no gainsaying how important these liaison relationships are to human intelligence collection in the war on terrorism. But with that said, for all of the problems and shortcomings in the American intelligence community, they pale in comparison to the problems that plague many foreign liaison services. For example, these foreign services suffer from a deep subordination to vested policy interests, ingrained bureaucratic and cultural resistance to "speaking truth to power," personal fears of delivering bad news to their superiors, as well as worldviews—especially pronounced in the Middle East—that greatly hamper objective and critical analytic thinking and intelligence. There is also a significant risk that liaison services skew their human intelligence reports shared with the United States to influence the direction of American foreign policy. These tendencies all underscore the critical need for the CIA to acquire its own unilateral intelligence sources.

The NSA is charged with the responsibilities for intercepting the communications of terrorist groups. The United States has had better collection performance in strategic intelligence from the NSA than the CIA. Tragically, however, NSA operations against Al Qaeda appear to have suffered a major blow when word leaked by August 1998 that the United States was listening to Osama bin Laden's satellite telephone conversations, and he stopped using the satellite phone shortly after U.S. cruise missile strikes against his camps in Afghanistan in retaliation for the bombings of two American embassies in Africa. More recently, Edward Snowden leaks have been even more damaging to NSA collection efforts.[15]

The NSA is now deeply embroiled in a domestic spying controversy with accusations that it was listening to American phone calls and emails domestically without the legal authority to do so.[16] Above and beyond today's news headlines, the NSA is up against the wall in reorienting its collection operations from the Cold War to the war on terrorism. Al Qaeda and other terrorist groups benefit enormously in the explosion in information and communication technology, and the NSA has had to work hard to keep pace. Al Qaeda can now purchase off-the-shelf encryption technology, making it difficult for NSA to crack their communications. Al Qaeda can hide its communications in the billions of emails and cell phone calls made daily. And Al Qaeda operatives can easily and readily replace cell phones, making it extraordinarily difficult for the NSA to keep apace of small, nimble, and adaptive terrorist cells.

The shortcomings of CIA human operations and NSA communication interception operations were made painfully clear in the aftermath of the 9/11 attacks. The joint House-Senate investigation found that the CIA had no human agent placed inside Al Qaeda in a position to steal secrets on the 9/11 conspiracy.[17] Although the NSA did intercept some Al Qaeda communications related to the conspiracy, the intercepts were not sufficiently specific and not translated into English before the attacks because the NSA lacked the resources to translate all the communications it manages to intercept.[18] But even if these communications had been translated before 9/11, they would not have been sufficiently detailed to have allowed U.S. officials to wrap up the Al Qaeda cell that orchestrated the attack.

Analyzing Terrorists' Intentions, Plans, and Capabilities

Intelligence analysis does not hold the public's fascination nearly as well as human intelligence operations and covert action, which are the stuff of spy novels and adventure movies, but it plays no less a critical role in the war on terrorism. Even the best human intelligence and superb intelligence from other sources will come to naught if not married with first-rate analysis.

The CTC has been the focal point for intelligence collection as well as analysis. The CTC was an exceptionally innovative organization that was created in the mid-1980s to grapple with the problems the United States was facing with Palestinian terrorism as well as Iranian-backed Hezbollah terrorism that was responsible for the bombings of the American embassy, the Marine Corps barracks in Beirut, and the kidnapping and killing of American citizens, such as the CIA's station chief in the 1980s.[19] The creation of the CTC was a remarkable bureaucratic innovation because it located in one office both CIA case officers charged with running HUMINT operations with the CIA's Directorate of Intelligence (DI) analysts. The CIA had traditionally fostered a bureaucratic barrier between case officers and analysts partly to protect disclosure of sources and methods, but the separation prevented the synergy of case officers working side by side with analysts. Analysts could identify blind spots and recommend avenues for case officers to gain access to individuals with access to information to fill intelligence gaps.

Despite these strengths, the CTC suffers from a lack of substantive analytic talent, a shortcoming that is a reflection of the CIA's entire analytic corps. The Senate-House inquiry discovered that

> the quality of counterterrorism analysis was inconsistent, and many analysts were inexperienced, unqualified, under-trained, and without access to critical information. As a result, there was a dearth of creative, aggressive analysis targeting Bin Ladin and a persistent inability to comprehend the collective significance of individual pieces of intelligence.[20]

Notwithstanding these profound weaknesses, the CTC did indeed provide strategic intelligence warning to President Bush of the September 11 attacks. The CIA, in its August 6, 2001, *President's Daily Brief*—a daily current intelligence document prepared for the president and his closest advisors—had warned Bush in an article titled "Bin Laden Determined to Strike in US."[21] The CIA's warning, however, was more a historical review than tactical intelligence needed to disrupt the conspiracy. In contrast, the FBI did have specific information coming from astute field offices in Arizona and Minnesota on suspected Al Qaeda members training on commercial aircraft, but Bureau headquarters lacked a robust analytic staff in Washington to "connect the dots."[22]

Although the strategic intelligence failure of 9/11 falls most heavily on the FBI, the CIA, for whatever reason, took the lion's share of public blame.

As is the case with many reforms, the 9/11 Commission recommended changes that "threw the baby out with the bathwater" and recommended a new center under the auspices of the DNI for doing counterterrorism analysis, a recommendation that President Bush accepted.[23] The new National Counterterrorism Center (NCTC), however, will likely be inferior to the old CTC because it will not benefit from shoulder-to-shoulder relationships with the CIA's case officers.

Covertly Killing and Detaining Suspected Terrorists

The collection of intelligence—via clandestine human sources, intercepted communications, and other means such as satellites and media monitoring—by far consumes the lion's share of the American intelligence community's budget, which now is running at $44 billion per year.[24] But public attention is captivated by covert action, which is designed to influence events abroad without exposing the hand of the United States, and special activities such as training foreign security services.[25]

These activities, which after many years tend to become publicly exposed, create political controversies in the United States and abroad. One of the largest covert action programs in the CIA's history was the military backing of the insurgency against the Soviet Union's occupation of Afghanistan during the Cold War. The CIA spent millions of dollars and provided tons of military arms and equipment to the Afghan insurgents over a period of years to substantially increase the costs of Soviet occupation and contributed to the Soviet decision to withdraw from Afghanistan. That less-than-covert war is heralded by CIA veterans as an exemplar of covert action that contributed to ending the Cold War. Other commentators are not so sanguine and argue that the covert action program gave military training, expertise, and battlefield experience to militant Islamic extremists, who later went on to found Al Qaeda. The truth probably lies somewhere in between, but it is important to note that the United States never dealt directly with bin Laden during the Afghan war. Bin Laden's direct sponsors and benefactors were intelligence services of Saudi Arabia and Pakistan.[26]

Covert action has taken on an increasingly important role in the war on terrorism, which the public gets glimpses of by leaks. The CIA did a superb job in facilitating the U.S. Special Forces entry into Afghanistan in the 2001 war.[27] Covert actions such as the ones carried out in Afghanistan are carried out by the CIA and need to be authorized by a presidential order called a "finding," which is shared with and approved by the House and Senate oversight committees to be legal in the American judicial system.

Traditionally, the presidents have banned American assassination of foreign leaders under executive orders, a practice that has been perpetuated since President Ford's Executive Order 12333, which prohibited assassinations, a move to stem the tide of public criticisms against the CIA and the IC during a tumultuous period of history in American intelligence.[28] When he was CIA director, Porter Goss told Congress in public testimony that the ban on assassinations by U.S. intelligence was still in force but that it does not prohibit the CIA from killing terrorists.[29]

The CIA appears to be effectively using armed unmanned aerial vehicles (UAVs) to kill Al Qaeda operatives. The CIA has used armed UAVs to kill operatives in Yemen and Pakistan as well as in Iraq. "Several U.S. officials confirmed that at least on 19 occasions since Sept. 11 in which Predators successfully fired Hellfire missiles on terrorist suspects overseas, including 10 in Iraq in one month in 2005, the Predator strikes have killed at least four senior Al Qaeda leaders, but also many civilians, and it is not known how many times they missed their targets." [30]

Some critics have faulted the CIA for failing to use the armed UAVs to target bin Laden or covert paramilitary operations to capture him prior to 9/11. The CIA's Directorate of Operations chief in 1998, for example, did not want to use his funds to sponsor a paramilitary operation to grab bin Laden from his farm in Afghanistan and "expressed concern that people might get killed" and that "the operation had at least a slight flavor of a plan for an assassination. Moreover, he calculated that it would cost several million dollars. He was not prepared to take the money "out of hide," and he did not want to go to all the necessary congressional committees to get special money." [31] Although civilians have been tragically killed in paramilitary operations, military strikes, or UAV attacks since 9/11, the strikes are probably still legitimate instruments of war—as long as there is a reasonable chance of killing Al Qaeda operatives and leaders who are sworn to kill as many American civilians and soldiers as they can as long as they live.

The CIA also used covert teams to locate suspected Al Qaeda operatives abroad—in areas where UAV attacks would not be politically viable options, such as in Europe—and in daring raids called "renditions," they swept them off the streets and brought them to other countries for detention and interrogations. These operations have been embroiled in controversies. Italy, for example, was in a political uproar because a CIA team took a person off Italian soil.[32] Other European and Asian countries were in uproars over the purported existence of a string of clandestine CIA detention facilities on their soil. The CIA also has been publicly condemned for blatant violations of the Geneva Conventions with the use of techniques that are commonly considered to be torture in its interrogations undertaken in U.S. military detention facilities in Afghanistan, Iraq, and Guantánamo Bay, Cuba.[33] These accusations include charges that the CIA used a technique called water-boarding, which made detainees believe they were drowning. Not only is this technique morally unacceptable, many professional interrogators judge that this technique produces bad intelligence because prisoners will say or make up anything to get interrogators to stop the water-boarding.[34]

The United States may have fallen victim to this intelligence pitfall. According to journalist James Risen, the information the CIA got from debriefing one high-level Al Qaeda operational commander was fabricated because he wanted to stop the water-boarding.[35] Another CIA detainee who was reportedly tortured after the CIA turned him over to Egyptian officials fabricated information on Iraq's links to Al Qaeda in the run-up to the 2003 Iraq war.[36]

Strengthening Intelligence Collection, Analysis, and Covert Action for the War on Terrorism

Lawyers could argue until the sun goes down whether water-boarding and other techniques the CIA used constitute the legal definition of "torture," but the average American using his or her common sense and moral compass would have little to no difficulty calling these techniques torture. And the American legalistic argument that Al Qaeda operatives are "enemy combatants" and not "prisoners of war" who are governed by the Geneva Conventions carries little weight with Americans and even less with the Middle Eastern populations, which the United States desperately needs to wean away from ideological support for Al Qaeda recruitment and operational support. Even the appearance of Geneva Conventions violations renders American calls for freedom and democracy in the Middle East as sheer hypocrisy and aids and abets our terrorist enemies by handing them ready-made justifications for their ruthless tactics, such as decapitating hostages. Even in its intelligence war on terrorism, the United States must uphold its own ethical standards.

The CIA's use of paramilitary operations was a success story in the 2001 war in Afghanistan. But in the wake of the war, the 9/11 Commission recommended—on not very deep analysis or consideration—that these functions should all be controlled by the Pentagon and that the CIA should get out of the business. The commission said, "Before 9/11, the CIA did not invest in developing a robust capability to conduct paramilitary operations with U.S. personnel. It relied on proxies instead, organized by CIA operatives with the requisite military training. The results were unsatisfactory."[37]

The spectacular SEAL team raid into Pakistan in 2011 that killed bin Laden and the subsequent calls for beefing up of American Special Operations Forces will likely work to further push the CIA out of paramilitary operations. The plan is to increase the number of special operations forces by 14,000 to about 64,000, the largest number since the Vietnam War, to fight small Al Qaeda cells dispersed across some 80 countries.[38] The Pentagon's new emphasis no doubt reflects in part the frustration over the initial lethargic response of the Special Forces to get into the 2001 Afghanistan war in comparison to the quick dispatch of CIA operatives into Afghanistan, which won high praise and respect from President Bush.[39] The push to remove the CIA from the paramilitary business will make sense as long as the Pentagon gives its Special Operations Forces room for operational ingenuity, a key ingredient of effective special operations. Unfortunately, creativity and ingenuity are often crushed by the weight of the Pentagon's bureaucracy.

The DNI, a post created by the president on the recommendation of the 9/11 Commission, will have his hands full trying to overcome the shortcomings of American strategic intelligence against terrorist groups. The DNI's activities so far have focused on recruiting a staff, leaving little time for substantive reforms to address strategic intelligence shortcomings all too evident to the American public in the aftermath of 9/11. The DNI, not the director of the CIA, is now the president's principal intelligence advisor. The DNI has established the National Clandestine Service, the Open Sources Center, and centers under his wing for counterterrorism and counterproliferation, as well as named IC collection managers for Iran and North Korea.[40] There is little evidence to show that these steps are anything more than renaming old organizations, however, and adding some new ones to respond to calls for reform, while in practice doing little to qualitatively improve America's intelligence performance in the war on terrorism.

These bureaucratic fixes run the risk of creating a false impression that the United States has "corrected" all of its strategic intelligence shortcomings in the war on terrorism. But the real root causes of past failures lie in the quality of human intelligence collection and analysis. The creation of the DNI and new national support offices does nothing directly to correct the bureaucratic culture and failed business practices that are stubbornly rooted at the grassroots level of the CIA. Until reforms and profound changes in managerial business practices change at this level, all the reorganizing and changing of the bureaucratic wiring diagrams at the senior-most rungs of the U.S. intelligence community will amount to little more than rearranging the deck chairs on the *Titanic*.

Notes

The views expressed are those of the author and do not represent the policy or position of the National Defense University, the Department of Defense, or the U.S. government.

1. For an insightful analysis of the political and military obstacles against moving to a war footing against Al Qaeda before 9/11, see Richard H. Shultz Jr., "Showstoppers: Nine Reasons Why We Never Sent Our Special Operations Forces after al-Qaeda before 9/11," *Weekly Standard* (January 26, 2004).

2. House Permanent Select Committee on Intelligence and Senate Select Committee on Intelligence, *Report of the Joint Inquiry into the Terrorist Attacks of September 11, 2001* (Washington, DC, December 2002), p. 40. Hereafter referred to as the Joint House-Senate Inquiry.

3. Ibid., p. 59.

4. Richard A. Clarke, *Against All Enemies: Inside America's War on Terror* (New York: Free Press, 2004), pp. 205, 210.

5. Anonymous [Michael Scheuer], *Through Our Enemies' Eyes: Osama bin Laden, Radical Islam, and the Future of America* (Washington, DC: Brassey's, 2002), p. xiv.

6. Greg Miller, "CIA Plans No Discipline over 9/11," *Los Angeles Times* (October 6, 2005), p. A10.

7. For the most authoritative study of state sponsorship of terrorist groups, see Daniel L. Byman, *Deadly Connections: States that Sponsor Terrorism* (New York: Cambridge University Press, 2005).

8. On policy deliberations, see Clarke, *Against All Enemies*, pp. 184–189.

9. Walter Pincus, "CIA to Retain Coordinator of Overseas Spying," *Washington Post* (October 13, 2005), p. A4.

10. John Diamond, "CIA's Spy Network Thin," *USA Today* (September 22, 2004).

11. Lindsay Moran, "More Spies, Worse Intelligence?" *New York Times* (April 12, 2005).

12. Robert Baer, *See No Evil: The True Story of a Ground Soldier in the CIA's War on Terrorism* (New York: Three Rivers Press, 2002), p. 86.

13. Cited in Michael Janofsky, "Bush Proposes Broader Language Training," *New York Times* (January 6, 2006), p. A15.

14. Joint House-Senate Inquiry, p. 109.

15. Glenn Kessler, "On Leaks, Relying on a Faulty Case Study," *Washington Post* (December 23, 2005), p. A3.

16. On the controversy, see James Risen and Eric Lichtblau, "Bush Lets U.S. Spy on Callers without Courts," *New York Times* (December 16, 2005), p. A1.

17. Joint House-Senate Inquiry, p. 90.

18. Ibid., p. 205.

19. For an account of the innovative creation of the CTC by its founding chief, see Duane R. Clarridge with Digby Diehl, *A Spy for All Seasons: My Life in the CIA* (New York: Scribner's, 1997), pp. 321–329.

20. Joint House-Senate Inquiry, 59.

21. *The 9/11 Commission Report* (New York: Norton, 2004), pp. 260–261.

22. See the Joint House-Senate Inquiry, pp. 325–335.

23. For the recommendation to establish the NCTC, see *The 9/11 Commission Report*, pp. 403–406.

24. The budget figure was revealed by a senior official in the DNI's office in 2005. See Scott Shane, "Official Reveals Budget for U.S. Intelligence," *New York Times* (November 8, 2005), p. A18.

25. For an insightful discussion of the differences between covert action and special activities, see William J. Daugherty, *Executive Secrets: Covert Action and the Presidency* (Lexington: University Press of Kentucky, 2004), pp. 12–16.

26. For a fascinating account of the CIA's covert action program in Afghanistan, see Steve Coll, *Ghost Wars: The Secret History of the CIA, Afghanistan, and bin Laden, from the Soviet Invasion to September 10, 2001* (New York: Penguin Press, 2004) and George Crile, *Charlie Wilson's War: The Extraordinary Story of How the Wildest Man in Congress and a Rogue CIA Agent Changed the History of Our Times* (New York: Grove Press, 2003).

27. See Gary C. Schroen, *First In: An Insider's Account of How the CIA Spearheaded the War on Terror in Afghanistan* (New York: Ballantine Books, 2005). For an excellent account of CIA paramilitary activities in the past decade of war, see Mark Mazzetti, *The Way of the Knife: The CIA, A Secret Army, and a War at the Ends of the Earth* (New York: Penguin Press, 2013).

28. For a concise history of congressional oversight of the CIA and covert action, see Loch K. Johnson, "Presidents, Lawmakers, and Spies: Intelligence Accountability in the United States," *Presidential Studies Quarterly* 34, no. 4 (December 2004), pp. 828–837.

29. Shaun Waterman, "Goss Says CIA Ban Excludes Terrorists," *Washington Times* (March 25, 2005), p. A5.

30. Josh Meyer, "CIA Expands Use of Drones in Terror War," *Los Angeles Times* (January 29, 2006), p. A1.

31. *The 9/11 Commission Report*, p. 113.

32. In a reflection of the anger surrounding the case, an Italian judge ordered the arrest of 13 suspected CIA officers who participated in the rendition operation in 2003. See Stephen Grey and Don Van Natta, "In Italy, Anger at U.S. Tactics Colors Spy Case," *New York Times* (June 26, 2005), p. A1.

33. For an insightful treatment of the CIA's covert activity and ethical dilemmas with maintaining prison facilities for renditioned individuals, see Dana Priest, "CIA Holds Terror Suspects in Secret Prisons," *Washington Post* (November 2, 2005), p. A1.

34. James Risen, *State of War: The Secret History of the CIA and the Bush Administration* (New York: Free Press, 2006), pp. 32–33. For details of the CIA's role in interrogations, see John Rizzo, "I Could Have Stopped Waterboarding before It Happened," *Politico Magazine* (5 January 2014).

35. Ibid., p. 33.

36. Douglas Jehl, "Qaeda–Iraq Link U.S. Cited Is Tied to Coercion Claim," *New York Times* (December 9, 2005), p. A1.

37. *The 9/11 Commission Report*, p. 415.

38. Greg Jaffe, "Rumsfeld Aims to Elevate Role of Special Forces," *Wall Street Journal* (February 18, 2006), p. A1.

39. Bob Woodward, *Bush at War* (New York: Simon & Schuster, 2002), pp. 53, 78–80, 88, 99.

40. John D. Negroponte, "Intelligence Reform: Challenges and Opportunities," 25th Jit Trainor Award Speech, Georgetown University, February 17, 2006.

CHAPTER SEVENTEEN

Counterterrorism, Fusion Centers, and the Importance of All-Source Intelligence

Jennifer Sims

FROM 1934 TO 1937, THE BRITISH GOVERNMENT collected suspicious communications from its monitoring station at Camberwell.[1] Peeling back the encryption with the help of a well-placed mole and several émigrés, the government discovered the existence of an illicit Soviet spying and covert action network operating on British soil. It appeared to involve senior politicians and established political organizations. Direction-finding equipment owned by the Army intercept station at Fort Bridgewoods, the Air Ministry at Waddington, and at the Royal Navy's receiver at Flowerdown established the location of the network's transmission sites. MI5 used this knowledge to begin surveillance of the broad-based network, penetrate it with human intelligence assets, and gain advance notice of illegal activities. These counterintelligence efforts eventually established that the illicit British cells were connected to Vienna, Shanghai, Prague, Copenhagen, Zurich, Paris, Spain, and the United States. All were directed by Moscow and coordinated through the operations of Comintern, or Communist International. According to British historian Nigel West, this huge counterintelligence operation, which intercepted a total of 1,571 messages, disrupted Moscow's efforts to influence British elections "on a massive scale."[2]

This is the story of MASK—the code name for MI5's penetration of the Communist Party of Great Britain during the period between the world wars. Although the details of the story are worth rereading in the post–September 11, 2001, political context, just the facts summarized above suggest three truths about counterintelligence operations directed against networks: first, they involve intrusive domestic operations, often against domestically based groups designed to "disappear" within the societies in which they operate; second, they require patient accumulation of data over a lengthy period of time; and finally, they depend on information fused from a variety of widely differing sources. These three ingredients, essential for such operations almost a century ago, are still important in the age of global, digitalized information flows and transnational threats. In fact, the new digital environment has made transnational crimes vastly easier to coordinate on a worldwide scale than was possible before World War II. It has also exacerbated a most serious challenge: governments (particularly democracies) attempting to stop terrorists are expected to do so without undermining the laws, representative principles, and informal confidences upon which a culture of democracy depends. Unfortunately, what Britain succeeded in doing against its domestic threat—to the satisfaction of the British public—was done even better within the militarized Nazi German state by Hitler's Gestapo and the Schutzstaffel, or SS ("Blackshirts"). If, as President Truman once promised the American people, we are not in the business of creating a Gestapo in this country, what are the proper limits of our counterintelligence business?

The purpose of this chapter is to examine the modern intelligence requirements for countering terror to appreciate this challenge in greater depth and develop a reasoned basis for balancing counterintelligence capabilities with civil liberties. What is meant by all-source data fusion in intelligence work, and how necessary is it against terrorists? How necessary are government-wide databases of digitalized information, and why does the idea of connecting them worry civil libertarians? If, as the post-9/11 commissions have suggested, one of the U.S. government's worst intelligence failures during this tragedy was the lack of adequate data fusion and analysis, what has been done about it, and can we do more without intolerable risks to our social and moral fabric?

To explore these questions, this chapter begins by considering the nature of the terrorists we face and the requirements for good intelligence operations against them. Historical examples will illustrate that there are lessons to be learned from the defeat of similar threats in the past, including the recurring ways in which challenges to civil liberties arise as democracies optimize intelligence in the name of security. Second, I run through the special opportunities and challenges modern technology presents. Third, I discuss an essential next step for democracies threatened by terrorists in their midst.

The Nature of Intelligence and Counterintelligence in the Age of Terror

As has been repeatedly pointed out, terrorism is a tool, not an adversary in and of itself. Yet adversaries who use this tool reveal much about themselves. They are ruthless, have strategies and tactics that require operational access to their victims, and they are able to organize in pursuit of their goals. Moreover, unless they are psychopathic, they use terror because they have no alternative that offers as much opportunity to win battles. Public access to national treasures and freedom to organize are integral to Western democracies' most vital interests. Democracies intent on fighting adversaries who exploit openness to kill massively, risk undermining themselves. Countering such adversaries at the strategic level may require understanding their larger purposes to deflect, overcome, or undermine them. But to defeat them at the tactical level, one must deny them access, disrupt their ability to organize, or deny them their "victories," even if their tactics succeed. One must know what they are doing and either catch them at it or refuse to flinch—ideally, both. Intelligence, in any case, is essential.

The Role of Intelligence

"Intelligence" is best understood as the collection, analysis, and dissemination of information by parties in conflict or competition. What turns the simple pursuit of information into the business of intelligence is its purpose: gaining competitive advantage over adversaries.[3] This goal fuels the desire for specific, urgent, and often secret knowledge as well as a systematic way of obtaining it in time to win the contest. Given that the context is competition, such decision advantages can be acquired in two ways: by getting better information for one's strategy than one's opponents gain for theirs, or by degrading the competitors' decision making through denial, disruption, deception, and surprise.[4] This latter category of activity is called "counterintelligence." More than just security, counterintelligence involves discovering what opponents think they need to know and then using this information to block, disorient, confuse, and ultimately beat them. In virulent or hostile competitions, increasing the speed of one's own decision making and the mobility of the decision makers may unbalance the opponent more than trying to discern and defend all the information believed to be critical to that opponent's strategy—a process that can actually slow decision making and cripple one's offense. Of course, the best way to protect an intelligence system is to own the adversary's intelligence system through the use of moles, double agents, and the like.

Gangs, bureaucrats, and football teams all use a form of intelligence to gain advantages over their competitors.[5] The more intense and lawless the competition, such as in international politics, the more secretive intelligence operations tend to become and the more decisive the potential advantages they offer. In fact, for states, intelligence can be more than a life or death enterprise; it can entail the end of nations and cultures.[6] For these reasons, secrecy is often viewed as a necessary component of national or transnational intelligence efforts. It is more accurate, however, to think of secrecy as an attribute of a relatively good intelligence effort—not an essential requirement for it. Some contestants' counterintelligence capabilities are so poor that they are not aware of what information they should protect to beat their adversaries. Or they believe their relative agility makes such protection unnecessary. Trying to defeat such opponents by only looking for secrets they protect would lead to failure. Intelligence must instead work to collect the information that provides the competitor with a decision advantage over opponents—whether or not that information is secret—and to assume adversaries are doing likewise.

Arguably, a preoccupation with secrets cost the United States much before the devastation of 9/11. Although the terrorists' plans were indeed closely held, their operations were boldly open. Most used their true names when making airline reservations, used common addresses, and communicated on the Internet, not through privileged diplomatic pouches or hidden radios. The trick to catching them would have been to combine what we knew from the efforts of the Central Intelligence Agency (CIA) to track them overseas with what we could have known from the surveillance and unclassified information collected at home by the Federal Bureau of Investigation (FBI). Using classified sources to tip off the FBI and discern the unclassified information crucial for counterterrorist decision making is a critical part of the domestic intelligence enterprise.[7]

Traditionally, U.S. intelligence has used three types of collection to target opponents: technical intelligence (TECHINT), human intelligence (HUMINT), and open-source or unclassified intelligence (OSINT). TECHINT includes the collection of imagery, intercepted communications, electronic signals emitted by equipment, engineering data from captured electronics or weapons systems, and data from equipment or materials in the environment that leave signatures of their presence (such as radiation, effluent plumes, and noise) that trained analysts can discern using pre-existing data as reference.[8] The productivity of any of these collectors against a particular target will depend on that collector's access to the target's most vulnerable point. For example, if a network of spies uses wireless radios, picking up their electronic emissions (TECHINT) will be an effective way to find them; if they use couriers, human agents secretly opening the letters and packages (HUMINT) is likely to work best; if the adversary believes he is unobserved, collecting the names of those he visits from a phone book or the sites he visits while traveling as an ostensible tourist (OSINT) would be useful.

In any case, the best intelligence is obtained when the capabilities of all these collectors are quickly combined. Just as newspaper editors like to see multiple sources corroborating articles even from their best reporters, directors of national intelligence have greater confidence in intelligence that comes from multiple collectors. Better than simply hearing that Osama bin Laden has been sighted on a road in Pakistan would be seeing imagery of his convoy and receiving intercepts from his communications that each independently confirm the initial report.[9] As long as an opponent runs reasonably complex operations, some collectors will work best against certain aspects of those operations, whereas others will work best against the rest. Thus "all-source" collection can yield many pieces of a puzzle that analysts can then assemble, jumble up, and reassemble as the adversary moves, reacts to countermoves, and moves again.

Beyond corroboration, however, is the concept of collection boosting, in which the productivity of one collector depends on input from others.[10] The most obvious example of boosting within a single discipline is "direction finding" (DF), which may involve the use of multiple antennae to triangulate on a signal so that it can be not only identified but also geolocated with some degree of precision.[11] During World War II, the SS paired up with the Gestapo and used DF to locate the wireless radios used by a network of Stalin's spies in Europe. To their great chagrin, these radios were found in Berlin—some next to the most sensitive government ministries.[12]

Of course, boosting also works among collection disciplines, such as the use of spies (HUMINT) to steal the codes of adversaries so that analysts working on intercepted communications (TECHINT) can overcome the encryption methods and read the content of the messages.[13] In fact, the more tightly integrated collectors are in the decision-making process, the more likely an adversary's spoofing of a collector will work to deflect or deceive one's own decision makers. Because securing collectors can be a costly and seemingly never-ending endeavor, one good way to compensate for inevitable vulnerabilities is to ensure collection is "constructively redundant"—that is, sufficiently all-source so that one collector's vulnerability to spoofing will not lead to misperception or miscalculation.

This kind of constructively redundant all-source collection was a linchpin of the Allied strategy to defeat Hitler during World War II; it was employed, for example, to determine whether covert and clandestine collection operations had been compromised and specifically in the running of the famous British counterintelligence operation known as the Double Cross System.[14] But the history of Double Cross also alerts us to the inherent dangers of redundant collection systems: Because collectors improve the reliability of each other's products by offering independent corroboration, they depend on good system-wide counterintelligence so an adversary can't defeat or spoof one of them and thus sow ambiguity, uncertainty, and confusion throughout an interlaced collection system. If systemic counterintelligence is weak, collectors have good reason not to share their "take" lest it become tainted. Poor counterintelligence can lead to system-wide failure, even when the majority of collection endeavors are robust and productive.[15]

U.S. Intelligence for Counterterrorism

In some respects, then, the business of all-source data fusion for countering terrorism follows what has been done in a traditional sense against other intelligence targets. What makes counterterrorism a particularly challenging endeavor is the terrorists' objective of committing stealthy crime—often on the victim's home soil. In the U.S. case, this means that law enforcement information, including information on residents or citizens living in close proximity to terrorists, may be important intelligence information that needs to be shared with decision makers at the federal level working to thwart terrorist activities on a nationwide scale. Law enforcement agents, dedicated to preserving the information for the purposes of arrest and prosecution, realize the need to pass the information over to these officials but do not always know the best and most secure ways to do so. At times, in fact, the most important decisions must be made very quickly by state and local officials if they are to prevent an impending attack. In these cases, circulating information to Washington for recycling into intelligence products could delay action rather than assist it. The problem thus becomes the very nontraditional one of fusing all-source intelligence for a cop on the beat.

In other words, what makes terrorists particularly difficult intelligence targets for intelligence systems in democracies is that they organize as networks, insinuate themselves into open societies, and kill suddenly. Whereas collectors during the Cold War were designed to penetrate governments or military deployments located on discrete battlefields, terrorists specialize in operating in small numbers and under the skins of their adversaries—that is, wherever they can do the most damage. They fashion themselves to look like their targets and burrow into society to lie in wait. In this sense, they occupy the same moral space as assassins but without an assassin's traditional limits on targeting. Deceit is part of terrorists' stock in trade, and innocents are their intentional victims. Often free of the vertical command structures of their more bureaucratic opponents, they achieve agility through compartmented operations, often using minimal communications. Their offensive operations are also crucial to their defense; by instilling fear and panic, terrorists create sufficient confusion to enable their swift escape. For many of these reasons, analysts have long argued that it takes a network to fight networked organizations, such as Al Qaeda.[16]

Unfortunately for democracies, counterterrorism requires gaining access to the enemy where he operates, including on one's own soil. And because terrorists do not operate against a national security establishment but against an entire society, they will not necessarily be focused on any particular city or on stealing secrets from traditional national security establishments. This means that it may be necessary but no longer sufficient to use forms of collection appropriate to the Cold War, when the enemy was a highly bureaucratized state, targeting Washington and using a command-and-control system stretching halfway around the world. To stop terrorists, information from traditional intelligence collectors will need to be combined with information collected by those disconnected to the traditional national security community. Hospitals may be the first to see a spike in disease associated with a biological weapons attack; police may be the first to bust a document forger or stop a car carrying explosives; customs agents at a port may be the first to notice discrepancies between the scan of a shipping crate and its official manifest; a landlord may be the first to notice his building's security system is detecting toxic gases; and a shopper may be the first to notice someone in a mall or store pushing a heavy baby carriage with no baby inside.

Against this kind of threat, time is of the essence, yet indications and warning may come from untrained people just doing their day jobs. The intelligence these domestic collectors acquire, moreover, will often need to be analyzed and provided back to them. After all, they are likely to be the decision makers best placed to stop the attack itself. The first 9/11 counterattack was, in fact, carried out by passengers on an airliner—once they knew from collecting intelligence over their cell phones what they were up against and what was at stake.

In the modern era of the Internet and the global reach of broadband communications, terrorists have new capabilities beyond the reach of any one country. By piggybacking on this information system, bolstered by highly effective private encryption, transnational terrorist groups can communicate instantaneously and largely anonymously, even to the extent of sending sensitive information embedded in pictures on websites or in emails, a practice known as steganography. For this reason, the intelligence gained by other states and their private sector collectors may be as potentially valuable as intelligence collected unilaterally; much depends on the confidence a state has in its liaison relationships—confidence that should fluctuate more with the capabilities of that state's counterintelligence capabilities than with the number of its perceived friendships.

The overall picture, then, is of proliferating intelligence sources, increasingly complex all-source analysis, and a maddeningly contingent list of those decision makers who not only need the results but must get them in record time. Preparation of a terrorist attack might take years, but its execution or prevention may take only hours or minutes. Most crucial: suicide terrorists are often first-time perpetrators training for just one mission; state-based intelligence systems cannot rely just on tracking and targeting known terrorists to stop these attacks. Instead, they must find unknown jihadists before they strike by looking for patterns of suspicious behavior among people who have not necessarily committed a crime. In the United States, for example, the Boston Marathon bombers of 2012 had no criminal profile.

As bad as this situation sounds, it is not all that new. As with today's terrorists, history's most notorious plotters have threaded themselves through the fabric of the societies they planned to attack. In the 16th century, Catholics, intent on assassinating the Protestant Queen Elizabeth I and installing her Catholic cousin, Mary, Queen of Scots, were distinguishable from Elizabeth's loyalists only by their faith and their suspicious associations. Sir Walsingham, Elizabeth's Secretary of State and chief spymaster, nonetheless caught them.[17] Kaiser Wilhelm's saboteurs infiltrated German immigrant communities in the United States prior to World War I so that they would have cover for their mission to blow up weapons depots, warehouses, and storage facilities. They, too, were countered—this time by a network of British liaison officers and U.S. law enforcement personnel, assisted by the intermittent incompetence of the saboteurs themselves.[18] Successful counterterrorist intelligence operations such as these have generally employed well-known principles: collect multisource intelligence, tighten borders, tap liaison services, conduct deception operations, and enlist law enforcement to detect anomalous behavior and interdict and "turn" those criminals, such as forgers and money launderers, often superficially aligned with terrorists.[19]

What makes the current, post-9/11 effort so much more difficult than in times past is the nature of modern technology. Technology has affected the counterterrorist mission in a number of ways. For example, advances in weapons technologies have rendered the scariest forms of attack—biologically engineered germs, toxins, and nuclear explosive or radiological devices—feasible for small numbers of people (even non-experts)—to execute. Perhaps less well understood among the general population is the extent to which advances in communications technology permit terrorist networks to exchange messages and plan attacks on a worldwide basis and to do so almost instantaneously.

The development of cyber and commercial surveillance technologies means that information on a developing terrorist attack that is acquired by private citizens or local businesses can in theory be handed off rapidly to local and state officials. Individuals outside the traditional national security community may therefore not only be the first to get critical information about a coming terrorist attack but be empowered with the critical ability to decide what to do with it. Obviously, the national intelligence community has a stake in such decisions, but, not surprisingly, it has neither a roadmap for building the kind of domestic alliances that would facilitate such cooperation or the deep and nuanced understanding of American culture that makes such a task so difficult for the federal government to implement.[20] Unfortunately, terrorists who recognize the upward trend in private sector surveillance and capacities to secretly monitor and upload surveillance products for access by anyone, may use cyber espionage and perhaps even cyber attacks to facilitate their plans—and do so from a safe distance. Furthermore, the distributed nature of the modern software and computer manufacturing industry makes modern information technologies deliberately invasive or inherently vulnerable.[21]

Aware of both the threat in the private sector and its inherent vulnerability, President George W. Bush decided immediately after 9/11 to circumvent established procedures for domestic counterterrorist surveillance in case rapid sampling of certain domestic communications could detect other plots or unknown terrorists still in the country.[22] Certain communications companies cooperated with the government and, when this subsequently came to light, suffered public criticism. Although subsequent legislation absolved them of any wrong-doing, recent revelations by Edward Snowden show how rapidly the domestic consensus can change from insistence on greater domestic intelligence post-9-11 to public dismay over reports of even legally authorized surveillance just 10 years later. American political culture has always demanded that the task of domestic intelligence gathering be difficult for the federal government to implement; so the pendulum appears to be swinging back, after the 9-11 jolt, to a pre-9-11 sensitivity to increasing government powers for finding plotters, as opposed to criminals. And while the government can withstand such swings and adapt, private companies have and will suffer significant losses that will likely make them less willing to partner in counterterrorism efforts in the future.

Unfortunately and for reasons explained above, the national intelligence community has a continuing need for private sector partnership in the counterterrorism effort. The U.S. government roadmap for building such cooperation, much of it sensitive and necessarily secret, is now in jeopardy.[23]

Data Fusion and the Age of Terror: Implications for Democracy

The prominent role all-source intelligence and advanced technology have in countering terrorism presents special difficulties for democracies. The media initially highlighted issues related to prisoner detention, rendition, and interrogation. After the Snowden leaks, they have energized the long-standing debates among civil libertarians, security officials, and private citizens over issues of bulk data collection, domestic surveillance, and privacy. It is hard for democracies to promote freedom and liberty as antidotes for terror while at the same time intruding more deeply into their own societies for the purpose of monitoring individuals and capturing fanatics before they act. Unfortunately, this is exactly the course that the U.S. was forced to take after 9-11. Balancing security and pre-emption with restraint and freedom is difficult; terrorists likely hope the conundrum will prove paralyzing.

While some commentators have suggested that privacy may be one area where Americans may be willing to cede added power to authorities, others, including this author, have noted that suspicion of excess power in the hands of the federal government runs deep in American political culture. Although the issues related to the rights of prisoners (now before the courts) are beyond the scope of this paper; these other issues of data fusion, control, and management are not.

The Domestic Context for Data Collection and Fusion for Intelligence Purposes

Throughout the Cold War, the CIA, FBI, and certain military services were involved in domestic intelligence collection. When they over-reached, they were subjected to new legal constraints. By 1978, when the Foreign Intelligence Surveillance Act (FISA) was passed, the essential framework for domestic spying in the U.S. had been established: on the one hand, the president's constitutional authority for the nation's defense gave him the prerogative to order domestic surveillance; on the other hand, his powers to spy on American citizens and residents were constrained by the requirement that the courts be convinced of these individuals' connections to foreign powers or terrorist causes in each case. It was understood, if not written into law, that information gathered in this secret way, that is, without the normal warrant process, was not to bleed into the criminal justice system to be used against citizens for other purposes—such as to convict them of a crime unrelated to espionage or terror. In this way, what has come to be called the "wall" between intelligence and law enforcement was deliberately and perhaps too impermeably erected.

After 9/11, lawmakers and national security experts criticized this framework as too tight a constraint on domestic intelligence gathering for counter-terror purposes. While the president had secretly reasserted his perceived prerogatives to spy against domestic national security threats, Congress passed the Patriot Act. This act increased the FBI's ability to track and monitor terrorists using communications systems far more elaborate than those available when the original FISA law was passed. In addition, the "wall" between intelligence and law enforcement was torn down in the interests of intelligence sharing between agencies. The president also decided to consolidate within the Department of Homeland Security (DHS), those agencies responsible for border control, emergency response, and domestic security. While eschewing a new domestic intelligence gathering function, DHS began to consolidate databases and to generate related intelligence reports. The president created the Terrorism Threat Integration Center to fuse intelligence from all relevant agencies both inside and outside the formal intelligence community. Following the endorsement of the idea of data fusion centers by the 9/11 Commission, Congress passed legislation creating the National Counter Terrorism Center, the director of which gained authorities over overseas operations as well. Subsequently, its sister center was created under the new Director of National Intelligence to handle intelligence on weapons of mass destruction.

While these changes were under way at the highest levels in Washington, debate has continued on what appears to be a serious gap: Unlike Britain, the U.S. federal government continues to lack an institution specifically charged with conducting true domestic intelligence gathering and forging the kind of domestic alliances for intelligence networking already described. Although the FBI has adopted a more self-conscious domestic intelligence role, its expertise continues to be law enforcement and defensive counterintelligence—both arts involving the use of surveillance for arrests. Although the FBI has made strides in developing a positive intelligence capability for counterterrorism, its core mission remains countering crime, not offensive counterintelligence for policy purposes such as strategic planning and the exploitation of decision advantages against hostile powers or terrorists.. With CIA HUMINT still very limited in what it can (and should) do domestically, intelligence activities to counter terror have turned to bulk data collection through the Internet and cyber space. Post Snowden, this capability may now be in jeopardy. Without a deep domestic intelligence capability and the domestic consensus necessary to institutionalize it, data collection and fusion at the federal level may remain inadequate to the counterterrorism task.[24]

Despite controversies at the national level, law enforcement officials in cities such as New York, Los Angeles, and Chicago have expanded their capabilities to investigate domestic groups; consolidate the data from global, national, and local sources; and thus organize new and improved intelligence systems themselves. Data fusion has become a grassroots business. For example, Los Angeles pioneered the Terrorism Early Warning Group, which fuses intelligence and directs it to first responders.[25] And New York City has established liaison offices overseas. In the wake of the collapse of a local cable company, Chicago's then mayor, Richard Daley, bought up its fiber optic network and hooked hundreds of video cameras to it. He also encouraged private companies to dump the returns from their surveillance cameras onto the network so that, for a fee, crimes could be rapidly reported to the city's police department.

Of course, the establishments wired for commercial security are becoming Chicago's platforms for law enforcement surveillance of criminal and gang-related behavior. The city's operations center has become the hub of a network for surveillance and monitoring in the name of citizen protection against crime and, simultaneously, natural disasters and terrorist attack. Not surprisingly, Chicago's innovation has been replicated in at least 150 other cities to a greater or lesser degree. New York, which reportedly has a network of more than 3,000 cameras, has sought to archive the video files indefinitely.[26] Baltimore, whose cameras may gain the ability to "talk," intends to deter crime as much as counter terrorists with its electronic network.[27]

Other first responders are adopting similar methods for different purposes. Hospitals have begun wiring themselves to keep track of the conditions of patients and the scarce medical equipment they may need to ensure efficiency of care. When more than one hospital participates, ambulances can make better decisions about where to transport emergency cases to ensure the swiftest medical care at emergency rooms. A system such as this, or the one in Chicago, could have assisted New Orleans in its efforts to respond to the emergency following Hurricane Katrina. It holds the promise of gathering data swiftly and analyzing it appropriately in the event of a terrorist attack as well.

Although public protests of increases in domestic surveillance at the local level have been light and sporadic, this level of tolerance has not been apparent when federal surveillance has been involved. National attention more readily focuses on federal moves, hesitant though they may be, to increase domestic surveillance. The case of Edward Snowden is only the most recent example. The president's expansion of the Defense Department's Counterintelligence Field Activity (CIFA), including its surveillance activities nationwide, has triggered protests, including at least one congressional intervention.[28] Although CIFA was created to protect military facilities and personnel worldwide, it has significantly ramped up its domestic operations in recent years for the purpose of fusing intelligence, identifying and assessing threats, and retaining the results in a Pentagon database.

Perhaps even more notorious was the abbreviated effort to link databases at the federal level for similar purposes. In 2003 Adm. John Poindexter spearheaded an effort to link U.S. government databases for the purposes of querying them and drawing inferences about terrorists' actions from their contents over time. The project, unfortunately dubbed Total Information Awareness (TIA), had an Orwellian quality that made many Americans' hair stand on end. Among them were a number of legislators who promptly killed the program. Along with it, they killed the only ongoing federally funded research in how to protect the privacy of citizens from advances in "inferencing" capabilities (discussed below), so crucial to anticipating, warning, and managing not just terrorist attacks but natural disasters and outbreaks of disease as well.

For reasons elaborated more fully elsewhere, Americans clearly have a particular distaste for federal government intrusion in their lives.[29] That the citizens of a small town in Vermont wire their streets with surveillance cameras or that Chicago and New York and Baltimore experiment in new law enforcement techniques does not mean that the American public will be willing to accept those kinds of domestic initiatives from the federal government. This attitude holds true even when the nation's security is arguably at risk. Although the relevant laws have been modified in the wake of 9/11, citizens are continuing to demand that constitutional protections against unwarranted intrusion by the federal government stay intact even as they willingly cede these rights to commercial firms and local law enforcement.

What Is to Be Done?

Britain's successful counterintelligence operation against communist infiltrators during the interwar period involved the use of domestic surveillance, communications intercepts, direction finding involving the military services, and the penetration of a domestic political party. Such an aggressive approach would be firmly resisted in the United States, constrained as it is by the electorate's deeply seated sense of domestic privacy and individual prerogatives. Yet without successful efforts to bring together all-source intelligence on domestic threats, a repeat of tragedy on the scale of 9/11 could bring the kind of domestic overreaction that leads to vigilantism and the undermining of the very constitutional protections that national security measures are meant to protect. So what can be done to balance the need for data collection and fusion with civil liberties?

Challenging as the technological political landscape seems, it also presents opportunities for domestic counterterrorist operations, provided secret breaching of democratically developed laws does not trigger public blowback. Terrorists have gained an advantage in operating within democracies because they have found ways to use technological innovations, such as the Internet and commercially available programs for communicating, hiding, and ferreting out new recruits. This penetration of liberal societies through the hijacking of the technologies they excel at creating is crafty. After all, American entrepreneurs rapidly employ their best commercial innovations in critical infrastructure, protecting them as national assets even as adversaries exploit them.

But technology is, by its nature, neutral. It is also constantly changing. The American public has proved itself both adaptable and tolerant of efforts to fuse intelligence for the purposes of interdiction, at least when done at the local level. The issue is whether those officials countering terrorism can be quicker and more innovative than the terrorists in recognizing what must be done in binding innovation to mission and whether citizens and officials at the local, state, and federal levels can find ways to embrace such innovation without doing violence to civil liberties.

Pursuing Total Information Awareness?

Although no one would suggest that American citizens should embrace an Orwellian world in which the federal government monitors their every move, most Americans probably do understand and even value society's ability to remember them when their lives and livelihoods are at stake. Insurers and pharmacists keep track of medical records; credit card companies and banks track credit histories so that people can borrow money to buy homes or send their kids to college.

What is at issue, especially after the Snowden revelations, is the government's ability to access and combine these pools of data to uncover patterns of activity indicating unknown terrorists are plotting harm. Though such pooling might lower the risks to society, it could have unfortunate consequences for individuals in specific instances: a personal medical history falling into the hands of prospective employers; fallacious patterns that seem to implicate an innocent person in the activities of a gang; or the confusion of a name and profile of a suspected terrorist with that of a law-abiding citizen. At the same time, failure to establish such patterns may allow terrorists free rein in a society increasingly wired for their purposes.

Two avenues seem open for addressing this dilemma: First, research institutions could delve more deeply into the question of data mining and analysis and educate the public about their results. Until recently, the general public has been poorly informed about the uses and limits of government held databases. Now public interest has spiked, opening opportunities for more funding and dissemination of careful research into how bulk data might be safely used for countering domestic terrorism. Second, the U.S. government might carefully and transparently piggyback on domestic initiatives to fuse data for crisis management in the private sector and for local law enforcement purposes so that national security can benefit from improved security at local levels. In return for encouraging and even subsidizing those initiatives that have found support among local citizenry, the federal government could thereby share federally researched techniques and standards for information processing and hand-off, while negotiating protocols for ensuring the threshold for federal access is appropriately restrictive. Both these approaches are briefly elaborated below.

Data Mining and Data Analysis: Thinking Ahead

Inside Washington, the topics of bulk data collection, data mining, and data analysis have been intensely researched and debated for years. Unfortunately, the Snowden revelations have added both confusion about what the Federal government can do and a rush to judgment about how it does it. This frenzied atmosphere reflects a debate rocked by serial revelations from Snowden and reactions mediated first by "instant" media, not deliberative U.S. political institutions or expert centers for public policy research. In fact, not only were the programs legal, but they were monitored by three branches of government. Snowden was, however, uncomfortable. The public blowback from his decision to leak these programs has led to a political tsunami against bulk collection in general.

This is the world as it is, not as intelligence managers or counter-terrorism officials might want it to be. The shadow of 9-11 is lightening and faith in government is low. In this context a serial leaker has been idolized while public servants, following laws, have suffered often underserved criticism. Much as intelligence experts may dislike all this, it is a good thing. Democracies are healthiest when they are based on strong political institutions and, ironically, lack of trust in them. Bulk data collection has enormously increased government power—a kind of power that, if turned on political enemies instead of terrorists, could destroy democracy itself. The public is right to be concerned but not to insist on having cake and eating it too. Without bulk data collection of some kind, a nuclear 9-11 is more likely than it would have been before Snowden did us all the favor of stealing and ruining our innovative defenses. So what now?

It is past time for USG institutions to get a grip on the challenges of the new world of bulk data collection and to guide the public debate on what to do about them. The American people need context: bulk data collection is happening throughout the private sector and by many hostile governments intent on finding and stealing U.S. industrial secrets, profiling American political trends, and sifting through U.S. phone records from afar for their own far more nefarious targeting purposes. Although terrorists might soon be able to master these tools as well, bulk data collection and analysis is one of the few areas where large corporations and governments have an edge over the thief or terrorist. And most are using that edge. While private firms are opting to profit from bulk data tools to do business, sell citizens' information, and defend their products, no one wants or expects public institutions in the United States to behave this way toward citizens or legal residents. Instead of running for political cover, political leaders should help frame the debate through hearings in Congress and frank dialogue with constituents. Realistically, however, the chances that this kind of public debate will raise public consciousness are few.

A better avenue for advancing public understanding might be private sector research and reporting. Over 10 years ago, the Center for Strategic and International Studies (CSIS) launched several initiatives to raise public awareness of the nature of the bulk data and data-mining problem. Its expert at that time, Mary De Rosa, conducted a careful study of the data fusion and management problem confronting counterterrorism analysts.[30] In her published report, De Rosa made important headway by drawing clear distinctions between data mining and data analysis.[31] Both techniques simply exploit data that are already accessible. Yet they also create new knowledge from these data faster and more accurately than human analysts can. Although these techniques can help attribute records to people, they begin by discovering patterns in metadata (data about data, not content) to establish connections between actions, places, and things. If such connections seem suspicious, additional steps can be taken to link patterns to individuals. Unless such techniques are completely eschewed, the civil liberty question turns on who has the "key" to unlock individual identity from patterns, how that key is provided, and when. Protecting civil liberties requires developing protocols related to the key—protocols that require hard legal and technical work to develop.

Through disciplined discussion, De Rosa thus raised important questions that still require thoughtful discussion, including issues that the Snowden debate has overlooked. For example, although analysts can infer from existing data the probable development of sleeper cells, they can discern less well those data that no longer require archiving. The absence of such self-laundering systems means that inappropriate associations among data sets may linger. That the government of the United States does not always purge mistakes from its databases is well known. Innocent civilians have been pulled out of lines at airports and have had difficulties renewing their driver's licenses. These are real practical problems of having government in the bulk data business.

The CSIS study thus engendered a well-rounded discussion of how to constrain analysts interested in bulk phone and Internet data as well as how to discipline a federal government notorious for finding data but forgetting records no longer of use to it but of interest to the private citizen. De Rosa concluded in 2005 that even if the problems of inappropriate associations among data—that is, the problem of false positives—could be overcome, government mechanisms remained inadequate for controlling the use of the results. Among the issues she urged be addressed were those related to mission creep, or the tendency to do more with information than the public had agreed to tolerate.

The CSIS report and others like it informed the process of constraining federal power as De Rosa and her colleagues testified before Congress about surveillance techniques, helping to improve congressional and judicial oversight. More work along these lines is now called for, and perhaps the media and the public will take greater interest in the results than in years past. After all, even far more aggressive techniques are being developed in the private sector by commercial firms interested in increasing profits by understanding markets; the general public is intermittently outraged, perplexed, or delighted with the impact of these developments on their personal transactions and so will likely keep alive the issue of privacy in the world of bulk data. Among such advances are anonymizing, auditing, inferencing, and "permissioning" technologies. Investors are funding anonymizing techniques to allow data on individuals to be processed without using names. Auditing allows those working on newly enabled data-processing techniques to be held accountable for their actions. Inferencing technologies help users discern new information from patterns of data. Permissioning technologies ensure that rules established for handling data are fully respected. How bulk data is handled in the private sector may advance not only data-mining techniques but also the technologies necessary for developing better keys and protocols for their use from which the government might benefit.

Enlisting the Private Sector: Smart Buildings?

Provided the public debate can be reasoned and productive through the two mechanisms discussed above, counterterrorism can still entail useful public–private partnerships. It is not much of a stretch, given advances in data processing and the steps already taken in Chicago and New York, to see that in the event of a terrorist attack, the federal government would have potentially wide-ranging interest in information being generated in localities. Doctors, hospitals, and private surveillance cameras could become the new collectors in a nationwide intelligence effort to learn what the terrorists have done, where they have gone, and where they might attack next.

If such a system were developed and automated, the advantages would flow to both local crisis managers and the federal government. Doctors and hospitals could concentrate on care of the victims while an impersonal data hand-off of symptoms and geographic distribution could be provided to authorities responsible for determining if terrorists and biological weapons were involved. This would enable a quick, nationwide response. For example, if San Francisco, Houston, and Seattle were also equipped, the federal government would have instantaneous information from across the country should simultaneous attacks—the hallmark of terrorist groups such as Al Qaeda—occur. The capacity to learn about attacks and their nature early on would make the difference in the federal government's capacity to respond to such events.

Hospitals are not the only wired domains that might be lashed to such a nationwide 911 system. Indeed, technological innovations are moving swiftly toward a city landscape likely to differ greatly from the cities of today. Nanotechnology promises to offer micro-energy systems embedded in the skins of buildings that use solar power as energy for wireless sensing, lighting, and maintenance devices. Buildings already equipped with fiber optic cables of the kind laced through Chicago may soon have the ability to sense and control not only environmental conditions within them but the air quality and environmental conditions outside. In the event of disasters, these buildings may someday have the "sense" to seal themselves, control and clean air flows, and monitor the health, location, and well-being of their residents while sending this information to first responders and, if necessary, the federal government.

At the point where technology turns buildings into allies, the need to evacuate cities in the face of many kinds of disasters may pass. The trick, of course, would be to ensure that technology stays friendly and in the right hands. If technology is moving in this direction, and indications are that it is, the local governments, not just the federal one, need to anticipate the wired society that is emerging and work to ensure that the protocols, access, and management of this information stays within the scope of tolerance for Americans not only protective of their families and well-being but also of their freedoms and privacy as well. The Federal government might then, and only then, collaborate to ensure that attacks happening simultaneously in several cities are countered nationally with the least amount of duplication and confusion. Such a legislative package would set the bounds for federal surveillance of domestic threats and the proper procedures for handing off information collected at local levels for civilian purposes to the federal level in times of crisis or elevated threat.

Conclusion

In recognition of the rapid tempo of decision making so necessary for interdiction of terrorists—especially those possibly equipped with weapons of mass destruction—the intelligence community has organized centers for counterterrorism and nonproliferation that marry analysts with operators and technology specialists so that they can more rapidly fuse intelligence data, analyze it, and act. The military has employed a form of this approach since the first Persian Gulf War with its creation of National Intelligence Support Teams and now Joint Intelligence Operations Centers that fuse all collected data from tactical- and national-level sensors to support commanders' operations in the field. It was in the same spirit that the U.S. government developed lawful partnerships with the private sector for collection of bulk data on telephone traffic and Internet communications to identify unknown terrorists and track known ones. Although the Snowden affair has snapped the government back from its more ambitious efforts, the public deserves the continued pursuit of methods that can keep them safe without risking liberties or threatening their rights.

The federal government should encourage additional research into the problem of bulk data and the keys or protocols for its use in the counterterrorism context. It should also attend to the initiatives taken in Chicago, New York, and other cities so that information can be handed off to the federal government under certain specified conditions, such as suspected biological, chemical, or nuclear attack.[32] Arguably, the best time to negotiate these solutions is now, before the next terrorist attack takes place and a spasm of reaction leads to measures not nearly as well considered as the American polity deserves.

To take these necessary steps, the United States needs to muster the will for a public debate on privacy—not seek to avoid it as a bothersome drag on the mission of law enforcement and counterterrorism experts. The need is now urgent. Between the great world wars of the last century, Britain succeeded in protecting its polity from the threats posed by an international network intent on penetrating and corrupting it. It did so by employing all-source data fusion—to include data from domestic sources still beyond the scope of what federal intelligence authorities are permitted under U.S. law. A great American debate awaits over the extent to which the federal government can ally with state and local governments and private industry to manage the new, secure information infrastructure that is already emerging. Burned as they may be in the post-Snowden political environment, domestic intelligence and counterterrorism authorities need to do their job, within the law, as Americans expect them to do.

Notes

1. Nigel West, *MASK: MI-5's Penetration of the Communist Party of Great Britain* (London: Routledge, Taylor and Francis, 2005). This description of MASK and its accomplishments are derived from West's excellent work on the subject.

2. Ibid.

3. This argument on the nature of intelligence is expanded in my draft article, "Smart Realism: A Theory of Intelligence in International Politics" (April 2006).

4. Surprise is properly understood as the extension of a counterintelligence effort because it involves learning how the opponent thinks and acts and then making a strategic or tactical move designed to exploit weaknesses in that decision-making process. Surprise can be achieved by simply getting inside the decision loop of the adversary: Even if intelligence provides warning, the victim cannot turn warning into effective action in time to stop his losses.

5. For more on the similarities of strategic decision making among gangs, mobs, and nation-states, see Thomas C, Schelling, *The Strategy of Conflict* (London: Oxford University Press, 1968), especially pp. 12–13.

6. I owe the insight on the connection between intensity of competition and the need for secrecy to enlightening discussions of intelligence theory with my friend and colleague Michael Warner, a Defense Department historian, over the winter of 2005–2006. Getting any of this wrong is, of course, my responsibility, not his.

7. Most literature on open-source intelligence focuses on the role cheap, unclassified information can play in limiting the burden on precious, classified collection systems. But this leaves the comparative advantage for democracies partially unexploited and a fixation on the primacy of secrets intact. Speed may be more important than data source when stopping terrorists in our midst—and sifting huge quantities of data takes time. Intelligence managers should consider how classified information could be exploited to help target unclassified sources and databases to get the jump on an adversary. Creativity—and sloughing off old prejudices—is needed in thinking about the role of open sources in intelligence.

8. This last form of collection is known as measurement and signatures intelligence, or MASINT.

9. The importance of all-source collection for these purposes is discussed in Steve Coll, *Ghost Wars* (New York: Penguin Press, 2004), pp. 492–493.

10. The concept of boosting is discussed in greater detail in Jennifer E. Sims, "Smart Realism: A Theory of Intelligence in International Politics," paper presented to the Georgetown Intelligence Salon, April 2006. For more on this concept, see Michael Herman, *Intelligence Power in Peace and War* (London: Cambridge University Press, 1996), pp. 65–66.

11. This is a widely known technique for locating radio signals. In fact, amateurs engage in DF competitions under the sponsorship of the International Amateur Radio Union. For more on the term *DF*, see http://en.wikipedia.org/wiki /direction_finding.

12. For more on the Gestapo's efforts against Stalin's spies in Europe, including the use of DF against HUMINT cells, see V. E. Tarrant, *The Red Orchestra* (London: Wiley, 1996).

13. Michael Herman writes: "Espionage can also help other collection activities. Human sources are sometimes needed to plant bugging devices. Cipherbreaking has often been assisted by obtaining copies of codes and cipher material through human sources. Acquiring agents with this kind of cryptographic access was always one of the KGB's highest priorities." Herman, *Intelligence Power*, pp. 65–66.

14. See J. C. Masterman, *The Double-Cross System: The Incredible True Story of How Nazi Spies Were Turned into Double Agents* (Guilford, CT: Lyons Press, 2000). Also see Anthony Cave Brown, *Bodyguard of Lies* (New York: Harper & Row, 1975).

15. For an excellent history of the dangers of weak counterintelligence in an interlaced collection system, see Leo Marks, *Between Silk and Cyanide: A Codemaker's War* (New York: Touchstone, 1998).

16. John Arquilla and David Ronfeldt (eds.), *Networks and Netwars: The Future of Terror, Crime, and Militancy* (Santa Monica, CA: RAND, 2001).

17. See Stephen Budiansky, *Queen Elizabeth I, Sir Francis Walsingham, and the Birth of Modern Espionage* (New York: Penguin, 2005).

18. Jeffrey T. Richelson, *A Century of Spies: Intelligence in the Twentieth Century* (New York: Oxford University Press, 1995), pp. 27–30.

19. Unfortunately, law-abiding citizens sometimes suffered discrimination, undeserved punishment, and retribution in the process.

20. The point about local empowerment may have been dramatically illustrated by the decisions of individual Finns to use their Nokia cell phones during the immediate aftermath of the 2004 tsunami in the Indian Ocean. Empowered by their individual communications devices, which offered a direct link back to Helsinki, Finnish citizens were able to provide critical information for their government's decision-making process. (Based on author's informal interviews with officials and Nokia personnel in Finland during June 2005.) The notion that U.S. intelligence has poor appreciation of domestic cultural issues related to its profession should not be controversial. After all, intelligence systems have long been suspect elements of democracies and, in any case, have focused their attentions against adversaries, not on deepening knowledge of the societies in which they operate. This may be changing now. For lengthier discussion of the American cultural context for intelligence, see Jennifer E. Sims, "Understanding Ourselves," in Jennifer E. Sims and Burton Gerber (eds.), *Transforming U.S. Intelligence* (Washington DC: Georgetown University Press, 2005).

21. James Gosler, "The Digital Dimension," in Jennifer E. Sims and Burton Gerber (eds.), *Transforming U.S. Intelligence* (Washington DC: Georgetown University Press, 2005), pp. 96–114.

22. Domestic procedures for lawful surveillance were established in 1978 when Congress passed the Foreign Intelligence Surveillance Act (FISA). This act limits the president's authority to conduct domestic wiretapping for national security purposes by requiring federal intelligence and law enforcement authorities to get warrants for such surveillance from a secret court. Some legal experts argue that the act is unconstitutional because it involved one branch of government (Congress) circumscribing the constitutional authorities of another branch (the president). In any case, many observers have noted that FISA had been widely regarded as settled law. After the initial disclosures of the Bush Administration's expansion of NSA authorities immediately after 9-11, oversight mechanisms for NSA domestic surveillance were subsequently debated in the context of Congressional passage of the USA-PATRIOT Act. This act amended previous domestic surveillance laws to post-9/11 circumstances. Although critics at the time argued that such open debate revealed too much of our counterintelligence concerns and capabilities to the adversary, the massive leak of documents

by Edward Snowden since 2012 had exposed these programs in detail to the world.

23. For more on the idea of domestic alliances for intelligence purposes, see Henry C. Crumpton, "Intelligence and Homeland Defense," in Jennifer E. Sims and Burton Gerber (eds.), *Transforming U.S. Intelligence* (Washington DC: Georgetown University Press, 2005).

24. Ibid.

25. John P. Sullivan, "Terrorism Early Warning Group and Co-Production of Counterterrorism Intelligence," paper presented to the International Studies Association conference in San Diego, March 21–25, 2006. Also presented to the Canadian Association for Security and Intelligence Studies, 20th Anniversary International Conference, Montreal, Quebec, Canada, Panel 5, October 21, 2005.

26. Constituent Works, "Court Hears NYPD Surveillance Camera Case," (March 27, 2006), available at http://www.officeoutlook.com/news/security/1147 .htm (accessed April 7, 2006).

27. Associated Press, "Baltimore's Latest Crime Tool Is the Talking Camera," available at http://www.policeone.com/police-products/investigation/video -surveillance/articles/121178 (accessed April 7, 2006).

28. Walter Pincus, "Pentagon Will Review Database on U.S. Citizens: Protests among Acts Labeled 'Suspicious,'" Washingtonpost.com (December 15, 2005), p. A01. Indeed, Senator Feinstein wrote a letter on January 10, 2006, to Secretary of Defense Rumsfeld requesting additional information on CIFA practices, including the retention of TALON reports on the activities of private citizens engaged in activities protected under the First Amendment.

29. The history of American skepticism of domestic surveillance is admirably covered by Christopher Andrew in his excellent history, *For the President's Eyes Only: Secret Intelligence and the American Presidency from Washington to Bush* (New York: HarperCollins, 1996).

30. Mary De Rosa, *Data Mining and Data Analysis for Counterterrorism* (Washington DC: Center for Peace and Security Studies, March 2004).

31. Ibid. The former is a process that "uses algorithms to discover predictive patterns in data sets"; the latter "applies models to data to predict behavior, assess risk, determine associations or do other types of analysis."

32. The Department of Homeland Security has provided some funding for these initiatives. However, the development of privacy protocols, called "appliances" under the now-defunct TIA initiative, has languished. For more information, see "Chicago Moving to 'Smart' Surveillance Cameras," available at http:// www.policeone.com/products.

Part V: Intelligence and Accountability

CHAPTER EIGHTEEN

Congressional Oversight of the CIA in the Early Cold War, 1947–1963

David M. Barrett

A DEMOCRATIC NATION-STATE IN A DANGEROUS WORLD faces two obvious dilemmas that might be labeled "openness versus secrecy" and "fair play versus dirty tricks." *Openness* is at the heart of democratic theory and practice. If a nation's government is not substantially open about what it is doing and how it is doing it, then that nation's citizens can hardly pass effective judgment about the government in periodic elections. However, in a world full of perils, any government must employ much secrecy about its military and intelligence capabilities and plans.

Meanwhile, many citizens and leaders of democratic nation-states—certainly the United States—consider themselves to believe in fair play. President George Washington's famous farewell address set a standard along these lines by calling for the U.S. government to follow "exalted virtue" in its dealings with other nations. This, he predicted, would ultimately lead other nations to become habituated toward doing the right thing in their foreign affairs.

This is not to say that U.S. foreign policy was consistently virtuous across the ensuing decades. A century and a half later, a secretive commission advising President Dwight Eisenhower explicitly parted company with Washington. The world had become uniquely dangerous, due to the expansionist, communist, and nuclear-armed Soviet Union, "an implacable enemy whose avowed objective is world domination by whatever means and whatever cost. . . . If the United States is to survive, longstanding concepts of 'fair play' must be reconsidered." The United States would have "to learn to subvert, sabotage, and destroy our enemies by more clever, more sophisticated, and more effective methods than those used against us." Dirty tricks were necessary.[1]

Solutions to these two dilemmas were and are imperfect, to say the least. Still, they are at least mitigated for the United States by having some constitutionally elected leaders know of and give direction to covert action, espionage, and other morally unsavory policies. Most obviously, the president—having the executive power and commander-in-chief roles—should carry out such duties. The U.S. Constitution, though, gives the Congress the law-making power (shared with a veto-endowed president), which includes the right to pass spending laws. In light of this, during Washington's presidency, Congress first asserted a constitutionally implied right to monitor and investigate executive branch agencies.

The Literature on Congress and the CIA in the Early Cold War Years

Writings on Congress and the Central Intelligence Agency (CIA) in the Truman-Eisenhower-Kennedy era have been very few in number. Harry Howe Ransom provided rare, early, and thoughtful scholarly treatments of legislative oversight in books and articles on the CIA, finding in 1958 that the agency operated "with only nominal legislative surveillance."[2] Despite his best efforts to learn details of CIA–Congress relations, Ransom was handicapped by the secrecy surrounding the agency. A later and more extensive (retrospective) treatment of the topic came from the Church Committee of the mid-1970s, named for its chairman, Senator Frank Church (D-ID). That committee came into being as a result of various published allegations in the *New York Times* and certain books concerning certain questionable actions of the CIA in previous decades. Though the committee's main focus was not on legislative oversight of the CIA, it did give substantially more attention to the topic than had occurred before. It found that "from the beginning," the House and Senate subcommittees charged with monitoring the CIA "were relatively inactive."[3] Newspapers and magazines in the United States sporadically paid attention to congressional oversight of the CIA in the early Cold War years. An early example was the Richmond *News-Leader*, which charged Congress in the early 1950s with ignoring the CIA's "free-wheeling" status.

In the 21st century, two books emerged which gave fairly detailed treatment to congressional oversight of the CIA in the early Cold War era: David M. Barrett's *The CIA and Congress: The Untold Story from Truman to Kennedy* (2005) and L. Britt Snider's *The Agency and the Hill: the CIA's*

Relationship with Congress, 1946-2004 (2008). Perhaps the most surprising things about those two published works were their evidence that there had been any such oversight at all.[4]

Working from the much fuller evidence that has become available in archives in the past decade or so, it is fair to say that the two adjectives that best describe congressional oversight of the CIA during the Truman, Eisenhower, and Kennedy eras are "limited" and "informal." This is especially so when that oversight is compared to the oversight that Congress instituted and has carried out from the mid-1970s through the early 21st century. In the modern era, there are many hundreds of interactions between Capitol Hill and the CIA per year; the House and Senate Intelligence Committees are large and have substantial staffs. By contrast, from 1947—when the CIA was created by President Truman and Congress—through the early 1960s, there were anywhere from eight to 30 hearings held each year.

There were scores of other interactions between individual legislators and CIA personnel annually. But the hearings and the smaller, more informal sessions were almost all carried out under conditions of extreme secrecy. The legislators who conducted them were mostly on four tiny House and Senate Appropriations and Armed Services subcommittees that were mandated to monitor the CIA. Those legislators were assisted in these tasks by a small number of staff assistants, none of whose jobs were exclusively devoted to intelligence affairs.

Still, most of the older literature on Congress and the CIA has been erroneous in asserting that there was virtually no intelligence oversight in the early Cold War era, especially by the late Eisenhower era. Claims are common that Director of Central Intelligence (DCI) Allen Dulles (1953–1961) only had jocular but shallow meetings with legislators. Dulles's own experience of legislative oversight is instructive: In 1958, he spent parts of at least 25 days on Capitol Hill. There, he met with 10 or more different committees or subcommittees. During his long tenure and afterward, he periodically claimed that legislative oversight of the CIA had been reasonably substantive, though few have taken his claim seriously.[5]

The political atmosphere was challenging for Dulles in a year like 1958. For example, many Congress members had publicly expressed doubts that the CIA had alerted President Eisenhower and others that (1) the Soviet Union was likely to launch an earth satellite in the autumn of 1957, (2) Venezuelans were likely to riot and almost kill Vice President Richard Nixon on a "good will" visit to that country, or (3) the pro-American government of Iraq would be overthrown by a coup, thus provoking American intervention in nearby Lebanon. Dulles was relatively honest with legislators in that year's secret hearings, responding that the CIA had alerted President Eisenhower and at least one congressional subcommittee that the USSR might launch an earth satellite in 1957, that the CIA had relied too much on Venezuelan security services for its intelligence on the dangers Nixon might face, and that the Agency had simply failed to anticipate the Iraqi coup. In the next few years, following the U-2 and Bay of Pigs incidents, the CIA's challenges on Capitol Hill would be greater.[6]

One element missing from most of the older literature on Congress and the CIA is treatment of a particular kind of accountability that existed: DCIs Roscoe Hillenkoetter (1947–1950), Walter B. Smith (1950–1953), Dulles, and John McCone (1962–1965) literally feared what congressional barons heading the CIA subcommittees might do to the Agency if its leader were discovered to have lied or refused directives received on Capitol Hill. (The intelligence directors met those powerful legislators privately more often than they did in subcommittee sessions. Such meetings were poorly documented, unfortunately.) When Vice President Lyndon Johnson warned McCone in 1962 that Armed Services Committee chair Richard Russell (D-GA)—who was the most knowledgeable senator about CIA affairs—could "destroy" the Agency and McCone if he were not responsive on a current controversy, the DCI was being told something that he already knew. By virtually all accounts of those who worked for the four directors, keeping the members (especially chairs and ranking minority members) of the CIA subcommittees satisfied was of prime importance.[7]

This is not to say that the Agency faced anything like systematic scrutiny by Congress over its first decade and a half. As CIA legislative liaison John Warner occasionally pointed out to colleagues, the leaders of the CIA subcommittee were often too busy to pay as much attention to the Agency as they should have.

Essential Features of CIA Oversight by Congress, 1947–1963

Within a year of the CIA's creation in 1947, the House and Senate Armed Services and Appropriations Subcommittees began emerging and holding informal hearings with Agency leaders present. The frequency of those sessions in the late 1940s was low, and they have never been well documented. It was inevitable that the Appropriations Subcommittees (not formally named, but occasionally referred to by members simply as the "CIA Subcommittees") would come into being, because the CIA needed funds, but no one at the Agency, on Capitol Hill, or at the White House wanted the full Appropriations Committees to have access to information on the new Agency. The CIA was already doing analysis and coordination of the writing of estimates; also, some of its personnel were doing espionage and covert action. Thus, during the Agency's first few years, no more than five Appropriations members at the House and fewer than three at the Senate knew any details about the CIA's budgets, which were moving upward toward the $100 million mark.[8]

The Armed Services Committees successfully asserted their claims as the relevant law-making bodies to deal with CIA-related issues. But their chairs had no more interest than the Appropriations leaders in having all Committee members interact with the CIA. The commonly expressed view—both in public and in private—was that the CIA's work was too important for it to be endangered by leaks to the press, which would, in turn, inform the Soviet Union of such information. The resulting subcommittees were also small and met as infrequently as one to four times per year in the late 1940s.

Though the frequency of hearings and other meetings of the CIA subcommittees grew substantially in the 1950s and 1960s, certain features remained constant across the Truman, Eisenhower, and Kennedy eras. One was the dominance of their chairmen and ranking minority members. In the Senate, the chairs of the committees also headed the CIA subcommittees. In the House, this was also the case until the late 1950s, when the Armed Services and Appropriations Committee chairs—Democrats Carl Vinson (GA) and Clarence Cannon (MO)—turned over their CIA subcommittee chairmanships to Paul Kilday and George Mahon, both Texas Democrats. Nonetheless, Vinson and Cannon usually attended subcommittee meetings.

There seems to have been greater knowledge on the part of chairs and ranking minority members than there was among the other subcommittee members. In the Appropriations Subcommittees, for example, a few years passed before leaders informed other members of the existence of the U-2 program, which sent spy flights across the Soviet Union. This conforms to what Stephen Horn later wrote: the chairs and ranking minority members of Senate Appropriations were "lord and masters" of the Committee.[9]

Another feature of the subcommittees' dynamics was the lack of partisanship. Relations between the majority and minority party leaders and members were trusting and respectful most of the time. This made it "a joy to work there," said Bill Darden, a leading staffer at the Senate Armed Services Committee. Also, on those occasions in the 1940s and 1950s when party control of Congress changed, most staffers who interacted with the CIA frequently (like Darden) stayed on in their jobs. There were not many such staff members, though. In any given year, fewer than 10 of them—from the four subcommittees and the occasional other committee that looked into CIA matters—were designated by their bosses to do such work. With few exceptions (especially Senator Styles Bridges [R-NH], who was an ally of powerful columnist Drew Pearson), neither staffers nor members of the CIA subcommittees leaked to the press.

Did Subcommittee Members Know the CIA's Intimate Secrets?

Covert Action

Contrary to what is commonly found in the literature, it is clear that subcommittee leaders and/or members knew a fair amount about covert action. This should not be surprising: Congress members, whether they were on CIA subcommittees or not, mostly favored aggressive action. Records that have been uncovered in recent years show that many legislators went to executive branch leaders and suggested covert action in various parts of the world. "Why don't we instigate a large program of stirring up guerrilla activity on the Chinese mainland?" asked one out-of-the-loop legislator in 1950. Indeed, such Congress members who were not knowledgeable about the CIA managed to pass an amendment in 1951 that handed $100 million to the Truman administration to try to "roll back" Soviet influence in Eastern Europe. The money was not used because it was not needed by the CIA, which was then funded by the House and Senate Appropriations CIA subcommittees at a level of almost half a billion dollars, much of it for covert action.[10]

Two of the best remembered covert actions of the early Cold War era were the removal of the left-leaning government of Guatemala in 1954 (during the Eisenhower presidency) and the wildly unsuccessful attempt to overturn Fidel Castro's government of Cuba in 1961's Bay of Pigs incident (during the Kennedy presidency). Did the CIA subcommittee members and/or other legislators have advance knowledge of those planned covert actions? The evidence regarding Guatemala is extremely fragmentary, but it is likely that at least the heads of the subcommittees and some other legislators knew of those plans in advance. Furthermore, leaders at the CIA and elsewhere in the executive branch felt heat from Congress, who feared a Latin American outpost of the Soviet Union enough to insist that the executive branch "do something" about Guatemala.

As for the Bay of Pigs invasion, two different documents made available at the end of the 20th century show that DCI Dulles and associates went before the full CIA Subcommittees of the House Armed Services and Appropriations Committees to tell them what the Agency was prepared to do in the coming weeks. Although the documents show only a little of what transpired in the secret hearings, it is clear that some questions of the feasibility of the planned operation were raised; but there is no evidence that any legislator advised the Agency's leaders not to intervene in Cuba. The more significant point, however, is that the Subcommittees' members were told in advance of the Cuba plans. Russell and some other members on the Senate side were almost certainly told in advance, but no documentation seems to have been declassified regarding this.[11]

It is also clear that the practice of giving details about past and future covert actions did not begin in the Eisenhower or Kennedy era. Documents from the Truman era are less plentiful, but some of them support memories of former Agency personnel that, for example, DCI Walter "Beetle" Smith occasionally gave detailed operational briefings to members of CIA subcommittees. On one occasion, when a legislator asked a vague question about operations around the world, Smith pulled out a list of all ongoing covert action programs and reviewed them with subcommittee members.[12]

In summary, in the sensitive area of covert action, CIA subcommittees had a fair amount of knowledge, resulting from some of the few hearings each subcommittee held each year. It is likely, however, that many (especially smaller) operations occurred without being highlighted to legislators.

Intelligence Estimates

The sharing of information with the subcommittees (and occasionally other congressional bodies) was considerable. More than anything else, what legislators of the early Cold War era wanted from CIA leaders were their estimates of political and other conditions in nations around the world, especially the Soviet Union. DCIs Hillenkoetter, Smith, Dulles, and McCone routinely gave spoken summaries of analyses that the CIA and other agencies had created. On the one hand, with the exception of the Joint Committee on Atomic Energy (JCAE)—which had a legal right to intelligence estimates on nuclear topics—the CIA rarely, if ever, gave copies of National Intelligence Estimates to committees, subcommittees, or their members to keep beyond the time of hearings. On the other hand, the CIA routinely prepared special estimates for legislators to keep.

One of the most sensitive topics treated by intelligence estimates came in the late summer and early autumn of 1962, when news media outlets and certain legislators (especially Senator Kenneth Keating [R-NY]) claimed that the Soviet Union was placing medium- or intermediate-range nuclear-armed missiles in Cuba. These claims contradicted U.S. intelligence estimates that called such a Soviet move unlikely. On such a topic, CIA subcommittee heads—who could be quite trusting and deferential toward the Agency during quiet times—became all business. As Deputy Director of Central Intelligence (DDCI) Marshall Carter noted on September 26, 1962, he had talked to Leverett Saltonstall, the ranking Republican on the Senate Armed Services CIA subcommittee, about the growing Soviet militarization of Cuba. "He said that he and Senator Russell considered this a very important matter and would like to be kept currently advised of whatever developed in the way of hard intelligence."

Over the ensuing weeks, during what became the Cuban missile crisis, Agency heads bent over backward to keep subcommittee leaders informed about the CIA's knowledge. Indeed, within 24 hours of President Kennedy being informed that the Soviets had missiles in Cuba, Russell summoned a nervous Carter and legislative liaison John Warner to his office to hear the full story. The CIA men knew that Kennedy had directed that the intelligence on missile sites be kept absolutely secret. Just after Carter and Warner greeted the Senator, Russell was called to a telephone and informed by the president that the CIA had important news for him. The briefers' task had been made immeasurably easier by the president's phone call, which apparently resulted from an alert to the White House by McCone concerning Russell's request for the latest intelligence.[13]

Counterintelligence

At certain points in the early Cold War, some legislative bodies pushed the CIA to share information about counterintelligence problems and controversies. Besides the CIA subcommittees, in the early 1950s, Republican Senator Joseph McCarthy's Permanent Subcommittee on Investigations harassed DCIs Hillenkoetter and Dulles about various (and sometimes nonexistent) problems. Also the House Un-American Activities Committee (HUAC) had interactions with the Agency on alleged infiltration of Soviet spies and sympathizers into the U.S. government. Few records of CIA-HUAC encounters seem to exist, though a tense encounter at a 1952 public hearing between DCI Smith and members of HUAC can be seen (in retrospect) to show the director choosing his words carefully to avoid any mention of the harm done to U.S. intelligence by British traitor Kim Philby (who in reality worked for the Soviet Union). However, Smith offered to be much more forthcoming with the Committee in a private hearing.[14]

A decade later, HUAC was more aggressive than the House Armed Services CIA Subcommittee in investigating the defection of two employees of the National Security Agency (NSA) in 1960. While the latter Subcommittee conducted a brief investigation accompanied by hearings, HUAC (under Chairman Francis Walter [D-PA]) pursued the topic for two years and forced certain reforms in personnel hiring, training, and clearance procedures at the NSA.[15]

Domestic Involvements of the CIA

The sensitive topic that the Agency may have withheld from the CIA subcommittees and other congressional bodies was that of periodic involvement in matters at home in the United States. The Church Committee and other mid-1970s investigations showed that the CIA sometimes spied on American citizens (such as peace activists), tested drugs on unwitting citizens, and illegally opened letters being handled by the U.S. Post Office. There are virtually no records even hinting that the CIA ever informed any congressional bodies or members of these activities in the 1950s or early 1960s. However, because only a handful of (usually partial) transcripts of CIA subcommittee hearings survive or have been declassified, and even detailed notes of such meetings are not plentiful, it is possible that the Agency did inform certain legislators about such legally questionable activities.

The "Other" Committees and the CIA

Nothing is clearer in the papers of President Dwight D. Eisenhower than his hostility toward congressional "meddling" in the affairs of the CIA. Eisenhower directed his anger not toward the little subcommittees on the CIA, though; despite occasional differences with them, he trusted men like Russell, Saltonstall, and Vinson to be discreet and responsible in their interactions with the Agency. Eisenhower's fury—there is no better word to describe it—was over the actions of other legislative bodies, whose leaders sometimes successfully insisted on having CIA leaders testify at hearings. Besides the Permanent Investigations Subcommittee and the HUAC, those bodies included the following.

The Senate Foreign Relations Committee

A few years before J. William Fulbright (D-AR) famously assumed the chairmanship of the committee in 1959, Foreign Relations had begun requesting testimony by Dulles on the CIA's analyses of worldwide political conditions and on its occasional intelligence failures. The frequency of such events is not well documented for all years, but—despite the unhappiness of Eisenhower over such Agency appearances on Capitol Hill—Dulles testified four or five times before the Committee or one of its subcommittees in 1958 and three times in 1959. Among the topics that the committee had Dulles analyze in their presence were Soviet military capabilities, the chances for Tibet to resist occupation by China, and the odds that Cuban leader Fidel Castro would turn out to be a communist.

Among the real or alleged intelligence failures committed by the CIA that DCI Dulles had to discuss with the Foreign Relations Committee in 1956–1960 were the Hungarian and Suez crises in 1956, the launch of *Sputnik* in 1957, the 1958 attacks on Vice President Nixon in Venezuela, the Iraqi coup that same year, and the U-2 incident in 1960. Although Dulles generally received high marks from Committee members, the Agency received many criticisms and warnings in those sessions.[16]

The Air Force and Preparedness Subcommittees of the Senate Armed Services Committee

In 1956–1957 hearings, the Air Force Subcommittee, headed by Stuart Symington (D-MO), was permitted by Committee Chair Richard Russell to examine charges and supposed "intelligence" showing that the Soviet Union was far ahead of the United States in bomber aircraft capabilities. Later, Russell designated the Preparedness Subcommittee, headed by Senator Lyndon Johnson (D-TX), to examine charges that the Soviets excelled in long-range missile capabilities in 1958–1960. But Symington, a member of Johnson's Subcommittee, often outdid the Texan in publicizing and identifying himself with the missile "gap."

The discreet Russell had mixed feelings about Symington, but the gap controversies were too fierce to be ignored. While Russell's own CIA Subcommittee could and did discuss the issues with Dulles and other Agency leaders, the Georgia Senator insisted that such hearings be kept secret. Thus, Symington's and Johnson's hearings, though held in "executive" (that is, secret) sessions, were much discussed in the press. Both senators readily discussed the hearings with journalists.

In testimony before the Air Force and Preparedness Subcommittees, Dulles denied Symington's charges that the Eisenhower administration had somehow misused intelligence or that the CIA itself had seriously underestimated Soviet military capabilities. The president himself responded in a 1960 press conference to Symington's charges that the administration had distorted intelligence as a means to reduce the size of the U.S. defense budget. In the words of a *New York Times* reporter, Eisenhower "appeared to control himself with effort." Such charges were "despicable," said the president, who added, "If anybody—anybody!— believes that I have deliberately misled the American people, I'd like to tell him to his face what I think about him." There was little doubt in anyone's mind about the identity of "him." Eisenhower was almost as angry, in private, against Dulles for "giving such detailed figures to the Congress."[17]

The Joint Committee on Atomic Energy

No committee of Congress angered Eisenhower more for its insistence on obtaining CIA estimates and testimony (on nuclear weapons topics) than the JCAE. President Harry S. Truman had been no fan of the Joint Committee either. On a good day, Truman might merely complain that "those fellows . . . think they are the board of directors" on atomic energy matters. When really angry (according to Atomic Energy Commission Chair David Lilienthal's diary), Truman "glared through his thickish glasses" and erupted over "those bastards on the Hill." Indeed, the JCAE was mandated by law to have full knowledge and substantial control over nuclear policies. In 1949, after the CIA failed to predict that the Soviet Union would conduct a successful test explosion of its first atomic bomb, the Joint Committee virtually skinned alive DCI Hillenkoetter in a secret hearing. In the 1950s, Dulles's usual responsiveness to JCAE requests for information and testimony was a chronic irritant in the DCI's relationship with the White House.[18]

The Waxing and Waning of Oversight

Records that have been declassified or otherwise made available in recent years show clearly that congressional oversight of the CIA varied from one year to the next. Why did the Agency appear before no more than a dozen hearings in 1955, but testify twice as often in 1958? There are two fairly obvious answers.

The Political Environment

In an influential 1984 article, political scientists Matthew McCubbins and Thomas Schwartz suggested that conditions in the American political environment largely determined whether Congress would aggressively investigate failures and wrongdoing by executive branch agencies or remain relatively passive and deferential toward them. As they point out, with the Legislative Reorganization Act of 1946, Congress mandated itself to engage in continuous, assertive oversight (what McCubbins and Schwartz called "police patrol" oversight). But the reality of the ensuing decades was that Capitol Hill became assertive only when "fire alarms" were set off by interest groups, the news media, the public, or others complaining that one or more agencies had somehow failed.[19]

On the whole, the fire alarms analysis fits well with the surviving evidence about Congress and the CIA in the early Cold War decades. An examination of the news in 1955 and 1958, for example, shows that there were many more alarms ringing in the latter year: a firestorm over *Sputnik's* launch late in the previous year, Nixon's encounter with South American rioters, and the coup in Iraq. There was enormous critical news coverage of the CIA that year—more than in any previous year—as well as letters from citizens to newspapers, Congress, and the White House. After the year ended, an aide to Dulles reflected in a work diary on the "ground swell developing for more frequent briefings of these committees on some systematic basis."[20]

Attributes of Legislators

Much as the level of controversy in the American political environment affected the amount of congressional oversight of the CIA, there can be no doubt that attributes of the legislators charged with carrying out such duties mattered, too. Consider the different approaches to CIA used by Representative John Taber (R-NY) and Senator Carl Hayden (D-AZ).

Taber chaired the House Appropriations Committee and its CIA Subcommittee during the two first years of the Eisenhower presidency, when the Republican Party held a majority of seats in Congress. By all accounts, he was not a likable man and had no real friends in the House, but he was tough and capable. As chair, Taber hired new staff to examine the budgets of the CIA and many other bureaucracies. The Subcommittee held more hearings annually with the CIA than had ever been the case. He obtained more detailed descriptions of CIA successes and failures in covert action than apparently had been given by Agency heads before. He placed limitations on both spending and new hires at the Agency, provoking widespread complaints there. A new verb joined the Washington lexicon—to "taberize" was to cut budgets. After Democrats regained control of Congress, Taber continued to show an active interest in CIA affairs.[21]

Hayden was genuinely popular and respected in the Senate, but by the time he assumed the chair of its Appropriations Committee in 1955, he was 77 years old. Though bright and hard-working, Hayden was overly busy. He had high regard for Richard Russell, the most senior of his colleagues on Appropriations. Since Russell chaired Armed Services and its CIA Subcommittee, Hayden and he agreed sometime around 1956 that they would combine their subcommittees' oversight of the CIA, under

Russell's leadership. Although this could have led to reasonably effective monitoring of the Agency, it did not, at least concerning budgetary matters. Hayden was the least effective of any heads of CIA subcommittees in the 1950s.

Scrutiny of proposed CIA budgets was far greater in the House, where Clarence Cannon (D-MO) chaired Appropriations from 1955 through his death in 1964. Cannon has been criticized in histories of the CIA as essentially an old fool who did no more oversight than to trade stories with Dulles and McCone and ask them if the CIA had "enough" money. The reality was different. For example, before anyone else in Washington, Cannon insisted in 1958 that Dulles answer a simple question: "How much does the United States government spend annually on intelligence activities?" Theoretically, a director of Central Intelligence managed the entire American intelligence establishment, but the reality was that agencies other than the CIA received almost no direction from Dulles or other early DCIs. It took months of work by the CIA and other agencies before Dulles could give Cannon a reasonably accurate response in 1958. They would have to give a fuller report the following year.[22]

Among the other legislators who interacted with the Agency, there were many who—even if respectful toward the CIA—were reasonably assertive, especially when alarms were going off. These included in the Senate: Symington, Bridges, John Stennis (D-MS), and Kenneth McKellar (D-TN). In the House, Francis Walter, chair of HUAC, was a periodic thorn in the side of Dulles. The two men actually argued in one telephone conversation, with the chairman hanging up on the DCI.[23] Also in the House, starting around 1957, Clarence Cannon appointed the widely respected George Mahon (D-TX) to head the Appropriations CIA Subcommittee. Cannon remained periodically active in relation to the CIA, but Mahon took more of the burden and stepped up the frequency and substance of hearings.

Similarly, Carl Vinson appointed the well-regarded Paul Kilday (D-TX) to head the Armed Services CIA Subcommittee and improve its work. Among other things, Kilday oversaw very secretive investigations of the CIA in 1959 and the NSA in 1960. Kilday attempted to increase examinations of the CIA's budget by the General Accounting Office (GAO), an arm of Congress. Vinson had long relied on Kilday for assistance on crucial work, but on the GAO issue, Vinson withdrew his support of Kilday, and the idea died.

Kilday believed that the appropriate subcommittees of Congress should monitor intelligence agencies, but Vinson wavered on this point. After Kilday retired in 1961, Vinson resumed chairing the Armed Services Subcommittee and actually told DCI McCone at the beginning of 1962 that "it was not necessary that the Subcommittee know everything concerning Agency affairs." (In fairness to Vinson, records show that when Congress was in session, his Subcommittee held hearings with CIA witnesses almost monthly in 1962 and 1963 and discussed topics that Agency censors were still "sanitizing" from documents released early in the 21st century.)[24]

Others in the House and Senate displayed the sort of deference that Vinson voiced. Saltonstall, the ranking Republican on Senate Armed Services, had such faith in Dulles and McCone—both actual friends of the Senator—that he seems to have only rarely pushed hard for information about the CIA.

In summary, although it is fair to say that congressional oversight of the CIA generally increased across the years from 1947 through 1963, the trend was not steady. In years when events seemed less threatening to U.S. national security, oversight was likely to decrease. Still, the rise and fall of oversight depended, too, on the attributes of those legislators on the CIA subcommittees or elsewhere in Congress.

Two Debates about the CIA's Accountability

On the floors of the House and Senate, members only occasionally discussed the CIA. When they did, it was usually because of some surprise in world politics. Occasionally, though, the Agency's place in the U.S. political system was the topic. Two of the most substantive debates about whether or not it was subject to direction from constitutionally elected leaders occurred in 1956, when Senator Mike Mansfield (D-MT) offered a resolution to create a joint congressional committee on intelligence, and in 1962, when the Senate debated President Kennedy's nomination of John McCone to become DCI.

The Mansfield Resolution

Mike Mansfield was an atypical politician—not a back-slapper, not long-winded, and not especially egotistical. He cared and thought about democratic governance. Though an early supporter in the House of the CIA, after entering the Senate in 1953, Mansfield came to believe that the Agency was free from reasonable controls by the White House and Congress. He could do little to make presidents give more attention to the Agency, but Congress (he thought) should become far more active in monitoring the CIA and other intelligence agencies.

The Montanan had been promoting his resolution since 1953. By early 1956, he had won many supporters, including a bipartisan majority of the members on the Armed Services Committee. In April debates, Mansfield said that everything about the Agency was "clothed in secrecy" and that this invited "abuse." Furthermore, it seemed likely that "all is not well with the CIA," in light of reports that Congress suffered from "a woeful shortage of information about the CIA."

On the first day of debate, the main defender of the existing oversight system was Leverett Saltonstall. The Massachusetts Senator stumbled badly in that role, though, speaking of the "difficulty in connection with asking questions and obtaining information . . . which I personally would rather not have, unless it was essential for me, as a Member of Congress, to have it." He had not said that he did not obtain sensitive information, but that was the impression he left.

Two days later, Richard Russell tried to make up for Saltonstall's weak defense. His CIA Subcommittee had asked Dulles "very searching questions about some activities which it almost chills the marrow of a man to hear about." Russell even claimed that the CIA faced more congressional oversight than most other government agencies. In light of that assertion, his pledge about the future may not have signified much: "I shall undertake to exercise as close supervision over this Agency as is ordinarily exercised by parent committees of the Congress in dealing with agencies which are responsible to them."

Mansfield was not helped by allies. Wayne Morse (D-OR) charged Saltonstall with supporting an "American police statesystem." Joseph McCarthy spoke of incompetence and communist infiltration at the CIA and complimented "the able senator from Montana," but the once fearsome McCarthy was in the late stages of alcoholism—"a piteous specter with a bloated face" that day, noted a Senate observer.[25]

Some senators who implied that the CIA needed more oversight were not willing to vote for it. One defended his surprising vote with the claim that to establish an intelligence committee with a significant staff would "dry up sources of information."

Though the debate over the CIA's functioning in a democratic system was notable, it probably had nothing to do with the outcome. Russell and his ally, Majority Leader Lyndon Johnson, marshaled votes, with an assist from the White House and Allen Dulles, and 59 senators voted "no." The CIA subcommittees, with periodic assists from other congressional bodies would—for better or worse—continue to be the system by which Congress monitored the Agency's performance.[26]

The McCone Confirmation Debate

When prior DCIs were nominated by Presidents Truman and Eisenhower, Senate debates were perfunctory and the voice votes unanimously favorable. When President Kennedy nominated Republican John McCone, a businessman who had served the two most recent presidents (among other things, heading the Atomic Energy Commission), it provoked serious debate and actual opposition. Part of this was a result of McCone's longtime substantial holdings in corporations that had major contracts with the United States or foreign governments, and part derived from his lack of direct experience in intelligence. But the nomination was also hostage to a serious conviction in the Senate that as Eugene McCarthy (D-MN) said, "There is no regular or normal procedure . . . by which committees of the Congress are consulted or informed of CIA activities." Sooner or later, the question of proper congressional oversight of the Agency and its questionable operations "will have to be the basis for a great debate. I think this is the proper time to start that debate."

Most disappointing to the Kennedy administration was the decision of Senator Fulbright to join McCarthy's fight against McCone. Fulbright said he could have voted for McCone as Secretary of State, for that position was subject to "constant review and exposure to criticism." A DCI clearly influenced policymaking, Fulbright claimed, but McCone had not been required to state his policy views when he had testified before the Armed Services Committee days before. In the face of assertions by CIA/McCone supporters that the Agency did not have a major influence over U.S. foreign policy, the Foreign Relations chair stated bluntly that this was "not in accord with the facts as I know them."

Senator Russell was horrified "that we air on the floor of the Senate all the things that the CIA is reputed to have done or not to have done in foreign countries." He avoided saying that CIA Subcommittee members often had specific knowledge of such things, but claimed, "No Director of Central Intelligence would think of undertaking any activities anywhere on the face of the earth without the approval and consent of the president." Furthermore, there had been "six or seven hearings" before the Senate Armed Services and Appropriations Subcommittees in 1961, so Fulbright's charge that the CIA was not accountable to Congress was inaccurate. Fulbright's real complaint (Russell charged) must be that "it is not all under his Committee."[27]

The fierceness of the opponents to the confirmation before and during the debates actually unnerved the usually tough McCone. While traveling abroad as director-designate, he wondered (in a wire to his associates at the CIA) if it would be best if his nomination were withdrawn. John Warner and a colleague cabled back, "The president retains fullest confidence in you. . . . We believe it unnecessary and undesirable to even consider withdrawal." An "overwhelming affirmative" vote was likely, they said, and they were correct. The vote was 71 to 12. As the *New York Times* noted, though, that numerical tally obscured the considerable "uneasiness about the agency's freedom from congressional supervision." Many of McCone's supporters were like Mike Mansfield, by then the Majority Leader in the Senate: they voted for the new DCI mostly out of loyalty to the president.[28]

CIA and Democratic Accountability, 1947–1963

Was the CIA responsive to constitutionally elected leaders in the Truman-to-Kennedy era? While CIA–White House relations are not the focus of this chapter, it is worth pointing out that the weight of scholarship in recent decades has suggested that rather than being a "rogue elephant," the CIA was substantially a tool of the White House.[29] What about Congress? Numerous documents from the CIA and Capitol Hill have only become available recently, after many decades with very little publicly available evidence to go on. In those years, there was no possibility of a large body of literature on the CIA's accountability to Congress. Even now, so much remains classified—or was destroyed or never committed to paper—that it is entirely possible we will never have a truly detailed documentary record of CIA–Congress interactions in the early Cold War decades.

Based on what has become available, however, a better debate can take place over who was right: Senators Mike Mansfield and Eugene McCarthy or Senators Richard Russell and Leverett Saltonstall? Was the CIA mostly free from accountability to anyone in Congress, as Mansfield and McCarthy charged, or did a select number of legislators usually know of bone-chilling Agency activities?

I argue that neither of those two stances was quite right. There were far more Agency appearances on Capitol Hill and many more descriptions of sensitive activities to the CIA subcommittees than Mansfield or McCarthy knew. Any future scholarly treatment of the CIA's democratic accountability in the early Cold War must take into account, especially, the documentary record of Allen Dulles's and John McCone's substantial time on Capitol Hill.

Regarding covert action, perhaps the most controversial realm in which the CIA was active, there is now substantial evidence to negate Mansfield's suggestions that such operations were done without knowledge or support on Capitol Hill.

There were even a few congressional investigations of the CIA: by Taber in 1953, Joseph McCarthy in the early 1950s, Kilday in 1959, and Stennis in 1963. There may have been others. Also, investigations headed by Johnson, Symington, and some others touched partly on the CIA.

To the extent that the subcommittees did not know of certain morally or legally questionable activities, though, it appears that the legislators were as much to blame as Agency leaders. Clearly, sometimes people like Vinson or Saltonstall did not want the subcommittees to know the CIA's darkest secrets, and they may have chosen not to hear them either in hearings or in private.

However, the available records hardly suggest support for Richard Russell's claim that the CIA was more extensively monitored than most other bureaucracies of the executive branch. In a typical year, each subcommittee on the CIA met with Agency leaders a few times. The leaders of those subcommittees were busy heading other important congressional bodies, and the staffers who assisted those subcommittee leaders always had to divide their time between work on CIA matters and that of other agencies such as the Department of Defense. It may be revisionist to suggest that oversight of some real substance occurred in the early Cold War years, but it would be bizarre to claim that such oversight was systematic or comprehensive.

Notes

1. William Leary (ed.), *The Central Intelligence Agency: History and Documents* (Tuscaloosa: University of Alabama Press, 1984), pp. 143–145.

2. Harry Howe Ransom, *Central Intelligence and National Security* (Cambridge, MA: Harvard University Press, 1958), p. 145.

3. Select Committee to Study Governmental Operations with Respect to Intelligence Activities, *Book 1: Foreign and Military Intelligence*, p. 150.

4. David M. Barrett, *The CIA and Congress: The Untold Story from Truman to Kennedy* (Lawrence: University Press of Kansas, 2005). Papers of over two dozen legislators who interacted with the CIA from 1947 to 1960—used in writing this chapter—are available in the David M. Barrett Research Files at the Richard Russell Library, University of Georgia. See also L. Britt Snider, *The Agency and the Hill: CIA's Relationship with Congress, 1946–2004* (Washington, D.C.: Center for the Study of Intelligence, 2008).

5. Barrett, *CIA and Congress*, p. 321, has brief treatment of numbers for autumn 1957 through autumn 1958. Specific documents on 1958 can be found in that year's folders of the Barrett Research Files at the Russell Library.

6. Barrett, *CIA and Congress*, chaps. 27–29.

7. McCone, "Meeting Attended by the President . . .," October 9, 1962, *Foreign Relations of the United States: Cuba, 1961–63*, vols. 10–12, microfiche. The memo closes with a description of the private LBJ-McCone meeting. A good example of a DCI's adherence to directives is in McCone, Memo for File, August 21, 1962, in Mary McAuliffe, *CIA Documents on the Cuban Missile Crisis* (Washington: CIA, 1992), p. 21. On Senator Russell, see also Snider, *The Agency and the Hill*, pp. 6, 8, 13, 14, 15, and 24.

8. Barrett, *CIA and Congress*, chap. 3. In one or two of those earliest years, it may have been only the chair of House Appropriations who knew budget details. See also Snider, *The Agency and the Hill*, pp. 161–164.

9. Stephen Horn, *Unused Power: The Work of the Senate Committee on Appropriations* (Washington, DC: Brookings, 1970). Horn's book features rare, early treatment of a CIA subcommittee; see pp. 38–40, 76, 97–100, 127, 135, 178, and 186.

10. Barrett, *CIA and Congress*, pp. 96, 103–112.

11. Barrett, *CIA and Congress*, pp. 438–446; Jack Pfeiffer, *Official History of the Bay of Pigs Operation*, vol. 3, pp. 194–195, CIA Miscellaneous Records, Box 1, JFK Assassination Records Collection, National Archives. See also Snider, *The Agency and the Hill*, pp. 259–268.

12. Interview with Walter Pforzheimer (CIA's first legislative liaison), September 30, 1994, Washington, DC. Pforzheimer receives substantial treatment in both the Barrett and Snider volumes.

13. Interview with John Warner, October 19, 1999, Washington, DC; Carter, memo for the record, September 26, 1962, CREST (CIA Records Search Tool), National Archives, College Park, MD; M. Bundy to President Kennedy (re: Russell request), October 17, 1962, document no. 654, Cuban Missile Crisis collection, National Security Archive, Washington, DC. See also Snider, *The Agency and the Hill*, pp. 193–198.

14. Barrett, *CIA and Congress*, pp. 127–134.

15. Ibid., p. 421; James Bamford, *The Puzzle Palace: A Report on America's Most Secret Agency* (Boston: Houghton Mifflin, 1982), pp. 81–85, 147–150.

16. Barrett, *CIA and Congress*, chaps. 25–29, 34, and 39.

17. Ibid., pp. 367, 369–370.

18. Ibid., pp. 51, 56–62, 142, 209, and 322.

19. Matthew McCubbins and Thomas Schwartz, "Congressional Oversight Overlooked: Police Patrols Versus Fire Alarms," *American Journal of Political Science* 28 (1984), pp. 165–179.

20. L. K. White, diary, February 4, 1959, quoted in Barrett, *CIA and Congress*, p. 322.

21. Barrett, *CIA and Congress*, chap. 15.

22. Ibid., pp. 317–318.

23. Ibid., p. 421.

24. Warner, memo for the record (Vinson), January 16, 1962, CREST. On Kilday, see Barrett, *CIA and Congress*, pp. 334–339, 391–392, 440–446;

on Mahon, Barrett, *CIA and Congress*, pp. 121–122, 296–297, 341–346, 453–455.

25. Richard Riedel, *Halls of the Mighty: My 47 Years at the Senate* (Washington: Robert B. Luce, 1969), p. 229.

26. Barrett, *CIA and Congress*, pp. 223–233; *Congressional Record*, April 9 and April 11, 1956, pp. 5891–5939, 6048–6068; Snider, *The Agency and the Hill*, pp. 11–17.

27. *Congressional Record*, January 29, January 30, and January 31, 1962. Quotations are from lengthy memoranda prepared by CIA personnel for McCone, obtained from CREST.

28. [Name censored] and Warner to McCone, undated (from late January 1962), CREST; *New York Times*, February 1, 1962, p. 9. See also Snider, *The Agency and the Hill*, pp. 333–334.

29. See, for example, Christopher Andrew, *For the President's Eyes Only: Secret Intelligence and the American Presidency from Washington to Bush* (New York: Harper Collins, 1995); Thomas Powers, *The Man Who Kept the Secrets: Richard Helms and the CIA* (New York: Knopf, 1979); and Don Bohning, *The Castro Obsession: U.S. Covert Operations Against Cuba, 1959–1965* (Washington: Potomac Books, 2005). Despite the Church Committee's view that congressional oversight of the CIA was severely lacking, it did not endorse the "rogue elephant" analogy.

CHAPTER NINETEEN

Washington Politics, Homeland Security, and the Struggle against Global Terrorism

Glenn Hastedt

Politics stops at the water's edge.
All politics is local.

NO GOLDEN RULE HAS YET BEEN FOUND that guarantees success in making American foreign and national security policy. Instead, we find the two competing imperatives presented in the epigraphs. According to the first, "politics stops at the water's edge": foreign and national security policy is made in response to events and forces beyond American borders. The nature of the situation confronting the United States, its internal logic and dynamics, and the actions of other international actors combine to establish the parameters of American foreign and national security policy. There is no room for partisan politics or bureaucratic infighting in shaping this policy. At best, partisans are distracters that lessen the effectiveness of a policy; at worst, they doom it to failure by injecting inconsistencies, unwarranted constraints, and contradictions into it. According to the second, "all politics is local": American foreign and national security policy is always made in response to domestic political considerations. It cannot be otherwise. Events beyond America's borders no more demand or dictate a certain policy response than do events inside it. Accordingly, foreign and national security policy does not operate according to a different set of political rules than does domestic policy. Success in each requires accommodating differences of opinion that are rooted as much in self-interest as in points of principle and building winning coalitions that are based on power considerations and not the elegance of an argument.

These two imperatives share an uneasy coexistence. They point in opposite directions, yet each contains elements of truth. Policymakers who fully embrace the reasoning of one imperative to the neglect of insights offered by the other risk policy failure. Intelligence policy is no exception. Conceptualizing intelligence solely in terms of unmasking conditions and threats beyond American borders so that the proper response can be crafted will not by itself ensure success in the struggle against global terrorism. Intelligence also needs to be understood in the context of the political dynamics that shape the policy process in Washington.

Conventional accounts of intelligence comfortably reside within the confines of the first imperative. Intelligence is discussed as a value-neutral activity whose defining purpose is to help policymakers better understand a situation by furnishing them with analyzed information. The most heated debates have been over whether the intelligence community correctly understands the capabilities and intentions of America's external enemies, whether it be international communism, the Soviet Union, Al Qaeda, or global terrorism. The most frequently employed framework for understanding how such judgments are arrived at is the intelligence cycle.[1] It breaks intelligence down into a series of functionally related steps beginning with setting "needs to know" and ending with the production of intelligence for policymakers.

Less common are accounts of intelligence that build on the second policymaking imperative. Viewed from this perspective, the essence of intelligence is its ability to enhance the political power of those who possess it. The most heated debates here have been over whether intelligence has become politicized. Obtaining an understanding of intelligence's internal dynamics from this second perspective requires a different analytical framework. Rather than see it as composed of a series of functionally related steps that follow one after the other, intelligence can be broken down vertically into a series of different political games or contests that are continuously being played out. Not all of these games are equally visible to the public owing to the level of secrecy that surrounds them, nor is the level of activity the same in each game. Some political contests may be relatively quiet and in a state of equilibrium, whereas others may be hotly contested.

In the following sections, four political games that are continuously played out within the intelligence policy area will be introduced:

symbolic, resource, agenda, and accountability politics. For each I discuss what is being contested and why; I also identify the key political actors. The struggle against global terrorism provides the necessary policy context for the discussion because, as the first policymaking imperative correctly notes, American foreign and national security policy is designed with an eye toward dealing with a problem. Policy problems and politics cannot be totally separated. Having introduced the four political games, in the last two sections of the chapter, I extend the analysis by illustrating how they help us better understand the Washington politics of revelations in 2005–2006 and 2013–2014 that the National Security Agency (NSA) was engaged in domestic spying on Americans.

Symbolic Politics

Words and images matter in politics. By setting and controlling the language of the political debate and the images that frame it, policymakers are able to provide an inherent advantage to certain policy options over others and favor certain political institutions and actors over others.[2] As such, the words and images used in policy debates are often contested, but the political contest over symbols is not an even one. By virtue of their ability to command media attention, presidents possess an inherent advantage should they choose to use it. This is especially true in foreign and national security policy, where the president is looked on as the spokesperson for the nation and as the commander-in-chief. Entering into the arena of symbolic politics is not without risk. Words and images not only serve to control and direct political activity, they also raise expectations and can come to entrap policymakers that employ them.

Post-9/11 intelligence policy in the struggle against global terrorism has been shaped by symbolic politics in at least four different ways. First, it created a political context that favored aggressive collection policies. The George W. Bush administration moved quickly to define the terrorist threat as a war. Employing this imagery was easily understandable and well received by the American public. Both the location of the terrorist attacks of September 11, 2001, and the scale of the death and destruction they brought stunned Americans and produced a deep and palpable desire to reach out and punish those responsible for it. As natural as the war imagery seemed to most Americans, it was not the only way in which to symbolically frame the response to 9/11. Speaking of the British experience with terrorism in Northern Ireland, Michael Howard observed "a struggle against terrorism . . . is unlike a war against drugs or a war against crime in one vital respect. It is fundamentally a battle for hearts and minds. . . . Terrorists can be successfully destroyed only if public opinion, both at home and abroad, supports the authorities in regarding them as criminals rather than as heroes."[3]

From a political perspective, however, the war imagery offered something to the Bush administration that criminal imagery could not. It firmly centered decision-making power and authority on counterterrorism in the White House. It allowed the president to cast himself as a "war president" and in the process, at least for a time, politically disarmed his opponents who, in embracing the war imagery, were obliged to speak in the language of national unity. Just as significantly—given the American approach to war, which sharply distinguishes periods of war and peace and favors unilateral action and is loath to accepting restraints on the use of force—the war imagery allowed and perhaps encouraged the administration to think of intelligence activities in expansive terms. Wars are won or lost and presidents are held electorally accountable. Above all, winning the war on terrorism required preventing another attack on the American homeland, and to this end any and all information on the subject that could be collected needed to be collected.

Second, symbolic politics has been used extensively to reassure the public that the administration was in charge, all is well, and that progress in the war against terrorism was being made in the area of intelligence policy. In introducing his plan for creating a Department of Homeland Security, a reorganization he was advancing against his will and out of political necessity only after Congress balked at letting him establish an Office of Homeland Security in the White House, Bush again turned to symbolism, asserting that his proposal represented the most extensive reorganization of the Federal government since the 1940s.[4]

President Bush used similarly expansive and symbolic language two years later in signing the Intelligence Reform and Terrorism Prevention Act of 2004 (IRTPA, for short) that created the position of Director of National Intelligence, or DNI, calling it the "most dramatic reform of our nation's intelligence capabilities since President Harry S. Truman signed the National Security Act of 1947. Under this law our vast intelligence enterprise will become more unified, coordinated, and effective."[5] Establishing the position of DNI had been one of the principal recommendations of the 9/11 Commission. In reality the Bush administration had shown little interest in having it come into existence; but now that it was a reality, the administration used it for symbolic purposes. DNI John Negroponte publicly released a new National Intelligence Strategy of the United States, observing that this document "shows Congress and the public our commitment to building an intelligence community that is more unified, coordinated, and effective."[6]

Third, symbolic politics was used by the Bush administration to deflect criticism for intelligence failures. One example involves the administration's unsubstantiated charge that Iraq possessed weapons of mass destruction (WMD), a charge that was central to the administration's case for involvement. Central to the administration's strategy to deflect criticism was restricting the terms of reference given to bodies looking into these intelligence failures. The Senate Select Intelligence Committee (SSCI) investigated and reported its conclusions in July 2004 and stated that nearly every finding in the National Intelligence Estimate released prior to the war was wrong. As part of the agreement by Republicans and Democrats on the Committee, the Senate's investigation was divided into two parts. Part One dealt with the quality of prewar intelligence. The investigation was not permitted to examine how intelligence was used by the Bush administration. The administration's handling of intelligence was to be Part Two of the investigation. Part Two remained uncompleted as Republicans and Democrats on the Committee sparred over the need to hear testimony from administration officials.

Also looking into this matter was the Commission on the Intelligence Capabilities of the United States Regarding Weapons of Mass Destruction, also known as the Silberman-Robb Commission. Bush initially resisted efforts to establish such a commission, arguing that creating a special panel to look into this issue was premature and should wait on a more exhaustive search for WMD. He changed his position in early February 2004 following the late January resignation of UN chief weapons inspector David Kay and his subsequent testimony to Congress that "we were almost all wrong" about Iraq's weapons program.[7] Now fearful that the White House would lose control over the issue, Bush endorsed a commission but indicated that it would look at intelligence on weapons programs in Libya, Iran, and North Korea as well. He also indicated that he would appoint all of its members.

Unlike the 9/11 Commission, whose deliberations the administration had failed to control, the Silberman-Robb Commission held closed-door hearings rather than public ones. It was also not authorized to examine how policymakers used the intelligence they received. The Commission concluded that the intelligence community was "dead wrong" in most of their assessments.[8] It mentioned the CIA 1,567 times, the White House eight times, and Vice President Dick Cheney twice.

Finally, symbolic politics can be used to place responsibility for future problems on others. Consumer safety alerts, foreign travel advisories, drug warning labels, and the like all say to citizens that the government is doing its job and now you must do yours. This is very much the case with issuing warnings about terrorist attacks. Lawrence Freedman notes that by communicating threat warnings, governments are able to shift responsibility for dealing with the risk of terrorism from governments to citizens, who are then the ones who make the decision on whether to ride the subways, go to work, or open their mail.[9]

As examples of this tendency, we have the October 2005 decisions to place police officers on every train, to have major shows of force at transportation centers in New York City, and to close the Baltimore Harbor Tunnel. All decisions were made in the aftermath of the London terrorist bombings in 2005, and the intelligence used consisted almost entirely of tips that a terrorist attack was possible in the immediate future. In the Baltimore case, the tip was described as uncorroborated. In the New York case, the threat was dismissed by Department of Homeland Security officials almost as soon as the alert was announced. On a more general level, we have the color-coded alert system put in place by the Department of Homeland Security. Six times between its introduction after 9/11 and the presidential election of 2004, the system went into an orange or elevated alert level. Although issuing warnings holds the potential for shifting responsibility away from policymakers, it also has risks—especially when threats fail to materialize. Under these circumstances, policymakers are again trapped by their own symbols and run the risk of being accused of politicizing a situation or alarmism.

For intelligence, three consequences follow from the desire of policymakers to protect themselves (at least at a symbolic level) from charges that they are not doing their jobs. First, policymakers will demand greater specificity from intelligence than is possible. They will want the intelligence community to engage in fortune-telling.[10] One can see this outlook in President Bush's comment that the August 6, 2001, *President's Daily Brief* titled "Bin Laden Determined to Strike in US" did not contain specific enough information to take action.[11] Second, in the absence of concrete intelligence, policymakers tend to place greater emphasis on worst-case speculation about potential vulnerabilities and what terrorists might do rather than on the limited intelligence on hand about what terrorists are doing or planning. Finally, it heightens the tendency to engage in "sweepstakes" intelligence, where the rush to a bottom-line conclusion takes precedence over sound analysis.[12] Taken together, these three tendencies work against the credibility of intelligence warnings about terrorist attacks, but they do address the political imperative of shifting blame.

Resource Politics

By its very nature and purpose, symbolic politics is a highly visible enterprise. Far less visible is the second political game or contest played out in Washington, DC: resource politics. Where the president is the principal political player in the symbolic politics arena, Congress and bureaucratic forces dominate resource politics. Successful symbolic politics actually provides a cover that shields this political game from public view by encouraging the general population to turn its attention to other matters because public statements, laws, investigations, or administrative reforms have taken place that have addressed the problem. The struggle against terrorism is no exception. Speaking of the 9/11 Commission's call to create a powerful Director of National Intelligence and locate the office in the White House, Congressman Jack Murtha (D-PA) commented in September 2004 that "public indifference will make Congress able to resist changes [to the intelligence community]."[13] Presidents traditionally have not been active players in these political arenas because they care less about reorganization than do legislators and bureaucrats and frequently employ them as bargaining chips.

Resource politics are concerned with the basic fiber of organizations: their structure, budgets, and areas of jurisdiction. All were key areas of contention in intelligence policy in Washington after 9/11 with the creation of the Department of Homeland Security and the post of DNI.[14] As noted in the discussion of symbolic politics, they both were hailed as significant accomplishments in improving the quality of intelligence and winning the struggle against global terrorism. Yet, as the reorganization process came to an end, no intelligence agency was abolished. Instead, the number of intelligence bureaucracies increased.

We can see the central role played by resource politics in setting up the Department of Homeland Security. The policy debate began over whether a Cabinet-level Department of Homeland Security or an Office of Homeland Security in the White House should be created. This is a structural issue, and at its heart was the ability of Congress to influence how its funds were spent and who would run the department. A White House Office of Homeland Security would be beyond its reach, but not a Department of Homeland Security. The language establishing the Department suggested a major intelligence role.[15] The reality proved to be quite different. One Senate aide close to the reorganization process stated that "there is real friction among these agencies. A lot of people want to put Homeland Security in a little box and not share much with them."[16] Moreover, the president may have done little to advance the intelligence reforms.[17]

As created, the Department of Homeland Security had three primary missions: (1) to prevent terrorist attacks within the United States, (2) to reduce the vulnerability of the United States to terrorism, and (3) to minimize the damage and assist in the recovery from terrorist attacks that do occur here. To accomplish these objectives, 22 different agencies with some 170,000 employees were brought together in the new department. The FBI and CIA were largely unaffected by the establishment of the Department of Homeland Security. Also remaining outside the new unit were the NSA, the Defense Intelligence Agency (DIA), and the Northern Command, which is charged with the defense of American territory.

From the very outset, FBI Director Robert Mueller and Director of Central Intelligence (DCI) George Tenet spoke out against any rapid, major overhaul of the intelligence community, as did senior active and retired intelligence officials. Their opposition, coupled with uncertainty in Congress over how to proceed, led to a decision to postpone intelligence reorganization and focus on reorganizing other aspects of Homeland Security, such as border and transportation protection, immigration, and disaster preparedness.

With intelligence agencies not subject to reorganization, the Department of Homeland Security became confined to the status of a consumer of intelligence and not a producer. Both the FBI and CIA pressed for strict limits on the information they had to share with the new Department. By the end of 2002, it was determined that the Secretary of Homeland Security would only have access to unevaluated raw intelligence when he could make a case for it under yet-to-be-determined procedures.

The 9/11 Commission issued its report on July 22, 2004. Its central recommendation was the establishment of the position of DNI. This individual would oversee all-source national intelligence centers, serve as the president's principal intelligence advisor, manage the national intelligence program, and oversee the component agencies of the intelligence community. Included in his powers would be the responsibility for submitting a unified intelligence budget, appropriating funds to the intelligence agencies, and setting personnel policies for the intelligence community. The DNI's office (ODNI) would be in the White House.

The proposal to create a DNI became part of IRTPA, enacted in 2004. The House and Senate passed different versions of the bill with the Senate bill more closely following the 9/11 Commission's call for a strong DNI. The House bill provided for a far less powerful director. Under the Senate bill, the CIA director "shall be under the authority, direction, and control" of the DNI. In the House version, the CIA director would only "report" to the DNI. The House bill also only gave the DNI the power to develop budgets and give "guidance" to intelligence community members. The Senate bill stated that he or she would "determine" the budget.

Visible bureaucratic opposition to the 9/11 Commission's version of a DNI emerged soon after its report was released. Ridge opposed the idea, stating, "We don't need an intelligence czar."[18] Along with Secretary of Defense Donald Rumsfeld and National Security Advisor Condoleezza Rice, he cautioned against moving too quickly. The chairman of the Joint Chiefs of Staff, Gen. Richard Myers, made the same point in a letter he sent to congressional leaders. He asserted that if the Pentagon were to lose control of its spy satellites, troops on the ground would be endangered.

By fall, the House and Senate were deadlocked. Key opposition came from House Republicans led by Duncan Hunter (R-CA), chair of the House Armed Services Committee, who was adamant that the Pentagon should not lose control over its intelligence budget and that the overall intelligence budget should remain secret.[19] And in the intelligence community, at the CIA and the FBI it was business as usual as these agencies went about their intelligence collection activities.[20] Further, CIA Director Porter Goss announced that he would not hold any current or former agency officials responsible for pre-9/11 intelligence failures.[21]

In its final version, IRTPA as signed by President Bush followed far more closely the restricted vision of the Pentagon and its allies than it did the 9/11 Commission in establishing the DNI. Title I of the act stipulated that the DNI not be located in the executive office of the president. It gave the DNI the power to "develop and determine" an annual budget for the national intelligence program based on budget proposals provided by the heads of intelligence agencies and departments.

Resource politics does not end in Washington with the passage of legislation but continues on a daily basis. In April 2005, the Silverman-Robb Commission, now acting as a private watchdog organization over intelligence reform, warned Bush to expect existing intelligence agencies to try to undermine the authority of the new DNI. Modernization plans being put forward by the FBI and CIA were described as a "business as usual approach to intelligence gathering."

Resource politics potentially also has a second but more varied impact on those who produce intelligence. Richard Stoltz, former head of the CIA's clandestine service, suggests that the process of adding more layers to the intelligence bureaucracy will lead to a wait-and-see and risk-averse attitude among intelligence officials.[22]

These are precisely the traits that drew so much criticism from the 9/11 Commission and other studies. At the same time, the process of redirecting resources, creating new units, and seeking to imbue them with a sense of urgency and purpose to their mission may also embolden some to act in ways that transgress the bounds of permissible behavior. After 9/11, the CIA came under pressure to capture members of Al Qaeda and their supporters. Renditions, the process of secretly capturing a suspect and transferring them to another country for interrogation, became a favored tool in the war on terrorism. Identifying candidates for rendition involved collaboration between analysts and operations officers sifting through tips and other pieces of circumstantial information as to a person's politics or identity. An estimated 3,000 people were captured. Unfortunately, not all of them had a connection with terrorism. Mistakes were made because of the fear of missing a case. And, in the process, the vetting and evaluating information suffered. It was "the Camelot of counterterrorism."[23]

Agenda Politics

Policymakers are attracted to intelligence out of self-interest. They want to succeed, and to the extent that intelligence helps them succeed, they seek it out and use it. As one former diplomat noted, "I could not afford to read intelligence papers because this or that intelligence agency was empowered to produce them. . . . I could only read intelligence products tailored to help me through my substantive schedule."[24] This basic truth holds several important implications for intelligence. First, intelligence does not determine policy. Intelligence professionals recognize this. It is one ingredient in the mix of factors that determine what U.S. foreign and national security policy will be. The struggle against global terrorism is no exception. As Lawrence Freedman notes in speaking of the Iraq war, "This was not an intelligence driven crisis. The [9/11] attacks changed the terms of the security debate . . . [policy] drew on intelligence information but could rarely be refuted or confirmed in a definitive manner."[25]

Second, intelligence is not always welcomed. Often it is inconvenient.[26] Typically policymakers seek to keep options open as long as possible, but the logic of intelligence is to close off options. Particularly problematic is intelligence that questions the wisdom of a policy after policymakers have publicly committed themselves to it. Intelligence may also be discounted when it suggests that a potential problem exists at a time when policymakers are focused on other issues. Again the struggle against terrorism provides examples. Planning within the State Department, the CIA, and nongovernmental organizations suggested that the rebuilding and occupation of Iraq would not follow the model of Germany or Japan after the Second World War (as administration officials suggested) but would be more difficult and require a much larger military force than was being planned for. These warnings were shunted aside.[27] The same can be said for the administration's response to doubts within the intelligence community about the soundness of the intelligence on which its pre-war policy rested; because the incoming Bush administration's agenda did not include terrorism as a prominent concern, attempts by Clinton administration holdover Richard A. Clarke and others to warn the administration about Al Qaeda fell largely on deaf ears.[28] For that matter, terrorism was also not a major issue in the Clinton administration. Prior to 9/11, the most comprehensive National Intelligence Estimate on terrorism was published in July 1995.

Third, the extent that policymakers disagree over policy intelligence will become contested and competitive. Not only will policymakers seek out intelligence that supports their policy positions or undermines that of rivals, they will also seek to control its distribution. In some cases this will mean denying rivals access to it. In other cases it will mean going public with intelligence. Efforts by Bush administration officials to seek out supportive evidence in the struggle against terrorism prior to the Iraq war are well chronicled. Vice President Dick Cheney regularly visited CIA headquarters and challenged analysts on their sources and conclusions. Retired CIA official Michael Scheuer comments that the CIA received repeated inquiries from Undersecretary of Defense Douglas Feith's office at the Pentagon about Iraq–Al Qaeda links, causing the CIA to review over 70,000 documents.[29] Rumsfeld and Feith established the Office of Special Plans within the Defense Department to provide an alternative source of intelligence that would support their position.

The administration also sought to control access to intelligence. Defending its Iraq policy in 2005, the Bush administration argued that Congress had seen the same intelligence the president enjoyed prior to the war. Yet the administration had far more intelligence available to it and did not share all it possessed. Doubts within the intelligence community were not shared, such as those expressed by the National Security Council four days before President Bush's 2003 State of the Union address, where he made the case for war against Iraq. The NSC had called for additional intelligence to support the claim that Saddam Hussein possessed chemical, nuclear, or biological weapons. In contrast to DCI George Tenet, who called the case for war "a slam dunk," the national intelligence officer for strategic and nuclear programs called the case "weak."[30] Similarly, doubts raised by a Defense Intelligence Agency analysis of the reliability of the administration's principal source establishing a link between Al Qaeda and Iraq were neither shared nor reflected in Bush's October 2002 statement that "we know Iraq and al-Qaeda have had high-level contacts going back a decade."

Beginning in August 2002 and continuing through to the eve of war, the administration began a sustained and well-orchestrated campaign to promote public support for war against Iraq.[31] Central to this campaign was the release of intelligence (or references to intelligence) that supported its case. A White House Iraq Group under the direction of Chief of Staff Andrew Cord was set up to ensure that a unified front was being given by the administration on the need for war. Cheney asserted that he was convinced Saddam Hussein possessed WMD, citing information from defectors (including Hussein's son-in-law). Bush announced that Iraq was reconstituting its nuclear weapons program and that satellite photographs supported this conclusion. And, speaking to the United Nations, Secretary of State Colin Powell told the United Nations that his presentation on Iraqi efforts to obtain nuclear weapons was based on "solid intelligence."

The fourth implication for intelligence of policymakers approaching it in a self-interested fashion is that they tend to view intelligence as a tool or instrument of policy. Intelligence is not supposed to have policy views of its own. It exists to serve policymakers, whose basic approach is that they want "more, better and faster."[32] But in reality, intelligence officials are no more united in their views than are policymakers. The dividing lines separating intelligence officials are not necessarily partisan in the sense of Republican versus Democrat, or realist versus neoconservative, although such differences do exist. They are more likely to be centered on questions of institutional perspectives, control over information, the proper analytical frameworks employed, and definitions of professionalism. Thus, just as with policymakers, it is often necessary to find common ground to advance policy. In the case of the struggle against global terrorism, this common ground was the charge that Saddam Hussein possessed WMD. As Paul Wolfowitz acknowledged, "only the WMD issue had legs."[33] It was the only issue around which the bureaucracy could agree.

The failure to recognize that intelligence is not by definition neutral in its origins or infinitely malleable in its uses, but rather that it reflects the thinking of individuals embedded in organizations that contain their own political dynamics, can set the stage for a particularly bitter brand of agenda politics—one that pits the White House against portions of the intelligence community. The primary weapons at the disposal of the disaffected segments of the intelligence community are leaks. The recipients of these leaks tend to be the media or members of Congress. Their purpose is to alter the complexion of the political landscape by bringing other groups into the political fray that might otherwise not be aware that a policy is being contested or even under discussion. In addition to principled disagreement over policy decisions, self-interest plays an important role in the decision to leak intelligence. Policymakers come and go, but intelligence agencies are permanent. Recalling the post-Vietnam experience of the American military, those who leak may fear that their agencies will bear the blame for policy failures, excesses, and illegalities long after the policymakers who ordered them have left Washington.

This is the pattern of Washington politics that emerged with the beginning of the occupation and reconstruction of Iraq. Leaks from the intelligence community and military personnel provided the impetus for revelations about Abu Ghraib prisons in that country, as well as the practice of secretly capturing and incarcerating suspected terrorist suspects abroad, the use of torture as an interrogation device, and electronic spying by the NSA on American citizens in the United States. In each case, these revelations succeeded in widening the circle of those participating in the policy debate. Most notably it brought renewed attention to Senator John McCain (AR), a former prisoner of war and a potential Republican presidential candidate who opposed the use of torture. Leaks also brought European leaders into the policy debate as information about secret CIA renditions in Eastern European countries occurred on the eve of Secretary of State Condoleezza Rice's 2005 trip there.

For its part, the Bush administration continued to make secret intelligence public on a selective basis to further its position. DNI John D. Negroponte released an inflammatory letter allegedly written by Ayman Al-Zawahari, an Al Qaeda leader, just as President Bush was giving a speech on Iraq defending the administration's policy. In an October 6, 2005, news conference, Bush announced that 10 unidentified Al Qaeda terrorist plots had been disrupted by the United States and allied intelligence agencies since 9/11. When pressed on the subject by reporters, the administration later released a list of those incidents. Intelligence officials commented off the record that the administration had overstated the gravity of those plots and that most were far from being in a position to be carried out.

Accountability Politics

To whom is intelligence responsible? As we have just suggested, from the point of view of policymakers, intelligence is responsible to them. They expect intelligence organizations to provide them with information and assessments that will allow them to succeed. The conventional wisdom in Washington is that Porter Goss (R-FLA) was made director of the CIA in 2004 to bring it under control and end the series of anti-administration intelligence leaks emanating from it. Goss would not be the first director posted to the CIA for that purpose. He brought with him highly partisan staffers from the House Permanent Select Intelligence Committee (HPSCI). In his first months in that position, between 30 and 90 senior CIA officials left, including some whom Goss had appointed to key positions; further, someone who worked on the Bush-Cheney election campaigns was placed in charge of the CIA's public affairs unit. Goss also issued a memo to CIA employees (soon leaked) in which he stated "as agency employees we do not identify with, support, or champion opposition to the administration or its policies."[34]

Intelligence officials are well aware that executive branch policymakers are not the only ones interested in the performance of the intelligence community. Congress, through its powers of the budget, appointment, and oversight, has a constitutionally defined role in evaluating and assessing its performance. The media is also interested in intelligence both for its ability to provide a good story and because of the media's "fourth estate" role as a watchdog for the people over governmental action. Also active in the area of oversight, but generally playing a much more limited role in holding intelligence agencies responsible for their actions, are private sector interest groups, such as the Electronic Privacy Information Center, which aggressively pursues national security-oriented freedom of information questions.

Secrecy is an obvious and major impediment to the ability of political actors, outside of the small group in the executive branch who make national security policy, to judge the performance of intelligence. But it is not the only factor affecting the ability and willingness of Congress, the media, or interest groups to scrutinize intelligence agencies and personnel and hold them accountable for their actions or inaction. Three other factors, all rooted in Washington politics, also play major if not more important roles: deference, partisanship, and self-interest.

The 9/11 Commission characterized congressional oversight of intelligence as "dysfunctional," a situation that can be traced to the three traits just noted.[35] Deference was long visible in the approach that Congress brought to oversight during the early years of the Cold War. The national consensus focused on the need to combat communism, coupled with the widely held view that intelligence was an instrument of foreign policy to be exercised by the president at his discretion. During this period, congressional oversight served more to protect the CIA and other agencies than make them accountable for their actions. It was only in the mid-1970s, after revelations of CIA involvement in the coup to bring down Salvador Allende's government in Chile and spying on American citizens inside the United States, that congressional oversight became aggressive with the establishment of the Church and Pike Committees in the Senate and House, respectively. In the wake of the investigations carried out by these panels, each body established Select Intelligence Committees for purposes of continued oversight. They largely followed a model that stressed bipartisanship and deference to the president and his use of intelligence, with investigations being restricted to examining problems only after they occurred rather than engaging in anticipatory or preventive oversight.

Deference to the president began to lessen during the Reagan years as the administration talked of "unleashing" the CIA and as its Central American policies increasingly divided Republicans and Democrats. During the Clinton presidency, Congress (with Republicans leading the way) forced unwanted programs on the administration in the form of appropriating money for covert action programs against Saddam Hussein. In both administrations, as well as during Carter's term, the opposition party openly and successfully challenged the president's nominee to head the intelligence community. Deference returned briefly in the wake of the 9/11 terrorist attacks but soon faded as the United States moved from war in Afghanistan to war in Iraq. Partisanship became particularly intense in the House. Porter Goss, who chaired the HPSCI and was himself a retired intelligence officer who served in the clandestine service, had long acted as a protector of the CIA. Now he moved aggressively to protect the president. He often described the CIA as a mismanaged bureaucracy. He publicly supported the administration's position on WMD, and he blocked investigations into pre-war intelligence and the treatment of prisoners at Abu Ghraib. He also belittled the notion of an investigation into the leaking of undercover CIA official Valerie Plame's name to the press (linked by a special prosecutor to Lewis "Scooter" Libby in Vice President Cheney's office). During the presidential campaign, Goss also criticized Democratic nominee John Kerry's stance on intelligence in a speech on the House floor.

The 9/11 Commission rejected calls for tinkering with the system of intelligence accountability and urged a wholesale change that would establish a strong oversight committee in each chamber or a single joint committee. Congress reacted warily to the proposed reforms, even while making support public statements. Of particular concern to legislators was the notion advanced by some of giving one committee power over both, setting program priorities and budget authority. This would produce a reduction in influence of the Appropriations, Armed Forces, and Foreign Relations committees. Senate Appropriations Chair Ted Stevens (R-AK) commented on the thrust of the 9/11 Commission calls for centralizing congressional authority: "I don't think it will fly."[36] House Appropriations

Committee Chair C. W. Young (R-FL) observed that combining spending and authorization powers in one committee "is not part of this proposal" in discussing the House's response to the 9/11 Commission's plans. A Republican aide stated more bluntly that any such plan "doesn't have a snowball's chance in hell" of taking effect.

The same three factors emerge in media oversight of intelligence. Deference can be seen in how the media reports on intelligence. What the public tends to focus on are the sensational headlines of domestic spying, renditions, and the treatment of prisoners. Less often noticed is that the media are frequently in contact with the administration about the details of these stories and are sensitive to its concerns. In a November 2005 story revealing the covert prison system set up to hold and interrogate suspected terrorists outside of the United States without restrictions, the *Washington Post* agreed with a request from senior administration officials not to identify the Eastern European countries involved.[37] The next month, the *New York Times* reported on the program of domestic spying that President Bush had secretly authorized following the 9/11 attacks.[38] The paper reported that it had delayed publishing the story for one year after meeting with the White House and that some information that administration officials had argued could be useful to terrorists was omitted. When it was released, charges of partisanship were quickly raised. The story surfaced just as the Senate was nearing a final vote on extending the USA-PATRIOT Act. A compelling case for self-interest in the timing of the story can be made by pointing to competition between the *New York Times* and the *Washington Post* in breaking such stories and the imminent publication of a book on domestic spying by the article's author, James Risen.

For a brief period of time, one public affairs interest group played a key role in accountability politics. Its behavior deviated from the pattern of deference, partisanship, and self-interest exhibited by Congress and the media. After its report was issued on July 22, 2004, the members of the 9/11 Commission disbanded and formed a nonprofit organization, the 9/11 Public Discourse Project, to fulfill what they saw as the Commission's original mandate of guarding against future terrorist attacks and promoting a national debate on how future attacks can be prevented. To that end, the 9/11 Public Discourse Project issued a series of report cards from September to December 2005 on the extent to which the Commission's recommendations had been acted on. While seeking to be nonpartisan, the negative tone of its evaluation (one A-, twelve Bs, nine Cs, twelve Ds, five Fs, and two incompletes) struck a partisan chord in Washington. The 9/11 Public Discourse Project ceased operation on December 31, 2005, with its ultimate impact on intelligence and the struggle against terrorism unclear.

A New Era of Intelligence Controversy

In the recent past the Washington politics of intelligence have twice centered on revelations of domestic spying on Americans as part of the War on Terrorism. Both cases provide us with additional insights into the domestic side of intelligence. In this section I review the Washington politics of intelligence that followed from a mid-December 2005 *New York Times* report based on information leaked to it, that in February 2002 President Bush signed a secret order authorizing the National Security Agency (NSA) to monitor phone calls and other communications (such as faxes and emails) inside the United States by Americans identified by the NSA as having some connection to Al Qaeda or potential terrorist activities.[39] In the following section, I examine the controversy following the release of secret NSA documents to the press by Edward Snowden in 2013.

According to the documents leaked in 2005, up to 500 Americans were being eavesdropped on at any one time and all told, the number of Americans spied on may have reached into the thousands. The NSA, in turn, provided information to the DIA and others for use in carrying out its surveillance of people inside the United States. President Bush reportedly was deeply involved in the oversight of the program, reviewing it every 45 or 60 days and reauthorizing it some 36 times.[40]

The *New York Times* story broke the day before the Senate was to vote on reauthorizing the USA-PATRIOT Act.[41] A key point of debate was whether the provisions of this act went far enough in protecting the civil liberties of Americans. The story appeared to have a significant impact, and many senators expressed concern about the warrantless wiretapping. The next day, by a vote of 52 to 47, with four Republicans voting with all but two Democrats, the Republican-controlled Senate refused to end the filibuster, signaling a setback for the act. Just days before, in an effort to ensure its passage, the Bush administration reversed its position and endorsed Senator McCain's bill to ban the cruel, inhumane, and degrading treatment of prisoners in its custody. After extensive debate in the new year, Congress passed the renewed USA-PATRIOT Act on March 9.

The controversy that raged was not primarily over the value of this intelligence-gathering effort, although such questions were raised by some. The core issue was President Bush's authority to authorize this program on his own. And this moved intelligence politics squarely into the arena of symbolic politics, with the outcome determining in large part which side would have the upper hand in the overall political contest. The President defended the program on the grounds that it was "limited," "a vital tool in the war on terrorism," and "critical to saving American lives." Most significant, he also stated that it was "consistent with U.S. law and the Constitution."[42]

In making this last assertion, Bush was echoing the position taken by Attorney General John Ashcroft, who signed a brief on September 22, 2002, stating that "the Constitution vests in the President inherent authority to conduct wireless intelligence surveillance of foreign powers or their agents and Congress cannot by statue extinguish that constitutional authority."[43] Ashcroft's argument made no distinction between U.S. citizens or suspected foreign agents. In 2005, Attorney General Alberto Gonzales asserted that the administration's domestic eavesdropping was derived from the September 14, 2001, joint resolution authorizing the president to use "all necessary and appropriate force" to defeat Al Qaeda and the president's inherent powers as commander in chief. The Justice Department continued this line of argument, stating that because espionage is "a fundamental incident in the use of military force," even though it was not specifically mentioned, it was authorized by the resolution.[44]

As the controversy grew, Bush engaged in symbolic politics again when he sought to redefine the program as "terrorist surveillance" and publicly presented an account of an al Qaeda plot to crash a commercial jetliner into a Los Angeles skyscraper after 9/11. The significance of the revelation was quickly countered by unnamed intelligence officials who questioned whether the plot was anything more than loose talk.

Opponents countered with an argument heavily rooted in symbolism as well: American civil liberties were being violated, the rule of law had been broken, and neither Congress nor the Constitution provided such powers to the president. The Fourth Amendment to the U.S. Constitution protects citizens from unreasonable searches and seizures and stipulates that warrants can only be issued with probable cause. Moreover, the Supreme Court has rejected the argument that national security considerations override this requirement. Opponents also challenged the stated limited nature of this program. The National Counterterrorism Center maintained a list of international terrorism suspects or those who might be providing them with aid. In early 2006, 325,000 names were on that list (although duplicates might have reduced the number to some 200,000).[45]

Opponents continued that the rule of law was violated by Bush's failure to obtain permission from the U.S. Foreign Intelligence Surveillance Court (FISC) to conduct surveillance on Americans inside the United States. This eleven-judge body, all of whose members were selected by the GOP-appointed Chief Justice of the Supreme Court, was set up by the Foreign Intelligence Surveillance Act (FISA) that was passed in 1978 after revelations of widespread spying on Americans by the military and the

NSA in the name of rooting out communist influence on the anti-Vietnam War movement. According to the Justice Department, in 2004 the secret court approved 1,754 warrants.

The Bush administration's position was that FISA was not relevant because the September 14, 2001, resolution constitutes a statute that, by the terms of the act, can override its provisions. One of the judges resigned in protest following revelations that the program existed, and the presiding judge of the secret court requested a briefing on why it was not consulted.

The political battle over what symbolic reference points were to be used in judging the appropriateness of this intelligence-gathering policy set the stage for a renewed round of accountability politics. As noted above, the FISC was ignored. Only its presiding judge was informed, and she raised concerns in private that this program could undermine the secret court's work if information so obtained was later used to acquire warrants on terrorist suspects. In fact, twice since 9/11, the FISC was told that information obtained by this program may have been improperly used to obtain wiretap warrants. Vice President Cheney informed leaders of both parties about the program after it started, and later, the administration informed key members of Congress.[46]

These congressional briefings are given to the Gang of Eight, the leadership of the House and Senate, and the intelligence committees. Staff members are not present, and those briefed are prohibited from discussing the information with other members of Congress, including those who serve on the intelligence committees. The administration contends that with these briefings, Congress gave its approval to the domestic spying program. After it became public, John D. Rockefeller IV (D-WV), the ranking SSCI Democrat, revealed that in 2003 he sent a letter to Cheney stating that the briefings were unsatisfactory. The letter stated, "Given the security restrictions associated with this information, and inability to consult staff or counsel on my own, I feel unable to fully evaluate, much less endorse, these activities."[47]

Although the content of these briefings is the subject of debate, it is clear that congressional oversight was carried out with deference to the administration and far more in the spirit of putting out fires (which had not yet occurred) than patrolling for dangers.[48] When the program became public, Congress quickly moved out of principle and self-interest to reassert its oversight powers, as both Democrats and Republicans called for hearings and previously secret correspondence was made public. Partisanship was not completely absent, as many GOP members of Congress staunchly defended the program and the president's right to implement it. Cheney went so far as to suggest that the debate over spying on terrorists ought be an issue in the upcoming congressional campaign.

In addition to maintaining its right to conduct such a surveillance program, the administration also sought to deflect attention away from the question of presidential authority by returning to symbolic politics. Bush asserted that the story of the day was not the domestic intelligence-gathering program but the war in Iraq.

Lying beneath the surface of this controversy we can also find resource politics. During the Cold War, the NSA collected intelligence on the Soviet Union through electronic intercepts and controlled much of the intelligence community's secret budget. This mission no longer exists. The war on terrorism provided an opportunity for the NSA to reinvent itself, but doing so was not without challenges. As a former NSA director observed, "We've gone from chasing a slow-moving, technologically inferior, resource poor nation-state to chasing a communications structure in which an al Qaeda member can go into a storefront in Istanbul and buy for $100 a communications device that is absolutely cutting edge, and for which he has had to make no investment for development."[49]

The NSA has long been authorized to monitor international phone calls and emails of American citizens without a warrant when they originate overseas. Secret NSA intelligence gathering in the United States was limited to communications intercepts involving foreign embassies and missions, as well as when an individual was suspected of being an "agent of a foreign power" or a member of a terrorist group—and only then with a warrant. Otherwise it generally fell to the FBI to carry out domestic eavesdropping operations. The expansion of the NSA's role after 9/11 was implemented with an eye to achieving results and not the imposition of accountability safeguards. It was mid-2004 before voices of concern were raised. At that time, elements of the program were suspended and others recast after concerns were raised by national security officials and the head of the Foreign Intelligence Surveillance Court (FISC).

This was not the only expansion in domestic intelligence-gathering activities after 9/11. Also in late 2005, it was revealed that the Defense Department's new counterterrorism agency, the Counterintelligence Field Activity (CIFA), had expanded its efforts from a coordinating and oversight body into one with operational responsibilities. Its Directorate of Field Activities became responsible for disrupting adversaries, running roving patrols around military bases, and conducting surveillance on potentially threatening people and organizations inside the United States. CIFA also manages data bases that include Talon reports, which consist of raw and unverified information collected by the military on suspicious activities. Talon reports are known to include information on peaceful civilian protests and demonstrations. In November 2005, the CIFA was given authority to task the domestic U.S. investigations and operations of the military counterintelligence units.

As promised by Senator Arlen Specter (R-PA), hearings on the NSA's domestic surveillance program began in February 2006 after Congress returned from its winter recess. An all-out White House lobbying campaign, plus a late-found willingness to brief House and Senate committees on the programs, slowed down the momentum that had built for an investigation. Through a procedural maneuver (which allowed time for a Republican working group appointed by Majority Leader Bill Frist, R-TN, to explore ways of changing the law to accommodate NSA's policy), the Senate rejected a Democratic attempt to launch an investigation into the matter. Democrats were quick to criticize the formation of an all-Republican committee.

Another Round of Controversy in 2013–2014

The controversy over NSA's secret surveillance program did not end in 2006, but it did fade from public view for a while, appearing only sporadically and in nuanced form. In 2012, just a year before Edward J. Snowden's leaked documents appeared in the press, senators Mark Udall (D-CO) and Ron Wyden (D-OR) made speeches in the Senate referencing its existence, and in a letter to Attorney General Eric H. Holder Jr., they wrote, "we believe most Americans would be stunned to learn the details of how these secret court opinions have interpreted Section 215 of the Patriot Act."

The story that again placed NSA's domestic surveillance program at the heart of Washington's intelligence politics broke on June 6, 2013, when the *Guardian* and the *Washington Post* revealed that the NSA had obtained a ruling from the FISC directing Verizon Business Network Services to provide it "on a daily basis" with all call logs "between the United States and abroad" or "wholly within the United States, including local telephone calls." The directive did not include the content of the communications but only what is referred to as metadata: the beginning and end points of a communication and its length. Snowden, a 29-year-old high school dropout working with NSA for the Booz Allen Hamilton (BAH) consulting firm, was identified as the source of the NSA leaks on June 9. In justifying his actions, Snowden declared, "the public needs to decide whether these programs and policies are right or wrong."

The White House initially declined to comment on the breaking story, but the following day, it was confirmed by DNI James R. Clapper Jr. He acknowledged that in the course of this data collection, NSA might "incidentally acquire" information about Americans and foreign residents, but it could not target any U.S. citizen, any other U.S. person, or anyone located within the United States. President Barack Obama quickly sought to reassure the American public and keep the issue off of the agenda by proclaiming that "nobody is listening to your telephone calls." Senate Majority Leader Harry Reid (D-NEV) further observed, "Everyone should just calm down and understand this isn't anything that is brand new." Congressional leaders indicated that the docket was too full for consideration of the issue.

A central feature of the Obama administration's reassurance strategy was to stress the legitimacy of the NSA's metadata programs and the presence of built-in safeguards that guaranteed political accountability. These efforts took several forms. First and foremost, the NSA programs were defended as legitimate because they were authorized by law and known to Congress. As part of his attempt to control the accountability game, Obama also promised to appoint members to a long-dormant Civil Liberties Board and make public previously classified FISC rulings. His administration also released a White Paper, entitled *Bulk Collection of Telephony Metadata under Section 215 of the USA Patriot Act,* that was intended to document the legality of the NSA's programs and firmly link the origins of the programs to the Bush administration.[50]

The SSCI and HPSCI leadership supported Obama's assertion that Congress had been informed about these operations and had been duly exercising its oversight responsibilities. Intelligence officials characterized the information on Americans collected and retained by NSA as part of these surveillance programs as "minuscule" and "incidentally acquired."

Critics in and out of Congress presented two broad challenges to these assertions. First, dissenting committee members described the typical hearing as being a one-side affair in which intelligence officials did not volunteer information unless asked, and then did not provide an insightful answer unless the question was asked with absolute precision. Rep. James Sensenbrenner (R-WISC) summed up these classified briefings as "rope-a-dope" operations.

Second, critics questioned the quality of oversight exercised by the FISC, whose approval was necessary for the NSA to conduct these operations. They charged that, contrary to the Obama administration's argument that the FISC was providing effective oversight, it had in fact become little more than a rubber stamp. While accounts of the number of cases that have come before the FISC vary slightly, over its entire history, the FISC is generally seen as having rejected only 11 out of some 34,000 warrant requests.

Accountability questions of a different sort were central to revelations that the NSA had engaged in secret intelligence gathering on the telephone conversations of foreign leaders. At the center of this controversy was the extent of Obama's knowledge about the surveillance program directed at German Chancellor Angela Merkel. Media accounts described an angry Merkel calling Obama and receiving assurances that she was not currently the target of a surveillance program and would not be in the future. A call to national security advisor Susan Rice from German officials produced a response to the effect that President Obama had not known about a surveillance program that targeted Chancellor Merkel.

Just as in the case of revelations about domestic surveillance, U.S. officials initially declined to comment. This denial was quickly negated by a new revelation that President Obama had been briefed on NSA spying on Merkel in 2010. Later, when it emerged that NSA operated a world leader surveillance program, the argument was made that Obama had only been informed of its scope in the summer and that most of the briefings based on it dealt with high threat items and not issues involving allies. Even this did not hold, as officials within the intelligence community, who now felt they were being made scapegoats, let it be known that the State Department and White House had signed off on the clandestine monitoring of phone calls of friendly leaders. Closure of sorts was brought to this controversy when DNI Clapper publicly stated that the NSA had kept senior officials informed of its secret overseas intelligence program and that the White House had long been aware of its broad outlines, but he stopped short of indicating that Obama had been told.

The administration's denial that Obama knew about the program forced NSA's supporters into the position of negating the impression that it was an out-of-control rogue organization. On grounds that the problems encountered were administrative in nature, the NSA put forward two sets of reforms. One imposed a two-man rule on system administrators such as Snowden, making it more difficult for them to gain unauthorized access to information. The second reduced the number of system administrators by 90 percent.

In addition to justifying the level of accountability over the NSA domestic surveillance program, supporters also employed highly symbolic language to keep attention on Snowden and away from the surveillance program. These symbols were directed at calling into question Snowden's character. Speaker of the House John Boehner (R-OH) identified him as a "traitor." Almost a month later, Senator Diane Feinstein (D-CA), the SSCI chair, repeated the charge, saying of Snowden's leaking of secret NSA documents: "I think it is an act of treason."

Later, as President Obama was preparing to announce his reform proposals, two HPSCI supporters of the NSA program released (with White House approval) portions of a classified DIA study highly critical of Snowden's actions. The Government Accountability Project (GAO), which serves as an advocacy organization for whistleblowers observed that this effort had the effect of shifting the spotlight from the dissent to the dissenter, "when what truly matters is the disclosure itself."[51]

A second line of symbolic rhetoric employed by NSA supporters to turn away any formal congressional consideration of reforms to the surveillance program was to invoke the danger of terrorist attacks and to stress the value of the metadata programs to U.S. national security. The NSA Director, Gen. Keith Alexander, argued that the programs had helped thwart dozens of potential attacks—a claim later rejected by SSCI and HPSCI members. FBI Director Robert Mueller indicated that a larger version of the program might have helped prevent the Boston Marathon attack. In 2013, Gen. Alexander and Rep. Peter King (R-NY) argued that the NSA programs would have prevented the 9/11 attacks, had they been in existence at the time. Critics challenged these assertions, claiming that no evidence had been produced to show how the NSA programs had played a major role in stopping terrorism. Defenders eventually cited as evidence of the program's success a 2009 plot to attack the New York Stock Exchange and the conviction of four Somali immigrants in San Diego of conspiring to support terrorism.

Increasingly, the Obama administration was now seen as struggling to gain control over the continuing revelations. President Obama held his first press conference in three months on August 9, 2013. He announced his intention to create a panel of outsiders to examine and assess the NSA program. He also outlined a series of reforms he would pursue. Numbered among them were working with Congress to establish an adversarial voice in FISC proceedings who would advocate privacy rights, and tightening the rules by which the NSA obtained access to the phone records of American citizens.

Resource games were an important, although often unreported, dimension to the question of how to deal with the NSA surveillance program. When such concerns did surface, it was often in the form of arguments that no alternative existed to the data collection program, or as DNI Alexander put it, one needed to have a haystack in order to find a needle.[52]

Haystacks are expensive and profitable. At the center of the rapid expansion of the post-9/11 intelligence community were private contractors who provided ready access to the information technology skills needed to conduct intelligence collection in a digital age. While originally seen as a surge capability, they have become a permanent fixture: 70 percent of the intelligence budget ($56 billion out of $80 billion) now goes to private contractors. An ODNI study concluded that 56 percent of private contractors provided unique skills that could not be found in-house. Snowden was one of some 1,000 system administrators working as contractors for NSA. BAH, for whom Snowden worked, is one such contractor. Of its 25,000 employees, 75 percent hold security clearances and 50 percent hold top secret clearances.

Links between private contractors and the intelligence community have come to resemble those existing between the military and defense contractors, leading some to speak of an industrial-intelligence complex. For example, Obama's DNI, James Clapper, is a former BAH executive. Mike McConnell, who served as President Bill Clinton's NSA director, left to work for BAH, later served as George W. Bush's DNI, and then returned to work for BAH. A six-month, five-company contract with NSA for a program known as "Trailblazer," designed to gather, sort, and analyze web traffic, was originally for $280 million. When the project was cancelled in 2006 because it failed to perform successfully, the cost had reached into the billions of dollars. In another case, a computer systems contract awarded to BAH by the Department of Homeland Security for $2 million escalated to $124 million. BAH continued to receive extensions on this contract because it was determined the intelligence community did not have the in-house capacity to carry out the assignment.[53]

Yet another resource game occurred in the political struggle over how to respond to the revelations over NSA domestic surveillance. This one involved the distribution of political resources, not economic ones. According to the statute that established the FISC, its judges were appointed solely and entirely by the chief justice of the Supreme Court. Critics argued this power was excessive and had resulted in a set of like-minded judges. Just days before Obama presented his reform proposals, Judge John Bates, whom Chief Justice John Roberts Jr. had appointed to present the position of the judicial branch on these reform proposals, warned that implementing many of them—including taking away Roberts's power—would have a negative impact on the FIS Court.

In December, President Obama's review group issued its report, *Liberty and Security in a Changing World*.[54] It concluded that the NSA surveillance program was legal but also presented 46 recommendations for how it might be changed. This report sent the political struggle over how to respond to Snowden's leaks into its final phase. On January 17, 2014, the president presented his reform agenda.[55] It steered a middle ground, trying to reassure the American public that their civil liberties were not being violated, but at the same time trying not to alienate NSA supporters.

Obama indicated that, in the future, the phone records contained in the data base would no longer be under the control of the NSA but would be maintained by a third party. He established a task force to report in late March of 2014 on how this should be accomplished. The NSA would now need to obtain permission for each query from the FISC. The data base would also be restricted as to what phone numbers could be accessed. Obama indicated that Congress would also be asked to establish a panel of public advocates to argue before the FISC on behalf of civil liberties and privacy when "novel issues of law" came before it. Additional restrictions on spying on American allies would be put in place as well.

There was also much that Obama did not say. He did not announce the end of NSA's bulk data collection program, only that it would end "as it currently exists."[56] His call for changes in how bulk data was collected and managed included a caveat that permitted NSA access in "case of a true emergency." He did not advocate changing how justices were appointed to the FIS Court. No independent advocate for civil liberties was created to argue before the court on a regular basis. Obama also failed to call for a halt in the NSA's efforts to subvert commercial efforts aimed at strengthening encryption policies.

Conclusion

A persistent and fundamental temptation exists in studies of intelligence to present this policy arena as one in which politics is absent and professional expertise governs decision making. As the case studies presented here illustrate, this is far from the case. Professional expertise is influential in deciding intelligence policy, but the dynamics of Washington politics also play an important role in making intelligence policy. Closer inspection reveals that four reoccurring patterns to politics can be found in intelligence policy: symbolic, resource, agenda, and accountability politics. These political games or contests are not self-contained. Activity in one feeds on and is influenced by the politics in the others; that is to say, the politics of agenda setting interacts with the politics of accountability. Moreover, the broader policy questions in which they operate, such as domestic surveillance, are linked together over time. Only by looking at intelligence policy as a stream of activity in which politics is ever present is it possible to gain a full understanding of how intelligence policy is formulated.

Notes

1. For a CIA statement describing the intelligence cycle, see http://www.odci.gov/cia/publications/facttell/intelligence_cycle.html.

2. Murray Edelman, *The Symbolic Uses of Politics* (Urbana: University of Illinois Press, 1964).

3. Michael Howard, "What's in a Name? How to Fight Terrorism," *Foreign Affairs* 81 (2002), pp. 8–13.

4. *Weekly Compilation of Presidential Documents* (June 21, 2002). From 2002 Presidential Documents online via GPO Access, http://www.gpo.gov/nara/nara003.html.

5. *Weekly Compilation of Presidential Documents* (December 17, 2004), from 2004 Presidential Documents online via GPO Access, http://www.gpo.gov/nara/nara003.html.

6. Office of the Director of National Intelligence, *The National Intelligence Strategy of the United States: Transformation through Integration and Innovation* (October 2005), Washington, DC.

7. http://www.Washingtonpost.com (January 28, 2004).

8. Katherin Shrader, "WMD Commission Releases Scathing Report," *Washington Post* (March 31, 2005), p. A1.

9. Lawrence Freedman, "The Politics of Warning: Terrorism and Risk Communication," *Intelligence and National Security* 20 (2005), pp. 379–418.

10. Shlomo Gazit, "Estimates and Fortunetelling in Intelligence Work," *International Security* 4 (1980), pp. 36–56.

11. See Dan Eggen, "Memo Not Specific Enough, Bush Says," *Washington Post* (April 12, 2004), p. A1.

12. Jack Davis, *Improving CIA Analytical Performance: Strategic Warning* (Washington, DC: Sherman Kent Center for Intelligence Analysis, Occasional Papers 1:1, Central Intelligence Agency, September 2002).

13. Charles Babington, "Hill Wary of Intelligence Oversight Changes," *Washington Post* (September 12, 2004), p. A5.

14. For a historical perspective on such politics, see Amy Zegart, *Flawed by Design: The Evolution of the CIA, JCS, and NSC* (Stanford, CA: Stanford University Press, 1999).

15. Walter Pincus, "Lesser Intelligence Role Seen for Security Dept.," *Washington Post* (July 18, 2002), p. A6.

16. Ibid.

17. Michael Turner, "Intelligence Reform and the Politics of Entrenchment," *International Journal of Intelligence and Counterintelligence* 18 (2005), pp. 383–397.

18. Dan Eggen and Dafna Linzer, "9/11 Commission Offers Critiques on Many Fronts," *Washington Post* (July 22, 2004), p. A1.

19. Helen Fessenden, "The Limits of Intelligence Reform," *Foreign Affairs* 84 (2005), p. 110.

20. Walter Pincus, "FBI, CIA Proposal to Retool Called 'Business as Usual,'" *Washington Post* (April 15, 2005), p. A6.

21. Dafna Linzer and Walter Pincus, "CIA Rejects Discipline for 9/11 Failures," *Washington Post* (October 6, 2005), p. A1.

22. Quoted in David Ignatius, "Danger Point in Spy Reform," *Washington Post* (October 21, 2005), p. A3.

23. Dana Priest, "Wrongful Imprisonment: Anatomy of a CIA Mistake," *Washington Post* (December 4, 2005), p. A1.

24. Robert D. Blackwill and Jack Davis, "A Policymaker's Perspective on Intelligence Analysis," in Loch K. Johnson and James Wirtz (eds.), *Strategic Intelligence: Windows into a Secret World* (Los Angeles: Roxbury, 2004), p. 122.

25. Lawrence Freedman, "War in Iraq: Selling the Threat," *Survival* 46 (2004), p. 38.

26. Jack Davis, *Strategic Warning: If Surprise Is Inevitable, What Role for Analysis?* (Washington, D.C.: Sherman Kent Center for Intelligence Analysis, Occasional Papers 2:1, Central Intelligence Agency, January 2003).

27. James Fallows, "Blind into Baghdad," *Atlantic Monthly* 293 (January/February 2004), pp. 52ff.

28. Richard Clarke, *Against All Enemies* (New York: Free Press, 2004).

29. Anonymous [Michael Scheuer], *Imperial Hubris* (Washington, DC: Brassey's, 2004).

30. The "slam dunk" remark is from Bob Woodward, *Plan of Attack* (New York: Simon & Schuster, 2004), p. 249; the "weak" remark from Walter Pincus, "Prewar Findings Worried Analysts," *Washington Post* (May 22, 2005), p. A1.

31. Glenn Hastedt, "Public Intelligence: Leaks as Policy Instruments—The Case of the Iraq War," *Intelligence and National Security* 20 (2005), pp. 419–439.

32. James Simon Jr., "Managing Domestic, Military, and Foreign Policy Requirements: Correcting Frankenstein's Blunder," in Jennifer Sims and Burton Gerber (eds.), *Transforming U.S. Intelligence* (Washington, DC: Georgetown University Press, 2005), p. 154.

33. Lawrence Freedman, "War in Iraq: Selling the Threat," *Survival* 42 (Summer 2004), p. 26.

34. Robert Dreyfuss, "The Yes-Man," *American Prospect* 16 (November 2005), pp. 18–24.

35. On congressional oversight see L. Britt Snider, "Congressional Oversight of Intelligence After September 11," in Jennifer Sims and Burton Gerber (eds.), *Transforming U.S. Intelligence* (Washington, DC: Georgetown University Press, 2005), pp. 239–258; and Loch K. Johnson, "Governing in the Absence of Angels: On the Practice of Intelligence Accountability in the United States," in Hans Born, Loch K. Johnson, and Ian Leigh (eds.), *Who's Watching the Spies?* (Washington, DC: Potomac Books, 2005), pp. 57–78.

36. This and the other quotations in this paragraph are from Charles Babington, "Hill Wary," p. A5.

37. David Johnston and Carl Hulse, "C.I.A. Asks Criminal Inquiry Over Secret Prison Article," *New York Times* (November 9, 2005), p. A18.

38. James Risen and Eric Lichtblau, "Bush Lets U.S. Spy on Callers Without Courts," *New York Times* (December 16, 2005), p. A1.

39. Eric Lichtblau and James Risen, "Spy Agency Mined Vast Data Trove, Officials Report," *New York Times* (December 24, 2005), p. A1.

40. Michael Hirsh, "The NSA's Overt Problem: So Many Conversations, So Few Clues to the Terrorist's Chatter," *Washington Post* (January 1, 2006), p. B1.

41. Dan Beltz and Claudia Deane, "Differing Views on Terrorism," *Washington Post* (January 11, 2006), p. A4.

42. Lisa Rein, "Bush Defends Spying Program as Necessary to Protect U.S.," *Washington Post* (January 2, 2006), p. A2.

43. Barton Gellman and Dafna Linzer, "Pushing the Limits of Wartime Powers," *Washington Post* (December 18, 2005), p. A1.

44. See "Legal Authorities Supporting the Activities of the National Security Agency Described by the President," *Department of Justice* (January 19, 2006).

45. Walter Pincus and Dan Eggen, "325,000 Names on Terrorism List," *Washington Post* (February 15, 2006), p. A1.

46. Suzzane Spaulding, "Power Play," *Washington Post* (December 25, 2005), p. B1.

47. Charles Babington and Dafna Linzer, "Senator Sounded Alarm," *Washington Post* (December 20, 2005), p. A10.

48. Dafna Linzer, "Secret Surveillance May Have Occurred Before Authorization," *Washington Post* (January 4, 2006), p. A3.

49. Quoted in Hirsh, "The NSA's Overt Problem."

50. Administration White Paper, *Bulk Collection of Telephony Metadata under Section 215 of the USA Patriot Act*, White House (August 9, 2013).

51. "GAP Statement on Edward Snowden and NSA Domestic Surveillance." Government Accountability Project, January 3, 2014. http://www.whistleblower.org/press/press-release-archive/2013/3125-gap-statement-on-edward-snowden-and-nsa-domestic-surveillance. Accessed January 4, 2014.

52. Charlie Savage and Michael Shear, "President Moves to Ease Worries on Surveillance," *New York Times* (August 10, 2013) p. 1.

53. Data for this section comes from Michael Scherer, "The Geeks Who Leak," *Time* (June 24, 2013) pp. 22–29.

54. *Liberty and Security in a Changing World,* President's Review Group on Intelligence and Communications Technologies. 2013. http://www.whitehouse.gov/sites/default/files/docs/2013-12-12_rg_final_report.pdf

55. "Transcript of President Obama's January 17 Speech on NSA Reforms."

56. http://www.washingtonpost.com/politics/full-text-of-president-obamas-jan-17-speech-on-nsa-reforms/2014/01/17/fa33590a-7f8c-11e3-9556-4a4bf7bcbd84_story.html Accessed January 18, 2014.

CHAPTER TWENTY

Prometheus Embattled

A Post-9/11 Report Card on the National Security Agency

Matthew M. Aid

THERE IS NO QUESTION THAT THE NATIONAL SECURITY AGENCY (NSA) is today one of the most important components of the U.S. intelligence community, if not the most important and powerful intelligence agency in the United States. Before September 11, 2001, the 32,000-strong NSA was struggling to reform and modernize itself with mixed success. Today, the Agency's manpower is rapidly climbing past 35,000 people, and its budget has reached about $11 billion. Its power, however, is not derived from its massive size and budget. Rather, it stems from the fact that the Agency produces the majority of the actionable intelligence coming out of the U.S. intelligence community today. Prior to the 9/11 disaster, approximately 60 percent of the intelligence information contained in the Top Secret Codeword *President's Daily Brief* (PDB) sent to the president of the United States every morning was based on signals intelligence (SIGINT) coming out of the NSA. Today, this number is even higher, as the NSA's access to global telecommunications has expanded dramatically in the five years since the 9/11 tragedy.[1] The NSA's standing with the White House and the Pentagon has been helped by the fact that the Central Intelligence Agency (CIA), formerly the NSA's chief competitor within the U.S. intelligence community, has been in a state of freefall since 9/11, with senior intelligence officials describing the current state of the Agency as being one of "chaos and disintegration."[2]

The slow but steady rise of the NSA to the top of the U.S. intelligence community can be traced back to the end of World War II in 1945, and the subsequent shift within the U.S. intelligence community to monitoring America's new principal global protagonist, the Soviet Union. Most of the NSA's accomplishments during the 40-year-long Cold War, of which there were many, remain classified; but two decades of research by the author indicates that, during the Cold War, the NSA and its foreign SIGINT partners provided more reliable intelligence on the Soviet Union and its allies than the rest of the U.S. intelligence community combined, with perhaps the exception of the spy satellites of the National Reconnaissance Office.[3]

And yet, despite its many accomplishments during the Cold War, it is now clear that the NSA, like the rest of the U.S. intelligence community, lost its way in the decade after the fall of the Berlin Wall and the collapse of the U.S.S.R. in 1991. The 10-year period from 1991 to 2001 inside the NSA was marked by declining fiscal and manpower resources, poor internal management, and a pervasive bureaucratic inertia that effectively stifled demands for change both from within and outside the Agency. Between 1991 and 1996, the NSA lost one-third of its staff, and its budget was slashed by 35 percent from $5.2 billion to less than $3.5 billion.[4] We now know that these cuts, especially the loss of so many of the Agency's most talented managers, had a devastating impact on the NSA's ability to perform its mission. According to a declassified congressional study: "One of the side effects of NSA's downsizing, outsourcing and transformation has been the loss of critical program management expertise, systems engineering, and requirements definition skills."[5] The NSA's inspector general, Joel F. Brenner, has written that the 1990s for the NSA was "a decade of underfunding and, in the view of some critics, indifferent management" that left the Agency "behind the curve" in terms of staying abreast of the dramatic changes then taking place in the global telecommunications infrastructure."[6] By the end of the 1990s, the Agency found itself swamped by millions of intercepted radio messages, telephone calls, and email messages, as well as millions of terabytes of digital data traffic, such as bank money transfer messages, which NSA overworked analysts just could not keep up with, much less digest.[7] The NSA also failed to adequately address itself to the rapid proliferation of new intelligence targets that it was required to confront in the post–Cold War era, such as international terrorism, narcotics trafficking, global economics and trade issues, and the proliferation of weapons of mass destruction (WMD) technology around the world. This was coupled with the inability on the part of senior Agency officials to come to grips with the dramatically changing nature of the global telecommunications infrastructure. The NSA's intelligence production declined precipitously during the 1990s, and the Agency's customers inside the U.S. government became increasingly unhappy with both the quantity and quality of the NSA's intelligence output. All in all, the NSA was in trouble and desperately needed someone to shake things up and bring much-needed change to an Agency that historically had resisted attempts at reform.[8]

General Hayden's Modernization and Reformation Effort

On February 23, 1999, the Pentagon announced that the new director of the NSA was to be U.S. Air Force Maj. Gen. Michael V. Hayden, who was finishing a tour of duty in Seoul, South Korea, as the deputy chief of staff of the United Nations Command and U.S. Forces in Korea. Gen. Hayden, age 52, was a veteran intelligence officer who had previously held a number of high-level intelligence and policy positions, including commanding the Air Intelligence Agency from January 1996 to September 1997. He had also previously served as the director of Defense Policy and Arms Control in the National Security Council (NSC) from September 1989 to July 1991.[9]

As noted above, Gen. Hayden inherited a deeply troubled organization. James R. Taylor, the deputy director for Operations, told Hayden a month after he took office: "We have good people [working] in a flawed system."[10] After considering all of his options, in October 2000 Gen. Hayden publicly unveiled an ambitious plan to completely reform and modernize the Agency.[11]

The price tag for Gen. Hayden's modernization programs was staggering, even by Washington standards. In 2000, NSA planners put a price tag of a whopping $12 billion on the full range of modernization options then being proposed. A review of the program reduced the price tag to $8 billion by the end of 2001, but everyone at the NSA knew that there was no way that Congress would approve this figure, even in the post-9/11 era. By mid-2002, the NSA had reduced the modernization price tag down to approximately $5 billion, with the costs of the program spread out over a 10-year period.[12]

Gen. Hayden moved quickly to implement the outlines of his modernization program. Dramatic changes took place at the NSA before the October 2000 reform plan had to be altered because of the tragic terrorist attacks on New York and Washington on September 11, 2001. Gen. Hayden completely restructured the NSA's senior management staff, fired or transferred a number of senior managers who opposed his reform plans, and cut the number of management committees involved in high-level policymaking down to just one. Gen. Hayden brought in a number of senior managers from the business world to help him reshape the Agency's management practices.

In February 2001, there was a dramatic reorganization of the internal operating structure of the NSA, which put "front-end" operations in the hands of just two organizations: the Signals Intelligence Directorate and the Information Assurance Directorate. All other nonoperational supporting functions were transferred to the director's office.[13] Hayden also immediately ordered a reduction in the size of the NSA's bloated workforce. In November 1999, the NSA cut its civilian personnel by 7.5 percent from 18,945 to 16,753 people, and the following year reduced the size of the Agency's military staff by 10 percent. The NSA also deactivated a number of older SIGINT collection sites, consolidated the Agency's plethora of mission support activities, worked more closely with outside commercial companies to develop new equipment and software for use by the NSA, ceased virtually all of its research and development work on obsolete SIGINT collection and processing systems, and overhauled and realigned its strategic funding relationships with its SIGINT partners at home and abroad.[14]

But critics inside and outside the Agency in interviews have described these changes as "superficial" or "window dressing." The critics noted that the reorganization of the NSA's internal structure did not result in greater efficiency or efficaciousness, especially within the Agency's senior management. There are now at the NSA 100 "super-grade" senior civilian managers trying to run an organization the size of an army corps, which the U.S. Army can run with eight to ten generals. The result, critics contend, is that the NSA's management structure remains bloated and top-heavy. More important, perhaps, a number of Agency insiders believe that Hayden's organizational changes did not resolve the central issue of dealing with the NSA's hide-bound bureaucracy. A recently retired NSA official quipped, "He's just shuffled the cards rather than getting a new pack."[15]

There is also considerable evidence that Gen. Hayden failed in his attempt to reform the Agency's faulty fiscal management practices. NSA insiders believe that the approach of the NSA's senior management in the 1999–2001 time period was to get the money from Congress "while the going was good" and then build a modernization package around the money they got, rather than the other way around. This inevitably led to serious clashes between the NSA and the congressional oversight committees. In October 2001, the Senate Armed Services Committee indicated that it intended to "put the brakes" on further spending on the NSA's modernization programs until the NSA "adopt[ed] a more comprehensive acquisition strategy." A committee report stated the "NSA appears to have made only modest progress in the area most important to its future: acquiring the technical ability to operate effectively against the emerging global effort." The Senate report also expressed concern that the "NSA is spending large sums of money on hundreds of in-house development activities, yet it cannot say how or whether these aid modernization." The committee concluded that "more money now, without further reform, will not succeed either."[16] Finally, in July 2003, a clearly frustrated Congress stripped the NSA of its ability to sign contracts with outside businesses, and in the process, transferred control of the NSA's hundreds of millions of dollars of modernization contracts to the Department of Defense to administer until the Agency proved that it could manage these programs in a fiscally responsible manner.[17]

The NSA has also experienced considerable difficulty since 2000 in hiring and retaining sufficient numbers of the technologically oriented engineering and computer science personnel that it needs in order to develop, operate, and maintain the new high-tech SIGINT collection and processing systems that are beginning to come online. In particular, the NSA has had significant trouble recruiting personnel with advanced technology degrees to work at Fort Meade, including systems engineers, software engineers, and program managers versed in computer hardware and software issues.[18] A current serving NSA manager stated the problem simply: "We can't afford to pay these kids anywhere near the amount of money they could get in private industry, much less offer them a decent benefits package or the stock options they would normally receive working for any decent high-tech company in California."[19]

Moreover, intelligence production at the NSA remained relatively flat in the two years after Gen. Hayden became director, with the quantity of intelligence reporting actually declining in some key areas as money was diverted to finance research and development work on new high-tech SIGINT collection and processing systems. Available SIGINT collection and analytic resources were gradually shifted away from older "legacy" targets, such as Russia, the former Soviet republics, Cuba, and the Balkans, to new higher priority global intelligence targets, such as international terrorism and nuclear proliferation. Gen. Hayden was forced to admit to a congressional committee looking into the 9/11 intelligence disaster that he felt "handcuffed" in that he was unable to "churn some $200 million into new age signals . . . because we were going to erode our coverage of [other intelligence issues] as part of this effort."[20]

More recently, reports have appeared in the press revealing that not everything has gone according to plan with Gen. Hayden's much ballyhooed multiyear, multi-billion-dollar NSA transformation and modernization effort. Two recent articles in the *Baltimore Sun* have revealed that the two key components of the NSA's modernization program, designated Groundbreaker and Trailblazer, as well as many of their supporting systems, are years behind schedule and hundreds of millions of dollars over budget.[21]

Both projects began relatively well. Initiated with much public fanfare in 1999, Project Groundbreaker was a 10-year, $2 billion program to completely rebuild and modernize the NSA's nightmarish internal information technology (IT) infrastructure.[22] One of the many problems the program was supposed to fix was to remedy the fact that the NSA had 68 different email systems, none of which could communicate with each other. This led Gen. Hayden to comment that it took "an act of God" for him to send an email to all of his employees.[23]

But the centerpiece of Gen. Hayden's modernization effort was a massive overhaul of the NSA's deeply troubled SIGINT collection and processing infrastructure. In January 2000, NSA Deputy Director for Operations Richard Taylor proposed a massive reorganization of the NSA's huge Operations Directorate that was designed to refocus the organization on its core mission, SIGINT collection, processing, analysis, and reporting. In addition to putting "our customers squarely front and center in our production process," Taylor proposed reorganizing the Operations Directorate into three functional SIGINT organizations: Collection, Exploitation, and Production; as well as the creation of an Advanced Analytic Techniques organization to "develop and spread the art of analysis." Taylor's proposal also called for removing from the directorate all nonmission functions, such as information technology, policy, budget, and logistics, as well as integrating more military support functions into all of the directorate's functional groups.[24]

The result of Taylor's proposal was the initiation of a highly ambitious program called Project Trailblazer. In January 2000, the NSA announced the initiation of the first phase of its SIGINT processing, analysis, and reporting modernization effort, called Project Trailblazer. According to an internal NSA document, the first phase of Trailblazer was supposed to "deliver tomorrow's analytic tools and functions to automate desktop processing and improve COMINT [communications intelligence] production. It will also provide us with the ability to profile customers' needs and requirements, and will modernize the dissemination process."[25] The classified objective of the Trailblazer program was to build an integrated series of state-of-the-art SIGINT collection and processing systems that would give the NSA the ability to eavesdrop on communications traffic being carried by email, fiber-optic cable, and cellular telephone systems around the world.[26]

The core focus of the first phase of Trailblazer was to design and build a system to attack the new global SIGINT target environment, which the NSA designated Digital Network Intelligence (DNI). The NSA defined DNI as "the intelligence from intercepted digital data communications transmitted between, or resident on, networked computers."[27] Trailblazer was to form the foundation for this attack by mapping "detailed Digital Network Exploitation (DNE) mission requirements to our cryptologic architecture and provide implementation focus. . . . Trailblazer 1 will build the SIGINT system we would want to build—if today's system didn't exist—to attack a tough, evolving DNE target." Among the different technologies being developed under Trailblazer were selection and filtering tools for NSA analysts, as well as hardware and software for "improved front-end access, collection, processing, and filtering" using web-based tools and techniques, a process that has become known within the NSA by the moniker "e-SIGINT."[28]

By October 2002, developmental work on the Trailblazer system was sufficiently advanced that the NSA awarded a contractor team headed by San Diego-based Science Applications International Corporation a $282 million contract to build a functional prototype of the system in only 26 months. But this was the last the public heard about the system for the next three years, which in retrospect should have been a red flag that things were not progressing as well as they should.[29]

As is usually the case, the warning signs of problems with these two multibillion-dollar programs were there for all to see. As early as 2000, NSA officials complained both publicly and privately that the Agency's reorganization and modernization plans were developed and constructed within segregated "stovepipes" rather than in an integrated and cohesive fashion. The Agency also suffered from an all-too-apparent lack of competent program management, which impaired its ability to effectively manage the various multi-billion-dollar modernization programs.[30] This problem was exacerbated by heavy turnover amongst senior management personnel, which resulted in a failure to reform the Agency's much-maligned contracting practices. As a result, today senior Pentagon and congressional officials are currently concerned that these programs, and related modernization efforts at the NSA, have not been well managed and may not yield the desired results when finally completed.[31]

The NSA in the Post–9/11 Era

Declassified documents, congressional reports, and the published record of the 9/11 Commission all indicate that the NSA did not commit any egregious errors in the days and months leading up to the attacks. A congressional investigative report concluded: "Prior to 11 September 2001, NSA had no specific information indicating the date, time, place, or participants in an attack on the United States."[32] There have, however, been recurring indications received from both retired and current U.S. intelligence officials that substantive problems with the Agency's performance prior to 9/11 have not yet been completely revealed because it involves highly classified information concerning the NSA's "sources and methods."[33]

Like the rest of the U.S. intelligence community, the searing events of 9/11 have dramatically changed the NSA, both for better and for worse. The Agency's budget has been dramatically increased every year since 2001, climbing to about $5 billion per annum.[34] NSA manpower has also been shooting upward at a 45-degree angle, with the NSA hiring 3,500 new civilian staff between 2002 and 2004 alone, which raised NSA manpower to about 35,000 military and civilian personnel. Press reports and interviews indicate the NSA intends to hire 12,000 additional civilian personnel between 2004 and 2011, bringing NSA manpower up to more than 40,000 military and civilian personnel by the end of the decade, after retirements and normal personnel attrition are factored in.[35] Moreover, the size of the entire U.S. Cryptologic System, including SIGINT personnel assigned to the CIA, the National Reconnaissance Office, and the military services, has grown to more than 60,000 military and civilian personnel since 9/11, making it by far the single largest component of the U.S. intelligence community. The NSA is in the process of opening new operations centers in San Antonio, Texas, Denver, Colorado, and Salt Lake City, Utah, which when completed will employ several thousand civilian and military staff.[36] In February 2006, Congress passed an emergency supplemental appropriations bill, which included $35 million to immediately expand the NSA's huge listening post at Menwith Hill in northern England, as well as another $700 million to construct new operational facilities at the Agency's large intelligence collection stations at Kunia, Hawaii, and Fort Gordon, Georgia.[37]

But despite the massive budget increases and unfettered operational discretion granted to the Agency since 9/11, the NSA still is not functioning as smoothly or efficiently as it should be. Senior U.S. intelligence officials believe that one of the signature results of the chaos produced by

9/11 is that the NSA, in its rush to respond to the Al Qaeda terrorist attacks on the United States, literally threw away its previous management reform plans. Critics of the Agency within the U.S. intelligence community point to the fact that since 9/11, the size of the NSA's multilayered bureaucracy has once again begun to mount, with a resulting decrease in operational efficiency caused by the retrenchment of stifling bureaucratic practices and procedures at the top levels of the Agency's management. The NSA has also been hurt by the loss of a number of veteran senior officials, who have either retired or quit the Agency in the past two years to take higher-paying jobs in the business world.[38] The result, according to the officials, is that in the years since 9/11, the NSA's relative effectiveness and efficiency have declined noticeably. In fact, interviews with senior intelligence officials suggest that the NSA's operational performance has declined somewhat in recent years, with officials pointing in particular to the Agency's disappointing performance to date in Afghanistan and Iraq, which is described in greater detail below.[39]

There is also evidence that NSA attempts to balance its spending between maintaining current SIGINT collection operations and at the same time developing new signals collection technologies for the 21st century have not gone well. In some instances since 2001, NSA SIGINT operations have suffered for lack of investment because available fiscal resources were being directed toward research and development on new technologies needed to allow the NSA to intercept and process signals in the new digital environment. But as noted above, the NSA's Groundbreaker and Trailblazer multi-billion-dollar modernization programs have not been effectively managed. Former NSA officials point to the fact that immediately after 9/11, the Agency abandoned a patient, long-term approach to modernization in favor of dubious, short-term "quick-fixes" that have only compounded the host of existing problems with the NSA's various multi-billion-dollar modernization programs.[40] Compounding these internal problems are the massive technological hurdles that the NSA has had to leap through over the past five years trying to develop and build the new high-tech equipment it needs to do its job. Much of the technology that the NSA desperately needs, such as powerful analytic software that is required to help NSA analysts sift through the immense amounts of data being intercepted every day by the Agency's listening posts, just does not exist today on the open market, which has meant that the NSA has had to spend hundreds of millions of dollars developing these systems in-house, and not always successfully.[41]

Moreover, the NSA was forced to make significant changes in its intelligence targeting in order to devote a substantial portion of its intelligence collection resources to the so-called global war on terrorism. This has forced the NSA to give short shrift to many previously important intelligence targets, such as the former Soviet Union, China, North Korea, Bosnia, and the national narcotics interdiction program. The same thing has happened in England. The British Parliament's Intelligence and Security Committee in its June 2003 annual report warned that the shift of precious intelligence collection resources from other targets to counterterrorism was creating a dangerous situation, stating: "These reductions are causing intelligence gaps to develop, which may mean over time unacceptable risks will arise in terms of safeguarding national security and in the prevention and detecting of Serious Organized Crime."[42] Sources note that the NSA's inability to dedicate sufficient resources to monitoring narcotics trafficking in the western hemisphere has forced the Drug Enforcement Administration (DEA)'s small SIGINT organization to largely take over this responsibility.[43] The increasingly important role of the DEA, the CIA, and the military services in the SIGINT field has led, in turn, to the diminishment of NSA control over the national SIGINT effort. The result has been that the NSA has lost somewhat the all-important "centrality of command" that it once enjoyed over the national SIGINT effort.

Interviews with intelligence officials in Washington suggest that the NSA has improved somewhat its customer relations with its consumers in Washington and elsewhere around the globe since 9/11. But apparently not everyone is happy. NSA officials contend that over the past five years, its ever-increasing number of customers in Washington have submitted conflicting requirements on the NSA, which has required years of oftentimes contentious negotiations in order to resolve the differing requirements levied on the agency. Interviews with intelligence officials reveal that there are still widespread complaints about the NSA's inability or unwillingness to share information with other government agencies. In particular, FBI officials complain about the lack of cooperation that they have received from the NSA since 9/11. The single largest barrier to the free flow of intelligence information appears to be the compartmentalized nature of the NSA itself, which has prevented an integrated approach to customer relations between the NSA and the rest of the U.S. intelligence community.[44]

The New Global Battlefield

The NSA found that its ability to effectively contribute to the global counterterrorism fight and concurrently support U.S. military forces in Afghanistan, which the United States invaded in November 2001, were hampered by the fact that it was not equipped to deal with unconventional intelligence targets operating in the less-developed countries of the world who typically do not use, much less own, computers connected to the Internet, cell phones, personal pagers, and digital assistants, such as the ubiquitous Blackberry, or even an iPod. One recent press report perhaps said it best that SIGINT today "is far less vital against an enemy that sleeps in caves and cellars, and communicates in whispers."[45] Moreover, the NSA's ability to collect SIGINT in Afghanistan was an extremely difficult proposition given the almost complete lack of linguists at the Agency who could speak the languages spoken in the country.[46] As of fall 2001, the NSA reportedly only had four linguists fluent in the languages spoken in Afghanistan (Pashto, Dari, Uzbek, and Turkmen), including only one who spoke Pashto, the primary language spoken in Pakistan and Afghanistan.[47]

In other words, the Agency's heavy investment in its multi-billion-dollar high-tech modernization efforts of the late 1990s, although badly needed, sadly may have left the NSA prepared to fight the "wrong war" in the 21st century. In fall 2001, chagrined U.S. intelligence officials discovered that the NSA's newly developed high-tech collection systems, which were designed to cover cellular telephones, the Internet, and communications traffic carried on fiber-optic cables, were largely worthless in the low-tech environment of Afghanistan and in northern Pakistan, where the remaining elements of Al Qaeda and their Taliban supporters operated.[48]

The NSA's underwhelming performance on the battlefield led to numerous complaints from the U.S. military services about the Agency's inability to provide adequate tactical SIGINT support to American military commanders in Afghanistan and to Special Operations Forces engaged in trying to hunt down terrorists in Pakistan and elsewhere around the world. Prior to 9/11, the U.S. Army had denuded its tactical SIGINT collection resources to practically nothing in the mistaken belief that such units were no longer needed in the post–Cold War geostrategic environment. The NSA's failure led the military services, especially the U.S. Army, to allocate over the past five years greater resources to building up their own dedicated tactical SIGINT collection resources that are largely independent of the NSA. As a result, U.S. Army SIGINT assets have now replaced the NSA in Afghanistan.

Over the past three years, U.S. military SIGINT assets in Afghanistan have been gradually reconfigured in order to work more efficiently in the extremely difficult Afghan environment, and more mobile and flexible SIGINT collection and processing systems have been added in recent years.[49] On the plus side of the equation, SIGINT has confirmed that former Taliban commanders based in the tribal areas of northern Pakistan have been orchestrating insurgent attacks against Afghan forces in southern and southeastern Afghanistan using satellite phones.[50] SIGINT has also been used effectively to counter Taliban rocket and mortar fire against U.S. military bases in southern and southeastern Afghanistan. By intercepting the walkie-talkie communications traffic of insurgent artillery spotters, forces have on more than one occasion been able to successfully destroy insurgent rocket and mortar pieces inside Afghanistan, and have forced insurgent forces instead to occasionally fire at outlying U.S. outposts and patrols along the Afghan–Pakistani border without the benefit of spotters inside Afghanistan.[51]

But problems continue to abound in the military's SIGINT collection programs in Afghanistan. Inhibiting the effectiveness of SIGINT in Afghanistan is the fact that the insurgent forces based in northern Pakistan have increasingly moved to the use of couriers and other noninterceptible means of communications rather than radio communications.[52] In addition, persistent shortages of trained linguists have severely hampered the effectiveness of SIGINT in Afghanistan. Since 9/11, the U.S. military has trained at great expense a small number of U.S.-born linguists in the Pashto, Dari, and Urdu dialects to process SIGINT intercepts. But reports from the field indicate that the competency levels of these linguists were so low that they only possessed "the ability to tell the difference between a burro and a burrito."[53] This has meant that the U.S. military today still largely relies on contract employees hired by the Department of Defense to provide U.S. intelligence units and combat units with linguistic capabilities in Urdu, Dari, and Pashto. But according to a 2003 U.S. Army report: "This develops into a big problem, because, not only do you have to have fluent linguists, but you also have to obtain one that can comprehend military terms and operations. . . . Laugh if you will, but many of the linguists with which I conversed were convenience store workers and cab drivers, most over the age of 40. None had any previous military experience."[54] Among the contract linguists hired on an emergency basis for the Department of Defense by Titan Systems Corp., a San Diego-based defense contractor, were a partner in a San Diego pharmaceuticals company, a software engineer from Texas, and an accountant from northern Virginia, who 20 years earlier had been a commander in the anti-Soviet *mujahedeen* forces.[55]

In addition, the NSA's accomplishments against international terrorist targets have slowed dramatically in recent years after a string of early successes immediately after 9/11. SIGINT's last notable success in the war on terror took place in February 2003, when intercepted emails and satellite telephone communications led U.S. and Pakistani security officials to the hideout in the Pakistani city of Rawalpindi of 9/11 mastermind Khalid Shaikh Mohammed. At 4:00 a.m. on March 1, 2003, heavily armed Pakistani security forces burst into Mohammed's hideout and arrested him and another key Al Qaeda operative, Mohammed Ahmed al-Hawsawi, while they slept.[56] But since 2003, SIGINT's successes against international terrorist targets have become fewer and further between as the surviving members of Al Qaeda and allied terrorist groups have learned not to trust electronic communications for communicating with each other. Spying on terrorist organizations is inherently difficult, and the same holds true for SIGINT. Testifying before Congress in 2002, NSA Director Gen. Michael Hayden admitted that "cracking into these targets is hard—very hard—and SIGINT operations require considerable patience—sometimes over years—before they mature."[57]

SIGINT and the War in Iraq

Reviews by both the House and Senate Intelligence Committees in 2004, followed by the Commission on the Capabilities of the United States Regarding Weapons of Mass Destruction (the Robb-Silberman Commission) in 2005, were all highly critical of the NSA's performance in the events leading up to the U.S. invasion of Iraq in March 2003. The NSA fared better than the CIA and the rest of the U.S. intelligence community in these investigations, but only because so much of the criticism of the Agency's performance was withheld from the public versions of these reports because of classification concerns.[58]

What was made public in these reports clearly shows that NSA SIGINT coverage of Iraq prior to the U.S. invasion in March 2003 was poor, especially on the question of whether Iraq was indeed pursuing weapons of mass destruction (WMD) programs. The reason for the NSA's poor performance was that virtually all high-level Iraqi government and military communications traffic was carried by buried fiber-optic cables and thus impervious to NSA radio interceptors. Then on March 18, 2003, only a few days before the invasion began, the Iraqi government switched off all telephone service across Iraq, and the use of satellite and mobile phones was banned by the Iraqi Ministry of the Interior. This closed off the last low-level source of SIGINT then available to the NSA about what was going on inside Iraq.[59]

These factors led a postwar review panel to conclude that for NSA SIGINT collectors, "changes in telecommunications technology have brought new challenges. This was the case in Iraq, where the Intelligence Community lost access to important aspects of Iraqi communications."[60]

As a result, the panel concluded that insofar as helping the U.S. intelligence community assess the nature and extent of the alleged Iraqi nuclear, chemical, and biological programs, SIGINT "on the whole was not useful."[61] For example, the panel concluded that "Signals Intelligence collection against Iraq's chemical activities was minimal, and much was of questionable value."[62]

What makes these revelations about the NSA's performance so disturbing was the fact that the U.S. government, in attempting to sell its vision of the danger posed by Saddam Hussein's Iraq in Secretary of State Colin Powell's presentation to the UN Security Council on February 5, 2003, depended to a very high degree on evidence obtained from SIGINT provided by the NSA. Powell used three communications intercepts during his February 5, 2003, presentation to the UN Security Council, which unfortunately did not provide tangible "smoking gun" proof for the Bush administration's case that Iraq possessed forbidden weapons of mass destruction.

Adding fuel to concern about the NSA's poor performance in Iraq were the revelations in the press that the NSA had been used by the Bush administration to intensively monitor the communications traffic of those countries or international bodies who opposed the Bush administration's Iraq policies. In January 2003, two months before the U.S.-led invasion of Iraq began, the NSA and GCHQ mounted an intensive effort to monitor the communications traffic of the foreign representatives to the UN Security Council, especially those members of the Security Council who publicly had expressed misgivings about the U.S. government's intentions to invade Iraq. This information was leaked to the press in early March 2003 by a GCHQ employee, who as a consequence was fired from her job.[63] The NSA was also tasked with monitoring the telephone calls and email communications of Mohamed El Baradei, the head of the United Nation's International Atomic Energy Agency (IAEA), because of the White House's intense dislike of his agency's policies with regard to Iraq, which oftentimes ran counter to what Washington wanted.[64]

Since the invasion of Iraq, NSA performance has been described as being disappointing by senior military commanders who have served there. Military and intelligence officials have confirmed that SIGINT has not been as helpful as it was hoped it would be in tracking down members of the insurgency movement in Iraq. Despite this fact, SIGINT is still the number one source of actionable intelligence on insurgent activities.

Sources confirm that SIGINT has been extremely useful in monitoring the activities of the Iranian and Syrian governments in Iraq. This effort, however, was badly hurt in 2004 by the compromise of these SIGINT efforts by Ahmed Chalabi.[65] Among the major complaints heard from many military officials returning from Iraq is that the NSA has emphasized SIGINT collection coverage against Iraq's neighbors, Iran and Syria, as well as the internal machinations of the Washington-backed Iraqi government. But SIGINT has not proven to be a meaningful or viable tool for helping root out Iraqi insurgents, who continue to bedevil U.S. and UN Coalition forces in Iraq despite the best efforts of the U.S. intelligence community.

The NSA Domestic Eavesdropping Scandal

The NSA currently finds itself at the center of a politically explosive domestic spying scandal that may very well have serious negative consequences for the Agency and the U.S. intelligence community as a whole. In December 2005, the *New York Times* revealed the outlines of the secret NSA eavesdropping program, the purpose of which was to locate Al Qaeda terrorist cells believed to be operating in the United States without referring the matter to the super-secret Foreign Intelligence Surveillance Activity Court for approval.[66]

The controversy over the legality and propriety of this still highly classified program rages on, exacerbated by the fact that neither the House nor the Senate Intelligence Committee has shown much inclination to examine the legal underpinnings of the program, much less ascertain the details of just how the program has been conducted.[67]

The controversy has proven to be particularly embarrassing to the NSA because former NSA director Lt. Gen. Michael V. Hayden told the House Intelligence Committee in April 2000 in no uncertain terms that the Agency did not engage in spying on U.S. citizens, describing this recurring area of concern an "urban myth." He assured the Committee that the NSA would assiduously abide by the legal strictures on such activities as contained in the 1978 Foreign Intelligence Surveillance Act (FISA).[68] In a March 2005 report to President George W. Bush on the U.S. intelligence community's performance against the Iraqi WMD programs, the NSA reported that FISA "ha[d] not posed a serious obstacle to effective intelligence gathering." It should be noted that at the time the NSA made this statement to the review panel, the Agency's secret domestic eavesdropping program, which deliberately bypassed the FISA Court, had been ongoing for almost three and a half years.[69] Since the *New York Times* broke the story of the NSA domestic eavesdropping program in December 2005, Gen. Hayden has become the Bush administration's most prominent defender of the legality and probity of the increasingly controversial program, while at the same time declaring publicly that the NSA had strictly abided by the terms of the law barring government spying on Americans. As he stated in a speech at the National Press Club in January 2006: "I've taken an oath to protect and defend the Constitution of the United States. I would never violate that Constitution, nor would I abuse the rights of the American people."[70]

As with all previous scandals involving the NSA, there were portents of what the NSA was up to. In April 2005, a political controversy erupted in Washington when it was learned that the Bush administration's nominee to be the ambassador to the United Nations, John R. Bolton, had requested from the NSA transcripts of intercepted conversations involving or pertaining to other U.S. government officials. The NSA admitted that it made copies of these transcripts, including the names of the American officials involved, available to Mr. Bolton.[71] A few weeks later, *Newsweek* revealed that since January 2004, the NSA had received between 3,000 and 3,500 requests for transcripts of intercepted communications involving American citizens from various U.S. government departments, 400 of which came from the State Department. The NSA had complied with all of these requests. The report indicated that the names of as many as 10,000 Americans were contained in the transcripts of the intercepts turned over to the various U.S. government agencies who had requested them.[72] It was later learned that Bolton personally had originated 10 requests since January 2004 for unredacted NSA intercept transcripts that mentioned the names of U.S. government officials or American citizens.[73]

Since the first article about the domestic eavesdropping program appeared in the *New York Times* in December 2005, further information about the nature and extent of the NSA domestic surveillance program has been slow in coming, but what has been revealed to date suggests that the program may have been far larger and more pervasive than initially indicated in the first press reports. In April 2006, an AT&T technician revealed that the telecommunications giant he worked for had allowed the NSA to place eavesdropping equipment inside its network switching centers in San Francisco and Atlanta, through which much of America and the world's email traffic passes. This may, in fact, be the tip of the iceberg, because a number of key American telecommunications companies other than AT&T have plaintively refused to answer questions from reporters about whether they too cooperated with the NSA's domestic eavesdropping effort.[74] These reports, taken together, all clearly indicated that the NSA had crossed the Rubicon and was engaged in doing something that it had not done since the days of Henry Kissinger in the late 1960s—give Bush administration officials intelligence products involving intercepted conversations involving U.S. citizens. Unfortunately, the Bush administration refused to turn over to Congress any details concerning these NSA operations, and Mr. Bolton was subsequently confirmed as the U.S. ambassador to the United Nations.

The fear among recently retired and active-serving NSA officers is that the Agency's domestic eavesdropping program, in addition to generating much unwanted negative publicity for the Agency, almost certainly diverted much-needed manpower and fiscal resources from the NSA's foreign intelligence gathering mission to what the Agency officers generally believe to have been a poorly considered and legally questionable domestic monitoring operation that apparently has produced little in the way of tangible results, despite claims to the contrary from the White House. The program has also only served to further exacerbate the NSA's already poor relations with the FBI, which for reasons passing easy comprehension was deliberately excluded from participation in the domestic eavesdropping program by the White House.

The Sum of All Its Parts

Today, the NSA remains a conundrum. It is by far the largest and most powerful intelligence agency within the U.S. intelligence community. It is today the principal intelligence collector for the entire U.S. intelligence community, accounting for the majority of the highest-level intelligence information going to the president of the United States.

And yet, like the community of which it is an integral part, it remains deeply troubled by a host of problems, many of its own making. NSA intelligence production, while rising in absolute numbers, has been declining in real terms in key areas, such as its ability to find insurgents in Afghanistan and Iraq. Gen. Hayden's internal reform measures at the NSA were left unfinished, in part because all reform measures were largely abandoned after 9/11. All of the NSA's major technical modernization programs are hundreds of millions of dollars over budget and years behind schedule. It has been left to Gen. Hayden's successor at the helm of the NSA, Lt. Gen. Keith Alexander, to try to put the NSA's various internal reform and modernization programs back on track while at the same time increase its productivity and good standing within the U.S. intelligence community.

Edward J. Snowden and NSA's Time of Troubles

Nothing terrifies us more than the unknown. That's what scares us so much about the NSA because so much about what the agency does and how it does it remains hidden behind a thick cloak of secrecy, much of it unnecessarily.

What we have learned about NSA's activities since the first news articles based on materials leaked to the press by former NSA contractor Edward J. Snowden began to appear in June 2013 have, whether deserved or not, only served to highlight and intensify these innate fears because the revelations have reminded us just how little we really know about what NSA does and how it does it.

No Longer Your Grandfather's Eavesdropping Agency

NSA today is a radically different organization than the somewhat bedraggled and dispirited spy agency that existed almost 13 years ago on the eve of the 9/11 terrorist attacks.

NSA has spent more than $40 billion of U.S. taxpayer money since 9/11 completely re-engineering and reorienting itself from the ground up. Leaked documents reveal that over the past nine years, NSA's manpower strength has risen from about 30,000 military and civilian personnel in 2004 to almost 35,000 today; and its budget has surged from approximately $7.0 billion in 2004 to $10.7 billion in 2013, which does not include the more than $4.0 billion being spent on SIGINT by other U.S. intelligence agencies, like the CIA and FBI, or the estimated $2.5 billion being spent on tactical SIGINT collection by the U.S. military.

The personnel makeup of the agency is completely different than what existed on 9/11, as most of the remaining Cold War era veterans have retired and been replaced by younger, more tech-centric men and women. NSA has hired more than 10,000 new employees, including thousands of mathematicians, computer scientists, software programmers, electronic engineers, and linguists; completely upgraded its formerly antiquated information technology (IT) infrastructure; and modernized the agency's SIGINT collection capabilities by buying billions of dollars of newly developed high-tech spy gear, data storage systems, processing equipment, and high-speed computer systems.

Reversal of Fortune

But most importantly, NSA has completely reversed its fortunes as an intelligence producer. Back on 9/11, NSA was the butt of jokes amongst Washington insiders. Many in the U.S. intelligence community and Congress, including senior NSA officials, believed that NSA was rapidly going deaf, dumb, and blind because the agency had fallen so far behind the technology curve after the end of the Cold War. Things were so bad that NSA's deputy director for operations in the late 1990s, James R. "Rich" Taylor, admitted in a secret interview with the 9/11 Commission that "NSA was a shambles."

But sources confirm that NSA is once again producing the best intelligence information available to the entire U.S. intelligence community, or at least it was before the first press reports based on leaked Snowden materials began appearing in the press. Today, there are a lot of question marks about how much damage to NSA's SIGINT collection capabilities have resulted from the articles that have appeared in the press over the past nine months.

Since 9/11, NSA has completely revamped the way that it collects intelligence information on overseas targets. It has largely scrapped its pre-9/11 dependence on radio intercept and brute-force supercomputer-based cryptanalysis, and re-engineered itself into a largely cyber-centric intelligence-gathering organization that now focuses primarily on foreign targets that now use the Internet to communicate.

NSA Now Lives on the Internet

If there is a signature development that has taken place at NSA since the 9/11 terrorist attacks, it is that the agency's newfound ability to intercept and exploit en masse email and other forms of electronic communications that use the Internet as their platform has changed, probably forever, the way NSA performs its SIGINT mission.

The advent of the Internet has proven to be the proverbial goose that laid the golden egg for NSA. National and transnational targets that NSA could not gain access to two decades ago, the agency can now relatively easily intercept because Internet-based communications media, such as emails and text messaging systems, are much easier to access than the old radio-based communications systems the agency use to depend on for its life blood.

So not surprisingly, since 9/11 the Internet has become the backbone of NSA's SIGINT collection efforts. Over the past nine months, we have learned that every minute of every day of the year, NSA's vast array of computers sweep the entire global Internet using almost exactly the same search and sweep techniques as Google, collecting vast amounts of both metadata and content on Internet communications around the world. The amount of metadata and message content that NSA collects off the Internet is nothing short of staggering. In an unclassified White Paper released on August 9, 2013, NSA revealed that it collects only 1.6 percent of the 1,826

Petabytes of traffic currently being carried by the Internet. To give one a sense of how much raw data this is, the entire Library of Congress collection, the largest in the world, holds an estimated 10 Terabytes of data, which is the equivalent of 0.009765625 Petabytes. In other words, NSA collects just from intercepted Internet traffic the equivalent of the entire textual collection of the Library of Congress 2,990 times every day. Of this amount, according to NSA, only 0.025 percent of the intercepted Internet material is selected for review by the agency's analysts. On paper this sounds reasonably manageable until you realize that the amount of material in question is the equivalent of 119 times the size of the entire Library of Congress collection that has to be sorted through every day.

We have also learned over the past nine months that getting at the vast and ever-growing volume of communications traffic being carried on the Internet is, from a technical standpoint, a relatively easy proposition for NSA. The majority of the world's Internet traffic transits through the U.S. via 32 fiber optic cable landing points or terminals in the U.S.—twenty on the east coast of the U.S. and twelve on the west coast. According to the consulting firm Telegeography in Washington, D.C., 56 different global fiber optic cable systems carrying Internet traffic to and from Europe, Asia, the Middle East, Africa, Latin America, and the Caribbean are connected to these 32 cable landing points.

NSA's ability to gain access to the Internet traffic carried on these fiber optic cables is made possible largely thanks to the agency's intimate relations with the three largest American telecommunications companies—AT&T, Verizon and Sprint. For the past 13 years NSA has had near-complete access to the roughly 80 percent of the world's Internet traffic that transits through the gateways, routers, or computer servers in the U.S. that are owned by these companies. In return for access to this traffic, NSA gives these three companies substantial amounts of cash—$278 million in 2013 alone. Leaked documents also show that NSA can access Internet communications traffic being carried by certain major British, Canadian, Australian, and New Zealand telecommunications companies, all of whom receive substantial cash payments ($56 million) from NSA in return for their cooperation and their silence.

Since September 2007, NSA has been able to expand and enhance its coverage of global Internet communications traffic through a program called PRISM, which uses court orders issued by the FISA Court that allow NSA to access emails and other communications traffic held by nine American companies: Microsoft, Google, Yahoo!, Facebook, PalTalk, YouTube, Skype, AOL, and Apple. Thanks to PRISM, for the past six years

NSA has been exploiting a plethora of communications systems besides emails that use the Internet as their platform, such as voice over Internet protocol (VoIP) systems like Skype, instant messaging and text messaging systems, social networking sites, and web chat rooms and forums.

The importance of the Internet as an intelligence source for NSA cannot be underestimated. National and transnational targets that the agency could not gain access to two decades ago, the agency can now readily monitor because the governments of virtually every developed nation in the world has shifted a large portion of their most sensitive political, military, and economic communications from encrypted radio systems to what they thought were secure web-based data transmission and communications systems. It turns out that in the past 13 years, NSA's engineers and computer scientists have discovered a number of somewhat ingenious methods of not only gaining access to this traffic, but exploiting en masse this huge volume of data. And the same thing is occurring within dozens of countries in the developing world, opening up a wide range of new collection options for the ever-opportunistic SIGINT collection managers at NSA.

The Dawn of NSA's Computer Hackers

Another somewhat surprising revelation stemming from the leaked Snowden documents is the fact that NSA uses a wide array of extremely sensitive non-cryptanalytic sources and methods to solve foreign government or commercial encryption systems, including computer hacking, interdiction of computer and computer security technologies, covert relationships with American and foreign manufacturers of computer security devices and software systems, and collaborative relationships with many other agencies comprising the U.S. intelligence community.

But by far the single most important resource available to NSA's cryptanalysts to facilitate the solution of foreign cipher systems, according to a recently retired U.S. intelligence official, are the computer hackers of NSA's cyber espionage unit, the Office of Tailored Access Operations (TAO). With NSA, these cyber espionage operations are not referred to as computer hacking, but rather as Computer Network Exploitation (CNE).

TAO's highly classified cyber espionage program, referred to in leaked documents by the codename GENIE, is conducted by a 1,600-person SIGINT collection unit at NSA headquarters at Fort Meade, Maryland, called the Office of Tailored Access Operations (TAO), whose 2013 budget amounts to more than $651 million.

Since TAO was created during the Clinton administration in the late 1990s, leaked documents indicate that the unit's hackers have managed to successfully penetrate tens of thousands of computers outside the U.S., including many in high priority countries like Russia, China, Iran, Syria, and Pakistan, to name but a few. The CIA has its own cyber espionage unit called the Office of Information Operations, whose budget is even larger than TAO's ($673 million) and whose operations include cyber-attack missions designed to cripple or destroy foreign computer networks.

NSA's substantial investment in the TAO computer hacking organization has paid robust dividends over the past 13 years. Over the past 12 years, TAO has been enormously successful in covertly inserting highly sophisticated spyware systems called "implants" into the hard drives of over 80,000 computer systems around the world which, according to sources, cannot be detected by currently available commercial computer security software. It has been suggested to me by a reliable source that "this is not an accident," with the insinuation being that many of the biggest commercially available computer security software systems made in the U.S. and overseas have been compromised by NSA, either covertly or with the knowledge and consent of the companies that manufacture these systems.

Former agency personnel confirm that the TAO implants have allowed NSA's analysts to copy and read all of the unencrypted documents stored on the targeted computer's hard drive, as well as copy every document and email message produced by the machine. In addition, TAO has helped solve several hundred foreign government encryption systems because these spyware implants, if properly inserted into the computer's programming files, can covertly alter the computer's security software as well as copy the encryption system's technical parameters, especially the system's encryption algorithm and access passwords, in a way that cannot be detected. These implants can compromise the encryption systems used by not only the targeted computer, but also all other computer systems that it communicates with using encryption technology.

In some cases, TAO works with the computer hacking units of a small number of foreign SIGINT organizations, particularly GCHQ in Great Britain, to conduct what are referred to as joint computer network exploitation operations against foreign computer system targets. In return for their cooperation, NSA provides financial subsidies and computer hardware/software technology to help these foreign intelligence entities with their CNE efforts.

NSA's Revitalized Cryptanalytic Capabilities

Documents leaked to the press since June 2013 reveal that NSA's code breaking efforts have become not only far more sophisticated than was the case prior to 9/11, but also far more successful. The more than 1,500 cryptanalysts, mathematicians, scientists, engineers, and computer technicians who today comprise NSA's elite cryptanalytic unit, the Office of Cryptanalysis and Exploitation Services (S31), have engineered a remarkably large number of cryptanalytic successes against foreign targets in the 13 years since the 9/11 terrorist attacks.

Many of NSA's code breaking successes over the past decade have been the direct result of traditional cryptanalytic methods, which exploit inherent design flaws or vulnerabilities in information security devices or encryption systems. Among the encryption systems solved over the past 12 years using this method are the ciphers used by a number of governments in North Africa, the Middle East, the Near East, and South Asia.

This method depends to a large degree on NSA's huge stable of supercomputers to break foreign encryption systems using what is referred to as "brute force methods," that is, using the super computers to run every cipher permutation until the message or messages in question become readable. It is a long, tedious, and costly process (NSA spends over $247 million a year to buy and maintain its state-of-the-art supercomputer systems just for cryptanalytic purposes), but it does work if there are inherent vulnerabilities or structural weakness in the cipher system being attacked or if the system's users do not practice proper communications security procedures, such as changing passwords frequently.

Other NSA cryptanalytic successes include solving a number of commercially available encryption systems made overseas. According to a now retired NSA official, the agency's cryptanalysts have been aided by the fact that many foreign governments, such as Russia and China, insist that commercial encryption systems made by indigenous companies or used by foreign companies operating in their countries be sufficiently weak that they can be exploited by the host nation's code breaking services. It is ironic that these weaknesses have been ruthlessly exploited by NSA. Sources report that the agency is also reading thousands of emails and data transmissions that were encrypted with a wide variety of commercially available encryption systems like PGP. How NSA's cryptanalysts solved these supposedly unbreakable encryptions in the years since the 9/11 terrorist attacks is one of the agency's most closely guarded secrets.

Most of NSA's focus with regard to commercial encryption systems has been in the developing world, where a number of foreign governments as well as large international organizations have been regular users of commercial off-the-shelf systems to try to protect their sensitive political and military communications. The details of these cryptanalytic efforts remain highly classified, but the suggestion has been made that NSA has had some success solving these systems using traditional code breaking methods, or perhaps using more unconventional techniques, such as computer network exploitation (computer hacking) or perhaps even using CIA operatives to compromise these systems from the inside.

Taken together, leaked documents and interviews with U.S. intelligence officials confirm that prior to the release of the first new report in June 2013, based on materials leaked by Edward Snowden, NSA was producing high-grade intelligence information on a multitude of national and transnational targets at levels never before achieved in the agency's history. Recall that on average, well over 60 percent of the information contained in President Barack Obama's top secret daily intelligence report, the *President's Daily Brief* (PDB), was derived from data supplied by NSA.

NSA's Uncertain Future

Despite NSA's numerous noteworthy cryptologic successes over the past 13 years, the agency today is facing an uncertain future. There is no question that the agency's political standing in Washington has been severely compromised by the political controversy stemming from the publication of one revelatory article after another about the means by which NSA and its foreign allies have been gathering intelligence information both at home and abroad.

The controversy has had its victims. Battered by the revelations appearing in the press, NSA's civilian deputy director, Chris Inglis, stepped down from his post in January 2014 several months before he was due to retire. And his boss, NSA director Gen. Keith Alexander, is scheduled to retire this spring and be replaced by Navy Adm. Mike Rogers. And sources report that there may be some more high-ranking NSA officials choosing to take early retirement in the coming months. NSA officials whom I have interviewed over the past six months admit that morale amongst the agency's workforce has plummeted since June 2013. The number of agency employees taking early retirement or resigning outright has risen dramatically, and the number of people applying for jobs at NSA has dropped by over one-third.

But there are a host of other more dangerous threats, both political and legal, that are looming on the horizon, which could potentially have an even greater impact on NSA SIGINT mission:

- In January 2014, President Barack Obama proposed making some limited, but still important, changes in the way the agency operates and whom it can spy on. But NSA's critics on Capitol Hill and elsewhere have made it clear that they do not think that the president's proposed changes to NSA's *modus operandi* go far enough. It remains to be seen just how serious the White House is about implementing the proposed changes, especially since many senior U.S. government officials and members of Congress make no secret of the fact they would prefer no changes at all in the way NSA operates.

- There are a number of bills currently pending in Congress that seek to impose new legal restrictions on NSA operations, which if enacted into law, will have a significant impact on the agency's SIGINT collection capabilities. But given the proclivity of the so-called "Do Nothing Congress" not to act on weighty issues, one has to wonder just how serious the threat to NSA's ability to perform its mission really is from these various congressional NSA reform proposals.
- Some of America's largest high-tech companies, such as Google, Yahoo! and Facebook, have loudly demanded substantive changes in the way NSA operates, in large part because these companies have lost hundreds of millions of dollars in overseas sales based on newspaper reports about their cooperation with NSA. Company executives make no secret of the fact that they believe President Obama's January 2014 proposals to reform NSA do not go far enough, and have been assiduously lobbying on Capitol Hill for tougher legislation that will buffer them from NSA demands for their customers' information.
- A number of lawsuits that challenge the constitutionality of NSA's operations are currently working their way through the federal appellate court system and will almost certainly eventually end up on the docket of the U.S. Supreme Court for its consideration. Depending on how the Supreme Court rules on these cases, there could potentially be some very significant changes coming down the road that will no doubt impact NSA's SIGINT collection and processing capabilities.
- According to sources, there is no question that the NSA political controversy has taken a severe toll on the formerly intimate relationships between NSA and the White House. NSA officials have privately complained in recent months about what they perceive as the lack of support they have gotten from the White House, particularly from President Obama. Agency officials also admit that relations with the State Department have cooled considerably in recent months because of complaints from a host of world leaders, such as German chancellor Angela Merkel, about news reports detailing NSA's spying on their communications.

But the "X Factor" that may, more than anything else, determine NSA's future is the media, which over the past nine months have kept alive and driven forward the public debate here in the U.S. and overseas about the agency's activities with periodic articles revealing new and hitherto unknown aspects of NSA's SIGINT collection operations. Each new article, to one degree or another, has created a political furor here in the U.S. and abroad, adding strength to those calling for substantive NSA reform, while at the same time dashing the hopes of NSA's supporters inside the White House and on Capitol Hill that the entire political controversy surrounding the agency's activities would disappear from the national political discourse. Given the state of things, this seems unlikely to happen at any point in the near future.

Notes

1. NSA/CSS, *Transition 2001*, December 2000, p. 33. The author is grateful to Dr. Jeffrey T. Richelson for making a copy of this document available.

2. David Ignatius, "The CIA at Rock Bottom," *Washington Post* (May 7, 2006), p. B7.

3. A detailed examination of the NSA's Cold War accomplishments and failures against the Soviet Union can be found in Matthew M. Aid, "The National Security Agency and the Cold War," in Matthew M. Aid and Cees Wiebes (eds.), *Secrets of Signals Intelligence During the Cold War and Beyond* (London: Frank Cass, 2001), pp. 27–66.

4. Matthew M. Aid, "The Time of Troubles: The U.S. National Security Agency in the Twenty-First Century," *Intelligence and National Security* 15 (Autumn 2000), p. 6. See also Statement for the Record by Lt. Gen. Michael V. Hayden, USAF, Director NSA/CSS Before the Joint Inquiry of the Senate Select Committee on Intelligence and the House Permanent Select Committee on Intelligence, October 17, 2002, p. 6.

5. Senate Report No. 107-351 and House Report No. 107-792, Report of the U.S. Senate Select Committee and U.S. House Permanent Select Committee on Intelligence, *Joint Inquiry Into Intelligence Community Activities Before and After the Terrorist Attacks of September 11, 2001*, 107th Congress, 2nd Session, December 2002 (declassified and released in July 2003), p. 76.

6. Heritage Lecture #851, Joel F. Brenner, *Information Oversight: Practical Lessons from Foreign Intelligence*, September 30, 2004, the Heritage Foundation, available at http://www.heritage.org/Research/NationalSecurity/hl851.cfm.

7. Michael Hirsh, "The NSA's Overt Problem," *Washington Post* (January 1, 2006), p. B1.

8. This troubled period in the NSA's history is covered in detail in Matthew M. Aid, "The Time of Troubles: The U.S. National Security Agency in the Twenty-First Century," *Intelligence and National Security* 15 (Autumn 2000), pp. 1–32.

9. Vernon Loeb, "General Named to Head NSA," *Washington Post* (February 25, 1999), p. A21; "Agency Welcomes New Director Lieutenant General Michael V. Hay-den," *National Security Agency Newsletter* (May 1999), p. 4.

10. Memorandum, Taylor to DIRNSA, *Thoughts on Strategic Issues for the Institution*, (April 9, 1999), p. 2, NSA FOIA.

11. Richard Lardner, "NSA Chief Pushes Ahead With Overhaul of Agency's Culture, Operations," *Inside Defense* (October 16, 2000); Vernon Loeb, "NSA's

Chief Unveils Restructuring," *Washington Post* (October 17, 2000), p. A31; Laura Sullivan, "Chief of NSA Begins Reforms," *Baltimore Sun* (October 17, 2000).

12. Confidential interview.

13. Vernon Loeb, "NSA Reorganization," *Washington Post* (December 19, 2000), p. A37.

14. NSA/CSS, *Transition 2001* (December 2000), p. 19.

15. Confidential interview.

16. Frank Tiboni, "Bill Calls for Pentagon to Monitor Spy Shop's Spending," *Defense News* (October 1–7, 2001), p. 6.

17. Ariel Sabar, "Congress Curbs NSA's Power to Contract With Suppliers," *Baltimore Sun* (July 20, 2003), p. A1.

18. Thomas R. Temin, "Defense Coders Are Fading Away," *Government Computer News* (May 6, 2002).

19. Confidential interview.

20. Senate Report No. 107-351 and House Report No. 107-792, Report of the U.S. Senate Select Committee and U.S. House Permanent Select Committee on Intelligence, *Joint Inquiry Into Intelligence Community Activities Before and After the Terrorist Attacks of September 11, 2001,* 107th Congress, 2nd Session, December 2002 (declassified and released in July 2003), p. 381.

21. Siobhan Gorman, "System Error," *Baltimore Sun* (January 29, 2006), p. A1; Siobhan Gorman, "Computer Ills Hinder NSA," *Baltimore Sun* (February 26, 2006), p. A1.

22. DIRgram-31: "Fixing NSA's IT Infrastructure" (January 6, 2000), NSA FOIA.

23. Neil King Jr., "Big Technology Players Vie to Upgrade NSA Computers," *Wall Street Journal* (March 13, 2001).

24. DIRgram-42, "DO Realignment and Transformation" (January 24, 2000), NSA FOIA.

25. DIRgram-37: "Transformation Begins With TRAILBLAZER" (January 14, 2000), NSA FOIA.

26. Confidential interview.

27. NSA Scientific Advisory Board, Panel on Digital Network Intelligence (DNI), Report to Director, (June 28, 1999), p. 20/61. The author is grateful to Dr. Jeffrey T. Richelson for making a copy of this document available.

28. DIRgram-45: "TRAILBLAZER I—A Progress report" (February 3, 2000), NSA FOIA.

29. SAIC Press Release, *SAIC Team Wins National Security Agency TRAILBLAZER Contract,* (October 21, 2002); Frank Tiboni, "NSA to Boost Range of Cryptologic Capabilities; Earmarks $282 Million for Eavesdropping Network," *Defense News* (January 20, 2003).

30. Senate Report No. 107-351 and House Report No. 107-792, Report of the U.S. Senate Select Committee and U.S. House Permanent Select Committee on Intelligence, *Joint Inquiry Into Intelligence Community Activities Before and After the Terrorist Attacks of September 11, 2001,* 107th Congress, 2nd Session, December 2002 (declassified and released in July 2003), p. 76.

31. Confidential interviews.

32. Senate Report No. 107-351 and House Report No. 107-792, Report of the U.S. Senate Select Committee and U.S. House Permanent Select Committee on Intelligence, *Joint Inquiry Into Intelligence Community Activities Before and After the Terrorist Attacks of September 11, 2001*, 107th Congress, 2nd Session, December 2002 (declassified and released in July 2003), p. 374.

33. For an assessment of NSA's performance prior to 9/11, see Matthew M. Aid, "All Glory Is Fleeting: SIGINT and the Fight against International Terrorism," *Intelligence and National Security* 18 (Winter 2003), pp. 72–120.

34. Confidential interview.

35. Ariel Sabar, "Want to Be a Spy? NSA Is Hiring," *Baltimore Sun* (April 10, 2004); Stephen Barr, "NSA Makes No Secret of Stepped-Up Recruitment Effort," *Washington Post* (April 22, 2004), p. B2; "A Good Spy Is Hard to Fund," *U.S. News & World Report* (November 22, 2004).

36. Sheila Hotchkin, "NSA Will Let Its Dollars Do the Talking," *San Antonio Express-News* (April 16, 2005); Mike Soraghan and Aldo Svaldi, "NSA Moving Some Workers, Operations to Denver Area," *Denver Post* (January 24, 2006); Robert Gehrke, "Key Spy Agency Expands to Utah," *Salt Lake Tribune* (February 2, 2006); Amy Choate, "NSA Seeks Linguists at BYU to Staff Utah Center," *Deseret Morning News* (February 24, 2006).

37. "Emergency War Supplemental Hides Millions," *UPI* (February 20, 2006).

38. Confidential interview.

39. Confidential interviews.

40. Michael A. Wertheimer, "Crippling Innovation—and Intelligence," *Washington Post* (July 21, 2004), p. A19.

41. Joab Jackson, "NSA Seeks Better Analysis Technologies," *Washington Technology* (November 11, 2004), available at http://www.wtonline.com.

42. CM 5837, Intelligence and Security Committee, *Annual Report 2002–2003* (June 2003), p. 20.

43. Confidential interview.

44. Memorandum, Zenker to Joint Tactical SIGINT Architecture (JTSA) Working Group, *Quarterly Meeting Minutes—December 2001*, (December 31, 2001). This document has since been reclassified and removed from the Internet site where the author originally found it.

45. Robert Little, "NSA Methods Lag in Age of Terror," *Baltimore Sun* (December 9, 2004).

46. Senate Report No. 107-351 and House Report No. 107-792, Report of the U.S. Senate Select Committee and U.S. House Permanent Select Committee on Intelligence, *Joint Inquiry Into Intelligence Community Activities Before and After the Terrorist Attacks of September 11, 2001*, 107th Congress, 2nd Session, December 2002 (declassified and released in July 2003), p. 336.

47. Ian Bruce, "Mistake in Translation Almost Proves Deadly," *Scotland Herald* (April 24, 2002).

48. Confidential interviews.

49. John L. Girardeau, "TSM Notes—Changes in Tactical Signals Intelligence and Electronic Warfare Forces During Operation Enduring Freedom," *Military Intelligence Professional Bulletin* (October–December 2003).

50. Paul Haven, "Taliban Plans Attacks From Pakistan," *Associated Press* (September 23, 2003).

51. Department of the Army, Center for Army Lessons Learned (CALL), *Newsletter No. 03-27: Project OUTREACH: Tactics, Techniques, and Procedures* (October 2003), p. 19.

52. B. Raman, "Sons' Killings Change Little in Iraq," *Asia Times Online* (July 31, 2003), available at http://www.atimes.com/atimes/Middle_East/EG31Ak03 .html.

53. Department of the Army, Center for Army Lessons Learned (CALL), *Newsletter No. 03-27: Project OUTREACH: Tactics, Techniques, and Procedures* (October 2003), p. 12.

54. Department of the Army, Center for Army Lessons Learned (CALL), *Newsletter No. 03-27: Project OUTREACH: Tactics, Techniques, and Procedures* (October 2003), p. 12.

55. Greg Miller, "Shortage of Linguists Initially Hampered U.S. Intelligence Mission," *Los Angeles Times* (July 28, 2002).

56. Kevin Johnson and Jack Kelly, "Terror Arrest Triggers Mad Scrammble," *USA Today* (March 2, 2003); Rory McCarthy and Jason Burke, "Endgame in the Desert of Death for the World's Most Wanted Man," *Observer* (March 9, 2003); Kevin Whitelaw, "A Tightening Noose," *U.S. News & World Report* (March 17, 2003).

57. Senate Report No. 107-351 and House Report No. 107-792, Report of the U.S. Senate Select Committee and U.S. House Permanent Select Committee on Intelligence, *Joint Inquiry Into Intelligence Community Activities Before and After the Terrorist Attacks of September 11, 2001*, 107th Congress, 2nd Session, December 2002 (declassified and released in July 2003), p. 380.

58. All information concerning the NSA's performance in the Iraqi WMD scandal was deleted from the report of the Senate Intelligence Committee on the U.S. intelligence community's performance prior to the invasion of Iraq, for which see: U.S. Senate, Select Committee on Intelligence, *Report on the U.S. Intelligence Community's Prewar Intelligence Assessments on Iraq*, 108th Congress (July 7, 2004), pp. 264–265.

59. "Iraq Shuts Down Phone Network to Thwart CIA Eavesdropping," *Associated Press* (March 19, 2003).

60. The Commission on the Intelligence Capabilities of the United States Regarding Weapons of Mass Destruction, *Report to the President of the United States* (March 31, 2005), pp. 15, 163–164.

61. Ibid., p. 65.

62. Ibid., p. 130.

63. Martin Bright, Ed Vulliamy, and Peter Beaumont, "Revealed: U.S. Dirty Tricks to Win Vote on Iraq War," *Observer* (March 2, 2003), p. 1.

64. Dafna Linzer, "IAEA Leader's Phone Tapped," *Washington Post* (December 12, 2004), p. A1.

65. Rupert Cornwell, "Chalabi Falls from Grace as U.S. Spy Row Erupts," *Independent* (June 3, 2004), p. A1.

66. James Risen and Eric Lichtblau, "Bush Lets U.S. Spy on Callers without Courts," *New York Times* (December 16, 2005), p. A1; Eric Lichtblau and James Risen, "Eavesdropping Effort Began Soon after Sept. 11 Attacks," *New York Times* (December 18, 2005), p. A1.

67. See, for example, the heated words exchanged between Republican and Democratic members of the House Intelligence Committee about the NSA's domestic eavesdropping program contained in U.S. House of Representatives, Report 109-411, *Intelligence Authorization Act for Fiscal Year 2007*, 109th Congress, 2nd Session (April 6, 2006).

68. *Statement for the Record of NSA Director Lt. General Michael V. Hayden, USAF Before the House Permanent Select Committee on Intelligence* (April 12, 2000). General Hayden's "urban myth" comment is contained in Neil King Jr., "U.S. Security Agency Defends Eavesdrop Use," *Wall Street Journal* (April 13, 2000).

69. The Commission on the Intelligence Capabilities of the United States Regarding Weapons of Mass Destruction, *Report to the President of the United States* (March 31, 2005), p. 375.

70. Scott Shane and Mark Mazzetti, "Top C.I.A. Pick Has Credentials and Skeptics," *New York Times* (May 6, 2006), p. A1.

71. Douglas Jehl, "Senator Asks U.N. Nominee to Explain His Security Requests," *New York Times* (April 14, 2005), p. A1.

72. Mark Hosenball, "Periscope: Spying—Giving Out U.S. Names," *Newsweek* (May 2, 2005).

73. Katherine Shrader, "Bolton Requested 10 Names in Spy Reports," *Associated Press* (June 27, 2005).

74. John Markoff and Scott Shane, "Documents Show Link Between AT&T and Agency in Eavesdropping Case," *New York Times* (April 13, 2006), p. A1.

CHAPTER TWENTY-ONE

The British Experience with Intelligence Accountability

Mark Phythian

The Emergence of Oversight

The momentum for establishing some form of legislative accountability of British security and intelligence agencies arose in part from a string of revelations and allegations during the 1970s and 1980s. Key to these was the belief, widespread on the Left, that in guarding against domestic subversion, the Security Service (MI5) was monitoring and interfering with legitimate political dissent. Left-wing critics argued that MI5 saw its primary allegiance as being to the Crown rather than the elected government of the day. There were suspicions that this extended to undermining Labour governments, reinforced by the revelations contained in former MI5 officer Peter Wright's memoir *Spycatcher*. There were other dimensions to the damage done to the reputation of the security and intelligence services during this period. The public exposure in November 1979 of Sir Anthony Blunt, surveyor of the Queen's Pictures and pillar of the establishment, as a former Soviet spy was quickly followed by the Prime and Bettaney espionage cases, all of which provided fertile ground for Wright's claim that former MI5 Director-General Sir Roger Hollis had been a Soviet spy. By the time of Paul Foot's 1989 book, *Who Framed Colin Wallace?*—at its core an account of the "cowboy" era of military intelligence in Northern Ireland in the early 1970s—it seemed that there was a reservoir of security and intelligence intrigue and scandal that was in no danger of running dry.

Notwithstanding this reservoir of intrigue and scandal, the most pressing impetus to act from the British government's perspective (although it did not concede this at the time) arose from the impact of European law on the British polity, in particular the European Convention of Human Rights (ECHR). Having fallen foul of this in 1984, the government enacted the Interception of Communications Act the following year. When former MI5 officer Cathy Massiter revealed that future Labour government Ministers Harriet Harman and Patricia Hewitt had been placed under surveillance as a consequence of working for the National Council for Civil Liberties, at that time classed by MI5 as a subversive organization, they prepared to take their case to the ECHR. The prospect of further adverse rulings led to the 1989 Security Service Act.

This established MI5 on a legal footing. It created a commissioner, "a person who holds or has held high judicial office," who would review the Home Secretary's exercise of his powers in signing warrants allowing for interference with private property and produce an annual report for the prime minister, who would lay it before Parliament after removing any material considered "prejudicial to the continued discharge of the functions of the Service." The Act also created a three-member tribunal to investigate complaints about MI5 from the public which, like the commissioner, had access to MI5 records and personnel. The tribunal would (in conjunction with the commissioner where allegations of property interference were involved) establish whether MI5 had conducted investigations into a complainant and, if so, establish whether the grounds for doing so were reasonable. If the tribunal found against MI5, it could order that any records relating to the complainant be destroyed, further investigations ended, and compensation paid. Out of over 100 cases investigated by the tribunal in its first three years of operation, it did not find for the complainant in a single one. Nevertheless, the commissioner, in his 1992 annual report, suggested that the very existence of the tribunal had acted as a spur to MI5 adopting a more cautious approach to warrants and surveillance.

In mid-1992, Prime Minister John Major, then embarked on a wider "open government" drive, broke with tradition by admitting that MI6 actually existed and undertook to put it on a statutory footing. Briefings to journalists suggested that parliamentary scrutiny was unlikely to be a feature of this opening, but when the Intelligence Services Bill was unveiled in 1993, tacked on to the end was provision for a form of parliamentary scrutiny of MI5, the Secret Intelligence Service (MI6), and the Government Communications Headquarters (GCHQ).

This was to be achieved via the creation of a committee of six parliamentarians (increased to nine—the only alteration made to the draft bill), hand-picked by the prime minister, who would meet in closed session and produce annual reports for the prime minister, who would lay them before Parliament after removing material considered prejudicial to the activities of the agencies. Hence, it was accountable to the executive and only through the executive was it accountable to the legislature. This arrangement would be a continual source of debate. At the outset the Labour opposition argued for scrutiny by a parliamentary select committee rather than the proposed hybrid. As Jack Cunningham, leading for the opposition, put it:

> It is proposed that the committee should not report to Parliament but to the Prime Minister. I do not regard that as parliamentary scrutiny or oversight, because the Prime Minister has the right to veto sections of its report—I call it prime ministerial oversight and scrutiny. If we are to have an effective parliamentary watchdog to oversee such matters and to probe and scrutinise, it should report to Parliament. It cannot legitimately be called a parliamentary committee unless it does so.[1]

Future members of the Intelligence Security Committee (ISC) were among those who expressed concern over the proposed form of oversight. Labour MP John Gilbert called it "far more timid than necessary." The advantages to the government in this arrangement, it was argued, lay in controlling the timing of publication of the report, and that the proposed committee would not have the same powers as a select committee to send for persons and papers. As future ISC member Allan Rogers put it, "The committee will be a charade, a pretence at accountability."[2] In general, the opposition made it clear that while voting for the bill, they favored select committee status. It would be two years later, with the increasing likelihood that they would form the next government, before the Labour Party began to distance itself from its earlier enthusiasm for genuine parliamentary oversight.

In response to fears that the proposed committee would be toothless, government minister Willam Waldegrave closed the debate by emphasizing the power that it would possess:

> Somebody asked earlier where the teeth were. The teeth consist of the fact that the committee . . . will have the right not to publish stuff that would damage national security—which it would not want to do—but to write a report saying, "We believe that things are not being handled properly, and that Ministers are not responding properly." No Government . . . would want to risk such criticism.[3]

Nevertheless, the ISC would first of all have to discover that things were not being "handled properly," and there remained concerns about its ability to do so. The final Intelligence Services Act stated that the ISC's requests for information would not be met if that information was deemed "sensitive" (and "sensitive" was broadly defined) or because the Home or Foreign Secretary "determined that it shall not be disclosed." As with the 1989 Act, a commissioner and tribunal were created, with the separate tribunals later supplanted by a single tribunal under the terms of the Regulation of Investigatory Powers Act 2000, which was introduced to keep pace with advances in European law.

Embedding Oversight

The ISC's first chairman was former Conservative Secretary of State for Defense and Northern Ireland Tom King, and the committee featured a Conservative Party majority. Its first report was an 11-paragraph interim report published in May 1995, reporting that "In general terms, we have been encouraged by the openness of the intelligence 'insiders' that we have come into contact with thus far, and in particular by the helpful approach of the Heads of the Agencies themselves."[4] The report set out the ISC's approach: ". . . concentrate on major issues rather than, for example, be drawn into every individual intelligence item of current excitement—unless they are of such significance and relevance as to merit exceptional consideration and report to you." The framing of the Committee's interpretation of its mandate inevitably involved a tussle over the question of investigating allegations of past abuses. An attempt by Allan Rogers to raise the question of the agencies' relationship with Soviet defector Oleg Gordievsky, in the context of his contemporaneous allegation that former Labour Party leader Michael Foot was regarded by the KGB as an "agent of influence," were defeated inside the Committee, with Lord Howe echoing Douglas Hurd's earlier intervention and arguing that the ISC should not involve itself in "political archaeology." However, in the United States, Canada, and Australia, the question of past abuses or scandals was among the first to be investigated by newly formed oversight committees. Having decided that the past was another country and interpreted its mandate as involving broad, strategic policy questions, in its first years of operation, the ISC focused on the implications for the agencies of the changed post-Cold War environment. Its second report, nine paragraphs long, concerned the decision to move MI5 into the fight against organized crime. Its first annual report was completed in December 1995 and published in March 1996.

There is no doubting the industry of the individual committee members in getting to grips with their task, nor the learning curve they faced. This first annual report revealed what became a pattern of at least weekly meetings and visits to the agencies and abroad (although the agencies had always stressed the limited utility of overseas experiences with accountability, instead emphasizing the unique character of MI5 and MI6). On the basis of its early experiences, the ISC felt able to reassure the prime minister that it considered its structure appropriate to the task. However, it would not be long before it requested the addition of an investigative capacity to assist it in its work.

One fundamental early aim of the ISC was to establish the confidence of the agencies themselves. King would subsequently refer to the initial Australian experience with intelligence oversight, where what he called the "awkward squad" was selected to sit on the oversight body, and consequently enjoyed little cooperation from the agencies. The ISC sought to reassure the agencies that any information they shared with committee members would be handled securely. In return, the ISC was keen that the agencies:

> Understand our needs and are sufficiently frank and open with a new oversight body with whom they have previously not had to relate. These mutual concerns must be met if the Committee is to command the confidence of parliament and the public. This is an essential foundation for our work, particularly if we were at any time required to deal urgently with some specially sensitive or difficult issue.[5]

In comparing the U.S. intelligence agencies' legal obligation to keep their oversight committees informed of their activities with the UK agencies' much more limited legal obligation to respond to ISC requests for information, the report later observed that the ISC "does expect to be kept properly and promptly informed." How fully the ISC succeeded in this area over the following years is very much an open question. Nevertheless, it is worth noting that this expectation represented something of an attempted expansion of its role—the Act was silent here. Similarly, its first annual report adopted an expansive interpretation of its financial oversight remit, arguing that this extended to "the clear responsibility to ensure that the Agencies have access to adequate resources for the tasks they are asked to undertake,"[6] and not just how cost-effectively such resources were used.

The second annual report, for 1996, was completed in December 1996 and published in February 1997. This reported that the Committee had faced the first challenges to its decision to focus on major issues (rather than feel obliged to address each and every controversy that might arise) in allegations concerning Menwith Hill and, separately, the alleged surveillance of a meeting between MPs and members of Sinn Fein inside the Palace of Westminster. Having asked the agencies about these matters, "we received . . . categorical assurances, which we accept, that the stories were without foundation."[7] Having no wider investigatory capability, the Committee had little option but to do so.

The third annual report was completed at the end of July 1998, a full 19 months after the previous one, the intervening period disrupted by the election of a Labour government in 1997 and the subsequent reorganization of the ISC to reflect political retirements and the parliamentary dominance of the Labour Party. King remained as chair of the Committee, reflecting the desire of the Labour government to reassure the agencies that the party's 1983 election manifesto was long forgotten. This period would be the only one to date where the committee chair was drawn from an opposition party rather than a party of government. Also during this period, the ISC came to see itself as having more of a public education role, opening its third annual report with a lengthy overview of the recent history of the agencies and the evolving nature of the threats they countered. The Committee assured the prime minister, Parliament, and the public that these new challenges were "real enough" and not "invented to justify the Agencies' continued existence," as some critics had asserted, and moreover that "intelligence and security capabilities cannot be turned on and off like a tap. To meet their responsibilities, they must be maintained, and funded in a sustainable way."[8] To some extent, the ISC was becoming involved in advocacy on the agencies' behalf.

Having taken an interest in the agencies' internal procedures, the now Labour-dominated ISC returned to these in the wake of the August 1997 revelations of former MI5 officer David Shayler, soon to be joined by those of former MI6 officer Richard Tomlinson. Frustrated by what he saw as an antiquated approach to management in general and personnel issues in particular, Shayler had gone public when he failed to secure what he felt was a fair hearing of his grievances internally. Among his revelations, Shayler disclosed the names of a few people on whom MI5 kept personal files, extending to the man to whom they were accountable, Home Secretary Jack Straw, and including other Cabinet members, thereby reviving an issue of particular sensitivity on the Labour left. He also alleged that MI6 had been involved in a plot to assassinate Libyan leader Col. Qaddafi. The ISC responded by returning to the question of personnel policies, vetting, and internal security at relative length.[9] However, it refused to meet or take evidence from Shayler and showed no interest in investigating his allegations of an assassination plot.

The Shayler revelations did, however, lead to a renewed interest in the issue of MI5's files. In its 1997–1998 report, the ISC confirmed that MI5 held approximately 250,000 hard copy personal files, with an additional 40,000 held on microfiche, and they outlined the process of opening, storing, and classifying these files—the first time this had been done. Concerned at Shayler's ability as an MI5 officer to call up the files of any politician or celebrity that took his fancy, the ISC recommended that access should be restricted to those "with a clear need to see them" and be accompanied by a detailed audit trail indicating who had seen any file, when, and for what purpose.

From the vantage point of the late 1990s, of even greater concern than MI5's historic maintenance of such an extensive number of personal files was the question of the destruction of those files. The ISC was able to bring considerable light to bear on MI5's approach to file retention/destruction. It revealed that until 1970, MI5 had a policy of weeding and destroying files. However, this had affected its ability to pursue a number of espionage cases. Hence, the policy shifted from destruction to microfiching. However, the ISC revealed that in 1992, MI5 "reconsidered its files policy again in the light of the changing nature of the threat with the end of the Cold War and the decline in the threat from subversion." As a result, MI5 began reviewing and destroying personal files on a case-by-case basis, destroying and concealing aspects of its own history in the process. As ISC member Yvette Cooper argued:

I accept that only the Security Service can make the operational decision whether it still needs to retain a file and continue to use it, but, once the service has decided that it does not need it, there is an historical—not operational—decision to be made. History is not an operational decision. There is absolutely no reason why only the Security Service should be capable of deciding whether something has historical significance for the future. In fact, for the sake of the credibility of history, someone other than the Security Service should make that decision.

It is controversial stuff. We have all heard the allegations about the monitoring of so-called subversives in the 1970s and 1980s. For all I know, none of it may have happened. On the other hand, all sorts of outrageous things may have happened. The point is that future generations have a right to know what happened and how the organs of the state behaved. They have a right to be able to learn from that and to know that what they are looking at is the entire record. They need to be confident about that. For the sake of credibility, it should not be the Security Service that decides that. Future historians should never be able to say that the service was given a licence to write its own history.[10]

By the time the ISC investigated the issue, 110,000 files had either been destroyed or marked for destruction, the "vast majority" of which related to subversion. The ISC found that "Ultimately, the judgment in respect of the review and destruction of individual files is made solely by the Security Service," and recommended that "some form of independent check should be built into the process, particularly in respect of files relating to subversion."[11]

In sum, the 1997–1998 report suggested a more assertive ISC, possibly a consequence of having developed greater self-confidence, possibly a consequence of its changed composition, but most likely a combination of the two. Having initially reassured the prime minister and Parliament that its structure was well suited to its task, the ISC had by this point become aware of the fact that it had no investigatory capability of its own, and without this it could not "make authoritative statements on certain issues." Hence, it argued that an investigatory arm would "reinforce the authority of any findings that we make, and be an important element in establishing public confidence in the oversight system."[12]

Two innovations followed from this report: firstly the government began the practice of producing a published response; secondly, it granted an annual parliamentary debate on the reports. In its first Response, the government rejected the ISC's proposal that some form of independent check should be built into the process by which MI5 files were reviewed for destruction. It also asserted that access to files was already restricted and subject to audit arrangements, raising the question of why the ISC, assumed to have access to information on such processes, made the recommendation in the first place. It also seemed to resist the introduction of an investigative arm.

There are two further noteworthy dimensions to this governmental response. First, while the ISC was reporting to the prime minister on its oversight of the agencies, in formulating its response, the government was clearly working closely with the intelligence agencies in framing their joint rejection of certain of the ISC's proposals. In other words, the government had established the ISC to oversee the agencies but joined forces with the agencies to reject recommendations arising from this oversight. The response found in favor of the agencies and its continued information monopoly rather than in favor of greater openness and accountability. Second, the timing of the government's response was significant. One of the weaknesses of the ISC structure highlighted in the debates over the Intelligence Services Bill had been that the executive would dictate the timing of publication. Here, a report that was published after a 19-month gap had to wait a further three months for a government response and parliamentary debate. Hence, Parliament was unable to debate the 1997–1998 annual report until November 1998.

This first parliamentary debate on an ISC report served to highlight concerns about the ISC on the part of its own members and the House of Commons in general, for example, about the implication for select committees' ability to oversee matters that now fell under the remit of the ISC. Henceforth, the existence of the ISC could allow governments to refuse to disclose information to select committees or to otherwise co-operate with them on the basis that this was now the business of the ISC. Indeed, governments would do precisely this—most significantly over the highly sensitive question of intelligence and the case for war in Iraq.

The linked question of the desirability of a move toward select committee status was also addressed in the debate. Allan Rogers referred to the ISC's own "strong debates on the possible adoption of a Select Committee style for our proceedings." Fellow ISC member Dale Campbell-Savours did not

> . . . believe that oversight is fully credible while the Committee remains a creature of the Executive—and that is what it is. The problem at the moment is that the Committee considers its relationship with the Prime Minister more important to its operation than its relationship with Parliament. I strongly dissent from that view and find the arguments in favour of Select Committee status utterly overwhelming.[13]

One reason why a narrow majority of ISC members at this point came to believe that select committee status was unnecessary was that they saw an alternative route via further evolution of the ISC; in particular, the establishment of an investigatory arm. As Yvette Cooper, one of the most articulate advocates of expanded oversight, argued:

> At the moment, information is provided by agency chiefs and by Ministers at their discretion, which raises a difficult point: how can we have proper oversight if the very people whom we are supposed to be overseeing are determining what information we get? That severely jeopardises the Committee's ability to pronounce with authority on important intelligence issues. Credibility demands knowledge and knowledge demands the power to verify—the power to check what is going on. Until now, the ISC has not had that power, and that reduces its credibility in the public mind, as well as in Parliament's mind.
>
> None of that means that I suspect the agencies of any wrongdoing; it means simply that we on the Committee lack the ability to pronounce with confidence that all is well. We cannot come to the House, put our hands on

our hearts and say that all is well, because we do not have the power to know.[14]

By the time the ISC produced its 1998–1999 report (in August 1999), the government had consented to the appointment of a single investigator, despite some agency unease at the prospect. The investigator, whose terms of reference were dictated by the prime minister rather than the ISC, occupied an interesting position, further inside the "ring of secrecy" than ISC members from whom he could well be obliged to withhold information. Before providing a report on an issue for the ISC, the investigator was required to consult with the agency involved, "so as to allow the Head of the Agency to determine whether any particular material should be withheld from the Committee."[15]

In its 1998–1999 annual report, the ISC returned to the question of MI5's personal files. Its earlier recommendations had contributed toward the creation of a degree of external scrutiny to help ensure that historically valuable documents were not being destroyed. However, the Committee learned that during the period between the Home Secretary undertaking to review the issue and the announcement that there would be external scrutiny in the future, rather than suspend file destruction, MI5 destroyed a further 3,000 files.[16] It also continued its campaign to bring greater transparency to the question of the agencies' budgets. In its response, the government continued to resist this.

The timing of the report's publication and the government's response was again tardy in the extreme. A report completed in August 1999 was only published in November 1999, the government's response was published at the end of January 2000, and the parliamentary debate finally held in June 2000, almost a year after the report was completed and just two months before the subsequent annual report was presented to the prime minister. The delay in publication, response, and scheduling of debate meant that this "annual" debate was held a full 20 months after the previous one.

Although the ISC was established as a self-tasking body, in September 1999, it agreed to the government's request to investigate the policy and procedures employed by the agencies in their handling of information acquired through Soviet defector Vasili Mitrokhin and the events that culminated in the publication of the first volume of his account of Soviet espionage, coauthored with Professor Christopher Andrew.[17] This was also interesting in that it had been made clear on establishing the ISC that "the past is another country." Now the ISC was being invited to investigate those parts of that country where it could be helpful to the government. Central to this case were issues of agency accountability to ministers and the degree to which ministers were kept informed about espionage issues. The key case was that of Melita Norwood, code-named HOLA, who the Mitrokhin papers allowed to be identified as a Soviet spy as long ago as 1992, but whom MI5 effectively decided against prosecuting without any wider consultation. In 1999, when the first volume of the *Mitrokhin Archive* was about to be published, MI5 asked for an opinion on a possible prosecution, only for the attorney general to advise that a court would be likely to view such a prosecution as an abuse of process, given that no action had been taken when Norwood's identity had first become known. The ISC concluded that

> . . . it was a serious failure of the Security Service not to refer Mrs. Norwood's case to the Law Officers in mid 1993. This failure to consult the Law Officers resulted in the decision whether or not to prosecute Mrs. Norwood effectively being taken by the Security Service. The Committee is concerned that the Service used public interest reasons to justify taking no further action against Mrs. Norwood, when this was for the Law Officers to decide. We also believe that the failure of the Security Services to interview Mrs. Norwood at this time prevented her possible prosecution.[18]

In a report highly critical of aspects of MI5's performance, the Committee also said that the Norwood case should have been kept under review between 1993 and 1998 and not allowed to "slip out of sight." That it did represented "a further serious failure." MI5 Director General Sir Stephen Lander would subsequently refer to this ISC report as representing a "public kicking" for the agency.[19]

The government had needed to be seen to launch some kind of investigation into the Mitrokhin/Norwood affair. The ISC was the ideal vehicle; given that original documents would remain within the ring of secrecy and not be made public, as was likely under alternative forms of inquiry. However, the ISC had made clear that to undertake the investigation, it needed full access to information, including the normally sacrosanct advice to ministers, a development that caused some concern within MI5. As the ISC reported, "Although there was some delay in reaching agreement about the papers, the request was eventually met in full." This access further emboldened the Committee. Nevertheless, despite working to achieve a high level of mutual trust with the agencies from 1994 onward, the Committee had not been informed of the Mitrokhin/Norwood issue, even after a decision had been taken to publish the *Mitrokhin Archive*. Hence, although this episode demonstrated that the ISC was not afraid to criticize the agencies, and that it was increasingly self-confident, it also left hanging questions about the degree of accountability it was achieving.

The 1999–2000 Report continued to provide evidence of some assertiveness. However, its analysis of the intelligence contribution to the 1999 Kosovo campaign was so heavily redacted as to be without meaning. Elsewhere, it advocated greater intelligence resources be applied to combating drug trafficking, recommended greater resources be committed to combat tobacco smuggling, and expressed concern at the scale of illegal immigration. Alongside greater assertiveness, then, it continued to act as an advocate for the agencies' interests.

The ISC produced an interim report in March 2001, in anticipation of the calling of a general election, marking the final contributions of a majority of the Committee, including Chairman King. The report reiterated the Committee's disappointment in the government's refusal to publish fuller agency budget figures (in its response the government again declined) and continued to press for the creation of an employment tribunal capable of hearing the grievances of agency staff to prevent the emergence of further Tomlinsons and Shaylers, something over which the government continued to drag its feet. In sum, the picture that emerged at the end of the Tom King era was of a Committee that had worked hard to establish itself, had reflected on its role and evolved its terms of reference, had gained a significant degree of trust from the agencies, had been critical of both government and agencies on occasion, and had probed government repeatedly in an attempt to secure access to a full range of information. In addition, King's seven-year stewardship had provided stability. The picture was also of a committee sometimes suspicious of the extent to which it had secured the full co-operation of the agencies, at other times more trusting, and of a committee trying to reconcile different aspects of its role; sometimes critic, at others advocate, but not really either. Yet in the nature of its responses and its handling of the reports, responses, and debates, the government inevitably had the upper hand.

The Question of Political Will

Following the 2001 general election, the government appointed a new ISC in August comprising five new members and chaired by one of these, Ann Taylor, a former Labour Chief Whip. Just weeks later, the events of September 11, 2001 (9/11), and the U.S. and international response to those events transformed the international and intelligence environments, so impacting on the environment in which intelligence oversight was conducted. It was to mark a shift of focus for intelligence oversight, away from the domestic, not simply toward the international, but toward an understanding that the dominant issues were "intermestic" in nature and that "foreign" and "domestic" issues could seldom in future be as neatly compartmentalized as had tended to be the case in the past. Neither the security and intelligence agencies nor the ISC were as quick to grasp the full implications of this shift as they might have been.

The most politically charged investigation that the ISC had handled to date followed, with the 2003 inquiry into pre-war UK intelligence on Iraq's WMD, which turned out not to exist. This represented the kind of controversial issue that for some observers would represent a litmus test of the ISC's ability to hold the agencies to account and deal objectively with an issue of great political sensitivity. How would the ISC deal with this?

The ISC sought "to examine whether the available intelligence, which informed the decision to invade Iraq, was adequate and properly assessed and whether it was accurately reflected in Government publications."[20] It did not consider the decision to go to war per se. It reported four months later that, based on the intelligence it had seen, there was convincing intelligence that Iraq had active chemical, biological, and nuclear programs and the capability to produce chemical and biological weapons. At the heart of the controversy over prewar intelligence on Iraq was a dossier produced by Downing Street in September 2002 and containing intelligence cleared by JIC Chairman John Scarlett. In its 2002–2003 annual report, the ISC had noted this and said that it "supports the responsible use of intelligence and material collected by the Agencies to inform the public on matters such as these." The question here, then, was how far this represented responsible use of the material, and how far it informed the public rather than misled it. However, the ISC did not rise to the challenge, offering no commentary on evidence that the political case was in advance of the intelligence case for war. For example, in a draft of Tony Blair's foreword to the dossier, it was acknowledged that there was no threat of nuclear attack on the United Kingdom, but this had been excluded from the published version. This denied the public available reassurance, removed an opportunity to bring some context to bear, and served to heighten the sense of threat posed by Iraq. In a tame criticism, the ISC contented itself with observing that "it was unfortunate that this point was removed from the published version of the foreword and not highlighted elsewhere."

The government's response constituted a further stage in the presentational game that had begun in earnest with the September 2002 dossier itself. It emphasized those aspects of the ISC report that appeared to support its conduct over the production of the dossier and rejected its criticisms. For example, with regard to the charge that the dossier was misleading, its response was that

. . . the dossier did present a balanced view of Iraq's CBW capability based on the intelligence available. The dossier made clear (paragraph 14, page 16) that the withdrawal of the United Nations Special Commission (UNSCOM) had greatly diminished the ability of the international community to monitor and assess Iraq's continued efforts to reconstitute its programmes. It also noted (paragraph 13, page 16) that UNSCOM was unable to account for significant quantities of agents, precursors and munitions.[21]

But the government could not have it both ways. Either—as this and the objective record both suggested—the intelligence picture on Iraq was characterized by a significant degree of uncertainty, or, as Blair wrote in his foreword, it was known that Iraq represented a "current and serious threat to the UK national interest." The ISC was dissatisfied with the government's response, as it

. . . emphasised only four key conclusions while either rejecting or failing to address fully many of our other conclusions and recommendations. We regard this as extremely unsatisfactory. . . . Our dissatisfaction was increased by the Government's decision to allow such little time for parliamentary debate. . .

on its Iraq and annual reports.[22] As a result, the government response to the 2003–2004 annual report began a practice of responding to each of the ISC's conclusions individually. However, it did not deal directly with the core question, simply stating, "We regret that the Committee found [the] response unsatisfactory."[23] This did not amount to effective oversight. Key questions had gone unanswered, and the ISC had effectively run out of options in the face of the government's refusal to engage with it. Its investigation had been limited, reflecting inadequate investigatory capacity, its findings dismissed by government, and its credibility damaged.

Subsequently, it emerged that although the ISC had stated that it had seen all JIC assessments on Iraq produced between August 1990 and September 2002 and the eight produced in the period October 2002 to March 2003, in fact eight had been withheld—five from the former period, three from the latter. Although the Committee was "satisfied that knowledge of them would not have led us to change the conclusions, including those that were critical, in our Report,"[24] earlier access would have allowed it to include further material, and its conclusions would have been more securely rooted in a fuller picture. While it accepted the cock-up rather than conspiracy explanation it was offered, this did affect confidence in the ISC and begged questions about just how full the cooperation being offered actually was. More widely, the episode begged questions about the degree of political will the Committee possessed in pursuing issues that had a clear political dimension and could embarrass the government. The Committee's decision to dispense with its only investigator, John Morrison, after he appeared on the BBC television programme *Panorama* and supported the view that Tony Blair had exaggerated the threat posed by Iraq in making the public case for war, only added to the sense that the ISC was a creature of the executive. Here, the problem of political will also impacted on that of investigatory capacity. As a result of this action, the ISC had no independent investigatory capacity from 2004-2008, in effect a case of oversight de-evolution.

Any assessment of the shortcomings of the ISC over the Iraq issue must also take into account the fact that were it not for a series of unpredictable events, its report would have represented the final word on UK intelligence on Iraqi WMD (this was clearly the intention of the Blair government), and there would have been no Butler report, which was to be more open about and critical of politicians' use of intelligence in making the case for war and much more forensic in its analysis of intelligence performance.

The question of political will was also writ large in the ISC's investigation of the July 7, 2005 (7/7), London suicide bombings and the question of whether this plot had been preventable and so represented a case of intelligence failure. At the time of the bombings, politicians and intelligence officials had claimed that the perpetrators were "clean skins" unknown to police or MI5. However, it later transpired that two of them, Mohammad Siddique Khan and Shazad Tanweer, had been monitored as part of a wider intelligence operation. The ISC concluded that the failure to monitor and investigate Khan and Tanweer more thoroughly prior to the bombings was a consequence of resource limitations and, in this context, was "understandable." As it wrote:

> It is possible that the chances of identifying attack planning and of preventing the 7 July attacks might have been greater had different investigative decisions been taken in 2000–2005. Nonetheless, we conclude that, in light of the other priority investigations being conducted and the limitations on Security Service resources, the decisions not to give greater investigative priority to these two individuals were understandable.[25]

However, the wider intelligence operation that Khan and Tanweer had seemingly stumbled onto the fringes of resulted in arrests and a high profile trial which, in April 2007, resulted in the conviction of five men who had plotted to explode ammonium nitrate fertilizer bombs at a range of heavily populated targets. With these convictions came the lifting of reporting restrictions, and with this lifting it became clear that surveillance of Khan and Tanweer had been more extensive than previously indicated.

This knowledge called into question the thrust of the ISC's earlier conclusions, raising once more the question of the extent of agency cooperation with the ISC. Prime Minister Tony Blair had earlier resisted calls for a public inquiry into the 7/7 bombings on the grounds that: "If we ended up having a full scale public inquiry . . . we would end up diverting a massive amount of police and security service time and I don't think it would be sensible."[26] However, an inquiry that sought to explain why the bombings had occurred would inevitably have had to consider the role of the decision to go to war in Iraq in radicalising young British Muslims, and so may have revealed a degree of governmental culpability. Instead, the government focused on the "what happened" question by producing a narrative account of the events of July 7, 2005. The decision to publish this alongside the ISC's report drew the ISC into the government's presentational strategy and had the unfortunate effect of giving the impression that the ISC was now an arm of the executive. With certain of that report's findings now being called into question, Blair still refused to hold the public inquiry that a growing number were demanding and instead asked the ISC to re-investigate the 7/7 attacks. In so doing, he implicitly accepted that their initial report had clear limitations and put the Committee in a Catch-22 situation that could only further undermine its credibility with Parliament and the public. Just as an alternative source of investigation had proved most thorough with regard to the Iraqi WMD issue (the Butler Inquiry), so the Coroner's Inquest into the 7/7 bombings provided a more thorough, and obviously independent, account of whether there were any failings on the part of MI5 in this case, making two recommendations that highlighted aspects of MI5 performance, both of which were fundamental to professional intelligence practice.[27]

The Normative Challenge

Questions of agency co-operation and investigatory capacity were raised again when the ISC turned to questions of abduction and torture raised by the prosecution of the post-9/11 "war on terror." In 2007, the Committee published its report on *Rendition*. One of the cases it considered was that of Binyam Mohamed, a British resident arrested in Pakistan and rendered to Morocco, where he claimed he was tortured, before being transferred to a U.S detention centre in Afghanistan and then to Guantánamo Bay. The ISC reported that no member of MI6 had any contact with Mohamed, but that one member of MI5 did interview him in Karachi in 2002 for three hours, and that the "interview was conducted by an experienced officer and was in line with the Service's guidance to staff on contact with detainees."[28] However, in August 2008 the High Court found that this interrogation was unlawful and ruled that MI5 "continued to facilitate" the interrogation of Mohamed after he was abducted from Pakistan and flown to Morocco, even though its officers "must also have appreciated" that he was being detained and interrogated by officials "of a foreign government." The Court concluded that: "The relationship of the United Kingdom government to the United States authorities in connection with [Mohamed] was far beyond that of a bystander or witness to the alleged wrongdoing."[29] In October 2008, the Home Secretary, Jacqui Smith, asked the attorney general to investigate possible criminal wrongdoing by MI5 and the CIA in relation to the detention and interrogation of Mohamed. While these developments clearly raised questions about MI5 compliance with human rights law, and hence the reliability of the ISC's report into extraordinary rendition, ISC Chair Margaret Beckett declined suggestions that the ISC should reinvestigate Mohamed's case, claiming that "individual cases are matters for the tribunal. The Intelligence and Security Committee investigates the policy and, indeed, the implementation of the policy by the agencies; the tribunal looks at individual cases."[30] However, there was nothing preventing the ISC from revisiting this case. Its *Rendition* report had itself focused on individual cases, while there was a further precedent in the Committee's 1999–2000 inquiry into the decision not to prosecute Soviet spy Melita Norwood.

By this time, the reputation of the ISC was at a low ebb. It had failed to get at the truth in successive cases it had investigated, which had raised fundamental questions of political will, investigatory capacity, and agency co-operation. The government's approach to the ISC had not helped either. During the 2005–2010 parliament, the Committee had three chairs, as the government came to see the post as a means of offering some consolation to those being dropped from the Cabinet, who then left the post when a return to the Cabinet or wider government was offered (see table below). This did nothing to improve perceptions of the Committee's independence from government and robbed the Committee of stable leadership and cumulative expertise at a particularly difficult time.

In 2010, the incoming coalition government headed by David Cameron established a judge-led inquiry into "whether, and if so to what extent, the UK Government and its intelligence agencies were involved in improper treatment of detainees held by other countries,"[31] to be led by former appeal court judge and Intelligence Services Commissioner Sir Peter Gibson. However, the opening of fresh police investigations into possible official complicity in renditions to Libya resulted in the government terminating the Gibson Inquiry and asking it to produce only a preparatory report. This

Table 21.1 Chairs of the ISC, 1994–2014

Years	Name	Previous Relevant Experience	Reason for Leaving ISC
1994–2001	Tom King	Secretary of State for Northern Ireland; Secretary of State for Defense	Retired as an MP
2001–2005	Ann Taylor	None	Retired as an MP
2005–2008	Paul Murphy	Secretary of State for Northern Ireland	Returned to the Cabinet as Secretary of State for Wales
2008 (Jan–Oct)	Margaret Beckett	Foreign Secretary	Returned to the Government as Minister of State for Housing & Planning
2008–2010	Kim Howells	Minister of State, Foreign & Commonwealth Office	Retired as an MP
2010–	Sir Malcolm Rifkind	Secretary of State for Defense; Foreign Secretary	

was published in December 2013. Contrary to the ISC, which had "found no evidence that the UK Agencies were complicit in any 'Extraordinary Rendition' operations,"[32] the Gibson report found evidence that the British Government and intelligence agencies had been involved in abduction (extraordinary rendition) and, in effect, torture. The report identified 27 separate issue areas that it would have gone on to explore had it not been terminated and that required answers in order to determine the full extent of British government and agency complicity in these practices. The report also raised questions about government and agency co-operation with the ISC during its Rendition inquiry, in light of clear evidence that relevant material was either withheld or not notified to the Committee.[33] This made the government's announcement, on the publication of the Gibson report, that it was handing further investigation over to the ISC somewhat surreal. Earlier, in announcing the establishment of the Gibson Inquiry, Prime Minister Cameron had explained that "I do not think for a moment that we should believe that the ISC should be doing this piece of work. For public confidence, and for independence from parliament, party and government, it is right to have a judge-led inquiry."[34] What had changed?

Reform

One thing that had changed between the announcement of the Gibson Inquiry and its report being published was that the ISC had been reformed in an attempt to restore sufficient public confidence for it to take on this kind of work for the government. Reform of the ISC was first mooted by the Labour government of Gordon Brown in 2007. By this time, just three constituencies believed that oversight was working well—the government, the agencies, and the ISC itself—and each realized that this state of affairs meant that, in reality, the ISC was failing. It was not delivering the public trust, and hence democratic legitimacy, that the agencies ultimately require. Subsequently, the ISC itself put forward proposals for reform which fed into the Justice and Security Act of 2013. This sought to make the Committee more independent, or at least give it this appearance. Certainly, some of the reforms involved less substantive concessions than they might at first glance have appeared. Previously criticized because it reported to the prime minister, the Committee would now report to Parliament. However, it would first need to send its report to the prime minister, who could exclude from it any information considered prejudicial to the continued work of the agencies. Hence, in terms of control over the content and timing of its reports, there was no substantive change here. In effect, the agencies still controlled what could be published about them by the ISC. Previously criticized because its members were appointed by the prime minister, now members would need to be approved by Parliament, but would have first to be nominated by the prime minister. Hence, Parliament still could not appoint to the ISC anyone the prime minister would not want to see there. The chair would then be chosen by the ISC, but this would not guarantee one commonly recommended reform; a chair drawn from an opposition rather than government party. Previously criticized because it had the power only to request information from the agencies, now the agencies were required to make any information available that the ISC asked for, unless this was vetoed by the Secretary of State on clearly defined grounds. This represented a shift from the earlier situation where the agency heads themselves were able to veto requests, although only time will tell whether in practice this change is more apparent than real, given the historically close government–agency co-operation in dealing with the ISC. Finally, the ISC's role in investigating operational matters, a role not explicitly stated in the 1994 Act but which had developed in the years since, was recognized through the new Act, though subject to prime ministerial approval.

Nevertheless, the reforms had the effect of giving the ISC of 2013 a clean slate. It was now up to its members to maximize the potential that existed in these reforms, which also addressed investigative capacity and staffing levels. However, this clean slate was rather messed up within weeks by the publication in *The Guardian* newspaper of NSA whistleblower Edward Snowden's revelations about widespread U.S. surveillance practices and the involvement of GCHQ in these. In response, the ISC issued a statement on GCHQ involvement providing assurance that GCHQ had complied with the law.[35] However, it seemed to many that it was the law—in this case the Regulation of Investigatory Powers Act of 2000 (RIPA)—that was the problem, and that a simple focus on legality would fail to deal with normative questions around the relationship between democratic values and the pursuit of security. At the same time, as the potential to hoover up vast quantities of electronic data had grown rapidly, there was a question as to whether RIPA remained an appropriate legislative base; as Yvette Cooper, a former ISC member and by now Shadow Home Secretary, argued; "strong powers need to be matched by strong checks and balances."[36] To its credit, the ISC quickly moved to announce that it would examine the "complex interaction" between RIPA, the Intelligence Services Act, the Human Rights Act, "and the policies and procedures that underpin them."[37] Addressing normative concerns, it subsequently announced an inquiry into the relationship between privacy and security which would invite written evidence from the public and so lead in the kind of public debate on this core issue that the government had studiously avoided. However, the newly reformed ISC found itself in a lose-lose situation over the NSA/GCHQ revelations. Either it knew about these prior to the Snowden revelations and did not flag up its concerns—thereby suggesting that it had a poor understanding of when the pursuit of security might be held to involve unacceptable levels of intrusion into personal privacy—or it was kept in the dark and did not know about them. Not surprisingly, ISC members conceded nothing either way in public, and the calls for further reform of the ISC were loud and came from across the political spectrum. In short, the ISC's relaunch was ruined by the timing of the Snowden revelations.

Conclusions

In light of the problems that have beset the ISC since the advent of the "war on terror," it is easy to overlook its achievements. Twenty years ago there was no legislative scrutiny of intelligence, and that this now seems an unthinkable state of affairs owes much to the work of the ISC in establishing and normalizing oversight. The ISC was tasked with performing intelligence from scratch, with no more guidance as to how to go about this in practice than that provided by the bare bones of the 1994 Intelligence Services Act. It put considerable flesh on these in subsequent years, expanding its remit in the process. Some of the reforms contained in the 2013 Justice and Security Act formalize a de facto situation brought about by the ISC's own initiatives, most significantly in terms of operational matters. Moreover, it introduced significant accountability with regard to the agencies' finances, previously an area of limited transparency even at the ministerial level.

However, if the period up to 2001 was marked by progress, the following decade was marked by serial setbacks. The ISC's seeming inability to get at the truth in inquiries into the biggest intelligence issues of the decade—the Iraqi WMD issues, the London 7/7 bombings, and the question of involvement in "war on terror" abduction and torture (whether due to a lack of political will, limited investigatory capacity, or limited government and agency co-operation)—severely damaged parliamentary and public confidence in it.

Perhaps another source of its difficulties is to be found in the tension inherent in the ISC's role. As then ISC member Richard Ottaway expressed it, in its most basic form, in July 2008:

> I feel most uncomfortable with the question about the precise role of the ISC. Is it with the agencies or against them? Does it provide oversight or a check or balance? The Committee's job is defined, as is the job of a Select Committee, as the provision of oversight of policy, finance and administration. That definition is wide and vague, and can be broadly or narrowly interpreted. During my time on the ISC, I have seen a narrow interpretation. A Select Committee has more freedom to range and is wide-ranging in its scope.[38]

The reality is that oversight of intelligence is inescapably political, and those conducting it must remember that they are engaged in contests of power in which the stakes are high. Different groups have had different interests in intelligence oversight, giving rise to competing understandings of its purpose. As Home Secretary Jacqui Smith explained in July 2008, from the government's perspective, "it is essential that Parliament and, through Parliament, the wider public can be assured that the security and intelligence agencies are fulfilling their lawful duties efficiently and effectively. That is the role of the Intelligence and Security Committee."[39] But this cannot be the ISC's only role. This interpretation begs obvious questions. What happens when the ISC finds evidence which is likely to further diminish trust in the agencies? Should it, or does it, consider how any shortcomings or criticisms should be revealed or aired so as to minimize any further erosion of public trust? Is this where the provision to communicate concerns in secret to the prime minister kicks in? If so, how is this to be reconciled with responsibility to Parliament? Given the non-linear reporting line it must follow, with which of these constituencies does the ISC see its primary responsibility lying?

By the end of 2013, the ISC was at a turning point. Taken together, the past failures of the ISC and the Snowden revelations demonstrated why the 2013 Justice and Security Act reforms were insufficient. The ISC needed (once again) to prove itself in the face of widespread skepticism and calls for further reform. In response, either the ISC will drive further reform from within, or it is likely to be imposed from outside. Either way, the Snowden revelations are likely to act as a catalyst in speeding up the next stage in what history will record as a slow march toward an appropriately powerful system of legislative oversight of intelligence. Will the ISC be a part of this? Possibly, but there is a limit to how many times a body can be reformed before logic suggests it is best replaced.

Notes

1. *Hansard* (February 22, 1994), col. 171.
2. *Hansard* (April 27, 1994), col. 351.
3. *Hansard* (February 22, 1994), col. 240.
4. *Interim Report of the Intelligence and Security Committee (ISC)*, Cm 2873 (May 1995), para. 8.
5. ISC, *Annual Report 1995*, Cm 3198 (March 1996), para. 7.
6. Ibid., para. 37.
7. ISC, *Annual Report 1996*, Cm 3574, para. 6.
8. ISC *Annual Report 1997–98*, Cm 4073 (November 1998), foreword.
9. Ibid, paras. 24–38.
10. *Hansard* (November 2, 1998), col. 612.
11. ISC, *Annual Report 1997–98*, para. 50.
12. Ibid, para. 69.
13. *Hansard* (November 2, 1998), cols. 596, 618.
14. Ibid, col. 610.
15. *Government Response to the Intelligence and Security Committee's Annual Report 1998–99*, Cm 4569 (January 2000), para. 34.
16. *ISC Annual Report 1998–99*, Cm 4532 (November 1999), para. 79.
17. Christopher Andrew and Vasili Mitrokhin, *The Mitrokhin Archive: The KGB in Europe and the West* (London: Allen Lane, 1999).

18. ISC, *The Mitrokhin Inquiry Report*, Cm 4764 (June 2000), para. 34.

19. Sir Stephen Lander, "The Oversight of Security and Intelligence," speech at Royal United Services Institute (London, March 15, 2001).

20. ISC, *Iraqi Weapons of Mass Destruction—Intelligence and Assessments*, Cm 5972 (September 2003), para. 11.

21. *Government Response to ISC Report on Iraqi Weapons of Mass Destruction—Intelligence and Assessments*, Cm 6118 (February 2004), para. 13.

22. ISC, *Annual Report 2003–04*, Cm 6240 (June 2004), para. 87.

23. *Government's Response to the Intelligence and Security Committee's Annual Report 2003–04*, Cm 6241 (July 2004), para. P.

24. ISC, *Annual Report 2003–04*, Cm 6240 (June 2004), para. 146.

25. ISC, *Report into the London Terrorist Attacks on 7 July 2005*, Cm 6785 (May 2006), para. 56.

26. "PM Defends Bomb Inquiry Decision," *BBC News* (December 14, 2005), http://news.bbc.co.uk/1/hi/uk/4527104.stm.

27. The Rt. Hon. Lady Justice Hallett, DBE, Report of the Coroner's Inquests into the London Bombings of July 7, 2005, May 6, 2011.

28. ISC, *Rendition*, Cm 7171 (July 2007), para.102.

29. Richard Norton-Taylor, "MI5 Criticised for Role in Case of Torture, Rendition and Secrecy," *The Guardian* (August 22, 2008).

30. *Hansard* (March 19, 2008), col. 469.

31. Cited in *The Report of the Detainee Inquiry* (London: TSO, December 2013), para. 1.11.

32. ISC, *Rendition*, p.64, para. E.

33. *Report of the Detainee Inquiry*, paras. 6.64–6.70.

34. Cited in Iain Cobain, Richard Norton-Taylor & Nick Hopkins, "MI5 and MI6 Face Questions over Torture of Terrorism Suspects," *The Guardian* (December 20, 2013).

35. ISC, Statement on GCHQ's Alleged Interception of Communications under the US PRISM Programme (July 17, 2013).

36. Yvette Cooper, "The Challenges of a Digital World to our Security and Liberty," Speech to Demos (March 3, 2014).

37. ISC, Statement on GCHQ's Alleged Interception.

38. *Hansard* (July 17, 2008), col. 483.

39. Ibid, col. 455.

The Organization of the U.S. Intelligence Community, 2014

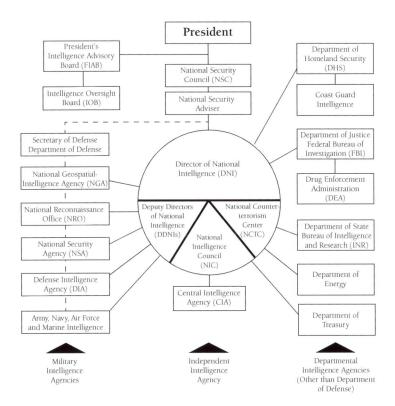

(From 1948 to 2004, a Director of Central Intelligence (DCI) led the Intelligence Community, rather than a Director of National Intelligence. The Department of Homeland Security and the Coast Guard did not become part of the IC until 2003; and the Drug Enforcement Administration, in 2006.).

U.S. Intelligence Leadership, 1947–2014

Directors, National Intelligence

2005–2007　John D. Negroponte
2007–2009　J. M. ("Mike") McConnell
2009–2010　Dennis C. Blair
2010–　　　James R. Clapper Jr.

Directors, Central Intelligence

1947–1950　Rear Adm. Roscoe H. Hillenkoetter
1950–1953　Gen. Walter Bedell Smith
1953–1961　Allen W. Dulles
1961–1965　John A. McCone
1965–1966　Vice Adm. William F. Raborn Jr.
1966–1973　Richard Helms
1973　　　　James R. Schlesinger
1973–1976　William E. Colby
1976–1977　George H. W. Bush
1977–1981　Adm. Stansfield Turner
1981–1987　William J. Casey
1987–1991　William H. Webster
1991–1993　Robert M. Gates
1993–1995　R. James Woolsey
1995–1997　John M. Deutch
1997–2004　George J. Tenet
2004–2005　Porter J. Goss

Chairs, Senate Select Committee on Intelligence

1976–1977　Daniel K. Inouye, Democrat, Hawaii
1977–1981　Birch Bayh, Democrat, Indiana
1981–1985　Barry Goldwater, Republican, Arizona
1985–1987　David Durenberger, Republican, Minnesota
1987–1993　David L. Boren, Democrat, Oklahoma
1993–1995　Dennis DeConcini, Democrat, Arizona
1995–1997　Arlen Specter, Republican, Pennsylvania
1997–2001　Richard C. Shelby, Republican, Alabama
2001–2003　Bob Graham, Democrat, Florida
2003–2006　Pat Roberts, Republican, Kansas
2006–2009　John D. Rockefeller IV, Democrat, West Virginia
2009–　　　Diane Feinstein, Democrat, California

Chairs, House Permanent Select Committee on Intelligence

1977–1985 Edward P. Boland, Democrat, Massachusetts
1985–1987 Lee H. Hamilton, Democrat, Indiana
1987–1989 Louis Stokes, Democrat, Ohio
1989–1991 Anthony C. Beilenson, Democrat, California
1991–1993 Dave McCurdy, Democrat, Oklahoma
1993–1995 Dan Glickman, Democrat, Kansas
1995–1997 Larry Combest, Republican, Texas
1997–2004 Porter J. Goss, Republican, Florida
2004–2006 Peter Hoekstra, Republican, Michigan
2007–2011 Silvestre Reyes, Democrat, Texas
2011–   Mike Rogers, Republican, Michigan

Glossary

ABM	anti-ballistic missile
ADCI/A&P	assistant director of Central Intelligence/Analysis and Production
ADCI/C	assistant director of Central Intelligence/Collection
AFIO	Association of Former Intelligence Officers
AFRICOM	Africa Command (U.S.)
AG	Attorney General
ASIO	Australian Security Intelligence Organization
A-12	U.S. spy plane
AWAC	airborne warning and control system (U.S. spy plane)
BDA	battle damage assessment
BMD	ballistic missile defense
BW	biological weapons
CA	covert action
CAS	Covert Action Staff
CB	chemical-biological
CBW	chemical-biological warfare
CE	counterespionage
CENTRCOM	Central Command (U.S.)
C4I	command, control, computer, communications, and intelligence
CHAOS	code name for CIA domestic spying operation
CI	counterintelligence
CIA	Central Intelligence Agency (the "Agency")
CIC	Counterintelligence Center (CIA)

CIG	Central Intelligence Group (CIA)
CINC	commander-in-chief (regional military commander)
CIPA	Classified Information Procedures Act (1980, U.S.)
CMS	Community Management Staff
CNC	Crime and Narcotics Center (CIA)
CNO	Chief of Naval Operations
COINTELPRO	Counterintelligence Program (FBI)
COMINT	communications intelligence
CORONA	codename for the first U.S. spy satellite system
C/O	case officer (CIA)
COS	chief of station, the top CIA officer in the field
CSIS	Canadian Security and Intelligence Service
CTC	Counterterrorism Center (CIA)
CW	chemical weapons
D	Democrat
DA	Directorate of Administration (CIA)
DAS	Deputy Assistant Secretary
DBA	dominant battlefield awareness
DCI	Director of Central Intelligence
DCIA or D/CIA	Director of the Central Intelligence Agency
DDA	Deputy Director for Administration (CIA)
DDCI	Deputy Director of Central Intelligence
DDCIA	Deputy Director for the Central Intelligence Agency
DDI	Deputy Director for Intelligence (CIA)
DDIC	Deputy Director for the Intelligence Community
DDO	Deputy Director for Operations (CIA)
DDP	Deputy Director for Plans (CIA)
DDS	Deputy Director for Support (CIA)
DDS&T	Deputy Director for Science and Technology (CIA)
DEA	Drug Enforcement Administration
DEC	Director's Environmental Center (CIA)
DHS	Department of Homeland Security
DI	Directorate of Intelligence (CIA)
DIA	Defense Intelligence Agency
DIAC	Defense Intelligence Agency Center
DIA/HUMINT	Defense HUMINT Service
DMA	Defense Mapping Agency (part of NGA)
DO	Directorate of Operations (CIA), also known as the Clandestine Services and the precursor to the NCS
DoD	Department of Defense

DoE	Department of Energy
DoS	Department of State
DMI	Director of Military Intelligence (proposed)
DNI	Director of National Intelligence
DoT	Department of Transportation
DP	Directorate of Plans (CIA), a precursor to the DO
DS	Directorate for Support (CIA, replacing the DA)
DS&T	Directorate for Science and Technology (CIA)
ELINT	electronic intelligence
E.O.	executive order
EOP	Executive Office of the President
EPA	Environmental Protection Agency
EURA	Office of European Analysis (CIA)
FAS	Federation of American Scientists
FBI	Federal Bureau of Investigation
FBIS	Foreign Broadcast Information Service
FISA	Foreign Intelligence Surveillance Act
FISC	Foreign Intelligence Surveillance Court
FSB	Federal Security Service (Russia)
FY	Fiscal Year
GATT	General Agreement on Trade and Tariffs
GEO	Geosynchronous Orbit
GEOINT	geospatial intelligence
GOP	Grand Old Party (the Republican Party)
GRU	Soviet Military Intelligence
HEO	highly elliptical orbit
HPSCI	House Permanent Select Committee on Intelligence
HUMINT	human intelligence (espionage assets)
I&W	indicators and warning
IC	intelligence community
ICBM	intercontinental ballistic missile
ICS	Intelligence Community Staff
IG	Inspector General
IM	Intelligence Memorandum
IMINT	imagery intelligence (photography), now known as GEOINT
INF	Intermediate Nuclear Force

INR	Bureau of Intelligence and Research (Department of State)
INTS	intelligence collection methods (as in "SIGINT")
IOB	Intelligence Oversight Board
IRTPA	Intelligence Reform and Terrorism Prevention Act (2004)
ISC	Intelligence and Security Committe (U.K.)
JCS	Joint Chiefs of Staff
JIC	Joint Intelligence Committee (U.K.)
JMIP	joint military intelligence program
JROC	Joint Reconnaissance Operations Center
JSOC	Joint Specials Operations Command
JSTARS	Joint Surveillance Target Attack Radar Systems
KGB	Soviet Secret Police and Foreign Intelligence: Committee for State Security
KH	Keyhole (satellite)
KIQs	Key Intelligence Questions
KJ	Key Judgment (NIE executive summaries)
KP	kitchen police (U.S. Army slang)
LEO	low earth orbit
MAGIC	Allied code-breaking operations against the Japanese in World War II
MASINT	measurement and signatures intelligence
MI	military intelligence
MIA	missing in action
MI5	British Security Service
MIP	Military Intelligence Program
MIRV	multiple, independently targeted, re-entry vehicle
MI6	Secret Intelligence Service (SIS—United Kingdom)
MIT	Massachusetts Institute of Technology
MRBM	medium-range ballistic missiles
MRC	major regional conflict
MX	Missile Experimental (a component of U.S. nuclear deterrence)
NAFTA	North American Free Trade Agreement
NASA	National Aeronautics and Space Administration

NATO	North Atlantic Treaty Organization
NBC	Nuclear, biological, chemical weapons
NCPC	National Counterproliferation Center (for the DNI)
NCS	National Clandestine Service (formerly CIA's DO)
NCTC	National Counterterrorism Center (for the DNI)
NEOB	New Executive Office Building
NFIP	National Foreign Intelligence Program (now NIP)
NGA	National Geospatial-Intelligence Agency
NGO	non-governmental organization
NIA	National Imagery Agency (proposed)
NIC	National Intelligence Council
NID	National Intelligence Daily; also, National Intelligence Director (a variation of DNI) and National Intelligence Directive
NIE	National Intelligence Estimate
NIO	National Intelligence Officer
NIMA	National Imagery and Mapping Agency
NIP	National Intelligence Program
NIT	National Intelligence Topic
NOC	nonofficial cover
NPC	Nonproliferation Center (CIA)
NPIC	National Photographic Interpretation Center (part of NGA)
NRO	National Reconnaissance Office
NSA	National Security Agency
NSC	National Security Council
NTM	National Technical Means
OBE	overtaken by events
OC	official cover
ODNI	Office of the Director of National Intelligence
OMB	Office of Management and Budget
ONE	Office of National Estimates (CIA)
OPEC	Organization of Petroleum Exporting Countries
OSINT	open-source intelligence
OSS	Office of Strategic Services
PDB	President's Daily Brief
PDD	Presidential Decision Directive
PFIAB	President's Foreign Intelligence Advisory Board (as of 2008, PIAB)

PIAB	President's Intelligence Advisory Board
PM ops	paramilitary operations
PNG	persona non grata
POW	prisoner of war
PRB	Publication Review Board (CIA)
PRC	People's Republic of China
QDR	Quadrennial Defense Review (U.S.)
R	Republican
RADINT	radar intelligence
RAF	Royal Air Force
RAND Corporation	a Washington, D.C. and California think tank
R & D	research and development
RMA	revolution in military affairs
RPG	rocket-propelled grenade
SAIS	School of Advanced International Studies (Johns Hopkins)
SAM	surface-to-air missile
SDO	support to diplomatic operations
SECDEF	Secretary of Defense
SHAMROCK	cryptonym for NSA domestic spying operations
SIG	Senior Interagency Group
SIGINT	signals intelligence
SLBM	submarine-launched ballistic missile
SMO	support to military operations
SNIE	Special National Intelligence Estimate
SOCOM	Special Operations Command
SOF	Special Operations Forces (DoD)
SOG	Special Operations Group (CIA)
SOVA	Office of Soviet Analysis (CIA)
SR-21	U.S. spy plane
SSCI	Senate Select Committee on Intelligence
START	Strategic Arms Reduction Treaty
SVR	Russian Foreign Intelligence Service (post-Cold War)
TCA	Technical Collection Agency (proposed)
TECHINT	technical intelligence
TELINT	telemetry intelligence
TIARA	tactical intelligence and related activities

TSA	Transportation Security Administration (U.S.)
TTAC	Technological Transfer Assessment Center (CIA)
TTIC	Terrorist Threat Integration Center
UAV	unmanned aerial vehicle (drone)
UK	United Kingdom
UN	United Nations
UNSCOM	United Nations Special Commission
USAF	United States Air Force
USAID	United States Agency for International Development
USC	United States Code
USG	United States Government
USIB	United States Intelligence Board
USSR	Union of Soviet Socialist Republics
USTR	United States Trade Representative
U-2	CIA spy plane
VX	a deadly nerve agent used in chemical weapons
WMD	weapons of mass destruction

About the Editor and Contributors

Editor

Loch K. Johnson is Regents professor of Public and International Affairs and Meigs distinguished professor at the University of Georgia; senior editor of the international journal *Intelligence and National Security*, and author or editor of thirty books on U.S. American foreign policy and national security, including: *American Foreign Policy and the Challenges of World Leadership: Power, Principle, and the Constitution* (Oxford, 2015); *National Security Intelligence: Secret Operations in Defense of the Democracies* (Polity, 2012); and *The Threat on the Horizon: An Inside Account of Intelligence Reform between the End of the Cold War and 9/11* (Oxford, 2011). Johnson served as special assistant to the chair of the Senate Select Committee on Intelligence in 1975–1976; staff director of the House Subcommittee on Intelligence Oversight in 1977–1979; and special assistant to Les Aspin, chair of the Aspin-Brown Commission on Intelligence, in 1995. He led the founding of the School of Public and International Affairs at the University of Georgia in 2001 and has been a Visiting Fellow at Oxford University (2003) and at Yale University (2005). In 2009, Johnson was named a Phi Beta Kappa Visiting Scholar; in 2012, he was selected as the inaugural recipient of the Southeast Conference Professor of the Year Award; and, in 2014, he was presented with the Distinguished Scholar Award by the Intelligence Studies Section of the International Studies Association.

Contributors

Matthew M. Aid is managing director in the Washington, D.C., office of Citigate Global Intelligence and Security. He is also co-editor of *Secrets of Signals Intelligence during the Cold War and Beyond* (2001) and author of *The*

Secret Sentry: The Untold History of the National Security Agency (Bloomsbury, 2009). Aid has been a Visiting Fellow at the National Security Archive at George Washington University.

James E. Baker serves as the chief judge of the United States Court of Appeals for the Armed Forces. He previously served as special assistant to the president, as well as legal advisor and deputy legal advisor to the National Security Council. He has also served as counsel to the President's Intelligence Advisory Board, an attorney-adviser at the Department of State, a legislative aide to Senator Daniel Patrick Moynihan, and a Marine Corps infantry officer. He is the author of *In the Common Defense: National Security Law for Perilous Times* (2007) and, with W. Michael Reisman, *Regulating Covert Action* (1992).

David M. Barrett is professor of political science at Villanova University and author of *Congress and the CIA* (Kansas, 2005).

William J. Daugherty is professor of government at Armstrong Atlantic State University in Savannah, Georgia. A retired senior officer in the CIA, he is also the author of *In the Shadow of the Ayatollah: A CIA Hostage in Iran* (Annapolis, 2001) and *Executive Secrets: Covert Action and the Presidency* (Kentucky, 2004).

Jack Davis is a former CIA analyst. The Agency named him a CIA TRAILBLAZER in recognition of his innovative work on analytic tradecraft.

Peter Gill is on the faculty for politics and security, Liverpool John Moores University, Liverpool, United Kingdom. He is co-author of *Introduction to Politics*, 2d. ed, (1988) and *Intelligence in an Insecure World* (2006).

Glenn Hastedt received his PhD in political science from Indiana University and is chair of the Justice Studies Department at James Madison University. He is the author of *American Foreign Policy: Past, Present, Future*, 7th ed. (2015) and many articles on intelligence.

Frederick P. Hitz, inspector general of the CIA from 1990 to 1998, is a lecturer at the University of Virginia School of Law.

Arthur S. Hulnick is professor of international relations at Boston University, a veteran of U.S. Air Force Intelligence and the CIA, and author of *Keeping Us Safe* (2004).

Jennifer D. Kibbe is associate professor of government at Franklin and Marshall College, as well as Department Head, and has been a postdoctoral fellow at the Brookings Institution.

Mark Phythian is professor of politics in the Department of Politics and International Relations at the University of Leicester, United Kingdom. His research interests are in the areas of intelligence, national security, and foreign policy. He is the author, as well as editor or co-editor, of thirteen books, most recently: *Intelligence in an Insecure World* (with Peter Gill, 2nd ed. Polity Press, 2012) and (as editor) *Understanding the Intelligence Cycle* (Routledge, 2013), along with numerous journal articles and book chapters.

Richard L. Russell is a professor of National Security Studies at the National Defense University. He previously served as a CIA political-military analyst and is the author of *Weapons Proliferation and War in the Greater Middle East* (2005).

Jennifer Sims served as director of Intelligence Studies and visiting professor in the Security Studies Program at Georgetown University's Edmund A. Walsh School of Foreign Service. Prior to this, Sims was research professor at Johns Hopkins University's Nitze School of Advanced International Studies in Washington, D.C. (2001–2003). Earlier in her career, she served as an aide to Senator John Danforth, a SSCI staff member, and deputy assistant secretary of state for Intelligence Coordination. In 1998, Sims was awarded the U.S. Intelligence Community's Distinguished Service Medal. Among her many writings is a book co-edited with Burton Gerber, entitled *Transforming US Intelligence* (Georgetown University, 2005).

John D. Stempel is senior professor of international relations at the University of Kentucky's Patterson School of Diplomacy and International Commerce, which he directed from 1993–2003. He came to Kentucky following a 24-year career in the U.S. Foreign Service, where he focused on political and military affairs. He holds a PhD from the University of California, Berkeley.

Stan A. Taylor, a professor of political science at Brigham Young University, has served as a staff member of the Senate Select committee on Intelligence (1976–1979). He has co-authored *America the Vincible: U.S. Foreign Policy for the Twenty-First Century* (1994).

Athan Theoharis is professor of history at Marquette University, and his research has focused on government secrecy, Cold War politics, and the history of the FBI. He is the author, co-author, and editor of eighteen books, including *The FBI and American Democracy* (2004), *Chasing Spies* (2002), *A Culture of Secrecy* (1998), and *The FBI: A Comprehensive Reference Guide* (1998). He has won the American Bar Association's Gavel Award.

Gregory F. Treverton served on the staff of the Church Committee as well as vice chairman and now chairman of the National Intelligence Council. He has also served as director, Center for Global Risk and Security, RAND, Santa Monica. He is the author of many articles and books on intelligence, including *Intelligence for an Age of Terror* (Cambridge, 2009).

Michael Warner serves as an historian in the Department of Defense and is the author of *The Rise and Fall of Intelligence: An International Security History* (Georgetown, 2014).

James J. Wirtz is dean of the School of International Graduate Studies at the Naval Postgraduate School, Monterey, California. He is the author of *The Tet Offensive: Intelligence Failure in War* (Cornell University Press, 1991, 1994) and has co-edited several books, including *Strategic Denial and Deception* (Transaction, 2002) and *Balance of Power: Theory and Practice in the 21st Century* (Stanford, 2004). He has served as section chair of the Intelligence Studies Section of the International Studies Association and the president of the International Security and Arms Control Section of the American Political Science Association; and he is general editor of the book series *Initiatives in Strategic Studies: Issues and Policies* (Palgrave Macmillan). He was a John M. Olin Fellow at the Center for International Affairs, Harvard University, and a visiting professor at the Center for International Security and Cooperation, Stanford University.

Amy B. Zegart is on the faculty at the Hoover Institute, Stanford University, and is the author of *Spying Blind: The CIA, the FBI, and the Origins of 9/11* (Princeton, 2007) and many articles on intelligence.

Index

Made in the USA
Columbia, SC
15 January 2021

30945536R00285